Advancing SMEs Toward E–Commerce Policies for Sustainability

Rajasekhara Mouly Potluri
Al Ghurair University, UAE

Narasimha Rao Vajjhala
University of New York Tirana, Albania

A volume in the Advances in Electronic Commerce
(AEC) Book Series

Published in the United States of America by
IGI Global
Business Science Reference (an imprint of IGI Global)
701 E. Chocolate Avenue
Hershey PA, USA 17033
Tel: 717-533-8845
Fax: 717-533-8661
E-mail: cust@igi-global.com
Web site: http://www.igi-global.com

Library of Congress Cataloging-in-Publication Data

Names: Potluri, Rajasekhara Mouly, 1967- editor. | Vajjhala, Narasimha Rao, 1978- editor.
Title: Advancing SMEs toward e-commerce policies for sustainability / Rajasekhara Mouly Potluri, and Narasimha Rao Vajjhala, editors.
Description: Hershey, PA : Business Science Reference, [2023] | Includes bibliographical references and index. | Summary: "This book will provide a fresh perspective on how small- and medium-sized enterprises can leverage e-commerce for sustainability considering how consumers have increasingly turned to digital options to bypass physical shopping environments"-- Provided by publisher.
Identifiers: LCCN 2022033897 (print) | LCCN 2022033898 (ebook) | ISBN 9781668457276 (hardcover) | ISBN 9781668457283 (paperback) | ISBN 9781668457290 (ebook)
Subjects: LCSH: Small business--Technological innovations. | Electronic commerce--Management. | Business enterprises--Environmental aspects.
Classification: LCC HD2341 .A38 2023 (print) | LCC HD2341 (ebook) | DDC 338.6/42--dc23/eng/20220823
LC record available at https://lccn.loc.gov/2022033897
LC ebook record available at https://lccn.loc.gov/2022033898

This book is published in the IGI Global book series Advances in Electronic Commerce (AEC) (ISSN: 1935-2921; eISSN: 1935-293X)

British Cataloguing in Publication Data
A Cataloguing in Publication record for this book is available from the British Library.

All work contributed to this book is new, previously-unpublished material. The views expressed in this book are those of the authors, but not necessarily of the publisher.

For electronic access to this publication, please contact: eresources@igi-global.com.

Advances in Electronic Commerce (AEC) Book Series

Mehdi Khosrow-Pour, D.B.A.
Information Resources Management Association, USA

ISSN:1935-2921
EISSN:1935-293X

MISSION

The impact of information technology on commerce is a dynamic and perpetually evolving field of research, most notably as electronic approaches for business transactions shift to the Internet and other telecommunication networks. Given the rapid advancements in the field, research addressing e-commerce and its related areas needs an outlet to reach its audience.

The **Advances in Electronic Commerce (AEC) Book Series** provides comprehensive coverage and understanding of the social, cultural, organizational, and cognitive impacts of e-commerce technologies. The series provides accounts from both the consumer perspective and the organization perspective. **AEC** aims to expand the body of knowledge regarding e-commerce technologies and applications, thus assisting researchers and practitioners to develop more effective systems.

COVERAGE

- Electronic Banking
- E-Tailing
- Online Transaction Processing
- Paid Content
- Online Marketplaces
- B2B and C2C Technologies
- Mobile Commerce
- Virtual Marketplaces
- Social Media and E-Commerce
- Mobile Banking

IGI Global is currently accepting manuscripts for publication within this series. To submit a proposal for a volume in this series, please contact our Acquisition Editors at Acquisitions@igi-global.com or visit: http://www.igi-global.com/publish/.

Titles in this Series

For a list of additional titles in this series, please visit: http://www.igi-global.com/book-series/advances-electronic-commerce/37141

Empirical Research for Futuristic E-Commerce Systems Foundations and Applications
Saurabh Bilgaiyan (Kalinga Institute of Industrial Technology (Deemed), Bhubaneswar, India) Jagannath Singh
(Kalinga Institute of Industrial Technology (Deemed), Bhubaneswar, India) and Himansu Das (Kalinga Institute
of Industrial Technology (Deemed), Bhubaneswa, India)
Business Science Reference • © 2022 • 344pp • H/C (ISBN: 9781668449691) • US $240.00

Handbook of Research on Social Impacts of E-Payment and Blockchain echnology
P.C. Lai (University Malaya, Kuala Lumpur, Malaysia)
Business Science Reference • © 2022 • 561pp • H/C (ISBN: 9781799890355) • US $435.00

Moving Businesses Online and Embracing E-Commerce Impact and Opportunities Caused by COVID-19
Tereza Semerádová (Technical University of Liberec, Czech Republic) and Petr Weinlich (Technical University
of Liberec, Czech Republic)
Business Science Reference • © 2022 • 275pp • H/C (ISBN: 9781799882947) • US $240.00

Handbook of Research on the Platform Economy and the Evolution of E-Commerce
Myriam Ertz (LaboNFC, University of Quebec at Chicoutimi, Canada)
Business Science Reference • © 2022 • 554pp • H/C (ISBN: 9781799875451) • US $325.00

Cross-Border E-Commerce Marketing and Management
Md. Rakibul Hoque (University of Dhaka, Bangladesh & Emporia State University, USA) and R. Edward Bashaw
(Emporia State University, USA)
Business Science Reference • © 2021 • 349pp • H/C (ISBN: 9781799858232) • US $215.00

Handbook of Research on Innovation and Development of E-Commerce and E-Business in ASEAN
Mohammad Nabil Almunawar (Universiti Brunei Darussalam, Brunei) Muhammad Anshari Ali (Universiti Brunei
Darussalam, Brunei) and Syamimi Ariff Lim (Universiti Brunei Darussalam, Brunei)
Business Science Reference • © 2021 • 738pp • H/C (ISBN: 9781799849841) • US $405.00

Impact of Mobile Services on Business Development and E-Commerce
Francisco Liébana (University of Granada, Spain) Zoran Kalinić (University of Kragujevac, Serbia) Iviane Ramos
de Luna (Open University of Catalonia, Spain) and Inma Rodríguez-Ardura (Open University of Catalonia, Spain)
Business Science Reference • © 2020 • 280pp • H/C (ISBN: 9781799800507) • US $230.00

701 East Chocolate Avenue, Hershey, PA 17033, USA
Tel: 717-533-8845 x100 • Fax: 717-533-8661
E-Mail: cust@igi-global.com • www.igi-global.com

EDITORIAL ADVISORY BOARD

Table of Contents

Detailed Table of Contents

Chapter 1
Significance of Brand Image on SME Survival in Digital Competition 1
    Esra Güven, Celal Bayar University, Turkey

With the digitalization of the world and the spread of social media, competition conditions are also changing, and SMEs must keep up with this rapid transformation. SMEs that use these digital platforms correctly and reflect their brand images properly will achieve their goals at a minimal cost. This chapter aims to give required descriptions and explanations about the significance of the brand image of an SME as well as the things to do to build a brand image in a sequence from the widespread content to the digital environments. Brand, image, and brand image concepts have been explained, respectively. The related topic has also elaborated on the kinds of brand image. Social media and its effect on brand image and the things to do to build a brand image in digital environments have been discussed in detail in the chapter. There are also some brand image development activity examples from successful SMEs worldwide.

Chapter 2
Digital Transformation of Small and Medium Businesses 19
    Aizhan Baimukhamedova, Gazi University, Turkey
    Malik Baimukhamedov, Social-Technical University Named After Aldymzharov Z.,
        Kazakhstan

This chapter examines the essence and importance of digital transformation in developing small and medium-sized businesses. It is noted that digitalization uses computer technology to reshape business so that all decisions are made based on data. The main objectives of the digital transformation of SMEs are shown. The technologies accelerating digital transformation include the internet of things, artificial intelligence, e-commerce, big data, cloud technology, blockchain, etc. The tasks of managing an organization in the context of digitalization include changing the company's business processes based on advanced digital technologies, maintaining a high level of knowledge of company management and specialists in the field of modern technologies, maintaining a high degree of preparedness for changes and challenges of the external environment. The authors consider the digital transformation of SMEs in the industrial, agricultural, and commercial spheres, as well as e-commerce.

During the last decades, we have seen building sustainable business models as an innovative part of the business strategy. Different economic sectors have used the concept to meet their economic objectives, and one of the leading business models with the highest growth in the last decade was e-commerce. It is not too much to emphasize the importance of sustainability in e-commerce in all its dimensions. We have seen several investigations on the subject covering a wide range of application areas. In this context, a systematic review of the bibliometric literature was carried out on the SCOPUS indexing database using the keywords "sustainability," "e-commerce," "electronic commerce," "B2C e-commerce", "business, management, and accounting" in the last decade (2012-2022). This study aims to understand how a sustainability strategy can leverage e-commerce.

India has one of the largest bases of small- and medium-sized enterprises around the world after China, and it provides several benefits to the Indian economy in terms of generating a vast range of employment opportunities, innovation of new self-reliance technologies, aiding export growth, socio-economic growth, and rural development, which supports the nation-building. Consumers are using the power of digital technologies and e-commerce; this is the time to measure the propensity of business-to-business (e-commerce) adoption among unorganized retailers. Some studies measured the e-commerce impacts on customers, impacts on organized retailers, and impacts on unorganized retailers. In addition, some other studies concentrated on assessing the unorganized retail SME performance, competition, issues, and challenges. However, studies related to measuring e-commerce acceptance by unorganized retailers are relatively low. This chapter aims to measure the nuances of business-to-business (e-commerce) propensity among unorganized retailers.

E-marketing is a strategic marketing approach that has revolutionized how marketing is executed by transitioning from traditional to internet-based platforms. It has significantly altered how firms interact with their customers. To provide insights and offer guidance for the growth and development of e-marketing among SMEs, the chapter explored the organizational, technological, and environmental elements that may drive the adoption of e-marketing, as well as models that can be implemented to enhance e-marketing. A thorough analysis of the literature revealed a significant positive association between sustainable marketing strategy and SME performance, indicating that sustainability is significantly influenced by the level of customer satisfaction, customer loyalty, and profitability.

Chapter 6

The Relevance of Supply Chain Preparedness on the Long-Term Sustainability of SMEs............... 111

Sefa Asortse, University of Nigeria, Enugu, Nigeria
Edna Mngusughun Denga, American University of Nigeria, Nigeria

The variety of risks and the frequency with which they can disrupt a supply chain are now vastly wider than ever, rendering heightened volatility the emerging norm for contemporary supply chains. Thus, resilience has grown in importance as a component of supply chain management. It is suggested that firms increase risk prevention and response strategies to inject resilience into supply chains. SMEs require resilient supply chains to anticipate potential changes, react to actual changes, and deliver superior value. By creating strategies that enable the supply chain to recover normal operations after a disruption, building supply chain resilience can assist in lessening and overcoming vulnerabilities to risks. The chapter aims to provide a detailed insight into the impact of one critical dimension of supply chain resilience, supply chain preparedness, which is aimed at boosting SME sustainability.

Chapter 7

Factors Hindering Small, Medium, and Micro Enterprise Business Growth in South Africa 134

Sfiso Nxele, Management College of Southern Africa, South Africa
Muhammad Ehsanul Hoque, Management College of Southern Africa, South Africa

Small, medium, and micro enterprises (SMMEs) are critical contributors to the gross domestic product (GDP) rise and the creation of employment opportunities. In South Africa, SMMEs receive funding for sustainability and job creation. The current SMMEs' contribution to the country's GDP and employment creation has, over the years, been on a decline. Therefore, the study aimed to explore the factors hindering SMME business growth. SMMEs experienced challenges of lack of financial assistance, lack of information, unavailable mentorship, unskilled administration, limited assessment within the various institutions, and access to financial support. Significant priority is placed on support institutions and government to create sector specific SMME assessment criterion instead of applying a blanket approach to all business sectors' support.

Chapter 8

Trust in E-Commerce From the Cultural Perspective: A Systematic Literature Review 152

Neslişah Özdemir, Kastamonu University, Turkey

The purpose of this study is to review the literature on e-commerce trust from a cultural perspective, analyze where and how research is conducted, and determine the research stream. For this purpose, a systematic literature review of 52 peer-reviewed articles published in the Scopus database on trust in e-commerce was performed. The findings indicate that there has been a rise, over time, in the number of publications that discuss trust in e-commerce across a variety of cultural contexts. Various methodologies have been employed in these studies, and e-commerce trust has been analyzed in several sectors. The articles on trust in e-commerce from the cultural perspective are under three categories: impact of culture on online trust, antecedents, and consequences of online trust. In this regard, this study contributes to the body of knowledge by evaluating the process of establishing trust in e-commerce and examining the antecedents and consequences of online trust from the cultural perspective.

Chapter 9

Thirunesha Naidu, Management College of Southern Africa, South Africa
Muhammad Hoque, Management College of Southern Africa, South Africa

Digital technology has developed over the years with numerous innovations that have improved how we live, communicate, and work. In business, such innovations have occurred predominantly at larger or newer organizations or e-commerce companies as resources are required to design, implement, and maintain bespoke digital technology solutions while other commercially available solutions and their integration into business operations have not been favored over the more traditional work methods. A business continuity plan is established when a company needs to quickly recover to maintain business operations following a disruption such as a pandemic. In this chapter, various business continuity planning initiatives that may occur during a pandemic, the types of digital technologies used by businesses, and their impact on business continuity during such occurrences are discussed. Recommendations are provided herein for businesses to continue successfully in the volatility, uncertainty, complexity, and ambiguity (VUCA) of this world.

Chapter 10

Aizhan Baimukhamedova, Gazi University, Turkey
Malik Baimukhamedov, Social-Technical University Named After Aldymzharov Z.,
Kazakhstan

E-government is based on electronic document management systems, state management automation systems, and other information and communication systems. A description of four e-government models—Continental European model, Anglo-American model, Asian model, and Russian model—are reviewed. The basis for the creation of the e-government portal is the Decree of the President of the Republic of Kazakhstan dated November 10, 2004, N° 1471 "On state program of formation of E-government in the Republic of Kazakhstan for 2005-2007." E-government supports the following goals: creating new forms of interaction between government agencies, optimizing the provision of government services to the public and businesses, supporting and expansion of citizens' self-service capabilities, increasing technological awareness and skills of citizens, and increasing the degree of participation of all voters in the processes of governance and management of the country.

Chapter 11

Edna Mngusughun Denga, American University of Nigeria, Nigeria
Sandip Rakshit, RMIT University, Vietnam

Contemporary marketing innovation embraces digital platforms, and irrespective of where SMEs operate, they are confronted with highly volatile, competitive, and dynamic market conditions. Research shows businesses cannot become profitable and competitive without implementing appropriate digital marketing strategies. By utilizing digital tools, SMEs can identify, engage, market, and successfully sustain consumer relationships. Therefore, the chapter analyzes literature to identify the various digital marketing strategies SMEs can adopt, the benefits they stand to gain, and the potential direct and indirect effects on SME performance.

E-commerce is one of the powerful tools in the business environment today. During the COVID-19 pandemic, various transactions like purchasing and selling products and services over e-commerce platforms hiked enormously. At the same time, it posed challenges for businesses to meet consumers' increased demands and expectations. The UAE consumers are enjoying the latest trends in e-commerce, like augmented reality to enhance the reality of online shopping, artificial intelligence, voice search, on-site personalization, chatbots, mobile shopping, multiple payment options, headless, and API-driven e-commerce. This chapter examines the trends and challenges of e-commerce posed by COVID-19 in the UAE and strategies to win the online marketplace.

Chapter 13

The most successful companies are the one that know their customers very well and can anticipate their needs. Good customer profiles at the fingertips have businesses improve marketing campaigns, targeting feature launches and product roadmaps. In this study, exploratory data analysis was done on the shopping mall data, and customer segmentation was done using k-means clustering. Two different clusters were done based on age vs. spending score and annual income vs. spending score. Four optimum clusters were obtained for age and spending scores using the elbow graph method, and five optimum clusters were obtained for annual income and spending scores. Firstly, for clusters based on age and spending score, people with higher age groups have less spending scores. Secondly, clusters based on annual income and spending scores had high annual income and very low spending scores. Thus, the mall can offer these cluster customers to attract them, thereby increasing its profits.

Chapter 14

The coronavirus outbreak is the latest world tragedy that has affected all sectors of the economy. The government's preemptive efforts to safeguard public health include lockdown, confinement, limited movement order, and social distancing. While recognizing the importance of the national order in preventing the immense spread of the virus, the authors contend that there are certain undiscovered impacts of the COVID-19 movement block and the role of digitalization on small and medium enterprises in Kurunegala District. In summary, the impacts of the COVID-19 movement block on SMEs are classified by five themes. Moreover, for the role of digitalization, the researcher used three built-in themes. The research recommends suggestions for future research work, business development agencies, and entrepreneurs.

Foreword

Global e-commerce is important for government policymakers and for small-to-medium-sized-enterprises (SME) to understand. The first reason this topic – and the book – are important, is due to economic value. Global e-commerce transaction value reached approximately $15 trillion USD by the time of writing, according to data I analyzed from the U.S. International Trade Association (USITA, 2022). I forecasted this to increase by 8% to $16.5 trillion by the end of 2023 (based on data from USITA, 2022). To make this clearer, figure 1 illustrates the projected global e-commerce value by region (in billions) on the primary x-axis, with a secondary axis depicting the year-on-year (YOY) percent increase (dotted yellow line). The data were added to the bottom of the chart, by region for the last decade (2013-2022, with 2023 being projected using a non-smoothed unadjusted linear trend equation).

The second reason these e-commerce value trends are important for policymakers and SMEs is concerned with which region has the dominant market share and growth. In figure 1, the Asia region consistently dominated the e-commerce market, with 80%-81% of the value. For example, the proportion for Asia was $12.2 trillion in 2022, which is roughly 81% of the $15 trillion I cited earlier. In fact, most of the Asian e-commerce market is controlled by the People's Republic of China (PRC), with a much smaller contribution from other Asian countries such as Japan, South Korea, Vietnam, etc. The faint red dotted line in figure 1 surrounding the Asia series is an exponential trend I created with a 98% effect size. That means Asia's e-commerce transaction value is growing exponentially, while the other regions are generally flat in terms of growth. If the reader is from USA or Europe, this means your policy administration or SME strategy can likely research only 3% (for Europe) to 12% (for North America dominated by USA), of the e-commerce market share. If you are a policy maker or SME in one of the other global regions, the market may seem impenetrable. However, if you are a stakeholder in Asia, your next steps are to continue innovating technology and addressing cybersecurity constraints to deliver e-commerce to your market and smile all the way to the bank where you will likely see those values increase.

Figure 1. Mixed line chart of global e-commerce transaction value by region with year-on-year increase

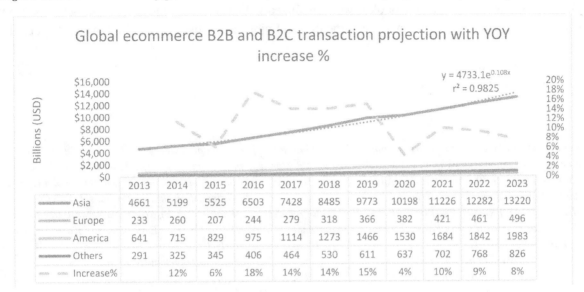

Global ecommerce B2B and B2C transaction projection with YOY increase %

$$y = 4733.1e^{0.108x}$$
$$r^2 = 0.9825$$

	2013	2014	2015	2016	2017	2018	2019	2020	2021	2022	2023
Asia	4661	5199	5525	6503	7428	8485	9773	10198	11226	12282	13220
Europe	233	260	207	244	279	318	366	382	421	461	496
America	641	715	829	975	1114	1273	1466	1530	1684	1842	1983
Others	291	325	345	406	464	530	611	637	702	768	826
Increase%		12%	6%	18%	14%	14%	15%	4%	10%	9%	8%

It does not matter which region your SME or planning administration agency are from you will have witnessed the drastic post-COVID-19 pandemic shift to online based transactions. The result of this post-pandemic e-commerce paradigm shift is a new breed of online software providers catering to SMEs with turn-key solutions. These solutions make it easy to transform a bricks-and-mortar style SME into a global e-commerce entrant. The reader will likely have noticed SME e-commerce solutions and partnerships being marketed by BigCommerce, Shopify, Wix, PrestaShop, and WooCommerce Blocks along with enhancements by market dominators PayPal and Apple Pay. These enhancements have made it easier for SMEs to get money from customers, using transfers or bitcoin.

These are fascinating topics addressed in much greater detail in this edited book. Most of the book contents address e-commerce strategies and theories for SME decision-makers and policymakers. There are chapters addressing SME digital transformation and e-commerce brand image development. Several chapters discuss ideas for developing sustainable e-commerce strategies. Although we are accustomed to studying e-commerce from an urban perspective, where there is a lot more value per capita, a few chapters investigate e-commerce concepts from a rural standpoint, which may be of interest to developing countries with less organized governance but widespread cellular adoption. Not surprisingly, some authors explore the supply chain dimension of e-commerce, along with its constraints and opportunities, particularly for developing countries. Consumer theories also make their way into the book, with several chapters tackling trust, market segmentation, and e-government issues in e-commerce. Interspersed within the literature reviews there are several interesting empirical case studies of e-commerce, which would be of interest to retail e-commerce policymakers and SME decision-makers in developing countries, particularly since the organizations serve as best practices from the Asian-dominated regions.

In conclusion, what makes this book a distinct mark above others is that it is an edited book, with chapters authored by authors around the world, and mostly not in the USA. This presents a refreshing non-USA global perspective of e-commerce. Additionally, many of the authors were from the European Union member countries, along with other authors from developing nations in Africa. This is a rare opportunity to read insights from such diverse constituencies. Finally, being an edited book, all chapters were double-blind peer reviews, which raises the bar for quality much beyond commercial books. I could also mention in closing that the book is well-organized with a subtle unstated theme progression from start to finish – see if you can understand the theme. Enjoy and I trust you will find the book valuable!

Kenneth David Strang
Independent Researcher, USA

Kenneth David Strang *is a research scientist and retired business/supply chain professor with 39+ years of experience and over 300 publications (http://kennethstrang.com). He has a doctorate in project management (operations research), an MBA (business strategy), BS (marketing), an AS (computer science), all with summa cum lade honors. Dr. Strang is a Certified Research Professional (IIPMR), a Fellow Life Management Institute with distinction (insurance/pensions, LOMA), a Project Management Professional (PMI), a Certified Supply Chain/Procurement Specialist (CS/CP), a Certified Network Administrator (Novel), and he is Certified for Research Ethics by the University of Miami. He is an emeritus Editor-in-Chief of a peer-reviewed journal, and an Associate Editor or reviewer on others. He has approximately 300 scholarly peer-reviewed publications. He received several citations, scholarships and honors including two Literati awards. He previously worked for IBM, Blue Cross, W3-Research, and several management consulting companies, while he taught at universities.*

REFERENCES

USITA. (2022). *ECommerce Sales & Size Forecast*. U.S. International Trade Association (USITA). https://www.trade.gov/ecommerce-sales-size-forecast

Preface

INTRODUCTION

People are increasingly inclined to shop online when traditional shopping becomes tricky or scary. In the first quarter of 2020, when the COVID-19 pandemic began to affect global markets, it became clear that it would test the resilience and performance of a rapidly growing e-commerce sector in every part of the globe. The entire world has witnessed the novel outburst of coronavirus and went into lockdown, forcing many businesses to shut down temporarily. Countries are gradually relaxing restrictions, but the future is still uncertain. Even companies reopening have rules enforcing social distancing, wearing masks, and limiting how many customers can enter a space at once. These limitations have forced the movements of world consumers and observed many difficulties in procuring all kinds of family requirements. These limitations, like government-imposed quarantines, social distancing, and fear of viruses, provide opportunities for the e-commerce business to thrive over the next few years. Consumers turn to digital options to bypass physical shopping environments, so the behavior change will undoubtedly influence longer-term buyer behavior. This book will help Small- and Medium-sized (SMEs) enterprises advance their e-commerce policies toward sustainability.

CHAPTER OVERVIEW

In Chapter 1, "Significance of Brand Image on Small- and Medium-Sized Enterprise (SME) Survival in Digital Competition," Esra Güven explains that the competition landscape is shifting because of the globalization of social media and the digitalization of society, and SMEs must adapt to this quick change. According to the author, SMEs can accomplish their objectives at a low cost if they use these digital platforms wisely and reflect their brand images. This chapter seeks to provide the necessary descriptions and explanations regarding the importance of a SME's brand image as well as the steps to take to develop a brand image in a sequential manner from widely distributed material to digital environments. The notions of brand, image, and brand image have all been described in this chapter. The types of brand image have also been covered in detail in the relevant topic. The chapter goes into great length about social media, its impact on brand image, and what can be done to develop a brand image in digital environments. Additionally, there are several case studies of brand image development activities from globally prosperous SMEs.

In Chapter 2, "Digital Transformation of Small and Medium Businesses," Aizhan Baimukhamedova and Malik Baimukhamedov discuss the purpose and significance of digital transformation in growing small and medium-sized organizations. The authors state that digitalization reshapes companies using computer technology so that all decisions are based on data. The primary goals of SMEs' digital transformation are outlined in this chapter. According to the authors, the Internet of Things, artificial intelligence, e-commerce, big data, cloud computing, blockchain, etc., are some of the technologies fueling digital transformation. This chapter lists some of the tasks involved in managing an organization in the era of digitalization: adapting the business processes of the company to cutting-edge digital technologies; maintaining a high level of expertise among company management and experts in the field of contemporary technologies and maintaining a high level of readiness for changes and challenges in the external environment. The authors consider e-commerce and the digital transformation of SMEs in the commercial, agricultural, and industrial realms.

In Chapter 3, "How a Sustainability Strategy Can Leverage E-Commerce," Albérico Travassos Rosário states that building sustainable business models has emerged as a cutting-edge component of corporate strategy over the past few decades. The idea has been applied to several economic sectors to achieve their goals, with e-commerce emerging as one of the most successful business models during the past ten years. According to the author, the significance of sustainability in e-commerce in all its forms cannot be emphasized enough. The author further states that numerous studies have been done on the subject, spanning various application areas. In this chapter, a thorough review of the bibliometric literature was conducted using the keywords "sustainability" along with the keywords "e-commerce," "Electronic Commerce," "E-commerce," "B2C E-commerce," and "Business, Management and Accounting" over the previous ten years in the SCOPUS indexing database (2012-2022). This chapter tries to comprehend how a sustainability approach can utilize e-commerce.

In Chapter 4, "The Propensity of E-Commerce Acceptance Among Unorganized Retail Small Medium Enterprises (SMEs)," Karthik Ram and Selvabaskar state that after China, India has one of the largest SME populations in the world. This benefits the Indian economy by creating a wide range of employment opportunities, innovating new self-sufficient technologies, and assisting export growth, socioeconomic growth, and rural development that supports nation-building. The authors explain that consumers are utilizing the power of digital technologies and e-commerce; now is the moment to assess the unorganized retailers' inclination to adopt business-to-business e-commerce. The authors explain that prior studies have examined the effects of e-commerce on consumers, organized retailers, and disorganized retailers. Additionally, some other research focused on analyzing unorganized retail SMEs' performance, rivalry, problems, and challenges. However, the authors posit that studies assessing the acceptability of e-commerce by independent retailers are scarce. This chapter considers the subtleties of unorganized retailers' tendency towards business-to-business e-commerce.

In Chapter 5, "Implementing E-Marketing in Small and Medium-Sized Enterprises for Enhanced Sustainability," Edna Mngusughun Denga points out that by switching from conventional to internet-based platforms, e-marketing has completely changed the way marketing is carried out. The author posits that e-marketing has dramatically changed how businesses communicate with clients. The chapter studied the organizational, technological, and environmental factors that may drive the adoption of e-marketing as well as models that can be used to enhance e-marketing to offer insights and direction for the growth and development of e-marketing among SMEs. A thorough examination of the literature in this chapter showed a significant positive correlation between sustainable marketing strategy and SME success, demonstrating that sustainability is greatly influenced by customer happiness, customer loyalty, and profitability.

In Chapter 6, "The Relevance of Supply Chain Preparedness on the Long-Term Sustainability of SMEs," Sefa Asortse and Edna Mngusughun Denga emphasize that greater volatility is becoming the new standard for modern supply chains because of the wide range of hazards and how frequently they can interrupt a supply chain. As a result, the authors state that resilience has become a crucial element of supply chain management. To strengthen supply chains' resilience, the authors advised that businesses boost their risk prevention and response measures. Through resilient supply chains, the authors encourage SMEs to foresee possible changes, respond to actual changes, and provide better value. Building supply chain resilience can help to decrease and overcome risk vulnerabilities by developing solutions that allow the supply chain to resume normal operations after an interruption. The chapter seeks to offer a thorough understanding of the effects of a critical aspect of supply chain resilience, supply chain readiness, which is intended to increase the sustainability of SMEs.

In Chapter 7, "Factors Hindering Small, Medium, and Micro Enterprise Business Growth in South Africa," Muhammad Ehsanul Hoque and Sfiso Nxele emphasize that Small, Medium, and Micro Enterprises (SMMEs) play a significant role in the growth of the GDP and the creation of new job opportunities. According to the authors, SMMEs in South Africa are given money for long-term success and employment generation. However, the contemporary SMMEs' contribution to the nation's GDP and job generation has decreased over time. This chapter's goal was to investigate the reasons preventing SMME business growth. The findings in this chapter identify some of the issues SMMEs, including a lack of funding, information, mentorship apart from incompetent management, inadequate assessment across numerous organizations, and access to funding. The authors recommend that the government and support organizations should provide significant attention to developing sector specific SMME assessment criteria instead of using a general approach to promote all business sectors.

In Chapter 8, "Trust in E-Commerce From the Cultural Perspective: A Systematic Literature Review," Neslişah Özdemir examines the research on e-commerce trust from a cultural viewpoint. This chapter adds to the body of knowledge in this area by analyzing the procedure for building trust in e-commerce and investigating the causes and effects of online trust from a cultural standpoint. In this chapter, 52 peer-reviewed publications on trust in e-commerce published in the Scopus database were systematically reviewed. The results show that there has been an increase over time in publications that cover e-commerce trust in various cultural contexts. These studies have used a variety of approaches, and they have examined e-commerce trust across a range of industries. The articles on online trust from a cultural perspective are divided into three groups: the influence of culture on online trust, its antecedents, and its effects.

In Chapter 9, "Impact of Technology on Business Continuity During COVID-19," Thirunesha Naidu and Muhammad Hoque list the numerous advancements in digital technology throughout the years that have transformed how we work, interact, and live. In business, such innovations have occurred predominantly at larger or newer organizations or e-commerce companies as resources are required to design, implement, and maintain bespoke digital technology solutions. Other commercially accessible alternatives have not been given preference over more conventional labor methods regarding integration into business processes. A business continuity strategy is created when a company needs to quickly recover to continue operating after a disruption like a pandemic. This chapter discusses potential business continuity planning initiatives that could take place during a pandemic, the kinds of digital technologies that firms utilize, and their effects on business continuity under such circumstances. Here are some suggestions for how businesses might survive and thrive in VUCA (volatility, uncertainty, complexity, and ambiguity).

In Chapter 10, "Electronic Government," Aizhan Baimukhamedova and Malik Baimukhamedov emphasize that electronic document management systems, state management automation systems, and other information and communication technologies are the foundation of e-government. Four types of "government models" are discussed in this chapter: the Russian model, the Asian model, the Continental European model, and the Anglo-American model. In this chapter, the authors describe the decree of the President of the Republic of Kazakhstan dated November 10, 2004, No 1471, "On state program of construction of e-government in the Republic of Kazakhstan for 2005-2007," that served as the foundation for the creation of the e-government portal. According to the authors, the following objectives are supported by government: fostering new modes of communication between agencies, enhancing the delivery of public services to individuals and businesses, fostering, and expanding citizen self-service capabilities, raising the level of technological literacy and competence among citizens, and enhancing the level of participation of all voters in national governance and management processes.

In Chapter 11, "Digital Marketing and the Sustainable Performance of Small and Medium Enterprises," Edna Mngusughun Denga and Sandip Rakshit explain that regardless of where SMEs operate, today's marketing innovation includes digital platforms, and they must deal with extremely unstable, competitive, and dynamic market conditions. According to the authors, companies cannot grow to be successful and competitive without using effective digital marketing methods. By leveraging digital tools, SMEs may successfully locate, engage, market, and sustain customer connections. In this chapter, the authors conduct a systematic review of the literature to determine the numerous digital marketing tactics SMEs can use, the advantages they stand to gain, and the potential direct and indirect consequences on SMEs' performance.

In Chapter 12, "Trends in E-Commerce During COVID-19: A Case of UAE," Rajasekhara Mouly Potluri and Sophia Johnson Thomas emphasize how effective e-commerce is as a tool in the current corporate environment. Various transactions, including as buying and selling goods and services on e-commerce platforms, increased significantly during the COVID pandemic. At the same time, it presented difficulties for companies to satisfy rising consumer demands and expectations. The authors state that consumers in the UAE are taking advantage of the newest e-commerce technologies, including augmented reality (AR), voice search, on-site personalization, chatbots, mobile shopping, numerous payment choices, and API-driven e-commerce. The tactics to succeed in the online market are examined in this book chapter, together with the trends and e-commerce issues COVID in the UAE has presented.

In Chapter 13, "Customer Segmentation of a Shopping Mall Users Using K-Means Clustering," Amit Kumar explains that the businesses that know their clients well and can foresee their demands are the most successful. The authors emphasize that with accurate consumer profiles at their fingertips, firms can focus feature launches and optimize product roadmaps and marketing campaigns. In this chapter, client segmentation was carried out utilizing k-means clustering and exploratory data analysis on the shopping mall data. Based on annual income vs. spending score and age vs. spending score, two separate clustering were performed. Using the elbow graph approach, four optimal clusters for age and expenditure scores were found, and five optimal clusters for yearly income and spending scores. First off, people in higher age groups had lower spending scores when grouped by age and expenditure score. Second, groups based on yearly income and spending scores had very low spending scores and high annual income scores. As per the findings in this chapter, the mall can provide these cluster customers with incentives to draw them in and boost its revenue.

In the book's final chapter, "Impact of COVID-19: Role of Digitalization on Small- and Medium-Sized Enterprises (SMEs) in Kurunegala District in Sri Lanka," Hasini Mekhala Rathnayake and Pratheesh

Pratheebha present the impact of digitalization on SMEs in the context of the pandemic in a case study in Sri Lanka. The authors state that the most recent global catastrophe impacting all economic sectors is the coronavirus pandemic. Lockdowns, incarceration, limited movement orders and social seclusion are a few of the proactive measures the government has taken to protect public health. The authors argue that there are some unrecognized effects of the COVID-19 mobility block and the influence of digitalization on small and medium firms in Kurunegala District while acknowledging the significance of the national order in avoiding the massive spread of the virus. In this chapter, five themes are used to group the effects of the COVID-19 Movement block on SMEs. Additionally, the authors employed three pre-existing themes to examine the role of digitalization. The authors recommend future research projects, business development organizations, and business owners in this chapter.

This book offers many benefits to academia spread in the world. Remarkably, the academia involved in research and teaching will receive confident inputs about the e-commerce situation during the pandemic and beyond. Furthermore, the book will highlight the proposed topic's influence of COVID-19 on consumer behavior in different parts of the world. The digital impact on sales of various products and services based on the changing trends of behavioral tendencies of consumers throughout the globe is emphasized in this book.

Rajasekhara Mouly Potluri
Al Ghurair University, UAE

Narasimha Rao Vajjhala
University of New York Tirana, Albania

Acknowledgment

I'm eternally grateful to my IGI Global Publishers and the team editorial board of the book, who made an extra effort to finish this book project. They are in constant touch with us in guiding us in this regard.

Although this period of my life was filled with many ups and downs, my time in the education industry was worth it. My time in higher education wouldn't have been possible without my family, Aruna (wife), Lohith (son), and Dr. Mouly (father). They helped and backed me up with their love, cooperation, and encouragement throughout my life.

A special thanks to all author contributors who were involved in sharp contact with the editorial team and strictly followed the deadlines of the entire project.

Rajasekhara Mouly Potluri

I want to thank my family members, particularly my mother, Mrs. Rajeswari Vajjhala, for her blessings and for instilling in me the virtues of perseverance and commitment.

A special note of thanks to my doctoral committee member, Professor Kenneth David Strang, for consistently motivating me to continue my research work and also for contributing a chapter to this book.

Narasimha Rao Vajjhala

Chapter 1
Significance of Brand Image on SME Survival in Digital Competition

Esra Güven

iD https://orcid.org/0000-0003-3233-9714

Celal Bayar University, Turkey

ABSTRACT

With the digitalization of the world and the spread of social media, competition conditions are also changing, and SMEs must keep up with this rapid transformation. SMEs that use these digital platforms correctly and reflect their brand images properly will achieve their goals at a minimal cost. This chapter aims to give required descriptions and explanations about the significance of the brand image of an SME as well as the things to do to build a brand image in a sequence from the widespread content to the digital environments. Brand, image, and brand image concepts have been explained, respectively. The related topic has also elaborated on the kinds of brand image. Social media and its effect on brand image and the things to do to build a brand image in digital environments have been discussed in detail in the chapter. There are also some brand image development activity examples from successful SMEs worldwide.

INTRODUCTION

Brand as a concept in the center of marketing is known to be a complex structure that hosts many different elements in itself. SMEs are in a great effort of developing strategies that will differentiate themselves from their rivals so that they can build their own brands as a face looking at the society and the consumers. At that point, they aim at analysing the consumer perceptions and creating favourable and striking images in the eyes of the consumers, because it is urgent for SMEs to have a positive brand images to be able to survive in today's competitive world. In this process, the attributes and the benefits as well as the consumer attitudes should be taken into consideration, as it wouldn't be impossible to understand

DOI: 10.4018/978-1-6684-5727-6.ch001

the consumer and create favourable images in the minds of consumers as long as the related factors effective in purchase preferences are handled unilaterally.

Throughout the history of marketing activities, marketers have always taken steps to build positive brand image in the eye of consumers so as to compete with the rival companies or brands. The advertising activities and promotion campaigns through TV, radio or other traditional methods have always aimed at coming to the fore in the preferences of consumers. In all this traditional process, a passive role of the consumer and the effort of the brands to give message actively have been regarded as the main characteristic of the consumer- brand communications.

The growth of digital marketing since the 1990s and 2000s has altered how companies and brands use technology for marketing. Digital marketing efforts are becoming more common and effective as more and more people use digital devices instead of going to physical stores and as digital platforms are integrated into marketing strategies and daily life (Desai, 2019). Together with the digital technologies surrounding everywhere, a great number of fundamental changes have been seen in every part of life. In this new world where internet is regarded as the most basic power to give direction to the life, traditional consumer profile has been replaced by digital consumer profile. Among too many alternatives, this new digital consumer profile prefers the brands which attract him or her the most, communicate in the best way, give fast and effective feedbacks, and for all, use the technology properly. Together with this digital transformation, the traditional passive consumers have become a completely active and self-confident ones.

Individuals have started to spend much of their time in social networking sites just after the introduction of social media platforms. The virtual environments such as Facebook, Instagram, YouTube, brand communities and fan groups and entertainment platforms have become indispensable platforms for leisure time activities. This great and extraordinary potential of social media and digital platforms has attracted the marketers and researchers in an unexpected manner. The digital environment has undergone changes. Traditional media has been rendered ineffectual and inefficient at introducing brands to consumers, due to the increased reliance of the customers on electronic media. The brands having been trying to affect the consumers bearing high costs have found opportunities to do marketing activities in much more inexpensive ways. We Are Social and HootSuite (2021) claim that the internet, which serves as the foundation for digital development (websites and social media), has touched more than half of the world's population (59.6%) and changed consumers' media consumption preferences. The saying "If a company cannot be located on Google, it does not exist" properly captures how modern consumers behave, and this tendency is in line with it (Suryani et al, 2021). It also highlights how important it is for businesses to use digital platforms, so that small and medium-sized businesses (SMEs) must keep up with technological changes in order to remain competitive (Taiminen and Karjaluoto, 2015).

It is often disregarded that there are some strategies for the SMEs about the move of the consumers into digital environments and the communication with them by joining the activities in digital platforms. The first thing to be seen in digital environments and create a difference there is that companies or brands should build a strong and consistent brand image in the minds of the consumers. While building this image, primarily the brand websites, social media platforms and other online environments should be analysed in detail. During this analysis, it should be known that the consumers are not the traditional ones any longer, and the contents created in these platforms should be handled carefully. Both in social media ads, viral videos and brand communities or consumer websites, the most important point is that the contents should be able to attract the consumers and make them listen to the given brand messages. It should also be known that advertising is not the only factor to affect the consumer purchase decision, and the new consumer profile is affected by many factors combined. Such kind of awareness will constitute the basis of a multi-dimensional brand image. The richness and abundance of data in this digital environment will help the SMEs and the brands reach the target consumer by the right messages in an accountable way.

To sum up, in this new digital age SMEs are in dire need of being aware of brand image concept first, and then they are supposed to know about the types of brand images to be able to position themselves in the right place in consumer minds. It must be taken into accunt in this process that the digital transformation of our age is not only an opportunity for SMEs but also a threat for the ones which cannot keep up with this transformation. As such, the main elements of this digital world to communicate with the consumers come to the fore for all SMEs. A good and effective website, internet ads and videos and all other social media platforms such as facebook, instagram, twitter or youtube should be adopted as the indispensable devices of this new digital age.

In this chapter, it is aimed to give required descriptions and explanations about the significance of brand image of a SME as well as the things to do to build a brand image in a sequence from the widespread content to the digital environments. When looked at the content in this context, it is seen that brand, image and brand image concepts have been explained, respectively. In accordance with the main theme of the chapter, the dimensions of brand images have been discussed from the point of views of various researchers. The kinds of brand image have also been elaborated following the related topic. After giving the required details and explanations about these given themes, the content of digital media and its content in terms of brand image concept. Social media, in particular, and its effect on brand image as well as the things to do to build a brand image in digital environments have been discussed in detail in the chapter. There are also some brand image development activity examples from successful SMEs across the world. This chapter about digital brand image will help the marketers, researchers and other shareholders see the differences between the brand image activities in the traditional and digital environments. In addition, the disambiguation of content of digital brand image concept having been discussed from the aspect of various researchers has been aimed in this chapter. SME owners and marketing managers are also thought to benefit from the content of the chapter.

BACKGROUND

The effects of brand image on brand image and consumer business is known as a subject to have been studied for many years (Hoffman, Al, at, 2021; Alrwashdeh et al., 2019; Bilgin,2018; Mohammed and Rashid, 2018). Building credibility and loyalty among current and potential customers requires a strong brand image (Thimothy, 2016). A brand must have fundamental principles that serve as guidelines for how the entire operation of the firm should be conducted. With the digitalization, the issue of brand image has started to be discussed in the context of digital platforms and studies have been started on the importance of brand image in terms of SMEs in the digital age (Juliana et al, 2021; Suryani et al, 2021; Ok and Bas, 2021). In many studies, many findings have been reached in different countries regarding the importance of brand image in terms of sustainability and survival of enterprises. In all these research, It is generally stated that customers with a favorable opinion of the brand have been found likely to make purchases, whereas those with a bad opinion may not be as likely to do so (Luong, Vo and Le, 2017).

Building the right brand image creates a higher awareness of the brand among consumers, which can lead to easier preferences among SME competitors (Ananda et al, 2018; Qalati et al, 2020). Effective use of websites in digital environments facilitates access to the consumer and effective positioning can be made in the consumer's mind (Wayne and Mogaji, 2020). Brand image building through social media platforms is also expressed as very effective methods in consumer preferences in many studies. In the studies conducted, especially the results of digital platforms such as Instagram and youtube, which the younger generation spends a lot of time on, are extremely effective environments for SME brand image studies, are very noticeable (Budiman, 2021; Hermanda, et al, 2019)

SMEs, BRAND AND BRAND IMAGE

Mall- and medium-sized businesses typically specialize in a specific constrained product range and use it to meet the needs and desires of a niche market. They are unable to compete by taking advantage of economies of scale, thus their prospects for competition lay in the creation of novel products or procedures. All of these point to the dilemma of developing new products and technology while under pressure to keep costs as low as possible. These characteristics encourage business owners to employ innovative and alternative marketing strategies, such as internet techniques, to get over resource limitations. Businesses that do not take advantage of digital marketing opportunities or implement the newest technologies are at a competitive disadvantage. These specific traits demonstrate the need for a distinctive examination of SMEs' competitiveness (Lanyi et al., 2021).

When consumers make their purchasing decisions, they use resources that we can call as past experiences, brand communications such as advertising or promotion, or environmental factors. In these decision-making processes, consumers remember the brand through the product they have experienced and can act more comfortably in their subsequent purchase decisions (Odabaşı and Oyman, 2013). As a result of this significance, brand managers, especially small and medium entreprises (SMEs) should concentrate on the perceptual position in which they want their brands to be perceived by consumers and be able to position their brands accordingly (Das et al., 2016). Because the expansion of the economy, development, and employment is widely acknowledged to depend on small and medium-sized businesses (SMEs). That's why the use of internet opportunities would give small and medium-sized businesses more competitive options.

It is seen that the connotations left by an entreprise in the consumer's mind through its products are not just the name of the brand. Thus, according to the American Marketing Association, brand aims to identify the products or services, to identify and to differentiate the products or services of competitors, used to differentiate the name, term, sign, symbol, design, shape, or a combination of all those (Odabaşı and Oyman, 2013). A brand is a collection of intellectual and emotional values that enable its stakeholders to have a distinctive and desired experience (De Chernatony (2002:116). It can be claimed that the consumers follow a hierarchical sequence in order to assess a brand. The consumer will present either rational or emotional values in this hierarchy. It will then move to the following level. Such moves signify a hierarchical structure in the brand knowledge of the consumer.

On the other hand, when looking at the concept and content of the image, it is known that this word comes from the word 'image', which is a French word by origin. Semantically, it means an image in Turkish language, and an image is defined by the Turkish Language Institution as 'an object and events that are perceived by the senses and appear in consciousness without the presence of a stimulus, or a dream' (TDK). Instead of looking at the concept of image from a single point of view, it should be known that this is a holistic concept that contains many different elements. It has a rich content ranging from verbal and nonverbal communications, appearance, thinking, listening, presentation and writing style, accumulations, charisma, self-confidence, self-esteem, potential and development (Harmancı, 2009). One of the most important reasons that make this phenomenon of image, which is so much in life, is its power in the life of individuals, institutions and small or large businesses. Because social life or business life has the potential to change according to the image they have (Sampson, 1995). This shows that the concept of image is a phenomenon that has the power to direct many moments of our lives, whether it is sometimes an attempt to find a job, sometimes an effort to convince, and sometimes just an attempt to make an impact on the other side, and many times to attract the potential customers of our SMEs.

Possessing a strong brand provides businesses an advantage over the competition and keeps potential clients from going to other businesses when making purchases. The related literature emphasizes the value of comprehending and controlling consumer perceptions and associations. Given its significance, SME managers should concentrate on the perception they want consumers to have of their brands and be able to position their brands to reflect this perception. They should be able to demonstrate holistic image management while doing so by taking into account the fact that a brand is made up of a variety of elements, including a name, logo, color, and packaging (Das et al., 2016:884)

The idea of "brand image" emerges when the concept of image is thought about in the context of consumption and branding. Technically, a brand image is a collection of ideas and impressions that people generate about a company when they hear or see its name. The content of this totality raises questions about how consumers interpret a specific brand, its implications, qualities, and how closely this mental formation resembles the company or brand (Aaker, 1991:87). The shared traits and benefits of products, people and connections, programs and ideals, and corporate reputation can all be evoked when creating a brand image. Any interaction a client has with a brand or company has the ability to influence these connections either directly or indirectly (Keller, 2000:118). A brand's image is evaluated holistically based on the total of functional, experimental, and symbolic benefits, varying in the strength and applicability (Salcuviene et al, 2007: 465). Increased brand sales and successful image management can arise from the total of pleasant connections and feelings that users develop after having positive brand experiences (Babayeva, 2020:34).

It should be noted that different academics highlight integrity in their definitions of the idea of brand image, which plays a significant role in how brands communicate with consumers and are perceived by them, despite the fact that they typically focus on different areas. Brand image is defined by Park et al. (1986: 135) as "a perceptual phenomenon impacted by the firm's communication activities, as well as the understanding that consumers get from the actions associated with the brand by the company as a whole." In another definition used by Dichter (1985:75), brand image is used to express a comprehensive view of of product, advertising, and more crucially, the consumer's propensity and the attitudinal screen he or she uses to make the observation.

The literature on brand image has a wide range of ideas and definitions. Some of these definitions that take the brand image's content into account are presented in Table 1. It can be seen in these definitions that while some academics view brand image as a term related to associations and perceptions, others consider it as a compilation of impressions with a comprehensive evaluation.

Table 1. Brand image definitions

Number	Researcher	Definition of Brand Image
1	Levy (1959), Martineau (1958)	Consumers typically perceive and associate non-functional and symbolic characteristics with brands in addition to functional benefits and traits.
2	Herzog (1963)	the sum of consumer perceptions from several sources that come together to form a brand personality.
3	Levy (1978)	The physical reality of the product and the beliefs, attitudes, and emotions connected to the product combine to form the brand image.
4	Ditcher (1985)	The brand image reflects all of the impressions that the product has left on consumers' minds in addition to describing the specific qualities of the product.
5	Park, Jaworski and MacInnis (1986)	It is the knowledge that customers gain through all of the company's connected actions.
6	Keller (1993)	It is the consumer's memories of the brand connotations that are reflected in their impressions of the brand.
7	Aaker (1996)	They are primarily a collection of associations that are usefully arranged.
8	VanAuken (2004)	A brand is the culmination of consumer impressions of the brand as well as knowledge and experience-based perceptions.
9	Salciuviene, Lee ve Yu (2007)	It is a holistic assessment based on the sum of functional, experimental and symbolic benefits that can vary in strength and suitability.
10	Bivainien (2007)	It is a versatile collection of both abstract and physical qualities that enables the customer to connect with the product. The brand image cannot be separated from communication because it is tied to customer attitudes and values as well as corporate attitudes and values.
11	Malone (2010)	Brand image is not everything. It is a single thing. Building relationships with customers and loyal customers is the way to win. It is also a WOM resource.
12	Popoli (2011)	Brand image is an important abstract resource that distinguishes between a brand and competition.
13	Ulusu (2014)	Brand image is the sum of consumer perceptions about brands and how consumers see the brand.

Source: Adapted from Das et al., 2016

Hogan (2005, cited by Wijaya: 2013:60) emphasizes that the brand image is an identity composed of all the information accessible about the product, service, or brand in his study in order to help us better grasp the content and dimensions of the brand image. There are two ways for consumers to get this information. Consumers first gain access to the knowledge that will shape a brand's perception in the context of their encounters with functional or emotional pleasure. The brand should strive to understand the consumer and match their demands by delivering the appropriate values in addition to working at its best to produce the best results possible. In exchange, the brand should be able to enhance relationships with customers. Second, customers can learn about a company's brand image through views that are intentionally established by the company at many touchpoints, including advertising, campaigns, public relations, logos, employee attitudes, and overall business performance. In this situation, consumers may associate various benefits with the atmosphere and perception that the brand provides to them. Both of these elements must be successfully handled and carried out in concert with one another in order to develop a brand image (Wijaya, 2013:60).

The associated literature presents several points of view when attempting to comprehend how different brand image dimensions are. Brand image dimensions are related to perceptions and associations since the majority of authors and academics think that the brand image dimension is a collection of perceptions and associations (Das et al., 2016:884). In the creation of a brand strategy, these brand associations are crucial. A consumer's brand association is their particular opinion of a company, whether it is actual or made up (Tiwari, 2010:423). Associations with a brand are broken down into distinct categories. The categories by Hankinson (2009) show numerous brand image models. The most popular models classify these relationships into two groups;

1.   Functional associations that reveal the specific properties of the product
2.   Symbolic or emotional associations that point to a product's intangible qualities

The specific traits of a brand can be expressed personally in the product and extend to diverse areas like packaging and warranty. These traits help to create consumer impressions of the brand's solid nature, which in turn helps to build a brand. In other words, specific traits show the distinction between levels of qualification that are seen as subjectively and those that are measured objectively. Brand associations that are unrelated to the specific features of the product are examples of abstract brand qualities. In this perspective, it is possible to assess the mascot's image that Marlboro Man conveys to consumers through Marlboro ads (Myers, 2003:42).

Different classifications and denominations based on various views are seen in the literature of brand image dimensions. It is noteworthy that when analyzing the aspects of the brand image, 'perceptions' and 'associations' come to the fore. Other scholars add experience as a third category in addition to perceptions and association. Associations are elements that trigger an internal demand or satisfaction for diversity and are related to consumer judgments when consuming a good or service. Positive WOM communications can result in benefits like an increase in purchase or customer retention when these viewpoints are applied by marketers. In circumstances where consumers will choose a brand based on its stronger brand image, there are no notable differences between products from other brands and their prices aside from these advantages (Das et al., 2016:872).

When discussing the elements of the brand image, Plummer (1985:28) highlights the personality and character of the brand and notes that the brand can be characterized by personality definitions such as young, colorful, or kind. These personality traits are categorized by Aaker (1991) into five categories: competence, sincerity, excitement, intellectuality, and solidity. In this regard, Chang et al. (2001:96) note out that if the brand personality is compatible with the consumer's self-image, the desired feelings toward the brand image can be delivered. In the perspective of customers, especially those with hedonistic attitudes and whose symbolic values shine out in their consumption, such harmony will be able to result in a successful brand image (Wijaya, 2013: 61). From this vantage point, it is possible to assert that brand identity and consumer-emphasized values are intimately tied to the phenomenon of brand image.

THE TYPES OF BRAND IMAGE

Three different categories of brands and brand images are mentioned by Doyle (2009:232);

1.   Qualified Brands and Qualified Brand Image

The brand image of qualified brands inspires consumer trust in the product's functional qualities. Consumers choose companies that have a track record of quality in today's markets since it is difficult for them to compare identical products and brands objectively when there are so many options. Beliefs about the merits of the brand are expressed by the safety of Volvo, the lowest price feature of Wall Mart, or the fact that Starbucks is the undisputed expert on coffee.

2. Passionate Brand Images and Passion Brands

These brand graphics are renowned for presenting a broad impression of the types of consumers who utilize the product. More than the commodity, this graphic conveys signals about a desired lifestyle. The fundamental tenet is that using such brands is correlated with celebrity or money. Such brand images respond to needs like prestige or awareness more than necessities or utility, as demonstrated by the rich professional image established by Rolex watches.

3. Experiential Brand Image and Experience Brands

An experience brand is renowned for displaying a certain connotation or emotional image. A set of concepts that promote uniqueness, personal growth, and vitality are expressed by brands that have been able to establish this kind of image. Nike's "just do it" mentality, Google's "don't be evil" emphasis on all of its endeavors, and Coca-strong Cola's focus on young people sharing their experiences are examples of brands with brand images that can be discussed in this light.

THE BRAND IMAGE IN DIGITAL WORLD AND SMEs

In order for a SME to developed, strengthen, and preserve its image in a market order where brands compete with their images, proper actions should be made promptly without falling behind the changing world. It has also been vital to adopt strategic actions in accordance with significant changes in the marketing world as a result of a variety of inventions that have entered social life throughout the history of marketing, which can be traced back to the dawn of humanity.

The advancement of technology and the widespread use of the Internet have, like all previous advances and changes, led to a diversification of marketing approaches, brand analyses, and brand image-related tools and strategies. Consumers have been forced to make an uncommon change in fundamental marketing principles, such as brand selection and purchase decisions, as a result of digitalization and the ensuing social media platforms. New dimensions of brands have started to emerge in today's digital environment, where new technologies are rapidly infiltrating our lives. These ideas, which can take on various forms like digital branding, digital brand identity, or digital brand image, are seen as strategic components for businesses to exist in the digital environment (Filkovskaia, 2017:11) Brands and businesses such as SMEs look to the digital platforms as constant instruments when determining their image in the eyes of consumers in this new environment, where the brand has little chance of surviving with a marketing strategy that is isolated from the digital world.

Brands can build strong communication with existing or future customers in digital platforms. Many research show that social media platforms where users generate content in digital environments are important for influencing consumer behavior as well as listening to and understanding them (Hartman et al., 2021). As such, the enterprises especially SMEs trying to compete with large corporations and wellknown brands need to use the digital platforms effectively. In today's competitive world, brand communications occur in the digital environment. While the methods used is the traditional, the content of digital media for the development and popularization of the domain are more widely used. Therefore, it can be said that traditional brand strategies and theories also remain valid in the planning and evaluation of communication activities that take place in digital environments (Koçak et al., 2020).

Digital marketing, or web-based marketing, mentioned above offers significant opportunity for businesses and brands to improve their brand perception. Particularly, social media platforms where users may publish material enable businesses to build strong relationships with current or potential customers (Islam, 2020:29). The research undertaken highlight the significance of digital settings where users can create content, both in terms of influencing consumer behavior and in terms of hearing and comprehending them (Hartman et al., 2021:6). Taking actions that can distinguish the SMEs in the eyes of consumers is considered as a must in this new digital world, which appears to be an integral component of brands and enterprises. Along with having the correct price and a quality product, one of the key requirements for achieving this differentiation is making sure that customers can interact with the SMEs swiftly and effortlessly. These speed and convenience aspects, which are among the major benefits of digitization, must be taken into account as crucial criteria for assessing the position and reputation of the brand in the eyes of the customer.

Keller (2013:236) identifies three brand image-building platforms related to digital marketing communications that brands and organizations should employ in building a brand image in digital age.

1. Web sites
2. Online advertising and videos
3. Social media

1. Websites

A website is a company's public relations tool that enables it to inform, market, and sell its goods and services (Kotler and Armstromg, 2007). In order for this to happen, one of the first stages for businesses using digital marketing strategies should be the design of an appealing website consistent with their goals and interests, develops interaction and captures users' attention while, above all, it should be useful (Alcaid et al, 2013). Utilizing websites has also been seen as a way to gain a competitive edge in a variety of activities (Mohammadi and Abrizah, 2013). Websites have all the features of traditional media advertising. it is the fastest growing area in terms of marketing activities of enterprises in a virtual environment in terms of providing a suitable environment (Dogan, 2002:131).

With the personalization tools used in websites, it is possible to provide personalized suggestions according to the visitor's behavior. It should be remembered that for the personalization that will be done in these media, all the behaviors that the visitor has done on the site should be stored and these behaviors should be analyzed. With the personalization tools, this analysis and suggestions can be done automatically or manually by the website administrator. With a real-time product recommendation, in cases where there is no information about the visitor, the products / contents that are most visited / viewed by other visitors are recommended at that time. In this way, suggestions are offered according to the behavior of the general audience of visitors on the site. Visitors who visit the Site for the first time and do not have any information about it can also be shown the most sold /read products /content. In such cases, since it is not known which category the visitor is related to, the most sold products are shown during the relevant period and the visitor is directed to the sale while determining the interests of the visitors. If a new product is added to any of the categories, a product proposal is made to visitors in the areas designated on the site. The fact that the new products are relevant to the categories that visitors are interested in may result in a sale of the visit. Displaying discounted products on the main page or in different areas designated on the site is another way that can attract visitors. Visitors who intend to purchase, but do not have enough budget, can be caught in this part.

2. Internet Ads and Videos

For brands and SMEs, there are numerous potential benefits of internet advertising. To begin with, online commercials are easier to track than traditional ads, and their influence can be seen more effectively than all other means. Furthermore, it offers the benefit of being able to reach the target demographic and directly appeal to potential buyers due to the ability to advertise based on certain criteria. Traditional advertising can also reach consumers faster using online and video advertising, which is not limited by time, space, or occasionally legal constraints (Jian and Yazdanifard, 2015). The crucial element to remember here is that advertising and video content may both lead customers to click and pique their curiosity. It is critical that the viral videos prepared here be thoroughly reviewed as well (Miller, 2010).

3. Social Media

Prior to the development of social media and social networks, mass communication platforms like TV and radio allowed brands to "speak to consumers" rather than listening to them, however social media has brought about a revolutionary change in the communication landscape. Consumers have now begun to interact with brands and talk about them as a result of this shift, and they have also selected a new era for the purpose's content, timing, and channel (Mangold and Faulds, 2009). While marketing with traditional media such as newspapers and television is about conveying a message, social media marketing is about talking to and relating to large audiences. In the past, marketing was a one-dimensional process, while today's marketing is expressed as a two-way process between the brand and its audience. Social media marketing is not just about giving a message and saying it. Rather, it is about taking those ideas and perceptions and exchanging them (Drury, 2008). Social media's viral nature can offer crucial chances for SME managers to connect with and guide customers who are planned to be captured by the brand image. The crucial thing to remember is that brand damage from improper actions in these settings, where the client has complete authority, can be much more severe than brand harm from conventional channels (Killian and Mcmanus, 2015:548).

Rowles de (2014:3) 21 argues that in the twenty-first century, the concept of the brand itself has evolved, and that social media fact now allows for two-way contact between the brand and the consumer in the modern day. In this context, it is made clear that brand management strategies that specifically target digital media and technology make a strategic contribution to the brand image. To do this, SMEs and brands should comprehend the distinctive digital traits and methodologies and deploy marketing communications in this context rather than sticking to traditional advertising concepts. Because consumer perceptions on online consumer comment platforms or social media interactions that might take place in online environments can have a significant impact on a SME's overall image.

Today, the vast majority of the world's population is inextricably linked to social media networks and is a prospective customer of any brand on one or more of these platforms. In brand communications, social media has become increasingly significant. It allows customers to share articles, photographs, music, and videos online and provides a unique marketing opportunity in this environment due to the breadth of the options it provides. Today, social media platforms such as Facebook, Twitter, YouTube, and Instagram provide a platform used by millions of people such as (Keller, 2013:238) who are aware of this wealth by creating a profile about your products, brands, and businesses on digital platforms to establish communication and share it (Islam, 2020:9).

Brands are actively attempting to take part in social media initiatives that enable them to connect with target audiences who identify with their themes. Utilizing material that can be interesting to users or fulfill their wants is important in order to do so in order to reach new consumers in this manner. It should be mentioned that brands and companies urge that their communications on various social media platforms contain the appropriate information. Visual appearance is also a very crucial and successful aspect in these communications in order to establish and maintain a strong brand image. Perkins (2014) claims that using colors, for example, consistently throughout social media platforms will help to ensure that customers are familiar with the brand. In order to increase brand awareness, the image in the consumer's head will be strengthened through visual consistency.

SMEs that want to achieve success on social media must have realistic expectations. After joining a social network and doing some advertising, they should not be in high income expectations. SMEs should always aim to get better on social networks. They should also aim to have a better following, not too much of a following. SMEs do not have as much budget and personnel power as large enterprises. For this reason, they should be fast, personal, flexible and effective in social media marketing. They should create strong, sincere relationships with their followers and be able to turn this into a business opportunity when the time comes. SMEs that handle most of the jobs within themselves should analyze this job with their in-house staff without getting outside services in social media marketing (Mestçi, 2013: 63).

Figure 1. SMEs and social media existence
Source: Ndiege (2019)

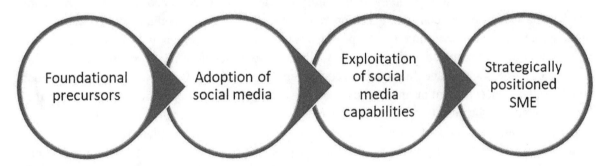

While trying to draw attention to social media use in converting an ordinary SME into the strategically positioned SME, while at the same time creating a strong brand image, Ndiege (2019) mentions a four step model as seen in figure 1. As seen in this figure, a SME needs some foundational precursors which refer to the readiness for and effective social media appearence such as organisational compatibility or infrastructure of the company. In the second step the SME needs to adopt and internalize the use of social media platforms in an agreement with all shareholders. In the third step, the right and effective use of social platforms are required. To be able to achieve this effective use, professionals and experts should be hired and employed. The management of the SME should be able to assess the outcomes in this process, and take the necessary steps to make up for the possible risks. In that way, a strategically located SME can be created and have a great advantage over the rival companies, and thus a strong digital brand image can be achieved.

SMEs or brands can reach new customers, uphold their brand image, and strengthen their presence in these environments as social media usage rises. To be able to observe the fine line between being able to forge deeper connections with the consumer, businesses must strengthen their presence in these environments. Brands may reach a larger audience and broaden their markets by using social media platforms. Once more, in these settings, they can benefit from the ability of their current customers to influence other consumers through word-of-mouth promotion. You can save money, time, or effort by using these new digital platforms, which is another benefit. Visual content can also be used to promote user interest in social media (Perkins, 2014:2). Pozinin (2014:1) asserts that messages with videos or images are shared substantially more frequently than ones devoid of any images. From this vantage point, businesses will benefit from a well-planned visual brand strategy for the sake of their brand image in social media contexts. The steps taken on these digital platforms should be carefully considered in order to accomplish this, and it should be remembered that doing so has the potential to improve the brand's value and reputation (Islam, 2020:9).

Failures that businesses have had in their first forays into social media might become a nightmare for them, deterring them from taking further moves. It should be noted, however, that customers increasingly live in a world that is split between the actual and digital worlds. As a result, brands must be stable and unable to abandon their marketing and communication efforts in social media settings. They will, nevertheless, be able to appeal to today's alternative-seeking consumers in this way (Laman and Topçu, 2019:11).

In order for a SME to create and develop a brand image in digital environments, Dayal (2000:78) states that design is an important step and mentions some design tools such as customization or personalization tools, cooperation tools, facilitating tools, self-service tools, self-design tools and dynamic pricing tools.

Customization tools can provide the opportunity to offer variations in accordance with the characteristics and wishes of the consumer, both on web pages and on social media or digital applications. Applications that enable consumers to be personally involved in the system and to cooperate with the enterprise in the communication that an SME will provide with the consumer are also an element that contributes to the brand image. In particular, consumers' support for SME's advertising efforts through WOM, friend advice, or viral means can be cited as an example of this cooperation. The tools that make it easier to buy are the ones that allow consumers to buy as quickly and easily as possible. In this context, the companies in Turkey trendyol.com, getir.com or yemek sepeti.com platforms can be shown as businesses that offer the consumer the opportunity to place the fastest and most effective orders. Again, other applications that allow consumers to design their own products or offer the opportunity to offer their own prices as in e-bay will strengthen the brand image of SME in the eyes of consumers, as well as provide an important competitive advantage. All these tools require a well-established social media appearance, for these platforms enable SMEs to act in a large diversity of communication ways to reach the customers, that's why an effective use of these platforms at the right time and then in the right place is required.

There are many SMEs trying to create and empower their brand image, thus catching a competition advantage over their competitors. Taking a glance at some of these SMEs and their stories in building a digital brand image in digital world will be helpful about startegical plannings of SMEs all around the world.

FRENZ HOTEL

Frenz Hotel needed to develop brand awareness in order to create a positive brand image. founded in 2010, this Kuala Lumpur hotel consists of 86 boutique-style rooms and suites and aims to combine elegance, modern technology and luxury. Acting on the motto 'Where guests are friends', this hotel is aimed not only at local customers with medium and high incomes, but also at customers who need it for a trip or a trip. Although Frenz Hotel has won many awards, such as Tripadvisor's 2012 Travelers' Choice, it has been noticed that this hotel has low customer awareness. For this purpose, the hotel has taken an important step to communicate with customers and fan groups by opening a profile on Facebook first and to increase brand awareness. In addition to social networks, the hotel administration has started advertising transit with local taxis, and the slogan "Stay with Frenz" has been implemented in these ads. The impressive visuals used in this advertisement also made a significant contribution to the awareness and image of the hotel. After these steps, which combine both digital media and traditional methods, Frenz has managed to increase hotel revenue by 15 percent within a year, and currently customers who want to stay at the hotel must make a reservation at least a week in advance to find a place.

MAES BEER

Despite being the second most popular beer in Belgium, Maes Beer was being outsold by the market leader four to one. They decided to employ creative people to develop a creative campaign on facebook to capture the market. They made the decision to contact their family, but not their actual family in order to get the help they needed. Given that 'Maes' is the third most popular last name in Belgium, they made the decision to attract every Mae there by offering them a free barrel of beer. All the residents of Maes were informed publicly that they would receive free beer with a little catch which had to be shared. A personalized invitation with a code to access their free barrel on Facebook was also sent to each Maes in Belgium. They had to organize an event at a location and invite twenty of their friends via Facebook. The initiative quickly gained popularity, and some people even changed their last name on their Facebook profile to qualify for free beer. Over 7,000 people changed their Facebook names to Maes at the conclusion of the campaign. In just six weeks, the SME's Facebook app attracted over 500,000 users, and in just one day, the brand added 75,000 new Facebook likes. One of each twenty Belgians visited the website of the brand and the amount of fans tripled in just one day. This popularity on social media provided Maes Beer with thousands of new costumers and thus a high familiarity in the country and the world.

CONCLUSION AND RECOMMENDATIONS

The new consumer profile of the digital world has now transformed from the role of a passive buyer into the identity of an active participant. SMEs, whose survival depends on attracting the attention of consumers and influencing them, they need to create an effective brand and be able to present this brand to the consumer with an influential image. The use of digital technologies, employee digital literacy, and digital transformation plans can all contribute to digital transformation, which in turn can enhance SMEs' performance. The primary element influencing this performance has been identified as the digital transformation plan. As Rogers (2016) stated in his research, 'digital transformation is not primarily a technology, but a strategy'. In order to achieve a competitive advantage in this respect, SMEs must be able to understand the concept of brand image correctly and take strategic steps in this regard. Nowadays, it seems extremely difficult for companies that do not have a existence on digital platforms to attract the attention of consumers. On the other hand, it is clear that businesses that can exist with an effective brand image on digital platforms such as social media can also be much more effective in reaching consumers. Proceeding from this, enterprises should first analyze the sector and its needs correctly and satisfy the consumer with a brand image that can meet these needs. In addition to the fact that the created brand image should be permanent and compatible with the products and services of the brand, it is necessary to be able to interact with the consumer with personalized digital applications that are appropriate for the target consumers. Social media platforms, websites, games and digital advertising should also be considered as unique platforms for businesses to reach their target audience. At this point, the projects carried out by Frenz Hotel and Maes Beers should be considered as motivating examples for all SMEs, and the digital world should be closely followed by SMEs to create similar opportunities.

REFERENCES

Aaker, D. A. (1991). *Managing Brand Equity*. Free Press.

Aaker, D. A. (1996). *Building strong brands*. Free Press.

Alcaide, J.C., Bernués, S., Díaz-Aroca, E., Espinosa, R., Muñiz, R., Smith, C. (2013). Marketing y Pymes. *Las principales claves de marketing en la pequeña y mediana empresa*.

Ali Qalati, S., Li, W., Ahmed, N., Ali Mirani, M., & Khan, A. (2020). Examining the factors affecting SME performance: The mediating role of social media adoption. *Sustainability*, *13*(1), 75. doi:10.3390u13010075

Ananda, A. S., Hernández-García, Á., & Lamberti, L. (2018). *SME fashion brands and social media marketing: From strategies to actions*. Academic Press.

Babayeva, N. 2020. *Perception of simplicity in brand image design by different generations* [Master Thesis]. Bahçeşehir Üniversitesi.

Bilgin, Y. (2018). The effect of social media marketing activities on brand awareness, brand image and brand loyalty. *Business & Management Studies: An International Journal*, *6*(1), 128-148.

Bivainien, L. (2007). Brand image conceptualization: The role of marketing communication. *Economics and Management*, *12*, 304–310.

Budiman, S. (2021). The effect of social media on brand image and brand loyalty in generation Y. *The Journal of Asian Finance. Economics and Business*, *8*(3), 1339–1347.

Chang, K. S., Park, J. Y., & Choi, I. H. (2001). The Influence of Self-Congruity Between Brand Personality and Self-Image on Attitude Toward Brand. *Korean Journal of Marketing*, *3*(2), 92–114.

Das, J. K., Prakash, O., & Khattri, V. (2016). Brand image mapping: A study on bathing soaps. *Global Business Review*, *17*(4), 870–885. doi:10.1177/0972150916645683

Dayal, S., Landesberg, H., & Zeisser, M. (2000). Building digital brands. *The McKinsey Quarterly*, (2), 42.

De Chernatony, L. (2002). Would a brand smell any sweeter by a corporate name? *Corporate Reputation Review*, *5*(2), 114–132. doi:10.1057/palgrave.crr.1540169

Dichter, E. (1985). What's in an image. *Journal of Consumer Marketing*, *2*(1), 75–81. doi:10.1108/eb038824

Dogan, K. (2002). *Modeling the impact of internet technology on marketing*. University of Florida.

Doyle, P. (2009). *Value-based marketing: Marketing strategies for corporate growth and shareholder value*. John Wiley & Sons.

Filkovskaia, J. (2017). *Influence of Visuals in Digital Brand Identity*. PIIK.

Hankinson, G., & Cowking, P. (1993). *Branding in action: Cases and strategies for profitable brand management*. McGraw-Hill.

Harmancı, M. (2009). *İş'te İmaj Faktörü*. Nesil Yayınları.

Hartmann, J., Heitmann, M., Schamp, C., & Netzer, O. (2021). *The power of brand selfies in consumer-generated brand imagery*. Columbia Business School Research Paper.

Hermanda, A., Sumarwan, U., & Tinaprillia, N. (2019). The effect of social media influencer on brand image, self-concept, and purchase intention. *Journal of Consumer Sciences*, *4*(2), 76–89. doi:10.29244/jcs.4.2.76-89

Herzog, H. (1963). Behavioral science concepts for analyzing the consumer. *Marketing and the Behavioral Sciences*, 76-86.

Hofmann, J., Schnittka, O., Johnen, M., & Kottemann, P. (2021). Talent or popularity: What drives market value and brand image for human brands? *Journal of Business Research*, *124*, 748–758. doi:10.1016/j.jbusres.2019.03.045

Hogan, S. (2005). Employees and Image: Bringing Brand Image to Life. In *The 2nd Annual Strategic Public Relations Conference*. Chicago: Lippincot Mercer.

Islam, M. (2020). *Digital Brand Management: Impact of Social Media Marketing on Brand Image*. Academic Press.

Jian, L. Z., & Yazdanifard, R. (2015). Which modern trend advertising methods are more effective in reaching certain outcome? A review on internet ads, mobile app ads, video ads, stealth ads and outdoor digital ads. *International Journal of Management*.

Juliana, J., Djakasaputra, A., Pramono, R., & Hulu, E. (2021). Brand Image, Perceived Quality, Ease Of Use, Trust, Price, Service Quality On Customer Satisfaction And Purchase Intention Of Blibli Website With Digital Technology As Dummy Variable. In *The Use Of Reviews*. Journal Of Critical Reviews.

Keller, K. L. (1993). Conceptualizing, measuring, and managing customer-based brand equity. *Journal of Marketing*, *57*(1), 1–22. doi:10.1177/002224299305700101

Keller, K. L. (2000). The brand report card. *Harvard Business Review*, *78*, 147–157.

Keller, K. L., Parameswaran, M. G., & Jacob, I. (2013). *Strategic brand management: Building, measuring, and managing brand equity.* Pearson Education India.

Killian, G., & McManus, K. (2015). A marketing communications approach for the digital era: Managerial guidelines for social media integration. *Business Horizons, 58*(5), 539–549. doi:10.1016/j.bushor.2015.05.006

Koçak, S., Varol, M. Ç., & Varol, E. (2020). Dijital Ortamda Marka İmaj Transferi ve İtibar Göstergeleri: Rolex-Roger Federer Örneği. *Uluslararası Kültürel ve Sosyal Araştırmalar Dergisi, 6*(2), 597–625.

Kotler, P., & Armstrong, G. (2007). *Marketing. Versión para Latinoamérica. Pearson Educación.* Atlacomulco.

Laman, İ., & Topçu, Ö. (2019). Sosyal Medyayla Birlikte Markanın Dijitalleşmesi. *Yeni Medya Elektronik Dergisi, 3*(1), 10–21. doi:10.17932/IAU.EJNM.25480200.2019.1/1.10-21

Lányi, B., Hornyák, M., & Kruzslicz, F. (2021). The effect of online activity on SMEs' competitiveness. *Competitiveness Review, 31*(3), 477–496. doi:10.1108/CR-01-2020-0022

Levy, S. J. (1959). Symbols for sale. *Harvard Business Review, 37*(July/August), 117–124.

Levy, S. J. (1978). *Marketplace behavior-its meaning for management.* Amacom.

Malone, T, (2010). *Branding in 2010, JCK.* Reed Business Information, a division of Reed Elsevier, Inc. Retrieved from https://www.jckonline.com/blogs/memo-to-merchandisers/2010/01/22/what-destination-location

Mangold, W. G., & Faulds, D. J. (2009). Social media: The new hybrid element of the promotion mix. *Business Horizons, 52*(4), 357–365. doi:10.1016/j.bushor.2009.03.002

Martineau, P. (1958). Sharper focus for the corporate image. *Harvard Business Review, 36*(6), 49–58.

Miller, C. C. (2010). YouTube ads turn videos into revenue. *New York Times,* 2.

Mohammed, A., & Rashid, B. (2018). A conceptual model of corporate social responsibility dimensions, brand image, and customer satisfaction in Malaysian hotel industry. *Kasetsart Journal of Social Sciences, 39*(2), 358–364. doi:10.1016/j.kjss.2018.04.001

Myers, C. A. (2003). Managing brand equity: A look at the impact of attributes. *Journal of Product and Brand Management, 12*(1), 39–51. doi:10.1108/10610420310463126

Odabaşı, Y., & Oyman, M. (2013). *Pazarlama İletişimi Yönetimi.* Mediacat Yayınları.

Ok, Ş., & Baş, M. (2021). Relationship Between Social Media Performance and Brand Image in Digital Branding Proces: Netflix Turkey. *İşletme Araştırmaları Dergisi, 13*(4), 3858-3872.

Park, C. W., Jaworski, B. J., & MacInnis, D. J. (1986). Strategic brand concept-image management. *Journal of Marketing, 50*(4), 135–145. doi:10.1177/002224298605000401

Perkins, M. (2014). *How to Develop a Strong Visual Brand on Social Media.* Available at: http://blog.hub-spot.com/marketing/strong-brand-voice-social-media

Plummer, J. T. (1985). How personality makes a difference. *Journal of Advertising Research*, *24*(6), 27–31.

Popoli, P. (2011). Linking CSR strategy and brand image: Different approaches in local and global markets. *Marketing Theory*, *11*(4), 419–433. doi:10.1177/1470593111418795

Pozin, I. (2014). Small Business Expert: Answers To Your Five Biggest Social Media Branding Questions. *Forbes*. Available at: https://www.forbes.com/sites/ilyapozin/2014/11/07/small-business-expert-an-swers-to-your-five-biggest-social-media-branding-questions/

Rogers, D. (2016). *The Digital Transformation Playbook: Rethink Your Business for the Digital Age*. Columbia University Press. doi:10.7312/roge17544

Rowles, D. (2014). *Digital branding: A complete step-by-step guide to strategy, tactics and measurement*. Kogan Page Publishers.

Salciuviene, L., Lee, K., & Yu, C. C. (2007). *The impact of brand image dimensions on brand preference*. Economics & Management.

Sampson, E. (1995). *İmaj Faktörü*. Rota Yayıncılık.

Suryani, T., Fauzi, A. A., & Nurhadi, M. (2021). Enhancing brand image in the digital era: Evidence from small and medium-sized enterprises (SMEs) in Indonesia. Gadjah Mada. *International Journal of Business*, *23*(3), 314–340.

Taiminen, H. M., & Karjaluoto, H. (2015). The usage of digital marketing channels in SMEs. *Journal of Small Business and Enterprise Development*. https://sozluk.gov.tr/

Thimothy, S. (2016). *Haettu 2017 osoitteesta Why Brand Image Matters More Than You Think*. https://www.forbes.com/sites/forbesagencycouncil/2016/10/31/why-brandimage- matters-more-than-you-think/#1d931feb10b8

Tiwari, M. K. (2010). Separation of brand equity and brand value. *Global Business Review*, *11*(3), 421–434. doi:10.1177/097215091001100307

Ulusu, Y. (2014). Effect of brand image on brand trust. *Journal of Yasar University*, *24*(6), 3932–3950.

Van Auken, H. (2004). The use of bootstrap financing among small technology-based firms. *Journal of Developmental Entrepreneurship*, *9*(2), 145.

Wayne, T., & Mogaji, E. (2020). *Academic branding and positioning through university's website profile*. Academic Press.

ADDITIONAL READING

Bilgin, Y. (2018). The effect of social media marketing activities on brand awareness, brand image and brand loyalty. *Business & Management Studies: An International Journal, 6*(1), 128-148.

Budiman, S. (2021). The effect of social media on brand image and brand loyalty in generation Y. *The Journal of Asian Finance. Economics and Business*, *8*(3), 1339–1347.

Juliana, J., Djakasaputra, A., Pramono, R., & Hulu, E. (2021). Brand Image, Perceived Quality, Ease Of Use, Trust, Price, Service Quality On Customer Satisfaction And Purchase Intention Of Blibli Website With Digital Technology As Dummy Variable. In *The Use Of Eviews*. Journal Of Critical Reviews.

Mohammed, A., & Rashid, B. (2018). A conceptual model of corporate social responsibility dimensions, brand image, and customer satisfaction in Malaysian hotel industry. *Kasetsart Journal of Social Sciences*, *39*(2), 358–364. doi:10.1016/j.kjss.2018.04.001

Suryani, T., Fauzi, A. A., & Nurhadi, M. (2021). Enhancing brand image in the digital era: Evidence from small and medium-sized enterprises (SMEs) in Indonesia. *Gadjah Mada International Journal of Business*, *23*(3), 314–340. doi:10.22146/gamaijb.51886

Taiminen, H. M., & Karjaluoto, H. (2015). The usage of digital marketing channels in SMEs. *Journal of Small Business and Enterprise Development*, *22*(4), 633–651. doi:10.1108/JSBED-05-2013-0073

KEY TERMS AND DEFINITIONS

Brand: A brand is a name, term, design, symbol, or any other feature that distinguishes one seller's good or service from those of other sellers.

Brand Image: A brand image is a collection of ideas and impressions that people generate about a company when they hear or see its name.

Internet Ads: Internet ads also known as online marketing, internet advertising, digital advertising, or web advertising, is a form of marketing and advertising which uses the Internet to promote products and services to audiences and platform users.

SME: A small and mid-size enterprise (SME) is a business that maintains revenues, assets or a number of employees below a certain threshold.

Social Media: Social media is a collective term for websites and applications that focus on communication, community-based input, interaction, content-sharing, and collaboration.

Chapter 2
Digital Transformation of Small and Medium Businesses

Aizhan Baimukhamedova
Gazi University, Turkey

Malik Baimukhamedov
Social-Technical University Named After Aldymzharov Z., Kazakhstan

ABSTRACT

This chapter examines the essence and importance of digital transformation in developing small and medium-sized businesses. It is noted that digitalization uses computer technology to reshape business so that all decisions are made based on data. The main objectives of the digital transformation of SMEs are shown. The technologies accelerating digital transformation include the internet of things, artificial intelligence, e-commerce, big data, cloud technology, blockchain, etc. The tasks of managing an organization in the context of digitalization include changing the company's business processes based on advanced digital technologies, maintaining a high level of knowledge of company management and specialists in the field of modern technologies, maintaining a high degree of preparedness for changes and challenges of the external environment. The authors consider the digital transformation of SMEs in the industrial, agricultural, and commercial spheres, as well as e-commerce.

INTRODUCTION

The Essence and Significance of Digital Transformation in The Development of Small and Medium-sized Businesses

Digital transformation is a restructuring of technologies, business models and processes that provide the formation of new values for customers and employees in a constantly changing business environment in order to develop the digital economy (Aubakirova, 2020). These processes place new demands on small and medium-sized businesses (SMBs), forcing them to adopt elements of digitalization. Their importance to business is clear, as they contribute to scientific and technological progress, and open up

DOI: 10.4018/978-1-6684-5727-6.ch002

opportunities for growth and sustainable competitiveness, affecting the entire production and supply chain. In addition, there is a direct correlation between the digitalization of business and its profitability. The McKinsey Global Institute estimates that productivity in digitized sectors of the economy is significantly higher because of data-driven business models. Therefore, companies around the world prefer digital technologies. Thus, according to experts' forecasts, 30% of companies from the Global 2000 list (the largest public companies in the world in 2020) will allocate at least 10% of revenues to finance their digital strategy.

Technologies accelerating digital transformation include

Internet of Things, artificial intelligence, e-commerce, big data, cloud technology, blockchain, etc. They help expand markets and export potential, often turning SMEs into micro transnational companies. Today, more and more businesses are digitizing their operations, thereby transforming their value chains and becoming more productive, competitive, and profitable.

BACKGROUND

Digitalization efforts are creating a new society where human capital is actively developing - the knowledge and skills of the future are nurtured from a very young age, business efficiency and speed are increasing through automation and other new technologies, and the dialogue of citizens with their states is becoming simple and open.

The challenges of managing an organization in a digitalized environment include the following:

- Changing the company's business processes on the basis of advanced digital technologies;
- Maintaining a high level of knowledge of company management and specialists in the field of modern technologies;
- Maintaining a high degree of readiness to changes and challenges of the external environment.

In today's environment, organizations should look at their own business in the context of the digital economy. Like it or not, the costs of research, development, consulting services, and employee training will inevitably rise as part of the digitalization of the company. Companies that are not ready for such developments will sooner or later leave the market. On the other hand, digitalization should not be an end. It is necessary to calculate the efficiency of these or those changes to be sure that the key processes at the enterprise will significantly improve because of digital technology implementation.

Companies that have already gone digital are facing the challenge of having to change their approach to organizational management to reflect the new digital reality. Digitalization should not be equated with automation: Automation is primarily the replacement of manual labor with the use of electronic machines. Digitalization is the use of digital computer technology to redesign a business so that all business decisions are based on data. It is not possible to digitalize a single part of a company. Digitalization cuts across the entire company, thereby achieving synergy between each area on a single digital platform. According to a study by the Boston Consulting Group (BCG), reflected in the article "Kazakhstan on its way to the digital economy," Kazakhstan ranked 50th out of 85 nations in 2016 in terms of the level of digitalization of the economy and is in the nascent digital economy group.

The digital gap between the leading countries and the lagging countries is increasing year by year. The key to maintaining the competitiveness of Kazakhstan's economy is the development of the digital component through the joint efforts of the state and business, including in such sectors as industrial, transport and logistics infrastructure, agriculture, subsoil use, energy, education, and healthcare.

That is why in 2017 the state program "Digital Kazakhstan", important for the development of modern Kazakhstan, was launched (Programma, 2017). It is designed for 2017-2022 and is of strategic importance for the country. The main goal of the program is to "improve the quality of life and competitiveness of Kazakhstan's economy through the progressive development of the digital ecosystem".

One of the areas of development of the state program - "Digital Kazakhstan" is the digital transformation of SMEs, since SMEs in the country account for more than 30% of the country's economy. Digital transformation of SMEs can contribute to the development of numerous forms of innovative processes:

1.   Mastering e-commerce by small and medium-sized enterprises will, for example, improve production efficiency by automating production processes and supply chains using intelligent machines or increasing data flow using radio-frequency identification technology.
2.   Big data analytics can provide important information about business processes and uncover opportunities to reduce costs and increase efficiency. This allows SMBs to reach specific customer segments and tailor product features more effectively to their customers' preferences. In addition to improving efficiency, big data analytics improves decision-making processes using financial and non-financial data as well as statistical methods.
3.   Business intelligence solutions, such as enterprise resource planning software, allow SMBs to improve their organizational processes and share information internally and within their supply chain in real time. This allows their employees to complete tasks more efficiently.
4.   Cloud computing provides SMBs with the ability to access business intelligence solutions without having to make the necessary investments in software, hardware and personnel to implement them in-house.
5.   Finally, small businesses can increase their visibility and global reach through e-commerce channels that provide access to a broader consumer base far beyond traditional market boundaries.

MAIN FOCUS OF THE CHAPTER

The main objectives of the digital transformation of SMEs:

1.   Ensuring continuity and sustainability of productivity in enterprises.
2.   Ensuring an integrated digital production structure, including management and production processes in enterprises.
3.   Ensuring business transformation with the outside world in digital harmony and digital interoperability.
4.   To prepare businesses for the transformation of Industry 4.0.
5.   Increase the capacity of digital transformation training and consulting services at the local level.
6.   Determine the performance levels of enterprises and ensure their readiness to apply the performance certificate.
7.   Train digital transformation practitioners (technology integrators) at the local level.

The new digital revolution is changing the way we produce, supply chains and value chains today. Industry 4.0, one of the drivers of the digital transformation of SMEs, is a concept of production organization where added value is provided by integrating physical objects, processes, and digital technologies, with real-time monitoring of physical processes, decentralized decisions, and interaction between machines and people.

The end-to-end digitalization of all physical assets and their integration provide the basis for the transition from mass production to mass customization, increased production flexibility, and shorter lead times for new products, allowing the implementation of new business models and a customized customer service approach. All this significantly increases the efficiency and competitiveness of SMEs.

A great variety of modern information and communication technologies constitute the infrastructure tools of the digital economy (Baimukhamedov, 2022) The digitalization of economic activity (the processes of creating, distributing, exchanging, consuming, and disposing of goods and services) is paying off for both large and small companies, the state and even individuals. The active implementation of digital tools (digital transformation or digitalization) has been taking place in all industries around the world for more than twenty years.

But if previously it was spontaneous and uncontrolled, now businesses and governments have realized the need for a structured approach. The development and implementation of digitalization strategies is now a priority for most companies, regardless of industry, business specifics or legislative regulation.

Information and communication technologies as a class include a huge number of tools and developments: from various state sensors to theories substantiating the areas of optimal application of a particular software architecture. When thinking about the digital economy, there are several defining technologies: the cloud, distributed computing, big data, and the Internet of Things. The second most important group of technologies includes blockchain, digital twins, augmented reality, additive manufacturing, robots and cognitive technologies (Nifantyev, 2020).

Below we explain what digital transformation of SMEs means (see Figure 1).

Figure 1. Digital transformation of SMBs

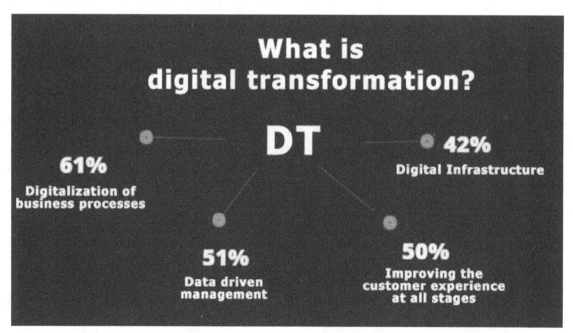

For SMBs, this means:

- Digitalization of business processes: doing more and faster with the same resources.
- Data-driven management: know the exact numbers and quickly remove the unprofitable.
- Improving the customer experience at all stages: fixing people's mistakes and making pre-sales.
- Digital infrastructure: use modern digital technologies and tools.

Digital transformation involves transforming existing companies into so-called "digital enterprises," which must operate on new business, economic and managerial principles that digital technology alone cannot realize. Digital transformation involves a fundamental rethinking of how an organization works and how it interacts with its environment, and all aspects of a company's activities, including strategy, operations, and technology:

1. The digital enterprise strategy focuses on defining the best customer experience, managing a unique business model and ecosystem, and managing change;
2. Operations involve continuous improvement, integrating physical and digital entities and creating a culture that encourages interactive innovation;
3. Technology involves the flexibility to leverage the full state-of-the-art of technology, including analytics, cognitive, mobility, etc.

SOLUTIONS AND RECOMMENDATIONS

Thanks to digitalization, SMEs can increase their competitiveness, be able to make quick decisions and ensure their own identity compared to other market participants, as well as learn more about support measures.

Digital transformation of business processes implies the following elements (Danchenok, Zaytseva, & Komlev, 2019):

1. Implementation. To ensure a successful strategy, organizations must have a clear understanding of how things are happening/changing in their business areas. Competitors need to be studied, and a market analysis needs to be done.
2. Outcome. The outcome of this phase will be a decision on whether to go digital or not with the necessary supporting documentation.
3. Analysis. An in-depth analysis of what organizations can do better with their current business processes should be conducted.
4. Recognition. In digital transformation, organizations need to identify the changes they can make to their processes/business to make it better. This requires several actions, such as:
    a) examining existing business processes (determine how to eliminate paper inputs and inputs, status updates, reminders);
    b) engage key stakeholders (customers, partners, employees);
    c) explore innovative technologies (explore recent technological innovations and their use and how they can help the business);
    d) identify technologies, technical products that can be used in the business.

e)   to review and improve the product, service offerings, if required, even the business model.

5.   Prioritization. Organizations need to rethink the changes identified, conduct a cost-benefit analysis, assess opportunities, resources, budgets, etc., and then prioritize based on that.

6.   Implementation. This step refers to the implementation of change. It includes obtaining the necessary budgets, identifying the teams responsible for implementation, redesigning the processes with the identified changes, and performing the technical implementation using the identified technologies and technical products.

7.   Deployment. The last step in the structure is to make the new system available for use. This also includes developing a clear deployment plan with clearly defined roles, responsibilities, and timelines.

Peter Weil and Stephanie Warner proposed a methodology for creating a digital business model to create the next generation company (Piter Vay & Stefani Vorner, 2015). According to the developers, digitalization pushes companies to change their business models in two ways:

1.   They are moving from controlled value chains to more complex networked systems;

2.   They are moving from a low awareness of the needs at various stages of customer life to an improved, deeper understanding of their requests, leading to a better contact with customers.

Assessing the importance of digital transformation in the development of SMEs, it should be noted that:

1.   Digital transformation can be defined as a strategic business transformation, were customer preferences and behavior drive enterprise technology decisions. It is an enterprise-wide, end-to-end transformation that affects all parts of the organization.

2.   Digital transformation involves streamlining and automating processes using digital technology. Business transaction data is digitized, and once it's digitized, algorithms, not humans, can start making decisions.

3.   SMEs are not yet fully ready for the digital transformation of business, so the government and banks should popularize this topic.

Sustainable growth of the organization is possible only through investment in all digital technologies.

4.   SMEs, today, to ensure the competitiveness and future digitalization of their own activities, have a strategic task consisting of three main positions:

a)   Building close relationships with suppliers and customers;

b)   stable growth of their own operating system;

c)   increasing the level of product competitiveness.

5.   A number of recommendations can be highlighted for the acceleration and success of digital transformation:

a)   it is necessary to maintain an internal audit of the state of digital technology;

b)   it is important to study the digital customer and take advantage of emerging opportunities;

c)   special attention should be paid to the level of training of employees, to engage in retraining;

d)   it is necessary to coordinate investments in digital technology with the goals of their own company.

Based on the above, we can say that today SMEs have all the necessary opportunities and prerequisites to improve their competitiveness by implementing advanced information technologies in the processes of their activities. Thanks to this implementation, business processes become simpler, more flexible, and companies are always ready for direct contact with customers. Digital transformation of SMEs does not necessarily require a radical transformation of the business model; the transformation can take place gradually and at different levels of change. The implementation of digital transformation will make companies more agile, leading to a more flexible allocation of resources.

The choice of strategy and success of digital transformation depends on various factors, such as the existing digital capabilities firms, learning culture, history of digital adoption, ability to evolve with supporting parties, etc. Regardless, digital adoption varies depending on many things, but three ways can be identified for shaping a digital transformation strategy for a business model:

1. Accelerating the transition to a more digital firm. This path is only suitable for a firm that is "ready to jump in" and become a digital firm. SMBs in this category can be said to be a "first mover" group and are seeking to instill a strategic sensitivity to identify weak signals of change before other firms can identify them. Digitalization was implemented quickly with the support of a group of dedicated teams working with a project-based approach. With this approach, each project has a specific goal and a specific time frame (Rachinger, 2019).

Digital technology is used in all organizational functions, but the depth of implementation varies depending on the functional tasks. Sales is the function with the most complete digitalization because digital technology was implemented before the pandemic began. When the pandemic began, the company expanded digitalization to various functions. It could be said that the pandemic acted as an external stimulus, threatening the firm's survival and forcing the firm to respond quickly by accelerating digitalization.

A rapid digital transformation offers a promising competitive advantage, which comes with a high risk. However, in a digital environment, this competitive position will not last long, as there is the potential for imitation by competitors. This type of transformation requires companies to create a framework for digital technology. This is coupled with a digital vision and strategy development, supported by a culture of learning, and achieving a certain level of digital literacy.

2. Digitalization of sales for firm survival. The second path is the most popular for SMEs, as evidenced by the fact that more than half of the firms fall into this group. Firms in this group are digitizing their sales functions to generate revenue in more creative ways, although there is some doubt that digital adoption will still be useful in the post-pandemic future.

The decision to pursue a digital transformation in sales helps firms generate revenue by creating customer experiences, and they expect it will save them from the brink of bankruptcy. In fact, firms in this group are interested in conducting a comprehensive digital transformation, but because of their low level of digital maturity they choose to digitize only the sales function.

Case study firms integrate product or service offerings through social networks that are equipped with a consumer and supported by a physical infrastructure for distribution, logistics and supply chain. All these strategies are designed to increase the organizational agility of firms.

3.   The search for digital partners to enter the market. The third path of business model transformation demonstrated changes in how SMBs interact with their partners. Two companies that lack digital literacy fall into this group and overcome their challenges by drowning in digital ecosystems that have many enthusiastic partners to collaborate. It has been proven that finding digital partners can solve problems arising from a lack of digital literacy, but this is considered a short-term solution, as companies need to balance their short-term solutions with their long-term plans.

At some point, firms in this group should be able to implement digital technologies without relying entirely on their partners. Partners manage and utilize digital technology according to the specific needs of the case study firm and help SMEs communicate with clients who need customized products.

Applications of Digital Transformation of SMEs

The development of small and medium-sized enterprises (SMEs) and the possibility of implementing entrepreneurial initiatives are the prerequisites for the successful development of a country. The development of small and medium sized enterprises (SMEs) is an essential requirement for the successful development of a country. SMEs have a very important advantage over large businesses in that they are mobile and flexible enough to take on new business initiatives. and medium-sized businesses have a very important advantage compared to large companies - they are quite mobile, adapt faster to changing market needs and implement organizational, technical, and other requirements.

One of the problems of modern small and medium entrepreneurship is not even so much the stage of creating and launching a business as it is the question of the functioning and development of the organization. This issue is important and relevant, especially now, in the era of digitalization. Established business models can no longer be competitive without the use of digital tools (McKinsey, 2022). In this context, the following digital technologies and applications have an important role to play in SMEs: ERP (Enterprise Resource Planning), MES (Manufacturing Execution Systems), software applications based on the IoT (Internet of Things) platform, 3D printing technology, Blockchain, Big Data, cloud computing, etc. These applications are run in an integrated way, to which every machine and equipment in the digitized enterprise can be connected using cloud computing technology. The authors will highlight the following key digital technologies.

Cloud Computing: An information technology concept that involves providing ubiquitous and convenient on-demand network access to the total amount of configurable computing resources that can be promptly allocated and released with minimal operating costs or recourse to the provider.

In layman's terms, cloud technology is access to remote data storage and remote computing resources that are made available to the user on demand and to the extent necessary.

Examples of resources include data networks, servers, storage devices, applications, and services, either together or separately. In other words, cloud technologies are data technologies in which computer resources are made available to an Internet user as an online service.

Cloud technology has many advantages over classic IT architecture:

- Savings on computing power;
- fault tolerance;
- high speed of data processing;
- savings on licenses and software;

- cheap server space;
- availability (limited only by availability/absence of Internet);
- resistance to DDOS attacks.

Big Data: A set of approaches, tools and methods designed to process structured and unstructured data (including from different independent sources) to obtain human-readable results. Big data is characterized by a significant volume, variety, and speed of updating, which makes standard methods and tools for working with information insufficiently effective.

Thus, Big Data technology is a tool for making decisions based on large volumes of information. This area of information technology began to actively develop in 2010. Today, there are many methods and comprehensive software products that allow processing Big Data, including those from IBM, Oracle, Microsoft, Hewlett-Packard, EMC, Apache Software Foundation, etc.

Examples of data sources that require Big Data methods are:

- logs of user behavior on the Internet;
- GPS signals from cars for the transportation company;
- transaction information of all bank customers;
- information on all purchases at a major retail chain;
- information from numerous city IP video cameras;
- information from sensors of a large production facility equipped with Industrial Internet technology, etc.

Internet of Things (IoT): Is a concept in which the Internet evolves from the association of computers and people to the association of (smart) objects/things. In its broadest sense, the term "Internet of Things" encompasses anything related to the Internet but is more commonly used to define objects that "talk" to each other. The Internet of Things allows devices connected to closed, private Internet connections to communicate with others, and connects those networks.

It enables devices to exchange data not only in tightly spaced nodes, but also between different types of networks, and creates a much more interconnected world. At the household level, the Internet of Things is represented by technologies and devices of the so-called "smart home" - motion sensors, smart outlets, switches and light bulbs, household appliances that can be controlled remotely and centrally using a smartphone. In industrial production nowadays, smart sensors are increasingly used on production lines, which control the production process and can increase its efficiency by reducing the amount of waste.

The Internet of Things is a concept that combines many technologies and implies that all devices (and things in general) are equipped with sensors and connected to the Internet, which allows remote monitoring, control, and management of processes in real time (including in automatic mode). Today, there are two major trends: the Internet of Things (IoT - Internet of Things) and the Industrial Internet of Things (Internet, Elektronnyy resurs, http://www.tadviser.ru/index.php). Instrumentally, these technologies are very similar, the key difference being the purpose: while the main task of the Internet of Things is to collect all sorts of data (which will be primarily used to build models and forecasts), the purpose of the Industrial Internet of Things is to automate production (by remotely managing resources and capacities according to sensor readings).

Building Information Modeling (BIM): Is the process of creating and managing information about a construction project throughout its life cycle. One of the key results of this process is a building information model, a digital description of every aspect of the constructed object. BIM integrates all information about each component of a building into a single whole and allows anyone to access this information for any purpose, for example, to better integrate various aspects of design. This reduces the risk of errors or inconsistencies and minimizes costs.

BIM data can be used to illustrate the entire life cycle of a building, from creation and design to demolition and material reuse. And with a conflict alert system, BIM prevents errors in the various stages of project development and construction itself. Computer modeling and design is actively used in construction and design these days, but often only in certain aspects of project work, so BIM is the future of design and long-term management of construction projects, as modern hardware, software and cloud technologies open up new possibilities for handling increasing volumes of raw data and information. The use of BIM soon, in our opinion, will become more common than today and will bring this industry to a fundamentally new, qualitative level of efficiency and cost-effectiveness.

Product Lifecycle Management (PLM): Is a comprehensive vision of managing all data related to the design, production, support, and final disposal of manufactured goods. PLM can be seen as (a) a repository of all information that affects a product, and (b) a process of communication between product stakeholders: mainly marketing, design, manufacturing, and maintenance. The PLM system is the place where all the information about a product comes together and from where it leaves in a form suitable for its production and further support. Some analysts use "PLM" as a general term that includes engineering CAD (computer-aided design systems).

But product information creation tools include word processors, spreadsheets and graphics programs, requirements analysis and market assessment tools, field accident reports, and even emails. In our view, a PLM tool focuses solely on managing data that spans the entire product lifecycle, regardless of how that data is developed. PLM can also serve as a central repository for secondary information such as catalogs, customer feedback, marketing plans, archived project schedules and other information generated during the product life cycle. PLM software can help people better understand how products are designed, manufactured, and maintained. Most users appreciate centralized access to all product information.

Cognitive Technologies: The name comes from the word cognition (Latin for "cognition"), that is, cognitive technologies are technologies that "work" with our cognition: assessing our attention, monitoring our condition, monitoring the work of the brain, and trying to "understand" the person.

The most promising directions in the development of these technologies are:

- Cognotropic drugs designed to enhance human capabilities, including the development of intelligence, memory;
- Cognitive assistants - systems of adaptive support in various situations (access control, autopilot);
- Virtual interfaces of the "brain-computer" type - intuitive, accessible to everyone ways of controlling computer systems.

According to IDC estimates, the global market for cognitive technology in the coming years will grow by an average of 55% annually, and by 2021 will reach $39.3 billion. At the same time, software applications for text analysis and other materials, search, machine learning, categorization, hypothesis generation, navigation, and cognitive platforms designed for development of intelligent programs will occupy more than 50% of the market. Almost 20% of global purchases of cognitive systems will come from the banking industry. In banks, they are used to detect fraud, automate the analysis and elimination of threats, and make recommendations. Trade, where cognitive systems ensure the work of automated customer service agents, merchandising, and healthcare, where they are used in diagnostic and treatment systems, rank second and third in terms of volume of purchases.

Customer Relationship Management, CRM: (Customer Relationship Management System) includes application software for organizations that serves to automate customer interaction strategies, to increase sales, optimize marketing policy and improve service quality by storing customer information and customer relationship history. In our opinion, a modern business needs to have a coherent CRM system, which will create a healthy communication between the organization and its customers.

Digital Transformation of SMEs in the Industrial Sphere: Kazakhstan's Experience

The driving force behind Kazakhstan's digitalization is the public sector. We are talking about the creation by the state of a favorable environment for the full development of innovations, financing the development of digital infrastructure, providing a legal framework for the digitalization of the business environment and the adaptation of industrial enterprises to the latest technologies. The emergence of the third platform (cloud, mobility, social networks, "big data") is precisely the milestone that marks the digital transformation. "The third platform" gets its name because it follows the third in a series of platform evolution. The first platform was implemented based on mainframes and terminals, the second on the PC and client-server architecture, and finally, the third platform is based on various, including mobile devices, mobile Internet, social networks, cloud technologies, which are the basis for building all kinds of smart economy solutions. All previous technologies only prepared the digital transformation.

Digitalization in industry marks the beginning of a new era of industrialization. It provides enterprises with a high degree of flexibility in shaping their business models and a broad coverage of their potential customer base by integrating CPS (Cyber-Physical System) and IoT (Internet of Things) into the production process. At the core of the implementation of new technologies is the desire to comprehensively improve efficiency and create the conditions for the successful operation of the enterprise. Digitalization in industry is a hot topic, marking the beginning of a new era of industrialization. It provides enterprises with a high degree of flexibility in shaping their business models and a broad coverage of their potential customer base by integrating CPS (Cyber-Physical System) and IoT (Internet of Things) into the production process. At the core of the implementation of new technologies is the desire to comprehensively improve efficiency and create the conditions for the successful operation of the enterprise.

For the digitalization of industry, the focus will be on the development of own technologies and competencies, ensuring coordination between the participants of the industrial-innovative ecosystem, removing barriers, popularizing digital technologies, and developing appropriate stimulating measures. It is planned to implement pilot projects to create model digital factories in small and medium-sized businesses, where technologies of Industry 4.0 will be implemented, which will serve as a demonstration of the effectiveness of digital technologies in production. Today there is a boom in Internet-connected devices around the world. No sector of the economy is taking advantage of it as effectively as the industrial sector (Figure 2). In the coming years, industrial manufacturers will spend tens of billions of dollars on the Internet of Things, incorporating the concept of the "Fourth Industrial Revolution" into their processes. Just as steam, electronics, and computers once caused a revolution in product manufacturing, the Internet of Things will cause the emergence of smart technologies that will accelerate and improve manufacturing today.

Figure 2. Industrial Internet of Things

This section includes technologies that can be used in digital enterprises, use-cases and alternative application levels. It is possible to produce application solutions at different levels for each usage scenario, and these levels naturally affect the application costs. Enterprise Resource Planning (ERP) application was commissioned and additionally Internet of Things, Cloud Computing, Big Data, Artificial Intelligence, Additive Manufacturing, Augmented Reality, Manufacturing Execution System (MES), Smart Logistics, Smart Warehouse, Product Lifecycle (PLC) etc.

Let's define the main stages of the installation of a "high-tech production line based on digital technology" for digitized industrial enterprises which will provide applied training to all processes of digital transformation. Therefore, a structure will be designed to show digitalization as an alternative from start to finish. A smarter product will be produced in the Digital Based High Technology Production Line than in the lean line (Figure 3). Machines, sensors, conveyor, assembly, testing etc. in accordance with the designed line. The technical specifications of devices such as the unit will be defined. Considering these features, a technical specification should be prepared.

Figure 3. Logical Flow Example in the Digitization of Lean Line

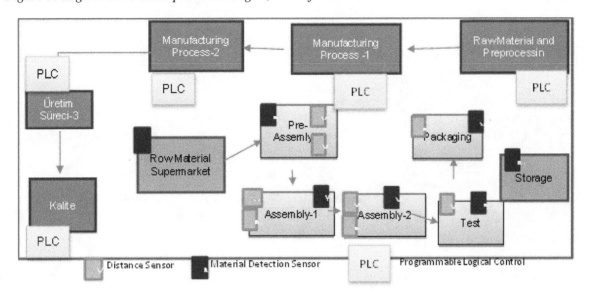

The Technologies That Can be Used in Digital Enterprises

Big Data Analytics and Artificial Intelligence Platforms: Data collection, aggregation and storage can be performed by IoT platforms or by big data platforms integrated with them. However, processing data and deriving value from it also often requires software packages for big data platform can be fully and seamlessly integrated with the IoT platform being used. The figure 4 below shows the uses of Big Data technology.

Figure 4. The uses of Big Data technology

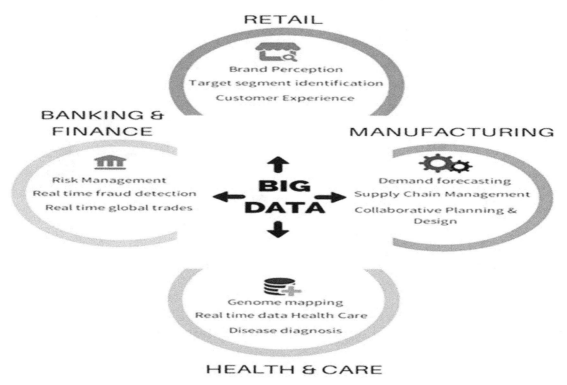

Data Collection from Machinery and Workbenches: Information that can be obtained from all possible machines and benches used in the factory; It includes receiving via PLC and/or sensors and transmitting it to the platform. Sensors and actuators to be used especially in assembly benches; It will be directly related to the selected product, process, and scenarios to be used. If the machines to be deployed within the MF can transfer data to the IoT platform, it should be preferred. In cases where this is not the case, it is very important in terms of digitalization that data can be drawn from the PLC of the machine.

Digital Work Instruction: With this application, operators' jobs and job details are displayed with the help of a screen. Operator information is obtained by reading the employee card on the same screens, and special work instructions can be presented to the operator when necessary. On the other hand, it is possible to control the employee availability status via this screen/device. It is important to use up-to-date and innovative technologies and techniques on human-computer-interaction.

For example, touch screens can be used to interact with the employee, as well as audio and visual interaction in more advanced solutions. With the camera system positioned on these screens, there is a chance for both image processing and image recording. The use case may extend beyond the fixed workstation scope to specific business processes such as maintenance operations.

Machine Line Monitoring: With the Machine Line Monitoring scenario, a usage scenario can be created that enables the realization of artificial intelligence applications such as "Predictive Maintenance", as well as increasing efficiency and quality, thanks to the increase in monitoring, control and auditability. In this usage scenario, which can be realized at different levels, it is possible to monitor each machine, machine and line in great detail, while monitoring can be performed only on the basis of the required parameters. Elements such as instantaneous alarm generation can be enabled in this usage scenario. Actions such as predictive maintenance, dynamic workflow change and effective intervention, thanks to the instantaneous analysis of many data with artificial intelligence applications, are also within the scope of this scenario.

Performance Monitoring and Evaluation: It also stands out as a usage scenario that enables easy detection of possible malfunctions by digitally monitoring, evaluating, and analyzing all performance metrics of the factory with different techniques. It can be monitored on a factory basis, or it can be applied as a use-case at the employee level. OEE calculations are considered within the scope of this use case.

Monitoring and evaluations are made based on factory, workshop, production line, workbench, machine, shift and operator, and production amount, scrap amount, quality rate, working and stopping rates, employee satisfaction, customer satisfaction, supplier satisfaction, etc. (Kudryashov,2018). It can be seen as a use case that can provide monitoring and evaluation with metrics.

Cycle Time Analysis and Evaluation: With this usage scenario, which is especially used in assembly lines, elements such as instant data in the workflow, transition times, cycle times and speed losses in workstations can be monitored and monitored. Dynamic line balancing is carried out by performing analyzes on historical data as well as instant tracking.

Since both shift, station and operator based analyzes can be made, it is possible to provide dynamic line balancing suggestions in line with the demand amount and production time constraint. It will also be able to alert production managers by generating alarms as the average cycle times are known. In addition, it allows for deeper analysis such as comparing the performance criteria of each operator and the same operator in different shifts.

Digital Kanban System: The Kanban system, which is one of the most important tools used in lean production techniques such as the Toyota Production System, is completely digitized, thus preventing time losses and possible human-induced errors (see figure 5). At the same time, Workflow management, which is the most important element that feeds material flow and inventory management, has an important place in the implementation of lean production techniques, and the Digital Kanban System, which will enable this to be realized, is among the indispensable parts of the digitalization of the lines. It stands out as an element that will pave the way for instant line balancing and workflow changes, that is, providing a dynamic structure.

Figure 5. Digital Kanban System

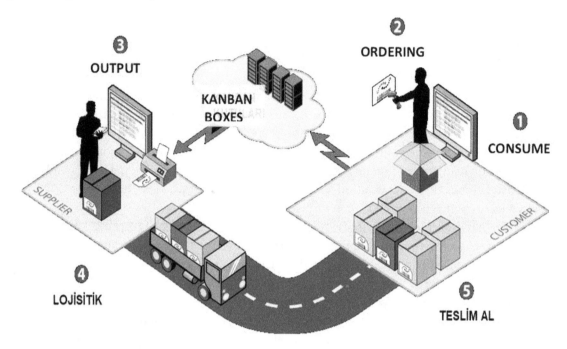

Cobot (Cobot) and Robot Applications: It is important to create examples of robot and/or cobot usage at some points within the digital enterprises. While the creation of a stacking robot example can be accomplished very easily, robot/cobot applications feeding the benches are among the tasks that need to be carried out with a little more cost and precision. Although there are different opinions about the fact that cobot applications are not yet mature enough, semi-autonomous cobots that can sense their environment, interact and work safely with humans in the same environment have started to take place in the industry. Although it is possible to use robots or cobots at various stages of production, it is useful to consider the costs and returns.

Digital Twin and Simulation: Today, with Digital Twin technologies, it is possible to make production simulations based on known values before installation and based on data collected during operation. In addition, with this method, the instant status of the factories can be monitored in the most detailed way. Applications developed in this direction contain very large differences. In addition to software capable of simulating an entire factory, it is also possible to come across Digital Twin applications that may be sufficient in terms of the Model Factory concept (training-consulting). In the selection of the Digital Twin and Simulation application to be used, financial adequacy and the functional adequacy of the application in terms of the Model Factory concept should be considered.

Additive Manufacturing: It is considered as a usage scenario where Additive Manufacturing technique can be exemplified. The production of a suitable part of the product being produced in the digital enterprise with this method will make a significant contribution to the training and consultancy processes related to the subject. It can be used for various purposes, from the production of the simplest part of the product to the production of an element that can transform the design into a personalized product.

Digital Quality Control: The digitalization of Quality Control systems can provide companies with significant gains. In this usage scenario, a paperless quality control scenario can be implemented to digitize the quality control measurement results and evaluate the measurement results. At this level, the measurement results can be transferred to the digital environment and the accuracy can be determined instantly, and it is decided whether the product will continue with the next processes.

In case of successive problem products from the measurements, an automatic alarm can be generated and/or the control of the production manager at the previous stations can be provided. At the next level of this usage scenario, it is possible to install quality control systems that can measure completely independent of people. Technologies such as image processing, robot/cobot, artificial intelligence can be used at this level, where the technique to be used is decided depending on the product.

Product Traceability (Product Genealogy Management or Digital Shadow)

Tracing the processes of each manufactured product at all stages is important not only in terms of quality assurance, but also in terms of identifying the sources of problems based on the product history and monitoring and evaluating the issue of compliance with the legislation. For this purpose, it is important to display this usage scenario, sometimes called Digital Shadow. While the developed products can be tracked at both the raw material, semi-finished product, and the final product's batch level, it is also possible to follow up on a product or piece basis from the points where the product identification process takes place.

The list of technologies associated with Industry 4.0: blockchain, augmented and virtual reality, unmanned devices, Internet of Things, three-dimensional printing, artificial intelligence, robots are not new technologies, but the expected synergistic effect of their implementation will open new horizons. To obtain this effect, they must be implemented in a production system that has the properties of computerization, networking, visibility, transparency, predictability, and adaptability.

Digitalization of the Industrial Enterprise

Before digitalization, business owners need to conduct in-depth research beforehand to know in advance how modern concepts and digital technologies can affect their business (Korablev, 2018). You need accurate data on capacity and capabilities, as well as the overall state of the enterprise, to set the right digital transformation goals and achieve a positive outcome in the end. To create a digitalization program for an industrial plant, the following questions must be answered in advance:

1. What can digitalization bring?
2. What are the goals for the enterprise?
    2. At what stage of digital transformation is the organization currently at, which of the technologies used can be retained?
    3. What digitalization work can the company perform by itself, and for which the help of specialists will be required?

Subsequently, the list of questions expands, there is a need to select the appropriate tools, software, and technical solutions. However, the first stage is to decide whether such a transformation can currently led to positive results for the company and whether such a transition will be economically justified.

Identification of Human Resources for Digitalized Enterprises

It is desirable that the human resources who will work at the level of manager, trainer and consultant for digital transformation in digitalized enterprises have theoretical and practical experience in lean manufacturing and digitalized production in the enterprise or its structural units: shops, sites, production lines, etc.

In this structure, when selecting human resources to take on responsibilities at manager, trainer, and consultant level in model factories, competencies in subjects that may fall within the scope of the digitalized enterprise, especially in lean manufacturing and digitalization, are needed (Pan'shin, 2019). This staff would benefit from early involvement in digital transformation projects.

The personnel who will work on the digital transformation of the enterprise can be defined as follows:

- Digital application trainer: full- or part-time employees who provide practical and theoretical training on model factories to increase the competence and capacity of enterprises in the field of digital transformation.
- Digital transformation consultant: full- or part-time employees who go to businesses and provide individual consultations in the process of digital transformation of businesses after undergoing applied training to increase the competence and capacity of enterprises. in the field of digital transformation.

The digital application trainer and the digital transformation consultant who will work in digitalized enterprises can be the same people, but it is recommended that they be different people. To ensure the sustainability of the enterprise, it is envisioned that it will be run by a board of directors with legal personality. On the other hand, it is also envisaged that the digital transformation applications implemented in the digitalized enterprises through training and consulting services will be networked to quickly spread throughout our country, share application experiences and exchange trainers and consultants. The Digital Enterprise Collaboration Network is supported through a web portal, and best practices and training presentations are also available on this portal, along with a pool of trainers and consultants.

Digital Transformation of SMEs in Agriculture

The digitalization of agricultural enterprises will help to increase the quality and volume of production, as well as to reduce human involvement in the production process. The digital transformation of SMEs in the agricultural sector envisages the following measures: The introduction of digital technologies in the enterprises of the agricultural sector of the economy, the creation of an agricultural portal in the district and regional centers of the country, the introduction of "precision farming" technology in several farms, including the use of meteorological stations. The management system "Precision Farming" allows farmers to monitor in real time the indicators of crops, moisture, nutrients, pests, probability of rainfall, etc.

To further develop SMEs in the agricultural sector of the country, it is planned to implement several measures aimed at automating the traceability of agricultural products with the inclusion of all the authorized organizations involved in the process, which will allow quantitative and qualitative accounting and trace the entire life cycle of production and origin of agro-industrial products. The implementation of the traceability system will have a direct impact on attracting investment in the industry and expanding both the line of export products and the geography of supply of agricultural products and deep processing products. The introduction of full monitoring with traceability system will also improve the quality standards of agricultural products, which will have a multiplicative effect on the attractiveness and competitiveness of Kazakh products in foreign markets.

To introduce "precision farming" a pilot project was conducted in several farms using elements of "precision farming", including the use of meteorological stations. Based on the results of the pilot project, the economic efficiency of wide application of "precision farming" was determined. Development and implementation of elements of precision farming in all regions of the Republic of Kazakhstan is expected to simplify activities, increase yields and productivity in the sector. Producer will be able to decide based on the array of data coming in real time on the state of crops, moisture, nutrients, nitrogen, potassium, phosphorus, pests, probability of rainfall. At the same time, introduction of precision farming elements will be carried out in conjunction with the acquisition of new agricultural equipment, implementation of agricultural technologies and as far as farmers are ready. Improving the competitiveness of domestic agricultural products and processed products is closely related to the need to promote and position domestic products on both the domestic and export markets. As part of solving these challenges, a platform for electronic trade between farmers, wholesale and distribution centers, trading networks and markets will be implemented to develop sales of agro-industrial products.

Digital Transformation of the Commercial Sphere, E-Commerce

The introduction of information technology has brought dramatic changes in all spheres of business activity and resulted in the appearance of its separate branch e-business. E-business (e-commerce) is a form of business transaction where the interaction of the parties is carried out electronically: via computer networks, via exchange of electronic documents. E-commerce may involve different types of transactions: wholesale and retail trade; supply and distribution of products; delivery, provision of information and other services; investments; insurance, banking services, etc. The objects of e- commerce are goods, manufactured products, securities, currencies, services, etc. The subjects of e-commerce are financial organizations, enterprises, individuals - consumers of goods and services. The basic models of interaction between the subjects of e-commerce are:

- B2B - Business-to-Business focused on the business partner;
- B2C - Business-to-Consumer focused on the end-user;
- C2C - Consumer-to-Consumer focused on the end-user.

B2B is a business model in which the interaction between the companies is done via computer networks. The basis of the B2C business model is retail trade, i.e., interaction between companies and consumers on the Internet.

C2C is a model of selling goods and services by one consumer to other consumers, i.e., consumers' interaction with other consumers on the Internet.

In addition, there are a few business models (B2A - Business-to- Administration, involving the interaction of companies with administrative authorities; C2A - Consumer-to-Administration, involving the interaction of consumers with the administration, etc.).

The increased reach and penetration of Internet access networks also stimulates the development of e-commerce in Kazakhstan. The Ministry of Trade and Integration plans to increase the share of electronic commerce to 20% by 2025 within the National Trade Development Project. In 2021 it is planned to increase the share of electronic commerce to 10.9%, which will amount to 1.4 trillion tenge. In 2025 - up to 20%, which is already 3.6 trillion tenge. According to Kazpost, the online commerce market more than doubled in 2020, exceeding 1.7 trillion tenge and reaching 10.7% of the total retail B2C commerce. In 2019, the figure was 5.7%.

It is planned to develop the e-commerce ecosystem with the help of three tools. The first is the stimulation of e-commerce and training for SMEs. The second is the development of delivery services and logistics services, and the third is the development of online cross-border trade.

As for the first direction, the specialized department is staking on improving literacy among university students and business entities. In April 2021, an educational program was launched to teach the peculiarities of the transition to e-business and its promotion. Webinars are conducted by leading independent experts, specialists from major international companies with extensive experience in areas such as Internet marketing, e-commerce, electronic payments, accounting, cash flow management. Seminars are organized by the USAID project on development of entrepreneurship and business environment, the Entrepreneurship Development Fund "Damu", Fintech Hub of MFCA and Mastercard international payment system. Participation in webinars is free of charge.

The Vice Minister of Trade and Integration, in her welcoming address to the participants of the first webinar, said that Kazakhstan plans to increase the share of e-commerce. "For this purpose, we should improve state regulation, improve e-commerce infrastructure, coordination of the state and business, and develop e-exports of Kazakhstani goods. It is very important to constantly develop the digital skills of businesses and the population in this process. I am sure that improving the digital and financial literacy of SMEs will help the further development of e-commerce in the country and the entry of our companies into other markets".

Much attention during the webinars is paid to digital promotion and types of digital advertising. Attendees are taught how to set up and mechanisms for advertising and image campaigns on the Internet, as well as how to evaluate their effectiveness. SMB representatives are told about the peculiarities of the transition to e-business: how to create a website and an online store, how to manage online orders and attract customers, how to make sales through retail marketplaces and popular social networks, such as Instagram. E-commerce is directly related to electronic payments, so special attention during webinars was paid to the topic of digital payments: how digital payments work, how they can be set up for an online business and how to ensure their security. Accounting and managing the cash flow of an online business are important aspects of an e-commerce enterprise. Therefore, entrepreneurs learned about the benefits and opportunities offered by accounting software for SMEs, how to issue invoices electronically for faster payment.

Another area that the Ministry of Trade and Integration is developing is access to international marketplaces. "We have held several rounds of negotiations on the three largest online marketplaces. Since May 2021, Kazakhstani citizens have been allowed to trade on such online marketplaces as Amazon, Ozon and eBay. This is an opportunity for our entrepreneurs to trade with more than 190 countries. In addition, since 2020, we have been actively supporting domestic producers in promoting exports on the online platform Alibaba. Already 100 domestic companies working on the platform as a "Golden Supplier" have signed export contracts worth 45 million dollars. Among them are such companies as "Aral Tuz", "Eurasian Foods", "Agro Product", "Aktobe Beef" and "Saumal".

In July 2021, Kazakhstan conducted a selection of companies to obtain "Gold Supplier" status on the largest international online trading platform Alibaba.com. In total, in 2021, according to QazTrade,

50 Kazakh suppliers of processed products will be selected to enter this platform. The application could be submitted online on the portal export.gov.kz.

Kazakh producers have also gained wider access to the Russian marketplace Ozon. "The giant of Russian e-commerce is a 16-million-strong base of regular customers and more than 80 million monthly users. "The marketplace features products in 20 different categories, from clothing and food to children's products and cosmetics. This has great potential for Kazakhstani entrepreneurs. Now any Kazakhstani manufacturer can offer its goods on this universal platform. It should be noted that Kazakh products (footwear, jewelry, and agricultural goods) have been represented on Ozon before, but in this case, to enter the site, domestic companies had to open branches in Russia. And this is extremely inconvenient and costly for business. "The entry of local businesses on Ozon was facilitated by improvements in logistics: from May 2021, our entrepreneurs can deliver goods directly to the client in Russia independently or with the help of third-party carriers.

The Eurasian Economic Community (EAEC) is launching a pilot project in the field of foreign electronic trade in B2C goods. The project is planned to be launched in January 2022. Preparatory work is under way. But there is already a preliminary agreement that all cross-border online goods that circulate between the EAEC countries will go through a single e-commerce operator within the pilot project. In the long term, the project will make it possible to significantly reduce people's expenses on customs fees and duty payments.

CONCLUSION

The purpose and significance of digital transformation in growing small and medium-sized organizations are examined in this chapter. It has been stated that digitalization reshapes company using computer technology so that all decisions are based on data. The primary goals of SMEs' digital transformation are outlined. The Internet of Things, artificial intelligence, e-commerce, big data, cloud computing, blockchain, etc. are some of the technologies fueling digital transformation. SMEs involved in e-commerce are exempt from income tax until 2024. But to qualify for this, a business must meet several conditions: transactions for the sale of goods must be completed electronically; payment for goods must be made by bank transfer; the entrepreneur must have his own delivery service or have a contract with cargo carriers or a courier or postal service. The tax legislation does not establish the procedure and conditions for the conclusion of contracts with individuals for the delivery of goods, as well as restrictions on the conclusion of such contracts.

REFERENCES

Aubakirova, G.M. (2020). Transformatsionnyye preobrazovaniya ekonomiki Kazakhstana. *Problemy prognozirovaniya, 1*, 155-163.

Baimukhamedov, M. F. (2022). *Metody i sredstva tsifrovizatsii i robotizatsii ekonomiki. Monografiya.* Master Reprint.

Danchenok, B. K., Zaytseva, T. B., & Komlev, M. O. (2019). Vliyaniye tsifrovykh kompetentsiy sub"yektov malogo i srednego predprinimatel'stva na razvitiye biznesa. *Ekonomika, predprinimatel'stvo i parvo*, 34-42. http://www.tadviser.ru/index.php

Korablev, A. YU. & Bobkin R.Ye. (2018). Informatsionnyye tekhnologii kak faktor povysheniya konkurentosposobnosti predpriyatiy malogo i srednego biznesa. *Azimut nauchnykh issledovaniy: ekonomika i upravleniye, 1,* 44-48.

Kudryashov, A. A. (2018). Infrastruktura tsifrovoy ekonomiki. *Aktual'nyye voprosy sovremennoy ekonomiki, 5,* 25-32.

McKinsey. (2022). *Digital transformation of economy*. https://www.mckinsey.com/industries/technology-media-and-telecommunications/our-insights

Nifantyev, A. N. (2020). Klyuchevyye tekhnologii tsifrovoy ekonomiki. *Molodoy uchenyy, 50,* 117-119.

Pan'shin B. (2019). Tsifrovaya ekonomika: ponyatiya i napravleniya razvitiya: teoriya. *Nauka i innovatsii, 3,* 48-55.

Programma «Tsifrovoy Kazakhstan». (2017). https://egov.kz/cms/ru/digital-kazakhstan

Rachinger, M. (2019). *Digitalization and its influence on business model innovation*. Institute of General Management and Organization.

Vay, P., & Vorner, S. (2015). Thriving in an Increasingly Digital Ecosystem. *MIT Sloan Management Review, 56*(4), 27–347.

KEY TERMS AND DEFINITIONS

Additive Technologies: Are technologies for creating objects by applying successive layers of material. Models made by the additive method can be used at any production stage - both for making prototypes and as finished products themselves.

Advanced Manufacturing Technologies: Technological processes (including machines, apparatus, equipment, and devices) based on microelectronics or computer-controlled and used in the design, manufacture, or processing of products.

Antivirus Tools: Are specialized programs designed to detect computer viruses, unwanted (malicious) programs and restore files infected (modified) by such programs.

Artificial Intelligence: Is a complex of technological solutions that allows you to simulate human cognitive functions (including self-learning and search for solutions without a predetermined algorithm) and to obtain, when performing specific tasks, results comparable, at least, to the results of human intellectual activity.

Artificial Intelligence Technologies: Technologies based on the use of artificial intelligence, including computer vision, natural language processing, speech recognition and synthesis, intelligent decision support and promising artificial intelligence methods.

Big Data: Technologies for collecting, processing, and storing significant arrays of heterogeneous information; are the basis for the development of machine learning and artificial intelligence algorithms, solving analytical problems and optimizing business processes.

Blockchain: Is a technology that combines several mathematical, cryptographic, and economic principles that support the existence of a ledger distributed among several participants.

Cloud Computing: Is an information technology model of providing ubiquitous and convenient access using the Internet to a common set of configurable computing resources (cloud), storage devices, applications and services that can be quickly provided and released from the load with minimal operating costs or virtually no participation of the provider.

Data: Presentation of information in a form suitable for automatic processing.

Data Transmission Channels: Are devices and means through which data (information) is transmitted at a distance.

Digital Economy: Is an economic activity in which digital data is a key factor in production, processing large volumes and using the analysis results of which, in comparison with traditional forms of management, can significantly increase the efficiency of various types of production, technologies, equipment, storage, sale, delivery of goods and services.

Digital Platform: represents 1) model of activities (including business activities) of stakeholders on a common platform for functioning in digital markets, 2) platform that supports a set of automated processes and model consumption of digital products (services) by a significant number of consumers, 3) an information system that has become one of the leading solutions in its technological niche (transactional, integration, etc.).

Ecosystem: Is an economic community that consists of a collection of interconnected organizations and individuals. The economic community produces goods and services of value to the consumer, which are also part of the ecosystem.

Electronic Commerce: Is a segment of the economy that includes the purchase and sale of goods, works, services, rights to use electronic content using electronic means of communication, primarily the internet.

Electronic Document Management (EDM): Is a document management system in which the entire array of created, transmitted, and stored documents is supported using information and communication technologies on computers united in a network structure, providing for the possibility of forming and maintaining a distributed database.

Electronic Signature: Is an analogue of a handwritten signature to give a document, issued in electronic form, legal force equal to the legal force of a paper document signed with a handwritten signature.

"End-to-End" Digital Technology: Is a part of the technological process for the production of goods, the provision of services and the performance of work, which is a set of processes and methods of searching, collecting, storing, processing, providing and disseminating information that provide services and work performance: improving the efficiency, accuracy or other significant characteristics of the technological process; improving the quality or other significant characteristics of the goods produced, the services provided and the work performed; reduction of costs in the production (supply) of goods, provision of services and performance of work.

Global Competitiveness Index: Characterizes the level of competitiveness of countries. Calculated by the World Economic Forum based on 12 parameters.

Global Cybersecurity Index: Characterizes the level of cybersecurity in the country, organizational measures in the field of cybersecurity, the presence of state educational and scientific institutions, partnerships, cooperation mechanisms, and information exchange systems that contribute to building capacity in the field of information security.

Industrial Internet: The concept of building information and communication infrastructures based on connecting industrial devices, equipment, sensors, sensors, process control systems to the information and telecommunication network of the internet.

Information and Communication Technologies (ICT): Are technologies that use microelectronic means for collecting, storing, processing, searching, transmitting and presenting data, texts, images, and sound.

Information Protection Means: Specialized software (anti-virus and / or anti-spam filters, electronic signature tools) designed to protect information when using.

International Digital Economy and Society Index (I-DESI): Is a derivative of the European Digital Economy and Society Index (DESI); aims to measure the progress of countries in the development of the digital economy and society in the following components: Connectivity, Human capital, use of the Internet, Integration of digital technologies, Digital public services.

Internet of Things: Is a concept of a computer network connecting things (physical objects) equipped with built-in information technologies for interacting with each other or with the external environment without human intervention.

Level of Digitalization: Is calculated as the ratio of the installed capacity of electronic exchanges to the total installed capacity of telephone exchanges.

Level of Innovative Activity of Organizations: Is usually defined as the ratio of the number of organizations that carried out technological, organizational, or marketing innovations to the total number of organizations surveyed for a certain period in a country, industry, region, etc.

Local Area Network: Connects two or more computers (possibly of different types), as well as printers, scanners, alarm systems (security, fire) and other production equipment or peripheral devices located within one or more neighboring buildings and does not use for this communication facilities of general purpose.

Neurotechnologies: Are technologies that provide monitoring of the activity of the brain of a person or other vertebrates and (or) control over it.

New Production Technologies: Include cyber-physical systems, sensor technologies, 3D printing, computer engineering, robotics, qualitatively different production resources (nanotechnology and new materials), etc. Their widespread introduction will optimize production processes, increase the efficiency of resource use, reduce downtime equipment and the cost of its maintenance.

Platform: Broadly defined as a communication and transactional environment, the participants of which benefit from interacting with each other.

Processing Large Amounts of Data: Is a set of approaches, tools, and methods for automatic processing of structured and unstructured information coming from a large number of different, including scattered or loosely coupled, information sources, in volumes that cannot be processed manually in a reasonable time.

Quantum Technologies: Are technologies that function by manipulating complex quantum systems at the level of their individual components.

Robotics and Sensorics: Are one of the main transforming technologies of the future, which in 5-10 years will be ubiquitous. These technologies, based on machine learning, the Internet of things and wireless communications, are aimed at maximizing the flexibility and efficiency of production, its complete automation and elimination of the "human factor".

Robotization: Is the use of intelligent robotic systems, the functional features of which are in a sufficiently flexible response to changes in the working area.

Sensorics: Technologies that allow interaction with a computer by touching its parts (contact interfaces) or by moving near the computer without touching it (contactless interfaces), and not by changing the position of its mechanical parts (keys, levers, etc.).

Virtual Reality: Is a world (objects and subjects) created by technical means, transmitted to a person through his sensations: sight, hearing, smell, touch, etc. Virtual reality imitates both impact and responses to exposure.

Virtual Reality Technology: Is a technology of non-contact information interaction that realizes the illusion of direct presence in real time in a stereoscopically presented "virtual world" using complex multimedia operating environments.

Website: Is a place on the Internet, which is determined by the address, has an owner, and consists of web pages. In statistical observation, an organization is considered to have a website if it has at least one page of its own on the Internet, on which information is published and regularly (at least once every six months) updated.

Chapter 3
How a Sustainability Strategy Can Leverage E-Commerce?

Albérico Travassos Rosário
https://orcid.org/0000-0003-4793-4110
GOVCOPP, IADE, Universidade Europeia, Portugal

ABSTRACT

During the last decades, we have seen building sustainable business models as an innovative part of the business strategy. Different economic sectors have used the concept to meet their economic objectives, and one of the leading business models with the highest growth in the last decade was e-commerce. It is not too much to emphasize the importance of sustainability in e-commerce in all its dimensions. We have seen several investigations on the subject covering a wide range of application areas. In this context, a systematic review of the bibliometric literature was carried out on the SCOPUS indexing database using the keywords "sustainability," "e-commerce," "electronic commerce," "B2C e-commerce", "business, management, and accounting" in the last decade (2012-2022). This study aims to understand how a sustainability strategy can leverage e-commerce.

INTRODUCTION

Over the past decade, the fast pace and scale of technological growth have significantly revolutionized the business industry, including the retail sector. There has been intense global growth in the electronic commerce (e-commerce) market, leading to increased retail sales and transactions conducted through online marketplaces or channels. Rao et al. (2021) demonstrates this growth by indicating that e-commerce has recorded an annual growth rate of 20% in the last decade, with the global e-commerce market size valued at 9 trillion in 2019. In addition, the scholars project that the e-commerce sector's growth from 2020 to 2027 will be at a compounded annual growth rate of 14.7%. Similarly, Escursell et al. (2021) weigh on this growth, indicating that e-commerce market penetration by 2026 will increase up to 25%, noting that online purchases increased from 32% in 2015 to 43% in 2018. The development of Information and Communication Technology (ICT) has played a critical role in this business revolution by providing resources and tools to facilitate online trading. For example, e-traders collect and analyze

DOI: 10.4018/978-1-6684-5727-6.ch003

customer information from multiple sources, including social media platforms, to guide and derive consumer decision-making (Sun et al., 2021). In addition, they can use data technologies and market research tools to evaluate consumer demand, behaviors, and preferences, allowing them to implement appropriate business and marketing strategies and processes. Research projects that e-commerce will continue to grow as technologies develop and evolve.

While the prospects of e-commerce look promising, there has been a global increase in the desire to address sustainability issues. Most consumers have begun to question what the growth of e-commerce means to the environment and whether it is more environmentally friendly than the traditional brick-and-mortar retail model (Ukko et al., 2019). As a result, adopting sustainable strategies has become a critical success factor in e-commerce, with companies devising ways of addressing climate change and environmental pollution issues. Sun et al. (2021) explain that most consumers worldwide pay attention to organizational activities and their sustainability initiatives, using these aspects to make purchasing decisions. Rao et al. (2021) contributes to this notion by stating that a recent study shows that environmental concerns influence busying decisions for approximately 50% of online consumers. This shift in consumer attitude towards sustainability is associated with increased awareness of the impact of lifestyle choices, industrialization, and economic development on the planet. In this regard, growing consumers in the virtual markets significantly depend on organizational sustainability efforts, ensuring competitiveness and success (Arora, 2019). This research essay specifies the interconnection between the e-commerce ecosystem and sustainability to illustrate how leveraging associated elements can lead to sustainable business growth and economic development. A systematic bibliometric literature review (LRSB) of 70 documents was used to gather and analyze data from e-commerce and sustainability literature. The study provides insights on how businesses can leverage the e-commerce ecosystem to promote and achieve sustainability.

METHODOLOGICAL APPROACH

A systematic bibliometric literature review (LRSB) methodology was used to comprehensively analyze the topics of e-commerce and sustainable strategies and how they intersect to promote sustainable business practices and economic development. The choice of LRSB was based on Donthu et al. (2021) description of the methodology as a helpful technique used for "deciphering and mapping the cumulative scientific knowledge and evolutionary nuances of well-established fields by making sense of large volumes of unstructured data in rigorous ways" (p.285). Given the popularity of both e-commerce and sustainability concepts, substantial research has been conducted to demonstrate how companies are applying them to achieve competitive advantage and promote sustainable production and consumption for the betterment of society and the environment. Thus, the approach was deemed more desirable.

The methodology used can build knowledge about the How A Sustainability Strategy Can Leverage E-Commerce. The use of the LRSB review process is divided into 3 phases and 6 steps (Table 1), as proposed by Rosário, (2021), Rosario and Dias, (2022).

Table 1. Process of systematic LRSB

Fase	Step	Description
Exploration	Step 1	formulating the research problem
	Step 2	searching for appropriate literature
	Step 3	critical appraisal of the selected studies
	Step 4	data synthesis from individual sources
Interpretation	Step 5	reporting findings and recommendations
Communicatio	Step 6	Presentation of the LRSB report

The database of indexed scientific and/or academic documents used was Scopus, the most important peer review in the scientific and academic world. However, we consider that the study has the limitation of considering only the Scopus decomposition database, excluding other scientific and academic bases. The literature search includes peer-reviewed scientific and/or academic documents published between 2012-2022 through June 2022.

The two main keywords used in the search are "sustainability" and "e-commerce" with exact keyword: Sustainability, Electronic Commerce, E-commerce, E-Commerces, E-Commerce, B2C E-commerce 310 document results were found in data base. Limiting the study to the subject area business, management, and accounting, 84 documents were obtained. Finally, it was limited to the documents published in the last decade 2012-2022, until June 2022, 70 documents were obtained. The researcher did a quick qualitative scan of the documents to ensure they have logical concepts that resonate and align with the main concepts and subjects of the research (Table 2).

Table 2. Screening methodology

Database Scopus	Screening	Publications
Meta-search	keyword: sustainability, e-commerce Exact keyword: Sustainability, Electronic Commerce, E-commerce, E-Commerces, E-Commerce, B2C E-commerce	310
First Inclusion Criterion	keyword: sustainability, e-commerce Exact keyword: Sustainability, Electronic Commerce, E-commerce, E-Commerces, E-Commerce, B2C E-commerce Subject area Business, Management and Accounting	84
	keyword: sustainability, e-commerce Exact keyword: Sustainability, Electronic Commerce, E-commerce, E-Commerces, E-Commerce, B2C E-commerce Subject area: Business, Management and Accounting Period: 2012-2022	70
Screening	keyword: sustainability, e-commerce Exact keyword: Sustainability, Electronic Commerce, E-commerce, E-Commerces, E-Commerce, B2C E-commerce Subject area: Business, Management and Accounting Period: 2012-2022 Published until June 2022	

Source: own elaboration

Content and theme analysis techniques were used to identify, analyze, and report the various documents as proposed by Rosário, (2021), Rosario and Dias, (2022). The 70 scientific and/or academic documents indexed in Scopus are later analyzed in a narrative and bibliometric way to deepen the content and possible derivation of common themes that directly respond to the research question (Rosário, 2021, Rosario & Dias, 2022). Of the 70 selected documents, 513 are Article; 12 Conference Paper; 4 Review and 3 Book Chapter.

PUBLICATION DISTRIBUTION

Peer-reviewed articles as sustainability strategy can leverage e-commerce (2012-2022) until Jun 2022. The year 2021 had the highest number of peer-reviewed publications on the subject, reaching 17.

Figure 1 summarizes the peer-reviewed literature published to period 2012-2022, Jun 2022.

The publications were sorted out as follow: Journal Of Cleaner Production (6) com 2 publicações (Emerald Emerging Markets Case Studies;

The publications were sorted out as follow: Journal Of Cleaner Production (6) with 2 publications (Emerald Emerging Markets Case Studies; IEEE International Conference On Industrial Engineering And Engineering Management; International Journal Of Logistics Research And Applications; International Journal Of Physical Distribution And Logistics Management; International Journal Of Quality And Service Sciences; International Review Of Retail Distribution And Consumer Research; Proceedings Of The 31st International Business Information Management Association Conference IBIMA 2018 Innovation Management and Education Excellence Through Vision 2020) and the remaining publications with 1 document. Interest in the topic has not had a positive evolution since 2016.

Figure 1. Documents by year
Source: own elaboration

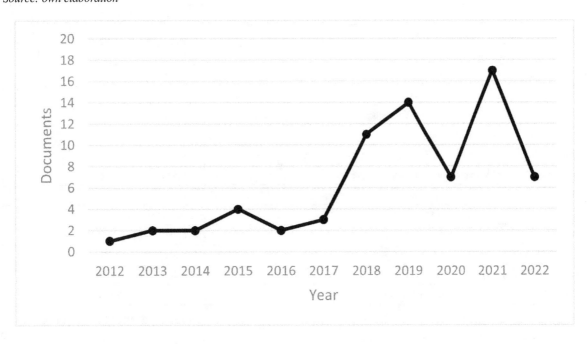

In Table 3 we analyze for the Scimago Journal & Country Rank (SJR), the best quartile and the H index by Manufacturing and Service Operations Management is the most quoted publication with 7,130 (SJR), Q1 and H index 92. There is a total of 20 publications on Q1, 11 publications on Q2 and 10 publications, Q3 and 1 publication on Q4. Publications from best quartile Q1 represent 34% of the 58 publications titles; best quartile Q2 represents 19%, best quartile Q3 represents 17%, and finally, best Q4 represents 2% each of the titles of 58 publications.

Finally, 16 publications without indexing data representing 28% of publications.

As shown in Table 3, most publications still do not have indexed data.

Table 3. Scimago journal & country rank impact factor

Title	SJR	Best Quartile	H index
Manufacturing And Service Operations Management	7,130	Q1	92
Journal Of Supply Chain Management	3,030	Q1	98
International Journal of Production Research	2,780	Q1	153
Business Horizons	2,380	Q1	97
Technological Forecasting and Social Change	2,340	Q1	134
International Journal of Operations and Production Management	2,290	Q1	146
Decision Support Systems	1,970	Q1	161
International Journal of Physical Distribution and Logistics Management	1,950	Q1	117
Journal Of Cleaner Production	1,920	Q1	232
Cities	1,660	Q1	102
International Journal of Logistics Management	1,500	Q1	80
European Management Journal	1,480	Q1	109
Electronic Commerce Research and Applications	1,370	Q1	82
International Journal of Logistics Research and Applications	1,060	Q1	38
Industrial Management and Data Systems	1,010	Q1	109
Journal Of Fashion Marketing and Management	0,970	Q1	56
Research In Transportation Business and Management	0,930	Q1	39
IEEE Transactions on Engineering Management	0,880	Q1	97
Total Quality Management and Business Excellence	0,770	Q1	87
Data Base for Advances in Information Systems	0,570	Q2	58
Journal Of Theoretical and Applied Electronic Commerce Research	0,570	Q2	33
International Journal of Engineering Business Management	0,540	Q2	25
Competitiveness Review	0,510	Q2	31
International Journal of Quality and Service Sciences	0,490	Q2	32
South Asian Journal of Business Studies	0,480	Q1	14
Journal Of Modelling in Management	0,470	Q2	32
International Review of Retail Distribution and Consumer Research	0,460	Q2	43
Logi Scientific Journal on Transport and Logistics	0,420	Q2	25

Continued on following page

Table 3. Continued

Title	SJR	Best Quartile	H index
Cogent Business and Management	0,410	Q2	23
Uncertain Supply Chain Management	0,360	Q2	19
Indian Journal of Marketing	0,320	Q3	11
International Journal of Logistics Systems and Management	0,320	Q2	32
Prabandhan Indian Journal of Management	0,310	Q3	9
International Journal of Grid and Utility Computing	0,290	Q3	22
International Journal of Technology Marketing	0,250	Q3	13
Emerald Emerging Markets Case Studies	0,230	Q3	7
World Review of Entrepreneurship Management and Sustainable Development	0,230	Q3	17
African Journal of Hospitality Tourism and Leisure	0,210	Q3	14
Gestao E Produção	0,200	Q3	18
International Journal of Networking and Virtual Organizations	0,200	Q3	20
Organization Development Journal	0,190	Q4	22
Rivista Di Studi Sulla Sostenibilita	0,150	Q3	12
IEEE International Conference on Industrial Engineering and Engineering Management	0	-*	21
Proceedings Of The 31st International Business Information Management Association Conference IBIMA 2018 Innovation Management and Education Excellence Through Vision 2020	0	-*	13
2021 IEEE International Conference on Industrial Engineering and Engineering Management IEEM 2021	0	-*	21
International Journal of Scientific and Technology Research	0	-*	22
Journal Of Asian Finance Economics and Business	0	-*	20
Journal Of Internet Banking and Commerce	0	-*	25
PICMET 2016 Portland International Conference on Management of Engineering and Technology Management for Social Innovation Proceedings	0	-*	9
Proceedings Of The 32nd International Business Information Management Association Conference IBIMA 2018 Vision 2020 Sustainable Economic Development and Application of Innovation Management from Regional Expansion to Global Growth	0	-*	10
Proceedings of the International Conference on Electronic Business ICEB	0	-*	9
Proceedings Of the Summer School Francesco Turco	0	-*	10
21st IAPRI World Conference on Packaging 2018 Packaging Driving a Sustainable Future	-*	-*	-*
International Journal of Professional Business Review	-*	-*	-*
Journal Of Retailing and Consumer Services	-*	-*	-*
Logforum	-*	-*	-*
Sustainable City Logistics Planning Methods and Applications Volume 2	-*	-*	-*
Sustainable City Logistics Planning Methods and Applications Volume 3	-*	-*	-*

Note: *data not available.

Source: own elaboration

The subject areas covered by the 70 scientific and/or academic documents were: Business, Management and Accounting (70); Decision Sciences (21); Engineering (19); Computer Science (14); Economics, Econometrics and Finance (13); Social Sciences (12); Energy (8); Environmental Science (8); Mathematics (2); Psychology (2); Arts and Humanities (1); Materials Science (1); and Medicine (1). The most quoted article was "A review of the environmental implications of B2C e-commerce: A logistics perspective" from Mangiaracina et al. (2015) with 95 quotes published in International Journal of Physical Distribution and Logistics Management 1,950 (SJR), the best quartile (Q1) and with H index (117), is "literature review on the topic of B2C e-commerce environmental sustainability, specifically from a logistics perspective".

In Figure 2 we can analyze the evolution of citations of the documents published until April 2022. The number of citations shows a positive net growth with R2 of 78% for the period £2012-2022, with 2021 reaching 321 citations.

Figure 2. Evolution of citations between 2012 and 2022
Source: own elaboration

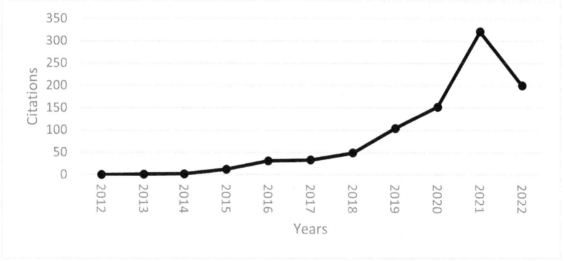

The h-index was used to ascertain the productivity and impact of the published work, based on the largest number of articles included that had at least the same number of citations. Of the documents considered for the h-index, 17 have been cited at least 17 times.

Citations of all scientific and/or academic documents from the period £2012 to April 2022, with a total of 905 citations, of the 70 documents 25 were not cited. The self-citation of documents in the period £2012 to April 2022 was self-cited 99 times.

In Annex I, citations of all scientific and/or academic documents from the period 2012 to 2022 are analyzed, with a total of 905 citations, of the 70 documents 23 not cited. Annex II examines the self-citation of the document during the period £2010 to 2021, 19 documents were self-cited 81 times, the document "Assessing the environmental impact of logistics in online and offline B2C purchasing processes in the apparel industry" by Mangiaracina et al. (2016) published in Electronic Markets has been cited 13 times.

The bibliometric study was carried out to investigate and identify indicators on the dynamics and evolution of scientific and/or academic information in documents based on the main keywords (Figure 3). the results were extracted from the scientific software VOSviewe, which aims to identify the main search keywords "Sustainability, Electronic Commerce, E-commerce, E- Commerces, E-Commerce, B2C E-commerce".

Figure 3. Network of all keywords

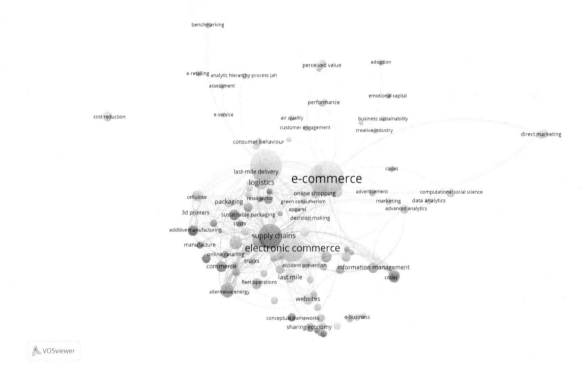

The research was based on scientific and/or academic documents on how A Sustainability Strategy Can Leverage E-Commerce. In Figure 4, we can examine the linked keywords, and thus, it is possible to highlight the network of keywords that appear together / linked in each scientific article, allowing to identify the topics studied by research and identify trends in future research. Finally, in Figure 5, a profusion of co-citation with a unit of analysis of the cited references is presented.

Figure 4. Network of linked keywords

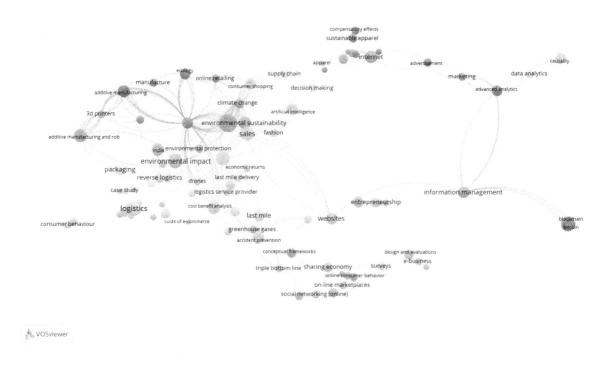

Figure 5. Network of co-citation

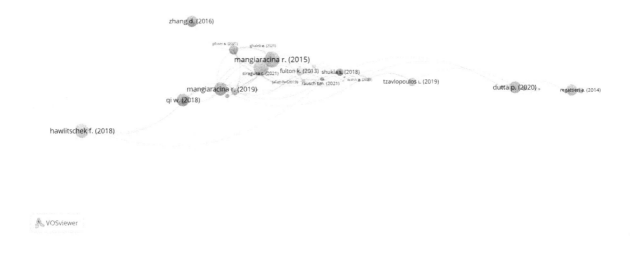

THEORETICAL PERSPECTIVES

The internet has been a revolutionary technology that has changed the way industries function by creating virtual markets and influencing consumer and business behavior and approaches to trade. Consumers have access to information and a wide range of products and services from competing firms, increasing levels of competition (Ahmadi et al., 2021). Similarly, companies now have access to critical information such as consumer needs and expectations that they utilize to innovate and improve their products and services. However, one major concern associated with this global reach is the need to achieve and maintain sustainability (Altuntaş Vural & Aktepe, 2021). For example, e-commerce shipment in business-to-consumer (B2C) distribution can lead to high gas emissions. Companies must consider whether their practices are sustainable to ensure that these technological and economic developments do not affect the ecosystem's ability to produce and recover (Andreopoulou et al., 2018). Failure to balance society's development needs and the planet's protection can have massive adverse consequences, such as environmental degradation and severe climate change (Walsh & Linzmajer, 2021). Hence, this study explores the e-commerce sector in relation to the three sustainability dimensions, environmental, economic, and social, to demonstrate how companies can develop sustainability strategies that leverage e-commerce for higher performance, competitiveness, and productivity.

Internet and E-commerce

The growth of e-commerce is hugely facilitated by the global increase in internet use and the development of communication technologies worldwide. The convergence of computer technology and telecommunications gave rise to the internet, which refers to a global system of computer networks (Arora & Singh, 2019). It consists of interconnected networks that allow users from any computer to directly communicate with or access information from other users. These new web technologies provided businesses unprecedented opportunities to improve strategic business models by integrating the internet and other ICT innovations into business processes and activities for higher efficiency and performance (Baglio et al., 2018). Research shows that internet penetration began to grow in the 1990s, leading to the growth of the e-commerce business model significantly. For instance, Kabugumila et al. (2016) indicate that the number of computers connected to the internet grew from 1 million to 20 million between 1993 and 1997, while in 2015, approximately 3.5 billion people worldwide were connected to the internet. These rapid developments influenced the evolution of digital technologies designed to enhance commercial transactions using the internet, enabling enterprises, customers, and governments to interact online effectively (Basu et al., 2022). The growing access to the internet in most countries, smartphones, tablets, and personal computers have continuously empowered consumers to engage in an online transaction, contributing to the expansion and evolution of e-commerce.

There are multiple definitions of e-commerce. E-commerce refers to the selling and buying goods and services using telecommunication and telecommunication-based tools such as the Internet (Chivandi & Sibanda, 2018). It can also be defined as using digital technologies to facilitate business processes and transactions. The e-commerce concept entails multiple aspects, including the electronic exchange of information within an organization or its external members and buying, selling, and exchanging products and services electronically (Costa & Castro, 2021). In this regard, e-commerce involves all electronic transactions, financial and non-financial, a company engages in to facilitate trade (Yen & Wong, 2019). For instance, e-commerce entails the purchasing transactions where customers buy and pay for products online and the engagements to respond to customer requests and pre-sale and post-sale activities (Dutta et al., 2020). Most customers today use the internet to gather more information about products and services before purchasing decisions (Bharucha, 2019). The e-commerce platforms allow them to compare competing product characteristics, including price, product use, and appropriate manufacturing information. Therefore, e-commerce has significantly changed how businesses are done and influenced consumer behaviors.

Companies operating under the e-commerce model deal with multiple types of third parties, leading to different kinds of e-commerce. The first type is business-to-business (B2B), which involves business transactions. It involves the electronic transfer of products and services among firms, especially the traditional industrial wholesale companies and producers (Jain et al., 2021). Business-to-Consumer (B2C) e-commerce refers to the trade between companies and customers. An example is the retail online shops and centers that sell consumer products such as groceries, computers, electronics, clothing, and accessories (Ersoy, 2021). Consumer-to-consumer (C2C) involves the electronic sale of goods and services among customers through an online transaction platform. Consumer-to-business (C2B) e-commerce is common among crowdsourcing-based companies that purchase consumer products or services on the internet (Escursell et al., 2021). For example, some graphic designers or artists usually share their work on social media platforms. A company can contact such internet users to purchase the graphics or portrait paintings from such as 'sellers' (Jain et al., 2021). Business-to-administration (B2A) is a type of e-commerce consisting of online transactions between the government and the firm, such as taxation, legal documentation, and records. Similarly, Consumer-to-administration (C2A) e-commerce involve transactions between individual internet users and the government, such as taxation, healthcare, education programs, and social security (Zhou et al., 2021). These transactions have significantly reduced the trading cycles and transaction costs since trading parties can communicate and engage online instead of traveling to specific geographical locations where physical shops, warehouses, manufacturing plants, and government agencies are located.

Facilitators of E-commerce

The evolution and growth of e-commerce can be attributed to multiple facilitating factors. These factors influence the business environment through innovations that companies must adopt to succeed in the markets. The facilitators discussed in this study include the internet, social media, payment gateway, and analytics.

Internet

The massive penetration of the internet has been a critical e-commerce driver. In the current society, smartphones and the internet have become part of everyday life by allowing people to interact and communicate, receive services, and buy products. Jain et al. (2021) note that ICT technologies and the internet and its services have fueled unprecedented economic growth in the past 15 years by creating new markets supported by substantial technological advancements. The increase in the number of internet users in the 1990s led to the gradual growth of virtual markets that connected companies to their target customers, eliminating some complexities in the supply chain (Febransyah & Camelia Goni, 2022). In addition, the emergence of the World Wide Web and the evolution of multimedia content led to increased online engagement, allowing firms access to user-generated content that is used to improve business processes, product quality, and customer service (Tsekouropoulos et al., 2014). Thus, e-commerce is powered by the internet since interconnected networks facilitate access to global markets, online transactions, communication, and critical information for innovation.

Social Media

The rapid development and adoption of social media platforms such as Facebook, Twitter, and Instagram have significantly influenced online consumer purchasing behaviors. The platforms allow customers to virtually interact to exchange purchasing experiences and opinions regarding various brands, influencing each other's purchasing decisions (Ghaleb & Balian, 2021). Research shows that customers are more likely to trust peer recommendations and opinions over a firm's promotional messages (Valerio et al., 2019). Thus, social media has become a critical source of information for purchasing decisions. In addition, social media has changed how businesses market their products and services (VidhyaPriya et al., 2017). Companies nowadays are leveraging social media platforms to increase visibility and create brand awareness in the modern-day competitive business environment. In this case, social media allows firms to drive traffic to their e-commerce platforms, boost sales, and provide social support to potential online customers.

Payment Gateway

An online payment gateway is a technology that facilitates electronic payment methods by authorizing a customer transaction. In this regard, an online payment gateway accepts, and processes online payments made through multiple systems, including debit cards, credit cards, online banking purchases, and transfers of electronic funds (Oo, 2019). In addition, the payment gateway provides secure, temporary storage of payment information, reconciliation reports, encryption services, flexible API and integration capabilities, and virtual terminal ability (Sausi et al., 2021). Payment gateway enhances e-commerce by streamlining checkout processes, encrypting data, and improving client experience by working between the payment processor and the website.

Analytics

Analytics as an e-commerce facilitator refers to the empirical technique of collecting, organizing, and analyzing customer data to enhance decision-making. Data technologies have increased companies' access to vast data volume, allowing them to understand the markets and client base for personalized experiences and promotions (Gupta et al., 2022). In this regard, data mining has become a critical process of analyzing the large volumes of data gathered from internet users to identify different perspectives and categorize helpful information for decision-making (VidhyaPriya et al., 2017). For example, companies can use data mining software to analyze data from multiple dimensions, classify it, and summarize relationships between variables to identify consumer behaviors' patterns or trends. These tools provide access to real-time insights needed to improve e-commerce platforms and service delivery.

SUSTAINABLE DEVELOPMENT AND SUSTAINABILITY

Despite the massive technological advancements achieved in the last two centuries, human survival is still hugely dependent on the natural systems' continued functioning. For example, the natural, biogeochemical cycles ensure that people have access to clean water, oxygen, carbon, and other essential elements (Barbosa et al., 2014). Plant life, directly and indirectly, ensures access to healthy food. While some technologies have been used to create artificial components that replace the natural, the economic costs involved in the processes are too high, and the world does not have adequate technological solutions to feed all the global populations (Brand & Rausch, 2021). Therefore, while economic development is critical in enhancing the quality of life, it is vital to ensure it is sustainable. Sustainable development protects the natural ecosystem and life (Haryanti & Subriadi, 2022). From these perspectives, the Bruntland Commission in the Our Common Future 1987 report defined sustainable development as "development that meets the needs of the present without compromising the ability of future generations to meet their own needs" (Emas, 2015, p.1). This definition provides a framework that encourages balancing development strategies with environmental policies by introducing the ethical principle of achieving fairness to present and future generations.

The Bruntland report centered on three primary principles: environmental protection, economic growth, and social equity. It advocated for alternative economic development strategies that met the economic needs of the world population without damaging the environment or reducing the natural resources to unsustainable levels (Carvalho et al., 2019). These aspects became the foundations for further definitions of the sustainable development concept. In 1991, the World Commission on Environment and Development provided various goals for sustainable development (Shadrina & Arviansyah, 2018). They included meeting the essential needs of the people, such as food, water, sanitation, energy, and jobs, protecting and conserving natural resources, renewable growth, risk management, and reorientation of technology (Barbosa et al., 2014). The main idea was to encourage the development of cities that provided opportunities and focused on meeting the needs of the people to improve their quality of life (de Araújo et al., 2018). These goals have further been classified in three broad perspectives; social, technological, and environmental. Therefore, the concept of sustainable development seeks to reconcile the aspect of economic growth and production with social justice and ecological sustainability.

Sustainability is the core idea behind sustainable development. The term refers to the efforts to create thriving, healthy, diverse, and resilient communities by integrating economic vitality, environmental protection, and social equity to benefit the current and future generations (Dhote & Zahoor, 2017). Sustainability recognizes that multiple issues in society are interconnected, and changes in one can influence the other. For example, massive economic growth can lead to environmental degradation. Sustainability recognizes that resources are finite and encourages conservative and wise use of these resources by prioritizing the long-term opportunities and consequences of continuous exploitation of these resources (Ferreira et al., 2020). It can also be defined as the process of living within the limits of current social, natural, and physical resources to allow long-lasting prosperity and create solutions to problems that threaten the stability and wellbeing of the planet and current and future generations (Fota et al., 2019). Therefore, sustainability advocates for a holistic systems approach that acknowledges the complexity of addressing the world's social, environmental, and economic issues.

Sustainability can be understood as both a goal to be attained and a process to achieve the goal. As a goal, sustainability can refer to various socioeconomic and environmental levels that must be completed to facilitate comfortable living (Frei et al., 2020). As a process, sustainability can involve multiple aspects, including political approaches to environmental problems, individual attitudes towards sustainability, organizational structures that influence sustainable strategies, consumption patterns, and economic structures. In this case, achieving sustainability requires acting deeply within these variables and structures to ensure that the overall system aligns with the sustainability and sustainable development goal (Fulton & Lee, 2013). Such an approach ensures that the sourcing, manufacturing, distribution, and consumption of existing resources are done in an ecologically viable, economically efficient, and socially appropriate way (Guo et al., 2019). Therefore, sustainability is a broad concept that requires diverse considerations when developing and implementing sustainable development approaches.

Pillars of Sustainability

The term sustainability is used to illustrate the need to satisfy fundamental human rights, protect genetic resources, conserve biodiversity, and ensure the functioning of ecosystems while facilitating production and economic growth. Consequently, the conceptual framework of sustainability is classified into three broad categories referred to as the pillars of sustainability; social, economic, and environmental subsystems.

Economic Sustainability

Economic sustainability is the sustainability dimension concerned with the economic system itself. It encourages creating an economic model that meets the consumption demands of the current population without compromising those of the future generations (Hassan et al., 2018). Economic sustainability involves adopting business practices that support economic growth without negatively affecting the society's environmental, social, and cultural aspects. Traditionally, economists believed that natural resource supply was inexhaustible (Hawlitschek et al., 2018). In addition, they argued that technological advancements would help refill or replace the natural resources destroyed during the production processes. However, modern-day economists and businesses have realized that natural resources are limited, and unsustainable production threatens the continuous output and the stability and wellbeing of current and future generations (Kauffman et al., 2017). This has led to concerns over the feasibility of consumption without bound and uncontrolled growth. As a result, economic sustainability has become a critical topic in the business world, encouraging businesses to adopt sustainable business models that protect and conserve natural resources by producing exact amounts needed to satisfy the consumption needs of current generations.

Environmental Sustainability

Environmental sustainability is concerned with protecting and conserving environmental resources to ensure that future generations have equal opportunities to use them to meet their needs. In addition, it involves engaging in human and business practices within the carrying capacity of the planet's supporting ecosystem (Liu & Sutanto, 2015). Therefore, it is critical to understand that environmental sustainability involves maintaining natural capital as the source of economic inputs and the absorber of the economic outputs. In this case, the environment as the source requires harvesting techniques to be kept within appropriate regeneration rates (Mangiaracina et al., 2016). The environment as the absorber demands that the amount of industrial waste emissions should not exceed the earth's capacity to assimilate them without damage. While all the pillars of sustainability are interconnected, environmental sustainability is often perceived as a more critical aspect (Niraj & Nageswara Rao, 2015). The socioeconomic dimensions of sustainability are heavily reliant on the environment. For example, the survival of human beings requires access to clean water, air, and productive land (van Duin et al., 2019). Similarly, the success of the economic systems is dependent on the environment for sufficient flow of material, energy, and environmental resources necessary for production. Therefore, the lack of a sustainable environment can lead to the failure of social and economic sustainability.

Environmental sustainability can take multiple forms, such as creating sustainable cities and eco-villages, developing green technologies, and using renewable energy. It can also involve adjusting individual lifestyles to minimize unnecessary consumption that leads to waste and reappraising the economic sectors through efforts such as sustainable architecture and green building (Paul Singh et al., 2019). Modern-day environmentalists and environmental organizations have realized that the earth's resources are used and damaged faster than they can be regenerated (Van Loon et al., 2015). As a result, environmental sustainability has become a global initiative concerned with protecting the long-term productivity and health of resources and species diversity and ecological structure while also preventing potential consequences of artificial worldwide warming and climate change (Pereira et al., 2022). Achieving these sustainable environmental goals requires collaboration between businesses, consumers, government, and non-governmental institutions to ensure creation and compliance with appropriate regulations and changes in attitudes and behaviors towards sustainability.

Social Sustainability

The dimension of social sustainability aims to answer the question, what are the social goals of sustainable development? Despite enormous literature on sustainable communities, social capital, and social cohesion, there is minimal research defining social sustainability and its parameters (Bacon et al., 2012). However, in the most basic perspective, social sustainability involves creating social organizations focused on poverty alleviation. As a people-centered dimension of sustainability, social sustainability involves identifying and managing business practices that negatively or positively impact people (Pfoser et al., 2021). The primary goal is to ensure that a business' activities contribute to the community it serves. In this regard, social sustainability values relationships and engagement with multiple stakeholders, including local communities, customers, employees, and other parties throughout the supply chain (Qi et al., 2018). Therefore, it encompasses ideas such as equity, empowerment, cultural identity, resource accessibility, societal participation and engagement, and institutional stability. Under sustainable development, issues such as the weak rule of law, poverty, and inequalities threaten business growth and operations (Rausch et al., 2021). In addition, social sustainability advocates for just, inclusive, and resilient societies that allows people to voice their concerns and ideas, and the government and other relevant institutions respond accordingly. These perspectives explain the rise in human rights advocates, the need for women empowerment, opportunities for people with disabilities, and other innovations aimed at solving social problems affecting global populations (Regattieri et al., 2014). Therefore, social sustainability is concerned with improving people's lives through social investments, public policies, and empowerment initiatives.

E-Commerce and Sustainability

In recent years, multiple people and institutions have raised concerns over the impact of e-commerce on the environment, society, and global economies. Issues such as environmental pollution and climate change have dominated economic discussions and debates, with individual customers, experts, and leaders questioning the sustainability of digital commerce (Ignat & Chankov, 2020). However, with the rapid rate of technological advancements, there has been a realization that technologies will keep evolving, and there is no going back to the traditional way of doing business (Varlese et al., 2020). As a result, companies are researching, developing, and implementing sustainable business strategies by considering all the three dimensions of sustainability (Schleiden & Neiberger, 2020). This section analyzes how environmental, social, and economic sustainability pillars relate to and affects e-commerce to derive insights on how it can be leveraged to support sustainable growth.

E-Commerce and Environmental Sustainability

Research shows that e-commerce has a lower carbon footprint compared to the traditional brick-and-mortar system. A study assessing the environmental impacts across an e-commerce supply chain, including energy consumption, transportation, warehousing, and packaging, found that e-commerce is more eco-friendly than traditional commerce (Rao et al., 2021). In addition, the scholars indicate that e-commerce is 35% less energy-intensive than the conventional retail business model. Proponents of e-commerce argue that the online retail hopping model uses optimized delivery techniques that reduce transportation emissions in online shopping compared to customer transportation in traditional physical shopping (Jafari, 2019). For instance, delivery trucks carrying packages for multiple customers are used to deliver goods ordered online (Singh et al., 2018). This approach minimizes the number of customers traveling from one place to another in search of desired products, thus reducing carbon footprints (Liu et al., 2017). Besides, e-commerce companies allow some of their employees to work online from home, reducing the number of commuters. Transportation is among the leading sectors in carbon dioxide emissions. Therefore, reducing the number of commuters has positive environmental impacts.

E-commerce involves paperless transactions, e-brochures, and catalogs that eliminate cutting down trees and associated environmental problems. The global online auctioning among internet users and businesses reduces and prevents waste by creating a market for secondary materials that would have otherwise turned into waste (Mangiaracina et al., 2015). For example, internet users can sell products they no longer use online, such as clothes, at lower prices instead of throwing them away. This strategy reduces the amount of waste that previously went to landfills, causing environmental pollution.

While the potential of e-commerce in saving material, reducing pollution, and energy use cannot be denied, it can also have multiple negative impacts on the environment. For example, customers using e-commerce tend to favor fast delivery, such as same-day home or few-hour deliveries (Mangiaracina et al., 2019). While this increases efficiency, customer satisfaction, and business performance, it can have multiple negative impacts on the environment, including an increase in energy use and fuel consumption. According to Rao et al. (2021), urban last-mile delivery in e-commerce is projected to grow by 78% by 2030, resulting in a 36% increase in delivery trucks in more than 100 cities worldwide. In this case, the environmental-related emissions are expected to increase by nearly one-third (Prajapati et al., 2022). Such notions indicate that although embracing online shopping can save the environment through reduced waste, minimal deforestation, and emissions from customer transportation, more energy is required to facilitate the functioning of the computers-intensive business model and may lead to higher transportation emissions in the long run. Therefore, further research and developments are needed to turn e-commerce into an eco-friendlier business model.

E-commerce and Economic Sustainability

Economic sustainability encourages firms to economize available resources to deliver higher value to stakeholders and maximize profits. In this case, the concept involves increasing efficiency throughout production while optimizing opportunities to grow profits (Priambodo et al., 2021). In e-commerce, the internet and advanced technologies are core facilitators of business processes and success. In this case, the use of interconnected systems increases efficiency, lowers operational and production costs, enhances convenience, and improves the ability to personalize information (Rossolov, 2019). For example, online inventory management reduces increases efficiency and reduces costs by decreasing the costs of handling and storing materials. Through inventory management software, companies can track inventory in real-time to determine the appropriate amount of stock to hold at any given time, thus avoiding overstocking that leads to higher storage costs (Shao & Liu, 2012). Advanced technologies integrated into the e-commerce system can be leveraged to improve economic sustainability. Multiple software programs and hardware allow companies to better allocate and utilize assets and control production and administration costs. In addition, they can be used to establish flexible mechanisms of responding to customer demands on time, leading to higher satisfaction and trust that build long-term customer relationships (Victor & Maria, 2018). E-commerce is characterized by multiple innovations and opportunities that can be leveraged to contribute to sustainable development and sustainability.

Economic sustainability in e-commerce is also concerned with promoting an eco-efficient, prosperous, and innovative economy that offers high-quality employment and improves society's living standards. It enables an economic model to prioritize people's wellbeing, long-lasting development, and economic and environmental harmony. In e-commerce, these aspects are promoted by prioritizing customer engagement and relationships, allowing businesses to gather critical information needed for innovation (Shukla et al., 2018). Besides, customers nowadays are aware of sustainable development and continuously share their opinions on sustainable business practices (Siragusa & Tumino, 2021). Consequently, e-commerce platforms use social media and the internet to connect and engage with existing and potential customers allowing them to share ideas that can be integrated to develop and implement sustainable business strategies (Tokar et al., 2021). Businesses have realized that sustainable development requires a collaborative approach, including their leaders and all the stakeholders across the entire supply chain. Therefore, this acknowledgment helps optimize data technologies in e-commerce to improve sustainability strategies and approaches.

E-commerce and Social Sustainability

The social dimension of sustainability involves investing in cultural development and human needs. Information and communication technologies (ICTs) have enhanced companies' capabilities to transfer information and communication globally and expanded their access to scattered markets worldwide through e-commerce (Tzavlopoulos et al., 2019). This expanded outreach has enabled companies to achieve social innovation, which involves meeting the people's social needs and improving their living conditions (Sodhi & Tang, 2021). One major strategy that corporations use to achieve social sustainability is corporate social responsibility (CSR), which defines an organization's policies and practices aimed at contributing to the goals of improving communities, the environment, and the economy (Oláh et al., 2018). CSR reflects an organization's willingness to take responsibility and accountability for its actions and consequent impacts on affected communities. Some goals that can be achieved through social sustainability include advocating for justice, eradicating poverty, improving access to educational and informational resources and facilities, preserving cultures, and supporting environmental protection initiatives (Velazquez & Chankov, 2019). Consumers in the modern world crave good health, better living conditions, a green environment, and socially responsible communities. E-commerce systems that prioritize social sustainability provide these desires by fostering innovations, creating high-quality jobs, and providing affordable, sustainable products and services that meet the needs of target consumers.

When creating sustainable strategies in e-commerce, it is critical to understand that all the three dimensions of sustainability, environmental, social, and economic, are interconnected. Unlike in the past, current consumers are aware of sustainable development and expect businesses to package their products and services sustainably. Therefore, basing major business decisions and actions on the three aspects of sustainability ensures that companies are sustainable enough to meet every stakeholder's expectation while contributing to the global efforts toward sustainable development.

CONCLUSION

Technological advancements in recent years have led to the significant growth of electronic commerce (e-commerce). E-commerce refers to a trading model in which customers purchase and pay for products online. With the internet and digital devices such as smartphones, tablets, or laptops, customers can buy products from any part of the world regardless of geographical boundaries. Other e-commerce facilitators include social media, data analytics, and payment gateway. These advanced technologies enabling e-commerce to have increased companies' access to real-time market information and trends, enhancing the planning and implementation of business strategies. Access to the customer has also increased their capability to provide customized services and innovative products based on customers' needs and expectations. However, while these developments have dramatically revolutionized the business environment, there have been increased concerns regarding e-commerce's impacts on sustainability. With the popularity of climate change and environmental pollution issues, businesses are under pressure from government and non-government institutions, customers, and other stakeholders to adopt sustainable practices. The sustainability issue is embedded in the global call for sustainable development goals that refer to the economic development and growth that satisfies the needs of current populations without compromising the capability of future generations to meet their own.

There are three dimensions of sustainability that must be considered when developing sustainable strategies, environmental, economic, and social sustainability. Although e-commerce does not entirely solve sustainability problems, enormous progress has been made in the retail e-commerce sector to achieve sustainability goals. For instance, e-commerce reduces transportation carbon emissions by reducing the number of customers commuting to physical stores. Instead, delivery trucks are used to deliver. One delivery truck can carry products ordered by multiple customers, reducing the number of cars on the roads. In addition, some e-commerce companies allow employees to work from home, further reducing commuters. The paperless structure reduces deforestation and associated environmental issues. The research found that e-commerce is more environmentally friendly than the traditional brick-and-mortar retail model. Economic sustainability in e-commerce involves using resources responsibly to increase production efficiencies and reduce costs to maximize profits. For instance, inventory management software prevents companies from overstocking, which may lead to waste when more than demanded products are stocked. The social aspect of e-commerce involves achieving social innovation by allowing the people to meet their social needs and enhancing their living conditions. In this regard, companies offer high-quality jobs, promote green consumerism, and support the creation of socially responsible communities. Sustainable strategies that leverage e-commerce must integrate environmental, social, and economic sustainability to achieve desired goals.

ACKNOWLEDGMENT

I would like to express gratitude to the Editor and the Arbitrators. They offered extremely valuable suggestions or improvements. The author was supported by the GOVCOPP Research Center of the University of Aveiro.

REFERENCES

Ahmadi, E., Wicaksono, H., & Valilai, O. F. (2021). Extending the last mile delivery routing problem for enhancing sustainability by drones using a sentiment analysis approach. *2021 IEEE International Conference on Industrial Engineering and Engineering Management, IEEM 2021*, 207-212. 10.1109/IEEM50564.2021.9672856

Altuntaş Vural, C., & Aktepe, Ç. (2021). Why do some sustainable urban logistics innovations fail? The case of collection and delivery points. *Research in Transportation Business & Management*, 100690. Advance online publication. doi:10.1016/j.rtbm.2021.100690

Andreopoulou, Z., Koliouska, C., Galariotis, E., & Zopounidis, C. (2018). Renewable energy sources: Using PROMETHEE II for ranking websites to support market opportunities. *Technological Forecasting and Social Change*, *131*, 31–37. doi:10.1016/j.techfore.2017.06.007

Arora, A., & Singh, S. (2019). Sustainability issues in freshfruggies: Hyperlocal fruits and vegetables delivery model. *Emerald Emerging Markets Case Studies*, *9*(2), 1–21. doi:10.1108/EEMCS-10-2018-0222

Arora, S. (2019). Devising e-commerce and green e-commerce sustainability. *International Journal of Engineering Development and Research*, *7*(2), 206–210.

Bacon, C. M., Getz, C., Kraus, S., Montenegro, M., & Holland, K. (2012). The social dimensions of sustainability and change in diversified farming systems. *Ecology and Society*, *17*(4), 41. doi:10.5751/ES-05226-170441

Baglio, M., Dallari, F., Garagiola, E., & Perotti, S. (2018). A model for assessing the quality and functionality of logistics buildings. *Proceedings of the Summer School Francesco Turco, 2018-September* 186-192.

Barbosa, G. S., Drach, P. R., & Corbella, O. D. (2014). A conceptual review of the terms sustainable development and sustainability. *Journal of Social Sciences*, *3*(2), 1–15. https://www.iises.net/download/Soubory/soubory-puvodni/pp-01-15_ijossV3N2.pdf

Basu, D., Chakraborty, K., Mitra, S., & Verma, N. K. (2022). Customer reciprocity in greening: The role of service quality. *International Journal of Quality and Service Sciences*, *14*(2), 238–257. doi:10.1108/IJQSS-08-2021-0116

Bharucha, J. (2019). Sustainability of Kirana stores in India: Reengineering physical with some digital. *World Review of Entrepreneurship, Management and Sustainable Development*, *15*(6), 751–764. doi:10.1504/WREMSD.2019.104866

Brand, B. M., & Rausch, T. M. (2021). Examining sustainability surcharges for outdoor apparel using adaptive choice-based conjoint analysis. *Journal of Cleaner Production, 289*, 125654. Advance online publication. doi:10.1016/j.jclepro.2020.125654

Carvalho, Y. A., Siqueira, R., Scafuto, I., & Silva, L. F. (2019). Sustainable marketplace project vendor selection criteria prioritization using AHP method [Utilização do método ahp para a priorização dos critérios de seleção de lojistas em um projeto de marketplace sustentável]. *International Journal of Professional Business Review, 4*(2), 114–123. doi:10.26668/businessreview/2019.v4i2.170

Chivandi, A., & Sibanda, F. (2018). An investigation of e-commerce adoption inhibitors in the tourism industry: A Zimbabwe national parks perspective. *African Journal of Hospitality, Tourism and Leisure, 7*(3), 1–15.

Costa, J., & Castro, R. (2021). SMEs must go online—E-commerce as an escape hatch for resilience and survivability. *Journal of Theoretical and Applied Electronic Commerce Research, 16*(7), 3043–3062. doi:10.3390/jtaer16070166

de Araújo, A. C., Matsuoka, E. M., Ung, J. E., Massote, A., & Sampaio, M. (2018). An exploratory study on the returns management process in an online retailer. *International Journal of Logistics Research and Applications, 21*(3), 345–362. doi:10.1080/13675567.2017.1370080

Dhote, T., & Zahoor, D. (2017). Framework for sustainability in E - commerce business models: A perspective based approach. *Indian Journal of Marketing, 47*(4), 35–50. doi:10.17010/ijom/2017/v47/i4/112681

Donthu, N., Kumar, S., Mukherjee, D., Pandey, N., & Lim, W. M. (2021). How to conduct a bibliometric analysis: An overview and guidelines. *Journal of Business Research, 133*, 285–296. doi:10.1016/j.jbusres.2021.04.070

Dutta, P., Mishra, A., Khandelwal, S., & Katthawala, I. (2020). A multiobjective optimization model for sustainable reverse logistics in Indian E-commerce market. *Journal of Cleaner Production, 249*, 119348. Advance online publication. doi:10.1016/j.jclepro.2019.119348

Emas, R. (2015). The concept of sustainable development: definition and defining principles. *Brief for GSDR, 2015*, 1-3. https://asset-pdf.scinapse.io/prod/2184349672/2184349672.pdf

Ersoy, Y. (2021). Equipment selection for an E-commerce company using entropy-based TOPSIS, EDAS and CODAS methods during the COVID-19. *Logforum, 17*(3), 341–358. doi:10.17270/J.LOG.2021.603

Escursell, S., Llorach-Massana, P., & Roncero, M. B. (2021). Sustainability in e-commerce packaging: A review. *Journal of Cleaner Production, 280*, 124314. doi:10.1016/j.jclepro.2020.124314 PMID:32989345

Escursell, S., Llorach-Massana, P., & Roncero, M. B. (2021). Sustainability in e-commerce packaging: A review. *Journal of Cleaner Production, 280*, 124314. Advance online publication. doi:10.1016/j.jclepro.2020.124314 PMID:32989345

Febransyah, A., & Camelia Goni, J. I. (2022). Measuring the supply chain competitiveness of e-commerce industry in Indonesia. *Competitiveness Review, 32*(2), 250–275. doi:10.1108/CR-05-2020-0059

Ferreira, J., Callou, G., MacIel, P., & Tutsch, D. (2020). An algorithm to optimize the energy distribution of data center electrical infrastructures. *International Journal of Grid and Utility Computing*, *11*(3), 419–433. doi:10.1504/IJGUC.2020.107625

Fota, A., Wagner, K., & Schramm-Klein, H. (2019). Is renting the new buying? A quantitative investigation of the determinants of the rental-commerce intention. *International Review of Retail, Distribution and Consumer Research*, *29*(5), 582–599. doi:10.1080/09593969.2019.1664616

Frei, R., Jack, L., & Brown, S. (2020). Product returns: A growing problem for business, society and environment. *International Journal of Operations & Production Management*, *40*(10), 1613–1621. doi:10.1108/IJOPM-02-2020-0083

Fulton, K., & Lee, S. (2013). Assessing sustainable initiatives of apparel retailers on the internet. *Journal of Fashion Marketing and Management*, *17*(3), 353–366. doi:10.1108/JFMM-11-2012-0071

Ghaleb, E., & Balian, P. (2021). Developing human potential within an e-commerce industry to leverage sustainability. *Organization Development Journal*, *39*(4), 34–46.

Guo, X., Lujan Jaramillo, Y. J., Bloemhof-Ruwaard, J., & Claassen, G. D. H. (2019). On integrating crowdsourced delivery in last-mile logistics: A simulation study to quantify its feasibility. *Journal of Cleaner Production*, *241*, 118365. Advance online publication. doi:10.1016/j.jclepro.2019.118365

Gupta, P., Bakhru, K. M., & Shankar, A. (2022). *Sustainable organizational performance management: Deciphering the role of emotional capital in e-commerce industry. South Asian Journal of Business Studies.* doi:10.1108/SAJBS-09-2021-0368

Haryanti, T., & Subriadi, A. P. (2022). E-commerce acceptance in the dimension of sustainability. *Journal of Modelling in Management*, *17*(2), 715–745. doi:10.1108/JM2-05-2020-0141

Hassan, R., Mahinderjit-Singh, M., Hassan, H., & Yuhaniz, S. S. (2018). Online Islamic business enhancer tool (OIBET) for young entrepreneurs. *Proceedings of the 31st International Business Information Management Association Conference, IBIMA 2018: Innovation Management and Education Excellence through Vision, 2020*, 687–701.

Hawlitschek, F., Teubner, T., & Gimpel, H. (2018). Consumer motives for peer-to-peer sharing. *Journal of Cleaner Production*, *204*, 144–157. doi:10.1016/j.jclepro.2018.08.326

Ignat, B., & Chankov, S. (2020). Do e-commerce customers change their preferred last-mile delivery based on its sustainability impact? *International Journal of Logistics Management*, *31*(3), 521–548. doi:10.1108/IJLM-11-2019-0305

Jafari, H. (2019). E-commerce logistics - contemporary literature. *IEEE International Conference on Industrial Engineering and Engineering Management*, 1196-1200. doi:10.1109/IEEM.2018.8607522

Jain, V., Malviya, B., & Arya, S. (2021). An Overview of Electronic Commerce (e-Commerce). *Journal of Contemporary Issues in Business and Government*, *27*(3), 666.

Kabugumila, M. S., Lushakuzi, S., & Mtui, J. E. (2016). E-commerce: An overview of adoption and its effective implementation. *International Journal of Business and Social Science*, *7*(4), 243–252.

Kauffman, R. J., Kim, K., Lee, S. T., Hoang, A., & Ren, J. (2017). Combining machine-based and econometrics methods for policy analytics insights. *Electronic Commerce Research and Applications*, *25*, 115–140. doi:10.1016/j.elerap.2017.04.004

Liu, X., Zhang, S., Lin, Y., & Xie, Y. (2017). Enhancing the health and sustainability of e-commerce ecosystem by bringing manufacturers online: Evidence from tao-factory. *PICMET 2016 - Portland International Conference on Management of Engineering and Technology: Technology Management for Social Innovation, Proceedings,* 815-823. doi:10.1109/PICMET.2016.7806756

Liu, Y., & Sutanto, J. (2015). Online group-buying: Literature review and directions for future research. *The Data Base for Advances in Information Systems*, *46*(1), 39–59. doi:10.1145/2747544.2747548

Mangiaracina, R., Marchet, G., Perotti, S., & Tumino, A. (2015). A review of the environmental implications of B2C e-commerce: A logistics perspective. *International Journal of Physical Distribution & Logistics Management*, *45*(6), 565–591. doi:10.1108/IJPDLM-06-2014-0133

Mangiaracina, R., Perego, A., Perotti, S., & Tumino, A. (2016). Assessing the environmental impact of logistics in online and offline B2C purchasing processes in the apparel industry. *International Journal of Logistics Systems and Management*, *23*(1), 98–124. doi:10.1504/IJLSM.2016.073300

Mangiaracina, R., Perego, A., Seghezzi, A., & Tumino, A. (2019). Innovative solutions to increase last-mile delivery efficiency in B2C e-commerce: A literature review. *International Journal of Physical Distribution & Logistics Management*, *49*(9), 901–920. doi:10.1108/IJPDLM-02-2019-0048

Niraj, S., & Nageswara Rao, S. V. D. (2015). Sustainability of E-retail in India. *Journal of Internet Banking and Commerce*, *20*(2). Advance online publication. doi:10.4172/1204-5357.1000107

Oláh, J., Kitukutha, N., Haddad, H., Pakurár, M., Máté, D., & Popp, J. (2018). Achieving sustainable e-commerce in environmental, social and economic dimensions by taking possible trade-offs. *Sustainability*, *11*(1), 1–22. doi:10.3390u11010089

Oo, K. Z. (2019). Design and implementation of electronic payment gateway for secure online payment system. *Int. J. Trend Sci. Res. Dev*, *3*, 1329–1334.

Paul Singh, S., Smith, K. D., Singh, J., & Rutledge, N. (2019). Packaging and logistics sustainability for the 21st century. *21st IAPRI World Conference on Packaging 2018 - Packaging: Driving a Sustainable Future,* 817-824.

Pereira, A. M., Moura, J. A. B., Costa, E. D. B., Vieira, T., Landim, A. R. D. B., Bazaki, E., & Wanick, V. (2022). Customer models for artificial intelligence-based decision support in fashion online retail supply chains. *Decision Support Systems*, *158*, 113795. Advance online publication. doi:10.1016/j.dss.2022.113795

Pfoser, S., Brandner, M., Herman, K., Steinbach, E., Brandtner, P., & Schauer, O. (2021). Sustainable transport packaging: Evaluation and feasibility for different use cases. *LOGI - Scientific Journal on Transport and Logistics, 12*(1), 159-170. doi:10.2478/logi-2021-0015

Prajapati, D., Chan, F. T. S., Daultani, Y., & Pratap, S. (2022). Sustainable vehicle routing of agro-food grains in the e-commerce industry. *International Journal of Production Research*, 1–26. Advance online publication. doi:10.1080/00207543.2022.2034192

Priambodo, I. T., Sasmoko, S., Abdinagoro, S. B., & Bandur, A. (2021). E-commerce readiness of creative industry during the COVID-19 pandemic in Indonesia. *Journal of Asian Finance. Economics and Business*, 8(3), 865–873. doi:10.13106/jafeb.2021.vol8.no3.0865

Qi, W., Li, L., Liu, S., & Shen, Z. M. (2018). Shared mobility for last-mile delivery: Design, operational prescriptions, and environmental impact. *Manufacturing & Service Operations Management*, 20(4), 737–751. doi:10.1287/msom.2017.0683

Rao, P., Balasubramanian, S., Vihari, N., Jabeen, S., Shukla, V., & Chanchaichujit, J. (2021). The e-commerce supply chain and environmental sustainability: An empirical investigation on the online retail sector. *Cogent Business & Management*, 8(1), 1938377. doi:10.1080/23311975.2021.1938377

Rausch, T. M., Baier, D., & Wening, S. (2021). Does sustainability really matter to consumers? assessing the importance of online shop and apparel product attributes. *Journal of Retailing and Consumer Services*, 63, 102681. Advance online publication. doi:10.1016/j.jretconser.2021.102681

Regattieri, A., Santarelli, G., Gamberi, M., & Mora, C. (2014). A new paradigm for packaging design in web-based commerce. *International Journal of Engineering Business Management*, 6(1), 1–11. doi:10.5772/58825

Rosário, A. T. (2021). The Background of articial intelligence applied to marketing. *Academy of Strategic Management Journal*, 20(6), 1–19.

Rosário, A. T., & Dias, J. C. (2022). Sustainability and the Digital Transition: A Literature Review. *Sustainability*, 14(7), 4072. doi:10.3390u14074072

Rossolov, A. (2019). Sustainable balance between e-commerce and in-store purchases. Sustainable city logistics planning: Methods and applications, 2, 61-84.

Sausi, J. M., Mtebe, J. S., & Mbelwa, J. (2021). Evaluating user satisfaction with the e-payment gateway system in Tanzania. *South African Journal of Information Management*, 23(1), 9. doi:10.4102ajim.v23i1.1430

Schleiden, V., & Neiberger, C. (2020). Does sustainability matter? A structural equation model for cross-border online purchasing behavior. *International Review of Retail, Distribution and Consumer Research*, 30(1), 46–67. doi:10.1080/09593969.2019.1635907

Shadrina, R., & Arviansyah. (2018). User interface and generations' preferences: Design and evaluation. *Proceedings of the 32nd International Business Information Management Association Conference, IBIMA 2018 - Vision 2020: Sustainable Economic Development and Application of Innovation Management from Regional Expansion to Global Growth*, 7882-7892.

Shao, T., & Liu, Z. (2012). How to maintain the sustainability of an e-commerce firm? From the perspective of social network. *International Journal of Networking and Virtual Organisations*, 11(3-4), 212–224. doi:10.1504/IJNVO.2012.048906

Shukla, S., Mohanty, B. K., & Kumar, A. (2018). Strategizing sustainability in e-commerce channels for additive manufacturing using value-focused thinking and fuzzy cognitive maps. *Industrial Management & Data Systems*, *118*(2), 390–411. doi:10.1108/IMDS-03-2017-0122

Singh, J., Srivastava, A., & Awasthi, M. K. (2018). Study of value chain of Indian textile handicrafts: A case of Lucknow Chikankari. *Prabandhan: Indian Journal of Management*, *11*(5), 28–41. doi:10.17010/pijom/2018/v11i5/123810

Siragusa, C., & Tumino, A. (2021). *E-grocery: Comparing the environmental impacts of the online and offline purchasing processes. International Journal of Logistics Research and Applications.* doi:10.1080/13675567.2021.1892041

Sodhi, M. S., & Tang, C. S. (2021). Supply chain management for extreme conditions: Research opportunities. *The Journal of Supply Chain Management*, *57*(1), 7–16. doi:10.1111/jscm.12255

Sun, M., Grondys, K., Hajiyev, N., & Zhukov, P. (2021). Improving the E-Commerce Business Model in a Sustainable Environment. *Sustainability*, *13*(22), 12667. doi:10.3390u132212667

Tokar, T., Jensen, R., & Williams, B. D. (2021). A guide to the seen costs and unseen benefits of e-commerce. *Business Horizons*, *64*(3), 323–332. doi:10.1016/j.bushor.2021.01.002

Tsekouropoulos, G., Vatis, S., Andreopoulou, Z., Katsonis, N., & Papaioannou, E. (2014). The aspects of internet-based management, marketing, consumer's purchasing behavior and social media towards food sustainability. *Rivista di Studi sulla Sostenibilità*, (2), 207–222.

Tzavlopoulos, I., Gotzamani, K., Andronikidis, A., & Vassiliadis, C. (2019). Determining the impact of e-commerce quality on customers' perceived risk, satisfaction, value and loyalty. *International Journal of Quality and Service Sciences*, *11*(4), 576–587. doi:10.1108/IJQSS-03-2019-0047

Ukko, J., Nasiri, M., Saunila, M., & Rantala, T. (2019). Sustainability strategy as a moderator in the relationship between digital business strategy and financial performance. *Journal of Cleaner Production*, *236*, 117626. doi:10.1016/j.jclepro.2019.117626

Valerio, C., William, L., & Noémier, Q. (2019). The impact of social media on E-Commerce decision making process. *International Journal of Technology for Business*, *1*(1), 1–9.

Van Duin, J. H. R., Enserink, B., Daleman, J. J., & Vaandrager, M. (2019). The near future of parcel delivery: Selecting sustainable alternatives for parcel delivery. Sustainable city logistics planning: Methods and applications, 3, 219-252.

Van Loon, P., Deketele, L., Dewaele, J., McKinnon, A., & Rutherford, C. (2015). A comparative analysis of carbon emissions from online retailing of fast moving consumer goods. *Journal of Cleaner Production*, *106*, 478–486. doi:10.1016/j.jclepro.2014.06.060

Varlese, M., Misso, R., Koliouska, C., & Andreopoulou, Z. (2020). Food, internet and neuromarketing in the context of well-being sustainability. *International Journal of Technology Marketing*, *14*(3), 267–282. doi:10.1504/IJTMKT.2020.111500

Velazquez, R., & Chankov, S. M. (2019). Environmental impact of last mile deliveries and returns in fashion E-commerce: A cross-case analysis of six retailers. *IEEE International Conference on Industrial Engineering and Engineering Management*, 1099-1103. 10.1109/IEEM44572.2019.8978705

Victor, V., & Maria, F. F. (2018). The era of big data and path towards sustainability. *Proceedings of the 31st International Business Information Management Association Conference, IBIMA 2018: Innovation Management and Education Excellence through Vision, 2020*, 561–568.

VidhyaPriya. (2017). Connecting social media to eCommerce using microblogging and artificial neural network. *International Journal of Recent Trends in Engineering and Research, 3*(3), 337–343. doi:10.23883/IJRTER.2017.3087.4IJNP

Walsh, G., & Linzmajer, M. (2021). The services field: A cornucopia filled with potential management topics. *European Management Journal, 39*(6), 688–694. doi:10.1016/j.emj.2021.10.002

Yen, B., & Wong, G. (2019). Case study: Cainiao and JD.com leading sustainability packaging in China. *Proceedings of the International Conference on Electronic Business (ICEB)*, 90-98.

Zhou, Z., Wang, M., Ni, Z., Xia, Z., & Gupta, B. B. (2021). Reliable and sustainable product evaluation management system based on blockchain. *IEEE Transactions on Engineering Management*. Advance online publication. doi:10.1109/TEM.2021.3131583

ADDITIONAL READING

Arnold, F., Cardenas, I., Sörensen, K., & Dewulf, W. (2018). Simulation of B2C e-commerce distribution in antwerp using cargo bikes and delivery points. *European Transport Research Review, 10*(1), 2. Advance online publication. doi:10.100712544-017-0272-6

Bergman, M. (2014). *7 qualities of inferences in mixed methods research: Calling for an integrative framework*. Advances in Mixed Methods Research.

Carrillo, J. E., Vakharia, A. J., & Wang, R. (2014). Environmental implications for online retailing. *European Journal of Operational Research, 239*(3), 744–755. doi:10.1016/j.ejor.2014.05.038

Denzin, N. K., & Lincoln, Y. S. (1994). Handbook of Qualitative Research. Academic Press.

Hong, I. B. (2018). Social and personal dimensions as predictors of sustainable intention to use Facebook in Korea: An empirical analysis. *Sustainability (Switzerland), 10*(8), 2856. Advance online publication. doi:10.3390u10082856

Kautish, P., & Dash, G. (2017). Environmentally concerned consumer behavior: Evidence from consumers in Rajasthan. *Journal of Modelling in Management, 12*(4), 712–738. doi:10.1108/JM2-05-2015-0021

Lee, W., & Benbasat, I. (2003). Designing an electronic commerce interface: Attention and product memory as elicited by web design. *Electronic Commerce Research and Applications, 2*(3), 240–253. doi:10.1016/S1567-4223(03)00026-7

Mangiaracina, R., Marchet, G., Perotti, S., & Tumino, A. (2015). A review of the environmental implications of B2C e-commerce: A logistics perspective. *International Journal of Physical Distribution & Logistics Management, 45*(6), 565–591. doi:10.1108/IJPDLM-06-2014-0133

KEY TERMS AND DEFINITIONS

Business to Administration (B2A): E-commerce model that takes place between the company and the administration.

Business to Business (B2B): E-commerce model that takes place between two companies.

Business to Consumer (B2C): E-commerce model that takes place between business and consumer.

Consumer to Administration (C2A): E-commerce model that takes place between the consumer and the administration.

Consumer to Business (C2B): E-commerce model that takes place between consumer and company.

Consumer to Consumer (C2C): E-commerce model that takes place between two or more consumers.

Sustainable and/or Sustainability: Is a characteristic or condition of a process or a system that allows it to remain, at a certain level, for a certain period of time.

APPENDIX

Table 4. Overview of document citations period ≤2012 to 2022

Documents		≤2012	2013	2014	2015	2016	2017	2018	2019	2020	2021	2022	Total
Sustainable vehicle routing of agro-food grains in the e-com ...	2022	-	-	-	-	-	-	-	-	-	-	1	**1**
The role of e-marketing and e-crm on e-loyalty ofindonesian ...	2022	-	-	-	-	-	-	-	-	1	1	2	**4**
Smes must go online-e-commerce as an escape hatch for resili ...	2021	-	-	-	-	-	-	-	-	-	-	8	**8**
Does sustainability really matter to consumers? Assessing th ...	2021	-	-	-	-	-	-	-	-	-	-	6	**6**
A guide to the seen costs and unseen benefits of e-commerce	2021	-	-	-	-	-	-	-	-	-	3	5	**8**
Examining sustainability surcharges for outdoor apparel usin ...	2021	-	-	-	-	-	-	-	-	-		6	**6**
Sustainability in e-commerce packaging: A review	2021	-	-	-	-	-	-	-	-	1	18	13	**32**
The e-commerce supply chain and environmental sustainability ...	2021	-	-	-	-	-	-	-	-	-	-	1	**1**
E-Commerce Readiness ofCreative Industry During the COVID-1...	2021	-	-	-	-	-	-	-	-	-	-	-	*5*
E-grocery: comparing the environmental impacts ofthe online ...	2021	-	-	-	-	-	-	-	-	-	2	3	**4**
Supply Chain Management for Extreme Conditions: Research Opp ...	2021	-	-	-	-	-	-	-	-	-	11	14	**25**
Product returns: a growing problem for business, society and ...	2020	-	-	-	-	-	-	-	-	-	3	7	**10**
Do e-commerce customers change their preferred last-mile dei ...	2020	-	-	-	-	-	-	-	-	1	10	6	**17**
A multiobjective optimization model for sustainable reverse ...	2020	-	-	-	-	-	-	-	-	13	23	16	**52**
An algorithm to optimise the energy distribution of data cen ...	2020	-	-	-	-	-	-	-	-	2	1	1	**4**
Does sustainability matter? A structural equation model for ...	2020	-	-	-	-	-	-	-	-		3	1	**4**
On integrating crowdsourced delivery in last-mile logistics: ...	2019	-	-	-	-	-	-	-	-	2	13	8	**23**
Determining the impact of e-commerce quality on customers' p ...	2019	-	-	-	-	-	-	-	-	5	13	8	**26**
Environmental Impact of Last Mile Deliveries and Returns in ...	2019	-	-	-	-	-	-	-	-	2	2	2	**6**
Innovative solutions to increase last-mile delivery efficien ...	2019	-	-	-	-	-	-	-	-	5	43	19	**67**
Is renting the new buying? A quantitative investigation oft...	2019	-	-	-	-	-	-	-	-	1	1	2	**4**
Quo vadis, (e-)service quality? Towards a sustainability par ...	2019	-	-	-	-	-	-	-	-	-	4	2	**6**
E-Commerce Logistics - Contemporary Literature	2019	-	-	-	-	-	-	-	-	-	1	-	**1**
Sustainability of kirana stores in India: Reengineering phys ...	2019	-	-	-	-	-	-	-	-	-	-	1	**1**
Consumer motives for peer-to-peer sharing	2018	-	-	-	-	-	-	-	8	22	24	17	*75*
Shared mobility for last-mile delivery: Design, operational ...	2018	-	-	-	-	-	-	2	9	12	24	13	**60**

Continued on following page

Table 4. Continued

Documents		≤2012	2013	2014	2015	2016	2017	2018	2019	2020	2021	2022	Total
Renewable energy sources: Using PROMETHEE li for ranking web ...	2018	-	-	-	-	-	-	3	10	12	17	5	47
An exploratory study on the returns management process in an ...	2018	-	-	-	-	-	-	-	-	1	2	2	5
Study of value chain of Indian textile handicraf\s: A case o ...	2018	-	-	-	-	-	-	-	1	1	-	-	2
The era of big data and path towards sustainability	2018	-	-	-	-	-	-	-	-	-	1	-	1
A model for assessing the quality and functionality of logis ...	2018	-	-	-	-	-	-	-	1	-	-	-	1
Strategizing sustainability in e-commerce channels for addit...	2018	-	-	-	-	-	-	1	3	8	8	1	21
Combining machine-based and econometrics methods for policy ...	2017	-	-	-	-	-	1	6	4	7	8	1	27
Framework for sustainability in E - commerce business models ...	2017	-	-	-	-	-	1	1	-	-	-	-	2
Enhancing the health and sustainability of e-commerce ecosys ...	2017	-	-	-	-	-	-	-	-	-	1		1
The effects of E-commerce on the demand for commercial real ...	2016	-	-	-	-	3	4	4	11	5	18	3	48
Assessing the environmental impact oflogistics in online an ...	2016	-	-	-	-	3	5	5	5	2	9	4	33
A comparative analysis of carbon emissions from online retai ...	2015	-	-	-	2	5	6	8	22	18	19	9	89
A review ofthe environmental implications of B2C e-commerce ...	2015	-	-	-		6	11	14	19	18	18	9	95
Online group-buying: Literature review and directions for fu ...	2015	-	-	-	1	2	2	-	2	3	1	2	13
A new paradigm for packaging design in web-based commerce	2014	-	-	-	1	1	1	2	3	2	1	2	12
The aspects ofinternet-based management, marketing, consume ...	2014	-	-	-	1	3	-	1	2	-	1	-	8
Assessing sustainable initiatives of apparel retailers on th ...	2013	-	-	-	4	3	2	-	3	4	7	41	27
(Reverse logistics in the e-commerce: A case study, Logístic. ..	2013	-	-	1	2	2	-	2	-	-	1	1	9
How to mai ntain the sustai nability of an e-commerce firm? fr ...	2012	-	1	1	1	3	-	-	1	-	-	1	8
	Total	-	1	2	12	31	33	49	104	152	321	200	905

Source: own elaboration

Table 5. Overview of document self-citation period ≤2012 to 2022

Documents		≤2012	2013	2014	2015	2016	2017	2018	2019	2020	2021	2022	Total
The role of e-marketing and e-crm on e-loyalty ofindonesian ...	2022	-	-	-	-	-	-	-	-	1	1	-	2
Smes must go online-e-commerce as an escape hatch for resili ...	2021	-	-	-	-	-	-	-	-	-	-	8	8
Supply Chain Management for Extreme Conditions: Research Opp ...	2021	-	-	-	-	-	-	-	-	-	2	2	4
Product returns: a growing problem for business, society and ...	2020	-	-	-	-	-	-	-	-	-	-	2	2
Value chain analysis of varanasi silk sarees and brocade	2020	-	-	-	-	-	-	-	-	-	-	1	1
A multiobjective optimization model for sustainable reverse ...	2020	-	-	-	-	-	-	-	-	1	1	2	4
An algorithm to optimise the energy distribution of data cen ...	2020	-	-	-	-	-	-	-	-	1	1	-	2
Environmental Impact of Last Mile Deliveries and Returns in ...	2019	-	-	-	-	-	-	-	-	1	-	1	2
Innovative solutions to increase last-mile delivery efficien ...	2019	-	-	-	-	-	-	-	-	1	3	2	6
Consumer motives for peer-to-peer sharing	2018	-	-	-	-	-	-	-	2	3	-	1	6
Shared mobility for last-mile delivery: Design, operational ...	2018	-	-	-	-	-	-	-	1	1	1	-	3
Renewable energy sources: Using PROMETHEE li for ranking web ...	2018	-	-	-	-	-	-	1	-	1	-	-	2
Strategizing sustainability in e-commerce channels for addit...	2018	-	-	-	-	-	-	-	-	1	1	-	2
Combining machine-based and econometrics methods for policy ...	2017	-	-	-	-	-	1	1	2	2	1	-	7
Assessing the environmental impact oflogistics in online an ...	2016	-	-	-	-	1	2	1	2	1	4	2	13
A comparative analysis of carbon emissions from online retai ...	2015	-	-	-	-	1	-	-	-	1	1	-	3
A review ofthe environmental implications of B2C e-commerce ...	2015	-	-	-	-	1	3	2	1	-	1	-	8
Online group-buying: Literature review and directions for fu ...	2015	-	-	-	-	1	-	-	-	1	-	-	2
A new paradigm for packaging design in web-based commerce	2014	-	-	-	-	1	-	-	1	1	1	-	4
	Total	-	-	-	-	5	6	5	9	17	18	21	81

Chapter 4
The Propensity of E-Commerce Acceptance Among Unorganized Retail Small-Medium Enterprises (SMEs)

Karthik Ram M.
SASTRA University (Deemed), India

Selvabaskar S.
SASTRA University (Deemed), India

ABSTRACT

India has one of the largest bases of small- and medium-sized enterprises around the world after China, and it provides several benefits to the Indian economy in terms of generating a vast range of employment opportunities, innovation of new self-reliance technologies, aiding export growth, socio-economic growth, and rural development, which supports the nation-building. Consumers are using the power of digital technologies and e-commerce; this is the time to measure the propensity of business-to-business (e-commerce) adoption among unorganized retailers. Some studies measured the e-commerce impacts on customers, impacts on organized retailers, and impacts on unorganized retailers. In addition, some other studies concentrated on assessing the unorganized retail SME performance, competition, issues, and challenges. However, studies related to measuring e-commerce acceptance by unorganized retailers are relatively low. This chapter aims to measure the nuances of business-to-business (e-commerce) propensity among unorganized retailers.

INTRODUCTION

India has one of the largest bases of Small and Medium-sized enterprises around the world after China, and it provides several benefits to the Indian economy in terms of generating a vast range of employment opportunities, innovation of new self-reliance technologies, aid export growth, socio-economic growth,

DOI: 10.4018/978-1-6684-5727-6.ch004

and rural development which supports the nation building. In addition, as the new MSME Annual report shows, the service sector holds a 33 per cent MSME share in India and generates 362.82 lakhs new jobs service sector (Government of India, 2021). Most of the service sector enterprise do retail business in India, and the AT Kearney's Global Retail Development Index shows that India holds the second rank in 2021 with a score of 64.4 (Smriti Tankha, 2021). Further, Indian retail is dominated by Unorganized retail with a share of 88 per cent, organized retail holds a share of 9 per cent, and E-Commerce holds a share of 3 per cent (IBEF - Indian Retail Industry Report, 2021). The retail sector growth in India is backed up by several factors like rapid urbanization, robust industrial policy, socio-economic and cultural development, Modern family structure, increase in income, rapid changes in consumer habits, supporting digital infrastructure, internet connectivity, and digital disruption in the retail organization.

BACKGROUND

Digital Transformation in Indian Retail

The Indian retail sector has undergone several transformations in recent years and is one of the most dynamic worldwide. In addition, Kearney's Global Retail Development reports show several insights into the Indian retail sector. First, it states that Indian E-Commerce is estimated at 41 billion dollars and will poise to grow 25 per cent in 2025. Second, E-Commerce Gross Value Added shows an increasing trend in India's Tier 2, 3, and 4 cities. In addition, it indicates that the Tier 2, 3 and 4 cities' consumers' behavior substantially moved towards branded products and accepts the E-Commerce offerings. Third, it states that India's Tradition trade share or unorganized retail share is anticipated to drop from 92 per cent to 82 per cent by 2025 (Smriti Tankha, 2021). Fourth, the report states that Indian consumers and retailers are taking up digital technology's solutions, and the pandemic further propels it.

Further, on the one side, E-Commerce giants are actively participating with Brick-and-Mortar retailers and trying to minimize the delivery time. On another side, Kirana stores are transforming their storefront with various digital technologies like contactless payments, rewards, and door delivery service through WhatsApp orders. In addition, Reliance, Flipkart, and Amazon has initiated offering digital technologies to Kirana stores and plans to digitize Kirana store. Further, Several E-tailers also use Artificial Intelligence and Data Analytics software to provide tailor-made services to their customers, enhancing the customer experience and satisfaction.

Indian government plays an anchor role in this transformation, and the Government of India is working hard to thrive retail sector by initiating several initiatives like ameliorating government policies, robust investment in digital infrastructure, creating a favorable business climate for retail enterprise, supporting startup business ideas in retail, promoting self-reliance technologies among the retailers and consumers. These players boarded the Unorganized retailers on their platforms, allowing them to utilize their services. Acceptance of these platforms by the unorganized retailers will provide multiple benefits in terms of minimizing their competition from E-tailers & organized retailers, maximizing their market share, revenues, and cost of purchase, enhance customer experience, satisfaction, and engagement. It would not be a distant reality right now that circumstances like pandemics & lockdowns modified the minds of customers and retailers to accept the E-Commerce technologies in their business and day-to-day purchases.

There are studies which measured the E-Commerce impacts on customers, impacts on organized retailers, and impacts on unorganized retailers. Further, certain studies measured the organized retailers' impacts on unorganized retailers, technology adoption by the organized retailers, customer experience in the organized retail format, and organized retailers' customer relationship management programmers. In addition, some other studies concentrate on assessing the unorganized retail SME's performance, competition, issues, and challenges. However, studies related to measuring the E-Commerce acceptance by unorganized retailers are relatively low. In this digital world, consumers are using the power of digital technologies and E-Commerce; this is the time to measure the propensity of Business-to-Business (E-Commerce) adoption among unorganized retailers. This chapter aims to measure the nuances of Business-to-Business (E-Commerce) propensity among unorganized retailers.

Technology Acceptance Theories

The adoption of Business to Business (E-Commerce) among unorganized retailers is considerably increased after the outbreak of Covid 19 in India (Adapt to the new Kirana zamana, 2022). Further, the second wave and intermittent lockdowns cause supply chain disruptions for the unorganized retail business. To overcome those barriers, unorganized retailers are adopting such Business-to-Business platforms to ensure their sustainability in the market. This is the time to identify their grievances in the Business to Business (E-Commerce) Platforms and sort out their adoption issues with the platforms. To fix those existing issues, we need a solid theoretical background to capture the determinants of Business to Business (E-Commerce) Platforms. There are several theories in Technology acceptance, and some of the familiar theories are the Technology Acceptance Model – 1,2 & 3, Technology, Organization and Environment, Diffusion of Innovation theory, Unified theory of Acceptance and Use of Technology 1 & 2, Institutional Theory, Resource-Dependency theory, and Transaction Cost Theory. These theories are measured the user's adoption intention and their problems with the respected technologies. Even though earlier technology acceptance theories are available to measure the adoption intention among the unorganized retail SMEs, a Literature survey shows that the Innovation Diffusion Theory, Technology, Organization and Environment theory were used by most of the researchers who intended to measure the Business to Business (E-Commerce) Platforms (Tan, 2007), (Alsaad A. M., 2017). Based on the literature survey, this study adopts these two theories to measure the Business to Business (E-Commerce) Platforms among unorganized retailers.

MAIN FOCUS OF THE CHAPTER

Research Model

Figure 1. Research model

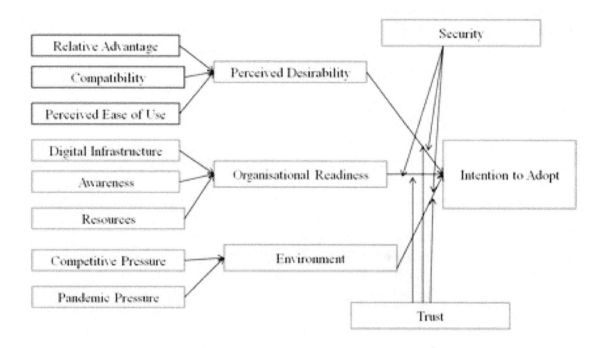

Perceived Desirability

Perceived desirability measures the retailers' readiness to adopt the Business to Business (E-Commerce) Platform. The retailers who adopt the technology have a higher level of desirability to adopt the Business to Business (E-Commerce) Platform (Alsaad A. M., 2017) (Alsaad A. M., 2015). Retailers' readiness will be significantly influenced after understanding the benefits of technology adoption, especially in the Business to Business (E-Commerce) Platform. Further, the studies unveiled that perceived desirability was influenced by Relative advantage, compatibility, and complexity. Finally, the intention to adopt Business to Business (E-Commerce) Platforms was influenced by perceived desirability.

Relative Advantage

Relative advantage is explained as the technology that creates a favorable perception among the adopters, and the technology is perceived as better than the existing notion or practice. In technology adoption literature, Relative Advantage is widely used in Business to Business (E-Commerce) Platforms research, and it is also a major influencing factor in Business to Business (E-Commerce) Platform studies (Alsaad A. M., 2015).

Compatibility

Compatibility aims to measure the Business to Business (E-Commerce) Platforms are how well they are suited for existing business operations. In other words, it measures the business compatibility between the technology and their business operations. Further, compatibility is positively influenced by technology adoption (Putra, 2020).

Perceived Ease-of-Use

Perceived Ease-of-Use is defined as an individual perception that the technology adoption requires the least amount of physical or mental exertion. Further, the technology used in the business is learnable, understandable, and flexible. Similarly, current research results indicate a robust positive relationship between perceived ease of use and attitude towards using (Islami, 2021).

Organizational Readiness

Organizational readiness is defined as how far the business of the unorganized retailers is equipped to adopt the Business to Business (E-Commerce) Platforms. Several study results unveiled that organizational readiness influences technology adoption (Fathian, 2008). Generally, these studies measure formal organization readiness. However, unorganized retail is a form of informal organization. It aims to measure the Business awareness level of the unorganized retailer and the resources of the organized retailer. Formal organizations invested a considerable amount in technologies, training programs and the like. However, in unorganized retail, retailers do their business for a significant source of their livelihood, earning a small profit. With that amount, unorganized retailers are unable to invest in the technologies. Further, this study identified three variables that measure the business readiness of unorganized retailers: Digital infrastructure, awareness, and resources are the sub-determinant measures of organizational readiness.

Digital Infrastructure

Digital Infrastructure is aimed to measure the level of internet & platform connectivity in their region among the potential adopters. Further, a higher level of digital infrastructure creates the notion among the retailers to adopt the Business to Business (E-Commerce) platform.

Awareness

Awareness is essential in this digital era, and it assists the adopters in responding to the Business to Business (E-Commerce) Platform appropriately and taking advantage of these changes. Further, awareness creates a notion of how well the Business to Business (E-Commerce) Platform works in their business. It also creates an idea about their potential suppliers' quality, price changes in the market, potential competitors, technical know-how and desirable demand level of a product.

Resources

Resources are essential in Business to Business (E-Commerce) Platform adoption among unorganized retailers. Resources aim to measure their organization's financial level and how well they can adopt a Business to Business (E-Commerce) Platform in their business.

Environment

The environment is another variable which influences technology adoption in existing studies. The environment aims to measure the situational factors that influence adopters in technology adoption. Several studies found that Competitive pressure influences technology adoption. This research wants to measure the pandemic impacts on the unorganized retail business.

Competitive Pressure

Competitive pressure is aimed to map the competitive pressure in the sector, and how far pushes the retailers to adopt Business to Business (E-Commerce) Platform in their business. Competitive pressures positively influence the adoption of Business to Business (E-Commerce) Platform among organizations.

Pandemic Pressure

Pandemic pressure in the world modified many organizations and their business operations. The extended lockdowns and social distancing norms foster the technology adoption among the unorganized retailers, which solves their business issues like supply chain disruption and changes in consumer behavior. The penetration of the Business to Business (E-Commerce) Platform is considerably high during this pandemic.

Trust

Trust is aimed to measure the emotional state of the unorganised retailer, whether he trusts the technology or not. It is a critical determinant in technology adoption studies, which builds a solid relationship to trust the Business to Business (E-Commerce) Platform (Koh, 2012). Several studies found trust mediating variables in the Business to Business (E-Commerce) Platform (Alsaad A. M., 2017).

Security

In Business to Business (E-Commerce), Platform adoption security aims to measure unorganized retailers' risk-free perception. Further, the current study result unveils that the platform's security determines the continuous usage of technologies. In addition, the Business to Business (E-Commerce) Platform needs to ensure the unorganized retailers' data and personal information will not reveal their information. Several studies show that security creates a negative effect on technology adoption (Moghavvemi, 2021)

Objectives

- To identify the determinants influencing the unorganized retailers SMEs to adopt Business to Business (E-Commerce) Platform.
- To assess the adoption of Business to Business (E-Commerce) Platform desirability among the unorganized retail SMEs.
- To evaluate the organizational readiness to adopt Business to Business (E-Commerce) technologies among unorganized retail SMEs.
- To identify the Environmental influence of adopting the Business to Business (E-Commerce) Platform among unorganized retail SMEs.
- To assess the relationship between the intention to adopt and trust & security.

RESEARCH METHODOLOGY

This study plans to develop an instrument to measure the Business to Business (E-Commerce) platform. In addition, it collects the data from the unorganized retail SMEs through a structured questionnaire. Further, this study adopts an experimental research design and uses a stratified random sampling method for data collection. The sample size is 250, and it collects the data from unorganized retailers. This study aims to validate the proposed research model through PLS-SEM analysis.

Hypothesis Development

H1: *PEOU (Perceived Ease of Use) has a significant influence on PD (Perceived Desirability)*

H2: *RA (Relative Advantage) Positively influence PD (Perceived Desirability)*

H3: *COMP (Compatibility) has a significant influence on PD (Perceived Desirability)*

H4: *PD (Perceived Desirability) Positively influence Behavioral Intention (BI)*

H5: *DI (Digital Infrastructure) Positively influence OR (Organizational Readiness)*

H6: *Aware (Awareness) creates a significant impact on OR (Organizational Readiness)*

H7: *RE (Resources) Positively influence OR (Organizational Readiness)*

H8: *OR (Organizational Readiness) has a significant influence on BI (Behavioral Intention)*

H9: *CP (Competitive Pressure) creates a significant impact on EN (Environment)*

H10: *PP (Pandemic Pressure) Positively Influence EN (Environment)*

H11: *EN (Environment) has a significant impact on BI (Behavioral Intention)*

H12: *SE (Security) has a significant impact on BI (Behavioral Intention)*

H13: *TR (Trust) creates a positive impact on BI (Behavioral Intention)*

Data Collection

This study was carried out among Tamil Nadu's unorganized retailers. Data was gathered through friends and family using a well-structured questionnaire. The data was gathered from unorganized retailers already utilizing Business to Business (E-Commerce) platforms, with a sample size of 250.

Table 1. Demographic profile of the respondents

Socio –Economic Profile	Demographics	Frequency	Percentage
Gender of the respondents	Female	35	13.89
	Male	215	86.11
Year of Birth	Above25-35	114	45.6
	36-45	73	29.3
	46- 55	60	24
	Above	3	1
Education	Diploma/HSC	125	50.0
	Graduate	25	10.1
	Postgraduate	78	31.2
	SSLC	22	8.7
Location	Rural	17	6.7
	Semi-Urban	78	31.2
	Urban	97	38.9
Retail shops	Apparel	50	20.2
	Grocery	75	29.8
	Footwear	4	1.4
	Vegetables	49	19.7
	Fruits	57	23.1
	Petty shops	15	5.8

(Source: - Primary Data)

It is clear from Table I that there are more women than men overall, with men making up around a third of the population. Furthermore, diploma- or higher-level-educated individuals make up half of the population. Most attendees are members of generation X, Y, and baby boomers. Most of the retailer's stores are in metropolitan and semi-urban areas. Most of the merchants that participated in the survey were owners of fruit, grocery, and apparel stores.

Figure 2. Structural path model for business to business (e-commerce) platform adoption

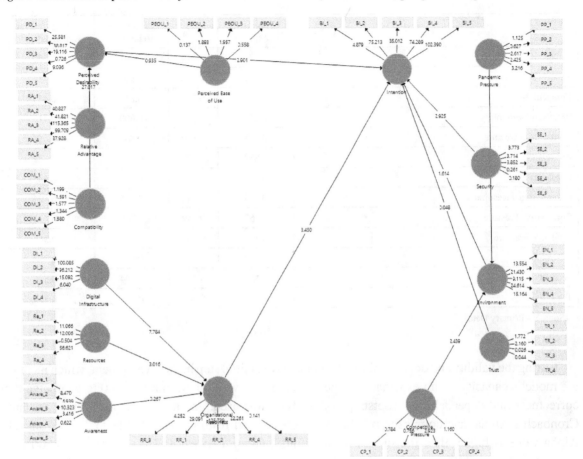

CMB (Common Method Bias)

To ensure that the collected data does not include Common Method Bias (CMB), the Harman's Single Factor Test was carried out using eight constructs (Ease-of-Use, Relative advantage, Compatibility, Perceived Desirability, Trust, Security, Awareness, Resources, Digital Infrastructure, Organizational Readiness, Perceived Desirability, Competitive Pressure, Pandemic Pressure, Environment, Behavioral Intention) (Salimon, 2021) (Alsaad A. M., 2015). The test findings show that the variation explained by the single factor maintains a value of 43.13 per cent, which is much less than the required value of 50 per cent, after these eight constructs had been loaded into a single factor (Podsakoff, 2012) (Fuller, 2016). Therefore, the collected data is valid and has no concerns in terms of Common Method Bias.

Table 2. Reliability and validity

Constructs	Cronbach's Alpha	rhea	Composite Reliability	Average Variance Extracted (AVE)
Perceived Ease of Use	0.877	0.919	0.901	0.570
Relative Advantage	0.881	0.887	0.900	0.414
Compatibility	0.728	0.737	0.814	0.425
Perceived Desirability	0.879	0.887	0.900	0.413
Digital Infrastructure	0.827	0.830	0.868	0.453
Awareness	0.852	0.853	0.910	0.772
Resources	0.858	0.863	0.894	0.586
Organisational Readiness	0.649	0.788	0.745	0.404
Competitive Pressure	0.767	0.789	0.829	0.412
Pandemic Pressure	0.826	0.833	0.863	0.368
Environment	0.852	0.853	0.910	0.772
Security	0.858	0.864	0.894	0.586
Trust	0.649	0.787	0.746	0.404

(Source: - Primary Data)

Testing the validity and dependability of a model is the initial step in its development, which increases the model's capacity for an explanation. The gathered data were input into PLS 3.0 to guarantee their correctness and dependability. Bootstrapping analysis was used, and the values for average variance, Cronbach's Alpha, and composite reliability were extracted from the data (table 1). The Cronbach's Alpha value is higher than the suggested threshold, ranging between 0.700 and 0.960. (0.600). The composite dependability rating is greater than the suggested value, ranging between 0.800 and 0.964. (0.600). The Average Variance Extracted value is larger than the suggested range of 0.500 between 0.500 and 0.863. These outcomes supported the validity and construct dependability of the data. Convergent validity is vital in model measurement since it determines if the various questionnaire items measure the same ideas. The average variance from the gathered data to test the convergent validity and the findings are shown in table 1. It shows that the Average Variance Extracted values are more than the proposed threshold value of 0.500, ranging between 0.555 and 0.854 (Mussel, 2018). These results affirmed that the collected data has adequate convergent validity.

Table 3. Regression value

Variable	R Square Value	Adjusted R Square
Environment	0.758	0.768
Intention	0.156	0.142
Perceived Desirability	0.88	0.823
Organisational Readiness	0.754	0.715

(Source: - Primary Data)

The regression values are shown in table 2 and were produced using the SMART PLS. Table 3 revealed that factors like the surroundings and perceived desirability significantly impacted intention. Additionally, the retailer preparedness regression values are also significantly affecting intention. However, the regression value of the intention shows that business-to-business technology penetration is relatively low. Business-to-business technology adoption is only getting started, and as knowledge is spread, the technology will also become popular with the unorganized.

The measurement model's values guarantee the multi-collinearity statistics' dependability, validity, and reliability. This study evaluates multi-collinearity statistics in addition to regression results, and it was discovered that the value of these statistics is far below the threshold value. Additionally, this strengthens the data's validity and reliability and supports this study's research tool.

This study uses structural path analysis and SMART PLS to analyze the relationships between the components to verify the research model. The results are shown below. This test determines the link between dependent and independent notions. Additionally, this test shows how the connected dimensions are interdependent, validating the study paradigm.

Table 4. Hypotheses test results

Hypothesis	Relationship	Standard Deviation	T-Statistics	P - Values	Test Result
H1	PEOU → PD	0.009	25.636	**0.000***	Supported
H2	RA → PD	0.031	1.750	**0.081***	Supported
H3	COMP → PD	0.016	0.875	0.382	Not Supported
H4	PD → BI	0.027	1.618	0.106	Not Supported
H5	DI → OR	0.017	7.456	**0.000***	Supported
H6	Aware → OR	0.016	2.967	**0.003***	Supported
H7	RE → OR	0.018	0.249	0.803	Not Supported
H8	OR → BI	0.008	2.370	**0.018***	Supported
H9	CP → EN	0.028	1.451	0.147	Not Supported
H10	PP → EN	0.016	16.701	**0.000***	Supported
H11	EN → BI	0.027	2.417	0.016*	Supported
H12	SE → BI	0.018	2.566	0.011*	Supported
H13	TR → BI	0.023	28.460	0.000*	Supported

(Source: - Primary Data)

After ensuring the accuracy and authenticity of the data, the structural route evaluation comes as the last phase. The measurement model must be tested to ensure that the measures are reliable and accurately measure the theoretical components. Five hundred re-samples must be used to bootstrap the path coefficients for this evaluation. Table 3 presents the findings of the hypothesis test. The findings supported that organizational readiness and environmental factors directly affect behavioral intention. Below is a discussion of the structural model's findings.

The structural path analysis results indicate the test results of hypotheses testing. The findings indicate that Ease-of-use & Relative Advantage has significantly influenced and positively affected Perceived Desirability among unorganized retailers. However, compatibility failed to influence Perceived Desirability, and Perceived Desirability is also insignificant to Behavioral Intention. Thus, the result shows that H1 ($\beta = 0.009$, t = 25.636 and p-value = 0.000) & H2 ($\beta = 0.031$, t = 1.750 and p-value = 0.081) are supported and H3 ($\beta = 0.016$, t = 0.875 and p-value = 0.382) & H4 ($\beta = 0.027$, t = 1.618 and p-value = 0.106) are insignificant. The second dependent construct is Organisational Readiness, significantly influenced by Digital Infrastructure and Awareness. Further, Organizational Readiness is insignificant to the Resources of the organisation. Thus, the result shows that H5 ($\beta = 0.017$, t = 7.456 and p-value = 0.000) & H6 ($\beta = 0.016$, t = 2.967 and p-value = 0.003) are supported. The third most important construct is the environment, which is significantly influenced by pandemic pressure. However, Competitive pressure failed to influence the environment. Hence, the result exhibits that H7 ($\beta = 0.018$, t = 0.249 and p-value = 0.803) & H9 ($\beta = 0.028$, t = 1.451 and p-value = 0.147) are insignificant. Finally, Behavioral Intention was substantially influenced by Trust, Security, Organizational Readiness and Environment. Thus, the result indicates that H8 ($\beta = 0.008$, t = 2.370 and p-value = 0.018), H10 ($\beta = 0.016$, t = 16.701 and p-value = 0.000), H11 ($\beta = 0.027$, t = 2.417 and p-value = 0.016), H12 ($\beta = 0.018$, t = 2.556 and p-value = 0.011) and H13 ($\beta = 0.023$, t = 28.460 and p-value = 0.000) are supported.

SOLUTIONS AND RECOMMENDATIONS

Impact of Perceived Desirability

The test result indicates that the Business to Business (E-Commerce) platforms are easy to use and have several benefits for unorganized retailers. However, some businesses do not have a business scope to enter the Business to Business (E-Commerce) platform adoption. The scope of the business is insignificant to perceived desirability in terms of its product, the volume of business, and even its location. Thus, it affects the retailer's readiness to adopt the Business to Business (E-Commerce) platform.

Impact of Organizational Readiness

The test results show that the unorganized retailers have contextual awareness, and Digital infrastructure is sufficient to install the Business to Business (E-Commerce) platform in their stores. However, the resources which are insignificant to Organization's Readiness. It indicates that the retailers lack in their technology and labor resources. Hence, this study suggested providing adequate resources for unorganized retailers to adopt the Business to Business (E-Commerce) platform in their stores.

Impact of Environment

The study results unveil that the unorganized retailers have more pandemic pressure than competitive pressure, and during the pandemic, several retailers face a massive loss in their business. Further, more than six lakh retailers were chucked out of business in India, especially during the first and second waves of a pandemic.

Impact of Trust & Security

The study results show that security and trust are significant to Business to Business (E-Commerce) platform acceptance behavior among unorganized retailers. Due to several awareness creation programs, they have sufficient awareness and create trust & security Awareness among the unorganized retailers. Finally, Trust & Security influences the Business (E-Commerce) platform's behavioral intention among unorganized retailers.

Practical Implications

From the analysis, this study found that the acceptance and penetration of the Business to Business (E-Commerce) Platform are still in their infancy in India. The study results unveiled that the unorganized retailers want to adopt technologies which require minimum physical effort while at the same time also render several benefits for their business. Unorganized retailers have massive acceptance and adoption behavior over advertisement-related technologies, which will create a brand image among their customers. Thus, it is strongly recommended that the Business to Business (E-Commerce) platform also concentrate on digitizing retail stores. Unorganized retailers are expected to adopt IoT, NFC and AI-based technologies in their business, which will assist them in providing a new way of customer experience among their customers. In addition, unorganized retailers also like the assistance of AI-based technologies, which helps them to make better management decisions in-store operations. Thus, this study strongly suggests that Business to Business (E-Commerce) platforms should develop AI, IoT, and NFC-based technologies to have a massive penetration among the unorganized retailers, which creates convenience among the unorganized retailers rather than compulsion.

Unorganized retailers will likely adopt inexpensive technologies requiring less exertion in their business. Mostly unorganized retailers like to adopt free digital tools & technologies; however, they are not incorporate those accessible technologies into their business instantly, and they adopt such technologies after considerable penetration in their location. While, in some cases, the self-efficacy of unorganized retail SMEs is considerably low, affecting the penetration of technologies. In addition, they will adopt such technologies instantly if the technology simultaneously creates competitive pressure and customer demand. Thus, this study strongly recommended that the Business to Business (E-Commerce) platform should target first tier 1 & tier 2 cities, and after the success of technologies, it will penetrate all other unorganized retail formats. In addition, the Business to Business (E-Commerce) platform should also segment and target its customers category-wise with certain rewards for joining and using Business to Business (E-Commerce) platforms. Further, the Business to Business (E-Commerce) platform should continuously run loyalty programs for unorganized retailers.

The government of India mainly concentrates on creating digital infrastructure and promoting digital payments among citizens. However, the focus on developing retail digital technologies is nascent, and laws relating to digital technologies are unavailable. Though the study results unveiled that unorganized retailers trust Business to Business (E-Commerce) platforms, privacy hinders the penetration of Business (E-Commerce) platforms among the unorganized retailers. Thus, this study strongly affirmed that the Government of India should concentrate on creating and promoting the Business (E-Commerce) platform among unorganized retailers, which will penetrate the Business (E-Commerce) platform across the nation. In addition, it has several benefits to the Government of India, such as generating revenues, eliminating unfair trade practices, price war, ensuring price stability in several commodities, measuring wholesale price index in real-time, and nation building.

CONCLUSION

The Business to Business (E-Commerce) platform considerably penetrates the unorganized retail SMEs, and this is the need of the hour to find out their determinants and eliminate the barriers to their adoption. Further, adopting the Business to Business (E-Commerce) platform creates a new business model (Q-Commerce), Quick Commerce. Finally, adopting the Business to Business (E-Commerce) platform assists the unorganized retail SMEs and supports the stakeholders around the unorganized retail business. Consumers are using the power of digital technologies and E-Commerce; this is the time to measure the propensity of Business-to-Business (E-Commerce) adoption among unorganized retailers.

REFERENCES

Alsaad, A. M. (2017). The moderating role of trust in business to electronic business commerce (B2B EC) adoption. *Computers in Human Behavior*, *68*, 157–169. doi:10.1016/j.chb.2016.11.040

Alsaad, A. M., Mohamad, R., & Ismail, N. A. (2015). Perceived desirability and firm's intention to adopt business-to-business e-commerce: A test of the second-order construct. *Advanced Science Letters*, *21*(6), 2028–2032. doi:10.1166/asl.2015.6194

Fathian, M. A., Akhavan, P., & Hoorali, M. (2008). E-readiness assessment of non-profit ICT SMEs in a developing country: The case of Iran. *Technovation*, *28*(9), 578–590. doi:10.1016/j.technovation.2008.02.002

Fuller, C. M., Simmering, M. J., Atinc, G., Atinc, Y., & Babin, B. J. (2016). Standard methods variance detection in business research. *Journal of Business Research*, *8*(69), 3192–3198. doi:10.1016/j.jbusres.2015.12.008

Government of India. (2021). *MSME Annual Report 2020 -2021*. New Delhi: Government of India, Ministry of Micro, Small and Medium Enterprises. www.msme.gov.in

IBEF - Indian Retail Industry Report. (2021). New Delhi: IBEF.

Islami, M. M., Asdar, M., & Baumassepe, A. N. (2021). Analysis of Perceived Usefulness and Perceived Ease of Use to the Actual System Usage through Attitude Using Online Guidance Application. *Hasanuddin Journal of Business Strategy*, *3*(1), 52–64. doi:10.26487/hjbs.v3i1.410

Koh, T. K., Fichman, M., & Kraut, R. (2012). trust across borders: Buyer-supplier trust in global business-to-business e-commerce. *Journal of the Association for Information Systems*, *13*(11), 886–922. doi:10.17705/1jais.00316

Lee, Y. K. (2021). Impacts of Digital Technostress and Digital Technology Self-Efficacy on Fintech Usage Intention of Chinese Gen Z Consumers. *Sustainability*, *13*(9), 5077. doi:10.3390u13095077

Moghavvemi, S. M., Mei, T. X., Phoong, S. W., & Phoong, S. Y. (2021). Drivers and barriers of mobile payment adoption: Malaysian merchants' perspective. *Journal of Retailing and Consumer Services*, *59*, 102364. doi:10.1016/j.jretconser.2020.102364

Mussel, P. R., Rodrigues, J., Krumm, S., & Hewig, J. (2018). The convergent validity of five dispositional greed scales. *Personality and Individual Differences*, *131*, 249–253. doi:10.1016/j.paid.2018.05.006

Podsakoff, P. M., MacKenzie, S. B., & Podsakoff, N. P. (2012). Sources of method bias in social science research and recommendations on how to control it. *Annual Review of Psychology*, *63*(1), 539–569. doi:10.1146/annurev-psych-120710-100452 PMID:21838546

Putra, P. O. (2020). Contextual factors and performance impact of e-business use in Indonesian small and medium enterprises. *Heliyon*, *6*(3), e03568. doi:10.1016/j.heliyon.2020.e03568 PMID:32211544

Report, C. (2022). *India B2B spending set to surge with rising recovery optimism – India Business Spend Indicator by American Express and Invest India.* https://s1.q4cdn.com/692158879/files/doc_news/2022/01/20/Final_Press-Release_India-Business-Spend-Indicator-Report_19.01.2022.pdf

Salimon, M. G., Kareem, O., Mokhtar, S. S. M., Aliyu, O. A., Bamgbade, J. A., & Adeleke, A. Q. (2021). Malaysian SMEs m-commerce adoption: TAM 3, UTAUT 2 and TOE approach. *Journal of Science and Technology Policy Management.*, *12*(4). Advance online publication. doi:10.1108/JSTPM-06-2019-0060

Smriti Tankha, P. G. (2021). *Leapfrogging into the future of retail, The 2021 Global Retail Development Index*. AT Kearney.

Tan, J. T., Tyler, K., & Manica, A. (2007). Business-to-business adoption of eCommerce in China. *Information & Management*, *44*(3), 332–351. doi:10.1016/j.im.2007.04.001

Chapter 5
Implementing E-Marketing in Small and Medium-Sized Enterprises for Enhanced Sustainability

Edna Mngusughun Denga
https://orcid.org/0000-0002-2121-242X
American University of Nigeria, Nigeria

ABSTRACT

E-marketing is a strategic marketing approach that has revolutionized how marketing is executed by transitioning from traditional to internet-based platforms. It has significantly altered how firms interact with their customers. To provide insights and offer guidance for the growth and development of e-marketing among SMEs, the chapter explored the organizational, technological, and environmental elements that may drive the adoption of e-marketing, as well as models that can be implemented to enhance e-marketing. A thorough analysis of the literature revealed a significant positive association between sustainable marketing strategy and SME performance, indicating that sustainability is significantly influenced by the level of customer satisfaction, customer loyalty, and profitability.

INTRODUCTION

Information technological advancements have revolutionized marketing initiatives and organizational approaches worldwide. Numerous enterprises are leveraging the Internet and other electronic channels to execute marketing campaigns culminating in e-marketing evolution as a novel marketing concept. E-marketing is a contemporary activity that involves utilizing the Internet and other electronic means to promote goods, services, information, and ideas (El-Gohary, 2010). E-marketing, according to Gao (2021), is the integration of electronic data and applications to organize and execute the invention, distribution, promotion, and pricing of ideas, goods, and services to generate exchanges that fulfill customer and organizational objectives. The practice of marketing has been reinvented in the era of the internet.

DOI: 10.4018/978-1-6684-5727-6.ch005

To compete effectively, businesses must establish an internet presence, most business organizations in all segments of the economy such as insurance companies, hotels, and education service providers have joined the online business community and incorporated the internet as a strategic management tool in their daily marketing efforts as a result of the popularity of personal computers, mobile smartphones, and enhanced access to internet service facilities. E-marketing is progressively gaining traction as a technique of attaining a competitive edge, which has significance for marketing practices. Businesses must embrace information technology, particularly the internet, to be successful in the twenty-first century. It is increasingly evident that countries, businesses, and consumers who neglect the internet will ultimately realize how challenging it is to survive without it, as the internet is redefining the relationship between trade partners and will continue to govern the entire exchange mechanisms.

BACKGROUND OF THE STUDY

Small and medium-sized enterprises (SMEs) are indispensable drivers of economic growth and development of several economies. A large percentage of businesses in the world are SMEs and are essential creators of employment and economic sustainability (World Bank,2021). They are responsible for up to 90% of enterprises and more than half of all job generation worldwide. In 2021, World Bank estimated that 600 million employments will be required to meet global demand for jobs by 2030, hence reasons why governments around the world must prioritize the growth of SMEs. The adoption of the internet for electronically facilitated exchanges (e-commerce) has proliferated in relation to the surge in commercial websites. Orders can be placed and filled, products and services provided, and have lowered international market entry barriers offering opportunities to multitudes of small and medium-sized businesses (SMEs) attempting to penetrate new markets by empowering them to effectively interact globally like any giant corporation. Notwithstanding the substantial contributions to the economy, SMEs encounter a range of obstacles, including limited access to finance, insufficient infrastructure, shortage of power supply, adverse taxation and government regulations, and most recently, the Coronavirus (COVID-19) pandemic.

The onset of the COVID-19 pandemic, as well as the subsequent widespread lockdown enforced by governments, inflicted a major blow to SMEs leading to difficulty to obtain raw materials for production and operational processes; the curfew and lockdowns deterred SMEs from gaining valuable customer patronage, and the high cost of productive materials resulted in financial disaster for most SMEs already suffering from the impacts of a shortage of finance. While the COVID-19 pandemic wreaked havoc on most SMEs, large-scale businesses like banking, telecommunications, and e-commerce experienced considerable improvements in profitability, sales, and performance during the pandemic. The integration of marketing and business operational processes into online channels and platforms was the single most significant success factor for these large-scale businesses, as it enabled them to continue marketing activities despite the lockdown, culminating in enhanced customer patronage, the volume of sales, and profit growth.

Marketing in small businesses differs from marketing in a large company as it is more instinctive, competence-based, concentrated on networking, and constrained by financial and human resources. While SMEs' traditional assets include their capability to serve specialty markets and create robust customer relationships, internet-enabled firms of any size weaken these capabilities to some extent. Due to the obvious reduced transaction costs associated with penetrating marketplaces dominated by SMEs, larger regional, national, and international firms pose a significant threat to entry. This creates a dilemma: either embark on the e-marketing adoption trend, possibly without fully comprehending all the implications, or delay and be left behind by competitors who are actively leveraging it. SMEs could benefit from incorporating online services into their marketing strategy by providing online quotes for products and services, advertising in more market segments cheaply, utilizing e-mail as a promotional tool, and lowering the costs of printing materials such as catalogs and glossy brochures. Additionally, businesses can strengthen their credibility by presenting a robust brand image through effective websites, answering inquiries about products and services in many languages, and conducting market research in foreign markets. Despite the anticipated advantages and benefits of implementing an e-marketing plan, SMEs are sluggish to adapt to the transformations driven by the internet and hence fail to make appropriate use of it. SMEs perceive the internet as a separate and distinct entity, rather than integrating it into their overall operations. it is incorporated impromptu, mostly as a supplementary promotional weapon rather than planning ahead for its long-term usage. Hence, instead of employing technology to create a competitive advantage, businesses are constrained to rely on the immediate operational benefits it provides in terms of marketing communications.

The practice of marketing philosophy has been redefined for the contemporary internet era. To maintain a competitive advantage, firms must establish an internet presence. With the surge in popularity of laptops, mobile smartphones, and enhanced access to internet service facilities, a percent of SMEs across all economic sectors (banks, insurance companies, hotels, airlines, and education service providers) have joined the internet marketing community and adopted the internet as a strategic instrument in their routine marketing efforts. E-marketing is rapidly gaining popularity as a technique for establishing a competitive edge, and this has implications for how SMEs conduct marketing. Hence, the book chapter aims to thoroughly discuss the concept of e-marketing, the drivers that influence SMEs' adoption of e-marketing, and the various strategic e-marketing models SMEs can leverage to achieve sustainability.

E-MARKETING CONCEPT

The technological era of the internet and the World Wide Web has revolutionized and computerized everything. E-marketing has replaced traditional marketing concepts, processes, and strategies. Marketing over the internet or e-marketing entails the usage of highly sophisticated and advanced instruments. It offers analytics and data accessible to organizations to enable them to coordinate their marketing and commercial strategies accordingly. E-marketing is the planning and execution of product and service creation, distribution, promotion, and pricing in a digitized, interconnected environment, like the Internet and the World Wide Web, to facilitate exchanges and meet customer expectations (Singh et al.,2021) Marketing as a concept is adaptive and flexible to remain abreast of technological advancements. Thus, traditional marketing did not rely on segmented customer expectations based on market categories. E-marketing aims to boost market share and business for organizations attributable to the advent of innumerable components such as advertising, products, distribution, and prices (Kor, 2020). Individuals, distribution, technology, and information are all required for the implementation of e-marketing, and these elements are avenues for generating new offers or attracting potential customers. E-marketing is focused on the utilization of technology and strives to boost revenues for businesses while also attempting to meet the particular demands of clients in an interactive and ongoing manner. As a result of technological advancements, the perception of e-marketing is now comparable to that of traditional marketing.

The use of digital interactive technologies and information technology to run a company's business is referred to as e-business. This term is frequently used interchangeably with e-commerce and e-marketing, but these latter concepts are basic components of those e-business operations (Roumieh et al.,2018). E-marketing employed those exact technologies as a logical extension of traditional market practices of building, communicating, and delivering value to customers. E-commerce, which is closely aligned with this, refers to the facilitation of transactions generated by a business's marketing efforts. Similarly, the phrases digital marketing and e-marketing are frequently interchanged and assumed to indicate the same thing. Digital marketing is a broad phrase that refers to all marketing efforts that take place on the internet. Email marketing, influencer marketing, SEO, mobile marketing, app adverts, paid social media advertising, and other strategies are among them. Digital marketing includes offline outlets such as electronic billboards. On the other hand, e-marketing is a more precise term that only relates to media that can be accessed via the Internet. Content marketing, search engine optimization, pay-per-click advertising, social media marketing, and other strategies fall under this category (Denga et al.,2022a) Other technologies that facilitate customer relationship management, enterprise resource planning, supply chain management, messaging services, bar code scanners, and digital television are also involved. E-marketing is distinguished by a variety of characteristics, the most notable are:

- **Addressability:** Visitors to a website can identify themselves and offer information about their product requirements and preferences leveraging Internet technology prior to making purchases (Ivoino & Migliaccio, 2019). Addressability refers to a firm's capacity to recognize prospective customers before they complete a transaction. It is the pinnacle of the marketing notion, with businesses being able to customize elements of the marketing mix more accurately to target customers with specific interests with the information gleaned from the Internet about individual customers. Addressability further makes it easier for businesses to track website visits and online purchasing behavior, simplifying data collection about specific customers and strengthening subsequent marketing efforts. Limiting access to some portions of their website to promote customer registration, offering contests and rewards in exchange for consumer information, and installing "cookies" on visitors' computers to track visitor usage and preferences are all strategies to attain addressability.

- **Interactivity:** Interactivity is the tendency for customers to actively express their preferences to businesses by responding to and interacting with marketing communications provided by these businesses, resulting in real-time connection with customers and greater market coverage at a reduced cost (Shaltoni et al.,2018) Interactivity empowers businesses to leverage the concept of community to assist customers to obtain the maximum benefits of their products and websites. Community connotes a sense of belonging or group membership by individual members of a group (Surer & Mutiu, 2015). Rather than clicking elsewhere, such sites encourage visitors to "hang out" and participate in the community as well as see the website's advertising. Communities have well-defined demographics and shared interests, hence are a desirable audience for businesses, which usually subsidize the upkeep of such sites.

- **Accessibility:** There is an extraordinarily large quantity of information available or handy on the internet. Accessibility refers to the ability to obtain it (Qashou & Saleh, 2018). Customers are considerably better informed about a firm's products and their proportional value than ever before since they can access in-depth details about competitor products, prices, ratings, blog viewpoints, and so forth. Customers thus will receive more extensive information about a firm's products and prices, as well as options to compare a set of products. As a result, businesses strive to improve their products focusing on the preferences of current customers while also attempting to reach out to prospective ones.

- **Control:** Customers' ingenuity to regulate the information they access, as well as the rate and sequence of their exposure to such information, is referred to as control in the context of e-marketing (Njoroge,2017). Since consumers select what they view on websites, the Web is usually described as a pull medium; website operators' capacity to manage what content users' access and in what sequence is restricted. Television, on the other hand, can be classified as a push medium as the broadcaster decides what the audience sees once they have chosen a station.
- **Memory:** Memory refers to a firm's capacity to access databases or data warehouses containing individual customers' profiles and purchase histories in real-time and tailor its marketing efforts to such customers (Maduku et al.,2016). A database is a collection of information that has been organized to allow for quick access and retrieval. Although businesses have had database systems for a long time, the information contained in these systems has only recently become readily available. While the user is still on the site, current software technology enables marketers to instantly identify a specific visitor to its website, locate that customer's profile in its database, and then display the customer's prior purchases or recommend new offerings based on previous purchases.
- **Digitalization:** The capability to portray a product, or a substantial portion of its attributes, as digital pieces of information, is known as digitalization (Tan, 2009). Firms can utilize the Internet to distribute, promote, and market those functionalities in addition to the actual item itself as an outcome of digitalization. Users with broadband Internet access can benefit from digitalization as quicker connections enable streaming audio and video as well as other new technologies. Digitizing a portion of a product's features facilitates new combinations of services and features to be generated rapidly and affordably, in addition to enabling distribution efficiencies (Waheed & Jianhua, 2018).

KEY DISTINCTIONS BETWEEN DIGITAL MARKETING AND E-MARKETING

A firm's success depends on implementing efficient marketing strategies, especially nowadays with consumers having numerous options for products and services both online and offline. SMEs frequently employ contemporary marketing strategies like e-marketing and digital marketing to promote their products. SMEs can improve their chances of success by understanding the differences between these marketing techniques, comparing and contrasting e-marketing with digital marketing, and outlining each approach's concept, salient features, and practical applications for SMEs. E-marketing is the term for electronic marketing strategies that are intended to interact with consumers in order to increase brand recognition and revenue (Lonial &Carter, 2015). Instead of static, non-targeted platforms like a billboard next to a highway, this strategy often utilizes outlets like social media or blogs that enable communication with SMEs' intended audience. Marketers seek to target a specific demographic by leveraging internet analytics and interacting with them via blogs, emails, and social media (Sheikh et al.,2018). E-marketing is regarded as a subset of digital marketing that concentrates on the internet rather than other digital platforms as it employs technology to advertise. Digital marketing is the domain of marketing that promotes goods and services utilizing the Internet and other online-based digital technology like desktop and mobile computers, as well as other digital media and platforms. Digital marketing strategies lay emphasis on building brand recognition across a variety of electronic platforms without anticipating any engagement from customers. Digital marketing is performed offline through electronic billboard ads or radio commercials, as well as online through social media or search engines. There are many similarities between e-marketing and digital marketing since the former is a subset of the latter (Ainin et al.,2015). The two methods do, however, differ significantly in key aspects. The majority of e-marketing takes place online, which is especially advantageous for SMEs as it allows them to engage with customers from across the globe. Customers can view electronic ads and social media posts anytime, anyplace, which gives online marketing greater freedom than offline marketing. A broader consumer base and more options for interaction with potential customers are two advantages that SMEs who employ e-marketing enjoy. Digital marketing offers greater versatility in the various ways a marketer can advertise as ads can display on internet platforms like apps and search engines or on physical platforms like billboards (Denga et al.,2022a)

Through online interaction, e-marketing seeks to establish a relationship with consumers. SMEs can build a loyal customer base through customer interaction and social media engagement by putting their efforts into e-marketing. But typically, the aim of digital marketing is to increase brand recognition by reaching as many people as feasible with information about their products and services, it rarely focuses on how customers interact with their promotions. E-marketing initiatives typically employ adverts that are relevant to target targeted audiences. Ad targeting enables SMEs to reduce the audience they are able to contact through online platforms in order to produce more targeted and interesting content, which boosts sales and creates a satisfied customer base (Gilmor et al.,2007). With digital marketing, the target audience's range of interests is frequently wider.

DRIVERS OF E-MARKETING ADOPTION AMONGST SMES

Iddris and Ibrahim (2015) assert that adopting innovative technology necessitates E-readiness in a research investigation on E-marketing adoption by SMEs. Businesses must possess the capacity to adopt, implement, and profit from innovation both internally and externally. This demonstrates how crucial both internal and external influences are to the acceptance of innovation. Tornatzky and Fleischer (1990) investigated the drivers of e-marketing from the technology-organization-environment standpoint. The paradigm pinpoints three aspects of a firm's context that impacts the adoption of technological advances: technological, organizational, and environmental context (TOE). Considering it incorporates a range of elements, TOE is depicted as a comprehensive approach to technology adoption (Ramdani et al., 2013).

1. Technological Context: This incorporates the internal and external innovations significant to firms. Equipment and procedures are both examples of technologies that deal with firms' existing technological capabilities. E-marketing is highly inclined to be adopted by firms with information technology infrastructure, knowledge, and electronic know-how. According to Coviello et al. (2003), the adoption of e-marketing is proportionate to firms' information technology orientation as it is employed by organizations to potentially enhance or revolutionize marketing efforts. These technologies may already be in use within an organization or be purchased in the market (Oliveira et al., 2014).

   ○ The *perceived relative advantage* reflects the degree to which an innovation is thought to be superior to the idea it replaces (Ahmad et al., 2019), The perceived advantages of adopting e- marketing describe the relative advantage SMEs stand to benefit. According to research, firms decide to adopt modern technology mostly because they believe it will profit them. If managers, who act as decision-makers in SMEs, perceive that adaptation will yield operational and strategic gains for a firm, they will be more inclined to support such change (Ramayah et al., 2016). The implication is that SMEs are increasingly likely to embrace e-marketing if they believe its supporting technologies offer superior advantages over existing approaches. Additionally, it is asserted that the adoption of a certain breakthrough or technology will be significantly slowed down by its bad perception. Much research has delved into the role of relative advantage and has shown that it has favorable effects on adoption. These include boosting sales and earnings, minimizing expenses, enhancing customer service, creating new market niches, and streamlining business operations (Zailani et al., 2015a, 2019).

○ The *perceived complexity* of adopting innovative technologies is viewed as a significant indicator in the process (Zailani et al., 2015b). Any technology that is perceived as being difficult to use is unlikely to be adopted (Alshamaila et al., 2013). Additionally, it is emphasized that these technologies must be simple and user-friendly to speed up their adoption. It suffices to say that technology has a greater probability of being embraced and deployed the easier it is to implement. Thus, the adoption of innovative technology might be greatly hampered by perceived complexity (Maroufkhani et al., 2020). Perceived complexity and the propensity to adopt an innovation are significantly correlated (Gutierrez et al., 2015). A technological innovation's complexity increases the risk associated with the decision to accept it because of the worries and suspicions around its possibility of failure. Investigations revealed complexity as a basic determinant in the adoption and implementation of these innovations in SMEs.

○ *Perceived Cost*: The perception of cost plays a fundamental role in embracing and implementing technology (Ramayah et al., 2016). Cost is seen as a paramount technological variable that can have a significant impact on SMEs' decision to embrace e-marketing techniques (Chatterjee & Kar, 2020;). There have been instances where the adoption of IT was not considerably influenced by cost. In general, every firm that adopts emerging technologies will incur considerable start-up costs. However, unlike any other IT-related adoption, numerous SMEs favor e-marketing adoption due to its low cost, dearth of involvement barriers, and simplicity. Since it facilitates direct interaction between customers and firms, many businesses actually prefer employing e-marketing if the cost is minimal (Ainin et al., 2015a). E-marketing is, on the whole, financially effective innovation and enables SMEs to interact with customers affordably.

○ *Perceived Competitive Pressure*: It is described as the pressure exerted by external rivals in the same industry which has a profound influence on the adoption of the technology. Thus, perceived heightening industry competitiveness pushes businesses to implement technological changes (Zainuddin et al., 2017). The prospect of sacrificing market shares and competitive edge in the marketplace is what fuels this pressure. SMEs are vulnerable to myriad competitors around the world in the era of globalization and adopting technology can benefit them strategically and dominate the market. Hence, the earlier a firm accepts this change, the more advantageous it will possess over competitors (Gangwar et al., 2015). It is evident that industry competitiveness influences the likelihood that technology will be adopted. Numerous studies have demonstrated that the propensity to embrace technology is significantly influenced by competitive pressure (Low et al., 2016).

  ◦ *Perceived Customer Pressure*: Customer pressure is a notable environmental component in analyses of technological adoption (Rahayu & Day, 2015). A significant correlation between adoption intention and consumer pressure has been shown in earlier studies on SMEs' adoption of technology (Matikiti et al., 2018). Compared to large businesses, SMEs are more vulnerable to pressure from customers to live up to expectations set by those customers. A firm will obediently adopt e-marketing under the influence of pressure put forth by customers, as has been successfully proven in relation to the implementation by SMEs.

2. **Organizational Context:** This dimension highlights the internal elements of SMEs that impact their decision to adopt any technology (Qashou & Saleh, 2018). The organizational context represents the organizational traits that drive SMEs to adopt technology and alludes to firms' characteristics and capabilities, such as size, centralization of authority, the structure of the organization, managerial hierarchical levels, human capital, slack resources, and personnel interconnections. In respect of technological incorporation, large businesses have various benefits over small businesses. Large businesses are more adept at tolerating the elevated risks associated with the initial substantial investments essential for e-marketing initiatives since they possess more slack resources. Furthermore, the larger a firm's scope, the greater the requirement for IT expenditures, and thus more probable the implementation of e-marketing (Chang et al., 2020).

3. **Environmental Context**: refers to elements such as the size and architecture of the industry, the firm's rivals, the macroeconomic setting, and the regulatory structure. If the preponderance of firms in a certain industry has embraced e-marketing, it is virtually guaranteed that additional firms will follow suit to prevent competitive deterioration. Consumer readiness, which is categorized as the combined effect of internet infiltration and consumer willingness to interact, is also a consideration. The spread of PCs and the internet in a nation's people is measured by internet penetration. If the preparedness intensity is increased, it may motivate businesses to utilize e-marketing (Singhal, 2021).

In their investigation founded on the TOE conceptual framework, Rahayu and Day (2015) highlighted the individual context as another aspect that influences e-marketing acceptance. The individual context speaks to the owners' creativity and ingenuity, IT expertise, IT knowledge, and anticipated e-marketing benefits. Adoption is also influenced by the advantages that an individual or a specific manager intends to gain from going online. E-marketing is increasingly prone to be adopted by those who perceive there are multiple advantages to implementing e-marketing. These elements create both limits and opportunities for the application of e-marketing. Corollary, they have an impact on how SMEs perceive the need for, search for, and embrace new marketing strategies. Furthermore, several proactive and reactive drivers for SMEs to utilize e-marketing efforts have been described in the literature. The possibility to minimize competitive threats of SMEs in peripheral areas, the opportunity to lower operational and marketing expenses, and the option to effectively promote their firm and diversify their comprehensive marketing mix strategy are all proactive factors (Habidi et al., 2015). Other factors include managerial enthusiasm, the prospect to grow sales, or the possibility to conduct a market survey. Increased rivalry from both local and larger enterprises, shrinking domestic markets, fear of competitive disadvantage, and merely joining on the tide are all examples of reactive reasons.

E-MARKETING STRATEGIES FOR SMES

To maximize e-marketing practice among SMEs, the following few models are:

Marketing Mix Model

The marketing mix is a grouping of marketing variables that SMEs utilize to effectively serve their target market. The phrase "marketing mix" was first coined in 1948 by James Culliton, but Jerome Mc-Carthy popularized it in the 1960s. McCarthy proposed four variables, which all start with the letter P, that describe the four approaches that SMEs should adopt to successfully increase brand awareness. The four Ps are promotion, price, place (distribution), and product. SMEs can vary the 4Ps of the marketing mix to satisfy their customers. E-marketing offers firms a variety of new chances to change up these conventional marketing mix elements. A product is a collection of advantages that organizations and customers are willing to trade money or other valuables for in order to satisfy their needs (Kotler, 2003). Product features including color, taste, style, product guarantee, package, design, and size are also included as a component of the marketing mix. Products should be evaluated for web-product compatibility in order to determine whether they are appropriate for online business and to prioritize them on the website. The degree of alignment between a product's attributes and those of the internet is known as web-product compatibility. E-marketing offers the chance to change the product online. Decisions made on online products can either affect the core product or the extended product. The term "extended product" refers to additional services and advantages that are developed around the core of the product and distinguishes it from the "core product," which is the primary item that the customer purchases to meet their needs (Chaffey et al., 2006). Price is the number of money customers is willing to spend on a product. In addition to considering supplier costs, seasonal discounts, competitor prices, and retail markup into account, it must establish a link between the price and the product's actual and perceived worth. E-marketing has an impact on pricing in SMEs as the issue of pricing transparency, for instance, enables prospective customers to compare prices before finalizing a purchase decision (Levenburg et al., 2015). Therefore, there is a propensity for products offered online to have lower prices. There are a number of pricing strategies used in e-marketing, including status quo pricing, differential pricing, price discrimination, and dynamic pricing. The component of the marketing mix known as place or distribution is delivering goods to clients in accordance with demand while reducing the price of inventory, shipping, and storage (Kotler, 2003). With e-marketing, a business can disintermediate, or avoid channel intermediaries and sell to customers directly (Viljoen et al., 2015). SMEs can sell directly to customers and offer customer service online by using the internet. Promotions are tactics employed to enlighten consumers about a firm and its product in an effort to persuade them to make purchases (Bearden et al., 2007). Through the application of e-marketing, SMEs can adopt banner ads, online sales promotions, public relations, direct marketing, e-mails, and testimonies to market their products to the general public. The goal of online marketers is to increase word-of-mouth or buzz about a product. This is crucial since many consumers perceive peer-to-peer recommendations to be their most reliable source when considering a purchasing decision.

Chaffey et al., (2006) additional 3Ps also indicate that e-marketing is relevant thus: The people element of the marketing mix deals with how SME employees interact with customers during the sales and after-sales activities. The people element of e-marketing refers to employees who respond to customer inquiries via phone calls, emails, or online chats. Consequently, SMEs must establish an online call center as soon as they go online. The tangible expression of the company and its offering is considered as physical evidence. Despite the fact that the majority of what the consumer is paying for is intangible, all products incorporate some tangible components. Physical evidence in e-marketing alludes to the customer's interaction with an SME on the website and associated support system (Chen & Huang, 2016). Customers can visit online and complete a successful transaction mostly through websites. Information content, website appearance, design, usability, and availability are examples of tangible evidence. Information should therefore be displayed in a manner that allows everyone to quickly and easily understand the message. The term "process" refers to the strategies and tactics SMEs employ to carry out all marketing-related tasks, including the creation of new products, advertising, sales, and customer service (Ifindo, 2011). New processes must be carried out in order to implement a firm's reorganization and the channel structures outlined for the product, price, place, and promotion. The ability of SMEs to provide a service, handle complaints, etc. is discussed, as well as customer service. Customers are more confident in the firm's ability to manage any situation when these are well-defined and efficient. With the advent of the Internet and e-marketing, several authors are increasingly taking into account additional Ps or marketing mix components, like privacy, customization, and performance (Gary, 2010).

4S Model

The 4S model furnishes SMEs with guidelines for establishing and sustaining an online presence. Online success requires creating a superior e-marketing strategy such that the SME's e-marketing efforts relate to its marketing goals and broader business goals to offer a structured framework. The 4S proposed model by Constantinides (2002) offers a thorough, all-encompassing approach for managing SMEs' internet presence. This demands the defining strategic goals, the categorization of possible competitors and site users, the evaluation of the SME's level of e-marketing preparedness, and the recognition of collaboration with other Internet partners outside the organization. The model can be beneficial to SMEs planning to adopt e-marketing. The model is categorized into four phases: Scope, Site, Synergy, and System. Scope largely discusses strategic decisions that SMEs must make in four areas. The online venture's strategic and operational goals, the market definition, which includes assessing the market's potential and classifying potential competitors, customers, and trends, the organization's level of openness to innovative ideas as the foundation for its e-marketing initiatives, and the strategic role e-marketing plays for the SMEs (Caniels et al.,2015). Identification of e-marketing objectives, which outline what the SME hopes to accomplish through the e-marketing campaign, is the key component. It outlines the SME's motivations for going online and enables it to gauge and track the success of its online marketing initiatives. It also serves as an incentive to concentrate on important areas and develop strategies of action to assist in achieving desired goals. Depending on their specific needs, small businesses may come up with different e-marketing goals. Site is the most crucial communication component of e-marketing, which serves as the primary customer experience driver and the SME's interaction with its audience (Agwu &Murry, 2014). The website acts as a virtual product display, sales and distribution point, price catalog, and basis of promotional materials in the online marketplace. As a result, it functions as the practical channel for interactions, transactions, and communication with web users. The site's main responsibilities include promoting the e-marketing program, informing customers and stakeholders about the business, effectively communicating SMEs' physical and online marketing campaigns, offering customer service and helpdesk functionality to increase customer loyalty and retention, providing lead generation and customer/market data, enabling customers to interact with the SME, and creating online communities

(Braojos- Gomez, 2015). Synergy is the merging of processes required to achieve the goals of SMEs adopting e-marketing. These synergies can emerge between the virtual team and third parties as well as between the networked team and the physical organization. The Front Office, the Back Office, and the Third Parties are three of the many topics covered by this synergy factor. The physical marketing strategy and marketing operations are integrated with the front office. The internet business must be integrated into the current support operations in order to deliver the fulfillment and back-office assistance that web customers expect (Lin & Lin, 2016). While third-party integration establishes networks of partners to support commercial, logistical, and other site activities, back-office integration focuses on the integration of the website with SME's procedures, legacy systems, and databases. By enabling online users to find and easily access the site, these partnerships can boost the exposure of the SMEs that adopts e-marketing in the marketplace. The system highlights the technical and site maintenance problems that require to be handled by SMEs. The primary areas where system-related decisions need to be taken are website administration, maintenance, and service, web server hosting and Internet Service Provider (ISP) selection, site building, content management, site security, transaction functionality, and system backup (Ramayah et al., 2016). The technical management of the site must regularly identify and assess innovative products and technologies that have the prospect to enhance the site's performance, customer experience, and operational efficiencies. Technical issues and system breakdowns must be resolved quickly with a minimal degree of operational disruption.

Cox and Koelzer Model

Cox and Koelzer (2004) investigated the management and upkeep of online presence from the viewpoints of choosing what to include on the site, how the site should look, and how the site should be structured and maintained. Choosing what will go on the website is the first step. Before beginning an e-marketing program, an SME must make this choice as time and resources may be wasted if the site content is not planned. The website's content should be determined by the intended audience and e-marketing goals. While aligned with the SME, commercial, and marketing goals and objectives, internet activities must pursue their own unique, well-stated strategic goals and objectives. By doing this, the online operation will be capable of contributing value and assisting the physical organization meets its goals for the SME. These goals may include generating revenue, promoting customer retention, boosting product and brand exposure among new groups, profit growth, strengthening the SME's image, and minimizing operational costs. The operation of the e-marketing strategy will be based on the online objectives. Prospective customers and product marketers make up an SME's target market and small firms must decide who their target market is in order to build an effective online presence. Then, learn about their demographics and psychographics, as well as what they want and how they want it. Hence, the web design must reflect the informational style, tone, and content that will appeal to consumers (Low et al., 2016). Deciding how the site should look hinges on the SME's goals for marketing its company or product, how it wishes to be viewed, whom it wants to attract, and what it wants visitors to do when they find the site all influence how the site should appear. In other words, it focuses on the positioning, target market, and objectives of an SME. Positioning is the term used to describe how customers view an SME and its offerings. Businesses and its product need to occupy a distinct market position in order to differentiate themselves from rivals. If not, prospective customers will not have any rationale to choose it over competitive offerings. The following questions must be addressed in terms of determining the position to create and capture with e-marketing: "What are we great at? What stances have other firms not yet adopted? Whom are we trying to draw in? What do we hope to achieve? For the target web audience to appreciate and recall an SME and its products, they must be seen as distinctive from other similar offerings. The importance of positioning cannot be overstated if SMEs desire to gain online market share. The firm's logo, product(s), list of services, price, and promotion are insufficient for a website; instead, the site must concentrate on establishing and reinforcing a certain identity, capability, traits, feature, benefit, or service.

Granitz and Greene Model

Additional e-marketing tactics were proposed by Granitz and Greene in 2003, including Customization and Personalization where SMEs should prioritize their relationships with consumers and other stakeholders since they are a valuable resource. E-marketing success depends on the utilization of online channels for data analysis with the goal of boosting the value provided to customers. Users communicate their needs to the supplier through regular feedback enabling SMEs to tailor information to a user's or customer's demands. The community concept entails developing a platform for user interaction and experience sharing. These interactions may attract more visitors to the firm's website and engage them with the offering. The numerous social media platforms assist SMEs in establishing these communities where immediate customer feedback can be leveraged to enhance the customer experience. Consumer tracking offers a wealth of information on consumer behavior. SMEs utilize website metrics to analyze data on elements like views, visitor location, date, time, length of viewing, links clicked, and other information. This information is designed to track and forecast consumer behavior as well as evaluate how effective a website is. Mixing Bricks and Clicks-Granitz and Greene (2003) emphasized three alternatives that are open to customers. When customers want to shop through different channels, the SME must be prepared to accommodate their needs. If customers differ between channels, the firm should cater to each segment's unique needs.

SUSTAINABILITY MARKETING STRATEGY AND SME PERFORMANCE

Sustainability is a hallmark of the contemporary business environment as the desire to preserve resources for the current and upcoming generations is ongoing. Firms are the most significant institution on planet earth and thus have a primary obligation to protect the environment. It is crucial to properly address the social and environmental issues that confront humanity (Hawken 2007). The UN Global Compact Accenture (2014) released a report on the opinions of 1,000 CEOs on sustainable business practices. The report revealed that, despite increased attention to environmental and other sustainability-related issues, the global economy is not moving as quickly as it should place society on a more serious sustainable path. Several CEOs concurred that sustainability is the only free path to future firms' performance, but many characterized it as a frustrated aspiration as the advantages are insufficient in comparison to the efforts made (Krunal et al., 2018). According to this research, McKinsey (2012) acknowledged that many firms are successfully incorporating sustainability principles into their operational processes, while many are unsure of the precise benefits that result. Companies all over the world are increasingly spending a significant amount of money on energy conservation, creating eco-friendly products, and motivating their workforce to accomplish long-term growth and add value to the business. Consumers and other stakeholders continue to exert pressure on firms to satisfy their increasing expectations.

Sustainable marketing deals with socially, ethically, and environmentally responsible actions that yield values that satisfy the immediate and long-term needs of customers, the firm, and wider society. Whereas marketing tactics acknowledge that businesses thrive by meeting the day-to-day needs of customers. In order to ensure responsible marketing action, sustainable marketing requires a well-functioning marketing approach where customers, businesses, policymakers, and other stakeholders collaborate (Kotler & Armstrong, 2014). The goal of a sustainable marketing strategy is to satisfy customers by choosing a unique series of tasks for businesses to accomplish and performing them effectively (Kumar & Meenakshi, 2013). When consumers identify a need that a product from an SME can fulfill then the marketing strategy is successful. SMEs must leverage e-marketing to position their products according to customers' likes and dislikes for their strategy to be effective. Firms that fulfill the desired image of a target market tend to be effective (Bhatia, 2013). SMEs that are sustainable add value to their customers by operating in a manner that is socially, environmentally, and economically responsible. Today's businesses have come to understand the importance of offering positive customer education, information, and protection. Customer-oriented marketing, customer value marketing, sense-of-mission marketing, inventive marketing, and societal marketing are the five sustainable marketing principles that must be adhered to in order for an SME's marketing to promote the optimum long-term performance of the marketing strategy (Kotler & Armstrong, 2014)

Consumer purchasing behavior can be influenced by the sustained performance of businesses SMEs (Krunal et al., 2018). Heck and Yidan (2013) assert that implementing e- marketing sustainable strategies results in situations where everyone wins, as well as the environment and business. The relationship between sustainability tactics and a firm's value is still not sufficiently quantified, though. Value generation for investors and consumers is the primary objective of every firm around the globe. There are three fundamental aspects of e-marketing sustainability—the social, economic, and environmental aspects are essentially integral to the fundamental notion of sustainability. The evolution of e-marketing has a variety of effects on sustainability dimensions, so each dimension needs to be thoroughly evaluated. From the perspective of the economic dimension of e-marketing sustainability, which is for many experts the most recognizable one, it highlights operational and innovation performance, superior methods to implement differentiation from competitors, decreased time to market products, advancements in asset utilization, and distinctive and better adaptability of businesses in their attempt to respond to customers' demands. To achieve a competitive advantage that is sustainable and hence improves firm performance, strategy adoption is justifiable (Bharadwaj et al., 2012). The goal of a sustainable e-marketing strategy is to boost the long-term financial performance of an SME while also ensuring customer satisfaction and retention. A sustainable e-marketing strategy is an effective tool for enhancing a firm's financial performance through the utilization of sustainable advantages. Superior long-term market and financial performance is a product of sustainability of positioning advantage (Owonte, 2016). SMEs need resourcefulness skills to be valuable, rare among rivals, hard to imitate, and without any strategically equivalent substitutes if they want to acquire a sustainable competitive edge. Firm performance is a strategic instrument for generating and sustaining long value in order to acquire a competitive edge and sustainability is favorably correlated to an SME's ability to maintain its competitive edge by attracting and retaining more customers by leveraging e-marketing.

Kotler and Armstrong (2014) postulated that SMEs need to thoroughly appreciate market value creation in order to offer customers more distinctive offerings than their rivals. This will give them a competitive advantage in attracting customers with effective and superior products and services. SMEs that are successful accomplish that by establishing market segments, creating and positioning products for those categories, and creating economic value by keeping their sustainability vision and expectations for 21st-century consumers in perspective (Owonte 2018). UN Global Compact-Accenture (2014) posited that "the millennial consumer is pushing new expectations of all institutions in society, notably business." The millennial consumer is coming of age economically and is empowered by new technology and social media. Consumers of today desire to improve their health and the well-being of their communities in addition to expecting direct utility from the products and services. Once more as a result of the global economic downturn, consumers have grown more "Mindful". Excessive spending and careless consumption are no longer enjoyable for consumers. They exhibit a new trend known as "Mindful Consumption," where customers buy fewer goods from fewer brands and undertake increasingly deliberate decisions (Seth et al., 2011). SMEs adopting sustainable marketing strategies must embrace a holistic business model transformation as their launching point as it necessitates engaging numerous stakeholders without sacrificing customer expectations (Grubor & Milovanor, 2017). The role of the marketing manager is essential given that consumers are at the center of all marketing activities and that marketing is criticized for relentlessly exploiting the planet's resources. As a result, the path for SMEs to adopt sustainable marketing practices is arduous (Krunal et al., 2018). There is a huge gap between firms and investors that impede the creation of lasting value from sustainability measures (Alexender, 2015).

The UN Global Impact Accenture report of 2013 revealed that 93 percent of CEOs view sustainability as an important determinant of their corporate business strategy. Furthermore, similar research conducted by the same organization in 2014 indicated that investors in firms were enthusiastic about sustainability activities and that 88% of investors believed that sustainable marketing techniques constituted significant drivers of competitive advantages. These investor and business perspectives highlight the critical need to establish more direct relationships between sustainability and firm performance. Some businesses are still dubious about how significantly sustainable marketing may boost the value of businesses-to-business (B2B) and end users (B2C). Oftentimes, customers only consider a product's price, delivery, and functionality; however, contemporary marketers contend that sustainable marketing practices should be an essential component of a firm's marketing mix in order to minimize the time spent in operational and delivery phases as this will inevitably assist firms to interact with customers more effectively and achieve organizational goal and value (Krunal et al., 2018). The World Business Council for Sustainable Development (WBCSD) research states that sustainable marketing is a whole strategy and not only the marketing department's purview. All those within an organization active in decision-making are recognized by an inclusive approach. The performance of a company depends on extensive research and development, customer loyalty, and customer satisfaction. Sustainable marketing techniques assists SMEs to get a competitive edge over rivals and boost sales as it exerts an impact on customers' satisfaction, loyalty, and profitability (Denga et al.,2022a).

SUSTAINABLE SMEs' PERFORMANCE AND E-MARKETING

Performance is typically the ultimate goal anticipated in business activities (Galdeano et al., 2018; Roespinoedji et al., 2019) and is the most fundamental concept in management. Firm performance is a firm's overall performance which is determined by aggregating the efficiency of its marketing, finance, and human resource functions over a specific period of time (Ahmed et al., 2018). Firms establish goals and objectives that must be accomplished in a certain amount of time. Performance gauges how well a firm is performing in relation to its goals. Thus, Firm performance is the ability of a company to achieve its objectives, such as significant profit margin, product quality, increased market share, and superior financial outcomes at a predetermined period and by implementing the appropriate strategy (Muhammad et al., 2019). There are several dimensions of firm performance that can be complex to quantify. Both financial and non-financial metrics have been adopted to measure performance (Ahmed et al., 2018). One of the most essential aspects of management research nowadays is SME performance, which compares a firm's actual output or outcomes to its projected outputs (or goals and objectives). The three specific categories of firms' outcomes identified by Richard et al. (2006) as constituting SME performance are (a) financial performance (profits, return on assets, return on investment, etc.); (b) product market performance (sales, market share, etc.); and (c) shareholder return (total shareholder return, economic value added, etc.). According to Waiganjo et al., (2012), the performance of SMEs can be evaluated in terms of a multitude of objectives, including profitability, employee satisfaction, productivity, and growth. A broader performance appraisal approach has been proposed by proponents of the balanced scorecard performance management system that considers both financial and non-financial measures like sales, profitability, return on investments, market share, customer base, product quality, innovation, and company attractiveness.

For SMEs to function globally and generate a sustainable competitive edge over competitors that are less specialized in e-marketing usage, information and communication technology adoption must be crucially linked with marketing operations. Additionally, by minimizing the expenditures of communication from "one to one" to "many to many," the Internet has made it feasible for the marketing departments to connect with current and prospective customers (Denga et el.,2022b). However, achieving large profit margins has proven challenging in knowledge-based economies owing to fierce market competitiveness and the vast amount of products offered. Since sales cycles and decision-making times have begun to shorten, it was necessary to quickly adapt to the demands of modern business, deploy integrated internet-driven marketing strategies, and integrate them into standard business processes. Previous research has yielded conflicting results about the direct impacts of e-marketing usage on long-term business performance. Nevertheless, some research suggests that e-marketing has a favorable effect on long-term business performance, such as "firm growth" (Premalatha, 2014), "financial gain," and "competitive edge." Given the sizes and regions, the advantages were uneven across a range of sectors (Johnston & Wright, 2004). However, SMEs derived benefits that are favorably related to the utilization of e- marketing.

All marketing efforts are aimed at ensuring consumer satisfaction. Satisfaction is the degree to which the perceived cost of service differs from the expected benefit of that service or product. Customer satisfaction refers to a customer's overall perception of a good or service, as well as their emotional response to the discrepancy between what they expect and what they get in satisfying their wants, desires, or objectives. It is an assessment of whether a firm's products and services meet or exceed its expectations. Satisfaction is a general retroactive assessment of how well expectations for a product or service have been realized. Oliver (2007) defined customer satisfaction as their response to being fulfilled. is an attitude like judgments after acquiring a good or service, Customers' emotional reactions, attributions, expectations, and perceptions of the product's quality and service features all have an impact. The premise that the customer is "king," and that marketing efforts are centered on attempting to meet their needs and wants, is what makes marketing programs successful. This justifies the existence of the marketing function (Owonte, 2020). Marketers must learn everything there is to understand about consumers to satisfy them (Kalu, 2012). Customer satisfaction is viewed as a significant differentiator in a market where firms compete for customers and is becoming an indispensable component of SMEs' strategy.

With the advent of web 4.0 and the proliferation of the internet, there has been a surge in customer interconnectivity which altered consumer decision-making and consumer behavior. Social interaction has evolved dramatically as a function of social network development for customer engagement and behavioral modification. SMEs undertake marketing operations to alter consumer behavior; hence, they must be aware of how customer values, attitudes, and beliefs impact the effectiveness of e-marketing campaigns. The emergence of e-marketing has afforded SMEs the opportunity to promote their goods and services globally and is among the most economical strategies to educate customers, which assist builds brand awareness and image. SMEs are also actively engaged in consumer engagement initiatives that are creating a distinctive brand image for long-term sustainable outcomes. Customers' satisfaction boosts SMEs' performance and offers them a competitive edge over rivals. Customers that are satisfied with a product or service are loyal and often recommend the product or service and spread the word about it. Higher levels of satisfaction lower turnover, minimize the cost of acquiring new consumers and enhance customer loyalty (Denga et al.,2022b).

Consumer loyalty is a firmly held commitment to repeatedly purchase or patronize a favorite brand of good or service in the future, leading to repeat same-brand or brand-set purchases (Oliver, 1999). Loyal customers may affect switching behavior despite contextual factors and marketing initiatives. This explains why customers exhibit unwavering devotion and attachment to SMEs' products despite the difficulties they encounter in attaining their objectives. Loyal consumers are thought to be the best ones as they are more eager to pay than other customers, while also spreading word-of-mouth about the firm. Gaining the loyalty of customers is one guaranteed strategy to increase profits (Denga et al.,2022b)). E-marketing is an excellent strategy for boosting consumer awareness, trust, and loyalty, which will draw in more prospective customers and generate high-quality referrals. Customer loyalty is essential for the long-term success of any SME, and it is one of the primary objectives of an e-marketing strategy. Profit is the fundamental objective of any organization. Every SME was started with the intention of making money for the investors. Reasonable profits are necessary to maintain stakeholders' interest in the operation of the firm and to improve the organization's capacity to serve customers (Hotst, 2013). Profitability is a metric that measures the rate of growth that an SME has over a specific time. Without the ability to generate a gain or advantage, a firm cannot sustain itself in the long run.

E-marketing has an impact on SMEs' performance as it enables them to strengthen their financial and non-financial performance by increasing their asset turnover, market share, revenue growth, and customer acquisition and retention. Additionally, e- marketing assists the suppliers and agents of SMEs in improving their marketing efforts and bridging the knowledge gaps regarding their products, promotions, prices, and competitors to their customers. E-marketing is a significant difficulty for SMEs given their marketing strategies differ from that of large firms (Lipiamen & Karjaluoto, 2013). Owing to their limited resources and expertise, SMEs are less prone than large companies to be successful in adopting e-marketing strategies (Barnes et al., 2012). Many SMEs have adopted e-marketing at the moment; therefore it would be vital to understand its impact on sales growth and profitability as it continues to be an option for SMEs to reach the market and boost awareness of their products and services. For SMEs to be more competitive, they must understand how to leverage e- marketing approaches to enhance customer reach (Olonade, 2017). Effective e-marketing is indispensable due to the extremely competitive marketplace. SMEs need to improve their online web presence through efficient search engine optimization. Websites often serve as a potential customer's initial impression of a firm, it is crucial to incorporate both internal and external links, with up-to-date content. By creating shared links to aid in customer marketing, SMEs can create excellent usage of electronic media. This will increase word-of-mouth through connections on Facebook, Twitter, and YouTube.

FUTURE RESEARCH DIRECTIONS

The models and ideas presented here are based on an in-depth review of the literature and to determine their impact on the performance of SMEs, thus future research should therefore focus on how each model affects SME performance and other marketing initiatives. Furthermore, employing different performance metrics, such as marketing and financial performance could aid in further exploring the effectiveness of the suggested models and their influence on specific performance outcomes. To further explain e-marketing it is also significant to investigate other influencing elements. Future research should focus on their role in a range of aspects, including technological orientation and innovation as it has been proposed that strategies like customer relationship management, e-service approaches, and customization are vital for maximizing the internet. As a result, their impact on e-marketing and ultimately on SMEs' performance may constitute another interesting avenue for investigation. Finally, in an attempt to compete with the fierce market rivalry, SMEs are incorporating sustainability into their marketing strategies as the contemporary era of marketing strategy has already begun. Future studies are required to examine the empirical evidence demonstrating how sustainability affects the performance of SMEs.

CONCLUSION

The internet is firmly entrenched as a revolutionary marketing tool with significant implications for the marketing of SMEs' products and services. The advent of e-marketing has offered marketers innovative technology to mass-customize and promote their products to a wider range of target audiences. It gives them inexpensive access to mass markets and enables them to adopt a customized marketing strategy. Additionally, it is relevant for the marketing mix that SMEs must employ to accomplish their marketing goals. The traditional 4Ps—product, price, place, and promotion—as well as the additional 3Ps—people, physical evidence, and process—are equally essential in e-marketing, but more Ps are required to handle the specific characteristics of this channel. In order to create effective e-marketing strategies, three extra Ps—privacy, customization, and performance—can be leveraged. Every element needs to be strengthened to the maximum potential as it is crucial to the overall strategy. Connectivity as an obstacle must be addressed by SMEs as managing and maintaining an internet presence is fundamental. It is not enough to merely be available online; the website and the purposes for which customers can access it must also be promoted and maintained. The e-marketing environment is dynamic and occasionally unpredictable, therefore updating is vital. When changes take place, they should be recognized as soon as possible. The issues of privacy and security are also quite important. It comprises protections against identity theft and hacking that might provide unauthorized users quick access to other people's data and bank accounts. In order to successfully implement e-marketing, SMEs must strive to surmount these major issues. SMEs must embrace the concept of e-marketing in order to be positioned to take maximum advantage of the possibilities presented by the digital revolution, evolving internet presence, and mobile connectivity to increase their competitiveness in terms of market share, sales growth, customer patronage, customer satisfaction, customer retention, customer loyalty, and market presence. Today, achieving sustainable organizational growth in terms of triple bottom line practices is a major concern for all SMEs, but most of them still struggle with market growth and lag behind in terms of sustainability and e-marketing implementation.

REFERENCES

Adede, O. A., Kibera, F. N., & Owino, J. O. (2017). Electronic marketing practices, competitive environment, and performance of telecommunications companies in Kenya. *British Journal of Marketing Studies*, *5*(5), 60–67.

Aderemi, T. A., Ojo, L. B., Ifeanyi, O. J., & Efunbajo, S. A. (2020). Impact of Corona Virus (COVID-19) pandemic on small and medium scale enterprises (SMEs) in Nigeria: A critical case study. *Acta Universitatis Danubius OEconomica*, *16*(4), 81–98.

Agwu, M., & Murray, J. P. (2014). Drivers and inhibitors to E-commerce adoption among SMEs in Nigeria. *Journal of Emerging Trends in Computing and Information Sciences*, *5*(3), 192–199.

Ahmad, S. Z., Rahim, A., Bakar, A., & Mohamed, T. (2015). Information Technology for Development: An Empirical Study of Factors Affecting e-Commerce Adoption among Small- and Medium- Sized Enterprises in a Developing Country. Advance online publication. doi:10.1080/02681102.2014.899961

Ainin, S., Parveen, F., Moghavvemi, S., Jaafar, N. I., & Mohd Shuib, N. L. (2015). Factors influencing the use of social media by SMEs and its performance outcomes. *Industrial Management & Data Systems*, *115*(3), 570–588. doi:10.1108/IMDS-07-2014-0205

Akyuz, M., & Ibrahim, A. A. (2020). Effect of electronic marketing on the performance of SMEs in Karu Local Government Area, Nasarawa State of Nigeria. *FUO Quarterly Journal of Contemporary Research*, *8*(2), 1–16.

Bearden, W. O., Ingram, T. N., & LaForge, R. W. (2007). *Marketing: Principles and perspective*. Mc-Graw- Hill Inc.

Braojos-Gomez, J., Benitez-Amado, J., & Llorens-Montes, F. J. (2015). How do small firms learn to develop a social media competence. *International Journal of Information Management*, *35*(4), 443–458. doi:10.1016/j.ijinfomgt.2015.04.003

Caniëls, M. C., Lenaerts, H. K., & Gelderman, C. J. (2015). Explaining the internet usage of SMEs: The impact of market orientation, behavioural norms, motivation and technology acceptance. *Internet Research*, *25*(3), 358–377. doi:10.1108/IntR-12-2013-0266

Chaffey, D., Ellis-Chadwick, F., Mayer, R., & Johnston, K. (2006). *Internet marketing: Strategy, implementation and practice*. Pearson Education Limited.

Chai, L. G. (2009). A review of marketing mix: 4Ps or more? *International Journal of Marketing Studies*, *1*(1), 1–15.

Chang, Y. W., Hsu, P. Y., Huang, S. H., & Chen, J. (2020). Determinants of switching intention to cloud computing in large enterprises. *Data Technologies and Applications*, *54*(1), 16–33. doi:10.1108/DTA-12-2018-0104

Chatterjee, S., & Kar, A. K. (2020). Why do small and medium enterprises use social media marketing and what is the impact: Empirical insights from India. *International Journal of Information Management*, *53*, 102103. doi:10.1016/j.ijinfomgt.2020.102103

Chen, Y. Y., & Huang, H. L. (2016). Developing and Validating the Measurement Scale of e-Marketing Orientation. In *Rediscovering the Essentiality of Marketing*. Springer International Publishing. doi:10.1007/978-3-319-29877-1_47

Constantinides, E. (2002). The 4s web-marketing mix model. *Electronic Commerce Research and Applications*, *1*(1), 57–76. doi:10.1016/S1567-4223(02)00006-6

Coviello, N. E., Brodie, R. J., Brookes, R. W., & Palmer, R. A. (2003). Assessing the role of e-marketing in contemporary marketing practice. *Journal of Marketing Management*, *19*(7-8), 857–881. doi:10.10 80/0267257X.2003.9728240

Coviello, N. E., Brodie, R. J., Brookes, R. W., & Palmer, R. A. (2003). Assessing the role of e-marketing in contemporary marketing practice. *Journal of Marketing Management*, *19*(7-8), 857–881. doi:10.10 80/0267257X.2003.9728240

Cox, B. G., & Koelzer, W. (2004). *Internet marketing*. Pearson Education Limited.

Denga, E. M., Vajjhala, N. R., & Rakshit, S. (2022a). The Role of Digital Marketing in Achieving Sustainable Competitive Advantage. *Advances in Business Strategy and Competitive Advantage*, 44–60. doi:10.4018/978-1-7998-8169-8.ch003

Denga, E. M., Vajjhala, N. R., & Rakshit, S. (2022b). Relationship Selling as a Strategic Weapon for Sustainable Performance. In J. D. Santos (Ed.), *Sales Management for Improved Organizational Competitiveness and Performance*. doi:10.4018/978-1-6684-3430-7.ch005

Dlodlo, N., & Dhurup, M. (2010). Barriers to e-marketing adoption among small and medium enterprises (SMEs) in the *Vaal Triangle. Acta Commercii*, *10*(1), 164–180. doi:10.4102/ac.v10i1.126

El-Gohary, H. (2010). E-marketing - a literature review from a small businesses perspective. *International Journal of Business and Social Science*, *1*(1), 214–244.

Gangwar, H., Date, H., & Ramaswamy, R. (2015). Journal of Enterprise Information Management article information. *Journal of Enterprise Information Management*, *28*(1), 107–130. doi:10.1108/JEIM-08-2013-0065

Gao, P., Meng, F., Mata, M. N., Martins, J. M., Iqbal, S., & Farrukh, M. (2021). Trends and future research in electronic marketing: A bibliometric analysis of twenty years. *Journal of Theoretical and Applied Electronic Commerce Research*, *16*(5), 1667–1679. doi:10.3390/jtaer16050094

Gilmore, A., Gallagher, D., & Henry, S. (2007). E-marketing and SMEs: Operational lessons for the future. *European Business Review*, *19*(3), 234–247. doi:10.1108/09555340710746482

Granitz, N., & Greene, C. S. (2003). Applying e-marketing strategies to online distance learning. *Journal of Marketing Education*, *25*(1), 16–30. doi:10.1177/0273475302250569

Grubor, A. & Milovanov, O. (2017). Brand strategies in the era of sustainability. *Interdisciplinary Description of Complex Systems, 15*(1), 78-88.

Gutierrez, A., Boukrami, E., & Lumsden, R. (2015). Technological, organisational and environmental factors influencing managers' decision to adopt cloud computing in the UK. *Journal of Enterprise Information Management*, *28*(6), 788–807. doi:10.1108/JEIM-01-2015-0001

Habibi, F., Hamilton, C. A., Valos, M. J., & Callaghan, M. (2015). E-marketing orientation and social media implementation in B2B marketing. *European Business Review*, *27*(6), 638–655. doi:10.1108/EBR-03-2015-0026

Hooley, G. J., Greenley, G. E., Cadogan, J. W., & Fahy, J. (2005, January). (20050. The performance impact of marketing resources. *Journal of Business Research*, *58*(1), 18–27. doi:10.1016/S0148-2963(03)00109-7

Ifinedo, P. (2011). An empirical analysis of factors influencing Internet/E-Business technologies adoption by SMEs in Canada. *International Journal of Information Technology & Decision Making*, *10*(4), 731–766. doi:10.1142/S0219622011004543

Iovino, F., & Migliaccio, G. (2019). E-Marketing and Strategy by Energy Companies. In *The Cross-Disciplinary Perspectives of Management: Challenges and Opportunities*. Emerald Publishing Limited., doi:10.1108/978-1-83867-249-220191011

Korir, E. J. (2020). *E-marketing strategies and performance of registered rated hotels in Nakuru County* [MBA thesis]. Kenyatta University.

Kotler, P. (2003). *Marketing management*. Pearson Education, Inc.

Kotler, P., & Armstrong, G. (2014). Principles of Marketing. Pearson Prentice Hall.

Krunal, T., Pooja, T., & Varidana. (2018). Sustainable Marketing Strategies: Creating business value by meet consumer expectation. *International Journal of Management, Economic, and Social Science*, *7*(2), 186–205.

Kumar, A., & Meenakshi, N. (2013). Marketing management (2nd ed.). Vikas Publishing House PVT Ltd.

Lawrence, D. O., & Lawrence, A. W. (2021). Assessment of some basic strategies towards managing COVID-19 crisis in micro/small-sized businesses. *International Journal of Business and Management*, *16*(8), 34–49.

Levenburg, N. M., Schwarz, T. V., & Motwani, J. (2015). Understanding adoption of Internet technologies among SMEs. *Journal of Small Business Strategy*, *16*(1), 51–70.

Lin, F. J., & Lin, Y. H. (2016). The effect of network relationships on the performance of SMEs. *Journal of Business Research*, *69*(5), 1780–1784. doi:10.1016/j.jbusres.2015.10.055

Lonial, S. C., & Carter, R. E. (2015). The Impact of Organizational Orientations on Medium and Small Firm Performance: A Resource-Based Perspective. *Journal of Small Business Management*, *53*(1), 94–113. doi:10.1111/jsbm.12054

Maduku, D. K., Mpinganjira, M., & Duh, H. (2016). Understanding mobile marketing adoption intention by South African SMEs: A multi-perspective framework. *International Journal of Information Management, 36*(5), 711–723. doi:10.1016/j.ijinfomgt.2016.04.018

Maroufkhani, P., Tseng, M. L., Iranmanesh, M., Ismail, W. K. W., & Khalid, H. (2020). Big data analytics adoption: Determinants and performances among small to medium-sized enterprises. *International Journal of Information Management, 54*, 102190. doi:10.1016/j.ijinfomgt.2020.102190

Matikiti, R., Mpinganjira, M., & Roberts-Lombard, M. (2018). Application of the technology acceptance model and the technology– organisation–environment model to examine social media marketing use in the South African tourism industry. *South African Journal of Information Management, 20*(1), 1–12. doi:10.4102ajim.v20i1.790

Nasiri, M., Ukko, J., Saunila, M., Rantala, T., & Rantanen, H. (2020). Digital-related capabilities and financial performance: The mediating effect of performance measurement systems. *Technology Analysis and Strategic Management, 32*(12), 1393–1406. doi:10.1080/09537325.2020.1772966

Njau, J. N., & Karugu, W. (2014). Influence of e-marketing on the performance of small and medium enterprises in Kenya: Survey of small and medium enterprises in the manufacturing industry in Kenya. *International Journal of Business & Law Research, 2*(1), 62–70.

Njoroge, W. W. (2017). *The relationship between e-marketing strategies and brand performance of large bookstores in Nairobi County* [M.Sc. thesis]. University of Nairobi.

Oliveira, T., Thomas, M., & Espadanal, M. (2014). Assessing the determinants of cloud computing adoption: An analysis of the manufacturing and services sectors. *Information & Management, 51*(5), 497–510. doi:10.1016/j.im.2014.03.006

Oliver, R. L. (1999). Whence consumer loyalty. *Journal of Marketing, 63*(4), 33–44. doi:10.1177/00222429990634s105

Owonte, H., & Amu, G. (2016). Price skimming strategies and marketing performance of electronic firms in Nigeria. *Journal of Business and Value Creation, 5*(2), 135–149.

Papadopoulos, T., Baltas, K. N., & Balta, M. E. (2020). The use of digital technologies by small and medium enterprises during COVID-19: Implications for theory and practice. *International Journal of Information Management, 55*, 102192. doi:10.1016/j.ijinfomgt.2020.102192 PMID:32836646

Qashou, A., & Saleh, Y. (2018). E-marketing implementation in small and medium-sized restaurants in Palestine. *The Arab Economics and Business Journal, 13*(2), 93–110. doi:10.1016/j.aebj.2018.07.001

Rahayu, R., & Day, J. (2015). Determinant factors of e-commerce adoption by SMEs in developing country: Evidence from Indonesia. *Procedia: Social and Behavioral Sciences, 195*, 142–150. doi:10.1016/j.sbspro.2015.06.423

Ramdani, B., Chevers, D., & Williams, A. D. (2013). SMEs' adoption of enterprise applications. *Journal of Small Business and Enterprise Development*. Advance online publication. doi:10.1108/jsbed-12-2011-0035

Roumieh, A., Garg, L., Gupta, V., & Singh, G. (2018). E-marketing strategies for Islamic banking: A case-based study. *Journal of Global Information Management, 26*(4), 67–91. doi:10.4018/JGIM.2018100105

Shaltoni, A. M., West, D., Alnawas, I., & Shatnawi, T. (2018). Electronic marketing orientation in the Small and Medium-sized Enterprises context. *European Business Review*, *30*(3), 272–284. doi:10.1108/EBR-02-2017-0034

Sheikh, A. A., Rana, N. A., Inam, A., Shahzad, A., Awan, H. M., & Wright, L. T. (2018). Is e-marketing a source of sustainable business performance? Predicting the role of top management support with various interaction factors. *Cogent Business & Management*, *5*(1), 1–22. doi:10.1080/23311975.2018.1516487

Singh, T., Kumar, R., & Kalia, P. (2021). E-marketing Practices of Micro-, Small- and Medium-sized Enterprises: Evidence from India. In *Strategic Corporate Communication in the Digital Age*. Emerald Publishing Limited., doi:10.1108/978-1-80071-264-520211012

Sürer, A., & Mutlu, H. M. (2015). The Effects of an E-marketing Orientation on Performance on Turkish Exporter Firms. *Journal of Internet Commerce*, *14*(1), 123–138. doi:10.1080/15332861.2015.1010138

Tan, K., Choy Chong, S., Lin, B., & Cyril Eze, U. (2009). Internet-based ICT adoption: Evidence from Malaysian SMEs. *Industrial Management & Data Systems*, *109*(2), 224–244. doi:10.1108/02635570910930118

Tornatzky, L. G., & Fleischer, M. (1990). *The process of technological innovation*. Lexington Books.

Tsiotsou, R. H., & Vlachopoulou, M. (2011). Understanding the effects of market orientation and e-marketing on service performance. *Marketing Intelligence & Planning*, *29*(2), 141–155. doi:10.1108/02634501111117593

Viljoen, K., Roberts-Lombard, M., & Jooste, C. (2015). Reintermediation strategies for disintermediated travel agencies: A strategic marketing perspective. *The International Business & Economics Research Journal*, *14*(3), 561. doi:10.19030/iber.v14i3.9216

Waheed, A., & Jianhua, Y. (2018). Achieving consumers' attention through emerging technologies: The linkage between e-marketing and consumers' exploratory buying behavior tendencies. *Baltic Journal of Management*, *13*(2), 209–235. doi:10.1108/BJM-04-2017-0126

Zailani, S., Iranmanesh, M., Sean Hyun, S., & Ali, M. (2019). Barriers of biodiesel adoption by transportation companies: A case of Malaysian transportation industry. *Sustainability*, *11*(3), 931. doi:10.3390u11030931

ADDITIONAL READING

Chaffey, D., & Smith, P. R. (2005). *E-marketing excellence; the heart of e-business* (2nd ed.). Heinemann.

Consoli, D. (2012). Literature analysis on determinant factors and the impact of ICT in SMEs. *Procedia: Social and Behavioral Sciences*, *62*, 93–97. doi:10.1016/j.sbspro.2012.09.016

Levenburg, N. M., Schwarz, T. V., & Motwani, J. (2015). Understanding adoption of Internet technologies among SMEs. *Journal of Small Business Strategy*, *16*(1), 51–70.

Santos, J. B., & Brito, L. A. L. (2012). Toward a subjective measurement model for firm performance. *Brazilian Administration Review*, *9*(6), 95–117. doi:10.1590/S1807-76922012000500007

Shaltoni, A. M., West, D., Alnawas, I., & Shatnawi, T. (2018). Electronic marketing orientation in the Small and Medium-sized Enterprises context. *European Business Review*, *30*(3), 272–284. doi:10.1108/EBR-02-2017-0034

KEY TERMS AND DEFINITIONS

Competitiveness: A company's capacity to successfully generate goods and services that meet the needs of the market.

E-Marketing: A technique of organizing and conducting the creation, distribution, marketing, and pricing of goods and services in an interconnected, computerized setting, such as the Internet and the World Wide Web, in order to promote transactions and satisfy customers' needs and wants.

Firm Performance: A measure of how well businesses are able to leverage their material and human resources to achieve their goals.

Marketing Mix: The combination of methods or strategies a business employs to promote its products or brands.

Marketing Strategy: The overall strategy used by a firm to attract potential customers and convert them into buyers of its goods or services.

Small and Medium Enterprises: Enterprises that maintain their assets, revenue, or employee count below a predetermined level. Each nation has its own definition of what small and medium-sized businesses are.

Sustainability: Generating long-term value by considering how organizations function in the ecological, social, and economic settings, with the underlying premise that implementing such tactics encourages business longevity.

Chapter 6
The Relevance of Supply Chain Preparedness on the Long-Term Sustainability of SMEs

Sefa Asortse
https://orcid.org/0000-0002-8166-345X
University of Nigeria, Enugu, Nigeria

Edna Mngusughun Denga
https://orcid.org/0000-0002-2121-242X
American University of Nigeria, Nigeria

ABSTRACT

The variety of risks and the frequency with which they can disrupt a supply chain are now vastly wider than ever, rendering heightened volatility the emerging norm for contemporary supply chains. Thus, resilience has grown in importance as a component of supply chain management. It is suggested that firms increase risk prevention and response strategies to inject resilience into supply chains. SMEs require resilient supply chains to anticipate potential changes, react to actual changes, and deliver superior value. By creating strategies that enable the supply chain to recover normal operations after a disruption, building supply chain resilience can assist in lessening and overcoming vulnerabilities to risks. The chapter aims to provide a detailed insight into the impact of one critical dimension of supply chain resilience, supply chain preparedness, which is aimed at boosting SME sustainability.

INTRODUCTION

A supply chain is a whole system of creating and delivering a product or service from the initial step of acquiring raw materials through the ultimate delivery of the product or service to end-users The management of the movement of goods and services is referred to as supply chain management, and it encompasses all procedures that transform raw materials into finished items. It entails actively simplifying a company's supply-side processes in order to increase customer value and achieve a competitive

DOI: 10.4018/978-1-6684-5727-6.ch006

advantage in the market. The increasing sophistication of managing supply chains and meeting ever-increasing customer demands has made businesses more conscious of their economic and operational vulnerability to dangers from the macro environment: every economic activity carries the risk of unanticipated disruptions, which can result in financial liabilities and, in some cases, firm closure. Terrorist attacks, pandemics, natural catastrophes, and regional power outages in recent years have all revealed numerous firms' lack of supply chain preparedness. Market disruptions and supply chain threats are at an all-time high, the COVID-19 pandemic is, of course, the most well-known of these. According to a poll conducted by the Institute for Supply Management in April 2020, 95 percent of businesses have faced operational issues because of the epidemic. Business executives all around the world believe that if they want to be more robust and competitive in the present market, they will need to modernize and make significant changes to their supply chain operations. Consequently, improving supply chain preparedness is essential, and a significant component of a supply chain disruption management strategy which may be required in periods of catastrophe. In a highly unpredictable environment, firms require proactive supply chain resilience methods to get ready for potential changes, detect changes, and adapt to actual changes in ways that generates value.

The contemporary business environment has been plagued by ever-increasing uncertainties and vulnerabilities; as a result, supply chain (SC) risk mitigation techniques and associated SC capabilities, known as SC resilience, have become increasingly important. SCs' resilience has been widely recognized as a key dynamic trait. The goal of SC resilience is to get operations back to an optimal or better state after a disruption, Thus, instead of adapting to changes through disruptions, SCs can survive disruptions while retaining connection and stability across processes through SC preparedness which refers to firms' ability to withstand the effects of potential changes (Bellow, 2016). Businesses' ability to innovate, manage their staff and customers, and recoup their initial investment are all indicators of a SME's sustainability (Pratiwi, 2018). This demonstrates that they are growth-oriented and continually explore opportunities to innovate. Cost savings, consumer demand, risk mitigation, leadership, tax incentives, staff retention, brand reputation, limited resources, sustaining competitiveness, and new profit prospects are just a few important strategies to accomplish business sustainability (Pratiwi, 2018). However, more than 50% of SMEs worldwide faced a slowdown because of the Covid-19 epidemic (International Trade Center, 2020). Considering SMEs make up 73 percent of all businesses in the globe; this is a considerable percentage (ILO, 2020), and the Covid-19 significantly affects their major lifeline, which is income. Thus, SMEs have been having difficulty sustaining growth, surviving the market, and achieving sustainability for the past two years.

Supply chain preparedness is essential in achieving sustainability as it emphasizes business attributes, risk awareness, risk protection, competitive advantage, innovation, and strategic management in the supply chain (Pettit et al., 2010). Hence, the concept of supply chain preparedness is extremely sufficient to gauge a firm's sustainability, especially for SMEs with constrained resources. Business contingency plans are developed by SC firms to ensure that a SC can withstand a variety of business scenarios. Supply chain preparedness, which is built through the development of contingency plans to protect core business value and the formation of interest synchronization across members of the supply chain to collaboratively resist risks and optimize the creation of value at the supply chain level, can help SMEs improve their performance. Firms can achieve the goal of competitive edge in a vibrant economy by preparing supply chains for potential changes.

BACKGROUND

A significant shift in the approach of enhancing competitive advantage has been largely shaped by the globalization. Supply chain preparedness is one of the variables that facilitate the achievement of a firm 's competitive advantage, notably while facing a volatile environment (Dittfeld et al.,2022; Jutter and Maklan, 2011). Notwithstanding this, there is still debate over the relationship between supply preparedness and firms' sustainability (Sarkar et al.,2022), particularly among small and medium firms (SMEs). One of the essential sectors that drives a nation's economy are SMEs. The proportion of labor force that is incorporated into the SMEs sector is a clear indication of this. Therefore, the performance of SMEs is essential to ensuring its sustainability, and also indirectly aid in maintaining the nation's work force. One approach to improve a performance of firms is to ensure that the supply chain is prepared. Additionally, SMEs profitability and strategic preparedness may suffer if its sustainability efforts fail (Juan et al.,2022). Businesses can enhance their resilience to disruption in two primary areas, according to research, both before and after it occurs (Ramos, 2021; Li et al.,2017). The contemporary business climate is plagued by ever-increasing uncertainty and the resulting vulnerabilities (Ambulkar et al., 2015). Supply chain (SC) risk mitigation measures and associated SC capabilities in form of SC resilience, have become more important in such volatile contexts as is widely recognized as a crucial adaptive capability (Pournader et al., 2020).

The intensifying complexity of managing global supply chains and satisfying rising customer demands has made businesses further cognizant of their economic and operational vulnerability to macroeconomic threats: each business investment has an inherent risk of unforeseen disruptions that can culminate in financial losses and, in certain scenarios, firm shutdowns (Denga et al.,2022b). Modern supply chains face an ever-increasing variety of risks and roadblocks that render it challenging for them to routinely accomplish performance goals (Mandal, 2019). For firms to attain long term sustainability, they must simultaneously manage external risks such as natural disasters and terrorist acts, as well as internal disruptions such as product life cycles, customer demand patterns, and supplier disruptions, and inability to properly address these, if they occur, can have disastrous consequences (Huong et al.,2016). Potential disruptions to supply chains' expected performance levels and creating a system with the appropriate culture and practices to deal with disruptions proactively is the holy grail of management teams. Supply chain resilience (SCRES) has risen to prominence as an approach for managing and mitigating supply chain sustainability (Cheng and Lu, 2017). Any potential or actual disruption in the movement of goods, materials, and/or services is known to as a supply chain disruption (Can et al.,2021). Firms utilize techniques such as interpretive structural modeling, analytical hierarchical process and fault tree analysis (Colicchia et al., 2019) to interact in traditional supply chain risk management, such as the detection and quantification of sources of risk to curtail the likelihood of disruption events (Wan et al., 2016). Simultaneously, disruptions increasingly been considered as unavoidable events in today's volatile business environment (Listou,2018). While conventional supply chain risk management mitigate certain risks, it cannot eliminate all disruptions. As a result, a proactive and comprehensive strategy to supply chain resilience that fosters adaptive capacity to cope with unanticipated events is necessary. By maintaining operations at the appropriate level of interconnectedness and control over architecture and functionality, resilience allows a supply chain to be prepared for events, lessen the impact of a disruption, and increase the ability to recover rapidly (Das, 2018)

By establishing techniques that enable the supply chain to restore to its original (or enhanced) functional condition following a disruption, SCRES assist to minimize and eliminate vulnerability (Roy, 2021).

It is core is returning operations to an optimal or enhanced state following a disruption (Wieland and Wallenburg, 2013). While SCRES research is gaining traction, a discipline-wide definition has yet to be agreed upon (Mandal, 2016). SCRES is defined by Juttner and Maklan (2011, p. 247) as the "capacity to cope with the effects of unavoidable risk occurrences in order to return to its original operations or shift to a new, more desirable state after being disrupted." The capability of supply chain networks and players to thrive in pre-disruption, disruption, and post-disruption environments is what SCRES is all about. The ability of a corporation to implement an SCRES plan depends on a robust SCM structure that facilitates for proactive and reactive responses (Queiroz et al., 2021). As a result, SCRES is reliant on an ostensibly contradictory combination of inherent robustness and agility, as both characteristics offer the breadth required to effectively deal with disruptions.

According to recent research, SCRES can be achieved through either proactive or reactive tactics. The proactive strategy focuses on the ability to avert, or resist being impacted by an event, whereas the reactive strategy highlights the competence to respond to event occurrences (Li et al., 2017). On preparedness, the proactive approach enhances supply chain resilience. A supply chain preparedness thrives during fluctuating situations rather than responding to the changes, it maintains the exact operational stability as before the alteration thus, making it proactive (Durach et al., 2015). Alertness and agility are two essential characteristics proposed by the reactive approach to supply chain resilience. Supply chain alertness is defined as the ability to detect shifts swiftly (Li et al., 2017), which is the fundamental phase in adopting responsive measures. Agility is the ability of a supply chain to adjust rapidly to change by rearranging supply chain operations (Maria et al., 2015). The proactive and reactive techniques are not mutually exclusive in terms of supply chain resilience, but rather complement each other. As a result, three dimensions define supply chain resilience: preparedness, alertness, and agility. A general definition of supply chain resilience based on these highlighted dimensions is "a supply chain's ability to cope with changes, which is generated through being prepared to endure future changes, being alert to changes, and being agile in response to changes."(Rigliett et al.,2021). Sustainability is becoming increasingly more significant as a shift in the business world's mindset has necessitated firms to engage in practices that are beneficial to both the environment and people. Sustainability is integrating long-term and sustainable values into a firm's strategy and value creation. This suggests that businesses that apply sustainability strategies are committed to treating all parties engaged in the business process fairly and with respect, in addition to harnessing natural resources responsibly. Overall, sustainability emphasizes long-term corporate growth through sustainable practices rather than immediate financial gains. Nowadays, implementing a sustainability strategy is fundamental to a firm 's survival rather than just being "nice to have." A focus on social and environmental impacts assures firms to generate long-term value considering the difficulties our planet faces. Sustainability promotes investment, brand reputation, revenue growth, cost reduction, and risk mitigation. A firm that adopts sustainability is securing its position in the economy of the future. While studies have examined the numerous dimensions of SC resilience (Li et al., 2017; Gu and Huo, 2017), there is currently a paucity of research on the impact of supply chain preparedness, as a proactive dimension of supply chain resilience on the long-term sustainability of SMEs'. Most of the sustainability research in business focuses on just a dimension of sustainability such as social or environmental sustainability. However, by addressing the broader concept of sustainability, the chapter contributes to the literature, notably in SMEs and supply chain preparedness. Thus, the book chapter aims to discuss in- depth the concept of supply chain preparedness and the essential drivers SMEs can leverage to attain competitiveness and sustainability.

SUPPLY CHAIN PREPAREDNESS

SC preparedness refers to the ability to withstand the effects of potential disruptions (Tang, 2006). Planning to ensure an effective response to disruptions, managing supply-chain resources, and establishing inter-organizational structures are all part of supply-chain preparedness. Business contingency plans are developed by SC firms to ensure that a SC can tolerate a variety of unexpected circumstances. Every SC firm has a series of procedures and processes that needs to be harmonized with one another in attempt to respond to changes in a rapid manner. Following widespread disruptions, supply chain managers ought to be proactive in preparing for events and lowering disruption vulnerability (Liu et al.,2021). In the face of disruptive events, Ivanov and Sokolov (2012) emphasized the significance of dynamic control and adaptive management. Within SCs, several standardized mechanisms for operational synchronization are practiced. First and foremost, SC partner selection practice and choosing how to communicate with them impacts the resilience of SC networks in unpredictable business situations due to partners' dependability and enthusiasm for collaboration (Cao and Zhang, 2011). Secondly, the real-time exchange of information with SC partners to guarantee transparency of projections, sales figures, and plans. Finally, with explicit policies and protocols, incentive programs can be rendered transparent to empower supply chain players to share risks, expenses, and improvement initiatives more equitably Truong & Azadivar, (2003) opines that supplier selection, partnership, inventory ownership, information exchange, commitment and trust are all essential parts of a strategic plan. Considering inter-organizational factors take time to establish and managing comprehensive supply chain ties is resource intensive, such cooperation is frequently assumed to be close and long-term (Chowdhury and Quaddus, 2015).

In creating dynamic control over the supply chain, preparedness (i.e. pre-emptive) capability is essential. Supply chains with a high degree of preparedness have the flexibility to implement alternate techniques to mitigate vulnerabilities (Pettit et al. 2013). To evaluate the proactive approach to resilience, SCRE studies focused on diverse preparedness capabilities such as flexibility, redundancy, collaboration, visibility, market strength, financial strength, diversity, and efficiency (Pettit et al. 2011). Likewise, Juttner and Maklan (2011) characterized SCRE as having dynamic capabilities including flexibility, velocity, visibility, and collaboration. In the same light posited flexibility, responsiveness, redundancy/back up, and collaborative partnerships as significant strategic alternatives for identifying opportunities and mitigating environmental risks. According to Hollnagel et al. (2006), a system's pre-emptive resilience capability is "described as the ability to recognize, anticipate, and defend against changing risk forms before adverse consequences occur". A supply chain, in a similar vein, must anticipate, identify risk, assess risk, monitor deviation, and detect early warning signals to mitigate disruptions (Pettit et al. 2011). Furthermore, if the disaster can be foreseen, recovery preparations can be made ahead of time, allowing firms to detect hazards in a timely manner. Risk identification initiative facilitates in identifying risk drivers (Christopher and Peck, 2004). As a result, precautions can be taken to avoid disruptions. Proactive techniques, such as early warning signal analysis, are also significant in that they provide advance information about the potential of disruptions (Pettit et al. 2011). To combat the uncertainty of business environments, firms require proactive capabilities. To overcome disruptive events and build resilience capability, supply chain preparedness is vital and in accordance with the existing literature, flexibility, visibility, velocity and collaboration are chosen as sub-dimensions of supply chain preparedness.

Key Drivers of Supply Chain Preparedness

Firms are becoming increasingly interested in supply chain preparedness, which is a concept that minimizes the impact of a disruption by proactively establishing alternative approaches that enable supply chains to react while restoring to its original or even superior functioning state (Jüttner and Maklan, 2011). This necessitates an examination of a firm's broad supply network's capabilities to survive, adapt, and thrive in the face of uncertainties and changes. Flexible, adaptable supply chain put a firm in a successful position. The supply chain is where firms will compete in the future because those who plan ahead for unforeseen setbacks or disasters will be capable of surviving. Redesigning supply networks with the following major drivers in mind will improve preparedness:

Collaboration

Collaboration in a supply chain refers to the ability of two or more independent firms to organize and execute supply chain processes in an effort to achieve shared objectives (Cao et al., 2010). Collaboration has been used to denote a wide range of activities in supply chain management, including such related but separate concepts as cooperation, coordination, and integration. The word encompasses a wide range of activities, from simple sharing of data to relational interconnectedness among supply chain players (Saqib & Zhang, 2021). The emergence of supply chain collaboration necessitates a focus on collaboration understanding at the intercompany stage to equip chain members to effectively establish collaborative initiatives (Lambert et al., 2004). It entails businesses collaborating to get a competitive edge and higher profits than they could achieve on their own (Cheng & Lu, 2017). Collaboration among supply chain actors is a crucial part of risk management strategies. A significant level of collaboration across supply chains mitigate vulnerability. The vulnerable linkage aspect of supply chains and networks, and the realization that a disruption in any link would trigger a disruption in the entire supply chain is a propelling force behind collaboration. The core of the collaborative supply chain framework (CSCF) is comprised of five features: Information exchange, decision synchronization, incentive alignment, collaborative performance system and integrated supply chain processes. Each element can be thought of as an enabler that makes collaborative effort easier and effective as a proactive approach of supply chain resilience.

- *Information Exchange-* The advancement in information technology is accountable for information sharing becoming a fundamental component of supply chain collaboration. Lee and Whang (2000) examine the most recent developments in chain member information exchange. Although information sharing by itself can boost performance, chain members frequently combine it with process improvements. Quick response, vendor-managed inventory (VMI) and efficient-consumer-response are all examples of supply chain processes driven by a seamless information system. The collaborative process relies significantly on information sharing. The Global Logistics Research team at Michigan State University (1995) defined information sharing as "the willingness to make strategic and tactical data available to other members of the supply chain." Information sharing has emerged extremely relevant in supply networks, attributable to automation and technological advances that are reshaping firms' supply chain structures (Kache and Seuring, 2017). In practice, innovative technologies render it easier and faster to collect and share extensive data and information, and supply chains are increasingly operating in an interconnected global environment. Information sharing refers to all partners' systems having access to private data that enables them to track the movement of products as they move through each process in the supply chain (Kaneberg et al.,2016). Effective choices allow chain members to respond to product flow difficulties more rapidly, allowing for a resilient demand planning. Advanced technology, such as the internet, can be utilized to provide real-time information on planning, product movement, workflow, expenses, and performance. Relevance, accuracy, timeliness, and reliability are some of the criteria leveraged to evaluate the significance of information sharing to supply chain integration (Leat and Revoredo – Giha, 2013). The interaction of information sharing with other framework features is fundamental for integrating other features into a cohesive whole. The actors of the chain are more concerned with the value of information sharing than with information in itself. The capacity to make informed decisions and take actions premised on increased visibility is what makes information sharing important to supply chain members (Colicchia & Strozzi, 2012). Information sharing, in combination with incentive alignment, offers visibility into the state of chain members' incentive scores (Kumar et al.,2015). Information sharing facilitates resilience because the capability to manage information risks at the supply chain level empowers firms and supply chains to achieve robust resilience, culminating in improved protection and security against threats and disruptions associated to information sharing. Collaboration through information sharing minimizes uncertainty and improves supply chain resilience in a proactive way (Liu et al., 2018).

- *Decision Synchronization*-The extent to which supply chain stakeholders are able to orchestrate crucial decisions at the planning and execution phases for optimizing supply chain profitability is known as decision synchronization (Simatupang et al., 2002). The activity entails developing collective decision-making mechanisms, as well as redistributing decision rights, in an attempt to synchronize supply chain planning and implementation to match demand and supply. The effects of successful decision synchronization on accurate response to customer needs (logistical benefits) and supply chain profitability (commercial benefits) are employed to assess its effectiveness (Listou, 2018)). The relevance of decision synchronization stems from the notion that supply chain members have varying decision powers and levels of competence (Mandal et al.,2016). The interaction of decision synchronization with other collaboration drivers is fundamental as it empowers chain members to coordinate their decisions to better achieve overall performance. Decision synchronization offers information on how performance indicators aid chain members in making appropriate decisions (Lotfi and Larmour, 2022)

- *Incentive Alignment*-The practice of distributing costs, risks, and benefits among supply chain players is referred to as incentive alignment (Liu et al.,2018). This scheme encourages members to act in ways compatible with their collective strategic objectives, such as making decisions beneficial to the whole supply chain and disclosing accurate confidential information. It encompasses cost, risk, and benefit calculations, along with incentive programs like pay-for-effort and pay-for-performance. Compensation fairness and self-enforcement can be utilized to assess the significance of incentive alignment.

- *Collaborative Performance System(CPS)* – CPS is the process of developing and leveraging performance metrics to aid chain members enhance their overall performance. The process also entails addressing two interrelated issues: who should be engaged in deciding the collective objective and what performance indicators should be set in relation to the mutual goal. The common objective shows the competitive advantages that can be achieved if the chain members work collaboratively. Competitive elements can take the shape of product and service advantages that the market recognizes as superior to competitors, such as customer service, quality, price, supply chain costs, and responsiveness. Simatupang and Sridharan (2004a) suggest three dynamic learning cycles to address this need. These cycles assist chain members to review their collaborative performance at various managerial levels, empowering them to enhance overall performance.

- *Integrated Supply Chain Processes-* The extent to which chain members construct efficient supply chain processes that deliver products to end consumers on time and at reduced costs is considered as integrated supply chain processes. This feature's explicit description aids chain members in synchronizing the whole sequence of integrated work activities required to deliver items that meet customer requirements (Croxton et al., 2001). The supply chain processes must be as flexible as possible in order to respond to a wide range of customer demands at the lowest possible cost in terms of supply capacity.

Flexibility

Flexibility has been defined as "the ability to bend easily without breaking" and thus been recognized as an essential component of supply chain resilience (Peck, 2005). In the context of SC, SC flexibility is characterized as a firm's capacity to adjust to uncertainties and consumer expectations without incurring unnecessary costs, time, or performance losses, both externally and internally in collaboration with key customers and suppliers (Yu et al., 2015). Several significant themes are addressed in this definition. First, SC flexibility refers to the ability to collaborate across and within firms to integrate internal, downstream, and upstream processes. Secondly, SC flexibility encompasses a set of various resources and procedures in the SC that empower firms to adapt to adjustments swiftly and effectively with their SC collaborators and deliver appropriate products and services, hence offering value to customers. Thirdly, capabilities are embedded in management procedures in responding to changes in the environment from the perspective of organizational capability (Tiwari et al., 2015). Finally, SC flexibility is a capacity that can be implemented in preparation to deal with potential disruption, flexibility thus integrates agility and adaptability (Lee, 2004).

Flexibility entails establishing dynamic capabilities to recognize emerging threats and responds rapidly. This not only strengthens a firm's resilience, but it also offers competitive edge in the industry. Critical components of every supply chain can attain flexibility: Material flows from suppliers then through a conversion phase, channels of distribution and innovative product introduction (Spiegler et al., 2012; Ivanov and Spiegler, 2012). While flexibility facilitates effective disruptive response, it must be evaluated against the requirement for efficiency. Moreover, supply chains strengthens their resilience by reorganizing making optimal utilization of current assets and infrastructures. (Mackay et al., 2019) with such reconfiguration competencies allowing firms to rapidly recover to its optimum desirable state. It is also noteworthy highlighting that recent SC resilience research has placed a great emphasis on flexibility which is the most frequently cited resilience metric in the literature (Fiksel et al. 2015). Firms with the capabilities to blend and reconfigure these processes and resources can thrive and compete in a disruptive environment more effectively and efficiently. Internal and externally focused capabilities are the key subdivisions of SC flexibility. External capabilities are built on a supply chain's internal competencies, according to Zhang et al. (2002), and supply chain network competences serve as the framework for external, customer-facing abilities. External capability to offer products and services while adjusting to a swiftly dynamic marketplace is referred to as market-oriented flexibility. As inter - organization networks are tactical resources that management teams build and establish over time to match their strategic goals, the capacity to alter supply or logistics networks over time in responding to highly competitive variations enable the supply chain to capitalize on opportunities to enhance operational performance (Angkiriwang et al., 2014). Flexible network facilitates in establishing a spectrum of external capabilities that can adapt rapidly to unforeseen occurrences and enhance performance. Internally focused flexible capabilities denotes the competence to adjust to uncertainties and consumer expectations by incorporating and utilizing internal knowledge and routines incorporated in internal functions (Liao et al., 2010). These dimensions are often known as "market-oriented" dimensions as they explicitly highlight a supply chain's capabilities to address the expectations of consumers (Oh et al., 2013). supply chain flexibility can be divided into two categories: Network- oriented flexibility and Market-oriented flexibility

- *Market-oriented flexibility* is a firm's abilities to modify operational processes across the supply chain, including manufacturing and delivery, in response to environmental uncertainty or disruption. Volume, mix, and delivery are the three categories of this flexibility. Volume flexibility is described as a firm's capability to function at varied levels of production outputs effectively and economically. While functioning profitably, volume flexibility assists firms to respond to significant variance in consumer demand levels (Jain et al., 2013). A firm with a considerable level of volume flexibility can achieve competitive edge by absorbing disruption when products are unexpectedly in high demand whilst maintaining lower level of inventory than rivals, translating to a negative effect on the bottom line (Goyal et al., 2018). It is a vitally important component that small and medium enterprises (SMEs) needs to continuously gain market shares. Mix flexibility is the ability of a firm to modify the range of products it produces (Turner et al., 2018). It denotes the ability to manufacture a wide array of goods or variations with minimal switching costs. Providing products with various features, quality levels, and price points is crucial to a firm's competitive edge (Campos et al., 2019). One of the foremost significant characteristics of a SME is its ability to be flexible in product mix, therefore the supply chain must be able to adapt with variations in specifications. Delivery flexibility is a capacity to efficiently deliver products to customers in response to uncertainties in anticipated delivery schedule, volume, and destination and volume. Delivery flexibility, according to Sethi and Sethi (1990), is an essential dimension of market-oriented flexibility, which comprises strategies for achieving flexibility in the location, time, size, and variety of deliveries in order to enhance consumer satisfaction (Angkiriwang et al., 2014).
- *Network-oriented flexibility* are capabilities firms possess that position them to respond to environmental unpredictability by structuring its supply chain and altering flow of information and material. In responding to supply chain environmental uncertainties or disruptions, supply networks, logistics networks, and spanning flexibility are all considered network-oriented flexibility (Yu et al., 2015). As consumer preferences evolve rapidly, firm's effort initiatives to respond promptly and deliver new products/services is connected with strategic complexities (Tiwari et al., 2015). The flexibility to change supply chain architecture for long-term and strategic perks is required to meet these objectives in the supply chain (Oh et al., 2013). Thus, to respond to the fluctuations, architectural flexibility must be embedded into the supply chain structure. Supply network is the capability to effectively and efficiently restructure supplier base in response to disruptions (Thome et al., 2014; Liao et al., 2010).

Visibility

Supply chain visibility (SCV) is the gathering and evaluation of supply chain information that aids in the control of supply chain disruption risks and facilitates decision making (Tohamy, 2003). It also is known as "the capacity to track down the sources of materials incorporated in a product" (Lee and Rammohan, 2017). SCV has evolved as a critical supply chain capacity for improving supply chain effectiveness and mitigating the effects of supply chain network disruptions. According to Barrat et al., (2007), SCV is the degree to which actors in a supply chain have accessibility to or share information that they regard to be critical or valuable to their operations and that they believe will be mutually beneficial is defined as supply chain visibility. It also entails having a good picture of upstream and downstream inventories, supply and demand situations, as well as production and procurement schedules. Information needs be readily accessible, accurate, timely, and in a manner that provides required information for supply chain visibility to be efficient. The visibility of the members of the supply chain extends beyond the firms. By sharing information such as current inventory levels, procurement status, production schedules, distribution dependability, order status, and demand projections, this knowledge contributes to supply chain confidence (Carvalho et al 2012). Furthermore, supply chain visibility (the capability to view from one end of the pipeline to the other) is critical for supply chain preparedness. SCV dimensions, according to Pettit (2008), includes information technology, information sharing, business intelligence gathering, and asset status knowledge. Information technology is the usage of computerized technologies to connect supply chain operations and offer visibility of internal operations and procedures. Internal integration entails cross-functional cooperation that allow the entire business to absorb and exploit information in approaches that improve flexibility. Information sharing is the degree to which information is disseminated amongst the supply chain's partners (Vilko, 2012). The sharing of sufficiently high-quality information is critical in the integration of operations within the supply chain to facilitate diverse activities and decision-making. Information exchange and, increasingly recently, supply chain visibility have received a considerable of emphasis in supply chain management research. Enhanced information accessibility, according to Wiliam et al. (2013), boosts a firm's capabilities to respond swiftly to disruptions in the marketplace. The capability to disseminate information among members of the supply chain is critical to enhancing SCV. Since information minimizes uncertainties and lessen the quantity of buffer inventory required, information sharing it considerably boosts its power (Tukumuhabwa et al. 2015). Business intelligence is undoubtedly an accelerator of speedy, effective decision making to sustain routine operations and especially in challenging times, SMEs are expected to have a stronger visibility of it.

Velocity

Velocity is the capacity to finish an activity as rapidly as feasible (Carvalho et al., 2012). The time it takes to transmit goods and materials from one side of the supply chain to the other, or end-to-end pipeline time, must be scaled back in attempt to enhance velocity as it is further expressed as distance over time. Supply chain recovery from a risk event is based on supply chain velocity, which emphasizes the rate of flexible adaptation (Tukumuhabwa et al., 2015). Supply chain empowerment, supply chain flexibility, supply chain speed, and supply chain innovations were recognized as dimensions of supply chain velocity by Dubey et al., (2014). Velocity places a significant emphasis on the supply chain's response and recovery efficiency. In this aspect, higher supply chain velocity tends to enhance the speed of recovery from disruptions (Wieland and Wallenburg, 2013) by allowing for speedier response to market changes or occurrences. To achieve the optimal velocity, supply chain empowerment of the workforce is crucial (Dubey et al, 2014). This can be done by choosing and training individuals who have the ability to plan, coordinate, act, and intervene when necessary. Pettit (2008) asserts that empowerment through activities that foster trust can potentially reveal ways to boost routine operational effectiveness. The capability to transparently share information and subsequently leverage the data in joint decision-making will benefit from developing trust with strategic partners. The ability of firms to adjust its strategy in response to changes in its environment and to seize new possibilities is referred to as supply chain adaptation (Yao & Meurier, 2012). One of the most important elements for obtaining and maintaining competitive edge in supply chain networks is adaptation. The demand for quick change and adaptability must go beyond boundaries of the firm to embrace the entire supply chain as firms compete not just against one another but also collectively with their suppliers, suppliers of suppliers, customers, and customers of the customers, i.e., the supply chains.

As a result, firms ought to have resilient supply networks (Giannoccaro, 2015). (Ponomarov, 2012). To manage and effectively respond to changes, SMEs must adapt their activities in the face of difficulties. Supply chain speed is the capacity to accomplish a task as rapidly as possible as there is a necessity to mitigate from unanticipated risks with a sustainable elimination of their vulnerabilities in the quickest timeframe and with the least number of resources. SMEs delays in the commercial supply chain are expensive in terms of productivity, customer satisfaction and profitability. Innovation in the supply chain is the creation, acceptance, and application of novel concepts, procedures, goods, or services. Continuously seeking out innovative knowledge that is unrelated to a firm's existing operational activity constitutes innovation. to address issues and obstacles in business. Vicente et al. (2015) opines that managers should alter routines and create an inventive culture that is structured to embrace significant internal change. Elevated innovative culture has a stronger competitive edge, allowing them to build on their successes. Successful innovations are those that lead to enhancements in effectiveness, efficiency, quality, or societal results.

SUSTAINABILITY

The term "permanence" was first adopted by Schumacher in 1972 to describe the concept of sustainability. According to Schumacher, "nothing makes economic sense unless its survival for a long period can be projected without running into absurdities" (Ashby et al., 2012). Sustainability is meeting the requirements of the present without compromising the needs of the future and ensuring a balance between economic growth, environmental protection, and social well-being. Today, sustainability is still a top priority for several investors who want to use impact investing to generate financial gains while promoting social harmony. Ensuring that future generations' potential is not jeopardized in any way is the underlying principle of sustainability. Three pillars—economic, environmental, and social also known colloquially as profits, planet, and people are frequently used to describe sustainability. A sustainable firm follows the triple bottom line, a concept that was first introduced in 1994 by John Elkington, the founder of the British Consultancy Sustainability. Profits, people, and the environment are the triple bottom line's three pillars. By conserving the usage of the planet's resources and being socially responsible, a sustainable business earns profit. The Triple Bottom Line (TBL) model, which is leveraged to analyze the significance of the role of people, planet, and profit for business, cannot be excluded from discussions about business sustainability (John Elkington, 2017). While all three elements are significant, the research is centered on the broader definition of sustainability as serving the needs of the present without compromising the future is essential for business sustainability in a competitive market. SMEs that embrace socially responsible business practices about how they relate to regional and global social, environmental, and economic issues are considered to be practicing sustainability. Today, the business community and all the major participants in the various supply chains are focusing a high priority on the multifarious concepts of sustainability because of the urgent concerns expressed about environmental, social, and economic challenges (Sancha et al., 2016). In this context, practitioners and researchers alike have shown a great deal of interest in the concept of sustainability, which describes proactive actions intended to contribute to sustainable supply chain equilibria (Linnenluecke et al., 2009). These equilibriums relate to the incorporation of socioeconomic and environmental performance factors, as well as underlying relationships inside and across the temporal dimension, while considering the organizational system as a whole and its important stakeholders (Lozano et al., 2015).

The phrase "economic sustainability" is used to describe several tactics that allow for the most efficient use of available resources. The goal is to encourage the responsible and effective use of those resources in a way that will likely result in long-term advantages. In the context of a business operation, it entails leveraging resources in a way that the firm can keep operating for a while continually making a profit (John Elkington, 2017). Economic sustainability is a broad collection of decision-making principles and corporate practices aimed to achieve economic growth without making the negative environmental trade-offs that traditionally go hand in hand with growth. sustainable growth creates operational systems that deplete natural capital (sometimes referred to as natural resources) gradually enough to guarantee the continued usage of those resources by future generations. economic sustainability in the economy is important to small business economic sustainability because it affords consumers the ability to actively engage in the marketplace, leading to profit for businesses (Laurelli et al., 2019). Likewise, when small businesses practice smart economic sustainability practices, they reinforce a higher standard of living and sustainability in their own community and the world. This contributes toward a positive cycle where small businesses focus on internal sustainability, which reinforces external sustainability in the economy, leading to an increase in consumers who can spend money in the marketplace (Sancha et al., 2016). As it encourages consumers to participate actively in the market and generates profit for firms, economic sustainability is crucial for small business sustainability. Small businesses that engage in intelligent economic sustainability practices contribute to a greater standard of living and sustainability in both their local communities and around the globe. This aid in creating a beneficial cycle where small firms prioritize internal sustainability, which strengthens external sustainability in the economy and increases the number of customers who can make purchases.

Environmental sustainability is described as appropriate interactions with the environment that promotes long-term environmental quality while eliminating resource depletion or degradation. Environmental sustainability is an approach that makes it possible to meet the needs of the current generation without endangering the ability of future generations to do the same (Roy, 2021). Businesses that practice environmental sustainability may have an advantage over their rivals in attracting prospective customers and investors. Modern consumers are aware of social and environmental issues and keep track of firms acting responsibly in the community. Investors are likewise aware of these problems, and a trend toward investing in environmentally friendly businesses is emerging. The fact that environmental sustainability has no detrimental effects on a business' ability to make a profit is what matters most when evaluating the value proposition for it. In fact, by lowering costs and raising competition, it is thought to increase profitability over the long term. Since they are the largest contributors and are able to have a considerable impact, businesses are expected to take the lead in the field of environmental sustainability (Johnson et al., 2013). Most firms have historically functioned without much consideration for or concern for how their actions affect the environment. Both large and small businesses are guilty of seriously harming the environment and indulging in unsustainable activities. However, several businesses are increasingly making a commitment to lessening their negative effects to have a positive impact on environmental sustainability.

Social sustainability is the identification and management of corporate impacts on people, both positive and negative. Firms' stakeholder engagement and relationship quality are crucial, hence influences customers, local communities, value chain workers, employees, directly or indirectly, making it fundamental to proactively manage impacts. The social sustainability initiatives implemented by businesses have a significant impact on their capacity to function. Additionally, a lack of social development, such as poverty, inequality, and a lax rule of law, might impede the growth and operation of businesses (Das, 2018). Actions taken to attain social sustainability may also open new markets, assist in retaining and attracting trading partners, or serve as a catalyst for the development of new product or service lines. Productivity, risk management, and company-community friction may all improve while internal morale and employee involvement may increase. Quality of life, equality, diversity, social cohesion, and democracy & governance are the four pillars of social sustainability (Laurelli et al., 2019). Business sustainability benefits the company, as well as the environment and society at large. Here are just few of the numerous advantages of running a more sustainable firm: provides competitive advantage, improves business' reputation, increases bottom line and reduces business costs

SMEs Supply Chain Preparedness and Sustainability

In the contemporary business environment, a firm's supply chain preparedness and subsequent sustainability are determined by one supply chain competing against other supply chains (Christopher, 1992). Modern supply chains now have higher levels of network complexity as a result of this strategy evolution. Owing to the cascading characteristics and nonlinear effects that characterize complex systems, "catastrophes" may be more likely to occur as supply chains can be particularly sensitive to minor disruptions from anywhere in the network (Choi et al., 2001). SMEs are particularly at risk from a lack of supply chain preparedness and eventually find it difficult to recover when subjected to supply shocks or disruptions that are sustained or recurrent. Given the variety and severity of risks that businesses may encounter, disruption is unavoidable; what sets one company apart from another is the capacity to withstand, adapt to, and grow stronger. supply chain preparedness is pivotal in enabling businesses take proactive, forward-looking actions to engage in sustainable practices to achieve long sustainability (Moon et al., 2012). The present epidemic has moved the focus from the sustainability of SMEs in an increasingly globalized environment to concentrating on their resilience especially supply chain preparedness. Resilience, broadly speaking, is the capacity to deal with adversity, which, in the context of SMEs, is the capacity of an organization to foresee, absorb, respond to, and recover from conditions that have the potential to endanger its existence. This includes heightened international competition brought on by globalization, technological advancements, altering consumer preferences, and environmental or ecological catastrophes like COVID. When discussing about SMEs and business, supply chain preparedness and sustainability are the new catchphrases, but their connections are seldom ever addressed (Roy, 2021). An organization must be able to proactively mitigate against change and adversity in order to be sustainable, it must be able to meet present demands without jeopardizing the future. When talking about these concepts, we frequently include an organization's internal environment, such as its capacity to endure structural change or financial difficulty.

To compete in the globalized market of the twenty-first century, SMEs must maintain their dominance as the engine of economic growth. The ability of a SME to innovate, manage its personnel and customers, and recoup its initial investment are all indicators of its sustainability. This demonstrates their commitment to growth and continual awareness of innovative options. Cost savings, consumer demand, mitigating risk, leadership, tax incentives, staff retention, brand reputation, limited resources, sustaining competition, and innovative profit prospects are just a few of the important approaches to accomplish SME sustainability (Saqib &Zhang,2021). However, SMEs endure downturns and are all directly slammed into their significant lifeline, which is their income, during disruptions like the current Covid -19. Consequently, SMEs struggle to continue their growth, stay competitive, and secure their sustainability. Understanding business growth is crucial considering it is one of the pillars of SMEs' sustainability. Corporate environment has an impact on business growth, thus for it to continue, businesses must adapt to shifting environmental conditions. Supply chain preparedness is just as vital as growth for achieving firms' sustainability and is focused on organizational attributes, risk awareness, risk protection, competitive edge, innovation and strategic management in the supply chain (Dittfeld et al.,2022) The key to long-term sustainability is resilience, which is at the center of sustainability, and it is embedded in the DNA of sustainability. Boosting SCRES not only facilitates a firm to adapt and withstand unavoidable disruptions but also to anticipate and accommodate the future with the alternative solutions. While majority of SMEs lack the knowledge or resources necessary to completely integrate quantifiable beneficial environmental and social effect into their operational strategies, the sustainability of small businesses continues to be unmet. SMEs' capacity is frequently constrained when it comes to optimizing and assessing their sustainable impact, even though they frequently hold the keys to the kingdom when it pertains to resilience and innovation to accommodate anticipated and expected disruption (Laurelli et al., 2019). Every supply chain management has a formidable challenge when attempting to strike a sustainable equilibrium between supply and demand in today's fiercely competitive market (Denga et al.,2022a). Recently, several firms have discovered the actual cost of their decisions to forgo diversification, supply chain technology, and supply preparedness measures. To critically illustrate its relevance on the sustainability of SMEs, the benefits of the key drivers of supply chain preparedness will be highlighted.

Supply Chain Velocity is the term used to describe the pace at which activities are accomplished within the supply chain as well as the speed at which orders progress through the supply chain from processing to delivery to customers. High supply chain velocity reduces lead times, speeds up supply chain operations, and shortens the order cycle time (Laurelli et al., 2019). In general, high supply chain velocity results in orders being delivered to customers with a relatively little turnaround time from order placement and delivery. High supply chain velocity gives a company a competitive edge and is essential to its survival. Here are just a few reasons how supply chain velocity improves the sustainability of SMEs: Increases in customer satisfaction, brand loyalty, and repeat business can all be attributed to a supply chain that operates efficiently enough to deliver finished goods to customers more quickly. As a result, customers are more likely to recommend the company, leave positive reviews, and make repeat purchases, all of which foster brand loyalty and boost the bottom line of the company (Sagone and Caroli, 2013).. Secondly, supply chain velocity increases profitability and reduces costs. When it comes to sales, being able to move goods along the supply chain swiftly can translate to increased sales and higher revenues (Yun et al.,2020). Internally, highly streamlined, and effective supply chain methods generally result in lower operating and workforce expenses as well as productivity improvements. SMEs can boost their profitability by lessening their operational costs or allocating the additional funds for other purposes. Finally, it gets operations prepared for unforeseen difficulties. A lean supply network and rapid order turnaround time make an agile supply chain more flexible than a slow supply chain. As a result, high velocity supply chains can readily be altered to avert supply chain disruptions and seize opportunities in the face of variability. If a supply chain can support high-velocity operations, it will typically be well-prepared to proactively manage potential disruptions or obstacles (Bellow, 2016).

Supply Chain Collaboration is the long-term partnership developed between supply chain participants to achieve mutual goals and benefits, such as reducing cost and risk and raising quality and market value. Long-term relationships ultimately result in increased revenues, and the gains of supply chain collaboration mirrors the benefits of customer retention (Bellow, 2016). This occurs, among other things, because business partners are better able to harmonize quality production and ethical working standards throughout their supply chains when enough time has been spent working together and understanding one another. Better collaboration with partners and customers also aids SMEs in production optimization, minimizing wastage of resources like time and money. Collaboration in supply chains, whether horizontal or vertical, can have significant advantages for businesses (Pham et al.,2021). Through multi-stakeholder collaboration, better ethical standards are being driven. Consumers and businesses alike are placing a higher focus on ethical and sustainable sourcing. But no matter how committed a firm may be to enhancing the status of environmental sustainability and human rights in a certain industry, one company can only do so much. In fact, it is generally acknowledged that multi-stakeholder collaboration is essential for driving significant and long-lasting change in global supply chains. By working collaboratively with supply chain partners, businesses can advance higher ethical and environmental standards, increase supply chain transparency, and have more influence over the areas of their supply chains that are resistant to change (Sagone and Caroli, 2013). Furthermore, Collaboration enhances the safety and quality of products. Every business strives to provide customers with safe, high-quality items since this is paramount to customer satisfaction. Working together with supply chain partners helps SMEs gain a deeper understanding of the issues affecting product quality and safety in an industry, issues with raw materials, updated rules for chemical control, and more. Additionally, collaborating with others to overcome these obstacles yields results faster and more effectively than each partner working on their own. In the end, benefits to customers, businesses, and the industry as a whole translating to sustainability (Schaltagger et al.,2016). Collaboration within the supply chain also reduces long-term costs. In any operation, one-off partnerships have their time and place. However, long relationships have the biggest effects on a firms' bottom line. Long-term supply chain collaboration has practical, straightforward, and day-to-day benefits. Simply put, working together for a longer period allows for a greater grasp of each other's strengths, weaknesses, and working methods, making it simpler to play to each other's advantages. Lastly, collaboration promotes partner and supply chain talent retention. Businesses today are aware of the importance of customer retention and the level of competition vying for brand loyalty (Denga et al.,2022b) Customers are not the only thing firms needs to succeed, they must ensure they can attract and retaining top talent as well as maintain long-term relationships with the most effective players to guarantee their survival (Das, 2018). It is undeniable clear that "supply chain talent management is undoubtedly the most challenging and particular of all business requirements," according to The Global Supply Chain Institute and the most significant benefits of supply chain collaboration efforts is the retention of talented supply chain participants and executives. The underlying tenet of supply chain collaboration as a preparedness strategy is the sharing knowledge and exchanging information along the chain that eliminate uncertainties, improve visibility

(Faisal et al., 2006), strengthen operational efficiency and effectiveness, and optimize customer support translating to SMEs sustainability (Schaltagger et al.,2016).

Supply Chain Visibility is paramount for SMEs to operate effectively, make swift decisions, cut costs, and proactively manage and minimize risk. Enhancing visibility contributes to boosting supply chain preparedness and agility as well as addressing the burgeoning demand for more robust sustainability. Firms may be at risk from disruption, the inability to predict demand, and failure to satisfy consumer expectations if a supply chain lacks near-complete visibility. Supply chain visibility is a critical component of the effective implementation of sustainability (Yun et al.,2020). Numerous large corporations have made the commitment to only transact business with suppliers who uphold social and environmental standards. Today, more than 90% of CEOs claim that sustainability is crucial to the success of their business (Golic et al., 2017). Consumer trust is strengthened as supply chain visibility increases. Every supply chain leader must be fully cognizant of sustainability. Investing in supply chain visibility is a crucial and effective way for businesses to win over customers' trust; it can even boost sales as transparency enhances customers' trust in both an organization 's products and in the business itself. When customers feel confident in a company, they are more inclined to make additional purchases from that company. To maintain their competitiveness, supply chain managers must comprehend the significance of leveraging supply chain visibility to boost sustainable supply chain operations, build customer trust, and raise profitability (Golic et al., 2017).

Supply Chain Flexibility—the potential to quickly modify production levels, raw material acquisitions, and transport capacity has enormous advantages compared to traditional supply chain management. The reduction in liabilities is a beneficial feature of a flexible supply chain. Due to the inherent risks and dangers involved in the production and distribution of products, certain parts of supply chain management for SMEs bear significant liability (Carvalho et al., 2012). Catastrophe like stolen or destroyed goods during shipping and disruptive occurrences like the COVID-19 epidemic are both possible and inevitable. SMEs that have flexible supply chains can respond to these disturbances quickly, minimizing liability, maximizing profit, and minimizing supply chain risks as they expand. Instead of wasting resources due to the inability to make swift changes, a flexible supply chain adapts to meet the natural ebb and flow of a business. In many situations, like with COVID-19, it will be important to adjust different supply chain components as well as have the flexibility to scale up or down to match demand in order to avoid missing out on potential revenue or incurring spoilage. The decrease in liability is a major additional benefit of supply chain flexibility. Given the inherent risks and dangers involved in the manufacture and delivery of goods, certain areas of supply chain management bear significant liability (ILO,2020). Accidents like lost or damaged products during shipping and disruptive occurrences like the COVID-19 epidemic are both possible and inevitable. Firms that have flexible supply chains can respond to these disturbances swiftly, minimizing liability, maximizing profit, and minimizing supply chain risks as they expand. Firms can benefit from supply chain preparedness, which is founded through the creation of contingency initiatives to prevent the core business value and the formation of interest alignment among supply chain participants in a bid to collaboratively resist risks and maximize value creation at the supply chain level (Carvalho et al., 2012). Firms can achieve the ultimate objective of competitiveness in a robust economy by preparing supply chains for potential disruptions (Pettit et al., 2013).

FUTURE RESEARCH DIRECTIONS

The four supply chain preparation drivers need to be empirically tested in subsequent research in attempt to determine whether firms can implement them and achieve sustainability. Other drivers that are not addressed in this chapter, including redundancy and backup capacity, also ought to be investigated in effort to evaluate how they might affect the sustainability of SMEs. The impact of supply chain preparedness practices on performance indicators like responsiveness, customer happiness, and operational effectiveness should also be the subject of future research. Redundant (human, physical, or organizational) network resources and their trade-offs with efficiency must be further investigated to explore the underlying supply chain processes that contribute to supply chain preparedness through flexibility, velocity, visibility, and collaboration. To determine how much efficiency a supply chain preparedness can withstand, it is also necessary to examine how such redundancies balance with efficiency.

CONCLUSION

The concept of supply chain preparedness in SMEs facilitates efficient and effective firm operations with the numerous advantages: Measures to lessen the likelihood of risky circumstances will be taken as a result of the identification of the risk factors that can disrupt the business in SMEs, making operations more effective and efficient; Activities will be more streamlined and profitable as a function of the analysis of specific risk variables involved in the process and several options to deal with such aspects, SMEs will become more productive and efficient making it feasible to properly analyze the outcomes in order to achieve superior strategic decisions(Gu & Huo, 2017). Efficiency has to do with choosing a plan of action that has a hundred percent chance of producing the intended outcomes. In several SMEs, supply chain activities are where there is the most possibility of loss and risk. Supply networks are particularly prone to risk since they are by their very nature geographically distributed and functionally complex. Supply chain preparedness lowers risk by offering firms SMEs real-time access to all network operations and the ability to optimize and modify their processes and logistics. Risk is frequently reduced and the capacity to invest in innovation and growth is enhanced with greater supply chain preparedness (Rigliett et al.,2021). Shorter product development processes and higher production capacity are advantages for SMEs who prioritized investment in supply chain preparedness. Recent occurrences like the Covid-19 have demonstrated further that operational risks are unavoidable and are far more prone to affect today's supply chains due to their enormous global span and complexities. Nevertheless, as emphasized by Christopher and Peck (2004), many firms are rarely cognizant of the necessity to incorporate their supply chains' preparedness into account. Instead, they appear to be more inclined to focus on the likelihood of negative occurrences in their supply risk management than the effect. The chapter makes a case for knowledge management and supply chain risk by highlighting how this can strengthen the four resilience capabilities and, in the end, lessen the negative effects of unavoidable risk. The benefit of supply chain preparedness for managers is dual. First off, the four resilience capabilities seem to be able to handle risk events originating from a variety of sources as constituents of the supply chain system. By tackling several risks at once, they eventually have a significant impact on a firm's supply risk portfolio. Secondly, notable research suggests that flexibility, collaboration, and visibility are unquantifiable dynamic supply chain capabilities that can avert supply chain disruptions and yield sustainability practices during normal, daily operating hours.

REFERENCES

Ambulkar, S., Blackhurst, J., & Grawe, S. (2015). Firm's Resilience to Supply Chain Disruptions: Scale Development and Empirical Examination. *Journal of Operations Management, 33-34*(1), 111–122. doi:10.1016/j.jom.2014.11.002

Angkiriwang, R., Pujawan, I. N., & Budi, S. (2014). Managing uncertainty through supply chain flexibility: Reactive vs. proactive approaches. *Production & Manufacturing Research, 2*(1), 50–70. doi:10 .1080/21693277.2014.882804

Apeji, U.D., & Sunmola, F.T. (2022). Sustainable supply chain visibility assessment and proposals for improvements using fuzzy logic. *Journal of Modelling in Management.* . doi:10.1108/JM2-08-2021-01

Brady, M. (2020). Realising supply chain resilience: an exploratory study of Irish firms' priorities in the wake of Brexit. *Continuity & Resilience Review*. doi:10.1108/CRR-06-2020-0020

Can Saglam, Y., Yildiz Çankaya, S., & Sezen, B. (2021). Proactive risk mitigation strategies and supply chain risk management performance: An empirical analysis for manufacturing firms in Turkey. *Journal of Manufacturing Technology Management, 32*(6), 1224–1244. doi:10.1108/JMTM-08-2019-0299

Carvalho, L. S., Stefanelli, N. O., Viana, L. C., Vasconcelos, D. S. C., & Oliveira, B. G. (2020). Green supply chain management and innovation: A modern review. *Management of Environmental Quality, 31*(2), 470–482. doi:10.1108/MEQ-12-2019-0283

Chowdhury, M. M. H., & Quaddus, M. A. (2015). A multiple objective optimization based QFD approach for efficient resilient strategies to mitigate supply chain vulnerabilities: The case of garment industry of Bangladesh. *Omega, 57*, 5–21. doi:10.1016/j.omega.2015.05.016

Christopher & Peck. (2004). Building the resilient supply chain. *International Journal of Logistics Management, 15*(2), 1-13.

Colicchia, C., & Strozzi, F. (2012). Supply chain risk management: A new methodology for a systematic literature review. *Supply Chain Management, 17*(4), 403–418. doi:10.1108/13598541211246558

Colicchia, C., Creazza, A., Noè, C., & Strozzi, F. (2019). Information sharing in supply chains: A review of risks and opportunities using the systematic literature network analysis (SLNA). *Supply Chain Management, 24*(1), 5–21. doi:10.1108/SCM-01-2018-0003

Denga, E. M., & Rakshit, S. (2022a). Supply Chain Logistics Risk Mitigation - Impact of Covid-19 Pandemic. In K. Strang & N.R. Vajjhala (Eds.), Global Risk and Contingency Management Research in Times of Crisis. Academic Press.

Denga, E. M., & Rakshit, S. (2022b). Risks in Supply Chain Logistics - Constraints and Opportunities in North-Eastern Nigeria. *International Journal of Risk and Contingency Management, 11*(1), 1–18. Advance online publication. doi:10.4018/IJRCM.295957

Di Maria, E. (2015). Environmental innovations and internationalization: Theory and practices. *Business Strategy and the Environment, 24*(8), 790–80. doi:10.1002/bse.1846

Dittfeld, H., van Donk, D. P., & van Huet, S. (2022). The effect of production system characteristics on resilience capabilities: A multiple case study. *International Journal of Operations & Production Management, 42*(13), 103–127. doi:10.1108/IJOPM-12-2021-0789

Durach, C. F., Wieland, A., & Machuca, J. A. D. (2015). Antecedents and dimensions of supply chain robustness: A systematic literature review. *International Journal of Physical Distribution & Logistics Management, 45*(1/2), 118–137. doi:10.1108/IJPDLM-05-2013-0133

Fiksel, J., Polyviou, M., Croxton, K. L., & Pettit, T. J. (2015). From risk to resilience: Learning to deal with disruption. *MIT Sloan Management Review, 56*, 79–86.

Golicic, S. L., Flint, D. J., & Signori, P. (2017). Building business sustainability through resilience in the wine industry. *International Journal of Wine Business Research, 29*(1), 74–97. doi:10.1108/IJWBR-02-2016-0005

Hale, T., & Moberg, C. R. (2005). Improving supply chain disaster preparedness: A decision process for secure site location. *International Journal of Physical Distribution & Logistics Management, 35*(3), 195–207. doi:10.1108/09600030510594576

Huong Tran, T. T., Childerhouse, P., & Deakins, E. (2016). Supply chain information sharing: Challenges and risk mitigation strategies. *Journal of Manufacturing Technology Management, 27*(8), 1102–1126. doi:10.1108/JMTM-03-2016-0033

ILO. (2020). *MSME Day 2020: the COVID-19 pandemic and its impact on small business.* https://www.ilo.org/empent/whatsnew/WCMS_749275/lang--en/index.htm

International Trade Center. (2020). SME Competitiveness Outlook 2020: COVID-19: The Great Lockdown and its Impact on Small Business. *The American Journal of Emergency Medicine, 38*(2).

Ishfaq, R., Davis-Sramek, B., & Gibson, B. (2021). Digital Supply Chains in Omnichannel Retail: A Conceptual Framework. *Journal of Business Logistics.*

Jafari, H. (2015). Logistics flexibility: A systematic literature review. *International Journal of Productivity and Performance Management, 64*(7), 947–970. doi:10.1108/IJPPM-05-2014-0069

Juan, S.-J., Li, E. Y., & Hung, W.-H. (2022). An integrated model of supply chain resilience and its impact on supply chain performance under disruption. *International Journal of Logistics Management, 33*(1), 339–364. doi:10.1108/IJLM-03-2021-0174

Jüttner, U., & Maklan, S. (2011). Supply chain resilience in the global financial crisis: An empirical study. *Supply Chain Management, 16*(4), 246–259. doi:10.1108/13598541111139062

Kaneberg, E., Hertz, S., & Jensen, L.-M. (2016). Emergency preparedness planning in developed countries: The Swedish case. *Journal of Humanitarian Logistics and Supply Chain Management, 6*(2), 145–172. doi:10.1108/JHLSCM-10-2015-0039

Kumar, S., Himes, K., & Kritzer, C. (2014). Risk assessment and operational approaches to managing risk in global supply chains. *Journal of Manufacturing Technology Management, 2*(6), 873–890. doi:10.1108/JMTM-04-2012-0044

Kumar, S., Liu, J., & Scutella, J. (2015). The impact of supply chain disruptions on stockholder wealth in India. *International Journal of Physical Distribution & Logistics Management, 45*(9/10), 938–958. doi:10.1108/IJPDLM-09-2013-0247

Laurell, H., Karlsson, N. P. E., Lindgren, J., Andersson, S., & Svensson, G. (2019). Re-testing and validating a triple bottom line dominant logic for business sustainability. *Management of Environmental Quality, 30*(3), 518–537. doi:10.1108/MEQ-02-2018-0024

Li, X., Wu, Q., Holsapple, C. W., & Goldsby, T. (2017). An empirical examination of firm financial performance along dimensions of supply chain resilience. *Management Research Review, 40*(3), 254–269. doi:10.1108/MRR-02-2016-0030

Listou, T. (2018). Samhandling, Preparedness and Supply Chains. In G.-E. Torgersen (Ed.), *Interaction: 'Samhandling' Under Risk. A Step Ahead of the Unforeseen* (pp. 501–516). Cappelen Damm Akademisk. doi:10.23865/noasp.36.ch27

Liu, X., Arthanari, T., & Shi, Y. (2021). Leverage risks for supply chain robustness against corruption. *Industrial Management & Data Systems, 121*(7), 1496–1521. doi:10.1108/IMDS-10-2020-0587

Lotfi, M., & Larmour, A. (2022). Supply chain resilience in the face of uncertainty: How horizontal and vertical collaboration can help? *Continuity & Resilience Review, 4*(1), 37–53. doi:10.1108/CRR-04-2021-0016

Mandal, S. (2019). The influence of big data analytics management capabilities on supply chain preparedness, alertness and agility: An empirical investigation. *Information Technology & People, 32*(2), 297–318. doi:10.1108/ITP-11-2017-0386

Mandal, S., Sarathy, R., Korasiga, V. R., Bhattacharya, S., & Dastidar, S. G. (2016). Achieving supply chain resilience: The contribution of logistics and supply chain capabilities. *International Journal of Disaster Resilience in the Built Environment, 7*(5), 544–562. doi:10.1108/IJDRBE-04-2016-0010

Durach, C. F., Wieland, A., & Machuca, J. A. D. (2015). Antecedents and dimensions of supply chain robustness: A systematic literature review. *International Journal of Physical Distribution & Logistics Management, 45*(1/2), 118–137. doi:10.1108/IJPDLM-05-2013-0133

Pham, L. D. Q., Coles, T., Ritchie, B. W., & Wang, J. (2021). Building business resilience to external shocks: Conceptualising the role of social networks to small tourism & hospitality businesses. *Journal of Hospitality and Tourism Management, 48*(June), 210–219. doi:10.1016/j.jhtm.2021.06.012

Ponomarov & Holcomb. (2009). Understanding the concept of supply chain resilience. *International Journal of Logistics Management, 20*(1), 124-139.

Queiroz, M. M., Fosso Wamba, S., & Branski, R. M. (2021). Supply chain resilience during the CO-VID-19: Empirical evidence from an emerging economy. *Benchmarking.* Advance online publication. doi:10.1108/BIJ-08-2021-0454

Ramos, E., Patrucco, A. S., & Chavez, M. (2021). Dynamic capabilities in the "new normal": A study of organizational flexibility, integration and agility in the Peruvian coffee supply chain. *Supply Chain Management.* Advance online publication. doi:10.1108/SCM-12-2020-0620

Riglietti, G., Piraina, M., & Trucco, P. (2021). *The contribution of business continuity management (BCM) to supply chain resilience: a qualitative study on the response to COVID-19 outbreak.* Continuity & Resilience Review., doi:10.1108/CRR-08-2021-0030

Roy, V. (2021). Contrasting supply chain traceability and supply chain visibility: Are they interchangeable? *International Journal of Logistics Management, 32*(3), 942–972. doi:10.1108/IJLM-05-2020-0214

Sagone, E., & De Caroli, M. E. (2013). Relationships between Resilience, Self-Efficacy, and Thinking Styles in Italian Middle Adolescents. *Procedia: Social and Behavioral Sciences, 92*, 838–845. doi:10.1016/j.sbspro.2013.08.763

Schaltegger, S., Hansen, E. G., & Lüdeke-Freund, F. (2016). Business Models for Sustainability: Origins, Present Research, and Future Avenues. *Organization & Environment, 29*(1), 3–10. doi:10.1177/1086026615599806

Saqib, Z. A., & Zhang, Q. (2021). Impact of sustainable practices on sustainable performance: The moderating role of supply chain visibility. *Journal of Manufacturing Technology Management, 32*(7), 1421–1443. doi:10.1108/JMTM-10-2020-0403

Sarkar, P., Mohamed Ismail, M.W., & Kachev, T. (2022). Bridging the supply chain resilience research and practice gaps: pre and post COVID-19 perspectives. Journal of Global Operations and Strategic Sourcing. . doi:10.1108/JGOSS-09-2021-0082

Skipper, J. B., & Hanna, J. B. (2009). Minimizing supply chain disruption risk through enhanced flexibility. *International Journal of Physical Distribution & Logistics Management, 39*(5), 404–427. doi:10.1108/09600030910973742

Spiegler, V. L., Naim, M. M., Towill, D. R., & Wikner, J. (2016). A technique to develop simplified and linearised models of complex dynamic supply chain systems. *European Journal of Operational Research, 251*(3), 888–903. doi:10.1016/j.ejor.2015.12.004

Tang, C. S. (2006). Robust strategies for mitigating supply chain disruptions. *International Journal of Logistics Research and Applications, 9*(1), 33-45.

Thome, A. M. T., Scavarda, L. F., Fernandez, N. S., & Scavarda, A. J. (2014b). Sales and Operations Planning and the Firm Performance. *International Journal of Productivity and Performance Management, 61*(4), 359–38. doi:10.1108/17410401211212643

Tiwari, A. K., Tiwari, A., & Samuel, C. (2015). Supply chain flexibility: A comprehensive review. *Management Research Review, 38*(7), 767–792. doi:10.1108/MRR-08-2013-0194

Wieland, A., & Wallenburg, C. M. (2013). The influence of relational competencies on supply chain resilience: A relational view. *International Journal of Physical Distribution & Logistics Management, 43*(4), 300–320. doi:10.1108/IJPDLM-08-2012-0243

Tukamuhabwa, B. R., Stevenson, M., Busby, J., & Zorzini, M. (2015). Supply Chain Resilience: Definition, Review and Theoretical Foundations for Further Study. *International Journal of Production Research, 53*(18), 5592–5623. doi:10.1080/00207543.2015.1037934

Vilko, J., Ritala, P., & Edelmann, J. (2014). On Uncertainty in Supply Chain Risk Management. *International Journal of Logistics Management*, *25*(1), 3–19. doi:10.1108/IJLM-10-2012-0126

Wan Ahmad, N. K., Rezaei, J., Tavasszy, L. A., & de Brito, M. P. (2016). Commitment to preparedness for sustainable supply chain management in the oil and gas industry. *Journal of Environmental Management*, *180*, 202–213. doi:10.1016/j.jenvman.2016.04.056

Wieland, A., & Wallenburg, C. M. (2012). Dealing with supply chain risks: Linking risk management practices and strategies to performance. *International Journal of Physical Distribution & Logistics Management*, *42*(10), 887–905. doi:10.1108/09600031211281411

Wieland, A., & Wallenburg, C. M. (2013). The influence of relational competencies on supply chain resilience: A relational view. *International Journal of Physical Distribution & Logistics Management*, *43*(4), 300–320. doi:10.1108/IJPDLM-08-2012-0243

Yun, J. J., Zhao, X., Park, K. B., & Shi, L. (2020). Sustainability condition of open innovation: Dynamic growth of alibaba from SME to large enterprise. *Sustainability (Switzerland)*, *12*(11), 4379. Advance online publication. doi:10.3390u12114379

ADDITIONAL READING

Baah, C., Opoku Agyeman, D., Acquah, I. S. K., Agyabeng-Mensah, Y., Afum, E., Issau, K., Ofori, D., & Faibil, D. (2022). Effect of information sharing in supply chains: Understanding the roles of supply chain visibility, agility, collaboration on supply chain performance. *Benchmarking*, *29*(2), 434–455. doi:10.1108/BIJ-08-2020-0453

Chowdhury, M. M. H., & Quaddus, M. (2016). Supply chain readiness, response and recovery for resilience. *Supply Chain Management*, *21*(6), 709–731. doi:10.1108/SCM-12-2015-0463

Juan, S.-J., Li, E. Y., & Hung, W.-H. (2022). An integrated model of supply chain resilience and its impact on supply chain performance under disruption. *International Journal of Logistics Management*, *33*(1), 339–364. doi:10.1108/IJLM-03-2021-0174

Liao, Y. (2020). An integrative framework of supply chain flexibility. *International Journal of Productivity and Performance Management*, *69*(6), 1321–1342. doi:10.1108/IJPPM-07-2019-0359

Scholten, K., & Schilder, S. (2015). The role of Collaboration in Supply Chain Resilience. *Supply Chain Management*, *20*(4), 471–484. doi:10.1108/SCM-11-2014-0386

Simatupang, T. M., & Sridharan, R. (2005). An integrative framework for supply chain collaboration. *International Journal of Logistics Management*, *16*(2), 257–274. doi:10.1108/09574090510634548

Waqas, F., Mohamed, S., & Zain, U. A. (2014). SMEs' Preparedness to Face Economic Crisis: A Proposed Framework for Malaysian SMEs. *World Applied Sciences Journal, 30*. Doi:10.5829/idosi.wasj.2014.30.icmrp.1

Li, Wu, Holsapple, & Goldsby. (2017). An Empirical Examination of Firm Financial Performance along Dimensions of Supply Chain Resilience. *Management Research Review*, *40*(3). Advance online publication. doi:10.1108/MRR-02-2016-0030

KEY TERMS AND DEFINITIONS

Collaboration: Mechanism to synchronize internal and external partners to maintain an optimum supply chain flow to effectively fulfill demand and guarantee on-time, full delivery.

Firm Performance: An economic metric that measures how efficiently organizations can leverage both human and material resources to accomplish their objectives.

Flexibility in Supply Chain: Possessing the ability to adapt to unexpected changes in supply or demand. of external disruptions as well as the adaptation to structural and strategic alterations in the environment.

Supply Chain Preparedness: The capacity of firms to withstand unexpected disruptions' impacts.

Supply Chain Resilience: The capacity of a firm to handle unforeseen supply chain disruptions employing its available capabilities. It is the capacity to respond to challenges and recover from them without adversely effecting operations or customer deadlines.

Sustainability: Managing and coordinating demands and concerns from the perspectives of the environment, society, and the financial framework to guarantee sustainable performance.

Visibility: The capacity to track products movement, providing shippers with a transparent picture of the inventory and activity, enabling them to enhance customer service and cost management through proactive status updates, managing inventory in motion, reducing disruptions, and risk mitigation.

Chapter 7
Factors Hindering Small, Medium, and Micro Enterprise Business Growth in South Africa

Sfiso Nxele
Management College of Southern Africa, South Africa

Muhammad Ehsanul Hoque
Management College of Southern Africa, South Africa

ABSTRACT

Small, medium, and micro enterprises (SMMEs) are critical contributors to the gross domestic product (GDP) rise and the creation of employment opportunities. In South Africa, SMMEs receive funding for sustainability and job creation. The current SMMEs' contribution to the country's GDP and employment creation has, over the years, been on a decline. Therefore, the study aimed to explore the factors hindering SMME business growth. SMMEs experienced challenges of lack of financial assistance, lack of information, unavailable mentorship, unskilled administration, limited assessment within the various institutions, and access to financial support. Significant priority is placed on support institutions and government to create sector specific SMME assessment criterion instead of applying a blanket approach to all business sectors' support.

INTRODUCTION

The high unemployment rate, Gini eco-efficiency and continued dependence on state support as reported by Stats SA (2021) has sparked the need for an assessment of the role of a funding mechanism and support for SMMEs and their intended solution. South Africa's growth potential has been linked to SMME development as a measure to reduce unemployment, increase GDP, and increase business growth, yet little impact and contribution are currently evident. SMME development has the potential to elevate the nation's status quo from a developing to a developed country whilst actively participating in the global market. The research sought to obtain clarity behind the delayed growth of SMMEs by

DOI: 10.4018/978-1-6684-5727-6.ch007

exploring financial support systems within the Ugu District area. An assessment of the SMME funding mechanism to determine the reasons behind their delayed growth and influence on reducing unemployment is imperative for this research.

A need to assess the delayed SMME growth in reducing unemployment has been influenced by numerous challenges experienced by SMMEs. Firstly, the slow growth rate is a result of the high concentration of power sitting within the government and large corporates that are creating more employment opportunities than SMMEs. Secondly, the challenges on access to funding by SMMEs, the shortage of skills and the red tape from regulatory bodies. (Small Business Institute, 2019). Mbedzi and Simatele (2020) revealed that microfinance and privately-owned development financial institutions still have high rationing levels as commercial banks with credit rationing decreasing with the size of the firm and amplified by race. This is a factor mainly contributing to the delayed growth of SMMEs and later reduced unemployment levels leading to the need to assess SMME funding mechanisms through this study.

Thirdly, SMMEs further experience challenges in business growth and creating employment which has resulted in the need for research on business finance as well as the intended contribution to a company gaining a competitive advantage. The barriers to entry by monopolistic or oligopoly firms and minimum wage regulations hinder any possible growth. The assessment of SMMEs sought to confirm such reports within the Ugu District Area. Another challenge faced by SMMEs is the limited innovative business programmes available for SMMEs to capitalise on their competitive advantages (OECD, 2015). Finally, international and national interests in promoting small business development, through an incubation strategy to tackle the high mortality rates are prevalent amongst start-up enterprises according to Masutha et al. (2014) which makes it critical to assess the SMME funding mechanism and its impact on employment opportunities.

The Ugu District Municipal vision states that "… by 2030 the Ugu District will be a leading tourism destination and the agricultural and manufacturing hub where jobs are created and everyone benefits equally from socio-economic opportunities and services" (Ugu DGDS, 2012: 05). The Ugu Growth and Development Strategy commits all stakeholders (public, private and civil society) to achieve a shared vision as well as address the challenges faced by the district. The district's underperformance towards GDP contribution has been linked with the growing unemployment and declining business growth and investment. The district area is characterised by a distinct spatial divide of a coastal zone that is resilient, comprising a diversified formal economy as well as a largely impoverished rural hinterland. The agriculture sector is the main economic contributor within the rural hinterlands of the district and recently experienced a high shed of jobs due to restrictive legislation on labour. The tourism sector is perceived to be the leading sector but has declined due to the inability of the district to offer attractive packages when compared to the northern and midland regions (Ugu DGDS, 2012).

The funding mechanism and support within the district have been established to respond to the status quo and the triple challenges of unemployment, poverty and inequality. Currently, the District Institutes (Local Municipalities and District Municipality) offer assistance through the purchasing of inputs and materials aimed at improving productivity as well as profits. Capacity building through training sessions and mentorship, business incubation and workshops are provided for SMME development whilst, business indabas and forums are held for networking purposes and support. Business fares are hosted within the districts to advertise and market local SMMEs and their product packages. Finance packages are offered through finance by the Small Enterprise Development Agency. Grants are offered to SMMEs for a maximum of R800 000 for tools, machinery and equipment. Business development and training intervention grants amounting to R200 000 are offered per eligible enterprise. The Black

Business Supplier Development Programme is a finance incentive scheme for black-owned or black-managed SMMEs within the district, with an annual turnover of R250 000 to R35 million. The agency further assists SMMEs in product exporting for business growth and entering the global market (Small Enterprise Development Agency (Seda), 2017). An assessment of the SMME financial interventions and mechanisms is important for obtaining a clear result of their intended impact. An understanding will assist to ensure that the district vision is achieved to create a conducive space for citizens within the district. This chapter contains a background to the identified topic, problem statement, aim of the study, literature review and research procedures which were undertaken to reach conclusions on the topic.

Problem Statement

With the current unemployment rate sitting at 30.1%, poverty and inequality remain unchanged. The onus is on the government, the public, private sector, foreign investors and SMMEs to address the current status quo (Business Tech, 2020). On 04 and 05 October 2018, South Africa hosted the job summit which approved the signing of a framework agreement to enable the creation of an estimated 275 000 jobs annually. The framework agreement committed to five objectives as drivers toward achieving the annual targets (Department of the Presidency, 2018).

The Small Business Institute (2019), however, states that the current contribution of 28% of job creation from SMMEs is very low and more needs to be done to achieve the National Development Plan goals. SMMEs are faced with various challenges mainly business finance, business innovation, business sustainability, competition, as well as creating sustainable employment opportunities. Minimal efforts are prevalent in addressing such challenges which further also hinders the intended economic growth projections of the country.

Aim of The Study

The study aimed to conduct an assessment of the SMME funding mechanisms and to identify the reasons behind the delayed SMME growth in reducing unemployment. Through this exercise. recommendations were developed and provided as a way forward to address the slow employment rate.

Significance of the Study

The findings of the study will assist the district's funding and support institutions to explore the development of new economic sectors within the district and will be beneficial in obtaining updated information concerning the ever-changing dynamics faced by SMMEs. It will contribute to the planning, due diligence, budgeting and needs assessment practices done by the district's funding and support institutions prior to assisting SMMEs. The study further advocates for a different approach or the recreation of SMMEs funding criteria, tailored for each economic sector and income level of SMME.

The study has academic importance as very little is known about the impact of financial interventions on SMME success. The study aimed to provide recent academic knowledge on SMME growth and development within the South African context in relation to the literature review. The research emphasizes the need to prioritize business development and business skill learning at academic institutions at various levels. Empirical research of this nature will assist in the decision-making processes during policy formulation. Holistically the study signifies the importance of improving the private sector within the district, around the province and nationally to provide a more capable and global competitive state.

An assessment of the SMME funding mechanisms and support through engagement with funding institutions is critical in understanding the unattained goals or targets which have been envisioned for SMMEs and employment creation within the Ugu district area. The output of the assessment will, therefore, provide an understanding of the failures and grant opportunities to provide recommendations towards seeing an impactful contribution from SMMEs regarding employment opportunities within the Ugu district areas.

LITERATURE REVIEW

Amra, Hlatshwayo and McMillan (2013) state that there is no agreed-upon definition or criteria on what constitutes small, micro and medium enterprises. The Department of Trade and Industry sought to define and categorise SMMEs through the elements of annual turnover and employee composition. SMMEs are defined differently and categorised different all over the world. South Africa, through the National Small Business Act No. 102 of 1996, adopted a similar approach. The Act describes them as small separate and distinct business entities that are owned and/or managed by one or more owner(s) that conduct relevant business in any sector and/or sub-sector of the national economy of South Africa (National Small Business Act, 1996).

The Act defined five categories of business in South Africa which are presented in Table 1. below:

Table 1. SA SMME categorisation

SMME Category	Description
Survivalist enterprise	The income generated is less than the minimum income standard or the poverty line and is associated with hawkers, vendors and subsistence farmers.
Micro enterprise	The turnover is less than the VAT registration limit of R150 000 per year. They employ no more than five people with examples being spaza shops, minibus taxis and household industries.
Very small enterprise	The enterprise usually employs less than 10 to 20 employees with an annual turnover of less than R200 000 to R500 000 depending on the industry.
Small enterprise	This enterprise employs up to 50 employees and is well established and exhibits more complex business practices.
Medium enterprise	These businesses employ a total number of 100 or 200 employees in the mining, electricity, manufacturing and construction sectors.

Source: National Small Business Act (1996).

SMME Performance

According to research, South African SMMEs have among the worst sustainability rates in the world (Ayandibu & Houghton, 2017; Bruwer, Hattingh & Perold, 2020). Previous studies present that approximately 75% of South African SMMEs fail within three years of existence (Swart, 2011; Bruwer *et al.*, 2020). The poor performance of SMMEs is said to be a result of the following (1) unconducive economic environment (2) scarce business skills (3) volatile and unfavourable exchange rates (4) increased cost of water and electricity (5) strict government legislation (6) high levels of crime (7) volatile suppliers and/ or demand for products and or services (Bruwer *et al.,* 2020).

SMME Job Creation & Human Capital

According to research, South African SMMEs contribute to approximately 60% of the national workforce as well as contributing to 50% of the country's Gross Domestic Product (Bruwer *et al.*, 2020). Bhorat, Asmal, Lilenstein and Van Der Zee (2018) presented that the education level of business owners increases systematically as a firm size increases with a lack of creating a major constraint for the SMMEs when they were profiled on their size.

COVID-19 Pandemic on SMMEs in SA

The COVID-19 pandemic has added to the already existing and unresolved challenges experienced by SMMEs. The pandemic has affected the supply and demand factors of daily business operations. The supply of labour has been affected by employees working remotely due to health hazards, regulations and the inability to remunerate workers (Nyawo, 2020). The pandemic affected the demand for business operations and services which has led to increased closures and decreased revenue (Zeidy, 2020 cited Nyawo 2020). Government intervention, under the Department of Small Business Development, through the Debt Relief Fund, has an aim to relieve existing debts, repayments and support for SMMEs in the purchasing of raw material, and remunerations of workers and also assistance for other operational costs (Nyawo, 2020).

RESEARCH METHODOLOGY

This was a literature review study. The literature review was conducted between March and September 2021 using Google Scholar and EBSCOHost search engine. The following keywords were used to search the literature: business growth, factors for business growth, internal factors, external factors, and technology adoption. Initially, a total of 435 abstracts were retrieved for relevance. After careful consideration, 56 articles were found suitable for the study. Based on the articles the followings were found to be factors for SMME growth.

Business Growth

Penrose (1959) originally defined business growth as the increase in a firm's size measured from one period to another. Recent literature refers to sustainable business growth which incorporates the environmental, social and economic aspects. Sustainable business growth is, therefore, defined as the company's appropriate pace of growth that increases its economic, social and environmental capital or at least one of these without decreasing any of these capital stocks (Schwab, Gold, Kunz & Reiner, 2017). According to Churchill and Lewis (1983), there are five stages to small business growth. Firstly, an existence which is concerned with garnering customers and delivering the product or service contracted. Secondly, the survival firm is the state where a company is barely making enough money for the firm to break even or stay in business. The third stage is the success stage where the business has the opportunity to expand or keep the business stable and profitable. The fourth stage highlights the take-off which is concerned with how to make the business grow rapidly and how to finance the growth. Lastly, the resource maturity stage is characterised by the company's advantage of size, financial resources, managerial talent and market performance. (Wickman 1998) cited in Eresia-Eke (2013) urges that due to the multifaceted nature of business, it is important to constantly view the growth and development of a business from the four perspectives of financial, strategic, structural and organisational capacity. SMMEs need to consider all four perspectives when planning for growth otherwise negative results might surface in the event of one being neglected.

Business Growth of SMME

SMME finance instruments are said to possess low levels of diversification of external finance sources, which indicates an over-reliance on cash flow and bank debt, for funding growth opportunities (Serrasqueiro, Leitão & Smallbone, 2018). The authors identified the following positive and negative determinates of SMME business growth, (1) cash flow and GDP are positive growth. Whilst debt, size, age, and the interest rate are negative determinants (Serrasqueiro *et al.*, 2018). Berger and Udell (1998) cited in Khan (2015) stated that SMME growth is delayed by finance constraints compared to large corporations. Further to this, less than 10% of SMMEs finance their investment from banks, compared to 20% of larger firms.

Yun, Jung and Yang (2015) provide four SMMEs sustainable growth strategies, firstly C-C-type SMMEs use closed innovation approaches from knowledge strategies. The business models are assumed to pursue development only within the technologies and business models. SMMEs usually do not survive for long because they are regarded as insensitive to consumer preferences, changes in market situations and the introduction of new knowledge and technologies. The second is the C-O-type SMMEs which are known to continuously produce new products and services that meet the markets' and consumers' demands, technologies and knowledge. These SMMEs are assumed to develop until they can build diverse business models within their knowledge and technologies. Thirdly, the O-C-type SMMEs are characterised by having a secured area and customer base to a certain extent in the market. SMMEs should be considered large medium enterprises and can survive until they can supply more efficient products through the introduction of newer knowledge and technologies to their market and customers. Finally, the O-O-type SMMEs actively change major products in accordance with customers' or markets' demands, as well as continuously secure the necessary knowledge and technologies from outside. They operate best in countries and regions, where knowledge ecosystems have been well established and where activities of technology-based venture companies are active (Yun *et al.*, 2015).

According to the OECD (2018) report, SMME participation in global markets presents an opportunity to improve business growth, especially within the production and innovation aspects. Global participation later has positive spill-offs of technology and managerial skilling being transferred. Internationally, more specifically in OECD countries, over 95% of enterprises are SMMEs, accounting for between 60%-70% of the working population and they contribute as much as 60% to GDP (OECD, 2018).

The Parliamentary Monitoring Group (2019), from its recent study of SMMEs within South Africa, shows that while 98.5% of the country's economy comprises small and medium-sized enterprises, they currently contribute to 28% of all jobs. The goal of the small business report is to deliver the facts needed to underpin policy interventions and strategic planning for small business development in South Africa as it currently represents a negative growth trajectory. The Small Business Report (2019) further revealed that despite good intentions, most small business policies and support initiatives developed over the years – by both the private and public sectors – fail since their assumptions and data have been incorrect. The report also found that the government has failed to apply a common definition of a small, very small, or medium business across its laws, regulations and key strategies. The definition of small enterprises was completely inconsistent across the 70 laws, regulations and key government strategies reviewed. This, therefore, creates a barrier to entry or are determinant of business closures due to the red tape and inconsistent regulations which affect SMME growth within South Africa (Small Business Report, 2019).

Factors for Business Growth

SMMEs have internal and external factors which they need to overcome when seeking effective business growth. This later contributes to employment and economic growth. The section provides a detailed literature review on the internal and external factors to business growth.

Internal Factors

Internal factors of business growth are internal business affairs or aspects within the control of the company, which need to be overcome towards the realisation of the business vision and growth. The following are internal factors for positive business growth.

Financial Literacy: Okello et al. (2017) state that financial literacy through business training results in the acquisition of financial knowledge and business skills important for the growth of SMMEs in developing countries. It is further mentioned as the skill to obtain, understand, and evaluate, the relevant information necessary to make financial decisions and choices on possible financial consequences to the business (Okello et al., 2017). A significant aspect to consider of SMMEs' growth is that financially literacy offers SMMEs an opportunity to compete locally and globally (Okello et al., 2017). The financial literacy program helps SMMEs with the management of loan portfolios to ensure that loan liability is minimized, and interest expenses minimized. Other achievements from the initiative include proper planning, resource allocation and utility derivation (Okello et al., 2017).

Innovation: Teneja, Pryor and Hayek (2016) explain innovation as an improvement anywhere within the business beyond products, services, and processes. It is an inclusion of business leadership, human resources, communication, organisation, marketing and any other activities. The process is said to be key for SMMEs to innovate for survival within a competitive environment. Innovation offers opportunities to increase productivity through reduced operational costs which yield positive results in profit and business growth. Product innovation offers SMMEs an opportunity to gain a competitive advantage as well as increase market shares in their respective business sectors. Innovation in production, marketing and branding strategies helps SMMEs to differentiate their products from competitors which also helps in global competitiveness (OECD, 2018). Innovation is defined as the creation, development and implementation of a new product, process or service, aiming at improving efficiency, effectiveness or competitive advantage. It further can be seen as the process that translates knowledge into economic growth and social well-being (Cruz-Cunha & Varajao, 2011). The process of innovation is said to possess continuous change, which involves constant updating and work process and social practices which will lead to new patterns of how an organisation organises itself. The process of continuous change results in improvising, translating and learning (Hayes, 2014).

Technology Adoption: Windrum and De Barranger (2002) state that information communications technologies have led to increased firm competitiveness either by raising the efficiency of internal communication and organisation and/or by supply chain relations or by facilitating the development of new, improved products and services. SMMEs' adaptation to new technologies can assist in improved business production or performance which indicates a progressive organisation, is well equipped to increase business growth (OECD, 2018). Technology, therefore, plays a significant role in the implementation of the business strategy of firms or businesses. E-business is the integration of the internet and related ICTs into the business organisation's two facets (1) integration of the supply chain and (2) the creation of new business models based on open systems of communications between customers, suppliers and partners (Windrum & De Barranger, 2002).

Management and Human Capital: Good management skills and human capital can contribute to business growth by motivating staff to be more effective and efficient in their day-to-day operations as well as advocating for sustained growth of the entire organisation (Locavon & Qasim 2013 cited in OECD, 2018). Increased investment in human capital yields positive returns often on indirect return or spill-over effects which help promote efficiency, knowledge and invention. That results in increased productivity and accelerates the growth of businesses (Maitra, 2016). Human capital can be defined as the value of individual knowledge and talent in an organisation that includes the know-how, capacity, competency, attitude, intellectual ability and creativity (Samad, 2013). Through the Department of Small Business Development, SMMEs are required to understand the factors accounting for the level of credit rationing they endure and thus must advance internal capacity development that reduce the credit rationing burden (Mbedzi & Simatele,2020). An SMME or business would not exist without productive human inputs, as well as without a proper product to service customer needs. It is, therefore, imperative that SMMEs hire and manage labour and other resources in a manner that promotes sustained growth (Mahadea & Pillay, 2008).

Intellectual Property: SMMEs can increase business growth and value through the copyrighting of intellectual property rights for sustained growth whilst eliminating competitors. Intellectual property rights can be used as collateral to access external funding aimed at business growth. According to Wickham (2008), there are four perspectives which are important to business growth, these being financial, strategic, structural and organisational.

External Factors

External factors are said to have a significant effect on the business's success, however, these are beyond the control of the business. They are cultural, political and economic conditions of the region which the business operates under.

Access to Finance: SMMEs require access to finance to facilitate the process of innovation and procurement of technologies aimed at bettering productivity and performance. Business growth is, therefore, dependent on access to finance in order to expand and compete locally and globally (OECD, 2018). SMMEs have two financing options, the first being equity financing which is provided in the form of venture capital. This method refers to the practice where a company issues a certain portion of its shares in return for money. The second form of finance system available for SMMEs is debt financing, which refers to the practice where companies get finance in the form of a loan from lending institutions with the repayment plan period linked with an interest rate. The author further states that South Africa, as well as other countries in the world, holds the misperception that a broad supply of debt financing to

SMMEs will address the challenges experienced. This is, however, contradictory as SMMEs without a proven recorded experience are declined when applying for debt finance (Osano & Languitone, 2016). The Department of Trade and Industry strategy 2005 emphasises access to better finances, skills and business training, and more flexible regulations as key strategic pillars of promoting entrepreneurship, strengthening the enabling environment and enhancing competitiveness and capacity at the enterprise level (Rogerson, 2008).

Access to Information: An understanding of the market and access to suppliers, and business partners abroad allow for SMME growth support for business growth. Access to information allows for SMMEs to be able to provide products and services which are satisfactory to customer needs (OECD, 2018). The flow of information in the financial market is said to be crucial for SMMEs and financial providers. Access to information relates to the awareness of SMMEs to funding opportunities available (Osano & Languitone, 2016).

Financial Growth: This perspective relates to the development of the business as a commercial entity, with its main focus on increased turnover, the cost and investment required to achieve the turnover and resulting profits. Increases in the assets register or assets database of a company result in the financial growth status of a company. The author used the following measurement of financial growth (1) changes in total assets (2) changes in capital (3) changes in turnover (4) changes in profit (Eresia – Eka et al., 2013). Financial performance measures are used to evaluate the organisational health of a firm to inform decisions on enhancing or sustained performance. The performance and growth are assessed through financial statements and financial ratios (Ngary, Smit & Juan-Pierre, 2014). The financial growth rate is calculated internally through an internal growth rate which is the maximum growth rate a firm can achieve without external financing of any kind. The sustainable growth rate referred to by the author is the maximum growth rate a firm can achieve without external equity financing while maintaining a constant debt-equity ratio. Ross, Westerfield and Jordan (2013) highlight the sustainable growth aspects used by bankers and external analysts used to assess a company's credit worthiness. The exercise consists of several sophisticated computer software packages that provide a detailed analysis of the company's past financial performance as well as its sustainable growth rate (Ross *et al.*, 2013).

Strategic Growth: Strategic growth relates to changes that occur in the way in which the organisation interacts with its environment as a coherent strategic whole. It is primarily concerned with the way business develops its capabilities to exploit a presence in the marketplace. It is the profile of opportunities which the venture exploits and the assets both tangible and intangible, acquired to create a sustainable competitive advantage. The measure used by the author to assess strategic growth was based on (1) changes in sales and/or production volumes (2) changes in the cost of sales/production (3) changes in customer base (Eresia – Eka et al., 2013). Beaver (2007) cited in Weber, Geneste and Connell (2015) argues that strategic growth is based on the business owner's perceptions, motivations and desires as opposed to only strategic planning. They state that business owners seeking greater profit will use strategic plans, whilst those concerned with self-fulfilment will not. On the other hand, Porter provides generic strategies for business growth which can be adopted and implemented The Theoretical and Conceptual Framework Section or Chapter for the DBA Thesisto realise the firm's vision and help gain a competitive advantage. These strategies have to deal with (1) overall cost leadership (2) differentiation (3) cost focus and (4) focus differentiation. Strategic growth is a whole process of management which organisationally aims to achieve and improve performance. Strategic control includes controls of factors such as production, inventory, quality, judgement, consumer satisfaction, market share, social responsibility and human factor and management of people towards business growth (Mullins, 2010). The balanced scorecard developed by Robert Kaplan and David Norton as a management system is used to measure the implementation of an organisation's strategy. The evaluation is based on the following financial and non-financial perspectives (1) financial (2) customer (3) internal business (4) innovation and learning (Levens, 2014).

Structural Growth: This aspect mainly relates to the changes in the way a business organises its internal systems, in particular, managerial roles and responsibilities, reporting relationships, communication links and resource control systems. A tool to measure the structural growth of an SMME firstly changes in the number of employees and secondly changes in the size and/or location of business premises (Eresia – Eka et al., 2013). According to Rodrik (2013), structural growth or transformation is the shift which contributes to positive production within the sector but further enables the reallocation of factors of production across sectors. An example given is the shift from a family farm business to formally registered firms.

Organisational Growth: The perspective deals with the changes in the organisation's process, culture and attitudes as it grows and develops. It highlights the changes that are required in the side of the business owner's role and leadership style as the business transforms from a small to a large business (Eresia – Eka et al., 2013). The Business Elite (2020) mentions four factors which require particular attention when seeking to grow one's business. These factors are (1) Business structure and management (2) External factors (3) Behavioural and personal traits and (4) location.

Business Structure and Management: There are different business structures such as functional, divisional or matrix structure which need to be considered when deciding on the best direction for higher levels of performance. Business structure can be comprised of many aspects which included the business ownership, export status, organisational structure, outsourcing and subcontracting practices (McCann & Oxley, 2013). Mol et al. (2009 attempted to discover the source of management innovation. The research stated that evident change in the following areas gives an SMME or firm, the ability to be an innovator - (1) the ability to change the implementation of advanced management techniques; (2) implementation of new or expressively changed organisational structure (3) significantly changing firms marketing concepts/strategies. Mahadea and Pillay (2008) state that an entrepreneur or manager who is well skilled in various functional areas of management and marketing can perform better than another less talented entrepreneur.

Behavioural and Personal Traits: A business owner's behaviour, personality and attitude can impact the growth of the business. It is, therefore, important to possess or apply the appropriate leadership style and behaviour to persuade positive performance, teamwork, staff retention and intended outputs. Organisational behaviour is an applied discipline which attempts to explain behaviour in organisations in terms of valid theories which are aimed at addressing challenges experienced daily by management. These theories advocate for the motivation of subordinates, managing effective performance, delivering superior customer service, coaching and integrating the work of self-managed teams and creating rewards that recognise individual achievement in an environment of employee empowerment which uses self-directed teams (Dailey, 2003).

Location: Depending on the business industry, location will have varying levels of impact on business growth. The SMMEs' growth in the 2018/19 financial year has reportedly risen by 35% from the previous 2017/18 financial year (SEFA, 2019). Kuratko (2016) provides certain aspects to consider when opening an SMME operating within the retail sector, them being (1) the potential of the trading area (2) can customers get to the location (3) judging the competition (4) can the location attract new business (5) cost of the location (6) type of community to locate a business within. The geographic location of a firm is an important determinant for joining Global Value Chains (GVCs) by SMMEs seeking to explore new opportunities for exporting and competing with larger firms (Kowalski et al., 2015).

Role of Government: The role of government and policymakers is to develop and adopt policies to improve the business environment for SMMEs through the reduced market and institutional constraints hindering their growth. Ullah's (2019) study emphasized the harmfulness of a country's level of corruption on SMMEs access to finance. Vermaak et al. (2014) state that governments around the world play an advisory role to SMMEs in the form of marketing, advertising, public relations, product design, computer services, business strategy, staff recruitment, financial management, taxation and legal services. The most significant advisory field with an impact on turnover growth includes business strategy, staff recruitment, taxation and financial management. The South African Government, through the Department of Small Business Development, emphasises the need to consider SMMEs growth as a stimulant towards economic growth as well as job creation for inclusive growth. The government must understand the credit rationing risk profiles experienced by SMMEs and then propose policies to address the risk whilst aligning government earmarked financing programmes to well-known SMMEs' credit rationing risk profiles. (Mbedzi & Simatele, 2020).

Support for Business Growth: Internationally countries have committed to assisting SMMEs with intentions to grow and expand GDP contribution whilst creating employment opportunities. As of September 2018, the Russian Federation had seen more than 5.9 million SMMEs accounting for about 22.3% of GDP and employing around 26.3% of the workforce. The country has provided a budget of RUB 154.7 billion between 2019 and 2017 (OECD, 2019).

SMMEs within South Africa constitute about 2.25 million, with 1.5 million being informal and concentrated in the trade (wholesale and retail) and accommodation sectors. In South Africa, government funding for SMMEs is provided through grants and financing by development finance institutions (DFIs). In 2017, SMMEs government loans amounted to 11.48 billion which accounted for 1.8% of all SMME loans. South Africa further offers SMMEs credit guarantees, with an amount of R297 million provided by the IDC and SEFA in 2017. R243 million was issued during the year 2016.

The Ugu District area has decentralised SMMEs support to local municipalities for efficient and effective implementation of the National Development Plan goals. The district area consists of four local municipalities (Umzumbe, Umuziwabantu, Umdoni and Ray Nkonyeni) that annually, through the Local Economic Development Units, provide assistance and support to local SMMEs. During the 2016 year Ugu District Municipality partnered with local municipalities and Esaydi TVET Colleges to train 64 students in welding, gate automation, plumbing and small appliance repairs to empower SMME development through human capital investment (Ugu DM, 2016).

Business incubation has been adopted and supported by the government and the private sector in developed and developing countries in response to different development challenges. These challenges are predominantly employment creation, poverty alleviation, technology transfer, acceleration of business growth, reduction of the mortality rate of SMMEs, empowerment of specific groups of entrepreneurs, creating value from various stakeholders, urban/rural regeneration and the revitalisation of local economies (Masutha et al., 2014).

Factors that Hinder Business Growth

Several factors and challenges have been identified by different authors, research organisations and writers on the factors that result in poor SMME growth and finance instruments.

Bottleneck in Infrastructure & Distance: The OECD (2018) mentioned bottlenecks in infrastructure and distance as a barrier to business growth. The geographical distance between trading partners sometimes creates challenges of transportation costs which have to be factored into the sales process. This limits potential growth with SMMEs running the risk of being replaced by SMMEs closely located and with no transportation cost factored in sales.

The second challenge is infrastructure mainly regarding roads, ports and airports. The quality or standard of these facilities affects the potential of business growth, especially when not maintained well or not operated efficiently. The electricity crisis within the country makes it difficult for businesses to operate, therefore, making it difficult for companies to invest within the market (SEFA, 2019). A community provides businesses with physical and social infrastructure that allows them to operate, as its utilities and labour force, and the homes, schools, colleges and hospitals serve the employee's needs. The absence of the physical and social infrastructure affects the envisioned growth potential of the business (Jones et al., 2017). The ability of a firm to enter foreign markets and participate in Global Value Chains is hindered by the quality of the physical infrastructure as well as the efficiency of procedures in the maintenance and operation of the infrastructure (Bernhofen et al., 2016).

The telecommunication infrastructure further plays a pivotal role in support of the value chains of physical goods and enables the creation as well as the trade in digital services which accounts for the growing share of total international transactions. The logistics infrastructure assists in reducing time and cost and business uncertainty related to the import and export of goods and services. The logistic infrastructure is more important for SMMEs than larger firms as the cost of trade is fixed irrespective of the size or revenue of the firm (OECD, 2018).

Failure to Innovate: SMMEs that do not innovate run the risk of being shut down and not being competitive. Lack of innovation restricts the ability for business growth as well as exploring and exploiting the gaps available in the market (OECD, 2018). Innovative practices or strategies are often not understood well or welcomed to be adopted by the entire institution. This results in the resistance to implementation and utilisation of innovative systems. The resistance creates wasteful expenditure on the side of management in the procurement of the business system and later closure of the business. The time wasted on convincing the staff of the benefits associated with business innovation also creates a barrier to the timeframes associated with the adopted goals (Hayes, 2014). Innovation is said to be a costly process that most SMMEs find difficult to procure as well as to be integrated into their day-to-day business process. Further to this new product development, innovation is not 100% guaranteed to yield successful results. Insufficient access to finance and risk capital, lack of internal capacity to innovate, insufficient expertise in applying ICT and high risk are the main barriers to innovation in the service and manufacturing sectors (Cruz-Cunha & Varajao, 2011). The author further speaks of four challenges experienced by SMMEs when it comes to innovation and their failure. Firstly inadequate or lacking technology results in failures to use ICT effectively. Secondly, evidence indicates that there are inconsistencies in turnover and patterns of economic growth. Innovation has effects on other variables such as turnover and economic growth which might seem minor from the outside but, there can be long-term impacts. Thirdly, multiple innovation channels are counterproductive and lastly lack of managerial and technical skills on the side of SMMEs with innovative ideas who have often found themselves without the capacity to develop or exploit their innovations (Cruz-Cunha & Varajao, 2011).

Cost of New Technology: The challenge SMMEs face, is the cost implication associated with the procurement of new technologies to be more competitive. Unskilled, as well as poorly managed SMMEs, create negative results for business growth. Funding institutions will find it risk-binding to support poorly managed SMMEs over well-capacitated and skilled businesses (OECD, 2018). Telecommunication infrastructure plays a significant role in aiding SMMEs to participate in the global market. However, cost implications hinder the ability to enter such markets (Kowalski et al., 2015). Surveys on new technologies show that 75% of all users find their ICT tools more stressful than relaxing which may lead to more negative business growth (Cruz–Cunha & Varajao, 2011). The old conventional entrepreneur often views information technology as extremely expensive which may result in the preferred use of none technological instruments in the business process (Mahadea & Pillay, 2008).

Access to Finance: The access to finance challenge makes it difficult for an SMME to grow, especially in instances where they want to invest in innovative processes as well as explore new products. SMMEs commonly neglect or are unaware of the business growth opportunities offered by various institutions as an aid for businesses to enter the international market (OECD, 2018). The mandate of SEFA is to increase access and the provision of finance to SMMEs and to contribute to job creation. This has, however, been another challenge faced by the organisation as the impairment rate remained high at 46% during the 2018/19 financial year report (SEFA, 2019). Khan (2015) mentions three sources available for SMMEs in developing countries. Firstly, the access to formal sources which include the banks and non-banking financial institutions. The hindrance of this financial source is that it holds the most finance which should be given to SMMEs. However, little is allocated to SMMEs. The second concerns the retained earnings/internal funds/equity. SMMEs are mainly comprised of relatively young individuals with informal setups which makes it difficult for them to raise adequate funds at a cheaper cost. The last source of SMME funding is from informal sources which include friends and family or credit from suppliers and advances from customers and others. Informal finance involves lengthy documentation, collateral, borrowing costs and other requirements. It is a very expensive form of finance. Dlova (2017) explained that lending criteria used by development finance as well as microfinance institutions were similar to those used by commercial banks. Financial institutions use asset-based lending, venture capital lending and asset finance lending technologies. SMMEs, however, find it difficult to acquire finance as most of them do not have assets to provide collateral or consistent audited financial statements.

SA's Economic State: In South Africa, SMMEs are further faced with the challenge of growing within a slowly recovering economy and the possibility of creating jobs whilst the GDP reached 0.8 in 2018. The country's inability to compete on a global scale further creates burdens for local SMMEs when overseas businesses enter the market (SEFA, 2019). SMMEs experience the challenge of not being able to achieve a competitive advantage in foreign markets due to the lack of capital and insufficient resources. Secondly, they experience difficulties in selecting reliable distributors to aid in the new entrance into a foreign market. Thirdly, concerns the lack of negotiating power to later provide competitive prices on the goods and services. According to the Worldbank (2020), South Africa is ranked No. 84 out of 190 countries in the world in terms of the countries with the ease of doing business report. The ranking is based on an assessment of the state of the following (1) starting a business (2) employing workers (3) dealing with construction permits (4) getting electricity (5) registering property (6) obtaining credit (7) protecting minority investors (8) paying taxes (9) trading across borders (10) contracting with government (11) enforcing contracts and (12) resolving insolvency. Despite the positive outcomes, SA has a considerable amount of work to be done to fast-track SMMEs development by providing a conducive environment for local and international businesses

Access to Information: Disbursement, or support to SMMEs with disabilities, poses another challenge which is an indication of the poor accessibility of programmes (SEFA, 2019). Access to information further deals with the response rate on the products' packaging and business assistance. SMMEs are faced with the challenge of engaging in international activities which may be hindered by limited information and understanding of foreign markets. The challenge of access to information limits the ability to customise products to the diverse needs of consumers and to meet product requirements and standards under local regulatory environments. Further, the lack of advanced telecommunication technology limits SMMEs to alleviate some of the knowledge gaps as foreign contracts are seen as essential for overcoming information barriers for SMMEs (OECD, 2018). The limited access to information results in SMMEs not understanding the laws that govern them as well as difficulties in determining policies and the legislation which applies to them (Rogerson, 2008).

Legislative & Regulatory Measures: The regulations in place pose serious challenges to SMME development despite the structural reforms which have led to some improvements. However, more is still required (Abor & Quartey, 2010). SMMEs legislation is in place, however, implementation of the programmes is not impactful (Rogerson, 2008). Customer and business regulations which differ in countries create a challenge for SMMEs to grow. In South Africa, the market regulations through the Consumer Protection Act have cost implications for the required standard and quality of goods and services to be provided by SMMEs looking to grow and participate in the market. Labour regulations, mainly the labour laws such as labour, employment equity and minimum wage regulations may prevent employers from hiring additional labour. The stringent legislation imposed on SMMEs by the labour market firstly prevents the market flexible and secondly, makes the process of hiring and firing costly. Tax laws in the country, with their high tax rates and complex tax administration, are a constraint to SMME development and may increase the prevalence of tax evasion or avoidance as a result of high payoffs from productive and non-productive activities of the business (Mahadea & Pillay, 2008).

Poor Business Management/Administration: Busuttil (2007), cited in Mboyane et al. (2011), explains that poor inventory control delays the growth of small businesses. The reasons behind the poor inventory are that small businesses lack daily contact with customers, provide no special promotions, change prices and lack new product features. Another hindering factor for small business growth is the lack of management skills that later result in the poor management actions taken by small business owners (Mboyane et al., 2011).

High Crime Rate: Crime from robbery, break-ins, vandalism and injured or traumatised employees as a result creates a hindrance that has financial implications. Operational costs and savings have to be redirected toward improving security or repairing damage and compensating the affected staff members in Bowes (2005) cited in (Mboyane et al., 2011). SMMEs in South Africa experience crime directly as a result of theft of property and money as well as indirectly reduced business confidence, loss of investments, and emigration, together with the steady erosion of the foundations upon which the economy is built (Mahadea & Pillay, 2008). Crime in the country hinders entrepreneurial activity, visibility and the profitability of the firm whilst also slowing down business development and growth of the economy.

Poor Public/Private Sector Support: Baporikar (2016) mentions slow growth or progress on external sources such as government and commercial banks on the granting of loans and support to SMMEs as another challenge to growth. The refusal to grant loans is mainly a result of the high-risk notion associated with SMMEs. Huges (2009), cited in Baporikar (2016), states that SMMEs experience difficulties in connecting their business to the right capital providers. Working capital is important because of the effect profitability, risk and value contribute to firm growth (Carcia-Teruel & Martinez-Salano, 2007, cited Baporikar, 2016).

Lack of Capacity Building: Entrepreneurial learning and knowledge are important factors which SMMEs lack and later affect business growth. The employment of the right personnel contributes positively to business growth and success (Bouazza et al., 2015 cited in Baporikar, 2016). Human capital in working order and tuned to its environment results in the organisation being well equipped to support growth, product innovation and gain a competitive advantage. However, without effective talent management and human capital, this places the organisation at risk of losing productivity (Schweyer, 2004). Mahadea and Pillay (2008) mention a hindrance to business growth time consumed and expenses incurred in the hiring and retention of skilled labour. An abundance of a skilled labour pool is less costly and less time-consuming during recruitment than in situations where there's limited skill presence within the labour pool of the area. Lastly, the authors spoke of the importance of skills required for starting up a business versus the skills required to manage a business. These two stages in the business development or growth process require proper skill and training to equip business owners with the necessary skills required to sustain growth.

CONCLUSION

SMME development has its hindrances which need to be addressed for effective business growth. This chapter further gives guidance on the need to provide additional research and updates on the operations of SMMEs in the current economic climate.

The mentioned financial mechanism would be able to assist SMMEs to be more sustainable through the provision of proper employment opportunities rather than temporary employment. The financial mechanism and support would be based on prior research practices which would benefit the institutions as well as assisted SMMEs. In essence, a combination of both financial and non-financial support contributes to the sustainable growth of SMMEs. An improvement of the financial mechanism would, therefore, be realised through a strong sector, specific research, and the appropriate sector-specific experiential mentorship.

ACKNOWLEDGMENT

This research received no specific grant from any funding agency in the public, commercial, or not-for-profit sectors.

REFERENCES

Abor, J., & Quartey, P. (2010). Issues in SME development in Ghana and South Africa. *International Research Journal of Finance and Economics*, *39*, 218–228.

Amra, R., Hlatshwayo, A., & McMillan, L. (2013). SMME Employment in South Africa. In *Biennial conference of the economic society of South Africa.* Available: http://b-ok.cc

Attract Capital. (2020). *Business growth.* Available: www.atractcapital.com

Baporikar, N., Nambira, G., & Gomxos, G. (2016). Exploring factors hindering SMEs growth: evidence from Namibia. *Journal of Science and Technology Policy Management, 7*, 190–21.

Bhorat, H., Asmal, Z., Lilenstein, K., & Van Der Zee, K. (2018). *SMMEs in South Africa: understanding the constraints on growth and performance.* Development and Policy Research Unit.

Bruwer, J., Hattingh, C., & Perold, I. (2020). *Probable measures to aid South African Small Medium and Micro Enterprises sustainability, post–COVID-19: A literature review.* Available: https://ssrn.com/abstract=3625552

Business Dictionary. (2020). *Business growth.* Available: www.businessdictionary.com

Business Elite. (2020). *Business growth factors.* Available: www.businesselites.co.za

Churchill, N., & Lewis, V. (1983). The five stages of small business growth. Business Review, 1-12.

Cruz-Cunha, M. M., & Varajao, J. (2011). *E-business issues, challenges and opportunities for SMEs driving competitiveness.* Business Science Reference. Available: http://b-ok.cc

Dlova, M. R. (2017). *Small Micro and Medium Enterprises access to credit in the Eastern Cape South Africa* [Unpublished doctoral thesis]. Johannesburg University of Witwatersrand.

Hayes, J. (2014). *The theory and practice of change management* (4th ed.). Palgrave Macmillan. doi:10.1007/978-1-137-28902-5

Khan, S. (2015). Impact of sources of finance on the growth of SMEs: Evidence from Pakistan. Indian Institute of Management. *Decision, 42.* Advance online publication. doi:10.100740622-014-0071-z

Levens, M. (2014). *Marketing defined, explained, applied* (2nd ed.). Pearson Education Limited.

Mahadea, D., & Pillay, M. K. (2008). Environmental conditions for SMME Development in South African Province. *South African Journal of Economic and Management Sciences, 11*(4), 431-448.

Maitra, B. (2016). Investment in human capital and economic growth in Singapore. *Global Business Review, 17*(2), 425–437. doi:10.1177/0972150915619819

Mbedzi, E., & Simatele, M. (2020). Small micro and medium enterprises financing: Cost and benefits of lending technologies in the Eastern Cape province of South Africa. *Journal of Economic and Financial Sciences, 13*(1), 1–10. doi:10.4102/jef.v13i1.477

McCann, P., & Oxley, L. (2013). Innovation, entrepreneurship, geography and growth. *Journal of Economic Surveys, 26*(3), 1–195.

Ngary, C., Smit, Y., Juan-Pierre, B., & Ukpere, W. I. (2014). Financial performance measures and business objectives attainment in fast food SMMEs in the Cape Metropolis: A preliminary liability and suitability analysis. *Mediterranean Journal of Social Sciences, 5*(20), 909–921. doi:10.5901/mjss.2014.v5n20p909

Nyawo, J. C. (2020). Evaluation of government responses and measures on COVID-19 in the tourism sector: A case of tour guides in South Africa. *African Journal of Hospitality, Tourism and Leisure, 9*(5), 1144–1160. doi:10.46222/ajhtl.19770720-74

OECD. (2018). *SME ministerial conference. Fostering greater SME participation in a globally integrated economy.* Available: www.oecg.org

OECD. (2019). *Financing SMEs and entrepreneurs 2019: an OECD scoreboard.* OECD Publishing. doi:10.1787/fin_sme_ent-2019-

Osano, H. M., & Languitone, H. (2016). Factors influencing access to finance by SMEs in Mozambique: Case of SMEs in Maputo central business district. *Journal of Innovation and Entrepreneurship.*, 5(13), 1–16. doi:10.118613731-016-0041-0

Parliamentary Monitoring Group. (2019). *Small business development review and recommendations report.* Available: www.pmg.org.za

Rodrik, D. (2013). *Structural change, fundamentals, and growth: an overview.* Available: www.harvard.edu

Rogerson, C. (2008). Tracking SMME development in South Africa: issues of finance, training and the Regulatory Environment. *Urban Forum, 19,* 61-81.

Ross, S. A., Westerfield, R. W., & Jordan, B. D. (2013). *Fundamentals of corporate finance* (10th ed.). McGraw Hill Irwin.

Samad, S. (2013). Assessing the contribution of human capital on business performance. *International Journal of Trade. Economics and Finance, 4*(6), 393–397.

Saunders, M., Lewis, P., & Thornhill, A. (2009). *Research methods for business students* (6th ed.). Pearson Education Limited.

Schwab, L., Gold, S., Kunz, N., & Reiner, G. (2017). Sustainable business growth: Exploring operations decision-making. *Journal of Global Responsibility, 8*(1), 1–17. doi:10.1108/JGR-11-2016-0031

Serrasqueiro, Z., Leitão, J. C., & Smallbone, D. (2018). Small- and medium-sized enterprises (SME) growth and financing sources: Before and after the financial crisis. *Journal of Management & Organization, 27,* 1–16. doi:10.1017/jmo.2018.14

Small Enterprise Finance Agency. (2019). *Annual Report 2018/19.* Centurion. Available: www.sefa.org.za

Statistics South Africa. (2021). *Unemployment rate.* Available: www.statssa.gov.za

Teneja, S., Pryor, M. G., & Hayek, M. (2016). Leaping innovation barriers to small business longevity. *The Journal of Business, 37*(3), 44–51.

Ugu District. (2020). *Unemployed youth benefit from portable skills program.* Available: www.ugu.gov.za

Ullah, B. (2019). Financial constraints, corruption, and SME growth in transition economies. *The Quarterly Review of Economics and Finance,* 1–33.

Weber, P., Geneste, L. A., & Connell, J. (2015). Small business growth: Strategic goals and owner preparedness. *The Journal of Business Strategy, 36*(3), 30–36. doi:10.1108/JBS-03-2014-0036

Wickham, P. (2008). *Strategic entrepreneurship* (4th ed.). London: FT Financial Times.

Windrum, P., & De Barranger, P. (2002). *The adoption of e-business technology by SMEs.* Available: www.unu.edu

Yun, J., Jung, W., & Yang, J. (2015). Knowledge strategy and business model conditions for sustainable growth of SMEs. *Journal of Science & Technology Policy Management, 6*(3), 246–262. doi:10.1108/JSTPM-01-2015-0002

ADDITIONAL READING

Achtenhagen, L., & Brundin, E. (2016). *Entrepreneurship and SME management across Africa context, challenges, cases*. Springer.

Chiloane-Tsoka, E. & Mbiza, J. (2014). Climate change patterns affecting SMMEs business sustainability in Buchbuckridge District Local Municipality, South Africa. *Academic Journal of Interdisciplinary Studies, 3*(6), 109–116.

Jaiyeoba, O. (2011). The impact of market orientation on SMMEs in developing economies: A case – study of Botswana. *International Journal of Business Administration, 2*(3), 132–139. doi:10.5430/ijba.v2n3p132

Jili, N. N., Masuku, M. M., & Selepe, B. M. (2017). SMMEs promoting Local Economic Development (LED) in Umlalazi Local Municipality, KwaZulu Natal. *African Journal of Hospitality, Tourism and Leisure, 6*(1), 1–10.

Mbonyane, B., & Ladzani, W. (2011). Factors that hinder growth of small businesses in South African townships. *European Business Review, 23*(6), 550–560. doi:10.1108/09555341111175390

Pucci, T., Nosi, C., & Zanni, L. (2017). Firm capabilities model design and performance of SMEs. *Journal of Small Business and Enterprise Development, 24*(2), 1–41. doi:10.1108/JSBED-09-2016-0138

Sukarmijan, S., & De Vega Sapong, O. (2013). *The importance of intellectual property for SMEs: challenges and moving forward*. International Agribusness Marketing Conference 2013. IAMC 2013, Kuala Laumpur, Selangor, Malaysia.

Ultanir, E. (2012). An epistemological glance at the constructivist approach: Constructivist learning in Dewey, Piaget, and Montessori. *International Journal of Instruction, 5*(2), 195–212.

Chapter 8

Trust in E-Commerce From the Cultural Perspective:
A Systematic Literature Review

Neslişah Özdemir

https://orcid.org/0000-0003-2380-6149

Kastamonu University, Turkey

ABSTRACT

The purpose of this study is to review the literature on e-commerce trust from a cultural perspective, analyze where and how research is conducted, and determine the research stream. For this purpose, a systematic literature review of 52 peer-reviewed articles published in the Scopus database on trust in e-commerce was performed. The findings indicate that there has been a rise, over time, in the number of publications that discuss trust in e-commerce across a variety of cultural contexts. Various methodologies have been employed in these studies, and e-commerce trust has been analyzed in several sectors. The articles on trust in e-commerce from the cultural perspective are under three categories: impact of culture on online trust, antecedents, and consequences of online trust. In this regard, this study contributes to the body of knowledge by evaluating the process of establishing trust in e-commerce and examining the antecedents and consequences of online trust from the cultural perspective.

INTRODUCTION

Electronic commerce (e-commerce), which is described as the acquiring and selling of goods, services, and ideas via the use of communication technology, most notably the Internet, has become a critical component of modern enterprises, especially in the COVID-19 era (Bhatti et al., 2020; Shahzad, Hassan, Abdullah, Hussain & Fareed, 2020). The coronavirus pandemic has impacted global e-commerce and consumer behavior. Due to the virus's containment, millions of people stayed home in early 2020, making digital channels the preferred shopping choice. In 2019, it was discovered that 1.92 billion people used the internet to shop (Statista, 2022). For common things like food, apparel, but also retail technology, demand was extremely high in June 2020, reaching a record 22 billion monthly visits. It is

DOI: 10.4018/978-1-6684-5727-6.ch008

expected that the number of people who purchase online will increase at a rapid rate around the world (Wang, Dang, Nguyen & Le, 2020).

It is asserted that the expansion of e-commerce has caused persistent and profound changes in the way that individual's shop. Even in countries where online shopping is already widespread, it is predicted that e-commerce will continue to grow. According to the Europe E-commerce Europe report, North America and Asia dominate the world e-commerce trade. In addition, it is seen that there is a serious interest in e-commerce in eastern European countries (E-commerce Europe, 2022). In that sense, as a critical enabler of successful e-commerce, the importance of developing, establishing, and maintaining trust between consumers and sellers is increasingly becoming acknowledged in both the academic and practitioner domains. Trust in e-commerce has been widely investigated in previous literature (Kolsaker & Payne, 2002; Corbitt, Thanasankit & Yi, 2003; Chen & Dhillion, 2003 Salam, Iyer, Palvia & Singh, 2005; Palvia, 2009; Abyad, 2017; Teo & Liu, 2017; Hallikainen & Laukkanen, 2018; Sullivan & Kim, 2018; Mumu, Saona, Mamun & Azad, 2021). Trust can be described as confidence in the trade partner's reliability and honesty. Concerns regarding an online store's trustworthiness are among the most critical variables distinguishing online purchasers from non-buyers (Hallikainen & Laukkanen, 2018). Since an online purchaser's decision is so complicated and intelligent, trust must be considered in the decision-making process (Constantinides, 2004; Lăzăroiu et al., 2020). When people shop online, privacy and security concerns might be paramount. Because consumers' views of privacy and security, as well as the quality of information, are significant predictors of trust, firms should be concerned about these variables in order to improve transaction volume (Kim, Ferrin & Rao, 2008).

Particularly important in e-commerce is trust, because not only do individuals have varying levels of trust in regards to e-commerce, but people from different national cultures also differ in their overall level of trust in regards to e-commerce (Hallikainen & Laukkanen, 2018). Indeed, cultural differences have been of interest to many e-commerce marketers attempting to comprehend how to influence consumers of various cultures. Abyad (2017) argues that the global nature of online transactions highlights the necessity of considering how trust and trust-building differ across cultures. In the pertinent literature, researchers have emphasized the relevance of investigating trust in e-commerce from a cultural perspective. For instance, Benamati, Özdemir, and Smith (2021) discovered that consumers in the United States and India have different perceptions of trust in e-commerce. In their study on students, Mosunmola et al. (2019) demonstrated that the interaction between perceived value dimension and individual culture has a significant effect on trust. Merhi, Hone and Tarhini (2019) found that the predictors of behavioral intention towards adoption of mobile banking services are different for Lebanese and English mobile banking users. Mensah (2020) found that culture has an effect on the willingness of African students in China to use e-government services. Moreover, process flexibility and perceived control are crucial factors in establishing online trust in China. E-commerce success, however, necessitates more than the strong IT and process design skills developed in Western countries (Huang, Ba, & Lu, 2014).

The success of e-commerce platforms is largely dependent on their ability to inspire trust. The creation and establishment of online consumer trust, as well as the manner in which it will be developed, depend on the cultural factors that influence the behaviors and beliefs of individuals. In that sense, it is essential to investigate the basic characteristics of the process of establishing trust in e-commerce, as well as the antecedents and consequences of trust in e-commerce across various cultures. Therefore, the purpose of this study is to conduct a systematic literature review on studies that examine trust in e-commerce from a cultural perspective. In this vein, this study firstly examines trust in e-commerce and then it endeavors to answer following questions: (1) What theories do these studies utilize? (2) Which methodological approaches are most preferred? (3) Which countries and industries are being researched the most? (4) Which variables were investigated with the concept of trust in these studies that evaluated e-commerce trust from the culture perspective? In this respect, this research contributes to the body of knowledge by providing the current status of studies dealing with online trust from the culture perspective and proposing future research directions based on the revealed gaps. Furthermore, the research flow in this field could be determined, and an integrated framework is provided by presenting the antecedents and consequences of trust in various cultures.

BACKGROUND

Trust in E-commerce

Trust is a psychological state that entails the decision to accept vulnerability based on positive expectations of another's intentions or actions under conditions of risk and dependency (Rousseau, Sitkin, Burt & Camerer, 1998: 395). It is also described as a set of precise beliefs largely concerned with the integrity, benevolence, and ability of the other party (Gefen, 2002:40). This conception of trust is also known as "trusting intentions" and "trustworthiness". It is founded on a set of ideas that others to whom one is linked will behave in a socially acceptable manner by displaying suitable integrity, benevolence, and ability (Gefen, Karahanna & Straub, 2003).

Trust is the readiness to rely on an exchange or trade partner. Confidence and reliability are key components of trust definitions (Corbitt, Thanasanbit & Yi, 2003). Lee and Turban (2001) argue that trustworthy connections can be made not only between individuals or between individuals and organizations, but also between individuals and computing systems or between individuals and shopping agents in today's world. In this sense, trust has become an even more important component of e-commerce, which is a novel kind of commercial activity that entails greater uncertainty and risk than traditional buying (Lee & Turban, 2001). From an e-commerce perspective, trust is defined as the anticipation that other parties will honor their obligations, bargain in good faith, and not take advantage even when the opportunity presents itself (Hosmer, 1995). The presence of trust is a crucial precondition that enables customers to deal with the ambiguities, risks, and uncertainties that are connected with online transactions. Trust also has a great influence on end-users when they decide whether to participate in e-commerce or not (Salo & Karjaluoto, 2007: 609).

Trust in the context of e-commerce is conceptualized in various ways (Table 1). It is conceptualized as a (1) general belief in equality that results in behavioral intentions; (2) as a combination of e-sellers' reliability, integrity, and benevolence that reduces risk for inexperienced consumers; (3) as beliefs in honesty, benevolence, and ability that lead to a general belief of trust; or (4) specific beliefs about ability, honesty, and predictability that lead to trusting intentions (Gefen, Karahanna & Straub, 2003: 55). Ability is a company's expertise and competence to keep its promises to customers. Benevolence is the company's willingness to put the needs of its customers ahead of its own. Integrity is how consistent, reliable, and honest the company's actions are (Qingyun, Xun and Zhuohao, 2009: 649).

Table 1. Trust conceptualization in e-commerce

Scholars	Trust Conceptualization
Jarvenpaa, Tractinsky & Saarinen (1999)	Willingness to rely when there is vulnerabiliy
Jarvenpaa, Tractinsky & Vitale (2000)	A governance mechanism in buyer-seller relationship
Gefen (2002)	Willingness to depend.
McKnight, Choudhury & Kacmar (2002)	Trusting beliefs dealing with benevolence, competence, honesty, and predictability that lead to a trusting intention

Source: (Gefen, Karahanna & Straub, 2003)

Trust in e-commerce or online trust is the readiness of customers to become dependent on and vulnerable to the acts of others in the belief that the other party will adopt accepted procedures and provide the promised items and services (Zendehdel, Paim, Bojei & Osman, 2011). Trust relates to consumers' opinions of the behavior of online retailers based on their skills, kindness, and integrity (McKnight & Chervany, 2001). Trust can minimize the fear of uncertainty in online purchases, as online transactions are regarded to be riskier; hence, it alleviates customers' psychological concerns over the behavior of e-retailers (Mohseni & Sreenivasan, 2014).

Online shopping requires trust for many reasons. Online buyers must provide personal information when buying goods or registering on websites. Customers fear this information will be shared with a third party for unjustified marketing. Second, consumers' perceived danger increases when they give bank account, debit/credit card, etc. credentials to an online service with no physical presence. The buyers may fear that their financial details may be leaked (Raman, 2019: 1140).

Trust is particularly crucial in e-commerce because not only do individuals have variable levels of trust in regards to e-commerce, but people from different national cultures also have varying levels of trust in regards to e-commerce (Hallikainen & Laukkanen, 2018). Many e-commerce marketers are interested in cultural differences to influence consumers of various cultures. Abyad (2017) argues that the global nature of online transactions highlights the necessity of considering how trust and trust building differ across cultures.

It is widely established in academic research that culture plays a significant part in determining the degree to which various facets of information technology are accepted and utilized (Mosunmola et al., 2019). It is well acknowledged that people's cultures have significant influences on the ways in which they communicate and engage with emerging technology. Both the occurrence of culture and the act of shopping are examples of social phenomena and practices. As a result, it is commonly acknowledged that cultural factors play a significant role in shaping social behaviors. It is also assumed that people's cultural backgrounds have some bearing on the ways in which they choose to make purchases. As a direct consequence of this, successful marketing tactics are increasingly acknowledging culture's role as a very significant factor in determining how customers behave in relation to the introduction of new technology. (Faqih, 2022). Therefore, whether and how online trust will be established depends on cultural factors (e.g., social norms, values, etc.) that guide people's behavior and beliefs (Teo & Liu, 2007).

METHODOLOGY

This is a descriptive study based on a systematic literature review (SLR). SLR is defined as a procedure that is methodical, exhaustive, and deductive in nature that permits the identification, appraisal, and synthesis of existing studies. Thus, it is argued that by examining the current status of the subject, future research in that field is directed (Yıldırım & Cerit, 2020; Özdemir & Özcan, 2022). A SLR aims to gain insight into a topic of study by evaluating previous scientific papers in a repeatable, scientific, and transparent manner (Siddaway, Wood & Hedges, 2019). For the purpose of conducting a SLR, this study used a three-stage research procedure described by Tranfield, Denyer and Smart (2003), which consisted of three steps, namely planning, execution, and reporting (Table 2).

Table 2. Process of SLR

Phase	Step	Description
Planning	Step 1	Consideration of the need for a review
	Step 2	Development of a review protocol
Execution	Step 3	Identification of research
	Step 4	Selection of studies
	Step 5	Data synthesis
Reporting	Step 6	Reporting findings and recommendations

Source: (Tranfield, Denyer & Smart, 2003)

In the planning stage, an Excel protocol form was created. The aforementioned form was completed using the following criteria: article title, author name, publication year, journal in which it was published, research design, industry, sample, data collection method, analysis techniques, and research findings. The database to be scanned was determined at the execution stage. Scopus was chosen as the database because it contains an extensive collection of peer-reviewed publications and includes intelligent tools for monitoring, analyzing, and visualizing research (Bhimani, Mention & Barlatier, 2019). Scopus is the most significant peer-reviewed platform in academia (Rosário, Raimundo and Cruz, 2022).

Table 3. Screening methodology

Database- Scopus	Screening	Articles
Inclusion Criteria	keyword: "trust" AND "e-commerce" OR "online shopping" OR "online marketing" AND "cultur*" Subject area: Business, Management, and Accounting Language: English	66
Screening	Published until July 2022 Irrelavant (5) and inaccessible (9) articles excluded	52

The data for this study were gathered from a Scopus dataset by applying the following query in the article title, abstract, and keyword search fields: "trust" AND "e-commerce" OR "online shopping"

OR "online marketing" AND "cultur*". The evaluation included only English-language articles; book reviews, book chapters, and conference papers were not included. Following that, the search results were narrowed down by subject (Business, Managemet and Accounting) and document type ("journal"), yielding 66 articles. As a consequence of the full-text analysis, it was found that five of these publications were irrelevant (concerning organizational culture, etc.) and were therefore omitted from the analysis. Due to the inability to access the full text of nine of the articles, they were eliminated from the evaluation, leaving 52 articles for analysis (Table 3). Following this stage, the reporting stage was initiated in accordance with the findings.

FINDINGS

Descriptive Overview of Publications

It has been observed that since 2007, there has been a rise in the number of articles that discuss trust in e-commerce in the context of different cultures (Figure 1).

Figure 1. Number of articles per year

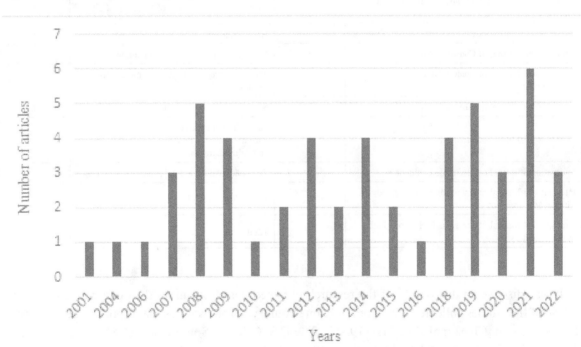

The year with the greatest number of publications was identified as 2021. Examining the distribution of the journals revealed that the Asia Pacific Journal of Marketing and Logistics (3 articles), Information and Management (3 articles), and Journal of Management Information Systems (3 articles) include more articles than the other journals (Table 4).

Table 4. Distribution of studies by journals

Journal	Number of Article	Journal	Number of Article
Academy of Strategic Management Journal	1	International Marketing Review	2
ACM Transactions on Management Information Systems	1	Journal of Applied Structural Equation Modeling	1
Asia Pacific Journal of Marketing and Logistics	3	Journal of Euromarketing	1
ABAC Journal	1	Journal of Global Fashion Marketing	1
Asian Journal of Business Research	1	Journal of Global Information Management	1
Business Process Management Journal	1	Journal of International Consumer Marketing	1
Emerald Emerging Markets Case Studies	1	Journal of International Marketing	1
European Journal of Information Systems	1	Journal of Internet Commerce	2
European Journal of Tourism Research	1	Journal of Islamic Marketing	1
Global Business Review	1	Journal of Management Information and Decision Sciences	1
Information and Management	3	Journal of Management Information Systems	3
Information Technology and Management	1	Journal of Research and Practice in Information Technology	1
International Entrepreneurship and Management Journal	1	Journal of the Academy of Marketing Science	1
International Journal of Business Information Systems	1	Knowledge and Process Management	1
International Journal of Consumer Studies	1	Marketing Intelligence and Planning	1
International Journal of Contemporary Hospitality Management	1	MIS Quarterly: Management Information Systems	1
International Journal of e-Business Research	2	Review of Marketing Science	1
International Journal of Electronic Business	1	Scientific Papers of the University of Pardubice, Series D: Faculty of Economics and Administration	1
International Journal of Electronic Commerce	1	Technological Forecasting and Social Change	1
International Journal of Knowledge, Culture and Change Management	2	Technology in Society	2
International Journal of Services, Technology and Management	1	Total	52

It was discovered that 41.2% of the research obtained data from more than one country, whereas 58.8% of the studies collected data from only one country. Of the studies that reported the country, in the Asia region, China ranks the first (19.2%). The U.S. (12.3%), South Korea (6.8%), Canada (4.1%), Germany (4.1%), Jordan (4.1%), Malaysia (4.1%), Pakistan (4.1%), and Thailand (4.1%) are among the countries where data is collected for studies assessing trust in e-commerce from a cultural perspective.

Table 5. Countries involved in e-commerce trust studies

Country	n	%	Country	n	%
China	14	19,2	Japan	2	2,7
U. S.	9	12,3	Nigeria	2	2,7
South Korea	5	6,8	Afghanistan	1	1,4
Canada	3	4,1	Australia	1	1,4
Germany	3	4,1	Chile	1	1,4
Jordan	3	4,1	Ireland	1	1,4
Malaysia	3	4,1	Netherlands	1	1,4
Pakistan	3	4,1	Poland	1	1,4
Thailand	3	4,1	Portugal	1	1,4
Colombia	2	2,7	Qatar	1	1,4
Egypt	2	2,7	Romania	1	1,4
Finland	2	2,7	Tunisia	1	1,4
France	2	2,7	UK	1	1,4
India	2	2,7	Italy	2	2,7

From the cultural perspective, the majority of the literature on e-commerce trust focuses on emerging countries. On the other hand, the U.S. is the country where online trust has been mostly studied from the culture perspective. In particular, comparisons have been made between emerging countries (such as South Korea, China, and Colombia) and the U.S. regarding the determinants and consequences of trust. In these nations, the effect of culture on trust is examined, and disparities are uncovered.

Methodological Trends

Table 6 shows the research designs of studies in terms of research method, data collection method, sample size, statistical analysis, and unit of analysis. Almost all of the studies in the online trust from a cultural perspective were quantitative in nature (92.3%). Among these quantitative studies, the survey was found to be the most preferred data collection method (83.3%). It has been observed that the most preferred range for the sample size in research is between 100 and 499, accounting for 54% of the total. To conduct their research, 38% of studies used a sample size of 500 or more people. The most popular statistical analysis in this literature is PLS-SEM.

Table 6. An overview of analyzed articles

Research design	Categories	N	%
Research method	Qualitative	2	3.8
	Quantitative	48	92.3
	Mixed (Quantitative + Qualitative)	2	3.8
Data collection method	Focus group/interview	3	5.5
	Survey	45	83.3
	Experiment	4	7.4
	Other (Case)	2	3.7
Sample size	<100	4	10
	100-499	27	54
	>500	19	38
Statistical analysis	PLS-SEM	27	51.9
	Content Analysis	2	3.8
	Other (Anova, regression, discriminant analysis)	23	44.2
Unit of analysis	Online shoppers/consumers/visitor/user	48	88.8
	Firm/Manager/e-business owners/sellers	6	11.1

Content analysis has rarely been used in studies examining trust in e-commerce from a cultural perspective (Phengkona, 2021). Few studies use the focus group/interview method (Shishany, Sarhan, Al-Turk & Albakjaji, 2020; Phengkona, 2021; Kitjaroenchai & Chaipoopiratana, 2022) and the experiment method (Cyr, Head, Larios & Pan, 2009; Furner, Racherla & Zhu, 2014; Fan et al., 2018; Broeder, 2022) as data collection methods. In these studies, it is seen that online shoppers or users have the largest share (88.8%) as the unit of analysis. When the studies are assessed based on the sector, it has been established that retail and service-related studies (48%) are the most prevalent. However, there are studies in the fields of information technology and systems (23%), websites (11%), hospitality and tourism (8%), and banking (4%) (Figure 2).

Figure 2. Distribution of industries examined trust in e-commerce from culture perspective

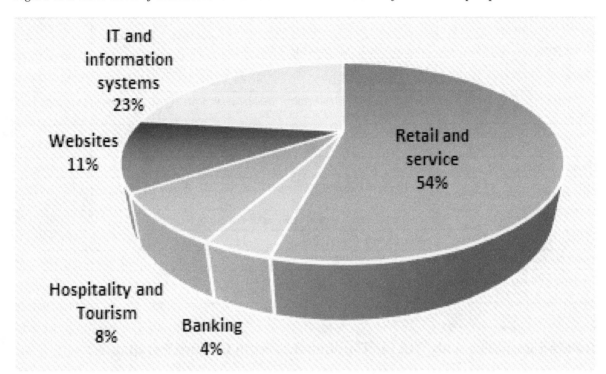

From the cultural perspective, Table 7 outlines the theoretical frameworks utilized to examine trust in e-commerce. Only a small fraction of articles are grounded in a particular theory (Dinev et al., 2006; Awad and Ragowsky, 2008; Furner et al., 2014). Among the theories used, the stimulus organism response (S-O-R) model, the theory of reasoned action (TRA), the theory of planned behavior (TPB), the technology acceptance model (TAM), and the Hofstede cultural dimensions theory are predominant. Some studies have combined trust with the technology acceptance model in various cultures (e.g., Yoon, 2009; Valencia et al., 2019).

Table 7. Theories used in at least one article

Theories	References	N	%
S-O-R model	Sohaib & Kang (2015); Nam, Cho & Kim (2021)	2	10
TRA	Yaobin & Tao (2007); Xu-Priour, Truong & Klink (2014); Park & Kim (2019)	3	15
TAM	Yaobin & Tao (2007); Yoon (2009); Ahmad, Ayyash & Al-Qudah (2018); Valencia et al. (2019)	4	20
Hofstede cultural dimensions theory	Dinev et al. (2006); Ahmad, Ayyash & Al-Qudah (2018); Faqih (2022)	3	15
Source credibility theory	Fan et al. (2018)	1	5
E-commerce and adoption theories	Tan, Tyler & Manica (2007); Marett, Pearson, Pearson & Bergiel (2015)	2	10
TPB	Yaobin & Tao (2007); Ashraf, Thongpapanl & Auh (2014)	2	10
Uncertainty reduction theory	Furner, Racherla & Zhu (2014)	1	5
Sociolinguistic theory	Awad &Ragowsky (2008)	1	5
Fukuyama's theory of trust and social capital theory	Dinev et al. (2006)	1	5

Related Variables with Trust in E-commerce from Culture Perspective

The research flow for studies examining online trust from a cultural perspective is divided into three categories. These are the effects of culture on online trust, online trust antecedents and consequences. Figure 3 depicts an overview of the links between online trust and related variables.

Culture Effects Online Trust

Trust is intricately linked to the cultural differences that exist across nations. Trust is a major feature of culture, connected with national cultural diversity (Hofstede, Neuijen, Ohayv & Sanders, 1990). According to a number of studies, culture has a role in the formation of trust. For instance, Qin, Qu, Zhang and Wu (2021) evaluated how masculinity, uncertainty avoidance, and long-term orientation influence platform trust for C2C vendors in China. They discovered that uncertainty avoidance negatively affected platform trust, whereas masculinity and long-term orientation positively affected platform trust. Moreover, in the research conducted by Xu-Priour, Truong and Klink (2014) in France and China, the effect of social interaction on the perception of trust and the influence of the perception of trust on the intention to use online shopping were greater among Chinese participants than among French participants.

The social conventions and tendencies toward trust that are prevalent in various cultures are not the same. Therefore, it is to be anticipated that people from different cultures will have varying levels of predisposition to participate in e-commerce (Greenberg, Wong-On-Wing & Lui, 2008). In that sense, examining the cultural factors influencing the adoption of online shopping in Egypt, Ramzy and Eldahan (2016) revealed that cultural factors, such as distrust and collectivism, had an effect on the spread of e-commerce. It has been confirmed that culture is the primary factor for Egypt's low e-commerce adoption. In their North American study, Awad and Ragowsky (2008) examined the cultural influence of gender on online word-of-mouth communication and e-commerce trust. The results reveal that the effect of trust on the inclination to shop online is greater among females than among males. In addition, they discovered that the influence of online word-of-mouth quality on online trust varies by gender. Greenberg and colleagues (2008) evaluated customer trust in online businesses in Hong Kong and the US. They analyzed security and privacy issues in product and service purchases. The results demonstrate that consumers from the two nations perceive online business risks and trust differently.

Antecedents of Online Trust

This review suggests that there are several antecedents of trust across diverse cultures. Website properties (Sohaib & Kang, 2015; Nam et al., 2021), technology acceptance factors (Yaobin &Tao, 2007; Bylok, 2021), risk factors (Yaobin & Tao, 2007), quality factors (Nam et al., 2021; Phengkona, 2021; Miao et al., 2021), personal variables (Micu et al., 2019; Shishany, Sarhan, Al-Turk & Albakjaji, 2020; Bylok, 2021) and brand related variables (Lee & Turban, 2001; Aeron, Jain & Kumar, 2019) are evaluated as the antecedents of trust in e-commerce in different cultural perspectives. Bylok (2021) identifies perceived personalization, communication quality, service quality, consumer satisfaction, benefits from relationships with the website, level of uncertainty, and ties to other online store customers as trust determinants for young e-consumers in Poland. Similary, Nam et al. (2021), in their study on university students in the U.S. and Korea, found that website design quality and responsiveness in e-service quality were strongly associated with trust in online clothing shopping, regardless of cultural differences. The results of this study indicate that trust is a crucial component in establishing the relationship between website design and responsiveness and online purchase intent in the two countries. On the other hand, the quality of customer service did not influence levels of trust in Pakistan (Miao et al., 2021).

Aeron et al. (2019) discovered that e-retailer ability, benevolence, integrity, consensus perception, and online familiarity affect trust in online transactions in India. According to research conducted by Phengkona (2021) in Thailand, e-wom is a significant source of information on which community-based tourism travelers can rely to inform their travel decisions. In terms of uncertainty avoidance, Shishany et al. (2020) compare how buyers view corporate processes employed by e-sellers in e-commerce in the UK and Jordan. Customers from the two cultures develop e-trust based on their belief in the credibility of the brands with which they interact. In addition, customers' previous contacts and experiences with firms build e-trust.

Trust in Nigeria is defined by perceived value dimensions, according to Mosunmola et al. (2019). The findings demonstrated that trust is greatly influenced by the interaction between the perceived value dimension and individual culture. Sohaib and Kang (2015) found that B2C web design affects trust and that this trust triggers online purchase intention in Australia and Pakistan. In this study, which is based on the Stimulus–Organism–Response (S–O–R) model, culture (individualism and uncertainty avoidance) plays a moderating role. Micu et al. (2019) compared the impact of customer experience on online trust in Romanian and Tunisian customers.

Sun (2011) studied experience and cultural propensity to trust in e-commerce and revealed that West Germans (a high-trust society) have more confidence in e-commerce than French (a low-trust culture) consumers. Only consumers without e-commerce experience have this cultural difference. Perceived usefulness, consumers' trust propensity, website security, and vendor reputation have significant effects on initial trust in China (Yaobin & Tao, 2007). Another study in China revealed that the trustworthiness of the Internet merchant is a primary positive factor of consumer trust in online commerce, although its effect is moderated by the consumer's trust propensity (Lee & Turban, 2001). A study in Egypt (high uncertainty avoidance) shows how important perceived familiarity and reputation are as the main factors that lead to online trust (El Said & Galal-Edeen, 2009).

Consequences of Online Trust

As a result of this review, trust in e-commerce in different cultures has an impact on online purchase intention (Yaobin & Tao, 2007; Awad & Ragowsky, 2008; Badrinarayanan, Becerra, Kim & Madhavaram, 2012; Hwang & Lee, 2012; Azam, Qiang, Abbas & Ibrahim Abdullah, 2013; Ashraf, Thongpapanl & Auh, 2014; Sohaib & Kang, 2015; Isa, Annuar, Gisip & Lajuni, 2020; Bylok, 2021), repurchase intention (Miao et al., 2021; Eine & Charoensukmongkol, 2021; Kitjaroenchai & Chaipoopiratana, 2022), loyalty (Cyr, 2008; Kassim & Abdullah, 2010; Olaleye, Salo & Ukpabi, 2018), intention to use e-commerce (Yoon, 2009; Capece et al., 2013; Xu-Priour, Truong & Klink, 2014), e-commerce adoption/diffusion (Tan et al., 2007; Ramzy & Eldahan, 2016; Valencia et al., 2019), willingness to use (Kim, 2008).

Bianchi and Andrews (2012) investigated the impact of perceived risk and trust on Chilean consumers' online buying behaviour. Despite the inherent risks, buyers in a collectivist Latin American nation with a culture of strong risk aversion are willing to shop online. Bylok (2021) in his study examining the effect of online trust on purchase intention found that trust in websites and positive experiences in relationships with an online store in the past positively affect young consumers' online shopping intentions in Poland. In addition, the study stated that among young Polish consumers, the level of online consumer trust is relatively high, which is related to the dominance of cultural individualism in Polish society. On the other hand, Mensah (2020) found that trust in the internet is not an important determinant of online shopping intention for university students in China.

Valencia et al. (2019) examined the factors of e-commerce adoption among university students in Colombia through the TAM by adding the perceived security and trust variables. Ease of use, perceived usefulness, and trust were determined to be the antecedents of online shopping intention. Ahmad et al. (2018), benefiting from TAM and Hofstede's cultural dimensions theory in their work in Jordan, found that trust and perceived risk affect the consumer's intention to use Arabic websites. Furthermore, cultural dimensions had moderator roles in the relationship between trust and intention to use websites.

Fan and colleagues (2018) proposed a cross-cultural comparison of consumers' different perceptions of trustworthiness and credibility perceptions in China and America when faced with online recommendations from different information sources (in-group and out-group). Due to their collectivistic nature, Chinese customers display more purchase intent when the recommendation comes from within the group as opposed to an outsider. Among the more individualistic American consumers, these distinctions are not noted.

Asraf et al. (2014) established an enhanced model of technology acceptance that combines trust and perceived behavioral control and tested it in non-U.S. contexts to better comprehend e-commerce adoption across cultures. In both the Pakistani and Canadian cases, trust played a crucial role in the adoption of e-commerce by influencing the intention to shop online. Xu-Priour et al. (2014) found that the effect of social interaction on the perception of trust and the effect of the perception of trust on the intention to use online shopping were stronger for Chinese participants than for French participants.

There was found to be no statistically significant correlation between trust and the level of consumer satisfaction in Thailand (Kitjaroenchai & Chaipoopiratana, 2022). Kassim and Asiah Abdullah (2010) investigated the link between trust and loyalty in Malaysian and Qatari e-commerce settings. The effects of trust on loyalty did not differ significantly between Qatari and Malaysian customers. The reason for this is that the individuals share a common cultural background. Yoon (2009) investigated the impact of national culture on Chinese consumers' acceptance of e-commerce. The findings indicated that uncertainty avoidance and long-term orientation moderated the link between trust and intention to use. The effects of power distance and individualism were insignificant. However, Capece et al. (2013) showed that power distance and individualism moderate the relationship between trust and the intention to use e-commerce in Italy. They compared this finding to a similar study conducted in China and highlighted the impact of national cultures on e-commerce acceptance. In their study of e-commerce use in Italy and the US, Dinev and colleagues (2006) analyze the moderating effect of culture. The authors discovered that corporate trust, privacy concerns, and perceived risk tend to be lower in Italian culture. Italy exhibited poorer connections between corporate trust and e-commerce use as well as perceived risk and corporate trust.

Studies also show that trust in e-commerce is among the factors that affect the spread and success of e-commerce at the company level. For instance, Chong, Shafaghi and Tan (2011) identified security and trust as critical success factors in B2B e-commerce in China. Similarly, Tan et al. (2007) demonstrate that a lack of internal trust is one of the factors hindering the acceptance and diffusion of e-commerce in a B2B environment.

Figure 3. Summary of research on trust in e-commerce from culture perspective

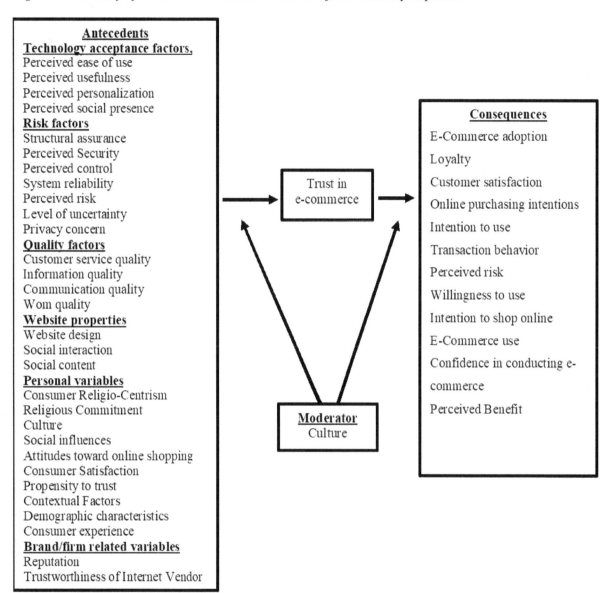

CONCLUSION AND DIRECTIONS FOR FUTURE RESEARCH

In this study, a systematic literature review of studies addressing online trust from a cultural perspective was conducted. It has been discovered that quantitative research designs are more frequently used, but qualitative and mixed design studies are rare. Numerous data collection methods and analysis techniques were utilized in these studies, which contributed to the richness of the research's methodological approaches. According to these studies, the most preferred industries are the retail and service sectors. In addition, websites that are used for online commerce and information systems are included in the scope of the research. In addition, variety was found in the nations from which the data was obtained, and the concept of trust in online transactions was investigated in the context of the countries of Europe and the US. However, the majority of the countries from whom data is obtained are emerging countries. Online trust is investigated frequently in China, one of the Asian nations. This is due to the rapid growth of e-commerce in emerging nations, which has led to an intensity of research in these nations. It was also discovered that the country comparison approach is the most popular approach in this literature for revealing the culturally diverse antecedents and consequences of online trust.

The articles considered for the systematic literature review are categorized by the topics they address. The first category includes studies examining the effect of culture on trust. Another category includes studies focusing on the antecedents of trust. This category identifies both the primary elements of the process of establishing trust in e-commerce and the cultural similarities and differences in this regard. Technology acceptance factors, risk factors, consumer variables, quality factors, and brand/firm related factors are determined as antecedents of online trust. People from different countries show differences in their online trust ancedents due to their national culture. The final category consists of articles that examine the results of trust. These studies examine the outcomes of online trust in a particular culture or compare the outcomes of trust in samples from nations with different national cultures.

To conclude, it is rather fascinating to examine the antecedents and consequences of online trust in the context of culture. Specifically, the antecedents of trust in various cultural contexts allow one to determine the relative relevance of the elements influencing trust. Understanding these elements is essential for creating effective trust-building methods. The consequences of trust in the context of cultural differences provide a clearer understanding of the importance of trust and its impact on online purchasing behavior.

In light of these findings, numerous suggestions for further research might be made. First, it can be suggested that qualitative design can be incorporated into research that explores online trust from a cultural perspective. Additionally, it may be suggested to complement quantitative studies with qualitative studies.

It was concluded that the countries for which data was collected were considered to be emerging countries. The developed or the underdeveloped countries could be the focus of future research. Other emerging nations other than China may be investigated. There is also a need to raise the number of online trust comparisons between developed, emerging and underdeveloped countries. It is also suggested to examine additional variables for brand/firm related variables, one of the antecedents of trust in e-commerce. In addition to culture, the role of other variables can also be investigated. Gender and culture can be used to compare the determinants and consequences of online trust. This study has a number of limitations. The articles included in this study were restricted to those from the Scopus database. In future research, the number of analyzed articles can be raised by evaluating these articles' citations or by integrating more databases. In addition, this study examined peer-reviewed articles on the topic of online trust. In future studies, the scope of the research can be broadened by including more publications, such as book chapters and papers.

REFERENCES

Abyad, A. (2017). Importance of consumer trust in e-commerce. *Middle East Journal of Business*, *12*(3), 20–24. doi:10.5742/MEJB.2017.92971

Aeron, P., Jain, S., & Kumar, A. (2019). Revisiting trust toward e-retailers among Indian online consumers. *Journal of Internet Commerce*, *18*(1), 45–72. doi:10.1080/15332861.2019.1567186

Ahmad, K., Ayyash, M. M., & Al-Qudah, O. M. A. (2018). The effect of culture values on consumer intention to use Arabic e-commerce websites in Jordan: An empirical investigation. *International Journal of Business Information Systems*, *29*(2), 155–182. doi:10.1504/IJBIS.2018.094691

Ashraf, A. R., Thongpapanl, N., & Auh, S. (2014). The application of the technology acceptance model under different cultural contexts: The case of online shopping adoption. *Journal of International Marketing*, *22*(3), 68–93. doi:10.1509/jim.14.0065

Awad, N. F., & Ragowsky, A. (2008). Establishing trust in electronic commerce through online word of mouth: An examination across genders. *Journal of Management Information Systems*, *24*(4), 101–121. doi:10.2753/MIS0742-1222240404

Azam, A., Qiang, F., Abbas, S. A., & Ibrahim Abdullah, M. (2013). Structural equation modeling (SEM) based trust analysis of Muslim consumers in the collective religion affiliation model in e-commerce. *Journal of Islamic Marketing*, *4*(2), 134–149. doi:10.1108/17590831311329278

Badrinarayanan, V., Becerra, E. P., Kim, C., & Madhavaram, S. (2012). Transference and congruence effects on purchase intentions in online stores of multi-channel retailers: Initial evidence from the U.S. and South Korea. *Journal of the Academy of Marketing Science*, *40*(4), 539–557. doi:10.100711747-010-0239-9

Benamati, J. H., Özdemir, Z., & Smith, H. J. (2021). Information privacy, cultural values, and regulatory preferences. *Journal of Global Information Management*, *29*(3), 131–164. doi:10.4018/JGIM.2021050106

Bhatti, A., Akram, H., Basit, H. M., Khan, A. U., Raza, S. M., & Naqvi, M. B. (2020). E-commerce trends during COVID-19 Pandemic. *International Journal of Future Generation Communication and Networking*, *13*(2), 1449–1452.

Bhimani, H., Mention, A. L., & Barlatier, P. J. (2019). Social media and innovation: A systematic literature review and future research directions. *Technological Forecasting and Social Change*, *144*, 251–269. doi:10.1016/j.techfore.2018.10.007

Bianchi, C., & Andrews, L. (2012). Risk, trust, and consumer online purchasing behaviour: A Chilean perspective. *International Marketing Review*, *29*(3), 253–275. doi:10.1108/02651331211229750

Broeder, P. (2022). Profile photos' impact in online reviews: The effect of cultural differences. *Review of Marketing Science*, 1-16.

Bylok, F. (2021). Examining the impact of trust on the e-commerce purchase intentions of young consumers in Poland. *Journal of Internet Commerce*, *21*(3), 364–391. doi:10.1080/15332861.2021.1978194

Capece, G., Calabrese, A., Di Pillo, F., Costa, R., & Crisciotti, V. (2013). The impact of national culture on e-commerce acceptance: The Italian case. *Knowledge and Process Management*, *20*(2), 102–112. doi:10.1002/kpm.1413

Chen, S. C., & Dhillon, G. S. (2003). Interpreting dimensions of consumer trust in e-commerce. *Information Technology and Management*, *4*(2), 303–318. doi:10.1023/A:1022962631249

Chong, W. K., Shafaghi, M., & Tan, B. L. (2011). Development of a business-to-business critical success factors (B2B CSFs) framework for Chinese SMEs. *Marketing Intelligence & Planning, 29*(5), 517–533. doi:10.1108/02634501111153700

Constantinides, E. (2004). Influencing the online consumer's behavior: The Web experience. Internet research. *Internet Research, 14*(2), 111–126. doi:10.1108/10662240410530835

Corbitt, B. J., Thanasankit, T., & Yi, H. (2003). Trust and e-commerce: A study of consumer perceptions. *Electronic Commerce Research and Applications, 2*(3), 203–215. doi:10.1016/S1567-4223(03)00024-3

Cyr, D. (2008). Modeling web site design across cultures: Relationships to trust, satisfaction, and e-loyalty. *Journal of Management Information Systems, 24*(4), 47–72. doi:10.2753/MIS0742-1222240402

Cyr, D., Head, M., Larios, H., & Pan, B. (2009). Exploring human images in website design: A multi-method approach. *MIS Quarterly: Management Information Systems, 33*(3), 539–566. doi:10.2307/20650308

Dinev, T., Bellotto, M., Hart, P., Russo, V., Serra, I., & Colautti, C. (2006). Privacy calculus model in e-commerce - A study of Italy and the United States. *European Journal of Information Systems, 15*(4), 389–402. doi:10.1057/palgrave.ejis.3000590

Ecommerce Europe. (2022). *European E-Commerce Report 2022.* https://ecommerce-europe.eu/wp-content/uploads/2022/06/CMI2022_FullVersion_LIGHT_v2.pdf

Eine, B., & Charoensukmongkol, P. (2021). A cross-cultural perspective on factors that influence the intention to repurchase in online marketplaces: A comparison between Thailand and Germany. *Asian Journal of Business Research, 11*(1), 20–39. doi:10.14707/ajbr.210097

El Said, G. R., & Galal-Edeen, G. H. (2009). The role of culture in e-commerce use for the Egyptian consumers. *Business Process Management Journal, 15*(1), 34–47. doi:10.1108/14637150910931451

Fan, A., Shen, H., Wu, L., Mattila, A. S., & Bilgihan, A. (2018). Whom do we trust? Cultural differences in consumer responses to online recommendations. *International Journal of Contemporary Hospitality Management, 30*(3), 1508–1525. doi:10.1108/IJCHM-01-2017-0050

Faqih, K. M. S. (2022). Internet shopping in the covid-19 era: Investigating the role of perceived risk, anxiety, gender, culture, and trust in the consumers' purchasing behavior from a developing country context. *Technology in Society, 70,* 1–15. doi:10.1016/j.techsoc.2022.101992

Furner, C. P., Racherla, P., & Zhu, Z. (2014). A multinational study of espoused national cultural and review characteristics in the formation of trust in online product reviews. *International Journal of Services Technology and Management, 20*(1-3), 14–30. doi:10.1504/IJSTM.2014.063586

Gefen, D. (2002). Reflections on the dimensions of trust and trustworthiness among online consumers. *ACM SIGMIS Database: The Database for Advances in Information Systems, 33*(3), 38–53. doi:10.1145/569905.569910

Gefen, D., Karahanna, E., & Straub, D. W. (2003). Trust and TAM in online shopping: An integrated model. *Management Information Systems Quarterly, 27*(1), 51–90. doi:10.2307/30036519

Greenberg, R., Wong-On-Wing, B., & Lui, G. (2008). Culture and consumer trust in online businesses. *Journal of Global Information Management*, *16*(3), 26–44. doi:10.4018/jgim.2008070102

Hallikainen, H., & Laukkanen, T. (2018). National culture and consumer trust in e-commerce. *International Journal of Information Management*, *38*(1), 97–106. doi:10.1016/j.ijinfomgt.2017.07.002

Hofstede, G., Neuijen, B., Ohayv, D. D., & Sanders, G. (1990). Measuring organizational cultures: A qualitative and quantitative study across twenty cases. *Administrative Science Quarterly*, *35*(2), 286–316. doi:10.2307/2393392

Hosmer, L. T. (1995). Trust: The connecting link between organizational theory and philosophical ethics. *Academy of Management Review*, *20*(2), 379–403. doi:10.2307/258851

Huang, L., Ba, S., & Lu, X. (2014). Building online trust in a culture of confucianism: The impact of process flexibility and perceived control. *ACM Transactions on Management Information Systems*, *5*(1), 1–23. doi:10.1145/2576756

Hwang, Y., & Lee, K. C. (2012). Investigating the moderating role of uncertainty avoidance cultural values on multidimensional online trust. *Information & Management*, *49*(3-4), 171–176. doi:10.1016/j.im.2012.02.003

Isa, N. F., Annuar, S. N. S., Gisip, I. A., & Lajuni, N. (2020). Factors influencing online purchase intention of millennials and gen Z consumers. *Journal of Applied Structural Equation Modeling*, *4*(2), 21–43. doi:10.47263/JASEM.4(2)03

Jarvenpaa, S. L., Tractinsky, N., & Saarinen, L. (1999). Consumer trust in an Internet store: A cross-cultural validation. *Journal of Computer-Mediated Communication, 5*(2), JCMC526.

Jarvenpaa, S. L., Tractinsky, N., & Vitale, M. (2000). Consumer trust in an Internet store. *Information Technology and Management*, *1*(1), 45–71. doi:10.1023/A:1019104520776

Kassim, N., & Abdullah, N. A. (2010). The effect of perceived service quality dimensions on customer satisfaction, trust, and loyalty in e-commerce settings: A cross cultural analysis. *Asia Pacific Journal of Marketing and Logistics*, *22*(3), 351–371. doi:10.1108/13555851011062269

Kim, D. J. (2008). Self-perception-based versus transference-based trust determinants in computer-mediated transactions: A cross-cultural comparison study. *Journal of Management Information Systems*, *24*(4), 13–45. doi:10.2753/MIS0742-1222240401

Kim, D. J., Ferrin, D. L., & Rao, H. R. (2008). A trust-based consumer decision-making model in electronic commerce: The role of trust, perceived risk, and their antecedents. *Decision Support Systems*, *44*(2), 544–564. doi:10.1016/j.dss.2007.07.001

Kitjaroenchai, M., & Chaipoopiratana, S. (2022). Mixed method: Antecedents of online repurchase intention of generation Y towards apparel products on e-commerce in Thailand. *ABAC Journal*, *42*(1), 73–95.

Kolsaker, A., & Payne, C. (2002). Engendering trust in e-commerce: A study of gender-based concerns. *Marketing Intelligence & Planning*, *20*(4), 206–214. doi:10.1108/02634500210431595

Lăzăroiu, G., Neguriţă, O., Grecu, I., Grecu, G., & Mitran, P. C. (2020). Consumers' decision-making process on social commerce platforms: Online trust, perceived risk, and purchase intentions. *Frontiers in Psychology*, *11*, 890. doi:10.3389/fpsyg.2020.00890 PMID:32499740

Lee, M. K. O., & Turban, E. (2001). A trust model for consumer internet shopping. *International Journal of Electronic Commerce*, *6*(1), 75–91. doi:10.1080/10864415.2001.11044227

Marett, K., Pearson, A. W., Pearson, R. A., & Bergiel, E. (2015). Using mobile devices in a high risk context: The role of risk and trust in an exploratory study in Afghanistan. *Technology in Society*, *41*, 54–64. doi:10.1016/j.techsoc.2014.11.002

McKnight, D. H., & Chervany, N. L. (2001). What trust means in e-commerce customer relationships: An interdisciplinary conceptual typology. *International Journal of Electronic Commerce*, *6*(2), 35–59. doi:10.1080/10864415.2001.11044235

McKnight, D. H., Choudhury, V., & Kacmar, C. (2002). The impact of initial consumer trust on intentions to transact with a web site: A trust building model. *The Journal of Strategic Information Systems*, *11*(3-4), 297–323. doi:10.1016/S0963-8687(02)00020-3

Mensah, I. K. (2020). Factors influencing the intention of international students to shop online in china. *International. Journal of Business Research*, *16*(3), 20–41.

Miao, M., Jalees, T., Zaman, S. I., Khan, S., Hanif, N., & Javed, M. K. (2021). The influence of e-customer satisfaction, e-trust and perceived value on consumer's repurchase intention in B2C e-commerce segment. *Asia Pacific Journal of Marketing and Logistics*, 1–23. doi:10.1108/APJML-03-2021-0221

Micu, A. E., Bouzaabia, O., Bouzaabia, R., Micu, A., & Capatina, A. (2019). Online customer experience in e-retailing: Implications for web entrepreneurship. *The International Entrepreneurship and Management Journal*, *15*(2), 651–675. doi:10.100711365-019-00564-x

Mohseni, S., & Sreenivasan, J. (2014). The impact of user characteristics in online purchase intention in tourism industry. *Reef Resources Assessment and Management Technical Paper*, *40*(1), 399–404.

Mosunmola, A., Adegbuyi, O., Kehinde, O., Agboola, M., & Olokundun, M. (2019). Percieved value dimensions on online shopping intention: The role of trust and culture. *Academy of Strategic Management Journal*, *18*(1), 1–20.

Mumu, J. R., Saona, P., Mamun, M. A. A., & Azad, M. A. K. (2022). Is trust gender biased? A bibliometric review of trust in E-commerce. *Journal of Internet Commerce*, *21*(2), 217–245. doi:10.1080/15332861.2021.1927437

Nam, C., Cho, K., & Kim, Y. D. (2021). Cross-cultural examination of apparel online purchase intention: S-O-R paradigm. *Journal of Global Fashion Marketing*, *12*(1), 62–76. doi:10.1080/20932685.2020.1845766

Olaleye, S. A., Salo, J., & Ukpabi, D. C. (2018). The role of reputation on trust and loyalty: A cross-cultural analysis of tablet E-tailing. *International. Journal of Business Research*, *14*(2), 61–75.

Özdemir, B., & Özcan, H. M. (2022). Islamic Work Ethic: A Content-Analysis Based Literature Review. In Religion and Its Impact on Organizational Behavior (pp. 42-64). IGI Global. doi:10.4018/978-1-7998-9319-6.ch003

Palvia, P. (2009). The role of trust in e-commerce relational exchange: A unified model. *Information & Management, 46*(4), 213–220. doi:10.1016/j.im.2009.02.003

Park, J., & Kim, R. B. (2019). The effects of integrated information & service, institutional mechanism and need for cognition (NFC) on consumer omnichannel adoption behavior. *Asia Pacific Journal of Marketing and Logistics, 33*(6), 1386–1414. doi:10.1108/APJML-06-2018-0209

Phengkona, J. (2021). Online marketing strategies for community-based tourism in the Andaman cluster of Thailand. *European Journal of Tourism Research, 28*, 1–5. doi:10.54055/ejtr.v28i.2046

Qin, L., Qu, Q., Zhang, L., & Wu, H. (2021). Platform trust in C2C e-commerce platform: The sellers' cultural perspective. *Information Technology Management*, 1–11.

Qingyun, J., Xun, H., & Zhuohao, C. (2009). Antecedents and consequences of consumers' trust in electronic intermediaries: An empirical study of hotel booking websites. *Frontiers of Business Research in China, 3*(4), 647–666. doi:10.100711782-009-0031-1

Raman, P. (2019). Understanding female consumers' intention to shop online: The role of trust, convenience and customer service. *Asia Pacific Journal of Marketing and Logistics, 31*(4), 1138–1160. doi:10.1108/APJML-10-2018-0396

Ramzy, O., & Eldahan, O. H. (2016). An empirical investigation of e-commerce in Egypt: The impact of culture on online purchasing. *Global Business Review, 17*(5), 1011–1025. doi:10.1177/0972150916656651

Rosário, A. T., Raimundo, R. J., & Cruz, S. P. (2022). Sustainable Entrepreneurship: A literature review. *Sustainability, 14*(9), 5556. doi:10.3390u14095556

Rousseau, D. M., Sitkin, S. B., Burt, R. S., & Camerer, C. (1998). Not so different after all: A cross-discipline view of trust. *Academy of Management Review, 23*(3), 393–404. doi:10.5465/amr.1998.926617

Salam, A. F., Iyer, L., Palvia, P., & Singh, R. (2005). Trust in e-commerce. *Communications of the ACM, 48*(2), 72–77. doi:10.1145/1042091.1042093

Salo, J., & Karjaluoto, H. (2007). A conceptual model of trust in the online environment. *Online Information Review, 31*(5), 604–621. doi:10.1108/14684520710832324

Shahzad, A., Hassan, R., Abdullah, N. I., Hussain, A., & Fareed, M. (2020). COVID-19 impact on e-commerce usage: An empirical evidence from Malaysian healthcare industry. *Humanities & Social Sciences Reviews, 8*(3), 599–609. doi:10.18510/hssr.2020.8364

Shishany, A. A., Sarhan, N. M., Al-Turk, A., & Albakjaji, M. (2020). The role of institutional mechanisms in creating online trust: Cross cultural investigation. *Journal of Management Information and Decision Sciences, 23*(4), 317–323.

Siddaway, A. P., Wood, A. M., & Hedges, L. V. (2019). How to do a systematic review: A best practice guide for conducting and reporting narrative reviews, meta-analyses, and meta-syntheses. *Annual Review of Psychology*, *70*(1), 747–770. doi:10.1146/annurev-psych-010418-102803 PMID:30089228

Sohaib, O., & Kang, K. (2015). Individual level culture influence on online consumer iTrust aspects towards purchase intention across cultures: A S-O-R model. *International Journal of Electronic Business*, *12*(2), 142–161. doi:10.1504/IJEB.2015.069104

Statista. (2022). *E-commerce Worldwide*. https://www.statista.com/topics/871/online-shopping/#dossierKeyfigures/

Sullivan, Y. W., & Kim, D. J. (2018). Assessing the effects of consumers' product evaluations and trust on repurchase intention in e-commerce environments. *International Journal of Information Management*, *39*, 199–219. doi:10.1016/j.ijinfomgt.2017.12.008

Sun, T. (2011). The roles of trust and experience in consumer confidence in conducting e-commerce: A cross-cultural comparison between France and Germany. *International Journal of Consumer Studies*, *35*(3), 330–337. doi:10.1111/j.1470-6431.2010.00938.x

Tan, J., Tyler, K., & Manica, A. (2007). Business-to-business adoption of eCommerce in China. *Information & Management*, *44*(3), 332–351. doi:10.1016/j.im.2007.04.001

Teo, T. S., & Liu, J. (2007). Consumer trust in e-commerce in the United States, Singapore and China. *Omega*, *35*(1), 22–38. doi:10.1016/j.omega.2005.02.001

Tranfield, D., Denyer, D., & Smart, P. (2003). Towards a methodology for developing evidence informed management knowledge by means of systematic review. *British Journal of Management*, *14*(3), 207–222. doi:10.1111/1467-8551.00375

Valencia, D. C., Valencia-Arias, A., Bran, L., Benjumea, M., & Valencia, J. (2019). Analysis of e-commerce acceptance using the technology acceptance model. *Scientific Papers of the University of Pardubice, Series D. Faculty of Economics and Administration*, *27*(1), 174–185.

Wang, C. N., Dang, T. T., Nguyen, N. A. T., & Le, T. T. H. (2020). Supporting better decision-making: A combined grey model and data envelopment analysis for efficiency evaluation in e-commerce marketplaces. *Sustainability*, *12*(24), 1–24. doi:10.3390u122410385

Xu-Priour, D., Truong, Y., & Klink, R. R. (2014). The effects of collectivism and polychronic time orientation on online social interaction and shopping behavior: A comparative study between China and France. *Technological Forecasting and Social Change*, *88*, 265–275. doi:10.1016/j.techfore.2014.07.010

Yaobin, L., & Tao, Z. (2007). A research of consumers' initial trust in online stores in China. *Journal of Research and Practice in Information Technology*, *39*(3), 167–180.

Yıldırım, C., & Cerit, A. G. (2020). Ulusal pazarlama kongresi yayınlarında stratejik pazarlama yazını analizi. *Pazarlama ve Pazarlama Araştırmaları Dergisi*, *13*(2), 379–408.

Yoon, C. (2009). The effects of national culture values on consumer acceptance of e-commerce: Online shoppers in China. *Information & Management*, *46*(5), 294–301. doi:10.1016/j.im.2009.06.001

Zendehdel, M., Paim, L., Bojei, J., & Osman, S. (2011). The effects of trust on online Malaysian students buying behavior. *Australian Journal of Basic and Applied Sciences, 5*(12), 1125–1132.

ADDITIONAL READING

Beatty, P., Reay, I., Dick, S., & Miller, J. (2011). Consumer trust in e-commerce web sites: A meta-study. *ACM Computing Surveys, 43*(3), 1–46. doi:10.1145/1922649.1922651

Broeder, P. (2020). Culture, Privacy, and Trust in E-commerce. *Marketing from Information to Decision Journal, 3*(1), 14–26. doi:10.2478/midj-2020-0002

Chen, J. V., Yen, D. C., Pornpriphet, W., & Widjaja, A. E. (2015). E-commerce web site loyalty: A cross cultural comparison. *Information Systems Frontiers, 17*(6), 1283–1299. doi:10.100710796-014-9499-0

Gao, Y., & Wu, X. (2010). A cognitive model of trust in e-commerce: Evidence from a field study in China. *Journal of Applied Business Research, 26*(1). Advance online publication. doi:10.19030/jabr.v26i1.275

Kolsaker, A., & Payne, C. (2002). Engendering trust in e-commerce: A study of gender-based concerns. *Marketing Intelligence & Planning, 20*(4), 206–214. doi:10.1108/02634500210431595

Lowry, P. B., Vance, A., Moody, G., Beckman, B., & Read, A. (2008). Explaining and predicting the impact of branding alliances and web site quality on initial consumer trust of e-commerce web sites. *Journal of Management Information Systems, 24*(4), 199–224. doi:10.2753/MIS0742-1222240408

Nica, E. (2015). Positive drivers of consumer trust in e-commerce. *Journal of Self-Governance and Management Economics, 3*(1), 60–65.

Oliveira, T., Alhinho, M., Rita, P., & Dhillon, G. (2017). Modelling and testing consumer trust dimensions in e-commerce. *Computers in Human Behavior, 71*, 153–164. doi:10.1016/j.chb.2017.01.050

KEY TERMS AND DEFINITIONS

Electronic Commerce: A term that refers the purchasing and selling of goods and services, or the transmission of payments or data, over an electronic network, most notably the internet.

Online Purchase Intention: A situation where a consumer is willing and intends to make online transactions.

Privacy Concern: An individual's apprehension towards the potential loss of privacy as a result of voluntary or covert information exposure to websites.

TAM: A theory of information systems that models how people adopt and utilize a technology.

Trust Propensity: A dispositional willingness to rely on others.

Uncertainty Avoidance: The degree to which a society, organization, or group relies on social norms, regulations, and processes to mitigate the unpredictability of future occurrences.

Website Quality: A term implies that a website is effective, user-friendly, and functional, as well as offering accurate and useful content.

Chapter 9
Impact of Technology on Business Continuity During COVID–19

Thirunesha Naidu

https://orcid.org/0000-0003-4037-0789

Management College of Southern Africa, South Africa

Muhammad Hoque

Management College of Southern Africa, South Africa

ABSTRACT

Digital technology has developed over the years with numerous innovations that have improved how we live, communicate, and work. In business, such innovations have occurred predominantly at larger or newer organizations or e-commerce companies as resources are required to design, implement, and maintain bespoke digital technology solutions while other commercially available solutions and their integration into business operations have not been favored over the more traditional work methods. A business continuity plan is established when a company needs to quickly recover to maintain business operations following a disruption such as a pandemic. In this chapter, various business continuity planning initiatives that may occur during a pandemic, the types of digital technologies used by businesses, and their impact on business continuity during such occurrences are discussed. Recommendations are provided herein for businesses to continue successfully in the volatility, uncertainty, complexity, and ambiguity (VUCA) of this world.

INTRODUCTION

The global COVID-19 pandemic lockdown disrupted business operations as many companies had to remain closed or only provide essential goods and services. Such disruptions should have been identified during the business continuity planning process. However, without the consideration of appropriate digital technology, companies would have had no choice but to remain closed if their business continuity plan

DOI: 10.4018/978-1-6684-5727-6.ch009

failed to meet the requirements promulgated for social distancing and working from home. The chapter details the literature reviewed for business continuity planning during a pandemic, the types of digital technologies used by businesses and their impact on business continuity during a pandemic.

The COVID-19 Pandemic

COVID-19 is a recent virus outbreak that was first identified in Wuhan, China in December 2019. The COVID-19 virus causes the coronavirus disease that can lead to severe illness and in some cases death (Centers for Disease Control and Prevention, 2020). The World Health Organization characterized the outbreak as a pandemic on 11 March 2020 as the number of infections increased. At the time there were more than 118 000 infected cases in 114 countries and 4 291 deaths (World Health Organization, 2020). As the virus spread, it has impacted economies and businesses so nations have attempted to contain the spread of the virus with lockdown measures (Jones, Palumbo & Brown, 2021).

Pandemics as an Interruptive Disaster

Cambridge University (2021) defines a pandemic as "… a disease that exists in almost all of an area or almost all of a group of people, animals or plants". Wallace and Webber (2017) indicate that pandemics differ from sudden disasters as these often last for extended periods as compared to other natural disasters such as hurricanes or severe snowstorms. Some of the techniques that are recommended for inclusion in the business continuity plan for a pandemic are social distancing, sanitation, communication, and timing. Pandemics faced in recent times include the Severe acute respiratory syndrome (SARS), Zika virus, Ebola virus, and Swine Flu (Wallace & Webber, 2017) and most recently COVID-19 which disrupted business operations globally.

From south African context, very little is known what strategies were used to continue operating businesses during the black swan events. Therefore, the objective of this study was to identify the types of technologies were used to operate businesses during covid-19.

LITERATURE REVIEW

COVID-19 Pandemic Impact on Business

The COVID-19 pandemic, thought by some researchers to be a black swan event, is regarded by theorist, Nassim Nicholas Taleb as rather being a white swan event as it had been foreseen by himself and others. The pandemic has impacted all sectors of the economy as it has caused challenges for management in trying to protect employees and minimize disruptions to their customers whilst managing revenue gaps, stabilizing financial liquidity, reducing working capital, and identifying other financial sources.

Patnaik (2020) adds that some businesses as a result will not survive the pandemic which has been likened to the Great Depression in the 1930s. Bloom, Bunn, Mizen, Smietanka and Thwaites, (2020) equated the onset of the COVID-19 pandemic as the largest economic shock since World War II considering the impact of capital and labor reallocation costs, social distancing, capital utilization and productivity, working from home and factor inputs, labor quality and business use of intermediate inputs on productivity. These impacts were considered during a survey conducted by Bloom *et al.* (2020) on around 3000 firms in which it was found that productivity will be reduced by an average of 3% by Q2 2021 in the United Kingdom.

With the unprecedented rate at which the coronavirus has spread, The World Economic Forum launched a report by Clift and Court (2020) to help businesses understand the emerging risks from the pandemic. The report was based on the views received as part of a survey of approximately 350 senior risk professionals. The preliminary outlook on COVID-19 risks and their implications are illustrated below. The top 10 dominating risks for companies were categorized as economic, societal, technological, or geopolitical.

Figure 1. Top 10 risks for companies

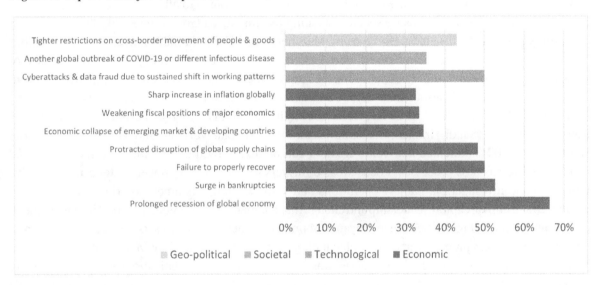

Govinden, Pillay and Ngobeni (2020) surveyed a total of 707 companies from various industries on the impact of the COVID-19 pandemic on companies of which 46.4% indicated that they had temporarily closed or paused their operations during the pandemic. When requested to indicate the measures taken for their workforce, 28.3% indicated that working hours had to be decreased and 19.6% were laying off staff, while 24.0% indicated that no measures were taken. When comparing the COVID-19 pandemic with that of the financial crisis of 2008-2009, most companies (65.0%), indicated that this pandemic is expected to be sustainably worse. However, 46.3% indicated that their workforce could meet their demands, as compared to the 43.0% that indicated that their workforce could not meet their requirements. Many companies indicated that more than 80% of their workforce was working at their normal place at work compared to those working remotely, although 64.8% indicated that their IT systems could handle more employees working from home.

Most of the companies that participated in the survey conducted by Govinden, Pillay and Ngobeni (2020) selected 'other' as their industry category, and these contributed 34.0% to the study. Testing, inspection, and certification (TIC) companies would also be classified in the 'other' category of industries due to the nature of their services provided to the various industries as opposed to manufacturing, retail, or transportation. According to Summers and Charrington (2020), the impact of COVID-19 on TIC companies was more negative for on-site testing, inspection, and audits, while for remote or digital testing and lab-based testing, the impact was less negative or positive. The negative impacts were attributed to the closure of customer facilities as these were classified as non-essential activities and the relaxed government regulations that rendered inspection audits as non-essential services.

Business Response to the COVID-19 Pandemic

The unprecedented nature of the COVID-19 pandemic might have been difficult to envisage during business continuity planning, regardless of how cautiously potential threats were identified. Companies such as TIC providers that were granted permission to operate during the lockdown had to comply with the requirements as promulgated by the South African Government for limited capacity at all business premises depending on the floor area. So companies were encouraged to allow their employees to work from home where possible to ensure social distancing (South Africa Government, 2020b).

A study published in Business Horizons by Margherita and Heikkila (2021) investigated the actions taken in response to the pandemic by 50 world-leading corporations to identify how opportunities for value creation were generated. These corporations represented organizations operating in different continents and countries and various industries. Companies included world-leading players such as Allianz, Amazon, Apple, AT&T, Bank of China, Berkshire Hathaway, BP, Daimler, Gazprom, General Electric, Royal Dutch Shell, Saudi Aramco, Samsung Electronics, Toyota, Verizon, and Walmart. Margherita and Heikkila (2021) indicated that value creation can be driven by transforming customer trends and by redesigning business processes. Focus areas or drivers for value creation were categorized into five groups for the investigation, namely operations and value system, customer experience and support, workforce and human capital, leadership and change management and community and social engagement.

The investigation highlighted the importance of immediate action protocols to which the implementation of agile business processes and digital technologies was recommended by Margherita and Heikkila (2021). The importance of technical reserves was also highlighted as organizations were forced to rely on their existing capabilities during the pandemic. However, the business analytic methods and tools adopted should be based on data gathering and capabilities monitoring. The ability to diversify is key to a faster recovery when a disaster disrupts business continuity.

Flexible Work Arrangements

Tripathi and Bagga (2020) indicated that work from home was adopted as part of the business continuity plan in response to the social distancing requirement promulgated to contain the spread of the coronavirus. Abulibdeh (2020) describes telecommuting or telework as a term describing a combination of technology, location, and time as a work platform. This flexible work arrangement allows employees to work outside the permanent work location with the use of information and communication technologies. The advantages of teleworking, according to Abulibdeh (2020), include improved productivity, better work-family balance, and increased job satisfaction for employees. Employers benefit from lower overhead costs, improved competitive advantages, and greater organizational efficiencies. Abulibdeh (2020) also noted that new complexities are created with the use of ICT to which practices such as smart work centers, work hubs and co-work centers can be used to overcome social and professional isolation tension among teleworkers due to work intensification and technostress. Summers and Charrington (2020) indicated that staffing was an operational challenge faced by TIC companies as laboratories had to operate with a skeleton crew as employees that could work from home were allowed to do so. Flexible work arrangements were also implemented by some TIC companies by reducing staff working hours in some laboratories.

Atiku, Jeremiah and Boateng (2020) investigated the perception of employees in the service industry in selected African countries during the lockdown on flexible work arrangements during the pandemic. The study found that flexible work arrangements had a significant influence on employee productivity and that information technology support was important for its effective implementation with no direct impact on employee productivity. This conforms with studies referenced by these authors that most workers surveyed prefer flexible work options. The study concluded that investment in technological innovation is also important for the employment of flexible work arrangements.

RESEARCH METHODOLOGY

This was a literature review study. Google scholar and Ebscohost search engine were used identify journal articles related to the objectives. The following words were used: Business continuity, business continuity planning, technology uses, digital technology infrastructure, and technology adoption. A total of 1364 articles were initially matched our objective. After going through the abstract, a total of 74 articles were selected for the study. Data were collected between January to March 2022.

RESULTS AND DISCUSSION

Use of Digital Technologies

Tripathi and Bagga (2020) indicated that the right communication medium is imperative for an effective work from home strategy. The lack of face-to-face interaction limits opportunities for employees who are working remotely to exchange information with their colleagues that are working from the office. Organizations can be categorized as not possible, possible at a cost, and highly possible based on their work from home adoption strategy, which is dependent on capital and operational costs. The additional capital and operational costs are attributed to the equipment or hardware, home office spaces, internet networks, conferencing, and collaboration tools requirements. These are the minimum requirements for employees to productively work from home. Tripathi and Bagga (2020) added that digital technology such as business intelligence solutions can also be leveraged to optimize work from home productivity.

Summers and Charrington (2020) indicated that resilience for TIC companies should be the immediate focus. However, opportunities that may arise should also be considered. According to the TIC Council (2021), many TIC providers quickly developed and integrated new types of services and delivery models in response to the COVID-19 pandemic, including remotely performed services, enhanced digitalization, increased automation, and diversification of supply chains. Summers and Charrington (2020) also added that the major players in the TIC industry considered cost-cutting measures to mitigate the impact of the COVID-19 pandemic on margins and cash flow. These measures include furloughing staff, decreasing leadership salaries, and deferring capital expenditure.

Business Continuity

Mäntylä (2020:16) described business continuity as "… having key resources supporting the essential business functions available at all times". Interruptive events or disasters ranging from physical, personnel, external criminal, information, economic and reputational crises, including natural disasters have an impact on business continuity, according to Herbane (2010), and thus the business continuity action plan should address each interruptive event or disaster by outlining the key resources to support the company's essential business functions. Laudon and Laudon (2018) also indicate that planning for business continuity is vital to ensure that critical business operations can be restored after a disruptive event.

A 2019 survey exploring the importance and awareness of business continuity planning at companies in the Bayhead Harbor Durban, South Africa by Poto (2019) found that half of the companies did not have a business continuity plan and 70% of those with a business continuity plan had not done any testing or rehearsal. Despite knowing the benefits of having a business continuity plan, a challenge for many companies is a lack of awareness or training.

Business Continuity Planning

The International Organization for Standardization (ISO) has developed the standard ISO 22031 template for business continuity management systems in response to the need for assurance that business continuity plays in mitigating the effect of disruptions on operations (ISO, 2019).

Business continuity management is described by ISO as a holistic approach to identifying potential threats or risks to business operations, assessing the impacts of those threats where realized, and then determining effective responses (ISO, 2019). The term risk is used by Wallace and Webber (2017) to refer to the potential of a disaster to interrupt business operations. Risks are categorized into five layers based on their potential impact as tabulated in Table 1 below:

Table 1. Risk categories

Layer 1	Layer 2	Layer 3	Layer 4	Layer 5
Natural and manufactured risks	Facilities and basic services risks	Data system risks	Individual department risks	Individual risks
Flooding, hurricanes, or severe snowstorms, rail, road, or airplane	Sites and everything on site Electrical power, and telephone access	Data network, information sharing or performing operational functions	Members of a department prevented from performing assigned work	Individuals not being able to perform their jobs timely

According to Wallace and Webber (2017), pandemics are categorized as a layer 1 external risk with wide area impacts like other natural disasters such as hurricanes, flooding, and severe snowstorms. All stakeholders, including the company, customers, suppliers and interested parties, are affected by layer 1 risks.

Bevan (2019) indicated that this holistic approach provides the organization with a framework to build resilience, respond to disruptions, and continue or resume operations following a disruption. A business continuity management system thus safeguards the organization's reputation and its brand, its value-creating activities, and the interests of its stakeholders. Refer to Figure 2 below for the components of business continuity, resilience, recovery, and continuity as a holistic approach for business continuity management.

Figure 2. Business continuity management components source
Source: Jones, (2018)

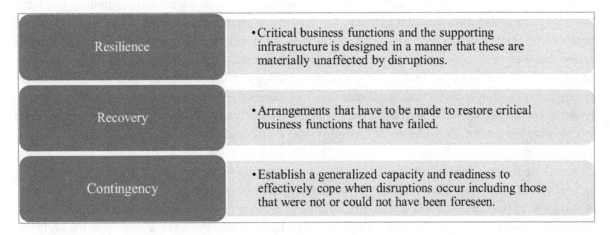

According to Bevan (2019), the business continuity planning system should consider all business processes, including support functions relevant to achieving its business objectives. These business processes, depending on the nature of the business, may include sales, manufacturing, and services. The support functions may include Human Resources, Information Technology, Finance, Customer Contact, Facilities and Purchasing. In the event of a disruption, business processes and support functions identified as critical should be prioritized.

Laudon and Laudon (2018) indicate that critical business processes and support functions are identified using a business impact analysis. This business impact analysis is performed during the business continuity planning process. For each impact identified, considerations are made during the business continuity planning process for the extent of the impact, the period for which the disaster will have an impact on critical business operations, and which of these critical business operations need to be restored first i.e., the order of priority. Tangen and Austin (2012) stated that information technology-led contingency planning responses have been used to mitigate the effects of natural disasters and terrorism since the 1980s.

Digital Technology Usage for Business Continuity

Technology is a well-known enabler of business. The International Labor Organization estimated that 340 million jobs could be lost worldwide by June 2020 because of the COVID-19 pandemic (ILO, 2020). Kundu (2020) indicated that businesses that had not invested in technology or e-commerce had struggled during the unprecedented COVID-19 lockdowns imposed to contain the spread of the coronavirus as compared to businesses that had invested in digital technology or e-commerce. Therefore, technology could be considered the heart of business continuity.

Jiles and Nathan (2020) indicated that the use of digital technologies for business continuity planning has been limited to temporary office setups during a disruption. The extent to which digital technologies are considered by businesses should have shifted since the H1N1 flu pandemic in 2009 and thereafter with the current COVID-19 pandemic. The advantages of using digital technologies include remote working, strengthening cyber security, enhancing network connectivity, leveraging analysis and increasing operational efficiency.

According to research and advisory company Gartner, digital technologies and capabilities influence business models and thus should affect business continuity planning. So, for strategic and systematic business continuity, Gartner proposes following the five-phase approach for companies; firstly, companies define their business model with a focus on their core customers, then secondly, identify any uncertainties through SWOT analysis. Thirdly, information technology infrastructure, applications and software systems are potential uncertainties and threats to which companies need to assess the potential impacts. Fourthly companies should design tentative strategies and lastly execute the changes once agreed upon by company leadership. Considerations for agility, speed and quality should be applied when executing changes to ensure the resilience of the business continuity plan (Gartner, 2020).

Resilience refers to the system's ability to resume and restore to normal after a disruption. According to Soufi, Torabi and Sahebjamnia (2018), the characteristics of resilience include robustness or ability to resist the impact of a disruption, rapidity, or time to recover to an acceptable level of functionality, resourcefulness, or the capability to monitor threats and act accurately and redundancy or the ability to substitute the damaged parts of the system. Even companies with resilient technology should re-imagine their systems for improvements post the COVID-19 pandemic, according to Lee (2020). An advanced technology provider to the banking industry, an industry which is known for resilient technology, despite the slow embrace of shared services, has noted a trend with companies considering the resilience of their technology for further digitalising of their processes. Lee (2020) indicated that these companies are also evaluating what data is available or accessible for their timely decision-making and what processes and costs will be associated. Research conducted by Ambasna-Jones (2020) on 825 enterprises based in Europe, the Middle East and Africa also showed that 41% believe managing information technology has become too complex, while 42% feel that migrating is too exhausting.

Burkitt-Gray (2021) reported that from Aryaka's 5th Annual Global State of the wide area network (WAN) survey of 1,350 networks and IT practitioners at global enterprises in various industries and across all regions, 21% of the organizations surveyed indicated that the pandemic meant that more than half of their employees will continue to work remotely in 2021 and between 25-50% of their employees will continue into 2022. Tripathi and Bagga (2020) indicated that after the disruptions caused by the COVID-19 pandemic, businesses will shift their focus from profit and wealth maximization to adopting business continuity best practices and analytic and business intelligence solutions. Burkitt-Gray (2021:1) further reported that a representative from Aryaka stated that "... traditional technologies are no longer cutting it" for remote working.

Papadopoulos, Baltas and Balta (2020) and Tripathi and Bagga (2020) listed mobile and collaborative technologies, the internet-of-things with next-generation telecommunication networks, big-data analytics, artificial intelligence for deep learning, blockchain technology and business intelligence solutions, as some of the digital technologies that were available for use by companies during business continuity disruptions such as the COVID-19 pandemic. Research conducted by Papadopoulos, Baltas and Balta (2020:2) on the use of digital technologies by small and medium enterprises during COVID-19 identified two main schools of thought, "technology-in-normal-use and technology-in-incident".

Niemimaa (2015) described technology-in-normal-use as the technology used routinely by an organization and which is implemented to support continuity and incident preparations. Technology-in-incident is the technology available in an organization during an incident that induces the need for additional or secondary technology. Therefore, technology-in-normal-use and technology-in-incident should be holistically considered when preparing for incidents and supporting continuity as these are closely connected.

Papadopoulos, Baltas and Balta (2020) indicated that the use of digital technologies by companies to strategically enhance competitiveness, productivity and performance is evident in the literature. However, the use of digital technologies by companies to deal with an interruptive event or disaster such as the COVID-19 pandemic is limited in the literature. The authors added that interruptive events or disasters impact efficiency, profitability and the survival of a business and this impact would be exacerbated with a global pandemic such as COVID-19. Tripathi and Bagga (2020) also indicated that how businesses respond to the COVID-19 pandemic, or how their business continuity plan is implemented, would be remembered as being crucial to coping with the impact of the pandemic and surviving the long-term effects. The role of the correct business intelligence solutions by business to inform decisions for challenges faced would also be vital.

Types of Digital Technology

The Internet-of-Things (IoT) refers to physical objects communicating, sensing or interacting with their internal states or external environment using embedded technology to form a network (Gartner, 2021). According to Cong, Li and Zhang (2021), the use of IoT empowers industries to be more efficient, increases interaction with customers for more personalized experiences, optimizes supply chain operations with the use of cloud computing, mobile telecommunications, big-data, and other technologies that integrate systems and become smarter. Refer to Figure 3 below for how IoT works to communicate or interact between systems.

Figure 3. How IoT works

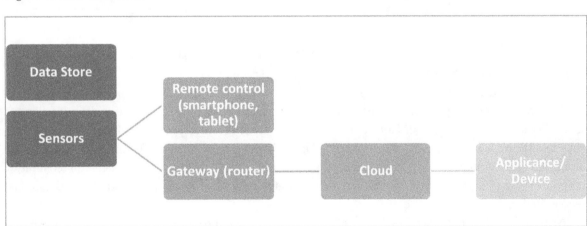

Telecommunications is defined as "the sending and receiving of messages over distance, especially by phone, radio, and television" (Cambridge University, 2021). According to Khan (2021), the use of telecommunications enables individuals and businesses to stay connected. During the COVID-19 pandemic, the use of telecommunications increased with the introduction of lockdowns, social distancing, quarantining, and working from home. Refer to Figure 4 for a corporate network infrastructure setup for sending and receiving messages.

Figure 4. Network infrastructure

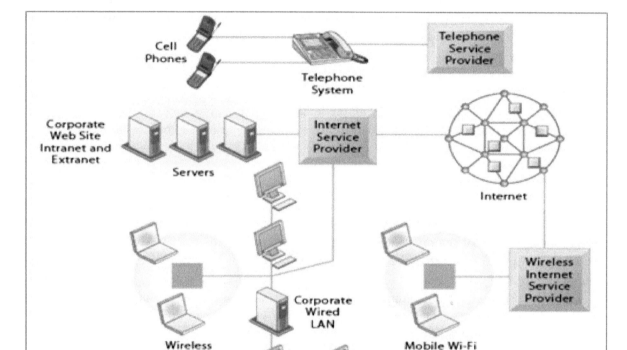

A blockchain is described as an expanding list of cryptographically signed, irrevocable transactional records that are shared by all participants in a network and each of these records contains a timestamp as well as a reference link to previous transactions (Gartner, 2021). Filipova (2018) indicated that the use of blockchain technology lowers the risk of fraud and unauthorized access to sensitive data. It improves reliability as a particular problematic device would not affect executed processes. It enhances transparency and the tracking of data that is trusted by all participants and increases efficiency at a lower cost as blockchains are automated and secure. According to Gilbert (2021), the uses of blockchain technology range from digital currency, accessing and sharing data, identity protection, track-and-trace, and data reconciliation.

Artificial Intelligence (AI) is defined as "the use of computer programs that have some of the qualities of the human mind, such as the ability to understand language, recognize pictures, and learn from experience" (Cambridge University, 2021). Agrawal, Gans, and Goldfarb (2020) indicated that AI or machine learning can be used by businesses to recognize patterns to make predictions that improve operations, enhance product appeal to customers, and make superior products. Analytics and business intelligence are described as applications, infrastructure and tools, as well as best practices that enable access to information, and the analysis of information to improve and optimize decisions and performance (Gartner, 2021). According to Lautenbach, Johnston, and Adeniran-Ogundipe (2017), the use of Business Intelligence and Analytics (BI&A) helps organizations to better position themselves to obtain value from data to support fact-based decision-making. Factors have found an influence on BI&A usage with data-related infrastructure capabilities, management support and external market influence.

According to PricewaterhouseCoopers International Ltd (2021), artificial intelligence, blockchain technology, the Internet-of-Things augmented reality, drones, robotics, virtual reality, and 3-D printing are listed as the essential eight technologies that have emerged that will revolutionize business.

A survey sponsored by IBM in the United States and Canada on the digital workplace found that 74% of 200 enterprise workers surveyed wanted a choice regarding work location, 74% also wanted the right work tools to work from anywhere, and 75% preferred to use company devices instead of their personal devices. Kleiner (2019) indicated that there was a general willingness of the workers surveyed to embrace artificial intelligence at work for human resource-related topics, scheduling meetings, information technology service desk support, and monitoring the health of work devices and their security.

Digital Technology Infrastructure

Wallace and Webber (2017) and Tripathi and Bagga (2020) indicated that the minimum infrastructure required for employees to work remotely instead of at their normal place of work are hardware, office space, internet network and conferencing and collaborative tools. Digital work tools help to reduce face-to-face contact during pandemics if these are already installed, and the users are familiar with the use of these tools and have been trained. According to the authors, the following digital work tools should be considered for remote working.

- The use of virtual private networks (VPNs) that enable employees working remotely to access the company network. This is ideal for those employees whose work involves electronic work objects such as documents.
- The use of virtual meetings that allow employees working remotely to communicate with others. This is ideal for those employees whose work involves attending meetings, presenting, and face-to-face communications.
- The use of cloud storage enables employees to work remotely using an alternative platform to store and share documents with others. This is ideal for those employees whose work involves reviewing or processing documents.
- The use of business intelligence solutions allows employees to work remotely and optimize productivity. This is ideal for those employees working remotely to maximize output to meet demands or expectations.

A survey conducted by Forbes Insight on executives and frontline employees worldwide grouped participants into a traditional workspace, a transitioning workspace, or a digital workspace. According to the report published by the Forbes team in 2017, employees in the digital workspace (54%) indicated that the use of applications has reduced the time spent on manual processes compared to the 29% in transitioning workspace and 12% in the traditional workspace. The importance of the use of applications in team collaboration was rated 67% by employees in the digital workspace, 56% by employees in the transitioning workspace, and 37% in the traditional workspace.

Employees in the digital workspace (63%) indicated that the use of applications increased their productivity compared to the 30% in the transitioning workspace and 14% in the traditional workspace. For future growth, 81% of the employees indicated that applications are important for the company (Forbes Insights, 2017).

According to Corrigan (2020), South Africa had the highest fixed broadband speed but was still behind the rest of the world. The compromising issue for ICT growth in Africa is affordability with most of the ICT financing on the continent provided by the private sector. Information and communication technologies (ICT) consisting of telephony and the internet are important contributors to any economy in the 21st century. Third generation (3G) technology was introduced early in the millennium, followed by fourth generation (4G) technology a decade later. The African Union envisaged the importance of ICT as a business, social interaction and governance tool and had thus included ICT as part of its continental development strategy for 2020-2030. As the current ICT infrastructure in Africa is inadequate it is unlikely to reap the benefits of the Fourth Industrial Revolution. In 2018, only 26.3% of Africans account for internet users as compared to the Arab States with 49.5%, Asia and the Pacific at 46.2%, Europe at 80.1%, Americas at 74.6% and the former Soviet Union States at 69.9%. In 2017, South Africa accounted for 56.2% of the continent's internet usage with Tunisia at 64.2% and Eritrea at 1.3% (ITU, 2021).

İrkey and Tüfekci (2021) stated that the business and financial losses further highlighted the importance of business continuity and knowledge management. Integrating knowledge management into the business continuity approach assisted companies that were adversely impacted by the pandemic and created a competitive advantage by improving their service delivery.

RECOMMENDATIONS

The business continuity plan should be reviewed holistically with digital technologies and should be tested to build resilience, improve responses to disruptions and continue with operations following a disruption. A continual evaluation of the business continuity plan will also enable newer employees to become familiar with the key resources available to support the company's essential business functions. Businesses should continually evaluate the use of digital technologies to keep current with the accelerated pace of innovative digital transformation, future risks, and cyber security and with the shift in working patterns. Investment in ICT infrastructure, in addition to training programs, must be aligned to improve digital literacy as workforce upskilling and investments in digital technology are linked.

CONCLUSION

The COVID-19 pandemic has created considerable awareness for companies regarding future risks and has accelerated the pace of innovative digital transformation. The adoption of digital technologies could be a cost-saving for companies that could also improve their operational efficiencies and productivity throughout the value chain if linked with investments in the workforce upskilling and in digital technology for their future success. In this chapter, various business continuity planning initiatives that may occur during a pandemic were discussed, the types of digital technologies used by businesses, and their impact on business continuity during such occurrences. Recommendations were provided herein for businesses to continue successfully in this Volatility, Uncertainty, Complexity and Ambiguity (VUCA) world.

FUNDING

This research received no specific grant from any funding agency in the public, commercial, or not-for-profit sectors.

REFERENCES

Abulibdeh, A. (2020). Can COVID-19 mitigation measures promote telework practices? *Journal of Labor and Society,* (23), 551–576.

Agrawal, A., Gans, J., & Goldfarb, A. (2020, September-October). How to win with machine learning. *Harvard Business Review*, 126–133.

Ambasna-Jones, M. (2020). *Between a cloud and a hard place: companies change applications tack.* Available: https://www.computerweekly.com/feature/Between-a-cloud-and-a-hard-place-companies-change-applications-tack

Atiku, S., Jeremiah, A., & Boateng, F. (2020). Perceptions of flexible work arrangements in selected African countries during the coronavirus pandemic. *South African Journal of Business Management, 51*(1), 1–10. doi:10.4102ajbm.v51i1.2285

Bevan, T. (2019). *ISO 22031 Implementation Guide. NQA Global Accredited Certification Body.* Available: https://www.nqa.com/medialibraries/NQA/NQA-Media-Library/PDFs/NQA-ISO-22301-Implementation-Guide.pdf

Bloom, N., Bunn, P., Mizen, P., Smietanka, P., & Thwaites, G. (2020). *The impact of COVID-19 on productivity.* Available: https://www.nber.org/papers/w28233%0D

Burkitt-Gray, A. (2021). *COVID means companies expect 'substantial' remote working by year-end.* Capacity Media. Available: https://www.capacitymedia.com/article/29otd15ias3ir9dx70jy8/news/covid-means-companies-expect-substantial-remote-working-by-year-end

Cambridge University. (2021). *Cambridge Dictionary.* Available: https://dictionary.cambridge.org/dictionary/english

Centers for Disease Control and Prevention. (2020*). About COVID-19.* Available: https://www.cdc.gov/coronavirus/2019-ncov/cdcresponse/about-COVID-19.html

Chegg Inc. (2022). *Networking and communication trends.* Available: https://www.chegg.com/homework-help/questions-and-answers/networking-communication-trends-compare-figure-71-diagrams-simple-computer-network-figure--q22389747

Clift, K., & Court, A. (2020). *How are companies responding to the coronavirus crisis?* World Economic Forum. Available: https://www.weforum.org/agenda/2020/03/how-are-companies-responding-to-the-coronavirus-crisis-d15bed6137/

Cong, L. W., Li, B., & Zhang, Q. T. (2021). Internet of Things: Business Economics and Applications. *Review of Business St. John's University, 41*(1), 15–29.

Corrigan, T. (2020). *Policy briefing 197: Africa's ICT infrastructure: its present and prospects.* Available: https://saiia.org.za/research/africas-ict-infrastructure-its-present-and-prospects/

Council, T. I. C. (2021). *The impact of COVID-19 on the TIC sector.* Available: https://www.tic-council.org/blog/impact-covid-19-tic-sector

Ecosystm. (2019). *What is IoT - Internet of Things?* Available: https://blog.ecosystm360.com/guides/iot-internet-of-things/

Filipova, N. (2018). Blockchain - an opportunity for developing new business models. Information Technologies. *D.A. Tsenov Academy of Economics, 20*(2), 75–92.

Forbes Insights. (2017). *The impact of the digital workforce.* Available: https://i.forbesimg.com/forbes-insights/vmware/impact-of-digital-workforce.pdf

Gartner. (2020). Gartner says organizations should follow a five-phase approach for resilient business continuity models during coronavirus disruptions. *Business Wire.* Available: http://search.ebscohost.com/login.aspx?direct=true&db=bwh&AN=bizwire.bw7241305&site=ehost-live

Gartner. (2021). *Gartner Glossary.* Available: https://www.gartner.com/en/information-technology/glossary

Gilbert, N. (2021). *51 critical blockchain statistics: 2021 data analysis & market share.* Finance Online. Available: https://financesonline.com/blockchain-statistics/

Govinden, K., Pillay, S., & Ngobeni, A. (2020). *Business impact survey of the COVID-19 pandemic in South Africa.* Available: http://www.statssa.gov.za/publications/Report-00-80-01/Report-00-80-01April2020.pdf

Herbane, B. (2010). The evolution of business continuity management: A historical review of practices and drivers. *Business History, 52*(6), 978–1002. doi:10.1080/00076791.2010.511185

İrkey, T., & Tüfekci, A. (2021). *The importance of business continuity and knowledge management during the pandemic period.* Academic Press.

ISO. (2019). *Business Continuity ISO 22301.* International Organization for Standardization.

ITU. (2021). *Statistics.* Available: https://www/itu.int/en/ITU-D/Statistics/Pages/stat/default.aspx

Jiles, L., & Nathan, B. (2020). *Technology and business continuity.* Strategic Finance. Available: https://sfmagazine.com/post-entry/june-2020-technology-and-business-continuity/

Jones, L., Palumbo, D., & Brown, D. (2021). *Coronavirus: how the pandemic has changed the world economy.* BBC News. Available: https://www.bbc.com/news/business-51706225

Jones, S. (2018). *Data integrity and planning for business continuity*. MSD. Available: https://slidetodoc.com/data-integrity-and-planning-for-business-continuity-april/

Khan, M. K. (2021). Importance of telecommunications in the times of COVID-19. *Telecommunication Systems, 76*(1), 1–2. doi:10.100711235-020-00749-8 PMID:33456275

Kleiner, A. (2019). *Digital workplace survey says what technology employees want*. Available: https://www.ibm.com/blogs/services/2019/03/05/survey-says-what-technology-employees-want/

Kundu, S. S. (2020). Technology: The heart of business continuity. *IMI Konnect, 9*(3), 21–29.

Laudon, K. C., & Laudon, J. P. (2018). Management information systems managing the digital firm. In Management Decision (5th ed.). Pearson Education Limited. doi:10.1108/eb000831

Lautenbach, P., Johnston, K., & Adeniran-Ogundipe, T. (2017). Factors influencing business intelligence and analytics usage extent in South African organisations. *South African Journal of Business Management, 48*(3), 23–33. doi:10.4102ajbm.v48i3.33

Lee, P. (2020). COVID-19 pandemic requires firms to re-imagine their tech. *Euromoney, 51*(612), 18.

Mäntylä, A. (2020). *Establishing business continuity management practices*. JMAK University of Applied Sciences. Available: https://www.theseus.fi/bitstream/handle/10024/355926/Opinnäytetyö_Mäntylä_Antti.pdf?sequence=2

Margherita, A., & Heikkila, M. (2021). *Business continuity in the COVID-19 emergency: A framework of actions undertaken by world-leading companies*. Kelley School of Business., doi:10.1016/j.bushor.2021.02.020

Niemimaa, M. (2015). Interdisciplinary review of business continuity from an information systems perspective: Toward an integrative framework. *Communications of the Association for Information Systems, 37*(1), 4. doi:10.17705/1CAIS.03704

Nurul, H., & Chandra, V. (2018). Blockchain, cryptocurrency and bitcoin. in Blockchain. *International Journal of Computer Engineering & Applications*. Available http://www.ijcea.com/blockchain-cryptocurrency-bitcoin-3/

Papadopoulos, T., Baltas, K., & Balta, M. (2020). The use of digital technologies by small and medium enterprises during COVID-19: Implications for theory and practice. *International Journal of Information Management, 55*, 102192. doi:10.1016/j.ijinfomgt.2020.102192 PMID:32836646

Pattnalk, S. K. (2020). COVID-19 and its impact on business continuity in Ghana: The role of government. *International Journal of Management and Leadership Studies, 2*(3), 171–180.

Poto, Z. V. (2019). *Awareness and importance of developing business continuity plans for disaster risks by companies at Bayhead Harbour, Durban, South Africa* [Master's dissertation]. University of the Free State. Available: https://www.ufs.ac.za/docs/librariesprovider22/disaster-management-training-and-education-centre-for-africa-(dimtec)-documents/dissertations/zukiswa-vallery-poto-mini-dissertation.pdf?sfvrsn=f4d39421_2

Pricewaterhousecoopers Int. Ltd. (2021). *The essential eight technologies.* Available: https://www.pwc.com/gx/en/issues/technology/essential-eight-technologies.html

Singularity University. (2021). *The exponential guide to artificial intelligence.* Available: https://su.org/resources/exponential-guides/the-exponential-guide-to-artificial-intelligence-2/

Soufi, H. R., Torabi, S. A., & Sahebjamnia, N. (2018). Developing a novel quantitative framework for business continuity planning. *International Journal of Production Research*, 1–23. doi:10.1080/00207543.2018.1483586

South Africa Government. (2020a). *Escalation of measures to combat Coronavirus COVID-19 pandemic.* Available: https://www.gov.za/speeches/president-cyril-ramaphosa-escalation-measures-combat-coronavirus-covid-19-pandemic-23-mar

Stedman, C., & Burns, E. (2021). *Business intelligence (BI), tech target.* Available: https://searchbusinessanalytics.techtarget.com/definition/business-intelligence-BI

Summers, B., & Charrington, H. (2020). *COVID-19 mindset: How pandemic times are shaping global consumers.* Fleishman Hillard. Available: https://fleishmanhillard.com/wp-content/uploads/2021/03/COVID-19-Mindset-How-Pandemic-Times-Are-Shaping-Global-Consumers.pdf

Tangen, S., & Austin, D. (2012). *Business continuity - ISO 22301 when things go seriously wrong.* ISO News. Available: https://www.iso.org/news/2012/06/Ref1602.html

Tripathi, A., & Bagga, T. (2020). Leveraging work from home for business continuity during covid-19 pandemic – with reference to BI solution adoption. *Indian Journal of Economics and Business*, *19*(1), 19–34.

Wallace, M., & Webber, L. (2017). *The disaster recovery handbook: a step-by-step plan to ensure business continuity and protect vital operations, facilities, and assets* (3rd ed.). AMACOM.

World Health Organization. (2020). *WHO Director-General's opening remarks at the media briefing on COVID-19 - 11 March 2020.* Available: https://www.who.int/director-general/speeches/detail/who-director-general-s-opening-remarks-at-the-media-briefing-on-covid-19---11-march-2020

ADDITIONAL READING

Aissaoui, N. (2021). *The digital divide: a literature review and some directions for future research in light of COVID-19.* Global Knowledge, Memory and Communication. doi:10.1108/GKMC-06-2020-0075

Council, T. I. C. (2018). *The new voice of the testing, inspection and certification (TIC) industry.* Available: http://www.ifia-federation.org/content/wp-content/uploads/Factsheet_TIC_Council.pdf

Dickey, C., Brogan, A., Everaard, R., & Haskell, T. (2020). *EY survey: impact of COVID-19 increases urgency of digital technology investments for oil and gas; skill gaps within the workforce hinder ROI.* Available: https://assets.ey.com/content/dam/ey-sites/ey-com/en_ro/news/2020/10/report-oil-gas-ey-ro.pdf

ILO. (2020). *ILO monitor: COVID-19 and the world of work. Fifth edition Updated estimates and analysis.* Available: https://www.ilo.org/wcmsp5/groups/public/@dgreports/@dcomm/documents/briefingnote/wcms_749399.pdf

PricewaterhouseCoopers Int. Ltd. (2020). *Driving digital transformation through digital adoption.* Available: https://www.pwc.co.za/en/publications/driving-digital-transformation-through-digital-adoption.html

Roese, J. (2021). *COVID-19 exposed the digital divide. Here's how we can close it.* World Economic Forum. Available: https://www.weforum.org/agenda/2021/01/covid-digital-divide-learning-education/

Schott, V., & Bindner, S. (2020). *Growth in the testing, inspection and certification (TIC) industry.* Ernest & Young Global Limited. Parthenon. Available: https://assets.ey.com/content/dam/ey-sites/ey-com/en_gl/topics/strategy/pdf/ey-a-steeper-ascent-growth-in-the-testing-tic-industry.pdf?download

South Africa Government. (2020b). *South Africa's response to Coronavirus COVID-19 pandemic.* Available: https://www.gov.za/speeches/president-cyril-ramaphosa-south-africas-response-coronavirus-covid-19-pandemic-23-apr-2020

KEY TERMS AND DEFINITIONS

Black Swan Event: This is a metaphor for a surprising change event with major implications. This theory is often used in finance and describes a negative occurrence that was impossible to predict. Nassim Nicholas Taleb, a Lebanese American former option trader and risk analyst, coined the term 'black swan'. He regards the COVID-19 pandemic as a 'white swan' event because it had been foreseen by him and others.

Blockchain: This is essentially a recording system that is difficult to hack and takes the form of a digital ledger of transactions. It can reduce compliance costs, speed up data processing, and provide secure transactions.

Business Continuity Planning: BCP is required in a company to prevent and recover from threats such as natural disasters or cyberattacks ensuring that both personnel and assets can function during and after such events. The process involves a risk assessment, business impact analysis, a continuity plan, strategic planning, and development and lastly to plan the testing and maintenance aspects.

Business Intelligence Solutions: These solutions comprise IT-based tools that enable the user to customize dashboards, generate data visualizations, combine multiple data sets, and share the results with other uses.

Internet of Things: This phrase, commonly used with the acronym IoT, refers to a system where ordinary items embedded with sensors, can be connected to the Internet. Examples of devices include smart microwaves and fridges, electric cars, fitness devices, and smart security systems.

SWOT Analysis: This term is generally used in project management forums and refers to the strengths, weaknesses, opportunities, and threats of a project. It is used when developing a strategic plan and frequently to evaluate a company's position in the market.

Teleworking: This term refers to remote or distance working where an arrangement with the employer is made concerning not having to commute to the office.

VUCA: This is a managerial acronym for volatility, uncertainty, complexity, and ambiguity. This expression would be used in boardroom discussions when there are uncertain issues raised. Managers would use this acronym when problem-solving and then decision-making.

Chapter 10
Electronic Government

Aizhan Baimukhamedova
Gazi University, Turkey

Malik Baimukhamedov
Social-Technical University Named After Aldymzharov Z., Kazakhstan

ABSTRACT

E-government is based on electronic document management systems, state management automation systems, and other information and communication systems. A description of four e-government models—Continental European model, Anglo-American model, Asian model, and Russian model—are reviewed. The basis for the creation of the e-government portal is the Decree of the President of the Republic of Kazakhstan dated November 10, 2004, N° 1471 "On state program of formation of E-government in the Republic of Kazakhstan for 2005-2007." E-government supports the following goals: creating new forms of interaction between government agencies, optimizing the provision of government services to the public and businesses, supporting and expansion of citizens' self-service capabilities, increasing technological awareness and skills of citizens, and increasing the degree of participation of all voters in the processes of governance and management of the country.

INTRODUCTION

Concept and Description

E-Government is a government that interacts with public authorities, citizens, organizations in an electronic format with minimal personal (physical) interaction. E-Government is based on electronic document management system, state management automation systems and other information and communication systems (Elektronnoye pravitel'stvo, 2017).

E-government Models

By 2017, 4 E-government models are known and applied in the world:

DOI: 10.4018/978-1-6684-5727-6.ch010

- ◦ Continental European model
- ◦ Anglo-American model
- ◦ Asian model
- ◦ Russian model

Continental European Model. This model is characterized by the presence of supranational institutions, whose recommendations must be implemented by all EU countries; a high degree of integration, which is manifested in a single currency, a single information space, in the preparation of a new single Constitution, etc.; legislation regulating information relations in the European information space. The application of technologies in this model is primarily focused on the needs of citizen users.

Anglo-American Model. The model is widely used in the US, Canada and the UK. The United States has created information superhighways that provide citizens with information about government. All services are open, transparent, and the government has a great responsibility to the population. In the UK program called "Electronic citizens, e-business, e-government.

The Strategic Concept of Serving Society in the" Information Age" focuses on solving the following problems: expanding the scope of services provided, the most efficient use of social information, creating conditions for full coverage. The main goal for the UK is to free civil servants from performing routine work.

Asian Model. This model has a specific type of control. The main emphasis is placed on meeting the information needs of the population and the introduction of information technologies in the system of culture and education. The creation of a single information space throughout the country not only strengthens the position of the state, but also puts into practice the basic principle of democracy: the people are the source and bearer of power.

Russian model. The main goals of the program are to increase the efficiency of the functioning of the economy, state and local government, create conditions for free access to information and receive the necessary services. In total, the program provides for development in nine areas, the main of which are ensuring openness in the activities of bodies and improving the activities of state authorities and local self-government.

The disadvantages of e-government models, especially at the early stages of its construction, include an overly "mechanical" way of transferring traditional state and municipal services to electronic form. The transition to an electronic form of public services usually does not include the identification of inefficient and outdated regulatory documents, the implementation of measures to cancel them, correct them and develop new laws, orders and regulations - as this requires the organization of a complex process of coordinating expert work and rule-making processes, and time for this job. E-government working groups are mainly funded from the budget, they are dominated by civil servants, and the search for a compromise with other participants in the ecosystem is not expected, or is difficult. Such a technocratic approach to the automation of public services, while undoubtedly increasing the convenience of their use by citizens and organizations, as a result, does not significantly improve the business climate and does not change the content of interaction between subjects (Malitikov E. M., 2009).

In the process of providing a number of public services, due to the impossibility of regulatory cancellation of the traditional "paper" workflow, there is a duplication of traditional and paper workflow, which leads to an increase in budget costs for supporting both processes and raises questions from experts about the economic efficiency and state feasibility of such an approach to automating them.

The idea to create an electronic government in Kazakhstan was initiated by the Head of State, Nursultan Nazarbayev.

In 2004, the Program for the Formation of the Electronic Government for 2005-2007 was approved (Ukaz Prezidenta, 2004). The implementation of the program involved the phased solution of the following tasks:

1. Information stage - publication and dissemination of information.
2. Interactive stage - the provision of services through direct and reverse interaction between a government agency and a citizen.
3. Transactional stage - interaction through the implementation of financial and legal transactions through the government portal.
4. Information society.

The e-government portal www.egov.kz is being developed by the national information technology operator of the Republic of Kazakhstan, JSC" National Information Technologies", and subsidiary National Info communication Holding" Zerde".

Today, three access points were created on the principle of "one-stop" window for the public and businesses in Kazakhstan in order to obtain government services. Namely saying, it is the E -government portal, public service and contact center. Formed for the current moment the E-government infrastructure allows Kazakhstanis to receive through E -government portal more than 570 services.

The basis for the creation of E-government portal is the Decree of the President of the Republic of Kazakhstan dated November 10, 2004 N° 1471 "On state program of formation of E-government in the Republic of Kazakhstan for 2005-2007".

Joint Stock Company "National Information Technologies" is directly involved in managing and supporting the portal of " E -government". E-government portal has been in operation since 2006.

The creation of E -government was necessary to make the work of government agencies more efficient, open, and accessible to citizens. Previously, each government agency "lived its own life" and had little contact with the rest, and citizens had to bypass many instances to collect all sorts of certificates, confirmations and other papers. All of this turned the process of obtaining one service into endless walking through institutions. Now that's over, thanks to E -government projects.

E-government is a single mechanism of interaction between the state and citizens, as well as state bodies with each other, ensuring their consistency through information technology. It is this mechanism that has made it possible to reduce queues at state bodies and to simplify and speed up the process of obtaining certificates, certificates, permits and much more. In other words, E -government is when only IIN is needed to obtain a license (and all other data is obtained through automatic requests), when you can pay for utilities and fines online, when you can get a certificate from the State Corporation "Government for Citizens" in order to obtain it, when you can register a business or to get a certificate on the portal of "E-government" in some 10-15 minutes, when you can find out the turn of the child in kindergarten at any time of the day or night.

BACKGROUND

Objectives of E-government

E-government supports the following goals (Baimukhamedov M.F., 2022):

1. creating new forms of interaction between government agencies.
2. optimizing the provision of government services to the public and businesses.
3. support and expansion of citizens' self-service capabilities.
4. increasing technological awareness and skills of citizens.
5. increasing the degree of participation of all voters in the processes of governance and management of the country.
6. reducing the impact of geographic location.

E-government provides:

- efficient and less costly administration;
- a radical change in the relationship between society and government;
- improvement of democracy and increased accountability of the government to the people.

In the context of the development of information and communication technologies, all areas of activity of state bodies in electronic form are in demand by citizens and organizations of various forms of ownership. The relevance of this direction is emphasized by the dynamic development of such areas as social, legal, economic, cultural, medical, municipal, etc.

The creation of E-government should provide not only more efficient and less costly administration, but also a fundamental change in the relationship between society and the government. Ultimately, this will lead to an improvement in democracy and an increase in the responsibility of the authorities to the people. Kazakhstan actively supports the initiative of "Open Government". Particularly, in 2013, there was launched an open data portal, dedicated to the accessibility of information disclosed by state bodies, national companies and other government agencies for the citizens of the Republic of Kazakhstan. Free access to government data of public character would make the governance process more transparent. Kazakhstan is in the process of transformation of both the public administration and the tools to ensure its effective operation. Such a tool is undoubtedly the electronic government and its next generation - Smart government. E-government has several definitions, it covers the processes of management, in which information and communication technologies (ICT) play an active role in the delivery of related management products and services.

The use of ICT in governance can lead to one of the following key changes:

- Improving the quality and standards of existing management products and delivered services.
- Provision of new government services and products to citizens/users.
- Strengthening citizens'/users' participation in making decision on what kind of products and state services should be provided and how.

- Introduction of the new social classes into the sphere of public administration, including those that are more likely to remain out of the spotlight, namely the poor, the illiterate, the disabled, migrants and internally displaced persons.

Today, the quality of public services is being improved by the development of two key tools: public service centers (PSC) and the " E -government" web-portal.

For the successful creation, development and modernization of automated public services, the development of E-government architecture is urgent and essential. This architecture consists of four levels: architecture of activities, architecture of data and information, architecture of application systems and architecture of technology.

Stages of maturity of the e-government are determined primarily by the stages of maturity of its architecture (EGA), namely:

1) the formation of the management bases for the development of EGA,
2) development of EGA elements,
3) completion of development of the EGA elements,
4) use of EGAs for changing the management system.

Key elements of the national e-government infrastructure have now been developed and are in operation, including:

- The Unified Portal of State and Municipal Services.
- A unified system of interagency electronic interaction.
- National platform for distributed data processing.
- Software and hardware for e-government includes the following elements:
- a server center of state bodies.
- a server room (data center) owned or owned by the operator of the information and communication infrastructure of E -government, designed to house the objects of informatization of e-government.
- local network of the external loop (hereinafter referred to as the external network of the subjects of informatization defined by the authorized body, referred to the external loop of the telecommunications network of the subjects of informatization, having connection with the Internet, access to which for the subjects of informatization is provided by telecommunications operators only through a unified gateway of access to the Internet.
- server room (data processing center) - a room designed to accommodate server, active and passive network (telecommunications) equipment and equipment of structured cable systems.
- crossover room - a telecommunications room designed to house interconnection, distribution points and devices.
- workstation - a stationary computer within a local network designed for solving application tasks.
- system software - a set of software to ensure the operation of computing equipment.
- application software (hereinafter referred to as "ASP") - a set of software for solving an application problem of a certain class of subject area.
- terminal system - thin or zero client to work with applications in a terminal environment or thin client programs in a client-server architecture.

- EGA has the following main objectives:
- the delivery of government services to the public and businesses.
- increasing the participation of all voters in the processes of governing and governing the country.
- supporting and enhancing citizens' self-service capabilities.
- increasing the technological awareness and skills of citizens.
- reducing the impact of the geographic location factor.

Thus, the creation of an EGA should provide not only a more efficient and less costly administration, but also a dramatic change in the relationship between society and government. Ultimately, this will lead to improved democracy and greater accountability of government to the people.

Key elements of the national E -government infrastructure have now been developed and are in operation, including:

- Single portal of state and municipal services.
- A unified system of interagency electronic interaction.
- A national platform for distributed data processing.
- Unified system of identification and authentication in the infrastructure that provides information and technological interaction of information systems used to provide state and municipal services in electronic form.
- The information system of the head certification

MAIN FOCUS OF THE CHAPTER

Classification of E-government Services

The classification of E-government services of the Republic of Kazakhstan is presented in table 1.

Table 1. Classification of E-government services

No.	Bodies of the government of the Republic of Kazakhstan	Services (functions)
1	Civil Service Agency of the Republic of Kazakhstan	Testing of civil servants, applicants for a vacant administrative state position and citizens entering the law enforcement service for the first time
2	Supreme Court of the Republic of Kazakhstan	Apostille of official documents originating from judicial authorities
3	General Prosecutor's Office of the Republic of Kazakhstan	Apostilization of official documents originating from the prosecutor's office, investigation and inquiry bodies. Issue of certificate of criminal record Obtaining of archive references and/or copies of archive documents within the archives of the Committee for Legal Statistics and Special Accounts of the Prosecutor General's Office of the Republic of Kazakhstan
4	Ministry of Internal Affairs of the Republic of Kazakhstan	Apostilization of archive certificates and copies of archive documents originating from the special state archive of the Ministry of Internal Affairs of the Republic of Kazakhstan and its territorial subdivisions Issuance of driving licenses Issue of a duplicate of the state registration license plate for a vehicle Issue of permits for foreign nationals and stateless persons for temporary residence in the Republic of Kazakhstan Issue of permission for foreigners and stateless persons for permanent residence in the Republic of Kazakhstan Issuance of certificates to stateless persons and residence permits to foreigners permanently residing in the Republic of Kazakhstan State registration, accounting and deregistration of certain types of vehicles under identification number of a vehicle as well as issuance of certificates of registration of vehicles and state registration license plates Registration of documents for leaving the Republic of Kazakhstan for permanent residence Primary registration of vehicles purchased from official dealers in the territory of the Republic of Kazakhstan Obtaining a passport, identity card Submission of information, confirming the registration at the permanent place of residence in the settlement of the border area Receipt and coordination of invitations for visas of the Republic of Kazakhstan Registration of children from 14 to 16 years old at the place of residence Registration by place of residence of the population of the Republic of Kazakhstan Deregistration at the place of residence of the population of the Republic of Kazakhstan

Continued on following page

Table 1. Continued

No.	Bodies of the government of the Republic of Kazakhstan	Services (functions)
5	Ministry of Industry and Infrastructure Development	Reimbursement of expenses for the development and/or expertise of a comprehensive plan of an industrial-innovation project Issuance of housing certificates Issue of information on state registration of mortgage of a vessel, small vessel or a vessel under construction Issuance of a permit to enter (exit) the territory (from the territory) of a foreign country to carriers of the Republic of Kazakhstan engaged in regular international passenger and baggage transportation by road Issuance of permission for passage through the territory of a foreign state to the Republic of Kazakhstan carriers in accordance with international treaties ratified by the Republic of Kazakhstan. Issuance of a permit for the transit of products subject to export control Issuance of a certificate of the right to perform flights (general aviation operator) Issuance of a certificate of vehicle approval for international carriage of dangerous goods Issuance of Air Navigation Service Provider Certificate Issuance of a special permit for heavy and/or oversized vehicles Issuance of a certificate of survey on determining the address of the property on the territory of the Republic of Kazakhstan Issuance of a certificate of admission to engage in international road transportation and issuance of a vehicle admission card State registration of title to a vessel under construction in the register of vessels under construction Privatization of housing from the state housing fund Coordination of the schedule of obligatory technical inspection of motor vehicles and their trailers within the region of operation Subsidizing losses of the carrier, associated with the implementation of road passenger transportation on socially important messages in the inter-district (intercity intraregional), intra-district, urban (rural) and suburban communications
6	Ministry of Foreign Affairs of the Republic of Kazakhstan	Issuance of application for investor visa for persons who are non-residents of the Republic of Kazakhstan and carrying out investment activities in the territory of the Republic of Kazakhstan Conclusion of an investment contract for the implementation of an investment project, providing for investments and investment preferences
7	Ministry of Information and Public Development of the Republic of Kazakhstan	Issuance of decision on approval of location of special stationary premises for distribution of religious literature and other informational materials of religious content, religious items Issuance of decision on re-profiling (change of functional purpose) of buildings (constructions) into buildings of worship (constructions) Issuance of decision on coordinating the location of premises for holding religious events outside religious buildings (constructions) Issuing a decision on the construction of religious buildings (structures), determining their location Conducting registration and re-registration of persons carrying out missionary activity Approval of activity of foreign religious associations on the territory of the Republic of Kazakhstan, appointment of heads of religious associations in the Republic of Kazakhstan by foreign religious centers

Continued on following page

Table 1. Continued

No.	Bodies of the government of the Republic of Kazakhstan	Services (functions)
8	Ministry of Culture and Sports of the Republic of Kazakhstan	Apostilization of archival certificates, copies of archival documents or archival extracts that come from state archives of the Republic of Kazakhstan and are sent abroad Issue of archival certificates, copies of archival documents or archival extracts Issue of permission for temporary export outside the Republic of Kazakhstan of documents of the National Archives Fund, which are in state ownership Payment of lifetime monthly material security to athletes and coaches Compensation payment to members of the national sports teams of the Republic of Kazakhstan (national sports teams) in case of sports injuries and maiming at international sports competitions Provision of housing for champions and prize-winners of Olympic, Paralympic and Deaflympic games and their use Assignment of sports titles and categories Assignment of sports categories: Candidate for Master of Sports of the Republic of Kazakhstan, 1st class athlete and qualification categories: coach of the highest level of qualification of the first category, trainer-teacher of the highest level of qualification of the first category, trainer-teacher of the average level of qualification of the first category, methodologist of the highest level of qualification of the first category, methodologist of the average level of qualification of the first category, trainer-sportsman of the highest level of qualification of the first category Assignment of sports categories: 2nd class athlete, 3rd class athlete, 1st class athlete, 2nd class athlete, 3rd class athlete and qualification categories Assignment of "specialized" status to sports schools and "specialized" status to branches of sports schools
9	Ministry of National Economy of the Republic of Kazakhstan	Provision of social support measures for specialists in health care, education, social welfare, culture, sports and agriculture, civil servants of the offices of akims of villages, settlements, rural districts who came to work and live in rural areas
10	Ministry of Defense of the Republic of Kazakhstan	Apostilization of archival certificates and copies of archival documents originating from the Central Archive of the Ministry of Defense of the Republic of Kazakhstan Issuance of military service cards or duplicates (temporary certificates replacing military service cards) for officers, sergeants and reserve soldiers Issuance of certificates of assignment to recruiting stations and duplicates of such certificates to conscripts Issuance of certificates to citizens leaving the Republic of Kazakhstan for permanent residence Issuance of certificates to veterans of the Great Patriotic War Providing information on a citizen's attitude towards military service
11	Ministry of Education and Science of Kazakhstan	Apostilization of official documents originating from educational organizations Appointment of social payments in case of loss of a breadwinner Registration of children of preschool age (up to 6 years old) for referral to preschool organizations Providing a letter of guarantee for those leaving for study as a Bolashak international scholarship recipient Establishing guardianship or custody over an orphaned child (children) and a child (children) left without parental care and assigning the payment of allowances to guardians or custodians for the maintenance of an orphaned child (children) and a child (children) left without parental care
12	Ministry of Emergency Situations of the Republic of Kazakhstan	Issuance of permits for the use of technologies used at hazardous production facilities, hazardous technical devices

Continued on following page

Table 1. Continued

No.	Bodies of the government of the Republic of Kazakhstan	Services (functions)
13	Ministry of Agriculture of the Republic of Kazakhstan	Issuance of phytosanitary certificate for export of regulated products outside the Republic of Kazakhstan State registration (deregistration) of pledge, registration of amendments, additions (including transfer of ownership to another person, assignment of claim, subsequent pledge (re-pledge) and termination of the registered pledge, as well as issuance of certificate or duplicate of state registration of pledge of tractors and self-propelled chassis and mechanisms made on their basis, trailers to them, including trailers with mounted special equipment, self-propelled agricultural, melioration and road construction machinery Production and issuance of certificates for land plots Coordination of the designed land plot with the graphical data of the automated information system of the state land cadastre Subsidizing of part of the expenses incurred by the subject of agricultural sector during the investment
14	Ministry of Labor and Social Protection of Kazakhstan	Reimbursement of expenses for home schooling of disabled children Issuance of information on the status and movement of social contributions to a member of the compulsory social insurance system Appointment of the state benefit to mothers with many children, awarded with pendants "Altyn alkya", "Kumis alkya" or previously received the title of "Mother-heroine", awarded the Order of "Maternal Glory" of I and II degree Appointment of state social allowance by age Assignment of state social security disability benefits Appointment of retirement benefits Assignment of mother's or father's allowance, adoption, tutor (guardian), who brings up a disabled child Appointment of social payments in case of loss of income in connection with pregnancy and childbirth, adoption of a newborn child (children) Assignment of social payment in case of loss of job Appointment of Social Security Disability Allowance Appointment of a special state benefit Registration of documents for the provision of sanatorium treatment to persons with disabilities and disabled children Registration of documents for providing disabled persons with special means of transportation Registration of documents for providing disabled persons with technical auxiliary (compensatory) means Registration of documents for the provision of individual assistant services to persons with disabilities of the first group, who have difficulties in movement Registration of documents for the provision of special social services in medical and social institutions (organizations) Obtaining information on the assignment of state basic pension payments Obtaining a certificate of pension deductions Registration of citizens who suffered as a result of nuclear tests at the Semipalatinsk nuclear test site, payment of lump-sum state monetary compensation, issuance of certificates

Continued on following page

Table 1. Continued

No.	Bodies of the government of the Republic of Kazakhstan	Services (functions)
15	Ministry of Finance of the Republic of Kazakhstan	Apostilization of official documents originating from structural subdivisions of the Ministry of Finance of the Republic of Kazakhstan and (or) their territorial subdivisions Inclusion in the register of owners of warehouses for storage of own goods Refund of income tax withheld at the source of payment Issue of the certificate on the amounts of the received incomes from the sources in the Republic of Kazakhstan and the withheld (paid) taxes Change of terms of execution of tax liability on payment of taxes and (or) payments Providing personal access to the taxpayer's registration data for viewing (for individuals) Receipt of tax forms for export (import) of goods in Eurasian Economic Union Suspension (prolongation, resumption) of tax reporting Assignment of a personal identification number (PIN) to producers (importers) of certain types of oil products and to producers and importers of certain types of excisable goods, aviation fuel and fuel oil Carrying out tax credits and refunds, payments to the budget, penalties, fines Review and payment of tax debts Registration of a person engaged in private practice Registration of taxpayers
16	Ministry of Digital Development, Innovation and Aerospace Industry of Kazakhstan	Issuance and revocation of the registration certificate of the NTC RK
17	Ministry of Ecology, Geology and Natural Resources of KR	Reimbursement of expenses for the establishment and cultivation of plantations of fast growing tree and shrub species, creation and development of private forest nurseries Issuance of an opinion on construction, reconstruction (expansion, modernization, technical re-equipment, re-profiling), operation, conservation, liquidation (postutilization) of facilities affecting the condition of water bodies Issuance of sturgeon caviar stamps for trade in the domestic market of the Republic of Kazakhstan Distribution of quotas for the withdrawal of wildlife on the basis of approved limits Approval of water protection measures aimed at preventing water bodies from depletion

Continued on following page

Table 1. Continued

No.	Bodies of the government of the Republic of Kazakhstan	Services (functions)
18	Ministry of Justice of the Republic of Kazakhstan	Updating the information in the Civil Registry Information System Annulment of records of acts of civil status Apostilization of official documents coming from judicial authorities and other state bodies, as well as notaries of the Republic of Kazakhstan Commencement of enforcement proceedings on the basis of a writ of execution upon an application of the claimant Issuance of a duplicate of the technical passport of real estate Issuance of copies of documents of the registration file certified by the registering authority, including the plan (scheme) of the objects of immovable property State re-registration of legal entities, record re-registration of their branches and representative offices State registration of amendments and additions to the constituent documents of the legal entity that is not a private business entity, as well as joint stock company, provisions on their branches (representative offices) State registration of legal entities, record registration of their branches and representative offices, taking into account the opening of a bank account and compulsory insurance of the employee against accidents in the performance of labor (job) duties Filing for a second certificate of marriage Applying for a repeated certificate on the change of name, surname, patronymic Submitting an electronic application for obtaining a technical passport of immovable property Filing an electronic application for the registration of a change of name, surname, patronymic Obtaining a certificate of marriage Obtaining certificate of name change, surname and patronymic Obtaining certificate of divorce Obtaining certificate of birth Birth registration, including making changes, additions and corrections to the civil status records Registration of death, including changes, additions and corrections to the civil status records

SOLUTIONS AND RECOMMENDATIONS

E-Government Projects of The Republic of Kazakhstan

E-licensing Information System

Project objective: The information system "State Database "E-licensing" was created in order to automate the processes of licensing, permits and to provide an effective, transparent mechanism of information interaction between government agencies - licensors and the business community of the Republic of Kazakhstan. The system was implemented as part of the Program for the formation and development of "e-government" in the Republic of Kazakhstan, and the State Program for Accelerated Industrial and Innovative Development of the Republic of Kazakhstan.

Unified Notary Information System "E-Notary"

The Unified Notary Information System "E-Notary" is a system designed to improve control over notary activities and optimize the work of notaries.

The system implies registration of notarial acts in an electronic registry and is of benefit to all participants in legal transactions. E-Notary allows notaries to check authenticity of documents, obtain data on real estate, register inheritance and wills, obtain electronic certificates from the e-government portal and check authenticity of powers of attorney. Citizens can be sure of the authenticity of data and the legitimacy and legality of a transaction when they contact a notary in this case (Nurgaziyeva B. G., 2020).

Open Government

The creation of Open Government began in 2013. To date, the Open Government continues to develop as part of the implementation of the Fifth Institutional Reform on the formation of an accountable state, including the implementation of 94 and 96-steps. Laws "On Access to Information" from 15.11.2015, "On Informatization" from 24.11.2015 were adopted.

Open government consists of such components as: open data, open NLAs (Normative legal acts), open dialogue, open budgets, as well as evaluation of the effectiveness of government bodies. In 2014, we launched Open Data and Open NPAs. In 2015, we launched Open Budget and Open Dialogue components. In 2017, we launched Assessment of the effectiveness of state bodies.

Goals of the Portals

- Open Data - to increase public awareness of the key and socially important activities of the state and provide the opportunity to create new applications, based on open data.
- Open budgets - to facilitate citizens' understanding of the concept of "budget" in the state and promote the development of active citizenship through public control over the spending of budgetary funds.
- Open NLAs - to ensure the participation of citizens in the consideration of draft regulations and concepts of bills of state bodies.
- Open dialogs - to provide citizens with the opportunity to interact directly with the first heads of state bodies.

Evaluating the effectiveness of government agencies - to provide citizens with information about the results of evaluating the effectiveness of government agencies, and to improve citizens' understanding of the evaluation system. The Open Data Portal is a platform where publicly available data from government agencies are posted in machine-readable form, allowing the public to receive reliable open data from the holders of information in a convenient form, including for re-use. The beta version of the open data portal was first launched in 2013. In addition, an application programming interface (API) is available on the portal, through which data can be accessed through queries. Based on open data, mobile applications and services are developed and placed for download on the portal thanks to an increase in the amount of data, as well as events such as contests and hackathons. The "Open NLAs" portal is a single platform for discussing draft laws, draft standards for state services and permits. Everyone can express their opinion and take part in the development of NLAs. Open NLAs allow every citizen to review a draft before it goes to a government agency and higher authorities for approval.

In 2015, the Open NLAs portal was launched, where not only the standards of public services under the Law "On Public Services" are publicly discussed, but with the adoption of the Law "On Access to Information," discussion of all draft regulations and concepts of draft laws became available.

Open dialogue is a platform for establishing effective feedback between the CS and society.

The purpose of the Internet portal "Open Dialog" is to provide citizens with the opportunity to interact with the government, through the tools of the portal.

This component includes:

- A blog platform for CSO leaders,
- An online conference with the CSO and IOI,
- The "Polls" system and
- Cellular Operator Service.

The procedure for submitting and reviewing appeals on the blog platform of heads of state agencies is spelled out in the law. According to paragraph 5 of Article 11 of the Law "On Access to Information", requests on the blog platform are equal to a written request. The request does not require signing, provided that there is an account on the e-government portal and a subscriber number is connected to it. Also, the component includes online conferences with members of Local Executive Bodies and Central Government Bodies, which have been held regularly since 2008 on the e-Government web portal.

The "Polls" system is a new service relative to other components of Open Dialog. The system is designed to create surveys, publish surveys on available "e-government" and "mobile government" channels, save and transmit survey results to clients. The system makes it possible to take surveys via SMS messages, mobile application, my Alpari, Open Dialog portal, as well as a social resource.

The "On Call" service provides citizens with several options, including filing an appeal with a cellular operator, identifying a cellular operator by phone number, and viewing the quality of cellular service by city (Kusherov N.S., 2015).

Open dialogue enables citizens to:

1. Send inquiries to the first leaders of government agencies.
2. Participate in a public discussion of the activities of state bodies from anywhere in the country.
3. Participate in surveys conducted by state authorities, social surveys, electronic and mobile government surveys.
4. To apply for Internet conferences conducted by state agencies on a desired topic.
5. Send feedback on the quality of cellular communication.

The purpose of the Internet portal "Open budgets" is to facilitate citizens' understanding of the concept of "budget" in the state and promote the development of active citizenship through public control over the expenditure of budgetary funds.

On the "Open budgets" portal, according to point 3, article 17 of the law "On access to information" there is publication and public discussion of draft budget programs and reports on the implementation of budget programs as well as budget reporting, consolidated financial statements and information about the results of state audit.

The "Open budgets" portal provides the following possibilities:

1. to get acquainted with the budget process of the country.
2. participate in the planning and execution process by commenting on draft budget programs and reports.
3. Use the published budget, consolidated financial statements, as well as the results of the state audit and financial control, for further study and analysis.
4. "eGov Mobile Application"

Project goal: The creation of a mobile government platform is aimed at providing public services and services to the population of the Republic of Kazakhstan through mobile devices, as well as creating an additional and effective channel of interaction between the population of the country and the state, to achieve sustainable social development.

The main components of the system include (Khasanshin I.A., 2013):

1. "Mobile application eGov Mobile" (iOS, Android) - designed to provide state services and e-government services through smartphones.
2. "SMS-gateway" - provides reception and sending of SMS messages to citizens on the provided public services within a short toll-free number "1414".
3. "Mobile Citizen Base" (MCB) - is designed to accumulate and store personal information about the user of e-government.
4. Chatbots in Telegram, Facebook and Vkontakte. Virtual consultant of the services provided by the Portal of E-Government, based on artificial intelligence (Chat-bot), was created to automate the consultation of the most frequently requested public services and services of the Portal of E-Government. A tool of information support in accordance with the interests of the target audience chat-bot functions on the e-government portal egov.kz, on the website 1414.kz, as well as in messengers Telegram, Facebook and Vkontakte. Chat-bot in 24x7 mode on user's request provides necessary information from ECC knowledge base, as well as a link to the sections of the website with complete information. Currently Chatbot has the ability to provide public services and E-government portal services via messengers.
5. Smart Bridge. The Smart Bridge project is a simplified integration process between the information systems of government agencies and the private sector.

The goal of the Smart Bridge project is:

• simplification of organizational procedures for integration, interaction of state bodies with business and development of a competitive environment (within the framework of the "Showcase of Services" platform of the "Smart Bridge" project).
• The "Service Showcase" platform ensures the solution of the following tasks:
• creation of a unified catalog of services of information systems of state bodies and private sector with provision of technical description of the service and contact data of the service owner and developer of the information system.
• automation of the processes of gaining access to the services published on the Services' Showcase portal via an "electronic government" gateway.

- creation of a system for monitoring the functioning of the information system services to exclude duplicating functions, as well as to determine the efficiency of introduction of information system
- automation of the process of creating new information system services via connectors (service builder).

Linking the E-government of The Republic of Kazakhstan with Foreign Governments

E-government of the Republic of Kazakhstan interacts quite actively with the governments of foreign countries. As part of such interaction the leaders of the republic take part in international meetings, symposiums, conferences, summits and other forums organized by the governments of international countries. As a rule, these forums are held in online format using Internet technologies and networks.

For example, the Astana Civil Service Hub and the State Examination Center of the Republic of Azerbaijan held an online conference on "Current Civil Service Reforms: Challenges and Prospects" on September 14, 2021. This conference was attended by heads of governments of both republics, the issues of civil service reform, ways to improve the work of state bodies, as well as the prospects for their interaction in solving problems of cooperation were discussed.

January 25, 2022 President Kassym-Jomart Tokayev attended the "Central Asia - China" summit, marking the 30th anniversary of the establishment of diplomatic relations between Kazakhstan and China. The event, initiated by the Chinese side, took place in the online format.

At the initiative of the UN, international experts carry out research on the level of development of e-government in various states every two years. In 2021, Kazakhstan ranked 29th among 193 UN member states.

Kazakhstan ranks first among the CIS countries, ahead of Russia, Belarus, Moldova, Ukraine, Azerbaijan, Uzbekistan and Armenia.

In terms of the online services index, it ranks third among Asian countries and 11th in the global ranking. In addition, Kazakhstan is ahead of such countries as Luxembourg, Israel, Bahrain, Belgium, China, Italy, Malaysia, Portugal and Romania.

According to the level of development of local online services Almaty is on the 29th place among 100 cities in the world.

Kazakhstan is an active member of the Economic and Social Commission for Asia and the Pacific (ESCAP). ESCAP is the most open intergovernmental platform in the Asia-Pacific region. The Commission promotes cooperation among its 53 member States in seeking solutions to sustainable development challenges. ESCAP is one of the five regional commissions of the United Nations. The ESCAP secretariat supports inclusive, sustainable and resilient development in the region by generating action-oriented knowledge and providing technical assistance and capacity-building services in support of national development goals, regional agreements and the implementation of the 2030 Agenda for Sustainable Development.

Kazakhstan is in a good position to become a digital hub for Central Asia by establishing a Digital Solutions Center (DSC). Kazakhstan has already made progress in digital transformation through a "whole-of-government" approach to e-government, following models such as South Korea's National Information Society Agency (NIA) and the government of Singapore, which are setting the pace in creating examples for the entire economy and society. The DSC will focus on evidence-based research and recommendations for decision makers to implement new digital technologies throughout the economy, in areas such as digital agriculture, industry 4.0 automation based on networked use and management of manufacturing process sensors and the Internet of Things, smart road networks and digital customs services, a national QR code for digitalizing financial services and payment systems, and the adoption of internationally recognized digital standards to promote digital commerce and investment.

The DSC will accelerate Kazakhstan's digital transformation across all sectors, including areas such as social welfare, intra-regulated healthcare, online education services for the COVID-19 pandemic, and progress toward achieving the Sustainable Development Goals, especially on green digitalization, renewable energy and energy conservation.

The Characteristics of E-government Organization in Kazakhstan

What are the characteristics of E-government organization in Kazakhstan? What needs to be improved?

1. Finance: Finance is the key issue. The national budget is the main source for implementing E-government. However, additional finances may come from local and multinational corporations, nongovernmental organizations, and international entities.
2. Regulation: The good functioning of E-government requires improvement of the regulatory and methodological basis of the project. When developing laws, it is also necessary to take into account the specifics of established regulatory mechanisms and the prospects for the development of transactional technologies.
3. Improve the infrastructure and organization (Dempsi D., 2003). It is necessary to ensure the improvement of the main components of the infrastructure of E-government. Given the integration of information subsystems of central and local government agencies, the government should be based on the use of common databases and activity algorithms, a "mechanism" that can be conventionally designated as the principle of E-government internal integrity.
4. Information security: A key aspect of electronic transactions is system and network security. When implementing interactive services, users must be assured of the authenticity of any part of the transaction process. This refers to the identification of the identity of the citizen, as well as characteristics such as education, professional qualifications, etc., i.e., information that can be requested and identified with common databases when accessing certain electronic services. However, this is necessary to guarantee a high level of information security and to ensure that the rights of E-government users are respected. Especially authentication plays an important role in the implementation of the financial transaction on the web portal.

CONCLUSION

Analysis of the current state of informatization in the field of public administration in Kazakhstan shows that, despite the impressive successes in the development of E-government, e-voting and e-document flow, further development will require the solution of many problems.

However, Kazakhstan is a dynamically developing country with a huge labor and innovative potential, to keep pace with scientific and technological progress. Therefore, the use of any new technologies that save time and money, is among the most important state tasks. E-government helps to save time, effort and to reduce corruption. Perhaps, that is why some structures are not in a hurry to implement it for fear of losing this source of income. In addition, e-government is more environmentally friendly: less paper waste, reduced load on auto transport - many operations can be done remotely.

REFERENCES

Baimukhamedov M.F. (2020). Etapy razvitiya elektronnogo pravitel'stva v Kazakhstane. *Problemy prava i ekonomiki, 3*, 45-53.

Dempsi Dzh. (2003). Elektronnoye pravitel'stvo i yego vygody dlya shirokikh mass. *Gosudarstvennoye upravleniye v perekhodnykh ekonomikakh, 1*, 67-74.

Elektronnoye pravitel'stvo. (2017). https://ru.wikipedia.org/wiki/

Khasanshin, I.A. (2013). *Sistemy podderzhki prinyatiya resheniy v upravlenii regional'nym elektronnym pravitel'stvom: monografiya*. Goryachaya liniya.

Kusherov, N.S. (2015). Razvitiye elektronnogo pravitel'stva v Kazakhstane. *Pravo i sovremennyye gosudarstva, 2*, 99-107.

Malitikov, E. M. (2009). Elektronnoye pravitel'stvo tsivilizatsionnaya neizbezhnost'. *Federal'naya gazeta, 1*, 4-5.

Nurgaziyeva, B.G. (2020). *Elektronnaya demokratiya*. http://www.osce.org/ru/odihr/77868?download=true

Ukaz Prezidenta Respubliki Kazakhstan ot 10 noyabrya 2004 goda "O Gosudarstvennoy programme formirovaniya «elektronnogo pravitel'stva" Respublike Kazakhstan na 2005-2007 gody.

KEY TERMS AND DEFINITIONS

Advanced Manufacturing Technologies: Technological processes (including machines, apparatus, equipment and devices) based on microelectronics or computer-controlled and used in the design, manufacture, or processing of products.

Artificial Intelligence: Is a complex of technological solutions that allows you to simulate human cognitive functions (including self-learning and search for solutions without a predetermined algorithm) and to obtain, when performing specific tasks, results comparable, at least, to the results of human intellectual activity.

Artificial Intelligence Technologies: Technologies based on the use of artificial intelligence, including computer vision, natural language processing, speech recognition and synthesis, intelligent decision support and promising artificial intelligence methods.

Big Data: Technologies for collecting, processing, and storing significant arrays of heterogeneous information; are the basis for the development of machine learning and artificial intelligence algorithms, solving analytical problems and optimizing business processes.

Blockchain: Is a technology that combines a number of mathematical, cryptographic, and economic principles that support the existence of a ledger distributed among several participants.

Cloud Computing: Is an information technology model of providing ubiquitous and convenient access using the Internet to a common set of configurable computing resources (cloud), storage devices, applications and services that can be quickly provided and released from the load with minimal operating costs or virtually no participation of the provider.

Data: Presentation of information in a form suitable for automatic processing.

Data Transmission Channels: Are devices and means through which data (information) is transmitted at a distance.

Ecosystem: Is an economic community that consists of a collection of interconnected organizations and individuals. The economic community produces goods and services of value to the consumer, which are also part of the ecosystem.

Electronic Commerce: Is a segment of the economy that includes the purchase and sale of goods, works, services, rights to use electronic content using electronic means of communication, primarily the internet.

Electronic Document Management (EDM): Is a document management system in which the entire array of created, transmitted, and stored documents is supported using information and communication technologies on computers united in a network structure, providing for the possibility of forming and maintaining a distributed database.

Electronic Signature: Is an analogue of a handwritten signature to give a document, issued in electronic form, legal force equal to the legal force of a paper document signed with a handwritten signature.

Global Competitiveness Index: Characterizes the level of competitiveness of countries. Calculated by the World Economic Forum based on 12 parameters.

Global Cybersecurity Index: Characterizes the level of cybersecurity in the country, organizational measures in the field of cybersecurity, the presence of state educational and scientific institutions, partnerships, cooperation mechanisms and information exchange systems that contribute to building capacity in the field of information security.

Industrial Internet: The concept of building information and communication infrastructures based on connecting industrial devices, equipment, sensors, sensors, process control systems to the information and telecommunication network of the internet.

Information and Communication Technologies (ICT): Are technologies that use microelectronic means for collecting, storing, processing, searching, transmitting, and presenting data, texts, images, and sound.

Internet of Things: Is a concept of a computer network connecting things (physical objects) equipped with built-in information technologies for interacting with each other or with the external environment without human intervention.

Level of Digitalization: Is calculated as the ratio of the installed capacity of electronic exchanges to the total installed capacity of telephone exchanges.

Level of Innovative Activity of Organizations: Is usually defined as the ratio of the number of organizations that carried out technological, organizational, or marketing innovations to the total number of organizations surveyed for a certain period in a country, industry, region, etc.

Neurotechnology: Are technologies that provide monitoring of the activity of the brain of a person or other vertebrates and (or) control over it.

New Production Technologies: Include cyber-physical systems, sensor technologies, 3D printing, computer engineering, robotics, qualitatively different production resources (nanotechnology and new materials), etc. Their widespread introduction will optimize production processes, increase the efficiency of resource use, reduce downtime equipment and the cost of its maintenance.

Platform: Broadly defined as a communication and transactional environment, the participants of which benefit from interacting with each other.

Processing Large Amounts of Data: Is a set of approaches, tools, and methods for automatic processing of structured and unstructured information coming from a large number of different, including scattered or loosely coupled, information sources, in volumes that cannot be processed manually in a reasonable time.

Robotization: Is the use of intelligent robotic systems, the functional features of which are in a sufficiently flexible response to changes in the working area.

Sensorics: Technologies that allow interaction with a computer by touching its parts (contact interfaces) or by moving near the computer without touching it (contactless interfaces), and not by changing the position of its mechanical parts (keys, levers, etc.).

Virtual Reality: Is a world (objects and subjects) created by technical means, transmitted to a person through his sensations: sight, hearing, smell, touch, etc. Virtual reality imitates both impact and responses to exposure.

Virtual Reality Technology: Is a technology of non-contact information interaction that realizes the illusion of direct presence in real time in a stereoscopically presented "virtual world" using complex multimedia operating environments.

Website: Is a place on the Internet, which is determined by the address, has an owner and consists of web pages. In statistical observation, an organization is considered to have a website if it has at least one page of its own on the Internet, on which information is published and regularly (at least once every six months) updated.

Chapter 11
Digital Marketing and the Sustainable Performance of Small and Medium Enterprises

Edna Mngusughun Denga

https://orcid.org/0000-0002-2121-242X

American University of Nigeria, Nigeria

Sandip Rakshit

RMIT University, Vietnam

ABSTRACT

Contemporary marketing innovation embraces digital platforms, and irrespective of where SMEs operate, they are confronted with highly volatile, competitive, and dynamic market conditions. Research shows businesses cannot become profitable and competitive without implementing appropriate digital marketing strategies. By utilizing digital tools, SMEs can identify, engage, market, and successfully sustain consumer relationships. Therefore, the chapter analyzes literature to identify the various digital marketing strategies SMEs can adopt, the benefits they stand to gain, and the potential direct and indirect effects on SME performance.

INTRODUCTION

Digital marketing describes a component of marketing that promotes products and services through the usage of internet and online-based digital technology like desktops and laptops, smart phones, along with other digital media and platforms (Denga et al.,2022). Its emergence in the 1990s and 2000s revolutionized the approach businesses and brands utilize technology effectively for marketing. People are increasingly adopting digital devices over physical locations as digital platforms have become highly interwoven into marketing strategies and day-to-day living. (Leeflang et al.,2014). The digitalization of marketing has been accelerated with technological advancements in recent times as marketing has attained a phase in its evolution where it is imperative it adapt to digital trends. The introduction of digital technology

DOI: 10.4018/978-1-6684-5727-6.ch011

has significantly altered human existence and amplifies new perspective in consumption patterns, have significant implications for products and brands. Consumers are devoting greater time on the internet than ever before. They exploit web services for surfing the web, storing, and playing music, emailing, connect directly to media platforms such as Twitter, Facebook, and applications with linked devices such as smart phones, tablets and laptops thus reshaping the manner the internet is being utilized (Alghizzawi, 2019a). Consumer behavior nowadays appears to be typified by the proverb, "If a firm cannot be found in Google, it does not exist." It is obvious that leveraging digital platforms is pivotal for businesses, and a measure SMEs must adopt to stay ahead of competition and expand (Le et al.,2021). Firms can reach a broader demographic with digital marketing than they could with traditional techniques, in addition to targeting prospects who are more inclined to purchase their service or product (Denga et al.,2022a). It is generally less expensive than traditional marketing and allows firms to track progress on a regular basis and adjust as appropriate. In today's Internet-driven society, digital marketing has become a priority, with over 3 billion Users around the globe, it appears having a website is a no-brainer for any business looking to be successful, grow, and raise income (Hofacker etal.,2020) To compete in today's rapidly dynamic environment, both large and small businesses require information. The Internet's proliferation has opened up a broad arena, offering firms, especially small and medium-sized organizations (SMEs), more opportunity to offer their products and services to a global consumer base than they could have reached through conventional approaches.

SMEs assume the internet world is out of their reach; perhaps they believe it is too expensive, or that reaching their target market is unattainable. The Internet has become an indispensable part of most people's lives, and shoppers are increasingly accustomed to researching products online and on social media before making purchases (Denga et al.,2022b). As a result, SMEs that employ digital marketing to promote their services or products have a significant competitive edge. Although implementing digital marketing tactics for SMEs can be difficult, it is worth the effort. These strategies, when implemented correctly, possess the ability to produce beneficial short- and long-term impacts. Firms' pools of potential customers grew significantly, and their influence much exceeded that of the analog era because of the advent of digitalization. Traditional marketing tactics, such as print and billboards, have taken a backseat as SMEs marketing strategies have evolved. SMEs are an important element of the global economy, research suggests that digitization in many forms is associated with small business growth, performance, and competitiveness as they leverage digital marketing to acquire prospective consumers and communicate effectively with existing ones. Thus, digital marketing is critical to the growth of SMEs as it aids them in increasing sales, revenue, and overall growth, as well as convert their audience into customers and generate additional revenue by selling their products or services.

BACKGROUND OF THE STUDY

Marketing is a vital component that affects a firm's performance and competitiveness (Sadiku-Dushi et al., 2019). In a marketing strategy, digital tools like the Internet, mobile devices, and social media exert a significant role. Businesses employ digital marketing tools like social media to enhance their performance, boost profitability, and achieve a competitive edge. Leveraging digital platforms is essential for expansion. However, a well-executed strategy is vital for digital marketing to be successful (Negoiță et al., 2018). The success of a business depends on its marketing expertise (Bacon & Schneider, 2019). Many small business owners, however, lack the marketing expertise that professional marketers possess as only business owners who are knowledgeable about efficient marketing tactics are skilled at attracting customers (Eryigit, 2017). By investing money in the activities that draw customers to sustain the firm, a great digital marketing strategy can minimize the likelihood of failure. Firms, particularly Small and medium-sized businesses (SMEs), are challenged with a great deal of changes that necessitate novel solutions. The creation of a competitive global market; trend toward an information-based economy; and the transition from mass production to a customer-driven economy are all examples of these problems. SMEs need to be efficient, innovative, and competitive to compete in today's global economy by respond speedily, commitment to quality, and execute mass-customization. SMEs can take advantage of new information, communication, and technology (ICT) to better fit into their environment, build more cooperative inter-organizational ties, and compete in worldwide markets. SMEs are widely regarded as the driving forces behind long-term domestic economic development around the world. They are the foundation of economies, stimulating private property and entrepreneurial capacities that can adapt quickly to market shifts, create employment, diversify economic activity, and contribute to exports and trade due to their flexibility. Numerous SMEs are struggling to succeed, according to research, because of their persistent susceptibility to economic shocks, constrained domestic markets, and knowledge gaps (Alleyne et al., 2017). Growth barriers, notably distance and time among businesses and their customers, are eliminated with the aid of digital technologies. For SMEs in small, vulnerable economies, regional obstacles exacerbate those challenges compounded with their failure to create robust digital marketing tactics to successfully ensure sustainability.

Therefore, digital marketing is essential for SMEs to expand as it assists to boost sales, revenue, and overall growth as well as convert audiences into customers and generate additional revenue by selling their products or services. The chapter intends to:

ü Describe Digital marketing and explain in detail the various types of digital Marketing options available to SMEs
ü Highlights the benefits SMEs stands to gain adopting digital marketing
ü Pinpoint how the implementation of digital marketing by SMEs can translate into competitiveness and performance

MAIN FOCUS OF THE CHAPTER

Digital Marketing Defined

Digital marketing is described as a marketing strategy that uses the internet to communicate with a target market through various digital media platforms and channels (Pandey et al., 2020). Digital marketing entails a wide range of marketing strategies and technology that are employed to reach out to customers over the internet. Non-Internet channels that extend digital media, like television, smart phones (SMS and MMS), callback, and on-hold mobile ring tones, are included in digital marketing, and is distinguished from online advertising by its expansion to non-Internet outlets. Marketing, in its broadest sense, is the act of recognizing and satisfying customer demands. In the commercial world, it is a critical function since effective marketing activities generate inbound prospects and attract a huge customer base. Market orientation, product mix, and business environment analysis are all part of traditional marketing cycle. Digital marketing is a relatively contemporary discipline, despite marketing deep origins in business culture and history. Businesses began experimenting with novel marketing strategies as a direct outcome of digital technologies, which included widespread and pervasive usage of computers and cellphones, as a result, the term "digital marketing" was coined (Omar and Atteya, 2020). Currently, digital marketing is just as essential as traditional marketing strategies, if not even more. This chasm appears to be widening overtime, as several businesses shift their marketing budgets from traditional to digital. Overall, it is imperative for firms to create and implement successful digital marketing strategies. A business's digital marketing tactics encompass leveraging websites, search engines, blogs, social media, video, email, and other avenues to connect with customers.

Unlike traditional marketing, that is fixed and commonly characterized as "one-way" communication, digital marketing is a dynamic approach that is constantly evolving (Lanyi et al.,2021). In other words, customers are incapable of engaging with a brand using billboards or print advertisement, whereas digital marketing facilitates two-way interaction between brands and its current or potential customers. screen usage is at an all-time peak nowadays, this phenomenon is exploited by digital marketing, which promotes business products and services through the internet. Thus, businesses enhance the likelihood of their marketing initiatives of reaching their customers by targeting them where they devote the significant amounts of time. From small to large businesses, a diversified digital marketing strategy can yield massive economic benefits. In the nutshell, digital marketing is a broad phrase that pertains to a variety of methods for promoting a business 's interests to potential customers. A successful digital marketing plan typically combines a variety of techniques, depending on the objectives and goals of the business as it is not a one-size-fits-all activity.

The 5D's Of Digital Marketing

It is essential to consider what target audience engagements businesses need to fully comprehend to appreciate the significance of digital marketing in the 21st century in any firm. Digital technology is at the heart of today's digital marketing, which covers far more than just website and email interactions with target audiences. The 5Ds are the cornerstones of digital marketing world in totality and identify the various ways customers engage with brands and SMEs reach and learn from their audiences along with providing insights on market behavior culminating in the development and execution of superior marketing strategies

The 5Ds:

- Digital devices,
- Digital platforms
- Digital media
- Digital data
- Digital Technology

Digital Devices are the devices that people harness practically on daily basis and are leveraged to promote targeted market segment (Alshaketheep, 2020). Different gadgets such as computers, laptops, tablets, and smartphones, as well as Smart TVs, smart watches, gaming devices and variety of connected gadgets forming the internet of things (IoT) which are employed to access digital services and also exploited to connect with target audience. Digital devices generate, create, transmit, share, communicate, receive, store, display, or process data and are used to interact with webpages, browsers, and online applications. Mobile devices are employed more regularly than laptop or desktop computers. According to research, 91.62 percent of the worldwide population own a smartphone in 2022, and 80 percent of smartphone users performed online transactions in the previous six months. When developing a digital marketing strategy, businesses must take this into consideration.

Digital Platforms are a diverse set of platforms that are employed in digital marketing tactics in a variety of ways, including gathering information about potential customers, such as their preferences and prior purchases, creating a brand's profile on an online platform, and promoting products (Bauman, 2020). Platforms are increasingly emerging as competitive imperative and the cornerstone for innovative value creation, thus businesses who do not integrate them risk being left on the outside peeking in. Several digital platforms have become an integral element of the business environment, and no longer just the domain of digital natives (Denga et al.,2022b). Effective platforms are built on technological excellence, but they cannot exist solely in the realm of technology. They rely primarily on buy-in and feedback from other parts of the business, which is best organized through a cross-functional collaboration that establishes success benchmarks and monitors performance. To do so, businesses post offers and information about themselves in a style that motivates people to visit their website. YouTube, Google, LinkedIn, Twitter, and Facebook are examples of digital platforms for browsers and applications. Customers begin their purchasing experience on search engines like Google, Bing, and Yahoo. People also utilizes such search engines to learn further about their problems and to seek solutions.

Digital Media is any type of media that is created, viewed, distributed, modified, listened to, and preserved on a digital electronics device It refers to any medium of communication that incorporates several encoded machine-readable data formats to operate (Negoita et al.,2018). Data represented by a sequence of digits is regarded as digital, whereas media refers to techniques of transmitting or disseminating such data. Digital media is to any medium that broadcasts digitized information through screens and/or speakers (Kapoor and Kapoor, 2021). In today's digital world, identifying the optimal ways to reach target audiences and increase marketing efforts is critical. Digital media is a fantastic tool to accomplish this. With the rapid advancements in technology, one cannot ignore the impact that digital media has on our way of life. It has a significant impact on how we educate, entertain, publish, and engage with one another on a regular basis. As a result of this effect, the business world is being pushed out of the industrial era and into the information age by digital media. People no longer converse with pens on paper, preferring instead to use digital devices. Owned media, paid media, and earned media are the three categories of digital media (Bacon and Schieider, 2019). Owned media refers to digital marketing medium over which a firm has entire control, such as a branded website and social media accounts. For online businesses, enhancing and leveraging owned media activities typically improves the effectiveness of paid and earned media. Earned media or free media is the publicity generated through promotional efforts other than branding or advertising. It is exposure achieved through tactics other than paid advertising. Earned media is basically online word of mouth, and it takes the form of 'viral' trends, retweets, shares, mentions, reviews, referrals, and content picked up by third-party sites. A blend of excellent organic search engine rankings and content disseminated by the brand is typically among the most powerful propelling forces of earned media. The most important factors are usually first page rankings and high-quality content. Paid media is an external marketing initiative that entail a paid placement, such as pay-per-click advertising, branded content, and display adverts. Paid media entails the purchase of advertisement inventory on a digital media channel or publisher site to disseminate a brand's message and reach its prospective customers (Sadiku-Dushi et al.,2019). It comprises sponsored content to market brands' goods or services and is an important part of online businesses' revenue growth and building brand awareness. Businesses can unveil new products, launches, sale, as well as employ social listening which monitors customer comments on postings featuring the brand name on digital media. They can also more readily discuss and edit content, which boosts brand awareness and social interaction. Digital media includes online advertising, social media marketing, search engines, messaging, and email marketing.

Digital Data is made up of all the required and relevant information on prospective customers that can be leveraged to persuade them to purchase or at the very least check out a brand's products or services (Alleyne, 2017). Data is a key digital marketing's cornerstones; in an effort to get additional prospects, build customer engagement, and monetize investments, businesses must put data into meaningful information, comprehend, and fully exploit it. Data reveals important details about a customer's behaviors, such as their preferences, tastes, and line of thinking. When it comes to tailoring the consumer experience, digital data is critical, consumers love to feel special, and will leave if they are bombarded with information or advertisements not specifically tailored to them (Dumitriu et al., 2019. With digital data, it has become feasible to personalize each communication content as well as the experiences of customers. To boost the conversion rate, each piece of content can be targeted and made to have a stronger impact on users. Personalization is the secret to every customer's confidence. Digital data can also be used to determine which kind of digital content, such as social media posts, polls, videos, or articles, customers are better inclined to respond to. Data collection aids businesses in storing and analyzing customer information. This information database enables them in retargeting and subsequent marketing efforts. Contests, Point - of - service, website contact forms, surveys, App installations, and event sign-ups are just a few of the ways to obtain digital data (Ozturk, 2016).

Digital Technology encompasses all electronic tools, automated processes, technical equipment, and resources that generate, process, or store information (Blazheska et al., 2020). Digital technology's continuous influence on marketing methods might be considered as a positive as businesses can expand their reach and strive to enhance their brand in terms of customer experience and awareness by developing a more comprehensive digital marketing approach that extends beyond social media and digital advertisements (Kaufman and Horton, 2015. It focuses on creating interactive experiences across multiple platforms, allowing businesses to provide a superior customer experience and market themselves more effectively. Devices and even types of social media were not available just a few years ago due to the rapid advancement of technology. In terms of digital marketing, what does this indicate? Businesses must be flexible to innovation and equipped for when it occurs to keep pace with new technological advancements. Millions of businesses are now adopting technology-driven marketing to elevate their brand. Artificial intelligence, internet of things, big data, cloud computing and virtual reality are commonly utilized digital technologies (Arbiet, 2017). Artificial intelligence, to put it simply, is the creation and efficiency of machines that can perform human tasks with little opportunity for error. Artificial intelligence is being adopted in nearly every business. Businesses are now leveraging its capabilities to improve the efficiency of AI-driven operations. When it comes to marketing, artificial intelligence is assisting businesses in gaining a better understanding of their customers by providing tools such as predictive search, chatbots and recommendation engines. It also makes it easier to communicate with customers in various nations. According to estimates, the cloud computing industry's revenue is expected to reach \$482 billion in 2022. This statistic is a good indicator of cloud computing's growth and how businesses are embracing it. The capacity for team members to share, access, and control data stored on a shared cloud has made it much easier for them to interact and cooperate. Furthermore, digital marketing team employs cloud services like google drive. A workforce of graphic designers, bloggers, and developers spread across the globe can effortlessly communicate with one another to provide the finest service to customers (Redjeki and Affandi, 2021). This simplicity of sharing data aids businesses in effectively planning their marketing campaigns. Businesses employ big data insights to learn what their customers prefer to increase their effectiveness. This might assist them in planning a successful marketing campaign. With technological advancements, it is now easier than ever to obtain the finest piece of data, which aids in deeper understanding of customers. This suggests that the chances of a marketing campaign succeeding are relatively high. The Internet of Things (IoT) is an internetworking of physical devices, electronic machines, and other devices that allow for seamless data transfer over the network without requiring real-time interaction (Smith,2012). IoT is being leveraged by business owners to achieve a clearer understanding of customer psychology and the purchase process. Brands have gone a step further by providing customers with virtual reality experiences. Big businesses like Audi have already begun to employ this technology to provide a better experience for their customers by allowing them to drive a new Audi Q5 in a massive virtual sandbox, giving them a real-time driving experience. Hence, their marketing tactics appears to be more inventive, effective, and notable.

Four Pillars of Digital Marketing

Digital marketing is indisputably the greatest and most effective tool for reaching out to prospective clients and customers, with roughly half of the world's population utilizing the Internet (Yamin, 2017). Businesses of all kinds and sizes must possess a basic knowledge of how to promote in the digital realm or risk losing customers to competition. Digital marketing, which is delivered via an Internet-enabled device or platform, empowers businesses to communicate directly with their intended audience, such as prospects, customers, employees, and other enthusiasts. The four pillars of digital marketing: content, communication, community, and commerce are built on this interactive connection, which separates it from non-digital marketing. Businesses actively sought novel strategies to broaden and integrate digital marketing with offline, non-digital techniques known as integrated marketing as it progresses and expands. Certain facets of digital marketing, such as content marketing, social media, search, email, and ecommerce, have evolved into specialized forms of marketing. Astute brands will leverage this top four pillars of digital marketing architecture to offer excellent content, establish a community of like-minded members, and provide valuable products and services to match current market demands (Veldman et al.,2015).

1.*Content*: Customers have difficulties concentrating in a message-rich and stimulating environment. As a result, businesses must explore information free of promotional campaign and strive to either entertain or fulfill their customers' demands and wants which is accomplished through high-quality content. More effectively, content marketing draws a specific audience as well as search robots while also offering the backdrop for their marketing message. Content marketing is the creation and dissemination of meaningful, valuable content to existing and prospective customers through blogs, newsletters, white papers, social media posts, emails, videos, and other channels (Ritz et al.,2019) This content, when performed effectively displays expertise and demonstrates that a business values customers to whom it sells. Consistent usage of content marketing builds and maintains relationships with both prospective and existing customers. When a business is viewed as a partner invested in their success and a valued source of information and guidance, the audience is more inclined to choose it when an opportunity to purchase present itself. The five core content types: foundational, FAQ, cyclical, crowd pleaser, and long-playing are at the basis of a well-balanced content marketing strategy. This contains all of a business's content, information, and data. It adds "intangibles," as Harvard Business professor Theodore Levitt put it, to a product or service's offering. To reduce content development efforts, businesses must convert content into many pieces of content marketing, including long form, medium form, and short form versions to optimize reach and distribution. Owned, social, and third-party media can all be exploited to distribute digital content (Alghizzawi,2019a). Content serves as the foundation for a series of strategies, processes, and tactics aimed at achieving business and customer growth. By serving, converting, retaining, attracting, and engaging genuine customers with the most relevant content. As cornerstones of content, blogs, podcasts, video, and social media sites are employed

2. *Community:* Digital marketing is all about communities, businesses can communicate with their intended audience using digital platforms such as social media and connected devices to surmount objections and minimize concerns (Holliman and Rowley, 2014). For many businesses, social media serves as a platform for fostering community. Facebook, Twitter, LinkedIn, YouTube, and Instagram all provide a range of alternatives for businesses to create outposts where their customers can spend some time. These communities provide a forum for customers to express their needs, as well as an opportunity for businesses to respond and make them feel cherished (Lamberton and Stephen, 2016). While other forms of marketing, such as advertising and public relations, are primarily concerned with attracting new customers, communities' focuses on maintaining relationships with existing customers. Everyone benefits from establishing and sustaining connections and relationships with current consumers through in-person or online communities. Customers would feel valued and more motivated to devote their loyalty to the business, while businesses can gain vital feedback on their products and a grip of their interactive online presence. Modern consumers desire more than an impersonal, one-sided interaction with the products and services they utilize, thus community marketing is an extremely important strategy to utilize in conjunction with social media. They anticipate having access to a customer support team that can answer their queries and address their problems. Businesses may provide them with precisely that by developing an efficient community marketing strategy that bridges the gap among brands and their customers, resulting in a deeper loyal customer base and a superior overall reputation. Organic and sponsored communities are the two types of communities in digital marketing (Salam et al.,2021). Customers could organically begin communicating with one another without the assistance of the brand by creating their own brand-specific message boards or communicate through Twitter and other social media platforms. A brand-sponsored community in a digital marketing campaign entails developing the appropriate social media platforms that assist customers to communicate not just with one another, but also with the brand. Businesses may cultivate loyal customers who perceive their brand as an ally by monitoring customer engagement and embracing it seriously, reacting to queries and concerns, and offering useful first-to-know information to their customer base. When utilized appropriately, these types of community marketing will connect existing customers with one another and with the business, fostering a loyalty and satisfaction-based engagement.

3. *Communication*: Communication is a key component of digital marketing as it acts as a channel for messaging. It is aimed at predefined target segments involved in the process of communication (Arbiet, 2017). Every communication flow has the potential to request for information or a response from the market. The ease with which digital technologies facilitate the flow of information is also the fundamental drawback of digital communication. Digital communications include email, messaging, texting, social media, and feeds. There are three ways to convey digital message: one-to-many communication, one-to-one communications and many-to many communications

4. *Commerce*: A lot of shopping starts online, irrespective of where the purchase is done. Over 40% of customers start their shopping research on Amazon, search engines, and retailer websites (Bauman, 2020). This implies that in attempt for businesses to enter the consideration set, they must provide the basic forms of content that customers constantly seek features of the product, customer questions, how to, customer stories, and customer fit to prospects, customers, and purchase influencers. Commerce generates a lot of money with the aid of digital marketing, since it facilitates the acquisition of loyal customers and significant boost in brand recognition. Customers are no longer reliant on advertisements; instead, they rely on content or word-of-mouth to decide whether to purchase a product or service. They read all of the product reviews on all of the platforms where the product is featured. Digital marketing commerce fulfills the needs of consumers as interconnected gadgets evolve and consumers adapt ways they search and purchase (Durkin et al.,2013). Websites, email, search (including voice), Apps, social media, and review sites are all examples of digital commerce points of entry.

STRATEGIES FOR EXECUTING DIGITAL MARKETING

SMEs can promote their businesses leveraging a wide range of diverse digital marketing tactics. A thorough knowledge of each of these digital marketing techniques is required to harness the best features of each and build a robust digital marketing strategy.

Search Engine Optimization (SEO): The technique of boosting the quantity and quality of search engine web pages or a website is known as search engine optimization (SEO). Instead of direct or paid traffic, SEO focuses on unpaid traffic termed "natural" or "organic" outcomes. Unpaid traffic originates from a range of searches, notably picture, video, academic, and news searches, as well as industry-specific vertical search engines (Atanassova and Clark, 2015). SEO examines how search engine's function, the computer-programmed rules that regulate search engine behavior, what individuals are searching, the original browse phrases or keywords entered into browsers and which search engines are favoured by target market as digital marketing tactics. SEO is conducted because websites ranking higher in search engine results page (SERP). attracts increased traffic in form of "visitors" from the search engine. Those visitors have the propensity of becoming consumers. The purpose of SEO is to foster a business's website to score high in Google search results, culminating in more traffic from search engines. To do so, SEO strategists look for phrases and words that people use to research for information on the web and include such terms into their own content. Strategies to boost a site's SEO include content indexing, good link structure, and keywords and keyword targeting.

Pay-Per-Click (PPC): PPC also termed cost-per-click (CPC)is a model of digital marketing where advertisers pay a premium every moment one of their advertisements is "clicked". Basically, it is a technique of purchasing website views rather than having to "earn" them naturally (Taiminen and Karjaiuoto, 2015). One of the most prevalent types of PPC is search engine advertising which enables advertisers to negotiate for ad placements in sponsored links of search engines anytime people search for keywords relating to their business offering. Since the pay-per-click approach is mostly focused on keywords, businesses that implement it conduct research and analysis on the keywords that are most relevant to their products or services. Investing in suitable keywords can manifest in more clicks and, ultimately, higher profitability. The most prominent PPC advertising platforms are Facebook Ads, Google Ads, and Twitter Ads.

Content Marketing: The Content Marketing Institute defines content marketing as "a strategic marketing approach focused on creating and distributing valuable, relevant, and consistent content to attract and retain a clearly defined audience and, ultimately, to drive profitable customer action"(Foroudi et al.,2017). Content marketing is an approach that involves developing and disseminating relevant articles, podcasts, video, and other media to attract, engage, and retain a target market. This approach generates expertise, boosts brand awareness, and maintains a business in the forefront of people's minds when they need to purchase what a brand offers (Nguyen et al.,2021). Content marketing is a long-term tactic that emphasizes developing a robust relationship with a target market by consistently providing them with high-quality content that is highly valuable to them. Customers' devotion to the brand is already established when they make a purchasing decision, enabling them to purchase a specific product or brand and prefer it to the alternatives offered by competitors. Unlike one-off advertising, content marketing demonstrates that a business cares about its customers. To interact and market, content marketing is employed in the awareness, consideration, and closing stages of a sales cycle.

Social Media Marketing (SMM): The utilization of social networks and social media to promote brand's products and services is referred to as social media marketing (Tuten and Solomon, 2015). Businesses leverage social media marketing to engage with existing consumers and connect with prospective ones while also promoting their intended culture, mission, or tone. Several social media platforms feature data analytics tools incorporated, allowing businesses to monitor ad campaign progress, performance, and engagement. Utilizing SMM, businesses interact with a wide range of stakeholders, including existing and prospective customers, actual and potential workforce, reporters, bloggers, and the public in general (Andersonand Wikstrom,2017). Businesses adopt SMM to better enable customers and internet users update user-generated content such as online comments and customer reviews, also widely recognized as "earned media."

When it comes to leveraging social media as a marketing tool, there are two primary approaches: Passive approach- social media can be a good source of market data and a means to discover what customers have to say. Individuals contribute their reviews and suggestions of brands, products, and services on blogs, content communities, and forums. Businesses utilize social media to tap and analyze customer voices and opinions for marketing rationales. In this way, social media is a low-cost source of market intelligence marketers and managers can maneuver to track and respond to consumer-identified problems and identify market possibilities (Siamagka et al.,2015). Active approach- social media can be considered as a channel of communication targeting relevant and engaging demographics, featuring social media influencers and social media personalities as powerful consumer engagement techniques. This strategy is also termed influencer marketing, Influencer marketing enables brands connect with their intended audience in a highly authentic, genuine fashion by promoting their product or service through a handpicked set of influencers (Itani et al.,2017).

Affiliate Marketing: Affiliate marketing is a form of performance-based marketing where a business compensates affiliates for every" visitor" or customer they attract in through their own marketing initiatives and efforts (Tiago and Verisimo, 2014). Affiliate marketing is the activity of advertising another individual or business's products or services in return for a commission on the transaction. Affiliate marketers sign up for affiliate programs, search for credible affiliate products to offer, and then inform their audiences about them. It is an advertising technique in which a firm pays third-party publishers to drive traffic or generate leads to their products and services. Affiliates are third-party publishers who are paid a commission to create new methods to promote the firm (Eryigit, 2017). Unattached affiliate marketing, related affiliate marketing, and involved affiliate marketing are the three major categories of affiliate marketing.

Email Marketing: Email marketing is a technique of direct marketing strategy which involves sending customized, bulk emails to leads to educate and persuade them to perform a specific behavior, such as purchases (Skard and Nysveen, 2016). It connotes s ending email messages with the goal of improving a brand's relations with existing or previous customers, inspiring customer loyalty and repeat purchases, acquiring new customers or persuading current customers to make an impulse purchase, and spreading third-party ads. Typically, email marketing tactics aim to accomplish one or more of three primary goals: loyalty, trust, or brand awareness. Email marketing has been around for quite long time, and for valid reason: it is the most direct and successful way to engage with prospects, nurture them, and convert them into customers, consistently outperforming all other marketing platforms. Email marketing can be done in a variety of ways, which include direct emails and transactional emails.

SOLUTIONS AND RECOMMENDATIONS

The Benefits of Digital Marketing for SMEs

The emergence of digital has transformed the fundamental fabric of marketing in ways that few other things have. The pool of prospective customers for SMEs in specifically surged enormously, and their reach far broader than in the previous, analog era. SMEs, especially those with a limited budget, have a plethora of options when it comes to marketing online. Digital marketing may be done on almost any budget and scaled up or down as the business expands to fulfill their goals. With the surge in smartphone and internet usage, a business's visible online presence is critical to its growth and customer reach. Digital marketing is a potent technique for online marketing and driving organic traffic to a website. SMEs gain more visibility as a result of the increased traffic, which drives higher sales and profitability. Increasingly, consumers nowadays search for a product or service online, emphasizing the necessity of digital marketing for SME 's performance.

1.   Build Lasting Customer Relationships

Digital marketing is absolutely essential in today's world for establishing and strengthening consumer relationships. The rising demand from customers for wide range of service alternatives has necessitated SMEs to be online and reachable at all times. Maintaining interactions with previous, existing, and prospective customers is what customer relationship is all about (Denga et al., 2022b). SMEs that effectively manage their customer relationships build a customer experience tactic that boosts customer retention and facilitates prospective customer acquisition. Customer relations involves a wide range of activities that can be proactive or reactive, ranging from aiding customers with day-to-day inquiries to developing long-term practices that drive customer satisfaction. Digital marketing results in beneficial outcomes such as enhanced consumer retention, enhanced customer lifetime value, and robust customer relationships when implemented effectively. The customer's journey encompasses all of their interactions with a business. It's about how they interacted with the brand on digital and non-digital platforms. A digital marketing approach enhances the consumer experience by ensuring that all points of interaction are functional and effective (Omar and Atteya, 2020). This also makes it easier for customers to purchase from a brand. Businesses may communicate directly to their target market with tailored message through digital marketing, which develops trust. Customers make purchasing decisions when they trust brands. Businesses that recognize the value of developing customer relationships form an emotional bond with customers and retain them for a long time. Building customer relationships is critical for a variety of reasons, including more prospective leads and improved customer retention rates. To make it easier to understand, here are the topmost advantages of developing strong customer relationships:

- *Boost Customer Loyalty:* Customer loyalty is described as a continuous preference for a brand's products and services over those of rivals (Skard and Nysveen, 2016). Customers that are loyal to a single provider are not easily influenced by price or availability. They would rather pay a higher price for the same high-quality service and product they are accustomed to. Customer loyalty is earned when a firm consistently meets and exceeds the expectations of its customers, which are founded on trust. To put it another way, loyalty is defined by likability and the ability to trust a product or a brand. Customers who have faith in the brands with whom they do business are more inclined to purchase from them again in the future (Denga et al., 2022a). Customer loyalty is difficult to achieve, but it is worth the effort and investment. Closing deals with consumers is fantastic, but its far better to keep them thereafter, as customers who are retained are more inclined to make additional purchases or suggest the brand to others, both of which assist boost sales. It's a great method to keep customers coming back for more and keep competitors at bay. Digital marketing, unlike many in-store purchasing experiences, does not end at the point of sale. It goes above and above to ensure that a purchasing consumer becomes a brand ambassador. In essence, loyal consumers are individuals that make repeat purchases, are uninterested in competitors, interact with the brand across diverse channels, share feedback on how a business can enhance its offerings, and advocate for a brand by recommending its products or services to others.

  ○ *Enhance Customer Satisfaction:* In today's marketing, customer satisfaction is a crucial notion. Customer satisfaction is regarded as the most essential marketing indicator in several businesses, because it is a primary driver of customer loyalty and financial performance. Customer satisfaction is often characterized as a person's reaction when an offering satisfies his or her expectations (Ozturk, 2016). Businesses that succeed at customer relationships create an environment where customers can freely express their opinions. A robust consumer feedback loop is critical to the success of SMEs. As they can effectively measure their consumers' demands by collecting feedback from them on a regular basis. Customer satisfaction levels inevitably rise when customers interact with a brand that values their comments and strives to enhance their experience.

  ○ *Enhanced Customer Lifetime Value:* One of the most important metrics to track as part of a customer experience program is customer lifetime value (CLV). CLV is a metric for determining how important a customer is to a business, not only for a single purchase but for the entire relationship (Blazheska et al.,2020) CLV is crucial to measure as it a well-known fact that attracting and converting potential customer costs more than retaining existing customers, thus boosting the value of existing customers is a fantastic method to generate growth. A high CLV indicates that each customer will generate more revenue. SMEs should make every effort to create great customer relationships when it comes to customer success.

  2. **Create Brand Awareness**

One of the most compelling benefits for SMEs to embrace digital marketing is to raise brand awareness. Building brand awareness is important for businesses since it allows them to generate more leads and conversions subsequently. Prospective customers can learn more about a brand through digital marketing (Lanyi, et al.,2021) Brand awareness is a marketing term that refers to how well a product's name is recognized by consumers. Brand awareness is an important stage in marketing a new product or revitalizing an old one. In an ideal scenario, brand awareness would include the traits that set the product apart from competitors. This could include customers who know what a brand is known for, social media users who know the adverts will be funny when they recognize it in their feed, customers choose a brand over others, even if there are cheaper alternatives, and search engine users types a brand name or other branded terms into search. Products and services with a high level of brand awareness are highly effective in generating sales. When given a choice, consumers are likely to choose a well-known brand than an unknown one. Pay-per-click (PPC) advertisements, for instance, can boost brand awareness by 80%. The following are some of the benefits of leveraging digital marketing to develop a brand awareness:

- *Recognition, Visibility, and Reach:* The internet has a global reach; brands can reach a much broader audience than a sales force or a physical store can on a daily or weekly basis. When a larger number of individuals can access a brand, product or service, awareness will be higher than when traditional techniques of building brand awareness are utilized. Being present on different digital channels increases brand awareness. The stronger the brand recognition, the more likely to be the brand of choice for prospective consumers. At the end of the day, all SMEs strive to develop brands that are remembered (Salam et al.,2021)

- *Credibility and Trust:* A trustworthy brand is one that is immediately identifiable, established for a long time, has a devoted following or consumer base, and keeps its promises. When a business is considered as a well-known, recognizable brand, its credibility rises both inside its industry and among its customers. Loyalty and community grow in tandem with credibility and trust. The knock-on effect is that as word-of-mouth marketing grows, so does the simplicity of buying (Durkin et al.,2013). This translates to increased online traffic, conversion rates, engagement with blogs and social media, and possibly higher rates of media interest in the digital domain. This has a direct bearing on an SMEs competitive edge.

- *Build a Community:* Community building has become much less labour - intensive and considerably easier as a function of the evolution of digital marketing components like media platforms and marketing automated tools than it was utilizing traditional community building tactics (Hofacker et al.,2020). Another benefit is word-of-mouth marketing. Consumers value recommendations and comments from friends and acquaintances more than they would if they saw a product advertisement. Reach increases as a brand community begins to anticipate and discuss upcoming products, and this organic reach is considered as contributing significantly to the brands' credibility. Additionally, creating a brand community enables SMEs to thoroughly understand their target audience.

- *Strengthen Brand Equity:* Brand equity is a commercial value derived from how customers perceive and feel about a brand, as well as how successfully a brand captures market share and profit within its industry. (Tuten and Solomon, 2015). SMEs' paid advertising costs connected with acquiring traffic or awareness will be reduced if their brand equity is higher. Consumers prefer stronger brands over those of competitors, therefore stronger brand equity is connected to a higher market share. Hence, a likelihood of moving toward a premium pricing mechanism.

3.   **Improves Conversion Rate**

Conversion rate is becoming an essential component of savvy firms' digital marketing strategies considering only a fifth of SMEs are satisfied with their conversion rates. The conversion rate in digital marketing refers to the percentage of website visitors who complete a desired behaviour, such as purchasing a product or signing up for a service (Leeflang et al.,2014). Although it is extremely uncommon, the ideal conversion rate is 100%. The excellent news is that there are numerous ways SMEs can leverage to enhance conversion rate. These methods make up the conversion rate optimization process (CRO), which consists of three main steps: finding out why site visitors are not converting, creating changes to the website to remove conversion roadblocks, and evaluating these changes to ascertain if they are effective. SMEs can implement those stages by utilizing these tried-and-true CRO strategies to satisfy customers (Anderson and Wikstrom, 2017):

- *Increase Page Speed-* Online customers today have high standards, Notably, they demand rapid website loads. Prospective shoppers may hit the "back" button and choose a competitor instead if there is even a brief delay. In fact, if a website takes longer than three seconds to load, 40% of visitors might leave. SMEs must keep website visitors on their page longer enough for it to load to increase conversions. So, a quick technique to boost SMEs' conversion rate is to expedite website loading.
- *Write a Compelling Headline-* About 80% of website visitors will read the headline of an SME web page, but only 20% will read any further content. Therefore, for a high conversion rate, the headline's phrasing must be perfect (Redjeki and Affandi, 2021). Their value proposition should be made crystal clear in the headline. Every word in a headline is important, so experiment with a few different iterations to find which one works the best. It's incredible how changing a few words in a SME's headline may have a significant impact on conversion rate.
- *Focus on Designing an Action-Inspiring Call-to-Action (CTA)* – CAT on a web page is another essential element in conversion rate optimization. As they go straight to the bottom of the conversion funnel, these are some of the most crucial on-site conversion marketing components and offer a wonderful "shortcut" to boost conversion rates. The users may be persuaded to adopt this shortcut with a catchy CTA and convincing. Effective CTA are: (i) *Actionable* a CTA's goal is to motivate visitors to take action, therefore SMEs must employ wording that encourages action, such as "Download Now" or "Yes, Give Me That Discount!". (ii) *Preceded by persuasive copy-* The value of a SME's product, service, or promotional offer must be explained in the persuasive content that comes before a CTA button in order to persuade website visitors to click on it. Describe how offerings (whether they be for a good or service, downloaded material, or a free trial) can assist them. SMEs will be far more likely to click on the call to action and convert if they craft their content appropriately by utilizing language that speaks to the target audience's concerns and resonates with them. (iii) *One to a page-* Even though SMEs may have several offers to share with website visitors, it is best to keep CTAs to one per web page. They can then adjust everything on the page to direct website visitors to this CTA in this fashion. Multiple, ambiguous CTAs will not convert as well as a single, focused CTA. *Easy to find* - Website visitors won't click on a firm CTA if they can't find it. CTA must also be simple to find. Utilize bold colors to help it stand out and place it in a prominent location on the page to catch the viewer's attention (Kaufman and Horton, 2015).

- *Create a Convincing, Attention-Grabbing, Authority-Building Content:* Content marketing is the thing of the present and the future. Possessing useful leads and excellent traffic, which include potential customers who are truly enthusiastic in what a firm has to say and offers, stem from generating high-quality, pertinent content that is beneficial to visitors (Alghizzawi, 2019b). Quality content not only enhance conversion rates but also customer engagement, site dwell time, bounce rate reduction, and search rankings. The degree of trust in an SME's products or services improves when the content is both distinctive in its value and authoritative. The greatest mechanism to ensure that their users finally convert is to cultivate this trust. If there is a solid foundation of trust, it is much simpler to convert an internet user on a firm 's website. Nobody likes to disclose their credit card details to a dubious website. Similar to this, many people will be hesitant to make an impulse purchase if there is no social proof. As always, well-written, well-researched content will continue to rank higher on Google and other search engines in 2022. A firm's organic traffic and, thus, its lead pool for conversion is significantly driven by these rankings.
- *Use Video to Engage Audience:* Video marketing is one of the best tactics for boosting conversion rates. Videos are effective in increasing audience engagement and disseminating relevant insights (Nguyen et al.,2021). When a video is included on a landing page, conversion rates go up by 80%. It's a straightforward but efficient method for assisting SMEs in raising their website conversion rate. By employing videos, firms can make it easier for audience to learn useful information. Reading long passages of text is far more difficult than watching a 30-second movie. It integrates visual components with important information to provide viewers a satisfying experience. SMEs can add videos to their pages to increase conversion rates and achieve more success with their pages. To encourage audience participation with their website and CTA, this is a tried-and-true conversion rate optimization strategy.
- *Create Dedicated Landing Pages for Paid Advertising Campaigns:* Making specific landing pages for paid ad campaigns is one of the top conversion marketing techniques (Foroudi et al.,2017). Every advertisement ought to include a landing page that emphasizes the commodity or service being marketed. If a user clicks on an advertisement for a certain good or service, they expect to find information about it on the landing page. A small business' landing page shouldn't be its homepage or a page with details about other products. A firm gets greater outcomes when it creates targeted landing pages and aids audiences in maintaining their attention on the good or service they first searched for.
    4. Elevated Return on investment (ROI)

Effective digital marketing strategies enable SMEs increase their brand value and revenue; digital marketing ROI is a very important business statistic that SMEs ought not to be disregarded. Similarly, when compared to traditional marketing, it aids in creating a higher return on investment (Denga et al.,2022a). Digital marketing methods are simple to track, allowing SME to assess the influence on their target demographic. The key to a successful digital marketing strategy is to generate a steady stream of traffic that can be converted into leads. The higher the traffic generated, the faster the return on investment. SMEs must focus on strategies that provide a high return on investment (ROI) to be successful in digital marketing across many platforms. Here are five examples of the best digital marketing tactics with the highest return on investment to drive revenue growth in 2022:

- *Conversion Rate Optimization-* Firms always place high premium on increasing website conversions, and for good reason it has significant effect on revenue. Profits can rise by 10% with just a 1% improvement in conversion rates. By ensuring that their website is user-friendly and responsive, SMEs can advance conversion rate optimization and by also removing obstacles in the customer's journey from "visitor" to "lead," such as excessively detailed forms or popups that interfere with digital experience (Pandey et al.,2020).
- *PPC Services-* "pay-per-click" is a form of internet marketing in which advertisers are charged a fee each time one of their ads is clicked. In essence, it is a technique for attracting website visitors or clicks rather than attempting to "earn" them naturally (Alshaketheep, 2020). One of the highly successful digital marketing platforms now accessible is paid search. It provides an immediate option of reaching the target market for SMEs, generating leads and sales.
- *SEO- Search Engine Optimization*, or SEO, is a digital marketing tactic that enables it easier for customers of SMEs to locate them online (Denga et al.,2022a). It focuses on boosting their ranking in search engine results for commercially relevant keywords. This robust technique boosts organic traffic to an SME's website and increases the possibility that prospective customers will discover it, which increases ROI. SEO initiatives frequently have ROIs in excess of 700 percent, but over the course of long-term sales growth, unlike PPC campaigns, which are noted for their quick returns. One advantage of SEO is that it functions continuously in the background, easily generating profits.
- *Email Marketing-* An effective digital marketing method for promoting SMEs' products or services is email marketing. It is one of the greatest opportunities to connect with target audience, engage them, and forge relationships with both prospective and existing customers. More than 50% of consumers prefer to receive updates from brands they follow by email (Le et al.,2021).
- *Social Media Marketing-* This marketing technique involves creating and disseminating content on social media sites like Facebook, Twitter, and Instagram. Leads increased by 66 percent for SMEs with effective marketing efforts that produce 16 or more pieces of content each month (Denga et al.,2022a). This is because social media is one of the most successful tactics to quickly reach prospective leads. With billions of consumers actively utilizing social media, investing in social media marketing is a remarkably successful mechanism to boost brand awareness, drive sales, and engage with target audiences through social listening. Additionally, social media marketing is among the most economical strategies for marketing budgets.

Direct and Indirect Effects of Digital Marketing on SMEs Sustainable Performance

It is fundamental to differentiate between the construct of firm performance and the larger concept of organizational effectiveness. Venkatraman and Ramanujan (1986) proposed an insightful diagram of three interrelated concentric circles, the greatest of which represented organizational effectiveness. The medium circle, which represents business performance, and the inner circle, which represents financial performance, make up the broadest realm of organizational effectiveness. Other components of the organization's functioning that are covered by organizational effectiveness include the paucity of internal pressure and faults, involvement in legitimate operations, resources procurement, and achievement of established goals (Cameron, 1986a). strategic(operational) and financial outcomes are covered by firm performance, which is a subcategory of organizational effectiveness.

Firm performance is a broad phrase that can be interpreted in a variety of ways provided as it applies to performance, functioning, and the outcomes of an organization activities. Typically, firm performance refers to an organization's overall performance, which includes product and service production, operation of the various units, employees' performance, and overall outcomes of their efforts. Firm performance is an economic metric that measures how efficiently a business fulfill its targets by leveraging human capital and material resources (Le, 2005). The efficiency of utilizing business means during the manufacturing and consuming processes is also considered when evaluating firm performance. Firm performance refers to an organization's actual output or results as compared to its expected outputs, goals, and objectives. According to Richard et al. (2009), it comprises three distinct areas of firm outcomes: (i)financial: earnings, returns on assets, and returns on investment (ii) product market performance: sales, market share; (iii) shareholder return: total shareholder return, economic value added. The process of determining the efficiency and effectiveness of an action is known as firm performance and it depicts the relationship between output results and input resources employed while executing business activities (Truong & Tran, 2009). Thus, strengthening firm performance necessitates specific metrics to determine the action's effectiveness and efficiency; these evaluations are sub-categorized into financial and strategic performance indices (Santos & Brito, 2012; Tarute & Gatautis, 2014).

SMEs Financial Performance

Financial performance is a comprehensive evaluation of a firm 's entire position in categories such as liabilities, assets, equity, expenditures, revenues, and profitability. Financial performance is a subjective indicator of a firm's ability to generate revenue from its core mode of operation. The phrase is frequently employed as a broad gauge of a firm 's overall financial health over time. It is calculated using a variety of business-related algorithms that enable users to compute precise statistics about a firm's prospective effectiveness. Financial performance is analyzed by internal users to ascertain the well-being and status of their respective firms, among other parameters. Financial performance is assessed for external users to assess prospective investment prospects and whether a firm is worth their time. It is regarded an efficient measure of firms' business operations and profitability when matched to the benchmarks return rate corresponds to the risk-adjusted weighted average of capital investments (Al-Matari et al., 2014). According to Santos & Brito (2012), it has three key dimensions of financial performance: market value, growth, and profitability.

Market Value is the external evaluation and expectation of firms' future performance is expressed by market value. It encompasses a relationship to a firm's historic growth and profitability levels, while also incorporating anticipated changes in the market and competitive maneuvers (Santos & Brito, 2014). Some indices of market value include market-share growth, asset growth, net revenue growth, net income growth, employees' growth number, earnings per share growth, stock price improvements, stock price volatility, Tobin's-Q (market value/replacement value of assets), and market value added. Growth reflects a company's previous potential to expand its size which culminate to increased absolute profit and cash generation, as well as expanded economic scales and market strength. Earnings per share, stock price appreciation, dividend yield, stock price volatility, market value added (market value / equity), market-share growth, asset growth, net revenue growth, net income growth, and employee growth are all examples of growth indicators. Profitability measures a firm's historical capacity to generate returns. Return on assets, return on investment, net income/revenues, return on equity, economic value added, Tobin-Q, and other metrics are all profitability indicators.

SMEs Strategic Performance

The strategic performance of a firm is a broad performance construct encompassing all non-financial components (Santos & Brito, 2012). Customers' happiness, employee satisfaction, environmental performance, and social performance are the four primary variables. Customer satisfaction is a metric that assesses how effectively a firm's products or services satisfy the needs of its customers. It is among the most crucial measures of customer loyalty and purchasing intentions. As a result, it aids in the forecasting of earnings and economic growth. Customers' satisfaction raises their willingness to pay, and consequently the firm's value (Barney & Clark, 2007). Experts proposed it aa a primary variable for evaluating a firm 's performance. Mix of products and services, frequency of complaints, repurchase rate, new customer retention, overall customer satisfaction, and amount of new product or services released are all indicators of customer satisfaction. social performance entails the effective conversion of a firm's purpose into practice in accordance with established social values is defined as. It describes how well businesses fulfills their declared societal goals and adds value to the people it intends to reach. Social performance is linked to an SMEs performance in relation to indirect stakeholders such as communities and government entities. It can be viewed of as a technique to delight communities (Chakravarthy, 1986). Some indices of social performance include minority employment, the quantity of cultural and social projects, and the percentage of lawsuits filed by personnel, consumers, and regulatory bodies. Employee satisfaction is a broad phrase that describes how contented or satisfied employees are with factors like their jobs, work environment, and the companies they work for. It is a crucial statistic for determining firms general wellbeing. Employee satisfaction is one of the most important stakeholders' indicators as it translates into attracting and retaining personnel, as well as a lower turnover of employees (Chakravarthy, 1986; Anne, 2020). Indicatives of a firm's employee satisfaction include staff turnover, investments in employee growth and retraining, fair remuneration, appropriate bonus programs, career ambitions, and overall employee satisfaction.). Environmental performance depicts how the firm operates in terms of environmental improvement and recovery. It is a crucial determinant of firm success and contains indications such as the amount of environmental improvement or recovery completed projects, pollution levels, utilization of recyclable materials, reuse of residuals and degree of recycling and total of environmental lawsuits.

FUTURE RESEARCH DIRECTIONS

Most SMEs are oblivious of the possibilities of leveraging digital platforms in their marketing campaigns. It appears that there is a necessity to improve awareness of how the multiple channels available can interact with one another and ways they can benefit SMEs. Researchers can support SMEs in keeping up with advancements in this area. To discover the best environment for SMEs owners and managers to adopt digital marketing and close the digital divide with large firms, more study is required. Lastly, investigating alternative drivers for owners and managers who conduct their own digital marketing efforts, such as higher cognitive variables like technology acceptance.

CONCLUSION

SMEs need to focus on several things, including how the marketing era which has now transitioned into the Marketing 5.0 era is developing. Digital marketing tools minimizes costs and increases transactions to strengthen the performance of their firm, digital marketing performs an increasingly significant role in enhancing the performance of SMEs. Firms develop their brands by harnessing consumer feedback obtained from digital media channels (Massey et al., 2004). For contemporary SME to survival, establishing an efficient digital marketing strategy for creating a distinctive and compelling brand is still indispensable. As recent research asserts that implementing a successful digital marketing roadmap guarantees competitive edge.

REFERENCES

Alghizzawi, M. (2019a). A survey of the role of social media platforms in viral marketing: The influence of eWOM. *International Journal of Information Technology and Language Studies, 3*(2).

Alghizzawi, M. (2019b). The role of digital marketing in consumer behavior: A survey. *International Journal of Information Technology and Language Studies, 3*(1).

Alshaketheep, K. (2020). Digital Marketing during COVID 19: Consumer's Perspective. *WSEAS Transactions on Business and Economics*, 831–841.

Andersson, S., & Wikström, N. (2017). Why and how are social media used in a B2B context, and which stakeholders are involved? *Journal of Business and Industrial Marketing, 32*(8), 1098–1108. doi:10.1108/JBIM-07-2016-0148

Anne, M. W. (2020). Digital marketing strategies and the marketing performance of top 100 small and medium enterprises (SMESs) in Kenya. *International Journal of Research in Management & Business Studies, 7*(3), 26–31.

Arbi, K. A., Bukhari, S. A. H., & Saadat, Z. (2017). Theoretical framework for taxonomizing sources of competitive advantage. *Management Research and Practice, 9*(4), 48-60. http://mrp.ase.ro

Atanassova, I., & Clark, L. (2015). Social media practices in SME marketing activities: A theoretical framework and research agenda. *Journal of Customer Behaviour, 14*(2), 163–183. doi:10.1362/14753 9215X14373846805824

Bacon, D. R., & Schneider, A. B. (2019). Exploring sources of marketing knowledge for small business decision-makers. *Journal for Advancement of Marketing Education, 27*(1), 1–12. http://www.mmaglobal.org

Bauman, A. A. (2020). How do entrepreneurs use social media? *Journal of Marketing Development and Competitiveness, 14*(2), 40–48. doi:10.33423/jmdc.v14i2.2832

Blazheska, D., Ristovska, N., & Gramatnikovski, S. (2020). The impact of digital trends on marketing. *UTMS Journal of Economics (Skopje), 11*(1), 48–58.

Chakravarthy, B. S. (1986). Measuring strategic performance. *Strategic Management Journal, 7*(5), 437–458. doi:10.1002mj.4250070505

Consoli, D. (2012). Literature analysis on determinant factors and the impact of ICT in SMEs. *Procedia: Social and Behavioral Sciences, 62,* 93–97. doi:10.1016/j.sbspro.2012.09.016

Denga, E. M., Vajjhala, N. R., & Rakshit, S. (2022a). The Role of Digital Marketing in Achieving Sustainable Competitive Advantage. *Advances in Business Strategy and Competitive Advantage,* 44–60. doi:10.4018/978-1-7998-8169-8.ch003

Denga, E. M., Vajjhala, N. R., & Rakshit, S. (2022b). Relationship Selling as a Strategic Weapon for Sustainable Performance. In J. D. Santos (Ed.), *Sales Management for Improved Organizational Competitiveness and Performance.* doi:10.4018/978-1-6684-3430-7.ch005

Durkin, M., McGowan, P., & McKeown, N. (2013). Exploring social media adoption in small to medium-sized enterprises in Ireland. *Journal of Small Business and Enterprise Development, 20*(4), 716–734. doi:10.1108/JSBED-08-2012-0094

Foroudi, P., Gupta, S., Nazarian, A., & Duda, M. (2017). Digital technology and marketing management capability: Achieving growth in SMEs. *Qualitative Market Research, 20*(2), 230–246. doi:10.1108/QMR-01-2017-0014

Hofacker, C., Golgeci, I., Pillai, K. G., & Gligor, D. M. (2020). Digital marketing and business-to-business relationships: A close look at the interface and a roadmap for the future. *European Journal of Marketing, 54*(6), 1161–1179. doi:10.1108/EJM-04-2020-0247

Holliman, G., & Rowley, J. (2014). B2B digital content marketing: Marketer's perceptions of best practices. *Journal of Research in Interactive Marketing, 8*(4), 269–293. doi:10.1108/JRIM-02-2014-0013

Itani, O. S., Agnihotri, R., & Dingus, R. (2017). Social media use in B2B sales and its impact on competitive intelligence collection and adaptive selling: Examining the role of learning orientation as an enabler. *Industrial Marketing Management, 66,* 64–79. doi:10.1016/j.indmarman.2017.06.012

Kapoor, R., & Kapoor, K. (2021). The transition from traditional to digital marketing: A study of the evolution of e-marketing in the Indian hotel industry. *Worldwide Hospitality and Tourism Themes, 13*(2), 199–213. doi:10.1108/WHATT-10-2020-0124

Lamberton, C., & Stephen, A. T. (2016). A thematic exploration of digital, social media, and mobile marketing: Research evolution from 2000 to 2015 and an agenda for future inquiry. *Journal of Marketing, 80*(6), 146–172. doi:10.1509/jm.15.0415

Lányi, B., Hornyák, M., & Kruzslicz, F. (2021). The effect of online activity on SMEs' competitiveness. *Competitiveness Review, 31*(3), 477–496. doi:10.1108/CR-01-2020-0022

Le, D., Nguyen, T.-M., Quach, S., Thaichon, P., & Ratten, V. (2021). The Development and Current Trends of Digital Marketing and Relationship Marketing Research. In Developing Digital Marketing. Emerald Publishing Limited. doi:10.1108/978-1-80071-348-220211001

Leeflang, P. S., Verhoef, P. C., Dahlström, P., & Freundt, T. (2014). Challenges and solutions for marketing in a digital era. *European Management Journal, 32*(1), 1–12. doi:10.1016/j.emj.2013.12.001

Nguyen, T.-M., Le, D., Quach, S., Thaichon, P., & Ratten, V. (2021). The Current Trends and Future Direction of Digital and Relationship Marketing: A Business Perspective. In *Developing Digital Marketing*. Emerald Publishing Limited., doi:10.1108/978-1-80071-348-220211011

Omar, A. M., & Atteya, N. (2020). The Impact of Digital Marketing on Consumer Buying Decision Process in the Egyptian Market. *International Journal of Business and Management*, *15*(7), 120. doi:10.5539/ijbm.v15n7p120

Öztürk, R. G. (2016, January). A New Approach for Reaching the Customer of the Digital age: Cross-Device Advertising. *Journalism and Mass Communication*, *6*(1), 19–25.

Pandey, N., Nayal, P., & Rathore, A. S. (2020). Digital marketing for B2B organizations: Structured literature review and future research directions. *Journal of Business and Industrial Marketing*, *35*(7), 1191–1204. doi:10.1108/JBIM-06-2019-0283

Redjeki, F., & Affandi, A. (2021). Utilization of Digital Marketing for MSME Players as Value Creation for Customers during the COVID-19 Pandemic. *The International Journal of Science in Society*, *3*(1), 40–55. doi:10.54783/ijsoc.v3i1.264

Ritz, W., Wolf, M., & McQuitty, S. (2019). Digital marketing adoption and success for small businesses: The application of the do-it-yourself and technology acceptance models. *Journal of Research in Interactive Marketing*, *13*(2), 179–203. doi:10.1108/JRIM-04-2018-0062

Salam, M. T., Imtiaz, H., & Burhan, M. (2021). The perceptions of SME retailers towards the usage of social media marketing amid COVID-19 crisis. *Journal of Entrepreneurship in Emerging Economies*, *13*(4), 588–605. doi:10.1108/JEEE-07-2020-0274

Santos, J. B., & Brito, L. A. L. (2012). Toward a subjective measurement model for firm performance. *Brazilian Administration Review*, *9*(6), 95–117. doi:10.1590/S1807-76922012000500007

Siamagka, N. T., Christodoulides, G., Michaelidou, N., & Valvi, A. (2015). Determinants of social media adoption by B2B organizations. *Industrial Marketing Management*, *51*, 89–99. doi:10.1016/j.indmarman.2015.05.005

Skard, S., & Nysveen, H. (2016). Trusting beliefs and loyalty in B-to-B self-services. *Journal of Business-To-Business Marketing*, *23*(4), 257–276. doi:10.1080/1051712X.2016.1250591

Smith, K. T. (2012). Longitudinal study of digital marketing strategies targeting millennials. *Journal of Consumer Marketing*, *29*(2), 86–92. doi:10.1108/07363761211206339

Tiago, M. T. P. M. B., & Veríssimo, J. M. C. (2014). Digital Marketing and Social media: Why bother? *Business Horizons*, *57*(6), 703–708. doi:10.1016/j.bushor.2014.07.002

Tuten, T. L., & Solomon, M. R. (2015). *Social Media Marketing* (2nd ed.). Sage.

Veldman, C., Van Praet, E., & Mechant, P. (2015). Social media adoption in business-to-business: IT and industrial companies compared. *International Journal of Business Communication*, *1*(23), 1–23.

Yamin, A. B. (2017). Impact of digital marketing as a tool of marketing communication: A behavioral perspective on consumers of Bangladesh. *American Journal of Trade and Policy*, *4*(3), 117–122. doi:10.18034/ajtp.v4i3.426

Yasmin, A., Tasneem, S., & Fatema, K. (2015). Effectiveness of Digital Marketing in the Challenging Age: An Empirical Study. *International Journal of Management Science and Business Administration*, *1*(5), 69–80. doi:10.18775/ijmsba.1849-5664-5419.2014.15.1006

ADDITIONAL READING

Kaufman, I., & Horton, C. (2015). *Digital Marketing: Intergating Strategy and Tactics with Values* (1st ed.). Routledge.

Ritz, W., Wolf, M., & Mc Quitty, S. (2019). Digital marketing adoption and success for small businesses: The application of the do-it-yourself and technology acceptance models. *Journal of Research in Interactive Marketing*, *13*(2), 179–203. Advance online publication. doi:10.1108/JRIM-04-2018-0062

Taiminen, H. M., & Karjaluoto, H. (2015). The usage of digital marketing channels in SMEs. *Journal of Small Business and Enterprise Development*, *22*(4), 633–651. doi:10.1108/JSBED-05-2013-0073

Tarutė, A., & Gatautis, R. (2014). ICT impact on SMEs performance. *Procedia: Social and Behavioral Sciences*, *110*, 1218–1225. doi:10.1016/j.sbspro.2013.12.968

KEY TERMS AND DEFINITIONS

Customer Life Value: Is the overall value of a customer to a company throughout the duration of their relationship.

Digital Marketing: The utilizing of internet and other digital communication channels to promote brands to reach prospective customers This comprises text and multimedia messages as well as email, social media, and web-based advertising as a marketing channel.

Firm Performance: An economic metric that measures how well organizations are able to leverage both human and material resources to achieve their goals.

Pay per Click: Is a technique for online advertising that is designed to increase website traffic. When an ad is clicked, a publisher typically a search engine, website owner, or network of websites gets paid.

Return on Investment: A prominent financial statistic for assessing the likelihood of profiting from an investment.

Search Engine Optimization: Enhancing a website to make it more visible when users search for goods or services relevant to a company on Google, Bing, and other search engines.

Small and Medium Enterprises: Autonomous, non-subsidiary businesses with fewer workers than a specific threshold.

Social Media Marketing: The usage of social media platforms where people create social networks and share information by building a company's brand, boosting sales, and increasing website traffic.

Chapter 12
Trends in E–Commerce During COVID–19:
A Case of UAE

Rajasekhara Mouly Potluri
iD https://orcid.org/0000-0002-6935-1373
Providence College of Engineering, India

Sophia Johnson Thomas
iD https://orcid.org/0000-0003-0912-634X
Providence College of Engineering, India

ABSTRACT

E-commerce is one of the powerful tools in the business environment today. During the COVID-19 pandemic, various transactions like purchasing and selling products and services over e-commerce platforms hiked enormously. At the same time, it posed challenges for businesses to meet consumers' increased demands and expectations. The UAE consumers are enjoying the latest trends in e-commerce, like augmented reality to enhance the reality of online shopping, artificial intelligence, voice search, on-site personalization, chatbots, mobile shopping, multiple payment options, headless, and API-driven e-commerce. This chapter examines the trends and challenges of e-commerce posed by COVID-19 in the UAE and strategies to win the online marketplace.

INTRODUCTION

Electronics commerce is the most influential and vibrant marketing tool in the current business map of the world. From a different point of view, the application of this marketing tool more extensively came into existence during the current pandemic because of lockdowns and other restrictions imposed worldwide in the last two-plus years. As a result, the UAE's widespread application of e-commerce platforms, such as Amazon, Noon, Ounass, Sharafdg, etc., has greatly grown its online retail business. Electronics commerce and electronic business are commonly interchangeable words in the business world, which

DOI: 10.4018/978-1-6684-5727-6.ch012

is imperatively powered by the Internet. For example, e-tail is recently widely applicable to online retail shopping transactional processes. The simple meaning of e-commerce is buying and selling goods and services or transmitting funds or data over an electronic network, primarily the Internet. These transactions occur as business-to-business (B2B), business-to-consumer (B2C), consumer-to-consumer or consumer-to-business. E-commerce has changed the way people shop and consumes their requirements. Most people in many parts of the globe are turning to their computers and smart devices to order goods, which can be tremendously enhanced during these pandemic days. This changing trend in the purchasing behavior of the public has forced many retailers to introduce online marketing or e-commerce in their marketing strategy, irrespective of their magnitude. For this changing trend, the existing pandemic situation and aftermath movement restrictions are the major and notable reasons widely considered by many businesses.

The most prominent country in the Middle East and Gulf Cooperation Council (GCC) countries, the United Arab Emirates, a city of malls, also enormously moved from traditional brick-and-mortar retailing to e-commerce due to the absolute development of all kinds of ways and means to design and develop online platforms. Because of all these efforts of the Federal and Emirati governments, the UAE is the e-commerce leader among GCC countries, where the market jumped by 53 percent in 2020 with a record of $ 3.9 billion in e-commerce sales, which constituted 10 percent of total retail sales (International Trade Administration, 2022) and forecasts to generate $ 8 billion in sales by 2025.

BACKGROUND

Though much of the dramatic growth in e-commerce was a reaction to Covid-19, and almost 100% of the UAE population enormously access the Internet and mobile phone access, consumers report an increased trust in purchasing products online. Undoubtedly, the current pandemic propels the UAE's e-commerce growth, which is a good sign, especially for the UAE where gradually reopening its economy and slowly lifting restrictions under strict precautionary safety and health measures. Even the middle-east's biggest retailers Carrefour and Lulu Group launched online shopping portals in the UAE. At the same time, e-government services are migrating to online platforms during the pandemic to offer their services, such as utility billing, traffic services, licensing, visa issuance, etc. The London-based professional services multi-national company Deloitte reiterated that the proliferation of e-commerce has drastically changed the global retail market, and significant drivers of e-commerce growth in the Middle East, especially in the Gulf region, would be a high spending potential-owing to a high per capita income, developed transport logistics networks, rising internet penetration levels and a growing tech-savvy youth population (Deloitte, 2018).

Yuldashev (2017) outlined the changes on the horizon for the UAE's online marketing and emphasized that there is no secret that e-commerce is gaining immense popularity by the minute in the UAE and through the GCC, with the retail sector witnessing a steady shift from conventional to a novel mode of shopping. E-Commerce platforms have become a mammoth trend among UAE businesspeople. The industry was anticipated to grow to $10 billion in 2018. The consequences of development in the sector have translated into various spillover effects, such as new goods and services, higher quality, and advanced technology. Before the pandemic, the UAE was already well established in digital trade (Andreev et al., 2020). The book chapter comprehensively presents the e-commerce situation before and after the pandemic with its significance in the UAE, trends, challenges during the current uncertain conditions, and unique strategies to be implemented to popularize e-commerce in the region. The pandemic in the last two years forced the world corporate sector, including governments looking to engage the world consumers, to invest in their e-commerce mode of business and boost innovation for in-shop experiences to keep them returning to the showrooms.

MAIN FOCUS OF THE CHAPTER

E-Commerce and its Significance

The term e-commerce was first coined and employed by Dr. Robert Jacobson, Principal Consultant to the California State Assembly's Utilities & Commerce Committee, in the title and text of California's Electronic Commerce Act, carried by the late Committee Chairwoman Gwen Moore (D-L.A.) and enacted in 1984. E-commerce typically uses the web for at least a part of a transaction's life cycle, although it may also use other technologies such as e-mail. Typical e-commerce transactions include the purchase of products (such as books from Amazon) or services (such as music downloads in the form of digital distribution such as iTunes Store) (Statista, 2016). There are three areas of e-commerce: online retailing, electronic markets, and online auctions. E-commerce is supported by electronic business (Subramani & Walden, 2001). The existence value of e-commerce is to allow consumers to shop online and pay online through the Internet, saving the time and space of customers and enterprises, significantly improving transaction efficiency, especially for busy office workers, and saving a lot of valuable time (Winclaw, 2013).

The corporate world keenly observes these growing numbers of e-commerce initiatives and progressively makes persistent decisions for substantial investments mandatory to participate in the budding online market. After identifying shopping as a weekend pleasure with their families, most people have shopped online for something at some point. The pandemic situation and aftermath movement restrictions again pushed all most all people towards e-commerce. So, it goes with saying that e-commerce is everywhere after Covid-19. Many companies in the e-commerce industry have gone through numerous changes since their inception, resulting in a great deal of evolution and creating a virtual marketplace for goods and services that consumers can easily access. Many novel technologies and an extensive dot. com boom have been propelling to make it easier for people and industry to get reciprocal and safest online transactions. Nowadays, people can connect with businesses through smartphones and other devices and by downloading apps to make purchases. The introduction of free shipping, multiple payment options, and safe and reliable online transactions has enhanced the confidence of both businesses and consumers by reducing all kinds of costs. Other supply-chain-related hick-ups helped e-commerce increase its popularity. E-commerce shows its significant mark on the lifestyles of all sorts of consumers irrespective of their cultural, social, geographical, demographical, and psychological aspects consumers throughout the globe.

E-commerce offers absolute convenience to place an order 24 hours a day, seven days a week, with an increased selection of the required goods and services. Even businesses can establish their startups with minimal cost with this kind of business model and sell their products and services throughout the globe with great ease to retarget customers. The crucial giant in the middle-east region, the UAE and its consumers are the most connected in this part of the world with 91 percent of Internet penetration, 66 percent smartphone penetration, 99 percent social media penetration, and on average here, people spend seven hours and forty-nine minutes daily in the Internet (Visa, 2020). The world wide web is recognized as one of the fastest growing publication mediums offering a broad range of growth opportunities for small and medium-sized enterprises (Potluri & Vajjhala, 2018). In most of the current emerging global economies, e-commerce has progressively become an emotional component of business strategy and a solid catalyst for economic development in a comprehensive manner. E-commerce has a great history since it was invested in May 1989, when Sequoia Data Crop introduced Compumarket, the first internet-based system for e-commerce (Digital Marketing Community, 2022). The increasing spread of e-commerce could reduce the pressure on inflation through increased competition, cost savings, and changes in sellers' pricing behavior. In the current pandemic days, irrespective of the magnitude of the business, from startups to small and medium-sized companies, large corporates can benefit from their online store, where they can sell their products and services. As we said earlier, the speedy influx of novel and innovative technology in the selling and buying experience has driven businesses and consumers of all ages to expect a convenient and connected experience that impeccably supports their daily routine lives.

Buekelaer (2020) penned an exciting article about the augmented opportunities for economies as Covid-19 halts all physical buying. She listed a handful of reasons economies need to shift their business online and the challenges they may face in the entire procedure. First, firms and companies must offer promotional products and discounts to start their online operations. Further, she states that consumers in the market should have balanced information about the company or business's new operations. This means that customers should be aware that their favored store offers their choice of products online; the store can make its operations more well-organized through formerly achieved market research. By prominence, the most in-demand products, more of its consumer base can be adequately targeted, and sales can be increased. In addition, customers should be prioritized in this pandemic by considering the financial constraints they are presently facing. That can be done by offering customers extendable payment invoices or payments after regular intermissions. This allows the company or store to reinstate consumer assurance as much of it was lost due to the reduction in employment and income. One more inference for the e-commerce market in UAE is the disruption of supply chain networks. A report published in the context of the global economy stated just how crucial it has become for economies to expand their supplier base (Ranney et al., 2020).

Nair (2020) informed of an unusual spike in online consumer demand after the commencement of Covid-19 in diverse categories of products. Likewise, Mansoor (2020) wrote an article that states the Dubai-based Majid Al Futtaim financial giant, which operates 24 shopping malls, stated an almost 60% rise in the demand for goods and services acquired through e-commerce facilities. Global companies have also experienced a similar surge in the online market and have had to make vital changes to their company operations. As per the extensive study by KPMG (2020), retailers worldwide have started to augment advanced technologies in their business operations to facilitate the consumer more effectively through virtual reality systems and AI. Retailers accumulate psychometric information and analytics to deliver the user a more customized and distinctive experience. For example, the product preference of the user is noted, and only comparable or pertinent products are shown to upsurge sales and amplify the reduced consumer number. Moreover, retailers have delivered users with a VR system to assess the effect more clearly and adequately.

The pandemic experience has revealed that companies need to become nimbler to familiarize themselves with abrupt fluctuations in consumer behavior. They must become more robust in the face of any expansion or drop in demand. This means that company procedures must be flexible enough to absorb shocks like the pandemic, says Mr. Chowhan. Staff needs to use more "design thinking," a customer-centered iterative process for problem-solving and innovation. Part of this involves working closely with consumers to gain real-time insights into their behavior and using suitable technology to support agile strategies. The second major lesson is the need for more innovation to engage consumers. This refers not just to creative online delivery but to in-store experiences too. "Innovation is not a choice anymore. You must innovate continuously, you need to do things far better and far faster," Mr. Chowhan says. Ms. El Khatib echoes this sentiment: "With the pandemic, we realized that we must speed things up and rush into offering more facilities on our online platforms. [But just as is important is] experience, experience, experience—physical spaces are here to stay." The ability to strike the right balance between online and in-store shopping experiences will determine which retailers succeed in the post-Covid era (The Economist Intelligence Unit Limited 2020).

In the current situation, like pandemics and most uncertain situations, the entire business world must develop dexterities to maintain a perfect balance between the effects of those uncertain conditions and its outcome. Only those companies who can develop skills to strike a balance between these situations survive in the highly competitive business environment because they can't manage macro environmental elements; instead, they can adjust their plans, policies, programs, procedures, and budgets. The world e-commerce industry has identified incredible growth in recent years. It is expected to keep growing, and the trend is more upward during and after pandemic situations in the market. According to official statistics, the number of digital buyers worldwide will grow to 2.14 billion in 2021 compared to 1.32 billion in 2014. This is a 62 percent increase in just four years. In 2019, e-commerce was responsible for around US$ 3.5 trillion in sales (Rochette, 2020). Covid-19 and global lockdown situations have inevitably changed how the corporate field looks at retail experiences of the markets and has changed consumer experiences and expectations entirely. Especially in the case of the UAE, the entire market relies heavily on the presence of tourists and due to diverse restrictions combined with the increase of retailers and service providers moving their offerings online means that the stage is firmly set for e-commerce to grow over the coming months and years (Mirza et al., 2020). According to Kearney, the results back up forecasts of the UAE's e-commerce market growth from US$10 billion in 2021 to US$17 billion in 2025. 74% of online shoppers said they would spend more online shopping in 2022. 19% expected to pay the same as in 2021, and just 6% expected to spend less (Zawya, 2022).

Trends of E-Commerce: Before and After the Pandemic in the UAE

When the COVID-19 pandemic began to affect global markets since its inception in the first quarter of 2020, it became clear that it would test the resilience and performance of a rapidly growing e-commerce sector in the Middle East and North Africa (MENA) region in general and the UAE. This paper closely examines how the pandemic impacted the growth and resilience of the e-commerce space in this crucial gulf country and its market. Before the pandemic, UAE's e-commerce sector was one of the fastest growing in the world. The UAE's digital economy before COVID-19 contributed 4.3 percent to the country's gross domestic product (GDP). In addition, the e-commerce industry in the country is set to reach $62.8 billion by 2023, according to the Dubai Future Foundation (Wamda-MIT Legatum Center, 2021). Today, more than eighty percent of young Arabs shop online frequently, compared to 71 percent in 2019. The coronavirus was the defining disastrous event that happened in 2020, which has severely affected the entire globe. Most countries, people, and corporates attempting to stymie the covid-19's impact has interrupted, distinguished, and repurposed their business and consumer practices. Even with a series of persistent efforts of many governments and companies, the e-commerce industry has identified changes in its regular operations with novel recommendations to advance in the current and future landscape.

In the last two years, UAE saw substantial declines in footfall and stricter controls imposed. Unfortunately, many shops persistently closed and finally became "permanently closed" due to a lack of online business transactions. This led to an opportunity for e-commerce in the country, as consumers switched to buying their requirements online. The pandemic resulted in a shift that accelerated this projected growth as early reports indicated that e-commerce in the UAE is winning the pandemic. With the dramatic and tremendous growth in the sector, e-commerce presents opportunities to transform the primary ways that economies work by reshaping consumer preferences and conventions in all most all sectors of the business. The present tech-driven renovation in the e-commerce sector has the power to shape ecosystems that invite small, medium, and local businesses into the value chain. Before the pandemic, the most identified e-commerce trends in the UAE were a shift towards localization, cross-border e-commerce, the effect of social media on e-commerce, technology advancement, digitalization in food delivery, and innovation in the e-commerce payments space (Deloitte, 2018).

In contrast, the impetus of e-commerce can drive the progress required in the country. Now only doubt in businesses' minds is whether the change in e-commerce due to the pandemic is a temporary or permanent momentum. Undoubtedly, Covid-19 propelled the growth of an already thriving e-commerce sector in the country, and within a short time, businesses that delayed digitalization shifted to meet consumers online. The industry also identified new consumers who came on board without much effort to access and purchase its indispensable requirements. Before the pandemic, e-commerce was the cornerstone of the concept of entrepreneurship, particularly in the MSME sector in the UAE, and has served a critical role in enabling the overall startup ecosystem. However, the country is occasionally panned for lack of innovation and a substantial dependence on the consumption-driven business model. Since its inception and before the pandemic, most e-commerce players in the country have progressively built the digital and physical infrastructure necessary to operate in the region. As a result, many startups in fintech and logistics would have struggled to manage and scale. Based on the current positive trend in the e-commerce sector, many investors who felt some sluggishness earlier are now ready to invest substantially in the region. Like other countries, the UAE is also recovering from the pandemic. Even many firms that opened their showrooms are still doing their business online. The e-commerce industry's quickening was also fueled by consumers' nervousness over physical contact like the condition covid-19 has created. Specifically in the UAE, many businesses who opted for an e-commerce mode of operations also received tremendous support from the supply-chain companies, supported by the Department of Economic Development's decision to exempt the e-commerce sector from the restrictions placed on commercial activity during Dubai's lockdown. All these efforts introduced, and support received from the authorities; the industry noticed a whooping success with a 176 percent rise in April 2020 compared to April 2019. The upsurge was also catalyzed due to the UAE's pre-existing presence in the e-commerce market when, in December 2019 alone, the country's e-commerce dissemination was at 4.2% - the highest in the MENA region compared to Saudi Arabia, which stood at 3.8%, and Egypt at 2.5%. The market has also been growing by 23% annually for the past three years. According to market research company IPSOS, the MENA region is expected to hit USD 200 billion by 2022. These prevailing situations, like marketing growth rate, strong government backup, changing consumer attitudes, mainly Gen Z and Gen Y, and solid support from the supply-chain industry, solidified by the UAE government's vision of prioritizing digital commerce. Specifically, as said by the academicians Potluri and others (2022), Gen Z – the first generation of true digital natives, is extensively enhanced throughout the globe and even in the Middle East and are more tech-savvy young generation who are crucial customer segment to prefer e-commerce.

Furthermore, a joint study conducted by the Dubai Economy and Visa authorities shows these growing strides because e-commerce allows for easy shopping and diverse purchases (Azman Free Zone, 2020). Along with the above, there is an enhanced trust in digital payments with the strong backup of enactments introduced by the Federal and Emirati governments, which is further emphasized by 30 percent of the UAEs population is made of digital-savvy millennials and Gen Z. This was the pre-pandemic situation of the e-commerce sector in the UAE. Moreover, the authorities predicted that the segment would multiply as robust online activities are expected to be sustained post-Covid-19 crisis. The Telecommunications Regulatory Authority (TRA) is the primary regulatory body regulating electronic transactions and commerce in the UAE. The TRA issued 196 licenses during May 2020 to the e-commerce retail business sector-the highest number of permits to be issued in a sector and observed a 300 percent hike in consumer demand recorded in the first five months of 2020 (Gowling Wlg, 2020). The Dubai Economy extraordinarily issued 943 trader licenses in Dubai to new businesses in the first three months of 2020 (a 179 percent increase from the first three months of 2019, and the UAE retail e-commerce market reached a record $3.9 billion in 2020, a 53 percent increase driven by the Covid-19 led digital shift (Emirates News Agency-WAM, 2022). Even though the e-commerce mode of marketing in the UAE is potentially lucrative, it also has given some unexpected setbacks, mostly limited customer service, lack of instant gratification, inability to touch and feel products, too much reliance on technology, and consumer wariness of the safety of e-commerce system, inadequate logistics, lack of unified address system, and higher competition (Investopedia, 2022). The pandemic is accelerating retailers' plans for digital transformation. Still, not all retail businesses can move online rapidly, offering scope, governments, and e-commerce platforms to step in with support. Post Covid-19, shoppers are returning to the malls but not at the same levels as before, as online shopping habits will have become more routine (Dubai Future Foundation, 2021). In a nutshell, 49 percent of more consumers have been shopping online, out of which 61 percent are using cards or digital wallets instead of opting for cash on delivery since the virus outbreak. At the same time, the post-Covid-19 outlook is that 43 percent will continue using contactless payments; 48 percent prefer digital payments online over cash on delivery for their e-commerce purchases (Visa, 2020).

Economies had to shut down primary operations and businesses to contain the infectious disease outbreak. Even so, the UAE has shown an enormous state-of-the-art capability to fight the financial crisis efficiently in a recessionary period. Although digitalization was becoming a budding trend in the UAE, the onset of COVID-19 acted as a catalyst and accelerated the call to action. E-Commerce became popular due to the need to do transactions during lockdown (Kim, 2020). Seetharaman et al. (2017) also reiterated the same. They said that e-commerce is now one of the most significant activities carried out over the Internet. Transaction costs include policing and search costs, which can be addressed by creating more awareness and holding various products. Therefore, regulations in favor of e-commerce retailers will motivate them to enter the market. It was also observed that the prevalence of mall culture is one reason there is no rapid growth in online retailing. So, the pandemic did nothing but speed up the progress of e-commerce in the UAE. UAE was strong-minded to be a powerhouse and the fastest growing Middle Eastern player in e-commerce (Seetharaman et al., 2017). Dubai has shown exclusively promising statistics regarding attracting online businesses and future start-ups. The UAE's e-commerce sales were estimated at $16 billion in 2019, and the expected growth rate is almost 25%, the highest in the entire MENA region (Ahmad et al., 2019). Similar kind of growth has been achieved by the sensational country UAE in the world either on its own or the pace of the transition also tremendously increased due to the pandemic. That has mainly been due to the security and framework UAE has implemented for making online transactions simple and easy. The market penetration rate of the UAE was ranked at 4.2% in 2019, followed by KSA's 3.8%. The convenience factor in e-commerce increased tremendously during the pandemic, not only in the composition of purchases but also in preferred retail channels. The residents of UAE have been moving to online shopping for years because of its convenience. Still, the trend enhanced during the lockdown, when it became the only option available for many products (The Economist Intelligence Unit Limited, 2020).

SOLUTIONS AND RECOMMENDATIONS

E-Commerce in the UAE: Post Pandemic

The terrific coronavirus pandemic evidently signals that e-commerce is a crucial business tool for consumers in times of health-related crises. Moreover, the fluctuations activated by Covid-19 can be a significant economic driver, particularly for small businesses. The COVID-19 pandemic could trigger further digitization of society and develop policies and rules to support online trade, given the digital economy's central role during this pandemic with the support of all the business stakeholders. At the commencement of the COVID-19 pandemic, governments instituted digital payments to reduce physical contact and the spread of coronavirus and successfully transformed their economy into a trust-based digital economy. Whenever customers identify the kind of confidence build-up digitalization in trading or e-commerce, without hesitation, they have shown great tremendous interest in the purchase of their requirements by using electronic and digital payments. As many countries reopened their economies after the pandemic, they never thought about eliminating the digital and electronic payment methods because the governments firmly created trust by implementing flawless policies. Even the UAE has successfully reinforced the same with its trust-based customer-friendly digitalization policies and enhanced the efforts to invite additional investments into the e-commerce sector.

The shown market confidence toward digital payments allowed the UAE federal government and seven Emirati governments to introduce more efficient and transparent business operations and accelerate the scale of technology-based ventures. The trivial setback in the application of mobile or electronic payments since the pandemic's beginning does not contradict e-payments' potential to be a great enabler. Suppose the UAE government investigates this issue. In that case, there will be a further chance to accelerate the adoption of mobile payments, which can bring other benefits like consumer demand for better and improved Internet and the creation of systems of digital identifications. At the same time, the UAE government also initiated efforts to reinforce market trust by implementing a customer fraud protection unit and law enforcement that can reassure customers of their complaints. During the pandemic, entrepreneurs and established companies experienced the uncontrollable external environment impact on their business operations. Therefore, these two needs more significant support from the governments after Covid-19 to survive the losses in the last two years and foster entrepreneurship by providing a solid infrastructure, especially for MSMEs, to access tools, resources, and markets. Most businesspeople in any part of the world always try to take back their investments as early as possible with the support of large markets.

The government here must take the initiative to create sizable geographic markets and customer base, and solid support for startups. Forming integrated customs would open e-commerce within the country and provide investors, entrepreneurs, and customers the capacity to contribute to more widespread and viable markets. Digitalization encourages financial flexibility, which is imperative for businesses to change to online operations. Even the UAE's small and medium entrepreneurs have intensified their efforts to introduce technology-based digitalization, allowing them to access local, regional, and international markets. As discussed above, the consumers' buying experience is persistently evolving due to the confident introduction of the latest technology considering UAE consumers' buying motives, spending patterns, and behavioral insights, confidently driving the future of e-commerce. The UAE e-commerce industry adopted most of the latest trends in developed countries. The UAE consumers are enjoying the latest trends in e-commerce like augmented reality to enhance the validity of online shopping, artificial intelligence, voice search, on-site personalization, chatbots, mobile shopping, multiple payment options, headless, and API-driven e-commerce, etc. (Big Commerce, 2021).

The coronavirus has positively affected the E-commerce industry as more retailers and consumers have shifted to online channels for their buying and selling activities in the UAE (Ghandour, A., & Woodford). Soon after the pandemic, Coibion et al. (2020) laid an introductory base contrasting the idea of digitalization and offered strong influences on any innovative capacity. This team of academicians stated that consumer demand would decline to a level at which firms and businesses would need to lay off workers. This would reduce the overall income levels; thus, even if retailers switched to e-commerce to provide goods and services, no consumer demand would exist due to diminished income levels. Consequently, the association between e-commerce and Covid-19 and its landscape varies. The UAE government would need to incentivize or subsidize production so that retailers can endure their businesses through e-commerce and more money circulation in the economy. Supply-side surprises are claimed to be more detrimental to growth levels as associated with a demand-side shock. This academic team stated that most businesses in the UAE operate under the concept that "Supply creates its demand." Therefore, supply chains and logistical operations must be adapted and digitalized so the economy can recommence without growing the rate of infections—the explicit recognition of the enhancing trend of e-commerce in the UAE. A PwC (2020) survey found that the proportion of people shopping for groceries online rose from 29% to 51% during a lockdown. Over 90% of survey respondents said that they are likely to continue shopping on smartphones even after social distancing measures are lifted. "People have tasted the flavor of online," with e-commerce platforms offering a massive variety of products, deals, and discounts, as well as convenience, says Shireen El Khatib, chief executive officer at Majid Al Futtaim shopping malls. People have also increasingly turned to the Internet for services like telemedicine and exercise classes, and some of these trends will stick, says Ms. Taki (The Economist Intelligence Unit Limited 2020). A&A Associate (2022) identified trends in the e-commerce sector in the year 2022 as follows: consumers will demand more eco-friendly packaging and contactless delivery and focus more on the sustainability of e-commerce operations; customers in the UAE are willing to share their purchase history in return for a more personalized feed when browsing through online stores; augmented reality is slowly making its mark in the UAE, allowing consumers to virtually try on pieces of apparel before purchasing them through e-commerce platforms. As mentioned above, the corporate sector and its stakeholders evidently identified various trends from both companies' sides and market size.

CONCLUSION

The story of the COVID-19 pandemic is almost over. After completing the three dreadful waves of Covid-19, the UAE observed thousands of demises. Now slowly creeping to normalcy with the strong backup of unwavering government support. Now prospects remain to flourish for e-commerce entrepreneurs, supply-chain companies, and financial institutions to revolutionize solutions that permit more people to access goods and services securely. E-commerce tendencies predictable to gain impetus with consumers include faster, benign, more instinctual, and personalized experiences, voice-activated shopping, contextual and social commerce, virtual instant reordering, and product subscriptions combined with conveniences such as same-day delivery and modest pricing will magnet more consumers to select e-commerce over conventional face-to-face channels. The e-commerce sector may not crack an imminent recession, but it unlocks undisputable replicas for retrieval. There is great hope for businesses and consumers on e-commerce business practices that getting reciprocal benefits will showcase the opportunity for digital adoption to unlock regional economic growth. Shopping through e-commerce will never replace the experience of physically interacting with a product, particularly in the UAE, because consumers here consider shopping a pleasureful activity with their family members. The country is called the country of malls, but with more people looking to opt online frequently, offering an additional framework through digital means is the thoughtful way to go further. Provided that the supply chain is adequately set up to back both online and physical stores, it's a winning strategy. There is no question that 2020 has brought unprecedented challenges to consumers and companies worldwide. Keeping on top of the trends can be overwhelming but can also be accomplished by reshaping and redefining your business strategy (Globalization Partners International, 2021). The UAE has magnificently shifted its physical business operations to online e-commerce channels while upholding consumer demand. However, some modifications must be implemented in the regulations and frameworks to stabilize supply-side factors and instill more confidence. Due to Covid-19, intercontinental supply chains have become dislocated due to the lockdowns of countries worldwide. Therefore, if UAE desires to arise as a front-runner in the world's e-commerce industry, it will have to prudently develop its supplier base by preparatory trade with new universal partners. This trend diversifies the UAE's trade and supply portfolio and supports future adversities resulting from supply chain inefficiencies. The e-commerce sector had been developing at a rapid rate before Covid-19. Finally, the pandemic made it vibrant that e-commerce can be an indispensable marketing tool for consumers in times of crisis and even in the corporate world.

REFERENCES

Ahmad, S. Z., Bakar, A. R. A., & Ahmad, N. (2019). Social media adoption and its impact on firm performance: The case of the UAE. *International Journal of Entrepreneurial Behaviour & Research*, *25*(1), 84–111. doi:10.1108/IJEBR-08-2017-0299

Andreev, O., The, C. P., Ghandour, A., & Gurova, T. (2020). Information technologies, e-commerce retail platforms and the impact on the regional economy. *Journal of Talent Development and Excellence*, *12*(2s), 4205–4216.

Azman Free Zone. (2020). *E-Commerce: Trends and Challenges During the Covid-19*. https://www.afz.ae/en/resources/blogs/2020/may/e-commerce

Buekelaer, O. D. (2020). *B2B e-commerce and Covid-19: challenges, solutions and opportunities*. Sana. https://www.sanacommerce.com/blog/b2b-E-Commerce-covid-19- challenges-opportunities/

Coibion, O., Gorodnichenko, Y., & Weber, M. (2020). *Labor markets during the COVID-19 crisis: A preliminary view* (No. w27017). National Bureau of Economic Research.

Commerce, B. (2021). *14 Ecommerce trends leading the way*. https://www.bigcommerce.com/articles/ecommerce/ecommerce-trends/

Deloitte. (2018). *Going digital-the nexyt fornier for Middle East retail*. https://www2.deloitte.com/xe/en/pages/about-deloitte/articles/we-are-25/e-commerce.html

Digital Marketing Community. (2022). *The importance of eCommerce for your business in 2022*. https://www.digitalmarketingcommunity.com/articles/importance-of-ecommerce/

Dubai Future Foundation (2021). *Life after Covid-19*. Author.

Ghandour, A., & Woodford, B. J. (2020, November). COVID-19 impact on e-commerce in UAE. In *2020 21st International Arab Conference on Information Technology (ACIT)* (pp. 1-8). IEEE.

Globalization Partners International. (2021). *A reshaped and redefined strategy for recovery post Covid-19: e-commerce and marketing in the UAE\Part 2*. https://www.globalizationpartners.com/2021/03/04/reshaped-strategy-for-recovery-post-covid-19-ecommerce-and-marketing-in-uae-part-2/

International Trade Administration. (2022). *United Arab Emirates – Country commercial guide*. eCommerce. https://www.trade.gov/country-commercial-guides/united-arab-emirates-ecommerce#:~:text=The%20UAE%20is%20the%20eCommerce,by%20a%20COVID%20digital%20shift

Investopedia. (2022). *Ecommerce defined: types, history, and examples*. https://www.investopedia.com/terms/e/ecommerce.asp

Kim, R. Y. (2020). The impact of COVID-19 on consumers: Preparing for digital sales. *IEEE Engineering Management Review, 48*(3), 212–218. doi:10.1109/EMR.2020.2990115

KPMG. (2020). *KPMG Embedding Resilience: Addressing the business Challenges Presented by the coronavirus*. https://home.kpmg/ae/en/home.html.

Mansoor, Z. (2020). E-commerce paving the way for the future of retail and more. *Gulf Business*. https://www.ey.com/eninlcovid-19/ecommerce-during-covid-19-preparing-for-now-next-and-beyond

Mirza, S., Elliott, S., & Beena, P. (2020). *United Arab Emirates: e-commerce in the UAE: Logistics (Part 4)*. https://www.mondaq.com/operational-impacts-and-strategy/987324/e-commerce-in-the-uae-logistics-part-4

Nair, D. (n.d.). *UAE residents switch to cost-effective online shopping during COVID-19*. Gulf News. Online at: https://gulfnews.com/yourmoney/community-tips/uae-residents-switch-tocost-effective-online-shopping-during-covid-19-1.1589210896861

Nicolas, R. (2020). *United Arab Emirates: setting up an e-business in the UAE – Why participate in the fastest growing e-commerce market of the Middle East.* https://www.mondaq.com/corporate-and-company-law/1045890/setting-up-an-e-business-in-the-uae-why-participate-in-the-fastest-growing-e-commerce-market-of-the-middle-east

Potluri, R. M., Johnson, S., & Koppalakrishnan, P. (2020). An exploratory treatise on the ethnocentric tendencies of Emirati Gen Z consumers. *Journal of Islamic Marketing, 13*(3), 763–780. doi:10.1108/JIMA-07-2020-0197

Potluri, R. M., & Vajjhala, N. R. (2018). A study on application of web 3.0 technologies in small and medium enterprises of India. *Journal of Asian Finance, Economics and Business, 5*(2), 73–79.

PwC. (2020). *How resilient Middle East consumers have responded to Covid-19.* https://www.pwc.com/m1/en/publications/images-new/gcis-2020/how-resilient-middle-east-consumers-have-responded-covid-19.pdf

Ranney, M. L., Griffeth, V., & Jha, A. K. (2020). Critical supply shortages—The need for ventilators and personal protective equipment during the Covid-19 pandemic. *The New England Journal of Medicine, 382*(18), e41. doi:10.1056/NEJMp2006141 PMID:32212516

Seetharaman, A., Niranjan, I., Saravanan, A. S., & Balaji, D. (2017). A study of the moderate growth of online retailing (ecommerce) in the UAE. *Journal of Developing Areas, 51*(4), 397–412. doi:10.1353/jda.2017.0109

Statista. (2016). *Retail e-commerce sales CAGR forecast in selected countries from 2016 to 2021.* Statista.

Subramani, M., & Walden, E. (2001, June). The Impact of E-Commerce Announcements on the Market Value of Firms. *Information Systems Research, 12*(2), 135–154. doi:10.1287/isre.12.2.135.9698

The Economist Intelligence Unit Limited. (2020). *The UAE's omni-channel consumer: striking a balance between online and in-store shopping experience.* https://impact.economist.com/perspectives/sites/default/files/eiu-uae-omni-channel-consumer.pdf

The Emirates News Agency-WAM. (2021). *Value of UAE retail e-commerce market hits record US$ 3.9bn in 2020.* https://www.wam.ae/en/details/1395302946511

Visa. (2020a). *The UAE eCommerce landscape 2020: Accelerated growth during turbulent time.* https://ae.visamiddleeast.com/dam/VCOM/regional/cemea/unitedarabemirates/media-kits/documents/visa_uae_ecommerce_landscape_2020_ppinion_paper_vf.pdf

Visa. (2020b). *UAE eCommerce sector to continue upward trajectory as digital payments boom during Covid-19.* https://ae.visamiddleeast.com/en_AE/about-visa/newsroom/press-releases/prl-09112020.html

Wamda-MIT Legatum Center. (2021). *How Covid-19 unlocked the adoption of e-commerce in the MENA region.* https://legatum.mit.edu/wp-content/uploads/2021/03/170321-MIT-Wamda-E-Commerce-COVID19-report-EN-01.pdf

Wienclaw, R. A. (2013). B2B Business Models. *Research Starters: Business.*

Wlg, G. (2020). *E-commerce in the UAE: is it the new normal? (Part 1).* https://gowlingwlg.com/en/insights-resources/articles/2020/e-commerce-in-the-uae-part-one/

Yuldashev, U. (2017). *The future of e-commerce in the UAE gulf business.* https://gulfbusiness.com/future-E-Commerce-uae/

Zawya. (2022). *New report finds that 74% of UAE's online shoppers expect to spend more online in 2022.* https://www.zawya.com/en/press-release/research-and-studies/new-report-finds-that-74-of-uaes-online-shoppers-expect-to-spend-more-online-in-2022-vxggzmwz

Chapter 13
Customer Segmentation of Shopping Mall Users Using K-Means Clustering

Amit Kumar

Andhra University, India

ABSTRACT

The most successful companies are the one that know their customers very well and can anticipate their needs. Good customer profiles at the fingertips have businesses improve marketing campaigns, targeting feature launches and product roadmaps. In this study, exploratory data analysis was done on the shopping mall data, and customer segmentation was done using k-means clustering. Two different clusters were done based on age vs. spending score and annual income vs. spending score. Four optimum clusters were obtained for age and spending scores using the elbow graph method, and five optimum clusters were obtained for annual income and spending scores. Firstly, for clusters based on age and spending score, people with higher age groups have less spending scores. Secondly, clusters based on annual income and spending scores had high annual income and very low spending scores. Thus, the mall can offer these cluster customers to attract them, thereby increasing its profits.

INTRODUCTION

The growth of the market has forced older companies to apply marketing strategies to stay competitive in the market as it has become more difficult to survive. Every day, the number of consumers increases significantly, and businesses find it difficult to cater for the needs of every customer. Thus, customer segmentation is used, which is the process of dividing customers into groups based on their common characteristics to target each group efficiently (Smith, 2016). The analysis allows companies to determine what their true customers are buying, thus allowing them to better serve their customers, resulting in customer satisfaction. The analysis also allows businesses to determine their target consumers and improve their marketing tactics to get more revenue. Successful marketing not only requires knowledge about who the customers are but also where exactly they are in the buying process and customer segmentation.

DOI: 10.4018/978-1-6684-5727-6.ch013

Customer segmentation was previously a challenging and time-consuming task that demanded hours of manual pouring over different tables and querying the data in hopes of finding ways to keep customers together. But, in recent years it has become much easier by the application of machine learning algorithms that tune statistical regularity and data to such problems (Dullaghan & Rozaki, 2017). Machine learning models can process customer data and discover recurring patterns across various features (Janakirman & Umamaheswari, 2014). In many cases machine learning algorithms can help marketing analyst find customer segment that would be very difficult to spot through intuitions and manual examination of data. Customer segmentation is a perfect example of how combination of machine learning and human intuition can create something that is greater than the sum of its parts (Ezenkwu, Ozuomba & Kalu, 2015).

There are few advantages of customer segmentation. The first advantage of customer segmentation is price optimization (Wilson-Jeanselme & Reynolds, 2006). Understanding the customer and financial status of the customers will assist the company to pace up with the price optimization accordingly and thus it helps in better allocation of resources which in return helps the companies to gain economics of scale. The second advantage is that it enhances competitiveness. The More the customer retention, more will be the revenue generated and all of this will enhance their competitiveness in the market. If a company segments the market, then it will know who are its customers and thus it can come up with new products or variations according to the changing preferences of the customers. If the company is vigilant enough then it may also have the first mover advantage. The third advantage is the brand awareness. By segmenting the customers, the company can make the customers well aware of its brand. Identifying the brand will help customers to directly purchase the product which will increase the company's goodwill in the market and the brand value which is established among other competitors. The fourth advantage is acquisition and retention of customer with a personalized connection and the customers which will help the company to win the satisfied customers. Satisfied customers are more likely to retain with the organization who regularly meet up with them. Better customer segmentation will lead to developing a better relationship with prospective customers. Customer segmentation allows the company to learn a great deal about its customers and thereby it can carter to their needs more effectively. The last advantage would be increased revenue and return on interest. By fine tuning the company's marketing message, there will be an increase in revenue because users will be more likely to make a purchase when they are delivered exactly what they need (Mirela & Stanica, 2009).

BACKGROUND

The Role of Data Mining in Customer Relationship Management (CRM)

Customer information can be analyzed using data mining techniques, but clustering and association rules mining are the most common. CRM data mining is based on the idea that past data can contain information that can be useful in the future. Rather than capturing random behavior, corporate data captures customer needs, preferences, propensities and treatments. Data mining aims to extract patterns from historical data. Identifying patterns can be challenging, as they are not always strong, and customer's signals can be confusing. The data mining process involves the separation of signal from noise, which is one of the most difficult things to do. Through data mining, for example, it is possible to reveal distinct customer segments that can be used to develop customized new products and services designed to better meet the specific needs of the customers. The process of data mining can be used to gain valuable customer insights, which can be used to make an effective CRM strategy. Analysis of data can help to personalize customer interactions, thereby increasing customer satisfaction and profitability. In addition to supporting an optimized customer lifecycle that includes acquisition, relationship building, attrition prevention and customer reacquisition, CRM can also support an optimized customer management process throughout the entire customer lifecycle. They are responsible for acquiring, developing and retaining customers. Through direct marketing campaigns, marketers reach their customers by mail, internet, phone and other means. Direct marketing campaigns are explained in the following stages (Kumar & Reinartz, 2018; Tsiptsis & Chorianopoulos, 2011).

1. Data should be collected and cleaned from different sources.
2. Identifying different groups of customers and segmenting them.
3. Selecting the right customers through targeted marketing campaigns.
4. In order to execute a campaign effectively, it must be executed by selecting the right channel, the right time, as well as the right offer.
5. Test and control groups are used to evaluate campaigns. Test and control groups are divided and positive responses are compared in the evaluation.
6. Analyzing campaign results and improving the campaign for the next round in terms of targeting, time, offer, product and communication.

All of these stages can benefit from data mining, particularly identifying the right customers to contact. Developing a data mining project is not an easy task. When engaged teams are not guided by a clear methodology framework, they may end up failing to meet high expectations. For successful implementations of data mining, Cross Industry Standard Process for Data Mining (CRISP-DM) which is a process model that serves as the base for a data science process, describes the following steps to be followed. The steps are as follows.

1. *Understanding of Business*: Analyzing the current situation and assessing problems should be the first steps in a data mining project. It is important to consider all the parameters of the project, including its resources and limitations. A data mining goal should be developed based on the business objective. An outline of the project plan and success criteria should be developed.
2. *Understanding of Data*: An investigation of the availability of required data is conducted during this phase, which involves understanding the data requirements in order to achieve the defined goal. A major part of this phase will include the initial collection of data and its exploration using summary statistics and visualization tools to better understand it and to identify possible issues with quality and availability.
3. *Preparation of Data*: A data mining model is prepared by identifying, selecting, and preparing the data to be mined. During this phase, data is collected, integrated, and formatted according to the project's needs. Following the consolidation of data, it must be cleaned and transformed appropriately, according to the algorithm requirements. To enrich customer information, to better summarize customer characteristics, and to enhance the performance of the models, new aggregation fields should be derived from the raw data, such as sums, averages, ratios, flags.
4. *Modeling the Data*: After the datasets are prepared, they are used to train the models. Depending on the business objective, analysts should choose the appropriate modeling technique. Models should be partitioned before training to ensure that the performance of the model is evaluated on a sepa-

rate dataset, especially when training predictive models. To determine which modeling algorithm and parameter settings yield the best results, alternative algorithms and parameter settings will be examined and compared. Once model results have been evaluated, the settings can be revised and fine-tuned.

5. *Evaluation*: In the evaluation phase, the models are evaluated not only with respect to technical measures but also with regard to the criteria set forth in the business understanding phase. An effective business model should address the initial business objectives, according to the project team. In that case, the model is approved and ready to be deployed.

6. *Deployment*: Upon completion of the project, the findings and conclusions are reported, but the project is not yet over. Any marketing model will fail if its results are not integrated and implemented into the organization's daily operations. To score the customers and update the results, a procedure should be designed and developed. In addition to distributing the model results and integrating them into the organization's databases and operations CRM system, the deployment procedure should allow the results to be distributed throughout the organization. As a final step, a maintenance plan should be created and the whole process should be analyzed. The next steps should be planned based on the lessons learned.

DATA MINING AND CUSTOMER SEGMENTATION

The process of segmenting customers consists of dividing them into distinct, meaningful and homogeneous groups based on their attributes and characteristics. As a marketing tool, it is used to differentiate products. As a result, organizations can build differentiated strategies based on an understanding of their customers (Kotler, 2005). Organizations traditionally segment their markets based on demographics and value information, regardless of the industry they operate in. Based on these simple business rule segments, organizations have developed their new products and services over the past few decades. Market research based on traditional surveys often provides a lot of information about a handful of people. Despite this, it is often necessary to understand the characteristics of all customers to use the results of market research effectively. Thus, market research could reveal interesting customer segments. In order to determine the impact on the existing customer base, it is necessary to use the data available. This is particularly true for behavioral data, which can typically be derived from transaction and billing histories. In order to understand the behavior of the market research participants, it is necessary to identify the customers in the market research. In considering the competitive nature of today's markets, this approach is no longer sufficient and efficient. In order to gain a competitive advantage, organizations must have a comprehensive view of their customers. Identifying the underlying segments requires them to analyze relevant data, including preferences, preferences, attitudes, behaviors and perceptions, as well as customer needs, wants, attitudes, abilities and behaviors. With the identification of unique groups, the organization will be able to create and deliver customized product offerings and promotions more effectively. Data mining with established customers is a popular application of customer segmentation. Defining business objectives is the first step in a segmentation project, and delivering differentiated marketing strategies is the end result. Depending on the criteria or attributes used for segmentation, there are many different types of segmentation. The value of a customer can be used to segment customers. In general, segmentation is dependent on the business objective (Tsiptsis & Chorianopoulos, 2011).

According to the segmentation criteria used, there are various types of segmentation. There are several factors that can be used to segment customers, such as their value, socio demographics, and life stages, as well as their behaviors, needs, and attitudes. Segmentation depends on the business objective and target market. For different situations and business objectives, different criteria and segmentation methods should be used. The behavioral segmentation process involves grouping customers based on their behaviors and usage patterns. Business rules can be used to create behavioral segments, but this method has inherent disadvantages. Due to the fact that it is based on the personal perceptions of a business expert, its objectivity can be questioned. However, it is able to handle only a few segmentation fields effectively. As an alternative, data mining can generate behavioral segments based on data. A clustering algorithm analyzes behavioral data, identifies customer groups naturally and suggests solutions based on observable patterns. In a properly developed data mining model, groups with distinct characteristics and profiles can be discovered, resulting in business-valued and meaningful segmentation schemes. When combining a large number of segmentation attributes, it is generally necessary to apply a cluster model. In contrast to business rules, a cluster model can manage a large number of attributes and reveal unknown segments based on data. In addition to segmentation schemes based on the current or expected value of a customer, data mining can also be used in the development of customer segmentation schemes. Customer segmentation helps prioritize marketing interventions and customer handling based on customer importance. Using clustering techniques described by Tan, Steinbach, and Kumar (2005) is one way to identify behavioral segments. As a result of these methods, clusters of similar customers are formed, but their relationship to the business may be unclear. It is more common for businesses to segment their customers into categories that are easy to understand. Subscription renewals or high spending levels are often used to build these segments. In this type of segmentation, decision tree techniques described are ideal (Maimon & Rokach, 2017). As part of marketing, segmentation is useful for the following reasons (Kotler, 2005).

- Identification of new marketing opportunities based on a better understanding of customers.
  - Development of new products/services tailored to the characteristics of each segment.
  - The design of customized product offering strategies for existing customers based on the needs and wants of each segment.
  - Rewards and incentives tailored to each customer's needs.
  - Choosing the right message and channel for advertising and communication.
  - Choosing the right sales and service channels.
  - Based on the specific characteristics of each segment, develop the brand image and key product benefits.
- Customer service can be differentiated according to the importance of each segment.
- Allocating resources more effectively based on the potential returns of each segment.
  - Prioritizing marketing initiatives intended to retain and develop customers according to their importance and value.

Consumer marketing can be optimized by using a variety of customer segmentation criteria. There are different types of segmentation based on the business situation, as discussed earlier in this chapter. According to Tsiptsis and Chorianopoulos (2011), the following customer segmentation types are widely used.

1. **Value Based**: A value-based segmentation groups customers based on their value. Identifying the most valuable customers and tracking value and value changes over time is one of the most important uses of this type of segmentation. A marketing initiative can also be optimized by using it to differentiate the service delivery strategy and allocate resource accordingly. Segmenting customers based on value is the process of dividing them into groups. A one-time task is not what this is. Tracking value changes across time is essential for the organization. To prevent downward migration and encourage upward migration, the organization should monitor and intervene if necessary. It is imperative to develop a credible and accurate methodology for determining the value of each customer, using day-to-day expenditures and revenues, prior to developing this segmentation scheme. An analysis of value-based segmentation does not require the use of data mining models. It is developed through simple computations. Customers are grouped by their binning and divided into equal value segments according to their value. Value segments are developed based on these groups in the form of low n%, medium n% and top n%.

2. **Behavior:** This type of segmentation is very useful and efficient. The availability of data from behavioral segmentation is minimal and hence it is widely used. Usually, the organization's databases store and make available ownership and utilization information about products. Behavioral and usage patterns of customers are identified and categorized. Customized product offering strategies as well as new product development, loyalty programs and new product development often use this type of segmentation. Data from a company's data warehouse or data mart are used to identify segments as part of behavioral segmentation. A high level of confidence can be achieved and the costs can be kept low when implementing behavioral segmentation. In addition to product usage and ownership, volume, type and frequency of transaction data, payment and revenue history can be used for behavioral segmentation.

3. **Propensity Based:** Customer segments are determined by propensity scores, which are calculated by classification models (propensity) based on churn, cross-selling and other factors. Customers are grouped into groups based on their propensity scores in this type of segmentation. There are three types of customers, such as bad, good and very good. Other segmentation schemes can also be used to enhance the targeting of marketing actions using propensity scores. Using propensities coupled with value segments, the value-at-risk segmentation scheme prioritizes retention actions based on risk. Based on the results of classification models, such as churn and cross-sales and upsells, propensity-based segmentation is developed. Customers are binned according to their propensity scores in this type of segmentation. The propensity scores can be used to create clusters of customers with similar future needs for specific products by applying cluster analysis. Compound segmentation schemes can be created by combining multiple propensity models and scores. Clustering models are typically used in this procedure. The clustering model can use the propensity scores as input fields once they have been estimated by the relevant models.

4. **Loyalty Based:** Segmentation based on loyalty involves identifying loyalty segments, such as loyal users and switchers/migrators. Those high value customers with disloyal profiles can be targeted for retention actions, while prospectively loyal customers can be targeted for cross-selling. By segmenting customers according to their loyalty status, it is possible to identify loyal customers from migrators/switchers. Based on survey or database information, simple business rules and/or cluster models are applied to create segments. Specific customer database attributes and loyalty segments can be associated with loyalty segments. As a first step, an organization can conduct a

market survey to identify loyalty segments and then build a classification model using the loyalty segments field.

5. **Socio-Demographic and Life-Stage:** Customer groups are determined based on socio demographic information, including gender, race, age, education, occupation, income and marital status. Segmentation of this kind is ideal for promoting products based on life stages and supporting life stage marketing. Demographic segmentation groups customers based on their demographic characteristics. As demographics are believed to have a strong influence on a customer's needs, preferences and consumption/usage behaviors, this segmentation is widely used. In many cases, however, people in the same demographic group may have different needs and wants.

6. **Needs/Attitudinal:** Market research data is typically used to segment customers according to their needs, wants, attitudes, preferences and perceptions regarding the company's products and services. New product development can be supported by it, as well as determining the brand image and key product features to communicate. Customer's needs, wants, attitudes, perceptions and preferences are examined using needs/attitudinal. A cluster model is typically applied to gathered questionnaire responses to identify the segments based on relevant information collected through market surveys. To enrich the profile of the revealed segments, the model provides insight into their qualitative characteristics and thus support the data mining framework, needs/attitudinal segmentation and is often used in conjunction with behavioral and value-based segments.

MAIN FOCUS OF THE CHAPTER

Objectives of the Study

1. The primary objective of this study is to use k-means clustering machine learning algorithm on a shopping mall dataset to achieve the customer segmentation.

2. To classify people based on age, annual income, and annual spending score to increase the profits.

In this study the primary objective is to find the most profitable customer groups within the entire pool of customers. The first step is creating a business case. The second step is preparing the data, the more the data, the merrier the results will be in this case. This is because the patterns and trends can be predicted with good accuracy. The preprocessing of the dataset will be done and removal of inconsistencies in data will eventually help in better data analysis. The third step is data analysis and exploration. This step is a crucial one as this will be useful to find some interesting relations and patterns in the data. With this step a better understanding of the customer's interest choices and purchasing pattern can be known. The fourth step is clustering analysis. In the context of customer segmentation, clustering analysis is the use of mathematical model to discover groups of similar customers based on finding the smallest variations among customers within each group. The goal of cluster analysis is to accurately segment customers in order to achieve more effective customer marketing via personalization. A common cluster analysis method is a mathematical one which is known as k-means clustering analysis (Hartigan & Wong, 1979; MacQueen, 1967). The cluster assistance better customer modeling and predictive analysis. The process is not based on any pre-determined threshold or rules, rather the data itself reveals the customer prototypes that inherently exist within the population of customers. The fifth step is choosing optimal hyper parameters. Choosing the best set of hyper parameters for an algorithm is called hyper parameter optimization or tuning. This is the next step because it helps to find the most accurate and rewarding customer groups based on previous work. The last step is visualization and interpretation. Finally, the visualization, findings and interpretation is done. The rest of the paper is organized as follows. The next section discusses the literature review. After that the methodologies section describes the dataset and methodologies used in the study. After the methodologies section, the next section contains the experimental outcomes. Finally, the last section summarizes and concludes the findings.

LITERATURE REVIEW

Two phase clustering was introduced by Namvar, Gholamian and Khakabi (2010) as a new method of segmenting customers. Based on recency, frequency, and monetary (RFM), demographic, and lifetime value (LTV) data, the authors constructed a new customer segmentation method. In order to segment customers, a two-phase method was developed. Based on RFM, customers were first clustered into different segments using K-means clustering. Secondly, the clusters were divided into new ones using demographic data. The final step was to create a profile for the customer based on the LTV. By combining demographic data with two phase clustering, Namvar, Gholamian and Khakabi (2010) found that the clustering was relatively better. Hruschka and Natter (1999) compared the performance of feed forward neural networks and k-means algorithms for cluster-based market segmentation. A data set was analyzed that analyzed how brands (product category and household cleaners) were used in various situations. Based on the proposed feed forward neural network model, proper tests confirmed that the solution was two segments. Alternatively, the k-means algorithm failed to discover a stronger cluster structure. Neural networks performed better than k-means algorithm at classifying respondents based on external criteria. Moreover, Wu and Lin (2005) studied cluster-based customer segmentation using credit card consumption data as the model building samples. They developed a modeling framework that utilized pattern-based clustering and signature discovery techniques to build segment level predictive models. Different modes of study were studied using monetary matrices and fluctuate rate matrices. Based on clustering on both matrices, the authors identified different customer characteristics. They use those characteristics to build a two-dimension consumption based customer segmentation model. Lee and Park (2005) surveyed customer satisfaction for satisfactory customer segmentation and based on the survey, the authors sought to provide an easy, efficient, and more practical alternative approach for segmenting profitable customers. A case study illustrating a profitable customer segmentation strategy for a motor company was presented. Data envelopment analysis (DEA), self-organizing map (SOM) and neural networks were used to support the segmentation of profitable customers using a multi agent based system. The system executed a customer satisfaction survey and performed mining of databases through the use of business intelligence tools.

Using data from more than 5800 airline passengers, Teichert, Shehu, and von Wartburg (2008) reported that segmenting customers into business and leisure does not sufficiently reflect the heterogeneity of consumer preferences, leading to a misunderstanding of consumer preferences. An alternative segmentation approach was proposed based on latent class modeling. Behavioral and socio demographic variables were used to profile the identified segments. To isolate and address customer segments receptive to tailored product packages, they combined their findings with observable consumer characteristics. Anderson Jr, Cox, and Fulcher (1976) analyzed customer segmentation in banking sector and its purpose of the survey was to determine whether certain factors influence people's choice of commercial banks. Using preliminary interviews, fifteen bank selection criteria were developed and significant demographic and socioeconomic cluster differences were found. The study showed that commercial banks serve a significant segment of the market that view banking services essentially as convenience goods and money as undifferentiated. Based on the results of the study, determinant attribute analysis acts as a useful tool for identifying and evaluating the relative determinants of bank selection criteria to provide a basis for market segmentation and the design of products/services that are focused on customer demographic differences. Lee and Park (2005) proposed a method where a retail supermarket was taken as the research object, data mining methods were then used to obtain association rules based on the Apriori algorithm for customer segments, and the rules were used to determine customer characteristics efficiently. Furthermore, the authors referred to the supermarket's marketing and management methods which helped in understanding the work more thoroughly. Data mining technique was used effectively to extract potential, useful and valuable information from the large number of historical and current data stored in the database which helped to locate the customers for a retail store.

A k-means clustering was used by several researchers (Aryuni, Madyatmadja, & Miranda, 2018; Bhade, Gulalkari, Harwani, & Dhage, 2018; Kansal, Bahuguna, Singh, & Choudhury, 2018) to segment customers. Aryuni, Madyatmadja, and Miranda (2018) segmented the customers of bank using k-means and k-medoids clustering methods. The internet banking data was used for the study where the customer profile data was fetched using RFM. The importance attributes for segmentation were the recent transactions of the customer, the frequency and the total amount of transaction within a period of one year. In their study they found that k-means clustering model outperformed k-medoids method. Bhade et al. (2018) proposed a systematic approach to target customers and provide maximum profit to organizations. The first step was to analyze the data from the purchase history and determine the parameters that had the highest correlation with sales. k-means clustering was used for customer segmentation and singular value decomposition was used to develop appropriate recommendations. Kansal et al. (2018) used a dataset that contained two features of 200 training samples taken from local retail shops. The two measurements which were used were the average amount of shopping by customers and the average number of times customers visit the shop annually. By applying clustering, five segments of the cluster were formed. They were careless, careful, standard, target and sensible customers. However, when mean shift clustering was applied, the authors found two new clusters labeled high buyers and frequent visitors and high buyers and occasional visitors. Wang, Zuo, Li, Chen, and Yada (2019) analyzed customer segmentation using broad learning systems which provide an alternative perspective on learning in deep structures. In addition to customer purchase behavior, RFID (Radio Frequency Identification) data was also collected, which is a reliable indicator of consumer behavior. In the work of Wang et al. (2019), the customer segmentation was analyzed using Broad Learning System (BLS). Furthermore, the authors collected customer behavior data from a real-world Japanese supermarket. RFID data was used to classify customers as a multi-label classification problem.

METHODOLOGIES AND DATASET

Methodology for Behavioral Segmentation

The methodology for behavioral customer segmentation consists of the following five steps (Thakare & Bagal, 2015; Sinha & Uniyal, 2005; Tsiptsis & Chorianopoulos, 2011).

1. *Segmentation Process Design and Business Understanding*: The first step in this phase is to understand the business requirements of the project. During this process, data miners and marketers involved in the project collaborate closely to assess the situation, define the specific business goal and design the entire data mining procedure. As part of this step, the business objective must be defined, segmentation criteria must be selected, segmentation population must be determined and segmentation level must be determined.
2. *Understanding, Preparing and Enriching Data*: For segmentation modeling, data acquisition, integration and processing follow the investigation and assessment of the available data sources. The data understanding and preparation phase is the most time consuming phase of this study. Activities in this phase include investigating data sources, defining the data to be used, integrating it and aggregating it and validating and cleaning it.
3. *Cluster Modeling for Segment Identification*: Cluster analysis divides customers into distinct segments. A cluster model assesses the similarities between the records/customers and suggests a way to group them based on the clustering fields, typically component scores. Before choosing the final segmentation scheme, data miners should test different combinations of inputs, models and model settings. Different clustering models will likely produce different segments. It is a recipe for disappointment to expect a unique and definitive solution. Different algorithms usually produce similar results, rather than identical results. There appears to be some convergence among them. It is important for analysts to evaluate which aspects of the different models are in agreement and which aspects are in disagreement. The existence of discernible groupings is generally indicated by high agreement levels between many cluster models. Prior to deploying the segmentation scheme, it is necessary to evaluate the modeling results.
4. *Analyzing and Profiling the Revealed Segments*: A segmentation scheme that best meet the needs of the organization is selected for deployment based on the modeling results. The solution suggested by one algorithm should not be blindly trusted by data miners. When selecting the most effective segmentation, they should explore different solutions and seek guidance from the marketers. The tasks in this step include technical evaluation of the clustering solution, profiling of the reveal segments, cluster profiling with supervised models, evaluating and enriching the behavioral segments based on marketing research information and labeling the segments accordingly.
5. *Deploying A Segmentation Solution, Designing and Delivering Differentiated Strategies*: In the final stage of the segmentation project, the segmentation solution is deployed and used to develop differentiated marketing strategies. Usually, three tasks are performed in this step: creating the customer scoring model for updating segments, creating a decision tree for scoring segments and disseminating segmentation information. Unlike behavioral segmentation, which usually examines multiple segmentation dimensions, value-based segmentation examines only one dimension, the customer value. Rather than the segmentation itself, computing a valid value measure to divide customers is the most challenging part of such a project.

Machine learning is divided into supervised, unsupervised and reinforcement learning. Since the customers should be segmented, clusters should be made by using unsupervised learning. Unsupervised learning is training of a machine using information that is neither classified not labelled and allowing the algorithm to add on that information without guidance. Due to the fact that there will be no indication of how the output values will appear, an unsupervised machine learning method cannot be directly applied to regression or classification problems. Here the task of machine is to group unsorted information according to the similarities patterns and differences without any prior training of data. Unsupervised learning can be classified into two categories of algorithms i.e., association and clustering. Learning association rules involves finding rules that describe large parts of the data, such as people who buy 'x' and also tend to buy 'y'. A clustering consists of discovering the inherent grouping in data, such as grouping customers based on purchasing behavior. Clustering may include types like hierarchical clustering, k-means clustering, principal component analysis, singular value decomposition or independent component analysis.

SOLUTIONS AND RECOMMENDATIONS

Centroid Based Clustering

The theoretical concepts behind this work include centroid-based clustering. Centroid based algorithms select a predefined number of points randomly, referred to as centroids, which indicates the number of clusters expected. Based on the closest centroid, each point is assigned to a cluster. After that, the positions of centroids are remapped to the mean position of their clusters. Iteratively, this process continues until all meaningful clusters are found. Several centroid based algorithms have been developed. Some of them are k-means, k-medoids, and fuzzy c-means; however, k-means is the most popular.

k-means algorithm is an iterative algorithm that tries to partition the datasets into 'k' predefined distinct non overlapping sub groups where each data point belongs to only one group. It tries to make the intra-cluster data points as similar as possible while also keeps the clusters as different as possible. It assigns data points to a cluster such that the sum of the squared distances between the data points and the clustered centroid is at the minimum. The smaller the variation within clusters, the more homogeneous the data points within the cluster will be. k-means is a popular way to quantize vectors. The goal of this algorithm is to group 'n' objects into 'k' clusters. Let $X = \{x_i\}$, $i = 1, 2, 3, ..., n$ be the set of n-dimensional points and $C = \{C_k, k = 1, 2, 3, ..., k\}$ where C is set of clusters. The centroid of cluster C_k is μ_k. According to equation 1, the squared error between μ_k and the points in cluster C_k must be minimized (Borlea, Precup, Dragan, & Borlea, 2017; Zhang, Zhang, & Xue, 2008).

$$J(C_k) = \sum_{X_i \epsilon C_k} \left\| X_i - \mu_k \right\|^2 \tag{1}$$

Equation-2 states that the goal of k-means is to minimize the sum of the squared error over all k clusters.

$$J(C_k) = \sum_{k=1}^{K} \sum_{X_i \epsilon C_k} \left\| X_i - \mu_k \right\|^2 \qquad (2)$$

The k-means algorithm works as follows:

i.   Initializes a random number of centroids within the data domain.
ii. Clusters the data into 'k' groups by assigning each data point to a centroid based on their distance from each other.
iii. Computes the average of all objects in each cluster and moves the centroid to that position.
iv. Repeats steps 2 and 3 until the same points are assigned to each cluster in successive iterations.

There are several distance metrics that can be used to calculate the minimum distance between any two points, such as the Euclidean distance, Manhattan distance, Chebyshev distance and Minkowski distance (Singh, Yadav, & Rana, 2013; Thakare & Bagal, 2015). The distance between two n-dimensional vectors X and Y can be calculated with Euclidean distance according to equation-3 and Manhattan distance according to equation-4.

$$D(X,Y) = \sqrt{\sum_{i=1}^{n} \left| X_i - Y_i \right|^2} \qquad (3)$$

$$D(X,Y) = \sum_{i=1}^{n} \left| X_i - Y_i \right| \qquad (4)$$

The number of clusters can be decided using "elbow method". Based on the distance between data points and their assigned clusters, the elbow method chooses an ideal value of 'k' by using the sum of squared distance (SSE) (Bholowalia & Kumar, 2014; Syakur, Khotimah, Rochman, & Satoto, 2018). A value of 'k' would be chosen where the SSE flattens out and an inflection point appears. The method's name arises from the fact that the graph looks like an elbow when visualized. In this study k-means classifier algorithm is used to classify different customers based on their age, annual income and spending patterns.

Dataset

The current supermarket mall work was completed utilizing the dataset which can be downloaded from the Kaggle website. After importing the dataset, several libraries like pandas, NumPy, scikit-learn, matplotlib and seaborn were imported in Jupyter notebook to perform descriptive analysis. In the original data set, there were totally 200 observations and 5 attributes as shown in Table 1. The attributes included Customer ID, Gender, Age, Annual Income(k$) and Spending Score (1-100) of the customers.

Table 1. Total number of observations in original dataset

	CustomerID	Gender	Age	Annual Income (k$)	Spending Score (1-100)
0	1	Male	19	15	39
1	2	Male	21	15	81
2	3	Female	20	16	6
3	4	Female	23	16	77
4	5	Female	31	17	40
...	...	...	...	...	...
195	196	Female	35	120	79
196	197	Female	45	126	28
197	198	Male	32	126	74
198	199	Male	32	137	18
199	200	Male	30	137	83

Exploratory Data Analysis

As shown in the Figure 1, the number of females in this data is more when compared to the number of males.

Figure 1. Gender distribution i.e., total number of males and females in the dataset

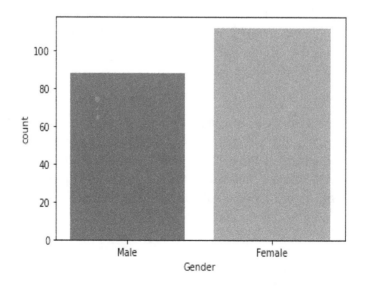

Distribution of Age, Annual Income ($) and Spending Score (1-100)

A distribution of age, annual income and spending score is plotted in Figures 2, 3, and 4. As shown in the Figure 2, most of the customers are aged between 26-35. Most of the customers have a spending score between 41-60 (Figure 3) and most of the customer's annual income lies between $60,001-$90,000 (Figure 4).

Figure 2. Bar plot of Age

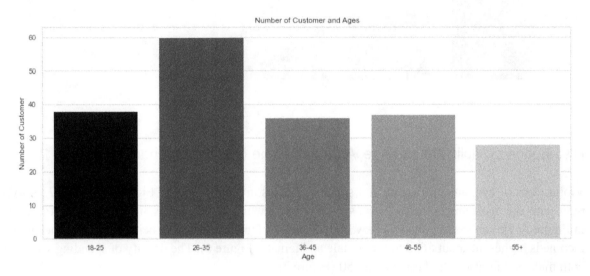

Figure 3. Bar plot of Annual Income (k$)

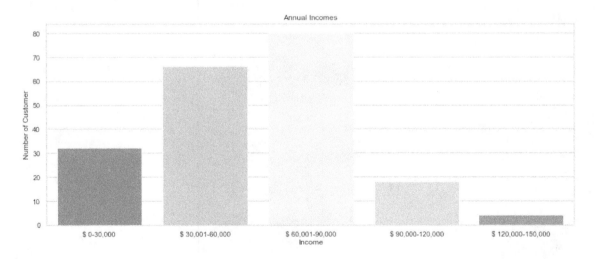

Figure 4. Bar plot of Spending Score (1-100)

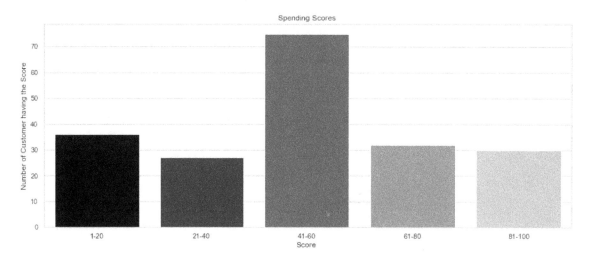

Distribution of Violin plots of Age, Annual Income (k$) and Spending Score (1-100)

Violin plots of age, annual income and spending scores are shown in the Figures 5,6, and 7. X-axis represents the age, annual income, sand spending score while Y-axis represents the gender. As shown in Figure 5, we can see that there is very high density of female whose age is in 30's, while the annual income is highest at about $65k for both male and female (Figure 6). The density of spending score for both male and female is highest at about 50 (Figure 7).

Figure 5. Age

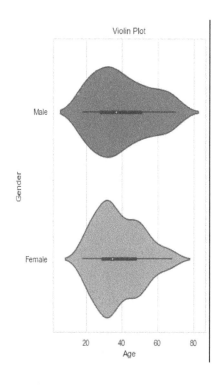

Figure 6. Annual Income (k$)

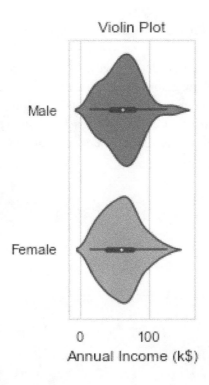

Figure 7. Spending Score

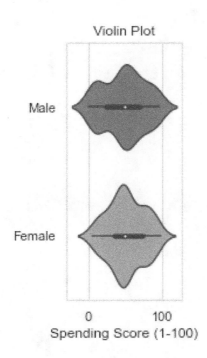

RESULTS AND DISCUSSION

Selection of Optimum Number of Clusters Based on Age and Spending Score

The optimum number of clusters that is needed for age and spending scores using within clusters sum of squares value is estimated using elbow graph. The bend in the elbow graph can be seen in the Figure 8. On x-axis, after a point i.e., 4, the graph is almost straight. Therefore, the optimum number of clusters chosen was 4. The scatterplots of the four clusters are as shown in Figure 9, where age is shown in x-axis and spending score is shown in y-axis. The blue dot in Figure 9 shows the centroid of each cluster.

Figure 8. Elbow Point 1

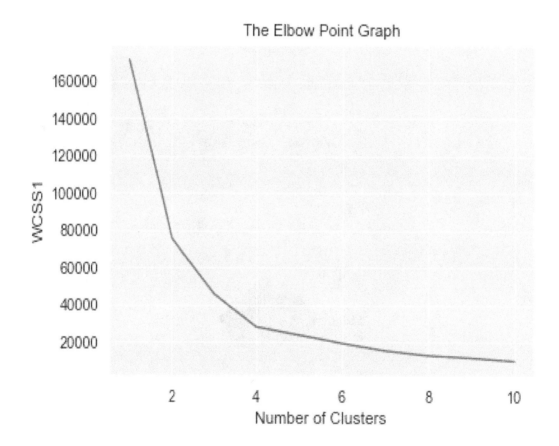

Figure 9. Customer groups based on age

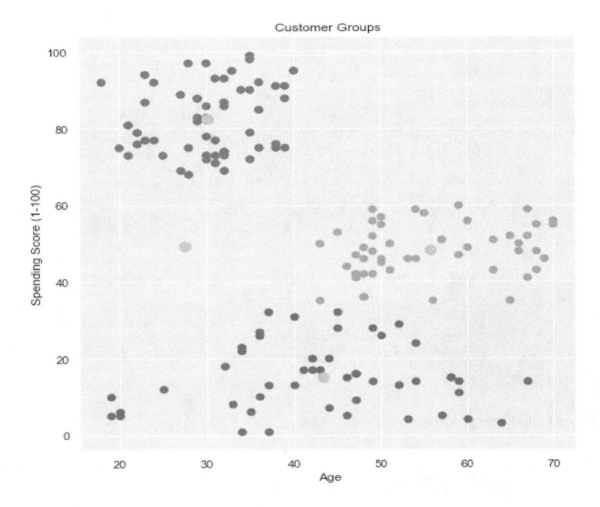

Selection of Optimum Number of Clusters Based on Annual Income and Spending Score

The optimum number of clusters that is needed for annual income and spending scores using within clusters sum of squares value is also estimated using elbow graph. The bend in the elbow graph can be seen in the Figure 10. On x-axis, after a point i.e., 5, the graph is almost straight. Therefore, the optimum number of clusters chosen was 5. The scatterplots of the five clusters is as shown in Figure 11 where annual income is shown in x-axis and spending score is shown in y-axis. The blue dot in Figure 11 shows the centroid of each cluster.

Figure 10. Elbow Point 2

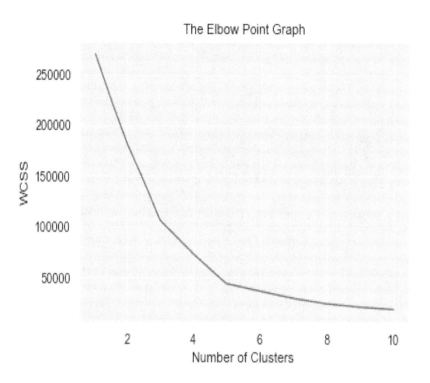

Figure 11. Customer groups based on annual income

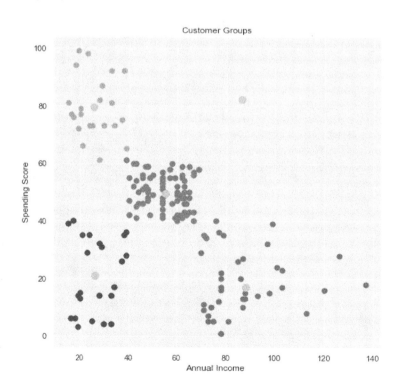

CONCLUSION

In this study an exploratory data analysis of the shopping mall data was done. Later, based on the age and annual income of the customers, by using k-means clustering, segmentation of customers was done. For clusters based on age and spending score, as shown in the Figure 5(b), the clusters in red can be seen as less aged people and they have high spending scores, cluster in yellow are less aged people and they are having moderate spending score and cluster in green and pink have less spending scores. Therefore, if the mall gives offers using some membership cards to the green and pink clustered customers then it can retain those customers by increasing the customer's satisfaction. For clusters based on annual income and spending score, as shown in the figures, the clusters in pink can be seen as having less annual income but they have high spending scores. Similarly, cluster in yellow have very high annual income and also very high spending score. Cluster in red have moderate annual income and also moderate spending score. Cluster in blue have very less annual income and also very less spending score. Cluster in green have very high annual income but very low spending score. Now, the mall can give offers using some membership cards to the blue and green clustered customers. Thus, by segmenting the customers the shopping mall can identify its potential customers and thus it can build some strategies which can eventually increase its profits.

REFERENCES

Anderson, W. T. Jr, Cox, E. P. III, & Fulcher, D. G. (1976). Bank Selection Decisions and Market Segmentation: Determinant attribute analysis reveals convenience-and sevice-oriented bank customers. *Journal of Marketing*, *40*(1), 40–45. doi:10.1177/002224297604000107

Aryuni, M., Madyatmadja, E. D., & Miranda, E. (2018). Customer segmentation in XYZ bank using K-means and K-medoids clustering. In *2018 International Conference on Information Management and Technology (ICIMTech)* (pp. 412-416). IEEE. 10.1109/ICIMTech.2018.8528086

Bhade, K., Gulalkari, V., Harwani, N., & Dhage, S. N. (2018). A Systematic Approach to Customer Segmentation and Buyer Targeting for Profit Maximization. In *2018 9th International Conference on Computing, Communication and Networking Technologies (ICCCNT)* (pp. 1-6). IEEE. 10.1109/ICCCNT.2018.8494019

Bholowalia, P., & Kumar, A. (2014). EBK-means: A clustering technique based on elbow method and k-means in WSN. *International Journal of Computers and Applications*, *105*(9).

Borlea, I. D., Precup, R. E., Dragan, F., & Borlea, A. B. (2017). Centroid update approach to K-means clustering. *Advances in Electrical and Computer Engineering*, *17*(4), 3–10. doi:10.4316/AECE.2017.04001

Dullaghan, C., & Rozaki, E. (2017). *Integration of machine learning techniques to evaluate dynamic customer segmentation analysis for mobile customers*. arXiv preprint arXiv:1702.02215.

Ezenkwu, C. P., Ozuomba, S., & Kalu, C. (2015). *Application of K-Means algorithm for efficient customer segmentation: a strategy for targeted customer services*. Academic Press.

Hartigan, J. A., & Wong, M. A. (1979). Algorithm AS 136: A k-means clustering algorithm. *Journal of the Royal Statistical Society. Series C (Applied Statistics), 28*(1), 100-108.

Hruschka, H., & Natter, M. (1999). Comparing performance of feedforward neural nets and K-means for cluster-based market segmentation. *European Journal of Operational Research, 114*(2), 346–353. doi:10.1016/S0377-2217(98)00170-2

Janakirman, S., & Umamaheswari, K. (2014). *A Survey on Data Mining Techniques for Customer Segmentation for Customer Relationship Management.* Academic Press.

Kansal, T., Bahuguna, S., Singh, V., & Choudhury, T. (2018). *Customer segmentation using K-means clustering. In 2018 international conference on computational techniques, electronics and mechanical systems (CTEMS).* IEEE.

Kotler, P. (2005). *Kevin Lane Keller-Marketing Management.* Prentice Hall.

Kumar, V., & Reinartz, W. (2018). *Customer relationship management.* Springer-Verlag GmbH Germany.

Lee, J. H., & Park, S. C. (2005). Intelligent profitable customer's segmentation system based on business intelligence tools. *Expert Systems with Applications, 29*(1), 145–152. doi:10.1016/j.eswa.2005.01.013

Li, Z. (2011, June). Research on customer segmentation in retailing based on clustering model. In *2011 International Conference on Computer Science and Service System (CSSS)* (pp. 3437-3440). IEEE.

MacQueen, J. (1967). Classification and analysis of multivariate observations. In *5th Berkeley Symp. Math. Statist. Probability* (pp. 281-297). Academic Press.

Maimon, O. Z., & Rokach, L. (2014). *Data mining with decision trees: Theory and applications* (Vol. 81). World scientific.

Mirela, D., & Stanica, A. M. (2009). Study of improving the customer relationship management by data mining applications. *Оптико-електронні інформаційно-енергетичні технології,* (1), 55-58.

Namvar, M., Gholamian, M. R., & Khakabi, S. (2010, January). A two phase clustering method for intelligent customer segmentation. In *2010 International Conference on Intelligent Systems, Modelling and Simulation* (pp. 215-219). IEEE. 10.1109/ISMS.2010.48

Singh, A., Yadav, A., & Rana, A. (2013). K-means with Three Different Distance Metrics. *International Journal of Computers and Applications, 67*(10).

Sinha, P. K., & Uniyal, D. P. (2005). Using observational research for behavioural segmentation of shoppers. *Journal of Retailing and Consumer Services, 12*(1), 35–48. doi:10.1016/j.jretconser.2004.02.003

Smith, W. R. (1956). Product differentiation and market segmentation as alternative marketing strategies. *Journal of Marketing, 21*(1), 3–8. doi:10.1177/002224295602100102

Syakur, M. A., Khotimah, B. K., Rochman, E. M. S., & Satoto, B. D. (2018). Integration k-means clustering method and elbow method for identification of the best customer profile cluster. *IOP Conference Series. Materials Science and Engineering, 336*(1), 012017. doi:10.1088/1757-899X/336/1/012017

Tan, P. N., Steinbach, M., & Kumar, V. (2005). *Introduction to data mining.* Addison-Wesley.

Teichert, T., Shehu, E., & von Wartburg, I. (2008). Customer segmentation revisited: The case of the airline industry. *Transportation Research Part A, Policy and Practice, 42*(1), 227–242. doi:10.1016/j.tra.2007.08.003

Thakare, Y. S., & Bagal, S. B. (2015). Performance evaluation of K-means clustering algorithm with various distance metrics. *International Journal of Computers and Applications, 110*(11), 12–16. doi:10.5120/19360-0929

Tsiptsis, K. K., & Chorianopoulos, A. (2011). *Data mining techniques in CRM: inside customer segmentation.* John Wiley & Sons.

Wang, Z., Zuo, Y., Li, T., Chen, C. P., & Yada, K. (2019). Analysis of Customer Segmentation Based on Broad Learning System. In *2019 International Conference on Security, Pattern Analysis, and Cybernetics (SPAC)* (pp. 75-80). IEEE. 10.1109/SPAC49953.2019.237870

Wilson-Jeanselme, M., & Reynolds, J. (2006). The advantages of preference-based segmentation: An investigation of online grocery retailing. *Journal of Targeting, Measurement, and Analysis for Marketing, 14*(4), 297-308.

Wu, J., & Lin, Z. (2005). Research on customer segmentation model by clustering. In *Proceedings of the 7th international conference on electronic commerce* (pp. 316-318). 10.1145/1089551.1089610

Zhang, Z., Zhang, J., & Xue, H. (2008). *Improved K-means clustering algorithm. In 2008 Congress on Image and Signal Processing* (Vol. 5). IEEE.

KEY TERMS AND DEFINITIONS

Centroid-Based Clustering: A centroid-based clustering method organizes the data into non-hierarchical clusters, as opposed to a hierarchical clustering method. K-means clustering is the most widely used centroid-based algorithm.

Chebyshev Distance: The Chebyshev distance calculation, also known as the "maximum metric" in mathematics, measures the distance between two points as the maximum difference between any two of their axis values.

Clustering: Clustering is the process of dividing a population or set of data points into a number of groups such that data points in the same group are more similar than those in other groups. Essentially, the objective is to categorize groups based on similar traits and assign them to clusters.

Customer Relationship Management (CRM): An organization's customer relationship management (CRM) system manages all interactions and relationships with customers and prospects. Ultimately, the goal is to improve business relationships. Using a CRM system can help businesses streamline processes, improve profitability, and stay connected to customers.

Customer Segmentation: A Customer Segmentation is a method of segmenting a customer or business market based on a set of common characteristics.

Elbow Method: The elbow method is a heuristic used in cluster analysis to determine the number of clusters in a data set. The method involves plotting the explained variation as a function of the number of clusters, then choosing the elbow of the curve as the number of clusters to use.

Euclidean Distance: The Euclidean distance between two points in Euclidean space is the length of a line segment between them. Based on the Pythagorean theorem, this distance can be calculated from the Cartesian coordinates of the points, so it is sometimes referred to as the Pythagorean distance.

K-Means: K-means clustering is a method of vector quantization, originally from signal processing, that seeks to partition n observations into k clusters in which each observation belongs to the cluster containing the nearest mean (cluster centers or cluster centroid), which serves as a prototype for the cluster.

Manhattan Distance: Manhattan distance is a distance metric between two points in an N-dimensional space. In geometric terms, it is the sum of the projections of a line segment between two points onto the coordinate axes. In other words, it is the sum of the absolute differences between two points in all dimensions.

Minkowski Distance: A Minkowski distance or Minkowski metric is a metric in a normed vector space that can be thought of as a generalization of both the Euclidean distance and the Manhattan distance. It was named after German mathematician Hermann Minkowski.

Unsupervised Learning: Unsupervised learning, also known as unsupervised machine learning, utilizes machine learning algorithms to analyze and cluster unlabeled data. Without human intervention, these algorithms identify hidden patterns or groups of data. Its ability to find similarities and differences in information makes it the ideal solution for exploratory data analysis, cross-selling strategies, customer segmentation, and image recognition.

Chapter 14
Impact of COVID–19:
Role of Digitalization on Small– and Medium–Sized Enterprises in Kurunegala District in Sri Lanka

Hasini Mekhala Rathnayake
Eastern University, Sri Lanka

ABSTRACT

The coronavirus outbreak is the latest world tragedy that has affected all sectors of the economy. The government's preemptive efforts to safeguard public health include lockdown, confinement, limited movement order, and social distancing. While recognizing the importance of the national order in preventing the immense spread of the virus, the authors contend that there are certain undiscovered impacts of the COVID-19 movement block and the role of digitalization on small and medium enterprises in Kurunegala District. In summary, the impacts of the COVID-19 movement block on SMEs are classified by five themes. Moreover, for the role of digitalization, the researcher used three built-in themes. The research recommends suggestions for future research work, business development agencies, and entrepreneurs.

INTRODUCTION

The Asian economy relies heavily on small and medium-sized businesses (SMEs). They make up more than 98% of all Asian businesses that provide two out of three private sector jobs in the region. As a result, having fully functional support measures for SMEs is critical for Asia's economic success (Taghizadeh-Hesary, 2016). SMEs constitutes for over 75% of the number of enterprises in Sri Lanka and contribute to 52% of the GDP of Sri Lankan economy (Roshan Rassool, 2021). SMEs are critical to the country's socio-economic development. It is estimated that SMEs contribute 52% to the GDP and are considered as the backbone of the economy. Small and medium-sized firms (SMEs) are estimated to account for over 90% of non-agricultural firms in Sri Lanka and 45 percent of overall employment. According to the Economic Census 2013/14 of the Department of Census and Statistics (DCS), the

DOI: 10.4018/978-1-6684-5727-6.ch014

number of SME firms is 1.017 million, employing roughly 2.255 million people in the non-agricultural sector (Gunawardana, 2020).

A Digital Transformation and Technology Adoption Program in Sri Lanka teaches and inspires entrepreneurs from regional SMEs in all industries and sectors about the need of embracing digital technology to expand their businesses (ICTA, 2021). The Sri Lanka Go Digital program is crucial in connecting national government activities, building regional digital economic and national export plans, and supporting the digital transformation of SMEs, all of which contribute to increased national exports. Small and medium firms are characterized by their exceptional flexibility, predisposition for entrepreneurial initiatives, lower production volumes, simple organizational structure, and informal internal communication (Lazarevic-Moravcevic, 2019). SMEs have been affected by the current crisis more severely than the large enterprises because of their sensitivity to the supply and demand shocks. The first registered cases COVID-19 appeared in Wuhan, China in December 2019. Between January and February 2020, the spread of the disease occurred in 31 provinces of mainland China with Wuhan being the epicenter of the epidemic. The Chinese government declared a state of emergency, with the highest-level enforcing measures such as self-quarantine, cancellation of public events, prohibition of crowd gatherings, closure of all businesses and sports facilities except food stores, and closure of highways, railroads, and flights across the country. Restriction measures imposed by the Chinese government were quickly followed by limitations imposed by other countries on travel to and from China. The outbreak of the pandemic has already had a significant impact on the Chinese economy (especially industries such as transportation, tourism, hospitality, entertainment, and financial services) by the end of January. The impact of the COVID-19 outbreaks, lockdowns, and travel ban on the confidence of both domestic and international companies, expected revenue loss, and cash flow challenges were among the findings of a survey of 761 business owners, mostly SMEs, conducted by the University of International Business and Economics in February. (Feng, 2020).

The COVID-2019 virus is mainly spread through droplets of discharge from the nose breathed by people who breathe in the droplets when an infected person coughs in close contact with others (Mutambisi, 2020). As a result, governments established social and physical barriers as a means of limiting the virus's spread. Lockdown has been applied in several countries to ensure the efficiency of social distancing. To restrict the spread of COVID-19, several impoverished countries are following the lead of wealthy ones by mandating strict lockdowns. They compel people to stay at home and restrict their economic activity outside of the home. In locations where health facilities are unable to handle an influx of patients because of the outbreak, lockdown can help relieve the burden of hospitalizing individuals.

Coronavirus disease 2019 (COVID-19) has been putting people's lives at danger. The SARS coronavirus 2 is thought to be spread primarily through close contact (Zhang, 2020). The infection risk in indoor environments is much higher than that in outdoor environments because of possible insufficient ventilation, long periods spent indoors, high close contact rate, and many frequently touched public surfaces (Zhang., 2019). For infection prevention and control, many nonpharmaceutical interventions have been introduced, with the goal of encouraging social distance and reducing exposure time and infection risk during close contact (Colbourn., 2020). In the absence of pharmaceutical therapies, human behavioral change is critical for preventing transmission (West R, 2020).

Infectious diseases have been a significant challenge in recent decades. Following the epidemics of SARS in China in 2002, Ebola in West Africa in 2014, and MERS in 2015, a novel coronavirus (COVID-19) outbreak signaled the start of 2020 (WHO, 2020). The COVID-19 virus, SARS-CoV-2, appears to be spreading mostly from person to person, readily and sustainably, causing respiratory sickness and death in older adults and people of all ages with major underlying medical disorders (CDC, 2020). In less than 3 months, after the first confirmed case in Wuhan, China (December 2019), COVID-19 has been swiftly spreading over the world, exploding into a pandemic that has affected 210 countries and claimed over 100,000 lives (WHO, 2020). Many countries, like Tunisia, have chosen a lockdown policy to restrict the spread of COVID-19 and protect their populations due to the lack of specialized vaccines or treatments. This strategy tries to slow the spread of the epidemic by socially isolating the whole population, closing schools and universities, and halting all non-essential economic operations (CDC, 2020). In 3 months, one-third of humanity was under COVID-19 lockdown. During a lockdown, residents are advised to stay at home and only go out to meet the most basic needs, such as purchasing food. Therefore, COVID-19 caused a drop in household consumption and a shift in their life and spending habits (Survey, 2020). It's fascinating to consider how people's actions have changed over time. Lockdown, on the other hand, has resulted in a reduction in energy and material use.

The income from the tourism industry has recorded US$ 3.59 billion in 2019 compared to US$ 4.38 billion (4.9% to GDP) in 2018 a drop of US$ 0.79 Billion mainly due to the Easter Sunday attack (Gunawardana, 2020). The outbreak of COVD-19, the closure of the Sri Lankan border for international passenger arrivals in mid-March, global travel restrictions, and finally the closure of the AirPort have resulted in significant losses, on top of the revenue loss experienced last year after the Easter Sunday assaults. Most SMEs in the apparel industry rely on textiles and accessories from China, and the supply chain disruption has had a significant impact on them. The micro-level clothing makers also get their raw materials from wholesalers that import the items in bulk, primarily from China and India, and the breakdown of their supply chain, along with the curfew's restrictions, has rendered them practically dormant.

The extremely labor-intensive footwear industry has the potential to be a big contributor to the country's economy. The diverse range of modern shoes like canvass and rubber boots, thongs, sports shoes, leather shoes, etc. are produced, using a variety of raw materials. In the MSME Footwear and Bags sector, the main raw material is genuine leather manufactured locally using a byproduct of the meat Industry (Gunawardana, 2020). Working capital, supply chain breakdowns, and marketing concerns are all prevalent concerns in this industry. In terms of production, consumption, export, and growth possibilities, the processed food industry in Sri Lanka is one of the most promising. Processed food sector consists of Dehydrated Fruits & Vegetables, Processed Gherkins & Cucumber, Herbal Tea, Frozen meat, Sauces, and Tomato ketchup and prepared foods and Dried Sprats, etc (Gunawardana, 2020). Many rural people, particularly women, rely on the traditional handloom and artisan industries for a living. In absence of real data, it could be estimated that there are around 10,000 handlooms in the country operated by the Private sector entrepreneurs, Provincial councils, and Cooperative societies (Gunawardana, 2020). While most handloom fabrics are produced for the domestic market, there are a few well-established companies who cater to the international market.

As we all know, the world is always changing. With the advent of technology and the globalization process, digital transformation with both digital and traditional economies is blossoming globally. Information and communication technology (ICT) contribute significantly to the growth and development of any economy, particularly in developing economies such as India, because it improves productivity and work efficiency by providing a platform for creativity and encouraging innovation, and, most importantly, it assists in entering and remaining in global markets (Debjani, 2021). The process of transforming information into a digital representation is known as digitization. The outcome is a series of integers that define a distinct set of points or samples that can be used to represent an object, image, sound, document, or signal. For the object, this is referred to as digital representation, and for the signal, it is referred to as digital form. In modern practice, digitized data is in the form of binary numbers, which facilitates processing by digital computers and other operations, but strictly speaking, digitizing simply refers to the conversion of analog source material into a numerical format, such as decimal or any other number system.

Because it "allows information of all kinds in all forms to be conveyed with the same efficiency and also intermingled," digitization is critical to data processing, storage, and transmission. Though analog data is more stable, digital data is easier to exchange and retrieve, and it can theoretically be propagated indefinitely without generation loss if it is transferred to new, stable formats as needed. Therefore, many organizations all around the world prefer it as a method of data preservation (McQuail, 2000). Digitaliza-tion is having a favorable impact on the boundaries between persons, businesses, and processes in every industry, while also upsetting the industry ecosystem. As technology pervades and infiltrates practically every aspect of people's lives, from buying groceries online to finding a life partner on a website, they are redefining the interaction between customers, workers, and employers (Muhleisen, 2005). By elimi-nating these barriers, digital transformation (DT) can enhance and help innovate products and service offerings and find proficient methods of working together.

Not only do new start-ups and technology emerge as a result of digital transformation. It also brings challenges to small and medium-sized enterprises. These changes are also reflected in the entire global supply chain of companies, as the nature of value creation has shifted away from classical physical products to "smart" products and data. Implementation of these products and data "in combination with other 'mega-trends' of digitalization, are expected to shape the (digital) supply chain of the future" (Pflaum, 2017).

MAIN FOCUS OF THE CHAPTER

Issues

The COVID-19 coronavirus outbreak is a human tragedy affecting billions of people in this world. The outbreak also imposed negative impacts on the global economy, industries, corporations and small and medium enterprises (SMEs) (Ahmad Raflis Che Omar, 2020). As a result, experts anticipate a slowing of economic activity starting in March 2020 and lasting until the end of the year (Segal, 2020). The lockdown, confinement, limited movement order, movement blocks and social distancing are amongst the preemptive governments' effort to safeguard the public health. Small and medium enterprises (SMEs) affected from this situation among this period in Sri Lanka as well as other countries.

With the discovery of the first Sri Lankan case and the closing of schools in mid-March2020, Sri Lanka saw the full effect of the pandemic. Following the discovery of an increasing number of infected individuals, particularly among those traveling from overseas, the government implemented a 14-day quarantine program for all those entering from foreign countries and those who come into contact with sick people. As the number of infected cases grew, new quarantine centers were opened, and a self-quarantine system was implemented. Subsequently, curfew and lockdown of some areas were introduced as a measure to control the spread of the virus. Curfews were occasionally lifted to allow people to get their daily needs met, and preventive measures such as Social Distancing, the wearing of mandatory face masks, and the usage of other personal protection equipment were implemented. With this situation, most of the economic activities were badly affected causing the MSMEs to undergo severe hardships.

The daily wage earners were the most affected and, in this scenario, and government offered several relief measures for their sustainability (Gunawardana, 2020).

Sri Lanka is a developing economy in the South Asian area, with a service-based economy. According to the Ministry of Industry and Commerce, SMEs account for more than 75% of the country's total number of businesses. SMEs provide such a significant contribution to the country's economic development that it is fair to say they are the country's backbone (Fatoki, 2011). Some countries utilize the number of employees, the amount of money invested, the turnover, or the nature of the business (Gamage, 2003). Even from a Sri Lankan standpoint, there are a variety of reasons to classify a company as a SME. For example, the Industrial Development Board of Sri Lanka (IDB) defines a small industry as a foundation with a capital investment in plant and machinery of less than Rs.4 million (US$ 42,000), and the Central Bank of Sri Lanka (CBSL) defines a small industry as a company with fewer than 50 employees. SMEs are defined as businesses with a capital investment of less than Rs.5 million (US$ 52,500) and fewer than 50 employees, according to the Department of Small Industries (DSI) (Ponnamperuma, 2000). To avoid any misunderstandings, we will use the Ministry of Industry and Commerce's definition of SME's, which was released in 2015. The Ministry of Industry and Commerce's National Policy Framework for SME Development in Sri Lanka defines SMEs based on yearly turnover and the number of persons employed, according to this report. Small businesses have 11-50 people and an annual revenue of Rs. 16-250 million, whereas medium businesses have 51-300 employees and an annual revenue of Rs. 251-750 million. Micro businesses, on the other hand, will have less than ten employees and a revenue of less than Rs.15 million per year. The Sri Lankan government considers SMEs as an important part of the economy, as they account for more than 75 percent of all businesses, employ 45 percent of the working population, and contribute 52 percent of the country's GDP (Gunawardana, 2020). In 2013/14, the Census and Statistics Department released its first economic census on the industry, trade, and services sector, confirming that the SME sector employs over 3 million people in Sri Lanka. It should be mentioned that the economic census found that over 90% of the operations are sole proprietorships (Satharasinghe, 2014).

Digitalization is attracting widespread interest along various industries and policies. "[The] ability to adapt existing products or services into digital counterparts, and hence give advantages over real products," according to the definition (parviainen, 2017). The significance of digitalization is growing all the time. (Kaiser, 2015) predicted in their contribution that in 2020 more than 50 billion devices will be connected to the Internet and (Diamondis, 2015) even forecasts that over 100 billion devices will be linked by the year 2025. This digital development is leading to a data revolution and permanent changes in customer needs, resulting in changes in customer and society (Waller, 2015). The need for digitalization is highly appreciated during the time of COVID-19 movement block. Most of the sectors promote work from home where the usage of digital devices is high among school students, teachers, managers, and all. in the context of SMEs, it is said that they are reluctant to adopt e-commerce in to their business due to certain owner/manager characteristics, existing literatures are mainly highlighting lack of knowledge in how to use technology and low level of computer literacy. Though Sri Lanka's overall literacy rate is high comparative to other developing countries, computer literacy among entrepreneurs is very low. Under firm characteristics, low level of technology usage is the main barrier. Still, most of the SMEs in Sri Lanka use primitive sources for production and marketing and use limited technology for these activities. Therefore, adoption of e-commerce has become very difficult (Thanigaseelan, 2020). In this background during covid-19 the usage of digital devises by SMEs are highly in question. Nowadays, the small and medium enterprises are highly affected by COVID-19 pandemic and movements block.

And, there is a very valuable role from the digitalization. For that reason, this research intends to assess the impact of COVID-19 movement block and role of digitalization on small and medium enterprises (with special reference to Kurunegala district).

Controversies

Objective 01

"To identify the impact of COVID-19 Movement Block on Small and Medium Enterprises in Kurunegala District"

Referring to the first objective "To identify the impact of COVID-19 Movement Block on Small and Medium Enterprises in Kurunegala District" several questions were made and answers of respondents were evaluated first theme analysis. Most scholars discussed COVID-19 pandemic in SME sector. But unfortunately, when considering the real situation in Kurunegala, not much discussing topic. The researcher previously mentioned that in the problem statement. Moreover, it is the most important requirement to identify the impact of COVID-19 movement block on small and medium enterprises located in Kurunegala District, 10 major questions were asked from the selected owners of small and medium enterprises.

Collected information was analyzed according to the selected themes which represent each objective in the study. To achieve the first objective researcher used five (5) themes that can elaborate on the impact of COVID-19 movement block on small and medium enterprises in Kurunegala.

Table 1. Themes which use to discuss the impact of COVID-19 movement block on small and medium enterprises in Kurunegala District

Ranking	Theme
1	Employee Absenteeism
2	Raw Material
3	Price Hike
4	Demand for products
5	Investments

Employee Absenteeism

Employee absenteeism is described as an employee's absence from work on a regular basis. This absence is frequently classified as a habitual absence, as it does not include approved leaves or paid vacation time. It is not easy to show up for work every day. Companies are aware of this and have leave plans in place for employees in the event of emergencies or health concerns. When those off days become regular, though, it becomes a concern and is referred to as absenteeism. Therefore, the researcher was analyzing the employee absenteeism is each SME that is very important for this study. According to the respondents, they stated that the employees are a main resource of their companies. Because of the employee absenteeism, they must face many problems during the COVID-19 movement block period.

"Now... one of the covid 19 spreads was that there were questions about their safety among the people. Therefore, every employee works with the covid in mind. It comes with a delay in the arrival of employees, efficiency issues because they work a little far away when they arrive on time, and then... then. if there is a covid patient in the family in the last few days, the employees will not come to the company because the family is quarantine. But as a first step in such a backdrop, covid is causing other aspects damage due to the lack of attendance of employees."

Respondent 01, Personal Interview, 2021

"Ah...employees suddenly have to quarantine. Then attendance decreases. Then the machine will lose employees to work. Then our daily output will decrease."

Respondent 04, Personal Interview, 2021

"Of course, during moment block, we can't find the necessary labor because especially at this moment, especially for the projects around Colombo because people are afraid to go to Colombo due to this covid thing."

Respondent 08, Personal Interview, 2021

"Yes... ah ... our business is usually affected by the fact that when doing any construction, many civilians want to build it. We work with a variety of people. As a team. If one or two members are absence of that team, maybe the right people, we'll not be able to do that. So sometimes we lose our operator because of covid and no one else can operate it. Sometimes they are quarantined because they are covid."

Respondent 11, Personal Interview, 2021

Raw Material

A raw material, also known as a feedstock, unprocessed material, or main commodity, is a basic substance used to manufacture goods, completed products, energy, or intermediate components that are utilized as feedstock for future finished products. The term "feedstock" implies that these commodities are bottleneck assets that must be used to make other products. Therefore, the researcher was analyzing the raw material is each SME that is very important for this study.

According to the respondents, the main resource is the raw materials in some SMEs. During this COVID-19 pandemic and movement block, they are unable to get their raw materials well. There is a shortage of raw materials. Because of that, the SMEs are facing many problems.

"Hmmm... our raw material network is spread all over the country. When importing all over the country ... we have gone to those institutions and informed them. But it has not yet returned to normal. The process is still at 50%, 60% compared to the previous year."

Respondent 01, Personal Interview, 2021

"A....We do business by buying goods from other suppliers. Then the amount we get decreases. Then the former travel shops will be closed. There is a shortage of raw materials to produce. Because of all of that, our monthly income will eventually decrease or decrease as we wait."

Respondent 03, Personal Interview, 2021

"Now we have locally available raw material. if they are our raw material, but they are their products. Then it indirectly affects us because of their raw material problems."

Respondent 04, Personal Interview, 2021

"In some villages there are our suppliers. They could not be downloaded due to lockdown."

Respondent 06, Personal Interview, 2021

Price Hike

A price hike is a general increase in an economy's pricing level over a period of time. When the general price level rises, each unit of currency buys less goods and services; as a result, inflation indicates a loss of purchasing power per unit of money – a real value loss in the economy's medium of exchange and unit of account. Therefore, the researcher was analyzing the inflation is each SME that is very important for this study. According to the respondents, they stated that because of inflation, they have to pay in additionally. Therefore, that SMEs will increase their prices of products. As a result of that, sales decrease.

"We had to unexpectedly increase the purchase value. We make coconut and coir-based products. We had to increase payments for that raw material to erase the loss of suppliers. These covid affiliates are the highest paid year in my business history. That price increase is approximately 75%."

Respondent 01, Personal Interview, 2021

"Actually, as a whole, as I said before, we deal with about 10 or 12 companies. In each company, they have increased their prices."

Respondent 03, Personal Interview, 2021

"When importing, our raw material has problems due to their price issues."

Respondent 04, Personal Interview, 2021

"Actually… If we take up to now, such foreign exchange rates have gone up and gone to very high price level."

Respondent 07, Personal Interview, 2021

"Mm… And so, due to the moment block in the international context and the freight charges have tripled for the at this moment, for example, earlier if a container is 900USD to deliver it to Sri Lanka, and now it's 3600USD, so that those are the main difficulties."

Respondent 08, Personal Interview, 2021=

Demand for Products

Product demand is a term that defines how much a company's product is desired by customers during a certain time. This could lead to price increases, as the greater the demand, the more people are ready to pay. When the demand decreases, the price tends to follow this downward trend. Therefore, the researcher was analyzing the decrease in demand is each SME that is very important for this study. According to the respondents, they stated that the customers are less frequent. Because of that the demand of products were decreased.

"Ah… our customers reduce their purchases. Lockdown, due to travel restrictions. The orders we receive are decreasing."

Respondent 04, Personal Interview, 2021

"Yes… It really affects my business because there are so many companies involved in this business. They are our main customers. Because of that now we have very low demand. We are doing this business together with them. But now we do not have that ability."

Respondent 09, Personal Interview, 2021

"Ah … usually our business is affected by the fact that people are less likely to hang out."

Respondent 10, Personal Interview, 2021

"Ah… Affects so the main one is the low number of customers. That means they're less likely to go out. Because of this, our demand will decrease."

Respondent 13, Personal Interview, 2021

Investments

An asset or object purchased with the intention of generating income or appreciation is referred to as an investment. Appreciation refers to an increase in the value of an asset over time. When someone buys something as an investment, the goal is not to consume it but to use it to build wealth in the future. Therefore, the researcher was analyzing the decline of investments is each SME that is very important for this study. According to the respondents, they stated that the investments are in very law level during COVID-19 pandemic. They have not money to invest because they want to balance the businesses and protect it.

"Mm... In such a situation no investor will take a second step. Because when there is so much risk, when there is not so much profit, why do we do this by trapping so much more wealth. Why take a risk on this."

Respondent 01, Personal Interview, 2021

"Ah ... we are not thinking about future business yet. Because the hope is to keep up with the current situation."

Respondent 03, Personal Interview, 2021

"Future business directions are clearly affected. Simply put, we think a business has gone backwards in 3 years. That situation has arisen."

Respondent 07, Personal Interview, 2021

Objective 02

"To identify the role of Digitalization on Small and Medium Enterprises during COVID-19 outbreak in Kurunegala District"

Referring to the first objective "To identify the role of Digitalization on Small and Medium Enterprises during COVID-19 outbreak in Kurunegala District" several questions were made and answers of respondents were evaluated first theme analysis. Most scholars discussed COVID-19 pandemic in SME sector. But unfortunately, when considering the real situation in Kurunegala, not much discussing topic. The researcher previously mentioned that in the problem statement. Moreover, it is the most important requirement to identify the nature of the role of Digitalization on Small and Medium Enterprises during COVID-19 outbreak in Kurunegala District, 10 major questions were asked from the selected owners of small and medium enterprises.

Collected information was analyzed according to the selected themes which represent each objective in the study. To achieve the second objective researcher used three (3) themes that can elaborate on the role of Digitalization on Small and Medium Enterprises during COVID-19 outbreak in Kurunegala District.

Table 2. Themes which use to discuss the role of digitalization in small and medium enterprises during COVID-19 pandemic in Kurunegala District

Ranking	Theme
1	Online Business
2	Communication
3	Work from Home

Online Business

Any type of company or commercial transaction that involves sharing information via the internet is referred to as online business or e-business. Commerce is the exchange of goods and services between firms, groups, and individuals, and it is one of the most important aspects of any company. Therefore, the researcher was analyzing the online business is each SME that is very important for this study. According to the respondents, they stated that the digitalization is the most important things in this COVID-19 pandemic, and some of them stated that there was not a change of about these days, they already use digitalization.

"Ah ... We usually work with digitalization. our real customers are buyers who export. Then the convenience of that system is to deal with a limited amount. There is no big difference between before and after digitalization."

Respondent 01, Personal Interview, 2021

"Ah... I used a lot for money transfers."

Respondent 04, Personal Interview, 2021

"Actually, yes. We have a few days. We got it fully digitalized, like we have an online shop available, and also customers."

Respondent 05, Personal Interview, 2021

"Mm... Yes. We developed the online business. We delivered goods to our customer's houses. Our company from Kurunegala did that very successfully. We received too many orders. We did them through Facebook, WhatsApp. A separate system was created for that. Separate employees were set aside to work in them. We planned it. Then the complaints decreased. That was a big advantage for us. Bookshop online all over the country. Despite the disadvantages of Covid, we took advantage of it."

Respondent 06, Personal Interview, 2021

Communication

The obvious answer to the unpleasant divisions between self and other, private and public, and inner thinking and exterior word is communication. Because it is widely used to refer to a wide variety of diverse actions, or to limit what can be included in the category of communication, as this definition demonstrates, communication is difficult to define in a consistent manner. The difficulty in defining communication, according to John Peters, stems from the fact that it is both a universal phenomenon and a distinct discipline of institutional academic study. Therefore, the researcher was analyzing the communication is each SME that is very important for this study. According to the respondents, they stated that the communication is very easy because of digitalization and also, they can decrease costs and save their time from it.

"At that time, it was really easy because some people sent the required document online and did those things. Without that we would have to touch a lot of those things if we were documentaries. A lot was controlled through this. If there was a problem, they could do those things with the system they had. So, it really benefited a lot."

Respondent 03, Personal Interview, 2021

"Mm... We can follow the whole process without visiting one of our showrooms. Our customers can inquire everything online. They can get the product specifications; everything is online and the productivity available steps."

Respondent 05, Personal Interview, 2021

"Actually, hmm... we haven't increased any digitalized processes because we have already been using the CIP systems and online meetings for, I think several years now we have. We had already realized the maximum extent that we could realize in, so it was no way to change."

Respondent 08, Personal Interview, 2021

Work from Home

Telecommuting, also known as remote working, distance working, telework, teleworking, working from home (WFH), mobile work, remote job, work from anywhere (WFA), and flexible workplace, is a work arrangement in which employees do not commute to a central office building, warehouse, or store. Therefore, the researcher was analyzing the work from home is each SME that is very important for this study. According to the respondents, they stated that they use digitalization very effectively to work from home during COVID-19 pandemic.

"Yes. Here it is. We did our works from home through online. We have 3 civil engineers. Most of the employees work under them. So, they get help where they need it."

Respondent 11, Personal Interview, 2021

"We do everything online. But work from home status is not yet in our business."

Respondent 15, Personal Interview, 2021

Problems

Employee Absenteeism

In the context of employee absenteeism, the researcher found out that the employees in the small and medium enterprises in Kurunegala District are the main human capital. Employee absenteeism highly affects the production process of businesses. Because of the COVID-19 movement block, employee absenteeism is increasing every day. Therefore, employee absenteeism is highly affected by the CO-VID-19 movement block. According to the (Matthew, 2020), As a result of their activity during the epidemic, specific categories of employees, such as health care workers and food production workers, may be at an increased risk of SARS-CoV-2 infection, according to public health surveillance and field research. The Occupational Safety and Health Administration has issued recommendations for protecting important critical infrastructure workers, which their employers should follow. In addition, in this and future pandemics, better surveillance is required to track industry- and occupation-specific morbidity and mortality. In May 2020, CDC (Centers for Disease Control and Prevention) revised its COVID-19 Case Report Form to record certain health care–specific occupations, as well as limited information on suspected workplace exposures and settings for essential critical infrastructure workers. Additional data on job factors could aid in better describing the occupational risk and impact of COVID-19, as well as informing intervention efforts.

Raw Materials

In the context of raw materials, the researcher found out that the raw materials in the small and medium enterprises in Kurunegala District are the main resources. The companies are unable to run their business without raw materials. Because of the COVID-19 movement block, there was travel restriction among Districts and some areas were lockdown. Some suppliers of SMEs were unable to supply their products because they were unable to get their raw materials. And some suppliers increase their prices of products because of shortage of raw materials. According to these problems the SMEs were unable to buy enough raw materials, and the suppliers of SMEs were unable to supply their products continually in Kurunegala District. According to (Kavindi B.G.H, 2021), the key reason for rising production prices for the Sri Lankan garment industry is that the COVID-19 has infected the primary source of raw materials suppliers in China. After China's instant shutdown, the garment industry's whole supply chain, which is fully reliant on China, was interrupted. Bangladesh, Myanmar, Sri Lanka, and Pakistan, the world's leading manufacturing countries, rely heavily on China for its raw resources. Because of the COVID-19 problem, which impacted timely shipment and receipt of items due to shortages and logistics bottlenecks, supplies failed, and raw material supply was unpredictable.

Price Hike

In the context of price hikes, the researcher found out that the price levels of goods and services are increasing during this COVID-19 pandemic on behalf of foreign exchange rates, labor shortage, raw material shortage. When the suppliers of SMEs increase their price levels of products, the SMEs in Kurunegala District should have to increase their products. The prices are increasing on behalf of the shortage of raw materials. Therefore, there is price hike in the Kurunegala District, as the COVID-19 movement block.

According to (Brent H. Meyer, 2020), the coronavirus pandemic has had a severe impact on the United States since mid-March 2020, with efforts to prevent the virus's spread leading to the shutdown of major sections of the economy. Business operations, sales activity, and supply chains have all been disrupted. The findings imply that, on average, businesses have perceived the crisis as a demand rather than a supply shock. Firms have dropped wages for a significant portion of their staff in response to the demand shock, expect further salary cuts by the end of 2020, and expect to lower selling prices shortly. Also, consistent with a demand shock, firms lowered their 1- year ahead inflation expectations. At the same time, household inflation expectations have risen considerably, indicating that households are focusing on key costs or are concerned about how vulnerable their nominal income is to the epidemic and their capacity to manage in the face of sharp food price increases. The transfer of lower-cost raw materials from China, according to (Kavindi B.G.H, 2021), led Sri Lankan enterprises to seek out new suppliers within the country. The new supplier's raw materials costs are much higher than the previous suppliers. So that is one reason for the increase in manufacturing costs of products. Before the covid-19, buyers ordered products in larger batch sizes. Currently, due to a lack of demand, buyers looking for products in smaller batch sizes, and that leads to higher manufacturing costs.

Demand for Products

In the context of the demand for products, the researcher found out that the customers in Kurunegala District did not go to shops or anything because of the COVID-19 movement block and the curfew. And they reduce their needs and wants. On the other hand, the price levels were increased and the buying power of the customers in Kurunegala District is very low because of decreasing their income levels. Because some individuals are lost their jobs, some individuals cannot do their businesses during CO-VID-19 pandemic period. According to (Kavindi B.G.H, 2021), the garment sector is heavily dependent on textiles, the supply of accessories from China, and supply chain disruption. Micro-scale garment makers also buy their raw materials in bulk from wholesalers, primarily in China and India, and have nearly gone out of business because of the supply chain collapse, which has been compounded by the curfew-imposed limitations. Many clients have postponed or lost orders, and some have deferred payments for exports. Many physical stores were closed because of this crisis, and European and Chinese buyers began canceling and suspending supplier orders. Asian manufacturers Outside of China, COVID-19 was initially considered an opportunity. Buyers were exploring for alternate sources as orders climbed. The virus began to have a negative economic impact on destinations.

Investments

In the context of investments, the researcher found out that the SMEs in Kurunegala District decrease and stop their future investments of their businesses and never go to new step in their business during the COVID-19 pandemic. The income levels of SMEs are very low during this period. They decide to carry on the business without any profits because they have to face a lot of problems and some SMEs have to stop their business. On behalf of those reasons, the SMEs in Kurunegala District did not plan about the future they only want to carry on their businesses during the COVID-19 movement block period.

Online Business

In the context of online business, the researcher found out that the SMEs in Kurunegala District is mostly using online business during the COVID-19 period for their daily businesses because the SMEs can get more income and, they were able to create and catch new customers from the business market as their benefit. Therefore, the SMEs in Kurunegala District get many benefits through online business. According to (Al-Ghraibah., 2020), businesses are today experiencing unprecedented hurdles because of COVID 19, and client retention has never been more critical. Customer retention is described as the process of converting new consumers into regular customers while maintaining a positive relationship with them. Most retailers were into the traditional way of conducting business. However, because of COVID 19, new clients and a new business model have emerged. This has two sides. On the one hand, it is an opportunity for businesses to broaden their reach and coverage, as well as their consumer base. On the other side, it is a threat and a challenge since it will raise the level of competitiveness.

His research found that the responsiveness of the services is one of the most important determinants of online client retention. Customers viewed rapid delivery as a good criterion to evaluate firms during COVID 19. Customers regarded fast delivery as a good criterion to evaluate businesses during COVID 19. The second important predictor of online customer retention is customer satisfaction. The satisfaction of the customer with the services or goods provided is essential. Ease of use is important for online activities. The ease of using the website and process of payment is critical for online customers. The final crucial determinant of online customer retention is an attitude toward the service.

According to (Kavindi B.G.H, 2021), at present many countries are still in a state of complete lockdown. Consumers have found it impossible to physically visit stores and meet their daily necessities because of the shutdown. These limitations have been implemented in several other nations, but people do not go to the stores because they are afraid of the corona, and the restrictions on the sale of items in shops have been removed because of government choices. Furthermore, these products' storage and shipping have been significantly impacted. As a result, people are increasingly resorting to the Internet for their demands, particularly in the case of Before Corona, which is unusual nowadays but gaining popularity. Another aspect to consider is that most garment companies have now adopted the "B to B" technique, which has evolved into the "B to C" methodology. Companies made only large-scale orders in the past, but now, even small-scale orders are handled by apparel companies. Apparel, as a medium, has a lot of potential in the Amazon and Alibaba e-market spaces these days.

Communication

In the context of communication, the researcher found out that all SMEs in Kurunegala District conduct all communications online. It is very fast, easy, and economical. And some customers sent the required document online and did those things. Without that SMEs would have to touch a lot of those things if they were documentaries. Therefore, digitalization is an essential service during the COVID-19 pandemic in Kurunegala District. According to (Ahmeti., 2021), many businesses have suffered worker aversion to going to work due to fear of infection. This shortcoming, in addition to other issues, has slowed economic activity even more. Companies that were more open to process digitization had a far easier time overcoming these communication issues during the pandemic. Before the epidemic, only a few of the organizations interviewed were using online team communication systems. They were compelled to transfer their interactions online because of the epidemic, including having business meetings, checking task completion, and coordinating projects with teams via the internet. Businesses that digitized their internal and external communication procedures transitioned to the new normal more smoothly. Even when the pandemic is ended, some businesses have stated that they will continue to use these digital technologies. The ability to work from home has had its benefits for employees; however, one major concern they have expressed about working remotely is surveillance. There appears to be a level of unease among employees who are required to use work laptops and communicate through the company's chosen platforms; they are unsure of the extent to which their employers can watch them.

Direct physical communication between buyers/consumers and businesses has been extremely difficult, resulting in a lack of accurate and timely information from buyers/consumers about business offers and products, as well as a decline in product purchases and interest. Business operations have shifted online because of fear and movement restrictions, highlighting the benefits of doing business online. With most of the consumption taking place online, social media platforms, company websites, and CRM platforms have become critical for business-to-consumer communication and value exchange. The world has learned to embrace this pandemic, adapting to a new normal way of living, and communicating mainly using digital tools to do so. We have yet to see how comfortable we will get with this new normal and whether, once the pandemic is gone, we will return to our old ways of doing things.

Work from Home

In the context of work from home, the researcher found out that the employees of some SMEs in the Kurunegala District work from home during this COVID-19 pandemic. But some SMEs do have not enough facilities and do not develop like that level for work from home system. Working from home has become the new normal, according to (Bawa., 2020), as many firms and workers struggle to stay operating under the social distancing limitations required to stop the spread of the COVID-19 virus. Working from home not only lowers social contact involved with commuting to and from work, but it also removes the potential spread of the virus at the workplace - between employees and between employees and consumers.

The limited evidence implies that workers are more productive when they work from home, but this assumes that their tasks are capable of being done from home in the first place. There is also a direct reduction in commuting times, potentially freeing up more time for productive tasks. Because most workers tend to work longer hours when they work from home, WFH may help workers to devote more time to work by more efficiently mixing work time with family and other non-work activities. A range of benefits from WFH has been identified for workers. These benefits include a direct reduction in commute time and associated travel costs, more control over start and finish times and work tempo, and more flexibility in balancing work and family obligations. That flexibility may be crucial in the COVID-19 context for workers who need to be at home to oversee their children and support them in homeschooling, or to provide support for elderly parents or other friends and relatives in need. Working from home reduces work-family conflict, according to some studies, and this has been cited as a factor for teleworking's growing popularity in the United States. Others argue that bringing work into the home to take up the same physical space, time, and resources that would otherwise be dedicated to family life exacerbates conflict and accentuates work's intrusion into family life.

SOLUTIONS AND RECOMMENDATIONS

The recommendation is the suggestions made by the researcher to improve or enhance the researched problem. In this study, the recommendation was also obtained from the respondents to validate the study with the true findings and essential solutions by the people experiencing the problem in addition to the researcher's recommendations. The small and medium enterprises should further promote work from system. Digitization is needed to move forward with new technology and avoid challenges. In this study, some of SMEs did not connect with digitalization. Because some of them haven't enough knowledge about new technology, and some of them did not think about it and it's uses. And, some respondents continue their tradition and the cultures. It also points out that small and medium enterprises have very low government intervention during COVID-19 periods. The SMEs stated that when request a corporation from government, then government will help. But without any request the government did not any corporation. But private companies have helped many times to small and medium enterprises during this COVID-19 pandemic. The small and medium enterprises are more concerned about the health of their employees. It needs to grow further. They also should be more concerned about the safety of their customers.

FUTURE RESEARCH DIRECTIONS

Obtaining additional samples and furthering this research would be more critical. If those studies can cover other SMEs, and other district SMEs can cover other district areas as well, the study's credibility will rise, and the generalizability of the research will be attained by extending the research in a quantitative method. The results will be more reliable if the interviews are conducted from multiple perspectives, rather than only semi-structured open-ended interviews. Increased reliability will also come from examining the results in different dimensions.

CONCLUSION

This study was conducted to identify impact of COVID-19 movement block and role of digitalization on small and medium enterprises in Kurunegala District. To that end, the researcher established two sub-objectives. These aims include addressing the impact of COVID-19 movement block on small and medium enterprises in Kurunegala District and role of digitalization on small and medium enterprises in Kurunegala District. To achieve the research objectives, the study was devised using a descriptive qualitative approach. Primary data were collected from 15 small and medium enterprises as per the sample from Kurunegala District for the validation purpose through semi-structured interviews. Secondary data were gathered through research articles, newspapers, articles, books, magazines and the internet. The analysis of collected data is done by the thematic analysis method by using NVivo 10 qualitative analysis software.

Referring to the selected sample it can be considered as a typical cross-section of owners in small and medium enterprises in Kurunegala District. This will enhance the representation of the population scope by the sample. According to the first objective in this research, identify the impact of COVID-19 movement block on small and medium enterprises in Kurunegala District, researcher built five major/parent themes such as employee absenteeism, raw materials, price hike, demand for products and investments. The identified second objective was identifying the role of digitalization on small and medium enterprises in Kurunegala District. Under that researcher identified three major themes, such as online business, communication, and work from home. Finally, the researcher found that small and medium enterprises in Kurunegala District are highly affected from COVID-19 movement block and there is a very valuable support from the digitalization to the small and medium enterprises in Kurunegala District.

ACKNOWLEDGMENT

First and foremost, I would like to express my deepest gratitude to my supervisor, Dr. (Mrs.) P. Pretheeba, Senior Lecturer, Faculty of Commerce and Management, Eastern University, Sri Lanka who has guided and supported me throughout the completion of this research project. Her gracious and tireless efforts were extended to me at all stages of the study's presentation. She gave me a lot of patience and important time, as well as unreserved assistance and helpful suggestions, all of which contributed to my effective completion of this report. I want to express my gratitude to her once more for her unwavering support and cooperation in my research study.

I express my sincere thanks to Dr. S. Jeyarajah, Dean, Faculty of Commerce and Management, Eastern University, Sri Lanka. And, I would like to express my gratitude to Dr. A. A. Arulrajah, the Head of the Department of Management, Faculty of Commerce and Management, Eastern University, Sri Lanka. I wish to thank you for the encouragement and support are given to me by the staff members in the Faculty of Commerce and Management, Library and Computer Unit and the English Unit are wholeheartedly acknowledged.

I express my sincere thanks to Owners, Managers, Directors of small and medium enterprises in Kurunegala District for their kind co-operation for providing the requested permission without any hesitation to collect data from their respected companies for this study. Furthermore, I would like to thank CEO of Wayamba Chamber of Commerce to provide me all details of SMEs in Kurunegala District. Moreover, I would like to thank my parents and friends, who have morally supported and take care of me especially those who work together and spent their valuable time.

Once again, I also wish to thank everyone who had helped me in numerous ways to carry on my research smoothly and make the study great success. I warmly thank them all.

REFERENCES

Ahmad Raflis Che Omar, S. I. (2020). The impact of covid-19 movement control order on SMEs' businesses and survival strategies. *Malaysian Journal of Society and Space*, 139-152.

Ahmeti, B. (2021). *Business Communication during the COVID-19 pandemic*. PECB University.

Al-Ghraibah., D. O. (2020). Online consumer retention in Saudi Arabia during COVID 19: The moderating role of online trust. *Journal of Critical Reviews*.

Bawa., M. D. (2020). *Working from Home in the COVID-19 Lockdown*. Bankwest Curtin Economics Centre Research Brief COVID-19 #5.

Brent, H., & Meyer, B. P. (2020). *The Impact of the COVID-19 Pandemic on Business Expectations*. Working Paper 2020-17a.

CDC. (2020, March 10). *Coronavirus (COVID-19)*. Retrieved from https ://www.cdc.gov/coron aviru s/2019-ncov/index .html

Colbourn., T. (2020). Extending pr relaxing distancing control measures. *COVID-19*, e236-7.

Debjani, S. A. (2021). Imperative role of Digitalization in the Indian economy During COVID-19. *International Journal of Advanced Research in Science, Communication and Technology.*

Diamondis, P. (2015). *The world in 2025: 8 Predictions fpr the next 10 years.* Singularity University.

Fatoki. (2011). The impact of human, social and financial capital on the performance f malland medium sized enterprises (SME's) in South Africa. *Journal of Social Science*, 193 - 204.

Feng, H. W. (2020). *Research Report on Companies' Survival and Development Strategy During a Novel Coronavirus Epidemic.* UIBE Press.

Gamage. (2003). *Small and Medium enterprises in Sri Lanka.* Academic Press.

Gunawardana. (2020, May). The Impact of COVID 19 to SME Sector in Sri Lanka. *COVID-19.*

ICTA. (2021). *ICTA adeas oriented.* ICTA.

Kaiser, D. H. (2015). *Wie das Internet der Dinge neue Geschaftsmodelle ermoglicht.* HDM Praxis der Wirschaftsmodelle.

Kavindi B.G.H, P. G. (2021). The effect of the covid 19 on overall firm performance in Sri lankan Apparel companies. *International Journal of Business, Economics and Law.*

Lazarevic-Moravcevic, M. (2019). *Characteristics of marketing communication strategy of a small enterprises.* Academic Press.

Matthew, G. S. (2020). *Increases in Health-Related Workplace Absenteeism Among Workers in Essential Critical Infrastructure Occupations During the COVID-19 Pandemic — United States.* Morbidity and Mortality Weekly Report.

McQuail. (2000). *McQuil's Mass Communication Theory.* Sage.

Muhleisen, M. &. (2005). *The long and short of the digital revolution.* IMF, Finance & Development.

Mutambisi, A. M. (2020). *The urban penalty of COVID-2019 lockdowns across the globe: manifestations and lessons for Anglophone sub-Saharan Africa.* Academic Press.

Parviainen, P. K. (2017). Tackling the digitalization challenge: How to benefit from dgotalization in practice. *International Journal of Information Systems and Project Management*, 5(1), 63–77.

Pflaum, C. K. (2017). *Toward the development of a maturity model for digitalization within the manufacturing industry's supply chain.* Academic Press.

Ponnamperuma. (2000). *SMEs in Competitive Markets.* Tokyo: Asian Productivity Organization.

Roshan Rassool, D. (2021). *Digital Transformation for Small & Medium Enterprises.* European - American Journals.

Satharasinghe. (2014). *Key indicators of industry trade and services sector.* Department of Census and statistics.

Segal, S. (2020). *The global economic impacts of COVID-19.* Center for Strategic and International Studies.

Survey, C. C. (2020, March 26). *Coronavirus consumer trends: Consumer electronics, pet supplies, and more*. Retrieved from https://www.crite o.com/insig hts/coron aviru s-consu mer-trend s/

Taghizadeh-Hesary, N. Y. (2016). *Major challenges facing small and medium seized enterprises in Asia and solutions for mitigationg team*. Asian Development Bank Institute.

Waller, M. R. (2015). *Digital to the Core: Remastering leadership for your industry, your enterprises and your self*. Bibliomotion Inc.

West R, M. S. (2020). *Applying principles of behavior change to reduce SARS-CoV-2 transmission*. Academic Press.

WHO. (2020, April 10). *Coronavirus disease (COVID-19) Pandemic*. Retrieved from https ://www.who. int/emerg encie s/disea ses/novel-coronavirus-2019

Zhang, S. Y. (2020). Asymptomatic and symptomatic SARS-Cv-2 infections in close contacts of CO-VID-19 patients. *COVID-19*.

Zhang., T. J. (2019). Human behavior during close contact in a graduate student office. *COVID-19, 29*, 577-90.

Compilation of References

Aaker, D. A. (1991). *Managing Brand Equity*. Free Press.

Aaker, D. A. (1996). *Building strong brands*. Free Press.

Abor, J., & Quartey, P. (2010). Issues in SME development in Ghana and South Africa. *International Research Journal of Finance and Economics*, *39*, 218–228.

Abulibdeh, A. (2020). Can COVID-19 mitigation measures promote telework practices? *Journal of Labor and Society,* (23), 551–576.

Abyad, A. (2017). Importance of consumer trust in e-commerce. *Middle East Journal of Business*, *12*(3), 20–24. doi:10.5742/MEJB.2017.92971

Adede, O. A., Kibera, F. N., & Owino, J. O. (2017). Electronic marketing practices, competitive environment, and performance of telecommunications companies in Kenya. *British Journal of Marketing Studies*, *5*(5), 60–67.

Aderemi, T. A., Ojo, L. B., Ifeanyi, O. J., & Efunbajo, S. A. (2020). Impact of Corona Virus (COVID-19) pandemic on small and medium scale enterprises (SMEs) in Nigeria: A critical case study. *Acta Universitatis Danubius OEconomica*, *16*(4), 81–98.

Aeron, P., Jain, S., & Kumar, A. (2019). Revisiting trust toward e-retailers among Indian online consumers. *Journal of Internet Commerce*, *18*(1), 45–72. doi:10.1080/15332861.2019.1567186

Agrawal, A., Gans, J., & Goldfarb, A. (2020, September-October). How to win with machine learning. *Harvard Business Review*, 126–133.

Agwu, M., & Murray, J. P. (2014). Drivers and inhibitors to E-commerce adoption among SMEs in Nigeria. *Journal of Emerging Trends in Computing and Information Sciences*, *5*(3), 192–199.

Ahmad Raflis Che Omar, S. I. (2020). The impact of covid-19 movement control order on SMEs' businesses and survival strategies. *Malaysian Journal of Society and Space*, 139-152.

Ahmadi, E., Wicaksono, H., & Valilai, O. F. (2021). Extending the last mile delivery routing problem for enhancing sustainability by drones using a sentiment analysis approach. *2021 IEEE International Conference on Industrial Engineering and Engineering Management, IEEM 2021*, 207-212. 10.1109/IEEM50564.2021.9672856

Ahmad, K., Ayyash, M. M., & Al-Qudah, O. M. A. (2018). The effect of culture values on consumer intention to use Arabic e-commerce websites in Jordan: An empirical investigation. *International Journal of Business Information Systems*, *29*(2), 155–182. doi:10.1504/IJBIS.2018.094691

Ahmad, S. Z., Bakar, A. R. A., & Ahmad, N. (2019). Social media adoption and its impact on firm performance: The case of the UAE. *International Journal of Entrepreneurial Behaviour & Research*, *25*(1), 84–111. doi:10.1108/IJEBR-08-2017-0299

Ahmad, S. Z., Rahim, A., Bakar, A., & Mohamed, T. (2015). Information Technology for Development: An Empirical Study of Factors Affecting e-Commerce Adoption among Small- and Medium- Sized Enterprises in a Developing Country. Advance online publication. doi:10.1080/02681102.2014.899961

Ahmeti, B. (2021). *Business Communication during the COVID-19 pandemic*. PECB University.

Ainin, S., Parveen, F., Moghavvemi, S., Jaafar, N. I., & Mohd Shuib, N. L. (2015). Factors influencing the use of social media by SMEs and its performance outcomes. *Industrial Management & Data Systems*, *115*(3), 570–588. doi:10.1108/IMDS-07-2014-0205

Akyuz, M., & Ibrahim, A. A. (2020). Effect of electronic marketing on the performance of SMEs in Karu Local Government Area, Nasarawa State of Nigeria. *FUO Quarterly Journal of Contemporary Research*, *8*(2), 1–16.

Alcaide, J.C., Bernués, S., Díaz-Aroca, E., Espinosa, R., Muñiz, R., Smith, C. (2013). Marketing y Pymes. *Las principales claves de marketing en la pequeña y mediana empresa.*

Alghizzawi, M. (2019a). A survey of the role of social media platforms in viral marketing: The influence of eWOM. *International Journal of Information Technology and Language Studies*, *3*(2).

Alghizzawi, M. (2019b). The role of digital marketing in consumer behavior: A survey. *International Journal of Information Technology and Language Studies*, *3*(1).

Al-Ghraibah., D. O. (2020). Online consumer retention in Saudi Arabia during COVID 19: The moderating role of online trust. *Journal of Critical Reviews*.

Ali Qalati, S., Li, W., Ahmed, N., Ali Mirani, M., & Khan, A. (2020). Examining the factors affecting SME performance: The mediating role of social media adoption. *Sustainability*, *13*(1), 75. doi:10.3390u13010075

Alsaad, A. M. (2017). The moderating role of trust in business to electronic business commerce (B2B EC) adoption. *Computers in Human Behavior*, *68*, 157–169. doi:10.1016/j.chb.2016.11.040

Alsaad, A. M., Mohamad, R., & Ismail, N. A. (2015). Perceived desirability and firm's intention to adopt business-to-business e-commerce: A test of the second-order construct. *Advanced Science Letters*, *21*(6), 2028–2032. doi:10.1166/asl.2015.6194

Alshaketheep, K. (2020). Digital Marketing during COVID 19: Consumer's Perspective. *WSEAS Transactions on Business and Economics*, 831–841.

Altuntaş Vural, C., & Aktepe, Ç. (2021). Why do some sustainable urban logistics innovations fail? The case of collection and delivery points. *Research in Transportation Business & Management*, 100690. Advance online publication. doi:10.1016/j.rtbm.2021.100690

Ambasna-Jones, M. (2020). *Between a cloud and a hard place: companies change applications tack*. Available: https://www.computerweekly.com/feature/Between-a-cloud-and-a-hard-place-companies-change-applications-tack

Ambulkar, S., Blackhurst, J., & Grawe, S. (2015). Firm's Resilience to Supply Chain Disruptions: Scale Development and Empirical Examination. *Journal of Operations Management*, *33-34*(1), 111–122. doi:10.1016/j.jom.2014.11.002

Amra, R., Hlatshwayo, A., & McMillan, L. (2013). SMME Employment in South Africa. In *Biennial conference of the economic society of South Africa*. Available: http://b-ok.cc

Ananda, A. S., Hernández-García, Á., & Lamberti, L. (2018). *SME fashion brands and social media marketing: From strategies to actions*. Academic Press.

Anderson, W. T. Jr, Cox, E. P. III, & Fulcher, D. G. (1976). Bank Selection Decisions and Market Segmentation: Determinant attribute analysis reveals convenience-and sevice-oriented bank customers. *Journal of Marketing*, *40*(1), 40–45. doi:10.1177/002224297604000107

Andersson, S., & Wikström, N. (2017). Why and how are social media used in a B2B context, and which stakeholders are involved? *Journal of Business and Industrial Marketing*, *32*(8), 1098–1108. doi:10.1108/JBIM-07-2016-0148

Andreev, O., The, C. P., Ghandour, A., & Gurova, T. (2020). Information technologies, e-commerce retail platforms and the impact on the regional economy. *Journal of Talent Development and Excellence*, *12*(2s), 4205–4216.

Andreopoulou, Z., Koliouska, C., Galariotis, E., & Zopounidis, C. (2018). Renewable energy sources: Using PROMETHEE II for ranking websites to support market opportunities. *Technological Forecasting and Social Change*, *131*, 31–37. doi:10.1016/j.techfore.2017.06.007

Angkiriwang, R., Pujawan, I. N., & Budi, S. (2014). Managing uncertainty through supply chain flexibility: Reactive vs. proactive approaches. *Production & Manufacturing Research*, *2*(1), 50–70. doi:10.1080/21693277.2014.882804

Anne, M. W. (2020). Digital marketing strategies and the marketing performance of top 100 small and medium enterprises (SMESs) in Kenya. *International Journal of Research in Management & Business Studies*, *7*(3), 26–31.

Apeji, U.D., & Sunmola, F.T. (2022). Sustainable supply chain visibility assessment and proposals for improvements using fuzzy logic. *Journal of Modelling in Management*. . doi:10.1108/JM2-08-2021-01

Arbi, K. A., Bukhari, S. A. H., & Saadat, Z. (2017). Theoretical framework for taxonomizing sources of competitive advantage. *Management Research and Practice*, *9*(4), 48-60. http://mrp.ase.ro

Arora, A., & Singh, S. (2019). Sustainability issues in freshfruggies: Hyperlocal fruits and vegetables delivery model. *Emerald Emerging Markets Case Studies*, *9*(2), 1–21. doi:10.1108/EEMCS-10-2018-0222

Arora, S. (2019). Devising e-commerce and green e-commerce sustainability. *International Journal of Engineering Development and Research*, *7*(2), 206–210.

Aryuni, M., Madyatmadja, E. D., & Miranda, E. (2018). Customer segmentation in XYZ bank using K-means and K-medoids clustering. In *2018 International Conference on Information Management and Technology (ICIMTech)* (pp. 412-416). IEEE. 10.1109/ICIMTech.2018.8528086

Ashraf, A. R., Thongpapanl, N., & Auh, S. (2014). The application of the technology acceptance model under different cultural contexts: The case of online shopping adoption. *Journal of International Marketing*, *22*(3), 68–93. doi:10.1509/jim.14.0065

Atanassova, I., & Clark, L. (2015). Social media practices in SME marketing activities: A theoretical framework and research agenda. *Journal of Customer Behaviour*, *14*(2), 163–183. doi:10.1362/147539215X14373846805824

Atiku, S., Jeremiah, A., & Boateng, F. (2020). Perceptions of flexible work arrangements in selected African countries during the coronavirus pandemic. *South African Journal of Business Management*, *51*(1), 1–10. doi:10.4102ajbm.v51i1.2285

Attract Capital. (2020). *Business growth*. Available: www.atractcapital.com

Aubakirova, G.M. (2020). Transformatsionnyye preobrazovaniya ekonomiki Kazakhstana. *Problemy prognozirovaniya*, *1*, 155-163.

Awad, N. F., & Ragowsky, A. (2008). Establishing trust in electronic commerce through online word of mouth: An examination across genders. *Journal of Management Information Systems, 24*(4), 101–121. doi:10.2753/MIS0742-1222240404

Azam, A., Qiang, F., Abbas, S. A., & Ibrahim Abdullah, M. (2013). Structural equation modeling (SEM) based trust analysis of Muslim consumers in the collective religion affiliation model in e-commerce. *Journal of Islamic Marketing, 4*(2), 134–149. doi:10.1108/17590831311329278

Azman Free Zone. (2020). *E-Commerce: Trends and Challenges During the Covid-19.* https://www.afz.ae/en/resources/blogs/2020/may/e-commerce

Babayeva, N. 2020. *Perception of simplicity in brand image design by different generations* [Master Thesis]. Bahçeşehir Üniversitesi.

Bacon, C. M., Getz, C., Kraus, S., Montenegro, M., & Holland, K. (2012). The social dimensions of sustainability and change in diversified farming systems. *Ecology and Society, 17*(4), 41. doi:10.5751/ES-05226-170441

Bacon, D. R., & Schneider, A. B. (2019). Exploring sources of marketing knowledge for small business decision-makers. *Journal for Advancement of Marketing Education, 27*(1), 1–12. http://www.mmaglobal.org

Badrinarayanan, V., Becerra, E. P., Kim, C., & Madhavaram, S. (2012). Transference and congruence effects on purchase intentions in online stores of multi-channel retailers: Initial evidence from the U.S. and South Korea. *Journal of the Academy of Marketing Science, 40*(4), 539–557. doi:10.100711747-010-0239-9

Baglio, M., Dallari, F., Garagiola, E., & Perotti, S. (2018). A model for assessing the quality and functionality of logistics buildings. *Proceedings of the Summer School Francesco Turco, 2018-September* 186-192.

Baimukhamedov M.F. (2020). Etapy razvitiya elektronnogo pravitel'stva v Kazakhstane. *Problemy prava i ekonomiki, 3*, 45-53.

Baimukhamedov, M. F. (2022). *Metody i sredstva tsifrovizatsii i robotizatsii ekonomiki. Monografiya.* Master Reprint.

Baporikar, N., Nambira, G., & Gomxos, G. (2016). Exploring factors hindering SMEs growth: evidence from Nambia. *Journal of Science and Technology Policy Management, 7*, 190–21.

Barbosa, G. S., Drach, P. R., & Corbella, O. D. (2014). A conceptual review of the terms sustainable development and sustainability. *Journal of Social Sciences, 3*(2), 1–15. https://www.iises.net/download/Soubory/soubory-puvodni/pp-01-15_ijossV3N2.pdf

Basu, D., Chakraborty, K., Mitra, S., & Verma, N. K. (2022). Customer reciprocity in greening: The role of service quality. *International Journal of Quality and Service Sciences, 14*(2), 238–257. doi:10.1108/IJQSS-08-2021-0116

Bauman, A. A. (2020). How do entrepreneurs use social media? *Journal of Marketing Development and Competitiveness, 14*(2), 40–48. doi:10.33423/jmdc.v14i2.2832

Bawa., M. D. (2020). *Working from Home in the COVID-19 Lockdown.* Bankwest Curtin Economics Centre Research Brief COVID-19 #5.

Bearden, W. O., Ingram, T. N., & LaForge, R. W. (2007). *Marketing: Principles and perspective.* McGraw- Hill Inc.

Benamati, J. H., Özdemir, Z., & Smith, H. J. (2021). Information privacy, cultural values, and regulatory preferences. *Journal of Global Information Management, 29*(3), 131–164. doi:10.4018/JGIM.2021050106

Bevan, T. (2019). *ISO 22031 Implementation Guide. NQA Global Accredited Certification Body.* Available: https://www.nqa.com/medialibraries/NQA/NQA-Media-Library/PDFs/NQA-ISO-22301-Implementation-Guide.pdf

Bhade, K., Gulalkari, V., Harwani, N., & Dhage, S. N. (2018). A Systematic Approach to Customer Segmentation and Buyer Targeting for Profit Maximization. In *2018 9th International Conference on Computing, Communication and Networking Technologies (ICCCNT)* (pp. 1-6). IEEE. 10.1109/ICCCNT.2018.8494019

Bharucha, J. (2019). Sustainability of Kirana stores in India: Reengineering physical with some digital. *World Review of Entrepreneurship, Management and Sustainable Development, 15*(6), 751–764. doi:10.1504/WREMSD.2019.104866

Bhatti, A., Akram, H., Basit, H. M., Khan, A. U., Raza, S. M., & Naqvi, M. B. (2020). E-commerce trends during COVID-19 Pandemic. *International Journal of Future Generation Communication and Networking, 13*(2), 1449–1452.

Bhimani, H., Mention, A. L., & Barlatier, P. J. (2019). Social media and innovation: A systematic literature review and future research directions. *Technological Forecasting and Social Change, 144,* 251–269. doi:10.1016/j.techfore.2018.10.007

Bholowalia, P., & Kumar, A. (2014). EBK-means: A clustering technique based on elbow method and k-means in WSN. *International Journal of Computers and Applications, 105*(9).

Bhorat, H., Asmal, Z., Lilenstein, K., & Van Der Zee, K. (2018). *SMMEs in South Africa: understanding the constraints on growth and performance.* Development and Policy Research Unit.

Bianchi, C., & Andrews, L. (2012). Risk, trust, and consumer online purchasing behaviour: A Chilean perspective. *International Marketing Review, 29*(3), 253–275. doi:10.1108/02651331211229750

Bilgin, Y. (2018). The effect of social media marketing activities on brand awareness, brand image and brand loyalty. *Business & Management Studies: An International Journal, 6*(1), 128-148.

Bivainien, L. (2007). Brand image conceptualization: The role of marketing communication. *Economics and Management, 12,* 304–310.

Blazheska, D., Ristovska, N., & Gramatnikovski, S. (2020). The impact of digital trends on marketing. *UTMS Journal of Economics (Skopje), 11*(1), 48–58.

Bloom, N., Bunn, P., Mizen, P., Smietanka, P., & Thwaites, G. (2020). *The impact of COVID-19 on productivity.* Available: https://www.nber.org/papers/w28233%0D

Borlea, I. D., Precup, R. E., Dragan, F., & Borlea, A. B. (2017). Centroid update approach to K-means clustering. *Advances in Electrical and Computer Engineering, 17*(4), 3–10. doi:10.4316/AECE.2017.04001

Brady, M. (2020). Realising supply chain resilience: an exploratory study of Irish firms' priorities in the wake of Brexit. *Continuity & Resilience Review.* doi:10.1108/CRR-06-2020-0020

Brand, B. M., & Rausch, T. M. (2021). Examining sustainability surcharges for outdoor apparel using adaptive choice-based conjoint analysis. *Journal of Cleaner Production, 289,* 125654. Advance online publication. doi:10.1016/j.jclepro.2020.125654

Braojos-Gomez, J., Benitez-Amado, J., & Llorens-Montes, F. J. (2015). How do small firms learn to develop a social media competence. *International Journal of Information Management, 35*(4), 443–458. doi:10.1016/j.ijinfomgt.2015.04.003

Brent, H., & Meyer, B. P. (2020). *The Impact of the COVID-19 Pandemic on Business Expectations.* Working Paper 2020-17a.

Broeder, P. (2022). Profile photos' impact in online reviews: The effect of cultural differences. *Review of Marketing Science,* 1-16.

Bruwer, J., Hattingh, C., & Perold, I. (2020). *Probable measures to aid South African Small Medium and Micro Enterprises sustainability, post–COVID-19: A literature review.* Available: https://ssrn.com/abstract=3625552

Budiman, S. (2021). The effect of social media on brand image and brand loyalty in generation Y. *The Journal of Asian Finance. Economics and Business, 8*(3), 1339–1347.

Buekelaer, O. D. (2020). *B2B e-commerce and Covid-19: challenges, solutions and opportunities.* Sana. https://www.sanacommerce.com/blog/b2b-E-Commerce-covid-19- challenges-opportunities/

Burkitt-Gray, A. (2021). *COVID means companies expect 'substantial' remote working by year-end.* Capacity Media. Available: https://www.capacitymedia.com/article/29otd15ias3ir9dx70jy8/news/covid-means-companies-expect-substantial-remote-working-by-year-end

Business Dictionary. (2020). *Business growth.* Available: www.businessdictionary.com

Business Elite. (2020). *Business growth factors.* Available: www.businesselites.co.za

Bylok, F. (2021). Examining the impact of trust on the e-commerce purchase intentions of young consumers in Poland. *Journal of Internet Commerce, 21*(3), 364–391. doi:10.1080/15332861.2021.1978194

Cambridge University. (2021). *Cambridge Dictionary.* Available: https://dictionary.cambridge.org/dictionary/english

Can Saglam, Y., Yildiz Çankaya, S., & Sezen, B. (2021). Proactive risk mitigation strategies and supply chain risk management performance: An empirical analysis for manufacturing firms in Turkey. *Journal of Manufacturing Technology Management, 32*(6), 1224–1244. doi:10.1108/JMTM-08-2019-0299

Caniëls, M. C., Lenaerts, H. K., & Gelderman, C. J. (2015). Explaining the internet usage of SMEs: The impact of market orientation, behavioural norms, motivation and technology acceptance. *Internet Research, 25*(3), 358–377. doi:10.1108/IntR-12-2013-0266

Capece, G., Calabrese, A., Di Pillo, F., Costa, R., & Crisciotti, V. (2013). The impact of national culture on e-commerce acceptance: The Italian case. *Knowledge and Process Management, 20*(2), 102–112. doi:10.1002/kpm.1413

Carvalho, L. S., Stefanelli, N. O., Viana, L. C., Vasconcelos, D. S. C., & Oliveira, B. G. (2020). Green supply chain management and innovation: A modern review. *Management of Environmental Quality, 31*(2), 470–482. doi:10.1108/MEQ-12-2019-0283

Carvalho, Y. A., Siqueira, R., Scafuto, I., & Silva, L. F. (2019). Sustainable marketplace project vendor selection criteria prioritization using AHP method [Utilização do método ahp para a priorização dos critérios de seleção de lojistas em um projeto de marketplace sustentável]. *International Journal of Professional Business Review, 4*(2), 114–123. doi:10.26668/businessreview/2019.v4i2.170

CDC. (2020, March 10). *Coronavirus (COVID-19).* Retrieved from https ://www.cdc.gov/coron aviru s/2019-ncov/index .html

Centers for Disease Control and Prevention. (2020*). About COVID-19.* Available: https://www.cdc.gov/coronavirus/2019-ncov/cdcresponse/about-COVID-19.html

Chaffey, D., Ellis-Chadwick, F., Mayer, R., & Johnston, K. (2006). *Internet marketing: Strategy, implementation and practice.* Pearson Education Limited.

Chai, L. G. (2009). A review of marketing mix: 4Ps or more? *International Journal of Marketing Studies, 1*(1), 1–15.

Chakravarthy, B. S. (1986). Measuring strategic performance. *Strategic Management Journal, 7*(5), 437–458. doi:10.1002mj.4250070505

Chang, K. S., Park, J. Y., & Choi, I. H. (2001). The Influence of Self-Congruity Between Brand Personality and Self-Image on Attitude Toward Brand. *Korean Journal of Marketing, 3*(2), 92–114.

Chang, Y. W., Hsu, P. Y., Huang, S. H., & Chen, J. (2020). Determinants of switching intention to cloud computing in large enterprises. *Data Technologies and Applications*, *54*(1), 16–33. doi:10.1108/DTA-12-2018-0104

Chatterjee, S., & Kar, A. K. (2020). Why do small and medium enterprises use social media marketing and what is the impact: Empirical insights from India. *International Journal of Information Management*, *53*, 102103. doi:10.1016/j.ijinfomgt.2020.102103

Chegg Inc. (2022). *Networking and communication trends*. Available: https://www.chegg.com/homework-help/questions-and-answers/networking-communication-trends-compare-figure-71-diagrams-simple-computer-network-figure--q22389747

Chen, S. C., & Dhillon, G. S. (2003). Interpreting dimensions of consumer trust in e-commerce. *Information Technology and Management*, *4*(2), 303–318. doi:10.1023/A:1022962631249

Chen, Y. Y., & Huang, H. L. (2016). Developing and Validating the Measurement Scale of e-Marketing Orientation. In *Rediscovering the Essentiality of Marketing*. Springer International Publishing. doi:10.1007/978-3-319-29877-1_47

Chivandi, A., & Sibanda, F. (2018). An investigation of e-commerce adoption inhibitors in the tourism industry: A Zimbabwe national parks perspective. *African Journal of Hospitality, Tourism and Leisure*, *7*(3), 1–15.

Chong, W. K., Shafaghi, M., & Tan, B. L. (2011). Development of a business-to-business critical success factors (B2B CSFs) framework for Chinese SMEs. *Marketing Intelligence & Planning*, *29*(5), 517–533. doi:10.1108/02634501111153700

Chowdhury, M. M. H., & Quaddus, M. A. (2015). A multiple objective optimization based QFD approach for efficient resilient strategies to mitigate supply chain vulnerabilities: The case of garment industry of Bangladesh. *Omega*, *57*, 5–21. doi:10.1016/j.omega.2015.05.016

Christopher & Peck. (2004). Building the resilient supply chain. *International Journal of Logistics Management, 15*(2), 1-13.

Churchill, N., & Lewis, V. (1983). The five stages of small business growth. Business Review, 1-12.

Clift, K., & Court, A. (2020). *How are companies responding to the coronavirus crisis?* World Economic Forum. Available: https://www.weforum.org/agenda/2020/03/how-are-companies-responding-to-the-coronavirus-crisis-d15bed6137/

Coibion, O., Gorodnichenko, Y., & Weber, M. (2020). *Labor markets during the COVID-19 crisis: A preliminary view* (No. w27017). National Bureau of Economic Research.

Colbourn., T. (2020). Extending pr relaxing distancing control measures. *COVID-19*, e236-7.

Colicchia, C., Creazza, A., Noè, C., & Strozzi, F. (2019). Information sharing in supply chains: A review of risks and opportunities using the systematic literature network analysis (SLNA). *Supply Chain Management*, *24*(1), 5–21. doi:10.1108/SCM-01-2018-0003

Colicchia, C., & Strozzi, F. (2012). Supply chain risk management: A new methodology for a systematic literature review. *Supply Chain Management*, *17*(4), 403–418. doi:10.1108/13598541211246558

Commerce, B. (2021). *14 Ecommerce trends leading the way*. https://www.bigcommerce.com/articles/ecommerce/ecommerce-trends/

Cong, L. W., Li, B., & Zhang, Q. T. (2021). Internet of Things: Business Economics and Applications. *Review of Business St. John's University*, *41*(1), 15–29.

Consoli, D. (2012). Literature analysis on determinant factors and the impact of ICT in SMEs. *Procedia: Social and Behavioral Sciences*, *62*, 93–97. doi:10.1016/j.sbspro.2012.09.016

Constantinides, E. (2002). The 4s web-marketing mix model. *Electronic Commerce Research and Applications*, *1*(1), 57–76. doi:10.1016/S1567-4223(02)00006-6

Constantinides, E. (2004). Influencing the online consumer's behavior: The Web experience. Internet research. *Internet Research*, *14*(2), 111–126. doi:10.1108/10662240410530835

Corbitt, B. J., Thanasankit, T., & Yi, H. (2003). Trust and e-commerce: A study of consumer perceptions. *Electronic Commerce Research and Applications*, *2*(3), 203–215. doi:10.1016/S1567-4223(03)00024-3

Corrigan, T. (2020). *Policy briefing 197: Africa's ICT infrastructure: its present and prospects*. Available: https://saiia.org.za/research/africas-ict-infrastructure-its-present-and-prospects/

Costa, J., & Castro, R. (2021). SMEs must go online—E-commerce as an escape hatch for resilience and survivability. *Journal of Theoretical and Applied Electronic Commerce Research*, *16*(7), 3043–3062. doi:10.3390/jtaer16070166

Council, T. I. C. (2021). *The impact of COVID-19 on the TIC sector*. Available: https://www.tic-council.org/blog/impact-covid-19-tic-sector

Coviello, N. E., Brodie, R. J., Brookes, R. W., & Palmer, R. A. (2003). Assessing the role of e-marketing in contemporary marketing practice. *Journal of Marketing Management*, *19*(7-8), 857–881. doi:10.1080/0267257X.2003.9728240

Cox, B. G., & Koelzer, W. (2004). *Internet marketing*. Pearson Education Limited.

Cruz-Cunha, M. M., & Varajao, J. (2011). *E-business issues, challenges and opportunities for SMEs driving competitiveness*. Business Science Reference. Available: http://b-ok.cc

Cyr, D. (2008). Modeling web site design across cultures: Relationships to trust, satisfaction, and e-loyalty. *Journal of Management Information Systems*, *24*(4), 47–72. doi:10.2753/MIS0742-1222240402

Cyr, D., Head, M., Larios, H., & Pan, B. (2009). Exploring human images in website design: A multi-method approach. *MIS Quarterly: Management Information Systems*, *33*(3), 539–566. doi:10.2307/20650308

Danchenok, B. K., Zaytseva, T. B., & Komlev, M. O. (2019). Vliyaniye tsifrovykh kompetentsiy sub"yektov malogo i srednego predprinimatel'stva na razvitiye biznesa. *Ekonomika, predprinimatel'stvo i parvo*, 34-42. http://www.tadviser.ru/index.php

Das, J. K., Prakash, O., & Khattri, V. (2016). Brand image mapping: A study on bathing soaps. *Global Business Review*, *17*(4), 870–885. doi:10.1177/0972150916645683

Dayal, S., Landesberg, H., & Zeisser, M. (2000). Building digital brands. *The McKinsey Quarterly*, (2), 42.

de Araújo, A. C., Matsuoka, E. M., Ung, J. E., Massote, A., & Sampaio, M. (2018). An exploratory study on the returns management process in an online retailer. *International Journal of Logistics Research and Applications*, *21*(3), 345–362. doi:10.1080/13675567.2017.1370080

De Chernatony, L. (2002). Would a brand smell any sweeter by a corporate name? *Corporate Reputation Review*, *5*(2), 114–132. doi:10.1057/palgrave.crr.1540169

Debjani, S. A. (2021). Imperative role of Digitalization in the Indian economy During COVID-19. *International Journal of Advanced Research in Science, Communication and Technology*.

Deloitte. (2018). *Going digital-the nexyt fornier for Middle East retail*. https://www2.deloitte.com/xe/en/pages/about-deloitte/articles/we-are-25/e-commerce.html

Dempsi Dzh. (2003). Elektronnoye pravitel'stvo i yego vygody dlya shirokikh mass. *Gosudarstvennoye upravleniye v perekhodnykh ekonomikakh, 1*, 67-74.

Denga, E. M., & Rakshit, S. (2022a). Supply Chain Logistics Risk Mitigation - Impact of Covid-19 Pandemic. In K. Strang & N.R. Vajjhala (Eds.), Global Risk and Contingency Management Research in Times of Crisis. Academic Press.

Denga, E. M., & Rakshit, S. (2022b). Risks in Supply Chain Logistics - Constraints and Opportunities in North-Eastern Nigeria. *International Journal of Risk and Contingency Management, 11*(1), 1–18. Advance online publication. doi:10.4018/IJRCM.295957

Denga, E. M., Vajjhala, N. R., & Rakshit, S. (2022a). The Role of Digital Marketing in Achieving Sustainable Competitive Advantage. *Advances in Business Strategy and Competitive Advantage*, 44–60. doi:10.4018/978-1-7998-8169-8.ch003

Denga, E. M., Vajjhala, N. R., & Rakshit, S. (2022b). Relationship Selling as a Strategic Weapon for Sustainable Performance. In J. D. Santos (Ed.), *Sales Management for Improved Organizational Competitiveness and Performance*. doi:10.4018/978-1-6684-3430-7.ch005

Dhote, T., & Zahoor, D. (2017). Framework for sustainability in E - commerce business models: A perspective based approach. *Indian Journal of Marketing, 47*(4), 35–50. doi:10.17010/ijom/2017/v47/i4/112681

Di Maria, E. (2015). Environmental innovations and internationalization: Theory and practices. *Business Strategy and the Environment, 24*(8), 790–80. doi:10.1002/bse.1846

Diamondis, P. (2015). *The world in 2025: 8 Predictions fpr the next 10 years.* Singularity University.

Dichter, E. (1985). What's in an image. *Journal of Consumer Marketing, 2*(1), 75–81. doi:10.1108/eb038824

Digital Marketing Community. (2022). *The importance of eCommerce for your business in 2022.* https://www.digital-marketingcommunity.com/articles/importance-of-ecommerce/

Dinev, T., Bellotto, M., Hart, P., Russo, V., Serra, I., & Colautti, C. (2006). Privacy calculus model in e-commerce - A study of Italy and the United States. *European Journal of Information Systems, 15*(4), 389–402. doi:10.1057/palgrave. ejis.3000590

Dittfeld, H., van Donk, D. P., & van Huet, S. (2022). The effect of production system characteristics on resilience capabilities: A multiple case study. *International Journal of Operations & Production Management, 42*(13), 103–127. doi:10.1108/IJOPM-12-2021-0789

Dlodlo, N., & Dhurup, M. (2010). Barriers to e-marketing adoption among small and medium enterprises (SMEs) in the *Vaal Triangle. Acta Commercii, 10*(1), 164–180. doi:10.4102/ac.v10i1.126

Dlova, M. R. (2017). *Small Micro and Medium Enterprises access to credit in the Eastern Cape South Africa* [Unpublished doctoral thesis]. Johannesburg University of Witwatersrand.

Dogan, K. (2002). *Modeling the impact of internet technology on marketing.* University of Florida.

Donthu, N., Kumar, S., Mukherjee, D., Pandey, N., & Lim, W. M. (2021). How to conduct a bibliometric analysis: An overview and guidelines. *Journal of Business Research, 133*, 285–296. doi:10.1016/j.jbusres.2021.04.070

Doyle, P. (2009). *Value-based marketing: Marketing strategies for corporate growth and shareholder value.* John Wiley & Sons.

Dubai Future Foundation (2021). *Life after Covid-19.* Author.

Dullaghan, C., & Rozaki, E. (2017). *Integration of machine learning techniques to evaluate dynamic customer segmentation analysis for mobile customers.* arXiv preprint arXiv:1702.02215.

Durach, C. F., Wieland, A., & Machuca, J. A. D. (2015). Antecedents and dimensions of supply chain robustness: A systematic literature review. *International Journal of Physical Distribution & Logistics Management, 45*(1/2), 118–137. doi:10.1108/IJPDLM-05-2013-0133

Durkin, M., McGowan, P., & McKeown, N. (2013). Exploring social media adoption in small to medium-sized enterprises in Ireland. *Journal of Small Business and Enterprise Development, 20*(4), 716–734. doi:10.1108/JSBED-08-2012-0094

Dutta, P., Mishra, A., Khandelwal, S., & Katthawala, I. (2020). A multiobjective optimization model for sustainable reverse logistics in Indian E-commerce market. *Journal of Cleaner Production, 249*, 119348. Advance online publication. doi:10.1016/j.jclepro.2019.119348

Ecommerce Europe. (2022). *European E-Commerce Report 2022.* https://ecommerce-europe.eu/wp-content/uploads/2022/06/CMI2022_FullVersion_LIGHT_v2.pdf

Ecosystm. (2019). *What is IoT - Internet of Things?* Available: https://blog.ecosystm360.com/guides/iot-internet-of-things/

Eine, B., & Charoensukmongkol, P. (2021). A cross-cultural perspective on factors that influence the intention to repurchase in online marketplaces: A comparison between Thailand and Germany. *Asian Journal of Business Research, 11*(1), 20–39. doi:10.14707/ajbr.210097

El Said, G. R., & Galal-Edeen, G. H. (2009). The role of culture in e-commerce use for the Egyptian consumers. *Business Process Management Journal, 15*(1), 34–47. doi:10.1108/14637150910931451

Elektronnoye pravitel'stvo. (2017). https://ru.wikipedia.org/wiki/

El-Gohary, H. (2010). E-marketing - a literature review from a small businesses perspective. *International Journal of Business and Social Science, 1*(1), 214–244.

Emas, R. (2015). The concept of sustainable development: definition and defining principles. *Brief for GSDR, 2015,* 1-3. https://asset-pdf.scinapse.io/prod/2184349672/2184349672.pdf

Ersoy, Y. (2021). Equipment selection for an E-commerce company using entropy-based TOPSIS, EDAS and CODAS methods during the COVID-19. *Logforum, 17*(3), 341–358. doi:10.17270/J.LOG.2021.603

Escursell, S., Llorach-Massana, P., & Roncero, M. B. (2021). Sustainability in e-commerce packaging: A review. *Journal of Cleaner Production, 280*, 124314. doi:10.1016/j.jclepro.2020.124314 PMID:32989345

Ezenkwu, C. P., Ozuomba, S., & Kalu, C. (2015). *Application of K-Means algorithm for efficient customer segmentation: a strategy for targeted customer services.* Academic Press.

Fan, A., Shen, H., Wu, L., Mattila, A. S., & Bilgihan, A. (2018). Whom do we trust? Cultural differences in consumer responses to online recommendations. *International Journal of Contemporary Hospitality Management, 30*(3), 1508–1525. doi:10.1108/IJCHM-01-2017-0050

Faqih, K. M. S. (2022). Internet shopping in the covid-19 era: Investigating the role of perceived risk, anxiety, gender, culture, and trust in the consumers' purchasing behavior from a developing country context. *Technology in Society, 70,* 1–15. doi:10.1016/j.techsoc.2022.101992

Fathian, M. A., Akhavan, P., & Hoorali, M. (2008). E-readiness assessment of non-profit ICT SMEs in a developing country: The case of Iran. *Technovation, 28*(9), 578–590. doi:10.1016/j.technovation.2008.02.002

Fatoki. (2011). The impact of human, social and financial capital on the performance f malland medium sized enterprises (SME's) in South Africa. *Journal of Social Science*, 193 - 204.

Febransyah, A., & Camelia Goni, J. I. (2022). Measuring the supply chain competitiveness of e-commerce industry in Indonesia. *Competitiveness Review*, *32*(2), 250–275. doi:10.1108/CR-05-2020-0059

Feng, H. W. (2020). *Research Report on Companies' Survival and Development Strategy During a Novel Coronavirus Epidemic*. UIBE Press.

Ferreira, J., Callou, G., MacIel, P., & Tutsch, D. (2020). An algorithm to optimize the energy distribution of data center electrical infrastructures. *International Journal of Grid and Utility Computing*, *11*(3), 419–433. doi:10.1504/IJGUC.2020.107625

Fiksel, J., Polyviou, M., Croxton, K. L., & Pettit, T. J. (2015). From risk to resilience: Learning to deal with disruption. *MIT Sloan Management Review*, *56*, 79–86.

Filipova, N. (2018). Blockchain - an opportunity for developing new business models. Information Technologies. *D.A. Tsenov Academy of Economics*, *20*(2), 75–92.

Filkovskaia, J. (2017). *Influence of Visuals in Digital Brand Identity*. PIIK.

Forbes Insights. (2017). *The impact of the digital workforce*. Available: https://i.forbesimg.com/forbesinsights/vmware/impact-of-digital-workforce.pdf

Foroudi, P., Gupta, S., Nazarian, A., & Duda, M. (2017). Digital technology and marketing management capability: Achieving growth in SMEs. *Qualitative Market Research*, *20*(2), 230–246. doi:10.1108/QMR-01-2017-0014

Fota, A., Wagner, K., & Schramm-Klein, H. (2019). Is renting the new buying? A quantitative investigation of the determinants of the rental-commerce intention. *International Review of Retail, Distribution and Consumer Research*, *29*(5), 582–599. doi:10.1080/09593969.2019.1664616

Frei, R., Jack, L., & Brown, S. (2020). Product returns: A growing problem for business, society and environment. *International Journal of Operations & Production Management*, *40*(10), 1613–1621. doi:10.1108/IJOPM-02-2020-0083

Fuller, C. M., Simmering, M. J., Atinc, G., Atinc, Y., & Babin, B. J. (2016). Standard methods variance detection in business research. *Journal of Business Research*, *8*(69), 3192–3198. doi:10.1016/j.jbusres.2015.12.008

Fulton, K., & Lee, S. (2013). Assessing sustainable initiatives of apparel retailers on the internet. *Journal of Fashion Marketing and Management*, *17*(3), 353–366. doi:10.1108/JFMM-11-2012-0071

Furner, C. P., Racherla, P., & Zhu, Z. (2014). A multinational study of espoused national cultural and review characteristics in the formation of trust in online product reviews. *International Journal of Services Technology and Management*, *20*(1-3), 14–30. doi:10.1504/IJSTM.2014.063586

Gamage. (2003). *Small and Medium enterprises in Sri Lanka*. Academic Press.

Gangwar, H., Date, H., & Ramaswamy, R. (2015). Journal of Enterprise Information Management article information. *Journal of Enterprise Information Management*, *28*(1), 107–130. doi:10.1108/JEIM-08-2013-0065

Gao, P., Meng, F., Mata, M. N., Martins, J. M., Iqbal, S., & Farrukh, M. (2021). Trends and future research in electronic marketing: A bibliometric analysis of twenty years. *Journal of Theoretical and Applied Electronic Commerce Research*, *16*(5), 1667–1679. doi:10.3390/jtaer16050094

Gartner. (2020). Gartner says organizations should follow a five-phase approach for resilient business continuity models during coronavirus disruptions. *Business Wire*. Available: http://search.ebscohost.com/login.aspx?direct=true&db=bwh&AN=bizwire.bw7241305&site=ehost-live

Gartner. (2021). *Gartner Glossary*. Available: https://www.gartner.com/en/information-technology/glossary

Gefen, D. (2002). Reflections on the dimensions of trust and trustworthiness among online consumers. *ACM SIGMIS Database: The Database for Advances in Information Systems, 33*(3), 38–53. doi:10.1145/569905.569910

Gefen, D., Karahanna, E., & Straub, D. W. (2003). Trust and TAM in online shopping: An integrated model. *Management Information Systems Quarterly, 27*(1), 51–90. doi:10.2307/30036519

Ghaleb, E., & Balian, P. (2021). Developing human potential within an e-commerce industry to leverage sustainability. *Organization Development Journal, 39*(4), 34–46.

Ghandour, A., & Woodford, B. J. (2020, November). COVID-19 impact on e-commerce in UAE. In *2020 21st International Arab Conference on Information Technology (ACIT)* (pp. 1-8). IEEE.

Gilbert, N. (2021). *51 critical blockchain statistics: 2021 data analysis & market share*. Finance Online. Available: https://financesonline.com/blockchain-statistics/

Gilmore, A., Gallagher, D., & Henry, S. (2007). E-marketing and SMEs: Operational lessons for the future. *European Business Review, 19*(3), 234–247. doi:10.1108/09555340710746482

Globalization Partners International. (2021). *A reshaped and redefined strategy for recovery post Covid-19: e-commerce and marketing in the UAE|Part 2*. https://www.globalizationpartners.com/2021/03/04/reshaped-strategy-for-recovery-post-covid-19-ecommerce-and-marketing-in-uae-part-2/

Golicic, S. L., Flint, D. J., & Signori, P. (2017). Building business sustainability through resilience in the wine industry. *International Journal of Wine Business Research, 29*(1), 74–97. doi:10.1108/IJWBR-02-2016-0005

Government of India. (2021). *MSME Annual Report 2020 -2021*. New Delhi: Government of India, Ministry of Micro, Small and Medium Enterprises. www.msme.gov.in

Govinden, K., Pillay, S., & Ngobeni, A. (2020). *Business impact survey of the COVID-19 pandemic in South Africa*. Available: http://www.statssa.gov.za/publications/Report-00-80-01/Report-00-80-01April2020.pdf

Granitz, N., & Greene, C. S. (2003). Applying e-marketing strategies to online distance learning. *Journal of Marketing Education, 25*(1), 16–30. doi:10.1177/0273475302250569

Greenberg, R., Wong-On-Wing, B., & Lui, G. (2008). Culture and consumer trust in online businesses. *Journal of Global Information Management, 16*(3), 26–44. doi:10.4018/jgim.2008070102

Grubor, A. & Milovanov, O. (2017). Brand strategies in the era of sustainability. *Interdisciplinary Description of Complex Systems, 15*(1), 78-88.

Gunawardana. (2020, May). The Impact of COVID 19 to SME Sector in Sri Lanka. *COVID-19*.

Guo, X., Lujan Jaramillo, Y. J., Bloemhof-Ruwaard, J., & Claassen, G. D. H. (2019). On integrating crowdsourced delivery in last-mile logistics: A simulation study to quantify its feasibility. *Journal of Cleaner Production, 241*, 118365. Advance online publication. doi:10.1016/j.jclepro.2019.118365

Gupta, P., Bakhru, K. M., & Shankar, A. (2022). *Sustainable organizational performance management: Deciphering the role of emotional capital in e-commerce industry*. *South Asian Journal of Business Studies*. doi:10.1108/SAJBS-09-2021-0368

Gutierrez, A., Boukrami, E., & Lumsden, R. (2015). Technological, organisational and environmental factors influencing managers' decision to adopt cloud computing in the UK. *Journal of Enterprise Information Management, 28*(6), 788–807. doi:10.1108/JEIM-01-2015-0001

Habibi, F., Hamilton, C. A., Valos, M. J., & Callaghan, M. (2015). E-marketing orientation and social media implementation in B2B marketing. *European Business Review, 27*(6), 638–655. doi:10.1108/EBR-03-2015-0026

Hale, T., & Moberg, C. R. (2005). Improving supply chain disaster preparedness: A decision process for secure site location. *International Journal of Physical Distribution & Logistics Management, 35*(3), 195–207. doi:10.1108/09600030510594576

Hallikainen, H., & Laukkanen, T. (2018). National culture and consumer trust in e-commerce. *International Journal of Information Management, 38*(1), 97–106. doi:10.1016/j.ijinfomgt.2017.07.002

Hankinson, G., & Cowking, P. (1993). *Branding in action: Cases and strategies for profitable brand management.* McGraw-Hill.

Harmancı, M. (2009). *İş'te İmaj Faktörü.* Nesil Yayınları.

Hartigan, J. A., & Wong, M. A. (1979). Algorithm AS 136: A k-means clustering algorithm. *Journal of the Royal Statistical Society. Series C (Applied Statistics), 28*(1), 100-108.

Hartmann, J., Heitmann, M., Schamp, C., & Netzer, O. (2021). *The power of brand selfies in consumer-generated brand imagery.* Columbia Business School Research Paper.

Haryanti, T., & Subriadi, A. P. (2022). E-commerce acceptance in the dimension of sustainability. *Journal of Modelling in Management, 17*(2), 715–745. doi:10.1108/JM2-05-2020-0141

Hassan, R., Mahinderjit-Singh, M., Hassan, H., & Yuhaniz, S. S. (2018). Online Islamic business enhancer tool (OIBET) for young entrepreneurs. *Proceedings of the 31st International Business Information Management Association Conference, IBIMA 2018: Innovation Management and Education Excellence through Vision, 2020,* 687–701.

Hawlitschek, F., Teubner, T., & Gimpel, H. (2018). Consumer motives for peer-to-peer sharing. *Journal of Cleaner Production, 204,* 144–157. doi:10.1016/j.jclepro.2018.08.326

Hayes, J. (2014). *The theory and practice of change management* (4th ed.). Palgrave Macmillan. doi:10.1007/978-1-137-28902-5

Herbane, B. (2010). The evolution of business continuity management: A historical review of practices and drivers. *Business History, 52*(6), 978–1002. doi:10.1080/00076791.2010.511185

Hermanda, A., Sumarwan, U., & Tinaprillia, N. (2019). The effect of social media influencer on brand image, self-concept, and purchase intention. *Journal of Consumer Sciences, 4*(2), 76–89. doi:10.29244/jcs.4.2.76-89

Herzog, H. (1963). Behavioral science concepts for analyzing the consumer. *Marketing and the Behavioral Sciences,* 76-86.

Hofacker, C., Golgeci, I., Pillai, K. G., & Gligor, D. M. (2020). Digital marketing and business-to-business relationships: A close look at the interface and a roadmap for the future. *European Journal of Marketing, 54*(6), 1161–1179. doi:10.1108/EJM-04-2020-0247

Hofmann, J., Schnittka, O., Johnen, M., & Kottemann, P. (2021). Talent or popularity: What drives market value and brand image for human brands? *Journal of Business Research, 124,* 748–758. doi:10.1016/j.jbusres.2019.03.045

Hofstede, G., Neuijen, B., Ohayv, D. D., & Sanders, G. (1990). Measuring organizational cultures: A qualitative and quantitative study across twenty cases. *Administrative Science Quarterly, 35*(2), 286–316. doi:10.2307/2393392

Hogan, S. (2005). Employees and Image: Bringing Brand Image to Life. In *The 2nd Annual Strategic Public Relations Conference*. Chicago: Lippincot Mercer.

Holliman, G., & Rowley, J. (2014). B2B digital content marketing: Marketer's perceptions of best practices. *Journal of Research in Interactive Marketing*, *8*(4), 269–293. doi:10.1108/JRIM-02-2014-0013

Hooley, G. J., Greenley, G. E., Cadogan, J. W., & Fahy, J. (2005, January). (20050. The performance impact of marketing resources. *Journal of Business Research*, *58*(1), 18–27. doi:10.1016/S0148-2963(03)00109-7

Hosmer, L. T. (1995). Trust: The connecting link between organizational theory and philosophical ethics. *Academy of Management Review*, *20*(2), 379–403. doi:10.2307/258851

Hruschka, H., & Natter, M. (1999). Comparing performance of feedforward neural nets and K-means for cluster-based market segmentation. *European Journal of Operational Research*, *114*(2), 346–353. doi:10.1016/S0377-2217(98)00170-2

Huang, L., Ba, S., & Lu, X. (2014). Building online trust in a culture of confucianism: The impact of process flexibility and perceived control. *ACM Transactions on Management Information Systems*, *5*(1), 1–23. doi:10.1145/2576756

Huong Tran, T. T., Childerhouse, P., & Deakins, E. (2016). Supply chain information sharing: Challenges and risk mitigation strategies. *Journal of Manufacturing Technology Management*, *27*(8), 1102–1126. doi:10.1108/JMTM-03-2016-0033

Hwang, Y., & Lee, K. C. (2012). Investigating the moderating role of uncertainty avoidance cultural values on multidimensional online trust. *Information & Management*, *49*(3-4), 171–176. doi:10.1016/j.im.2012.02.003

IBEF - Indian Retail Industry Report. (2021). New Delhi: IBEF.

ICTA. (2021). *ICTA adeas oriented*. ICTA.

Ifinedo, P. (2011). An empirical analysis of factors influencing Internet/E-Business technologies adoption by SMEs in Canada. *International Journal of Information Technology & Decision Making*, *10*(4), 731–766. doi:10.1142/S0219622011004543

Ignat, B., & Chankov, S. (2020). Do e-commerce customers change their preferred last-mile delivery based on its sustainability impact? *International Journal of Logistics Management*, *31*(3), 521–548. doi:10.1108/IJLM-11-2019-0305

ILO. (2020). *MSME Day 2020: the COVID-19 pandemic and its impact on small business*. https://www.ilo.org/empent/whatsnew/WCMS_749275/lang--en/index.htm

International Trade Administration. (2022). *United Arab Emirates – Country commercial guide*. eCommerce. https://www.trade.gov/country-commercial-guides/united-arab-emirates-ecommerce#:~:text=The%20UAE%20is%20the%20eCommerce,by%20a%20COVID%20digital%20shift

International Trade Center. (2020). SME Competitiveness Outlook 2020: COVID-19: The Great Lockdown and its Impact on Small Business. *The American Journal of Emergency Medicine*, *38*(2).

Investopedia. (2022). *Ecommerce defined: types, history, and examples*. https://www.investopedia.com/terms/e/ecommerce.asp

Iovino, F., & Migliaccio, G. (2019). E-Marketing and Strategy by Energy Companies. In *The Cross-Disciplinary Perspectives of Management: Challenges and Opportunities*. Emerald Publishing Limited., doi:10.1108/978-1-83867-249-220191011

İrkey, T., & Tüfekci, A. (2021). *The importance of business continuity and knowledge management during the pandemic period*. Academic Press.

Isa, N. F., Annuar, S. N. S., Gisip, I. A., & Lajuni, N. (2020). Factors influencing online purchase intention of millennials and gen Z consumers. *Journal of Applied Structural Equation Modeling, 4*(2), 21–43. doi:10.47263/JASEM.4(2)03

Ishfaq, R., Davis-Sramek, B., & Gibson, B. (2021). Digital Supply Chains in Omnichannel Retail: A Conceptual Framework. *Journal of Business Logistics.*

Islam, M. (2020). *Digital Brand Management: Impact of Social Media Marketing on Brand Image.* Academic Press.

Islami, M. M., Asdar, M., & Baumassepe, A. N. (2021). Analysis of Perceived Usefulness and Perceived Ease of Use to the Actual System Usage through Attitude Using Online Guidance Application. *Hasanuddin Journal of Business Strategy, 3*(1), 52–64. doi:10.26487/hjbs.v3i1.410

ISO. (2019). *Business Continuity ISO 22301.* International Organization for Standardization.

Itani, O. S., Agnihotri, R., & Dingus, R. (2017). Social media use in B2B sales and its impact on competitive intelligence collection and adaptive selling: Examining the role of learning orientation as an enabler. *Industrial Marketing Management, 66*, 64–79. doi:10.1016/j.indmarman.2017.06.012

ITU. (2021). *Statistics.* Available: https://www/itu.int/en/ITU-D/Statistics/Pages/stat/default.aspx

Jafari, H. (2015). Logistics flexibility: A systematic literature review. *International Journal of Productivity and Performance Management, 64*(7), 947–970. doi:10.1108/IJPPM-05-2014-0069

Jafari, H. (2019). E-commerce logistics - contemporary literature. *IEEE International Conference on Industrial Engineering and Engineering Management,* 1196-1200. doi:10.1109/IEEM.2018.8607522

Jain, V., Malviya, B., & Arya, S. (2021). An Overview of Electronic Commerce (e-Commerce). *Journal of Contemporary Issues in Business and Government, 27*(3), 666.

Janakirman, S., & Umamaheswari, K. (2014). *A Survey on Data Mining Techniques for Customer Segmentation for Customer Relationship Management.* Academic Press.

Jarvenpaa, S. L., Tractinsky, N., & Saarinen, L. (1999). Consumer trust in an Internet store: A cross-cultural validation. *Journal of Computer-Mediated Communication, 5*(2), JCMC526.

Jarvenpaa, S. L., Tractinsky, N., & Vitale, M. (2000). Consumer trust in an Internet store. *Information Technology and Management, 1*(1), 45–71. doi:10.1023/A:1019104520776

Jian, L. Z., & Yazdanifard, R. (2015). Which modern trend advertising methods are more effective in reaching certain outcome? A review on internet ads, mobile app ads, video ads, stealth ads and outdoor digital ads. *International Journal of Management.*

Jiles, L., & Nathan, B. (2020). *Technology and business continuity.* Strategic Finance. Available: https://sfmagazine.com/post-entry/june-2020-technology-and-business-continuity/

Jones, L., Palumbo, D., & Brown, D. (2021). *Coronavirus: how the pandemic has changed the world economy.* BBC News. Available: https://www.bbc.com/news/business-51706225

Jones, S. (2018). *Data integrity and planning for business continuity.* MSD. Available: https://slidetodoc.com/data-integrity-and-planning-for-business-continuity-april/

Juan, S.-J., Li, E. Y., & Hung, W.-H. (2022). An integrated model of supply chain resilience and its impact on supply chain performance under disruption. *International Journal of Logistics Management, 33*(1), 339–364. doi:10.1108/IJLM-03-2021-0174

Juliana, J., Djakasaputra, A., Pramono, R., & Hulu, E. (2021). Brand Image, Perceived Quality, Ease Of Use, Trust, Price, Service Quality On Customer Satisfaction And Purchase Intention Of Blibli Website With Digital Technology As Dummy Variable. In *The Use Of Reviews*. Journal Of Critical Reviews.

Jüttner, U., & Maklan, S. (2011). Supply chain resilience in the global financial crisis: An empirical study. *Supply Chain Management*, *16*(4), 246–259. doi:10.1108/13598541111139062

Kabugumila, M. S., Lushakuzi, S., & Mtui, J. E. (2016). E-commerce: An overview of adoption and its effective implementation. *International Journal of Business and Social Science*, *7*(4), 243–252.

Kaiser, D. H. (2015). *Wie das Internet der Dinge neue Geschaftsmodelle ermoglicht*. HDM Praxis der Wirschaftsmodelle.

Kaneberg, E., Hertz, S., & Jensen, L.-M. (2016). Emergency preparedness planning in developed countries: The Swedish case. *Journal of Humanitarian Logistics and Supply Chain Management*, *6*(2), 145–172. doi:10.1108/JHLSCM-10-2015-0039

Kansal, T., Bahuguna, S., Singh, V., & Choudhury, T. (2018). *Customer segmentation using K-means clustering. In 2018 international conference on computational techniques, electronics and mechanical systems (CTEMS)*. IEEE.

Kapoor, R., & Kapoor, K. (2021). The transition from traditional to digital marketing: A study of the evolution of e-marketing in the Indian hotel industry. *Worldwide Hospitality and Tourism Themes*, *13*(2), 199–213. doi:10.1108/WHATT-10-2020-0124

Kassim, N., & Abdullah, N. A. (2010). The effect of perceived service quality dimensions on customer satisfaction, trust, and loyalty in e-commerce settings: A cross cultural analysis. *Asia Pacific Journal of Marketing and Logistics*, *22*(3), 351–371. doi:10.1108/13555851011062269

Kauffman, R. J., Kim, K., Lee, S. T., Hoang, A., & Ren, J. (2017). Combining machine-based and econometrics methods for policy analytics insights. *Electronic Commerce Research and Applications*, *25*, 115–140. doi:10.1016/j.elerap.2017.04.004

Kavindi B.G.H, P. G. (2021). The effect of the covid 19 on overall firm performance in Sri lankan Apparel companies. *International Journal of Business, Economics and Law*.

Keller, K. L. (1993). Conceptualizing, measuring, and managing customer-based brand equity. *Journal of Marketing*, *57*(1), 1–22. doi:10.1177/002224299305700101

Keller, K. L. (2000). The brand report card. *Harvard Business Review*, *78*, 147–157.

Keller, K. L., Parameswaran, M. G., & Jacob, I. (2013). *Strategic brand management: Building, measuring, and managing brand equity*. Pearson Education India.

Khan, M. K. (2021). Importance of telecommunications in the times of COVID-19. *Telecommunication Systems*, *76*(1), 1–2. doi:10.100711235-020-00749-8 PMID:33456275

Khan, S. (2015). Impact of sources of finance on the growth of SMEs: Evidence from Pakistan. Indian Institute of Management. *Decision*, *42*. Advance online publication. doi:10.100740622-014-0071-z

Khasanshin, I.A. (2013). *Sistemy podderzhki prinyatiya resheniy v upravlenii regional'nym elektronnym pravitel'stvom: monografiya*. Goryachaya liniya.

Killian, G., & McManus, K. (2015). A marketing communications approach for the digital era: Managerial guidelines for social media integration. *Business Horizons*, *58*(5), 539–549. doi:10.1016/j.bushor.2015.05.006

Kim, D. J. (2008). Self-perception-based versus transference-based trust determinants in computer-mediated transactions: A cross-cultural comparison study. *Journal of Management Information Systems*, *24*(4), 13–45. doi:10.2753/MIS0742-1222240401

Kim, D. J., Ferrin, D. L., & Rao, H. R. (2008). A trust-based consumer decision-making model in electronic commerce: The role of trust, perceived risk, and their antecedents. *Decision Support Systems*, *44*(2), 544–564. doi:10.1016/j.dss.2007.07.001

Kim, R. Y. (2020). The impact of COVID-19 on consumers: Preparing for digital sales. *IEEE Engineering Management Review*, *48*(3), 212–218. doi:10.1109/EMR.2020.2990115

Kitjaroenchai, M., & Chaipoopiratana, S. (2022). Mixed method: Antecedents of online repurchase intention of generation Y towards apparel products on e-commerce in Thailand. *ABAC Journal*, *42*(1), 73–95.

Kleiner, A. (2019). *Digital workplace survey says what technology employees want.* Available: https://www.ibm.com/blogs/services/2019/03/05/survey-says-what-technology-employees-want/

Koçak, S., Varol, M. Ç., & Varol, E. (2020). Dijital Ortamda Marka İmaj Transferi ve İtibar Göstergeleri: Rolex-Roger Federer Örneği. *Uluslararası Kültürel ve Sosyal Araştırmalar Dergisi*, *6*(2), 597–625.

Koh, T. K., Fichman, M., & Kraut, R. (2012). trust across borders: Buyer-supplier trust in global business-to-business e-commerce. *Journal of the Association for Information Systems*, *13*(11), 886–922. doi:10.17705/1jais.00316

Kolsaker, A., & Payne, C. (2002). Engendering trust in e-commerce: A study of gender-based concerns. *Marketing Intelligence & Planning*, *20*(4), 206–214. doi:10.1108/02634500210431595

Korablev, A. YU. & Bobkin R.Ye. (2018). Informatsionnyye tekhnologii kak faktor povysheniya konkurentosposobnosti predpriyatiy malogo i srednego biznesa. *Azimut nauchnykh issledovaniy: ekonomika i upravleniye*, *1*, 44-48.

Korir, E. J. (2020). *E-marketing strategies and performance of registered rated hotels in Nakuru County* [MBA thesis]. Kenyatta University.

Kotler, P. (2005). *Kevin Lane Keller-Marketing Management.* Prentice Hall.

Kotler, P. (2003). *Marketing management.* Pearson Education, Inc.

Kotler, P., & Armstrong, G. (2007). *Marketing. Versión para Latinoamérica. Pearson Educación.* Atlacomulco.

Kotler, P., & Armstrong, G. (2014). Principles of Marketing. Pearson Prentice Hall.

KPMG. (2020). *KPMG Embedding Resilience: Addressing the business Challenges Presented by the coronavirus.* https://home.kpmg/ae/en/home.html.

Krunal, T., Pooja, T., & Varidana. (2018). Sustainable Marketing Strategies: Creating business value by meet consumer expectation. *International Journal of Management, Economic, and Social Science*, *7*(2), 186–205.

Kudryashov, A. A. (2018). Infrastruktura tsifrovoy ekonomiki. *Aktual'nyye voprosy sovremennoy ekonomiki*, *5*, 25-32.

Kumar, A., & Meenakshi, N. (2013). Marketing management (2nd ed.). Vikas Publishing House PVT Ltd.

Kumar, V., & Reinartz, W. (2018). *Customer relationship management.* Springer-Verlag GmbH Germany.

Kumar, S., Himes, K., & Kritzer, C. (2014). Risk assessment and operational approaches to managing risk in global supply chains. *Journal of Manufacturing Technology Management*, *2*(6), 873–890. doi:10.1108/JMTM-04-2012-0044

Kumar, S., Liu, J., & Scutella, J. (2015). The impact of supply chain disruptions on stockholder wealth in India. *International Journal of Physical Distribution & Logistics Management*, *45*(9/10), 938–958. doi:10.1108/IJPDLM-09-2013-0247

Kundu, S. S. (2020). Technology: The heart of business continuity. *IMI Konnect*, *9*(3), 21–29.

Kusherov, N.S. (2015). Razvitiye elektronnogo pravitel'stva v Kazakhstane. *Pravo i sovremennyye gosudarstva, 2*, 99-107.

Laman, İ., & Topçu, Ö. (2019). Sosyal Medyayla Birlikte Markanın Dijitalleşmesi. *Yeni Medya Elektronik Dergisi, 3*(1), 10–21. doi:10.17932/IAU.EJNM.25480200.2019.1/1.10-21

Lamberton, C., & Stephen, A. T. (2016). A thematic exploration of digital, social media, and mobile marketing: Research evolution from 2000 to 2015 and an agenda for future inquiry. *Journal of Marketing, 80*(6), 146–172. doi:10.1509/jm.15.0415

Lányi, B., Hornyák, M., & Kruzslicz, F. (2021). The effect of online activity on SMEs' competitiveness. *Competitiveness Review, 31*(3), 477–496. doi:10.1108/CR-01-2020-0022

Laudon, K. C., & Laudon, J. P. (2018). Management information systems managing the digital firm. In Management Decision (5th ed.). Pearson Education Limited. doi:10.1108/eb000831

Laurell, H., Karlsson, N. P. E., Lindgren, J., Andersson, S., & Svensson, G. (2019). Re-testing and validating a triple bottom line dominant logic for business sustainability. *Management of Environmental Quality, 30*(3), 518–537. doi:10.1108/MEQ-02-2018-0024

Lautenbach, P., Johnston, K., & Adeniran-Ogundipe, T. (2017). Factors influencing business intelligence and analytics usage extent in South African organisations. *South African Journal of Business Management, 48*(3), 23–33. doi:10.4102ajbm.v48i3.33

Lawrence, D. O., & Lawrence, A. W. (2021). Assessment of some basic strategies towards managing COVID-19 crisis in micro/small-sized businesses. *International Journal of Business and Management, 16*(8), 34–49.

Lazarevic-Moravcevic, M. (2019). *Characteristics of marketing communication strategy of a small enterprises.* Academic Press.

Lăzăroiu, G., Neguriţă, O., Grecu, I., Grecu, G., & Mitran, P. C. (2020). Consumers' decision-making process on social commerce platforms: Online trust, perceived risk, and purchase intentions. *Frontiers in Psychology, 11*, 890. doi:10.3389/fpsyg.2020.00890 PMID:32499740

Le, D., Nguyen, T.-M., Quach, S., Thaichon, P., & Ratten, V. (2021). The Development and Current Trends of Digital Marketing and Relationship Marketing Research. In Developing Digital Marketing. Emerald Publishing Limited. doi:10.1108/978-1-80071-348-220211001

Leeflang, P. S., Verhoef, P. C., Dahlström, P., & Freundt, T. (2014). Challenges and solutions for marketing in a digital era. *European Management Journal, 32*(1), 1–12. doi:10.1016/j.emj.2013.12.001

Lee, J. H., & Park, S. C. (2005). Intelligent profitable customer's segmentation system based on business intelligence tools. *Expert Systems with Applications, 29*(1), 145–152. doi:10.1016/j.eswa.2005.01.013

Lee, M. K. O., & Turban, E. (2001). A trust model for consumer internet shopping. *International Journal of Electronic Commerce, 6*(1), 75–91. doi:10.1080/10864415.2001.11044227

Lee, P. (2020). COVID-19 pandemic requires firms to re-imagine their tech. *Euromoney, 51*(612), 18.

Lee, Y. K. (2021). Impacts of Digital Technostress and Digital Technology Self-Efficacy on Fintech Usage Intention of Chinese Gen Z Consumers. *Sustainability, 13*(9), 5077. doi:10.3390u13095077

Levenburg, N. M., Schwarz, T. V., & Motwani, J. (2015). Understanding adoption of Internet technologies among SMEs. *Journal of Small Business Strategy, 16*(1), 51–70.

Levens, M. (2014). *Marketing defined, explained, applied* (2nd ed.). Pearson Education Limited.

Levy, S. J. (1959). Symbols for sale. *Harvard Business Review, 37*(July/August), 117–124.

Levy, S. J. (1978). *Marketplace behavior-its meaning for management.* Amacom.

Lin, F. J., & Lin, Y. H. (2016). The effect of network relationships on the performance of SMEs. *Journal of Business Research, 69*(5), 1780–1784. doi:10.1016/j.jbusres.2015.10.055

Listou, T. (2018). Samhandling, Preparedness and Supply Chains. In G.-E. Torgersen (Ed.), *Interaction: 'Samhandling' Under Risk. A Step Ahead of the Unforeseen* (pp. 501–516). Cappelen Damm Akademisk. doi:10.23865/noasp.36.ch27

Liu, X., Zhang, S., Lin, Y., & Xie, Y. (2017). Enhancing the health and sustainability of e-commerce ecosystem by bringing manufacturers online: Evidence from tao-factory. *PICMET 2016 - Portland International Conference on Management of Engineering and Technology: Technology Management for Social Innovation, Proceedings,* 815-823. doi:10.1109/PICMET.2016.7806756

Liu, X., Arthanari, T., & Shi, Y. (2021). Leverage risks for supply chain robustness against corruption. *Industrial Management & Data Systems, 121*(7), 1496–1521. doi:10.1108/IMDS-10-2020-0587

Liu, Y., & Sutanto, J. (2015). Online group-buying: Literature review and directions for future research. *The Data Base for Advances in Information Systems, 46*(1), 39–59. doi:10.1145/2747544.2747548

Li, X., Wu, Q., Holsapple, C. W., & Goldsby, T. (2017). An empirical examination of firm financial performance along dimensions of supply chain resilience. *Management Research Review, 40*(3), 254–269. doi:10.1108/MRR-02-2016-0030

Li, Z. (2011, June). Research on customer segmentation in retailing based on clustering model. In *2011 International Conference on Computer Science and Service System (CSSS)* (pp. 3437-3440). IEEE.

Lonial, S. C., & Carter, R. E. (2015). The Impact of Organizational Orientations on Medium and Small Firm Performance: A Resource-Based Perspective. *Journal of Small Business Management, 53*(1), 94–113. doi:10.1111/jsbm.12054

Lotfi, M., & Larmour, A. (2022). Supply chain resilience in the face of uncertainty: How horizontal and vertical collaboration can help? *Continuity & Resilience Review, 4*(1), 37–53. doi:10.1108/CRR-04-2021-0016

MacQueen, J. (1967). Classification and analysis of multivariate observations. In *5th Berkeley Symp. Math. Statist. Probability* (pp. 281-297). Academic Press.

Maduku, D. K., Mpinganjira, M., & Duh, H. (2016). Understanding mobile marketing adoption intention by South African SMEs: A multi-perspective framework. *International Journal of Information Management, 36*(5), 711–723. doi:10.1016/j.ijinfomgt.2016.04.018

Mahadea, D., & Pillay, M. K. (2008). Environmental conditions for SMME Development in South African Province. *South African Journal of Economic and Management Sciences, 11*(4), 431-448.

Maimon, O. Z., & Rokach, L. (2014). *Data mining with decision trees: Theory and applications* (Vol. 81). World scientific.

Maitra, B. (2016). Investment in human capital and economic growth in Singapore. *Global Business Review, 17*(2), 425–437. doi:10.1177/0972150915619819

Malitikov, E. M. (2009). Elektronnoye pravitel'stvo tsivilizatsionnaya neizbezhnost'. *Federal'naya gazeta, 1,* 4-5.

Malone, T, (2010). *Branding in 2010, JCK.* Reed Business Information, a division of Reed Elsevier, Inc. Retrieved from https://www.jckonline.com/blogs/memo-to-merchandisers/2010/01/22/what-destination-location

Mandal, S. (2019). The influence of big data analytics management capabilities on supply chain preparedness, alertness and agility: An empirical investigation. *Information Technology & People, 32*(2), 297–318. doi:10.1108/ITP-11-2017-0386

Mandal, S., Sarathy, R., Korasiga, V. R., Bhattacharya, S., & Dastidar, S. G. (2016). Achieving supply chain resilience: The contribution of logistics and supply chain capabilities. *International Journal of Disaster Resilience in the Built Environment, 7*(5), 544–562. doi:10.1108/IJDRBE-04-2016-0010

Mangiaracina, R., Marchet, G., Perotti, S., & Tumino, A. (2015). A review of the environmental implications of B2C e-commerce: A logistics perspective. *International Journal of Physical Distribution & Logistics Management, 45*(6), 565–591. doi:10.1108/IJPDLM-06-2014-0133

Mangiaracina, R., Perego, A., Perotti, S., & Tumino, A. (2016). Assessing the environmental impact of logistics in online and offline B2C purchasing processes in the apparel industry. *International Journal of Logistics Systems and Management, 23*(1), 98–124. doi:10.1504/IJLSM.2016.073300

Mangiaracina, R., Perego, A., Seghezzi, A., & Tumino, A. (2019). Innovative solutions to increase last-mile delivery efficiency in B2C e-commerce: A literature review. *International Journal of Physical Distribution & Logistics Management, 49*(9), 901–920. doi:10.1108/IJPDLM-02-2019-0048

Mangold, W. G., & Faulds, D. J. (2009). Social media: The new hybrid element of the promotion mix. *Business Horizons, 52*(4), 357–365. doi:10.1016/j.bushor.2009.03.002

Mansoor, Z. (2020). E-commerce paving the way for the future of retail and more. *Gulf Business.* https://www.ey.com/eninlcovid-19/ecommerce-during-covid-19-preparing-for-now-next-and-beyond

Mäntylä, A. (2020). *Establishing business continuity management practices.* JMAK University of Applied Sciences. Available: https://www.theseus.fi/bitstream/handle/10024/355926/Opinnäytetyö_Mäntylä_Antti.pdf?sequence=2

Marett, K., Pearson, A. W., Pearson, R. A., & Bergiel, E. (2015). Using mobile devices in a high risk context: The role of risk and trust in an exploratory study in Afghanistan. *Technology in Society, 41*, 54–64. doi:10.1016/j.techsoc.2014.11.002

Margherita, A., & Heikkila, M. (2021). *Business continuity in the COVID-19 emergency: A framework of actions undertaken by world-leading companies.* Kelley School of Business., doi:10.1016/j.bushor.2021.02.020

Maroufkhani, P., Tseng, M. L., Iranmanesh, M., Ismail, W. K. W., & Khalid, H. (2020). Big data analytics adoption: Determinants and performances among small to medium-sized enterprises. *International Journal of Information Management, 54*, 102190. doi:10.1016/j.ijinfomgt.2020.102190

Martineau, P. (1958). Sharper focus for the corporate image. *Harvard Business Review, 36*(6), 49–58.

Matikiti, R., Mpinganjira, M., & Roberts-Lombard, M. (2018). Application of the technology acceptance model and the technology– organisation–environment model to examine social media marketing use in the South African tourism industry. *South African Journal of Information Management, 20*(1), 1–12. doi:10.4102ajim.v20i1.790

Matthew, G. S. (2020). *Increases in Health-Related Workplace Absenteeism Among Workers in Essential Critical Infrastructure Occupations During the COVID-19 Pandemic — United States.* Morbidity and Mortality Weekly Report.

Mbedzi, E., & Simatele, M. (2020). Small micro and medium enterprises financing: Cost and benefits of lending technologies in the Eastern Cape province of South Africa. *Journal of Economic and Financial Sciences, 13*(1), 1–10. doi:10.4102/jef.v13i1.477

McCann, P., & Oxley, L. (2013). Innovation, entrepreneurship, geography and growth. *Journal of Economic Surveys, 26*(3), 1–195.

McKinsey. (2022). *Digital transformation of economy.* https://www.mckinsey.com/industries/technology-media-and-telecommunications/our-insights

McKnight, D. H., & Chervany, N. L. (2001). What trust means in e-commerce customer relationships: An interdisciplinary conceptual typology. *International Journal of Electronic Commerce, 6*(2), 35–59. doi:10.1080/10864415.2001.11044235

McKnight, D. H., Choudhury, V., & Kacmar, C. (2002). The impact of initial consumer trust on intentions to transact with a web site: A trust building model. *The Journal of Strategic Information Systems, 11*(3-4), 297–323. doi:10.1016/S0963-8687(02)00020-3

McQuail. (2000). *McQuil's Mass Communication Theory.* Sage.

Mensah, I. K. (2020). Factors influencing the intention of international students to shop online in china. *International. Journal of Business Research, 16*(3), 20–41.

Miao, M., Jalees, T., Zaman, S. I., Khan, S., Hanif, N., & Javed, M. K. (2021). The influence of e-customer satisfaction, e-trust and perceived value on consumer's repurchase intention in B2C e-commerce segment. *Asia Pacific Journal of Marketing and Logistics*, 1–23. doi:10.1108/APJML-03-2021-0221

Micu, A. E., Bouzaabia, O., Bouzaabia, R., Micu, A., & Capatina, A. (2019). Online customer experience in e-retailing: Implications for web entrepreneurship. *The International Entrepreneurship and Management Journal, 15*(2), 651–675. doi:10.100711365-019-00564-x

Miller, C. C. (2010). YouTube ads turn videos into revenue. *New York Times*, 2.

Mirela, D., & Stanica, A. M. (2009). Study of improving the customer relationship management by data mining applications. *Оптико-електронні інформаційно-енергетичні технології*, (1), 55-58.

Mirza, S., Elliott, S., & Beena, P. (2020). *United Arab Emirates: e-commerce in the UAE: Logistics (Part 4).* https://www.mondaq.com/operational-impacts-and-strategy/987324/e-commerce-in-the-uae-logistics-part-4

Moghavvemi, S. M., Mei, T. X., Phoong, S. W., & Phoong, S. Y. (2021). Drivers and barriers of mobile payment adoption: Malaysian merchants' perspective. *Journal of Retailing and Consumer Services, 59*, 102364. doi:10.1016/j.jretconser.2020.102364

Mohammed, A., & Rashid, B. (2018). A conceptual model of corporate social responsibility dimensions, brand image, and customer satisfaction in Malaysian hotel industry. *Kasetsart Journal of Social Sciences, 39*(2), 358–364. doi:10.1016/j.kjss.2018.04.001

Mohseni, S., & Sreenivasan, J. (2014). The impact of user characteristics in online purchase intention in tourism industry. *Reef Resources Assessment and Management Technical Paper, 40*(1), 399–404.

Mosunmola, A., Adegbuyi, O., Kehinde, O., Agboola, M., & Olokundun, M. (2019). Percieved value dimensions on online shopping intention: The role of trust and culture. *Academy of Strategic Management Journal, 18*(1), 1–20.

Muhleisen, M. &. (2005). *The long and short of the digital revolution.* IMF, Finance & Development.

Mumu, J. R., Saona, P., Mamun, M. A. A., & Azad, M. A. K. (2022). Is trust gender biased? A bibliometric review of trust in E-commerce. *Journal of Internet Commerce, 21*(2), 217–245. doi:10.1080/15332861.2021.1927437

Mussel, P. R., Rodrigues, J., Krumm, S., & Hewig, J. (2018). The convergent validity of five dispositional greed scales. *Personality and Individual Differences, 131*, 249–253. doi:10.1016/j.paid.2018.05.006

Mutambisi, A. M. (2020). *The urban penalty of COVID-2019 lockdowns across the globe: manifestations and lessons for Anglophone sub-Saharan Africa.* Academic Press.

Myers, C. A. (2003). Managing brand equity: A look at the impact of attributes. *Journal of Product and Brand Management, 12*(1), 39–51. doi:10.1108/10610420310463126

Nair, D. (n.d.). *UAE residents switch to cost-effective online shopping during COVID-19*. Gulf News. Online at: https://gulfnews.com/yourmoney/community-tips/uae-residents-switch-tocost-effective-online-shopping-during-covid-19-1.1589210896861

Nam, C., Cho, K., & Kim, Y. D. (2021). Cross-cultural examination of apparel online purchase intention: S-O-R paradigm. *Journal of Global Fashion Marketing*, *12*(1), 62–76. doi:10.1080/20932685.2020.1845766

Namvar, M., Gholamian, M. R., & Khakabi, S. (2010, January). A two phase clustering method for intelligent customer segmentation. In *2010 International Conference on Intelligent Systems, Modelling and Simulation* (pp. 215-219). IEEE. 10.1109/ISMS.2010.48

Nasiri, M., Ukko, J., Saunila, M., Rantala, T., & Rantanen, H. (2020). Digital-related capabilities and financial performance: The mediating effect of performance measurement systems. *Technology Analysis and Strategic Management*, *32*(12), 1393–1406. doi:10.1080/09537325.2020.1772966

Ngary, C., Smit, Y., Juan-Pierre, B., & Ukpere, W. I. (2014). Financial performance measures and business objectives attainment in fast food SMMEs in the Cape Metropolis: A preliminary liability and suitability analysis. *Mediterranean Journal of Social Sciences*, *5*(20), 909–921. doi:10.5901/mjss.2014.v5n20p909

Nguyen, T.-M., Le, D., Quach, S., Thaichon, P., & Ratten, V. (2021). The Current Trends and Future Direction of Digital and Relationship Marketing: A Business Perspective. In *Developing Digital Marketing*. Emerald Publishing Limited., doi:10.1108/978-1-80071-348-220211011

Nicolas, R. (2020). *United Arab Emirates: setting up an e-business in the UAE – Why participate in the fastest growing e-commerce market of the Middle East*. https://www.mondaq.com/corporate-and-company-law/1045890/setting-up-an-e-business-in-the-uae-why-participate-in-the-fastest-growing-e-commerce-market-of-the-middle-east

Niemimaa, M. (2015). Interdisciplinary review of business continuity from an information systems perspective: Toward an integrative framework. *Communications of the Association for Information Systems*, *37*(1), 4. doi:10.17705/1CAIS.03704

Nifantyev, A. N. (2020). Klyuchevyye tekhnologii tsifrovoy ekonomiki. *Molodoy uchenyy, 50*, 117-119.

Niraj, S., & Nageswara Rao, S. V. D. (2015). Sustainability of E-retail in India. *Journal of Internet Banking and Commerce*, *20*(2). Advance online publication. doi:10.4172/1204-5357.1000107

Njau, J. N., & Karugu, W. (2014). Influence of e-marketing on the performance of small and medium enterprises in Kenya: Survey of small and medium enterprises in the manufacturing industry in Kenya. *International Journal of Business & Law Research*, *2*(1), 62–70.

Njoroge, W. W. (2017). *The relationship between e-marketing strategies and brand performance of large bookstores in Nairobi County* [M.Sc. thesis]. University of Nairobi.

Nurgaziyeva, B. G. (2020). *Elektronnaya demokratiya*. http://www.osce.org/ru/odihr/77868?download=true

Nurul, H., & Chandra, V. (2018). Blockchain, cryptocurrency and bitcoin. in Blockchain. *International Journal of Computer Engineering & Applications*. Available http://www.ijcea.com/blockchain-cryptocurrency-bitcoin-3/

Nyawo, J. C. (2020). Evaluation of government responses and measures on COVID-19 in the tourism sector: A case of tour guides in South Africa. *African Journal of Hospitality, Tourism and Leisure*, *9*(5), 1144–1160. doi:10.46222/ajhtl.19770720-74

Odabaşı, Y., & Oyman, M. (2013). *Pazarlama İletişimi Yönetimi*. Mediacat Yayınları.

OECD. (2018). *SME ministerial conference. Fostering greater SME participation in a globally integrated economy.* Available: www.oecg.org

OECD. (2019). *Financing SMEs and entrepreneurs 2019: an OECD scoreboard.* OECD Publishing. doi:10.1787/fin_sme_ent-2019-

Ok, Ş., & Baş, M. (2021). Relationship Between Social Media Performance and Brand Image in Digital Branding Proces: Netflix Turkey. *İşletme Araştırmaları Dergisi, 13*(4), 3858-3872.

Oláh, J., Kitukutha, N., Haddad, H., Pakurár, M., Máté, D., & Popp, J. (2018). Achieving sustainable e-commerce in environmental, social and economic dimensions by taking possible trade-offs. *Sustainability, 11*(1), 1–22. doi:10.3390u11010089

Olaleye, S. A., Salo, J., & Ukpabi, D. C. (2018). The role of reputation on trust and loyalty: A cross-cultural analysis of tablet E-tailing. *International. Journal of Business Research, 14*(2), 61–75.

Oliveira, T., Thomas, M., & Espadanal, M. (2014). Assessing the determinants of cloud computing adoption: An analysis of the manufacturing and services sectors. *Information & Management, 51*(5), 497–510. doi:10.1016/j.im.2014.03.006

Oliver, R. L. (1999). Whence consumer loyalty. *Journal of Marketing, 63*(4), 33–44. doi:10.1177/00222429990634s105

Omar, A. M., & Atteya, N. (2020). The Impact of Digital Marketing on Consumer Buying Decision Process in the Egyptian Market. *International Journal of Business and Management, 15*(7), 120. doi:10.5539/ijbm.v15n7p120

Oo, K. Z. (2019). Design and implementation of electronic payment gateway for secure online payment system. *Int. J. Trend Sci. Res. Dev, 3*, 1329–1334.

Osano, H. M., & Languitone, H. (2016). Factors influencing access to finance by SMEs in Mozambique: Case of SMEs in Maputo central business district. *Journal of Innovation and Entrepreneurship., 5*(13), 1–16. doi:10.118613731-016-0041-0

Owonte, H., & Amu, G. (2016). Price skimming strategies and marketing performance of electronic firms in Nigeria. *Journal of Business and Value Creation, 5*(2), 135–149.

Özdemir, B., & Özcan, H. M. (2022). Islamic Work Ethic: A Content-Analysis Based Literature Review. In Religion and Its Impact on Organizational Behavior (pp. 42-64). IGI Global. doi:10.4018/978-1-7998-9319-6.ch003

Öztürk, R. G. (2016, January). A New Approach for Reaching the Customer of the Digital age: Cross-Device Advertising. *Journalism and Mass Communication, 6*(1), 19–25.

Palvia, P. (2009). The role of trust in e-commerce relational exchange: A unified model. *Information & Management, 46*(4), 213–220. doi:10.1016/j.im.2009.02.003

Pandey, N., Nayal, P., & Rathore, A. S. (2020). Digital marketing for B2B organizations: Structured literature review and future research directions. *Journal of Business and Industrial Marketing, 35*(7), 1191–1204. doi:10.1108/JBIM-06-2019-0283

Pan'shin B. (2019). Tsifrovaya ekonomika: ponyatiya i napravleniya razvitiya: teoriya. *Nauka i innovatsii, 3*, 48-55.

Papadopoulos, T., Baltas, K. N., & Balta, M. E. (2020). The use of digital technologies by small and medium enterprises during COVID-19: Implications for theory and practice. *International Journal of Information Management, 55*, 102192. doi:10.1016/j.ijinfomgt.2020.102192 PMID:32836646

Park, C. W., Jaworski, B. J., & MacInnis, D. J. (1986). Strategic brand concept-image management. *Journal of Marketing, 50*(4), 135–145. doi:10.1177/002224298605000401

Park, J., & Kim, R. B. (2019). The effects of integrated information & service, institutional mechanism and need for cognition (NFC) on consumer omnichannel adoption behavior. *Asia Pacific Journal of Marketing and Logistics*, *33*(6), 1386–1414. doi:10.1108/APJML-06-2018-0209

Parliamentary Monitoring Group. (2019). *Small business development review and recommendations report.* Available: www.pmg.org.za

Parviainen, P. K. (2017). Tackling the digitalization challenge: How to benefit from dgotalization in practice. *International Journal of Information Systems and Project Management*, *5*(1), 63–77.

Pattnalk, S. K. (2020). COVID-19 and its impact on business continuity in Ghana: The role of government. *International Journal of Management and Leadership Studies*, *2*(3), 171–180.

Paul Singh, S., Smith, K. D., Singh, J., & Rutledge, N. (2019). Packaging and logistics sustainability for the 21st century. *21st IAPRI World Conference on Packaging 2018 - Packaging: Driving a Sustainable Future*, 817-824.

Pereira, A. M., Moura, J. A. B., Costa, E. D. B., Vieira, T., Landim, A. R. D. B., Bazaki, E., & Wanick, V. (2022). Customer models for artificial intelligence-based decision support in fashion online retail supply chains. *Decision Support Systems*, *158*, 113795. Advance online publication. doi:10.1016/j.dss.2022.113795

Perkins, M. (2014). *How to Develop a Strong Visual Brand on Social Media.* Available at: http://blog.hub-spot.com/marketing/strong-brand-voice-social-media

Pflaum, C. K. (2017). *Toward the development of a maturity model for digitalization within the manufacturing industry's supply chain.* Academic Press.

Pfoser, S., Brandner, M., Herman, K., Steinbach, E., Brandtner, P., & Schauer, O. (2021). Sustainable transport packaging: Evaluation and feasibility for different use cases. *LOGI - Scientific Journal on Transport and Logistics, 12*(1), 159-170. doi:10.2478/logi-2021-0015

Pham, L. D. Q., Coles, T., Ritchie, B. W., & Wang, J. (2021). Building business resilience to external shocks: Conceptualising the role of social networks to small tourism & hospitality businesses. *Journal of Hospitality and Tourism Management*, *48*(June), 210–219. doi:10.1016/j.jhtm.2021.06.012

Phengkona, J. (2021). Online marketing strategies for community-based tourism in the Andaman cluster of Thailand. *European Journal of Tourism Research*, *28*, 1–5. doi:10.54055/ejtr.v28i.2046

Plummer, J. T. (1985). How personality makes a difference. *Journal of Advertising Research*, *24*(6), 27–31.

Podsakoff, P. M., MacKenzie, S. B., & Podsakoff, N. P. (2012). Sources of method bias in social science research and recommendations on how to control it. *Annual Review of Psychology*, *63*(1), 539–569. doi:10.1146/annurev-psych-120710-100452 PMID:21838546

Ponnamperuma. (2000). *SMEs in Competitive Markets.* Tokyo: Asian Productivity Organization.

Ponomarov & Holcomb. (2009). Understanding the concept of supply chain resilience. *International Journal of Logistics Management*, *20*(1), 124-139.

Popoli, P. (2011). Linking CSR strategy and brand image: Different approaches in local and global markets. *Marketing Theory*, *11*(4), 419–433. doi:10.1177/1470593111418795

Potluri, R. M., Johnson, S., & Koppalakrishnan, P. (2020). An exploratory treatise on the ethnocentric tendencies of Emirati Gen Z consumers. *Journal of Islamic Marketing*, *13*(3), 763–780. doi:10.1108/JIMA-07-2020-0197

Potluri, R. M., & Vajjhala, N. R. (2018). A study on application of web 3.0 technologies in small and medium enterprises of India. *Journal of Asian Finance, Economics and Business*, 5(2), 73–79.

Poto, Z. V. (2019). *Awareness and importance of developing business continuity plans for disaster risks by companies at Bayhead Harbour, Durban, South Africa* [Master's dissertation]. University of the Free State. Available: https://www.ufs.ac.za/docs/librariesprovider22/disaster-management-training-and-education-centre-for-africa-(dimtec)-documents/dissertations/zukiswa-vallery-poto-mini-dissertation.pdf?sfvrsn=f4d39421_2

Pozin, I. (2014). Small Business Expert: Answers To Your Five Biggest Social Media Branding Questions. *Forbes*. Available at: https://www.forbes.com/sites/ilyapozin/2014/11/07/small-business-expert-an-swers-to-your-five-biggest-social-media-branding-questions/

Prajapati, D., Chan, F. T. S., Daultani, Y., & Pratap, S. (2022). Sustainable vehicle routing of agro-food grains in the e-commerce industry. *International Journal of Production Research*, 1–26. Advance online publication. doi:10.1080/00207543.2022.2034192

Priambodo, I. T., Sasmoko, S., Abdinagoro, S. B., & Bandur, A. (2021). E-commerce readiness of creative industry during the COVID-19 pandemic in Indonesia. *Journal of Asian Finance. Economics and Business*, 8(3), 865–873. doi:10.13106/jafeb.2021.vol8.no3.0865

Pricewaterhousecoopers Int. Ltd. (2021). *The essential eight technologies*. Available: https://www.pwc.com/gx/en/issues/technology/essential-eight-technologies.html

Programma «Tsifrovoy Kazakhstan». (2017). https://egov.kz/cms/ru/digital-kazakhstan

Putra, P. O. (2020). Contextual factors and performance impact of e-business use in Indonesian small and medium enterprises. *Heliyon*, 6(3), e03568. doi:10.1016/j.heliyon.2020.e03568 PMID:32211544

PwC. (2020). *How resilient Middle East consumers have responded to Covid-19*. https://www.pwc.com/m1/en/publications/images-new/gcis-2020/ how-resilient-middle-east-consumers-have-responded-covid-19.pdf

Qashou, A., & Saleh, Y. (2018). E-marketing implementation in small and medium-sized restaurants in Palestine. *The Arab Economics and Business Journal*, 13(2), 93–110. doi:10.1016/j.aebj.2018.07.001

Qingyun, J., Xun, H., & Zhuohao, C. (2009). Antecedents and consequences of consumers' trust in electronic intermediaries: An empirical study of hotel booking websites. *Frontiers of Business Research in China*, 3(4), 647–666. doi:10.100711782-009-0031-1

Qin, L., Qu, Q., Zhang, L., & Wu, H. (2021). Platform trust in C2C e-commerce platform: The sellers' cultural perspective. *Information Technology Management*, 1–11.

Qi, W., Li, L., Liu, S., & Shen, Z. M. (2018). Shared mobility for last-mile delivery: Design, operational prescriptions, and environmental impact. *Manufacturing & Service Operations Management*, 20(4), 737–751. doi:10.1287/msom.2017.0683

Queiroz, M. M., Fosso Wamba, S., & Branski, R. M. (2021). Supply chain resilience during the COVID-19: Empirical evidence from an emerging economy. *Benchmarking*. Advance online publication. doi:10.1108/BIJ-08-2021-0454

Rachinger, M. (2019). *Digitalization and its influence on business model innovation*. Institute of General Management and Organization.

Rahayu, R., & Day, J. (2015). Determinant factors of e-commerce adoption by SMEs in developing country: Evidence from Indonesia. *Procedia: Social and Behavioral Sciences*, 195, 142–150. doi:10.1016/j.sbspro.2015.06.423

Raman, P. (2019). Understanding female consumers' intention to shop online: The role of trust, convenience and customer service. *Asia Pacific Journal of Marketing and Logistics*, *31*(4), 1138–1160. doi:10.1108/APJML-10-2018-0396

Ramdani, B., Chevers, D., & Williams, A. D. (2013). SMEs' adoption of enterprise applications. *Journal of Small Business and Enterprise Development*. Advance online publication. doi:10.1108/jsbed-12-2011-0035

Ramos, E., Patrucco, A. S., & Chavez, M. (2021). Dynamic capabilities in the "new normal": A study of organizational flexibility, integration and agility in the Peruvian coffee supply chain. *Supply Chain Management*. Advance online publication. doi:10.1108/SCM-12-2020-0620

Ramzy, O., & Eldahan, O. H. (2016). An empirical investigation of e-commerce in Egypt: The impact of culture on online purchasing. *Global Business Review*, *17*(5), 1011–1025. doi:10.1177/0972150916656651

Ranney, M. L., Griffeth, V., & Jha, A. K. (2020). Critical supply shortages—The need for ventilators and personal protective equipment during the Covid-19 pandemic. *The New England Journal of Medicine*, *382*(18), e41. doi:10.1056/NEJMp2006141 PMID:32212516

Rao, P., Balasubramanian, S., Vihari, N., Jabeen, S., Shukla, V., & Chanchaichujit, J. (2021). The e-commerce supply chain and environmental sustainability: An empirical investigation on the online retail sector. *Cogent Business & Management*, *8*(1), 1938377. doi:10.1080/23311975.2021.1938377

Rausch, T. M., Baier, D., & Wening, S. (2021). Does sustainability really matter to consumers? assessing the importance of online shop and apparel product attributes. *Journal of Retailing and Consumer Services*, *63*, 102681. Advance online publication. doi:10.1016/j.jretconser.2021.102681

Redjeki, F., & Affandi, A. (2021). Utilization of Digital Marketing for MSME Players as Value Creation for Customers during the COVID-19 Pandemic. *The International Journal of Science in Society*, *3*(1), 40–55. doi:10.54783/ijsoc.v3i1.264

Regattieri, A., Santarelli, G., Gamberi, M., & Mora, C. (2014). A new paradigm for packaging design in web-based commerce. *International Journal of Engineering Business Management*, *6*(1), 1–11. doi:10.5772/58825

Report, C. (2022). *India B2B spending set to surge with rising recovery optimism – India Business Spend Indicator by American Express and Invest India.* https://s1.q4cdn.com/692158879/files/doc_news/2022/01/20/Final_Press-Release_India-Business-Spend-Indicator-Report_19.01.2022.pdf

Riglietti, G., Piraina, M., & Trucco, P. (2021). *The contribution of business continuity management (BCM) to supply chain resilience: a qualitative study on the response to COVID-19 outbreak.* Continuity & Resilience Review., doi:10.1108/CRR-08-2021-0030

Ritz, W., Wolf, M., & McQuitty, S. (2019). Digital marketing adoption and success for small businesses: The application of the do-it-yourself and technology acceptance models. *Journal of Research in Interactive Marketing*, *13*(2), 179–203. doi:10.1108/JRIM-04-2018-0062

Rodrik, D. (2013). *Structural change, fundamentals, and growth: an overview.* Available: www.harvard.edu

Rogers, D. (2016). *The Digital Transformation Playbook: Rethink Your Business for the Digital Age.* Columbia University Press. doi:10.7312/roge17544

Rogerson, C. (2008). Tracking SMME development in South Africa: issues of finance, training and the Regulatory Environment. *Urban Forum, 19*, 61-81.

Rosário, A. T. (2021). The Background of articial intelligence applied to marketing. *Academy of Strategic Management Journal*, *20*(6), 1–19.

Rosário, A. T., & Dias, J. C. (2022). Sustainability and the Digital Transition: A Literature Review. *Sustainability*, *14*(7), 4072. doi:10.3390u14074072

Rosário, A. T., Raimundo, R. J., & Cruz, S. P. (2022). Sustainable Entrepreneurship: A literature review. *Sustainability*, *14*(9), 5556. doi:10.3390u14095556

Roshan Rassool, D. (2021). *Digital Transformation for Small & Medium Enterprises*. European - American Journals.

Rossolov, A. (2019). Sustainable balance between e-commerce and in-store purchases. Sustainable city logistics planning: Methods and applications, 2, 61-84.

Ross, S. A., Westerfield, R. W., & Jordan, B. D. (2013). *Fundamentals of corporate finance* (10th ed.). McGraw Hill Irwin.

Roumieh, A., Garg, L., Gupta, V., & Singh, G. (2018). E-marketing strategies for Islamic banking: A case-based study. *Journal of Global Information Management*, *26*(4), 67–91. doi:10.4018/JGIM.2018100105

Rousseau, D. M., Sitkin, S. B., Burt, R. S., & Camerer, C. (1998). Not so different after all: A cross-discipline view of trust. *Academy of Management Review*, *23*(3), 393–404. doi:10.5465/amr.1998.926617

Rowles, D. (2014). *Digital branding: A complete step-by-step guide to strategy, tactics and measurement*. Kogan Page Publishers.

Roy, V. (2021). Contrasting supply chain traceability and supply chain visibility: Are they interchangeable? *International Journal of Logistics Management*, *32*(3), 942–972. doi:10.1108/IJLM-05-2020-0214

Sagone, E., & De Caroli, M. E. (2013). Relationships between Resilience, Self-Efficacy, and Thinking Styles in Italian Middle Adolescents. *Procedia: Social and Behavioral Sciences*, *92*, 838–845. doi:10.1016/j.sbspro.2013.08.763

Salam, A. F., Iyer, L., Palvia, P., & Singh, R. (2005). Trust in e-commerce. *Communications of the ACM*, *48*(2), 72–77. doi:10.1145/1042091.1042093

Salam, M. T., Imtiaz, H., & Burhan, M. (2021). The perceptions of SME retailers towards the usage of social media marketing amid COVID-19 crisis. *Journal of Entrepreneurship in Emerging Economies*, *13*(4), 588–605. doi:10.1108/JEEE-07-2020-0274

Salciuviene, L., Lee, K., & Yu, C. C. (2007). *The impact of brand image dimensions on brand preference*. Economics & Management.

Salimon, M. G., Kareem, O., Mokhtar, S. S. M., Aliyu, O. A., Bamgbade, J. A., & Adeleke, A. Q. (2021). Malaysian SMEs m-commerce adoption: TAM 3, UTAUT 2 and TOE approach. *Journal of Science and Technology Policy Management.*, *12*(4). Advance online publication. doi:10.1108/JSTPM-06-2019-0060

Salo, J., & Karjaluoto, H. (2007). A conceptual model of trust in the online environment. *Online Information Review*, *31*(5), 604–621. doi:10.1108/14684520710832324

Samad, S. (2013). Assessing the contribution of human capital on business performance. *International Journal of Trade. Economics and Finance*, *4*(6), 393–397.

Sampson, E. (1995). *İmaj Faktörü*. Rota Yayıncılık.

Santos, J. B., & Brito, L. A. L. (2012). Toward a subjective measurement model for firm performance. *Brazilian Administration Review*, *9*(6), 95–117. doi:10.1590/S1807-76922012000500007

Saqib, Z. A., & Zhang, Q. (2021). Impact of sustainable practices on sustainable performance: The moderating role of supply chain visibility. *Journal of Manufacturing Technology Management*, *32*(7), 1421–1443. doi:10.1108/JMTM-10-2020-0403

Sarkar, P., Mohamed Ismail, M.W., & Kachev, T. (2022). Bridging the supply chain resilience research and practice gaps: pre and post COVID-19 perspectives. Journal of Global Operations and Strategic Sourcing. . doi:10.1108/JGOSS-09-2021-0082

Satharasinghe. (2014). *Key indicators of industry trade and services sector.* Department of Census and statistics.

Saunders, M., Lewis, P., & Thornhill, A. (2009). *Research methods for business students* (6th ed.). Pearson Education Limited.

Sausi, J. M., Mtebe, J. S., & Mbelwa, J. (2021). Evaluating user satisfaction with the e-payment gateway system in Tanzania. *South African Journal of Information Management*, *23*(1), 9. doi:10.4102ajim.v23i1.1430

Schaltegger, S., Hansen, E. G., & Lüdeke-Freund, F. (2016). Business Models for Sustainability: Origins, Present Research, and Future Avenues. *Organization & Environment*, *29*(1), 3–10. doi:10.1177/1086026615599806

Schleiden, V., & Neiberger, C. (2020). Does sustainability matter? A structural equation model for cross-border online purchasing behavior. *International Review of Retail, Distribution and Consumer Research*, *30*(1), 46–67. doi:10.1080/09593969.2019.1635907

Schwab, L., Gold, S., Kunz, N., & Reiner, G. (2017). Sustainable business growth: Exploring operations decision-making. *Journal of Global Responsibility*, *8*(1), 1–17. doi:10.1108/JGR-11-2016-0031

Seetharaman, A., Niranjan, I., Saravanan, A. S., & Balaji, D. (2017). A study of the moderate growth of online retailing (ecommerce) in the UAE. *Journal of Developing Areas*, *51*(4), 397–412. doi:10.1353/jda.2017.0109

Segal, S. (2020). *The global economic impacts of COVID-19.* Center for Strategic and International Studies.

Serrasqueiro, Z., Leitão, J. C., & Smallbone, D. (2018). Small- and medium-sized enterprises (SME) growth and financing sources: Before and after the financial crisis. *Journal of Management & Organization*, *27*, 1–16. doi:10.1017/jmo.2018.14

Shadrina, R., & Arviansyah. (2018). User interface and generations' preferences: Design and evaluation. *Proceedings of the 32nd International Business Information Management Association Conference, IBIMA 2018 - Vision 2020: Sustainable Economic Development and Application of Innovation Management from Regional Expansion to Global Growth*, 7882-7892.

Shahzad, A., Hassan, R., Abdullah, N. I., Hussain, A., & Fareed, M. (2020). COVID-19 impact on e-commerce usage: An empirical evidence from Malaysian healthcare industry. *Humanities & Social Sciences Reviews*, *8*(3), 599–609. doi:10.18510/hssr.2020.8364

Shaltoni, A. M., West, D., Alnawas, I., & Shatnawi, T. (2018). Electronic marketing orientation in the Small and Medium-sized Enterprises context. *European Business Review*, *30*(3), 272–284. doi:10.1108/EBR-02-2017-0034

Shao, T., & Liu, Z. (2012). How to maintain the sustainability of an e-commerce firm? From the perspective of social network. *International Journal of Networking and Virtual Organisations*, *11*(3-4), 212–224. doi:10.1504/IJNVO.2012.048906

Sheikh, A. A., Rana, N. A., Inam, A., Shahzad, A., Awan, H. M., & Wright, L. T. (2018). Is e-marketing a source of sustainable business performance? Predicting the role of top management support with various interaction factors. *Cogent Business & Management*, *5*(1), 1–22. doi:10.1080/23311975.2018.1516487

Shishany, A. A., Sarhan, N. M., Al-Turk, A., & Albakjaji, M. (2020). The role of institutional mechanisms in creating online trust: Cross cultural investigation. *Journal of Management Information and Decision Sciences, 23*(4), 317–323.

Shukla, S., Mohanty, B. K., & Kumar, A. (2018). Strategizing sustainability in e-commerce channels for additive manufacturing using value-focused thinking and fuzzy cognitive maps. *Industrial Management & Data Systems, 118*(2), 390–411. doi:10.1108/IMDS-03-2017-0122

Siamagka, N. T., Christodoulides, G., Michaelidou, N., & Valvi, A. (2015). Determinants of social media adoption by B2B organizations. *Industrial Marketing Management, 51*, 89–99. doi:10.1016/j.indmarman.2015.05.005

Siddaway, A. P., Wood, A. M., & Hedges, L. V. (2019). How to do a systematic review: A best practice guide for conducting and reporting narrative reviews, meta-analyses, and meta-syntheses. *Annual Review of Psychology, 70*(1), 747–770. doi:10.1146/annurev-psych-010418-102803 PMID:30089228

Singh, A., Yadav, A., & Rana, A. (2013). K-means with Three Different Distance Metrics. *International Journal of Computers and Applications, 67*(10).

Singh, J., Srivastava, A., & Awasthi, M. K. (2018). Study of value chain of Indian textile handicrafts: A case of Lucknow Chikankari. *Prabandhan: Indian Journal of Management, 11*(5), 28–41. doi:10.17010/pijom/2018/v11i5/123810

Singh, T., Kumar, R., & Kalia, P. (2021). E-marketing Practices of Micro-, Small- and Medium-sized Enterprises: Evidence from India. In *Strategic Corporate Communication in the Digital Age*. Emerald Publishing Limited., doi:10.1108/978-1-80071-264-520211012

Singularity University. (2021). *The exponential guide to artificial intelligence*. Available: https://su.org/resources/exponential-guides/the-exponential-guide-to-artificial-intelligence-2/

Sinha, P. K., & Uniyal, D. P. (2005). Using observational research for behavioural segmentation of shoppers. *Journal of Retailing and Consumer Services, 12*(1), 35–48. doi:10.1016/j.jretconser.2004.02.003

Siragusa, C., & Tumino, A. (2021). *E-grocery: Comparing the environmental impacts of the online and offline purchasing processes. International Journal of Logistics Research and Applications*. doi:10.1080/13675567.2021.1892041

Skard, S., & Nysveen, H. (2016). Trusting beliefs and loyalty in B-to-B self-services. *Journal of Business-To-Business Marketing, 23*(4), 257–276. doi:10.1080/1051712X.2016.1250591

Skipper, J. B., & Hanna, J. B. (2009). Minimizing supply chain disruption risk through enhanced flexibility. *International Journal of Physical Distribution & Logistics Management, 39*(5), 404–427. doi:10.1108/09600030910973742

Small Enterprise Finance Agency. (2019). *Annual Report 2018/19*. Centurion. Available: www.sefa.org.za

Smith, K. T. (2012). Longitudinal study of digital marketing strategies targeting millennials. *Journal of Consumer Marketing, 29*(2), 86–92. doi:10.1108/07363761211206339

Smith, W. R. (1956). Product differentiation and market segmentation as alternative marketing strategies. *Journal of Marketing, 21*(1), 3–8. doi:10.1177/002224295602100102

Smriti Tankha, P. G. (2021). *Leapfrogging into the future of retail, The 2021 Global Retail Development Index*. AT Kearney.

Sodhi, M. S., & Tang, C. S. (2021). Supply chain management for extreme conditions: Research opportunities. *The Journal of Supply Chain Management, 57*(1), 7–16. doi:10.1111/jscm.12255

Sohaib, O., & Kang, K. (2015). Individual level culture influence on online consumer iTrust aspects towards purchase intention across cultures: A S-O-R model. *International Journal of Electronic Business, 12*(2), 142–161. doi:10.1504/IJEB.2015.069104

Soufi, H. R., Torabi, S. A., & Sahebjamnia, N. (2018). Developing a novel quantitative framework for business continuity planning. *International Journal of Production Research*, 1–23. doi:10.1080/00207543.2018.1483586

South Africa Government. (2020a). *Escalation of measures to combat Coronavirus COVID-19 pandemic.* Available: https://www.gov.za/speeches/president-cyril-ramaphosa-escalation-measures-combat-coronavirus-covid-19-pandemic-23-mar

Spiegler, V. L., Naim, M. M., Towill, D. R., & Wikner, J. (2016). A technique to develop simplified and linearised models of complex dynamic supply chain systems. *European Journal of Operational Research*, *251*(3), 888–903. doi:10.1016/j.ejor.2015.12.004

Statista. (2016). *Retail e-commerce sales CAGR forecast in selected countries from 2016 to 2021.* Statista.

Statista. (2022). *E-commerce Worldwide.* https://www.statista.com/topics/871/online-shopping/#dossierKeyfigures/

Statistics South Africa. (2021). *Unemployment rate.* Available: www.statssa.gov.za

Stedman, C., & Burns, E. (2021). *Business intelligence (BI), tech target.* Available: https://searchbusinessanalytics.techtarget.com/definition/business-intelligence-BI

Subramani, M., & Walden, E. (2001, June). The Impact of E-Commerce Announcements on the Market Value of Firms. *Information Systems Research*, *12*(2), 135–154. doi:10.1287/isre.12.2.135.9698

Sullivan, Y. W., & Kim, D. J. (2018). Assessing the effects of consumers' product evaluations and trust on repurchase intention in e-commerce environments. *International Journal of Information Management*, *39*, 199–219. doi:10.1016/j.ijinfomgt.2017.12.008

Summers, B., & Charrington, H. (2020). *COVID-19 mindset: How pandemic times are shaping global consumers.* Fleishman Hillard. Available: https://fleishmanhillard.com/wp-content/uploads/2021/03/COVID-19-Mindset-How-Pandemic-Times-Are-Shaping-Global-Consumers.pdf

Sun, M., Grondys, K., Hajiyev, N., & Zhukov, P. (2021). Improving the E-Commerce Business Model in a Sustainable Environment. *Sustainability*, *13*(22), 12667. doi:10.3390u132212667

Sun, T. (2011). The roles of trust and experience in consumer confidence in conducting e-commerce: A cross-cultural comparison between France and Germany. *International Journal of Consumer Studies*, *35*(3), 330–337. doi:10.1111/j.1470-6431.2010.00938.x

Sürer, A., & Mutlu, H. M. (2015). The Effects of an E-marketing Orientation on Performance on Turkish Exporter Firms. *Journal of Internet Commerce*, *14*(1), 123–138. doi:10.1080/15332861.2015.1010138

Survey, C. C. (2020, March 26). *Coronavirus consumer trends: Consumer electronics, pet supplies, and more.* Retrieved from https://www.crite o.com/insig hts/coron aviru s-consu mer-trend s/

Suryani, T., Fauzi, A. A., & Nurhadi, M. (2021). Enhancing brand image in the digital era: Evidence from small and medium-sized enterprises (SMEs) in Indonesia. Gadjah Mada. *International Journal of Business*, *23*(3), 314–340.

Syakur, M. A., Khotimah, B. K., Rochman, E. M. S., & Satoto, B. D. (2018). Integration k-means clustering method and elbow method for identification of the best customer profile cluster. *IOP Conference Series. Materials Science and Engineering*, *336*(1), 012017. doi:10.1088/1757-899X/336/1/012017

Taghizadeh-Hesary, N. Y. (2016). *Major challenges facing small and medium seized enterprises in Asia and solutions for mitigationg team.* Asian Development Bank Institute.

Taiminen, H. M., & Karjaluoto, H. (2015). The usage of digital marketing channels in SMEs. *Journal of Small Business and Enterprise Development*. https://sozluk.gov.tr/

Tang, C. S. (2006). Robust strategies for mitigating supply chain disruptions. *International Journal of Logistics Research and Applications*, *9*(1), 33-45.

Tangen, S., & Austin, D. (2012). *Business continuity - ISO 22301 when things go seriously wrong*. ISO News. Available: https://www.iso.org/news/2012/06/Ref1602.html

Tan, J. T., Tyler, K., & Manica, A. (2007). Business-to-business adoption of eCommerce in China. *Information & Management*, *44*(3), 332–351. doi:10.1016/j.im.2007.04.001

Tan, K., Choy Chong, S., Lin, B., & Cyril Eze, U. (2009). Internet-based ICT adoption: Evidence from Malaysian SMEs. *Industrial Management & Data Systems*, *109*(2), 224–244. doi:10.1108/02635570910930118

Tan, P. N., Steinbach, M., & Kumar, V. (2005). *Introduction to data mining*. Addison-Wesley.

Teichert, T., Shehu, E., & von Wartburg, I. (2008). Customer segmentation revisited: The case of the airline industry. *Transportation Research Part A, Policy and Practice*, *42*(1), 227–242. doi:10.1016/j.tra.2007.08.003

Teneja, S., Pryor, M. G., & Hayek, M. (2016). Leaping innovation barriers to small business longevity. *The Journal of Business*, *37*(3), 44–51.

Teo, T. S., & Liu, J. (2007). Consumer trust in e-commerce in the United States, Singapore and China. *Omega*, *35*(1), 22–38. doi:10.1016/j.omega.2005.02.001

Thakare, Y. S., & Bagal, S. B. (2015). Performance evaluation of K-means clustering algorithm with various distance metrics. *International Journal of Computers and Applications*, *110*(11), 12–16. doi:10.5120/19360-0929

The Economist Intelligence Unit Limited. (2020). *The UAE's omni-channel consumer: striking a balance between online and in-store shopping experience*. https://impact.economist.com/perspectives/sites/default/files/eiu-uae-omni-channel-consumer.pdf

The Emirates News Agency-WAM. (2021). *Value of UAE retail e-commerce market hits record US$ 3.9bn in 2020*. https://www.wam.ae/en/details/1395302946511

Thimothy, S. (2016). *Haettu 2017 osoitteesta Why Brand Image Matters More Than You Think*. https://www.forbes.com/sites/forbesagencycouncil/2016/10/31/why-brandimage- matters-more-than-you-think/#1d931feb10b8

Thome, A. M. T., Scavarda, L. F., Fernandez, N. S., & Scavarda, A. J. (2014b). Sales and Operations Planning and the Firm Performance. *International Journal of Productivity and Performance Management*, *61*(4), 359–38. doi:10.1108/17410401211212643

Tiago, M. T. P. M. B., & Veríssimo, J. M. C. (2014). Digital Marketing and Social media: Why bother? *Business Horizons*, *57*(6), 703–708. doi:10.1016/j.bushor.2014.07.002

Tiwari, A. K., Tiwari, A., & Samuel, C. (2015). Supply chain flexibility: A comprehensive review. *Management Research Review*, *38*(7), 767–792. doi:10.1108/MRR-08-2013-0194

Tiwari, M. K. (2010). Separation of brand equity and brand value. *Global Business Review*, *11*(3), 421–434. doi:10.1177/097215091001100307

Tokar, T., Jensen, R., & Williams, B. D. (2021). A guide to the seen costs and unseen benefits of e-commerce. *Business Horizons*, *64*(3), 323–332. doi:10.1016/j.bushor.2021.01.002

Tornatzky, L. G., & Fleischer, M. (1990). *The process of technological innovation*. Lexington Books.

Tranfield, D., Denyer, D., & Smart, P. (2003). Towards a methodology for developing evidence informed management knowledge by means of systematic review. *British Journal of Management, 14*(3), 207–222. doi:10.1111/1467-8551.00375

Tripathi, A., & Bagga, T. (2020). Leveraging work from home for business continuity during covid-19 pandemic – with reference to BI solution adoption. *Indian Journal of Economics and Business, 19*(1), 19–34.

Tsekouropoulos, G., Vatis, S., Andreopoulou, Z., Katsonis, N., & Papaioannou, E. (2014). The aspects of internet-based management, marketing, consumer's purchasing behavior and social media towards food sustainability. *Rivista di Studi sulla Sostenibilità*, (2), 207–222.

Tsiotsou, R. H., & Vlachopoulou, M. (2011). Understanding the effects of market orientation and e-marketing on service performance. *Marketing Intelligence & Planning, 29*(2), 141–155. doi:10.1108/02634501111117593

Tsiptsis, K. K., & Chorianopoulos, A. (2011). *Data mining techniques in CRM: inside customer segmentation.* John Wiley & Sons.

Tukamuhabwa, B. R., Stevenson, M., Busby, J., & Zorzini, M. (2015). Supply Chain Resilience: Definition, Review and Theoretical Foundations for Further Study. *International Journal of Production Research, 53*(18), 5592–5623. doi:10.1080/00207543.2015.1037934

Tuten, T. L., & Solomon, M. R. (2015). *Social Media Marketing* (2nd ed.). Sage.

Tzavlopoulos, I., Gotzamani, K., Andronikidis, A., & Vassiliadis, C. (2019). Determining the impact of e-commerce quality on customers' perceived risk, satisfaction, value and loyalty. *International Journal of Quality and Service Sciences, 11*(4), 576–587. doi:10.1108/IJQSS-03-2019-0047

Ugu District. (2020). *Unemployed youth benefit from portable skills program.* Available: www.ugu.gov.za

Ukaz Prezidenta Respubliki Kazakhstan ot 10 noyabrya 2004 goda "O Gosudarstvennoy programme formirovaniya «elektronnogo pravitel'stva" Respublike Kazakhstan na 2005-2007 gody.

Ukko, J., Nasiri, M., Saunila, M., & Rantala, T. (2019). Sustainability strategy as a moderator in the relationship between digital business strategy and financial performance. *Journal of Cleaner Production, 236*, 117626. doi:10.1016/j.jclepro.2019.117626

Ullah, B. (2019). Financial constraints, corruption, and SME growth in transition economies. *The Quarterly Review of Economics and Finance*, 1–33.

Ulusu, Y. (2014). Effect of brand image on brand trust. *Journal of Yasar University, 24*(6), 3932–3950.

Valencia, D. C., Valencia-Arias, A., Bran, L., Benjumea, M., & Valencia, J. (2019). Analysis of e-commerce acceptance using the technology acceptance model. *Scientific Papers of the University of Pardubice, Series D. Faculty of Economics and Administration, 27*(1), 174–185.

Valerio, C., William, L., & Noémier, Q. (2019). The impact of social media on E-Commerce decision making process. *International Journal of Technology for Business, 1*(1), 1–9.

Van Auken, H. (2004). The use of bootstrap financing among small technology-based firms. *Journal of Developmental Entrepreneurship, 9*(2), 145.

Van Duin, J. H. R., Enserink, B., Daleman, J. J., & Vaandrager, M. (2019). The near future of parcel delivery: Selecting sustainable alternatives for parcel delivery. Sustainable city logistics planning: Methods and applications, 3, 219-252.

Van Loon, P., Deketele, L., Dewaele, J., McKinnon, A., & Rutherford, C. (2015). A comparative analysis of carbon emissions from online retailing of fast moving consumer goods. *Journal of Cleaner Production*, *106*, 478–486. doi:10.1016/j.jclepro.2014.06.060

Varlese, M., Misso, R., Koliouska, C., & Andreopoulou, Z. (2020). Food, internet and neuromarketing in the context of well-being sustainability. *International Journal of Technology Marketing*, *14*(3), 267–282. doi:10.1504/IJTMKT.2020.111500

Vay, P., & Vorner, S. (2015). Thriving in an Increasingly Digital Ecosystem. *MIT Sloan Management Review*, *56*(4), 27–347.

Velazquez, R., & Chankov, S. M. (2019). Environmental impact of last mile deliveries and returns in fashion E-commerce: A cross-case analysis of six retailers. *IEEE International Conference on Industrial Engineering and Engineering Management*, 1099-1103. 10.1109/IEEM44572.2019.8978705

Veldman, C., Van Praet, E., & Mechant, P. (2015). Social media adoption in business-to-business: IT and industrial companies compared. *International Journal of Business Communication*, *1*(23), 1–23.

Victor, V., & Maria, F. F. (2018). The era of big data and path towards sustainability. *Proceedings of the 31st International Business Information Management Association Conference, IBIMA 2018: Innovation Management and Education Excellence through Vision*, *2020*, 561–568.

VidhyaPriya. (2017). Connecting social media to eCommerce using microblogging and artificial neural network. *International Journal of Recent Trends in Engineering and Research*, *3*(3), 337–343. doi:10.23883/IJRTER.2017.3087.4IJNP

Viljoen, K., Roberts-Lombard, M., & Jooste, C. (2015). Reintermediation strategies for disintermediated travel agencies: A strategic marketing perspective. *The International Business & Economics Research Journal*, *14*(3), 561. doi:10.19030/iber.v14i3.9216

Vilko, J., Ritala, P., & Edelmann, J. (2014). On Uncertainty in Supply Chain Risk Management. *International Journal of Logistics Management*, *25*(1), 3–19. doi:10.1108/IJLM-10-2012-0126

Visa. (2020a). *The UAE eCommerce landscape 2020: Accelerated growth during turbulent time*. https://ae.visamiddleeast.com/dam/VCOM/regional/cemea/unitedarabemirates/media-kits/documents/visa_uae_ecommerce_landscape_2020_ppinion_paper_vf.pdf

Visa. (2020b). *UAE eCommerce sector to continue upward trajectory as digital payments boom during Covid-19*. https://ae.visamiddleeast.com/en_AE/about-visa/newsroom/press-releases/prl-09112020.html

Waheed, A., & Jianhua, Y. (2018). Achieving consumers' attention through emerging technologies: The linkage between e-marketing and consumers' exploratory buying behavior tendencies. *Baltic Journal of Management*, *13*(2), 209–235. doi:10.1108/BJM-04-2017-0126

Wallace, M., & Webber, L. (2017). *The disaster recovery handbook: a step-by-step plan to ensure business continuity and protect vital operations, facilities, and assets* (3rd ed.). AMACOM.

Waller, M. R. (2015). *Digital to the Core: Remastering leadership for your industry, your enterprises and your self*. Bibliomotion Inc.

Walsh, G., & Linzmajer, M. (2021). The services field: A cornucopia filled with potential management topics. *European Management Journal*, *39*(6), 688–694. doi:10.1016/j.emj.2021.10.002

Wamda-MIT Legatum Center. (2021). *How Covid-19 unlocked the adoption of e-commerce in the MENA region*. https://legatum.mit.edu/wp-content/uploads/2021/03/170321-MIT-Wamda-E-Commerce-COVID19-report-EN-01.pdf

Wan Ahmad, N. K., Rezaei, J., Tavasszy, L. A., & de Brito, M. P. (2016). Commitment to preparedness for sustainable supply chain management in the oil and gas industry. *Journal of Environmental Management*, *180*, 202–213. doi:10.1016/j.jenvman.2016.04.056

Wang, C. N., Dang, T. T., Nguyen, N. A. T., & Le, T. T. H. (2020). Supporting better decision-making: A combined grey model and data envelopment analysis for efficiency evaluation in e-commerce marketplaces. *Sustainability*, *12*(24), 1–24. doi:10.3390u122410385

Wang, Z., Zuo, Y., Li, T., Chen, C. P., & Yada, K. (2019). Analysis of Customer Segmentation Based on Broad Learning System. In *2019 International Conference on Security, Pattern Analysis, and Cybernetics (SPAC)* (pp. 75-80). IEEE. 10.1109/SPAC49953.2019.237870

Wayne, T., & Mogaji, E. (2020). *Academic branding and positioning through university's website profile*. Academic Press.

Weber, P., Geneste, L. A., & Connell, J. (2015). Small business growth: Strategic goals and owner preparedness. *The Journal of Business Strategy*, *36*(3), 30–36. doi:10.1108/JBS-03-2014-0036

West R, M. S. (2020). *Applying principles of behavior change to reduce SARS-CoV-2 transmission*. Academic Press.

WHO. (2020, April 10). *Coronavirus disease (COVID-19) Pandemic*. Retrieved from https ://www.who.int/emerg encie s/disea ses/novel-coronavirus-2019

Wickham, P. (2008). *Strategic entrepreneurship* (4th ed.). London: FT Financial Times.

Wieland, A., & Wallenburg, C. M. (2012). Dealing with supply chain risks: Linking risk management practices and strategies to performance. *International Journal of Physical Distribution & Logistics Management*, *42*(10), 887–905. doi:10.1108/09600031211281411

Wieland, A., & Wallenburg, C. M. (2013). The influence of relational competencies on supply chain resilience: A relational view. *International Journal of Physical Distribution & Logistics Management*, *43*(4), 300–320. doi:10.1108/IJPDLM-08-2012-0243

Wienclaw, R. A. (2013). B2B Business Models. *Research Starters: Business*.

Wilson-Jeanselme, M., & Reynolds, J. (2006). The advantages of preference-based segmentation: An investigation of online grocery retailing. *Journal of Targeting, Measurement, and Analysis for Marketing, 14*(4), 297-308.

Windrum, P., & De Barranger, P. (2002). *The adoption of e-business technology by SMEs*. Available: www.unu.edu

Wlg, G. (2020). *E-commerce in the UAE: is it the new normal? (Part 1)*. https://gowlingwlg.com/en/insights-resources/articles/2020/e-commerce-in-the-uae-part-one/

World Health Organization. (2020). *WHO Director-General's opening remarks at the media briefing on COVID-19 - 11 March 2020*. Available: https://www.who.int/director-general/speeches/detail/who-director-general-s-opening-remarks-at-the-media-briefing-on-covid-19---11-march-2020

Wu, J., & Lin, Z. (2005). Research on customer segmentation model by clustering. In *Proceedings of the 7th international conference on electronic commerce* (pp. 316-318). 10.1145/1089551.1089610

Xu-Priour, D., Truong, Y., & Klink, R. R. (2014). The effects of collectivism and polychronic time orientation on online social interaction and shopping behavior: A comparative study between China and France. *Technological Forecasting and Social Change*, *88*, 265–275. doi:10.1016/j.techfore.2014.07.010

Yamin, A. B. (2017). Impact of digital marketing as a tool of marketing communication: A behavioral perspective on consumers of Bangladesh. *American Journal of Trade and Policy*, *4*(3), 117–122. doi:10.18034/ajtp.v4i3.426

Yaobin, L., & Tao, Z. (2007). A research of consumers' initial trust in online stores in China. *Journal of Research and Practice in Information Technology, 39*(3), 167–180.

Yasmin, A., Tasneem, S., & Fatema, K. (2015). Effectiveness of Digital Marketing in the Challenging Age: An Empirical Study. *International Journal of Management Science and Business Administration, 1*(5), 69–80. doi:10.18775/ijmsba.1849-5664-5419.2014.15.1006

Yen, B., & Wong, G. (2019). Case study: Cainiao and JD.com leading sustainability packaging in China. *Proceedings of the International Conference on Electronic Business (ICEB),* 90-98.

Yıldırım, C., & Cerit, A. G. (2020). Ulusal pazarlama kongresi yayınlarında stratejik pazarlama yazını analizi. *Pazarlama ve Pazarlama Araştırmaları Dergisi, 13*(2), 379–408.

Yoon, C. (2009). The effects of national culture values on consumer acceptance of e-commerce: Online shoppers in China. *Information & Management, 46*(5), 294–301. doi:10.1016/j.im.2009.06.001

Yuldashev, U. (2017). *The future of e-commerce in the UAE gulf business.* https://gulfbusiness.com/future-E-Commerce-uae/

Yun, J. J., Zhao, X., Park, K. B., & Shi, L. (2020). Sustainability condition of open innovation: Dynamic growth of alibaba from SME to large enterprise. *Sustainability (Switzerland), 12*(11), 4379. Advance online publication. doi:10.3390u12114379

Yun, J., Jung, W., & Yang, J. (2015). Knowledge strategy and business model conditions for sustainable growth of SMEs. *Journal of Science & Technology Policy Management, 6*(3), 246–262. doi:10.1108/JSTPM-01-2015-0002

Zailani, S., Iranmanesh, M., Sean Hyun, S., & Ali, M. (2019). Barriers of biodiesel adoption by transportation companies: A case of Malaysian transportation industry. *Sustainability, 11*(3), 931. doi:10.3390u11030931

Zawya. (2022). *New report finds that 74% of UAE's online shoppers expect to spend more online in 2022.* https://www.zawya.com/en/press-release/research-and-studies/new-report-finds-that-74-of-uaes-online-shoppers-expect-to-spend-more-online-in-2022-vxggzmwz

Zendehdel, M., Paim, L., Bojei, J., & Osman, S. (2011). The effects of trust on online Malaysian students buying behavior. *Australian Journal of Basic and Applied Sciences, 5*(12), 1125–1132.

Zhang, S. Y. (2020). Asymptomatic and symptomatic SARS-Cv-2 infections in close contacts of COVID-19 patients. *COVID-19.*

Zhang., T. J. (2019). Human behavior during close contact in a graduate student office. *COVID-19, 29,* 577-90.

Zhang, Z., Zhang, J., & Xue, H. (2008). *Improved K-means clustering algorithm. In 2008 Congress on Image and Signal Processing* (Vol. 5). IEEE.

Zhou, Z., Wang, M., Ni, Z., Xia, Z., & Gupta, B. B. (2021). Reliable and sustainable product evaluation management system based on blockchain. *IEEE Transactions on Engineering Management.* Advance online publication. doi:10.1109/TEM.2021.3131583

About the Contributors

Rajasekhara Mouly Potluri is a Professor of Management/Marketing with thirty years of industry/teaching experience in various universities on many continents. He has taught both marketing and management courses on BBA, MBA, EMBA, MS (Management), and Ph.D. programs. Dr. Raj earned his Ph.D. in Marketing from Shivaji University in India and held four Master's degrees in Business Administration (Marketing), Commerce (Banking), Philosophy (Human Resources), as well as an MBA in Islamic Marketing from the International Islamic Marketing Association in the U.K. He has published more than eighty research articles, book chapters, and case studies in internationally ranked peer-reviewed journals indexed in Scopus, ABDC, SSCI, and KCI. Dr. Raj has won eleven Best Research Paper Awards and ten Academic Service Excellence Awards in different International Conference presentations in Egypt, South Korea, Malaysia, USA, and UAE. He has extensive teaching and research experience in multi-cultural and multi-ethnic environments in India, Ethiopia, Kazakhstan, South Korea, Nigeria, and the United Arab Emirates. His research interests are Marketing, Islamic Marketing, CSR, HRM & OB, and Entrepreneurship.

Narasimha Rao Vajjhala is working as an Associate Professor at the Faculty of Engineering and Architecture at the University of New York Tirana, Albania. He is a senior member of ACM and IEEE. He is the Editor-in-Chief of the International Journal of Risk and Contingency Management (IJRCM). He is also a member of the Risk Management Society (RIMS), and the Project Management Institute (PMI). He has over 20 years of experience teaching programming and database-related courses at both graduate and undergraduate levels in Europe and Africa. He has also worked as a consultant in technology firms in Europe and has experience participating in EU-funded projects. He has supervised several undergraduate senior design projects and graduate theses. He has completed a Doctorate in Information Systems and Technology (United States); holds a Master of Science in Computer Science and Applications (India), and a Master of Business Administration with a specialization in Information Systems (Switzerland), and an undergraduate degree in Computer Science (India).

* * *

Sefa Asortse is a Ph.D. candidate in the Faculty of Business Administration at the University of Nigeria Enugu Campus, Enugu. His primary research interests are in supply chain and logistics management and green management practices.

Malik Baimukhamedov was born on March 6, 1945. In 1968 he graduated with honors from the Kazakh Polytechnic Institute with a degree in Automation and Telemechanics. In 1975 he defended his Ph.D. thesis, and in 1995 his doctoral dissertation. He works as Vice-Rector for Science at the Kostanay Social and Technical University, scientific and pedagogical experience is 55 years. He has published more than 300 scientific and methodical works in English, Russian and Kazakh languages. Among them are 16 monographs, 43 textbooks and teaching materials, 8 scientific patents, and more than 220 scientific articles. He is a member of the International Academy of Informatization, International Economic Academy of Eurasia. He speaks fluently English and French.

Aizhan Baimukhamedova is an Assistant Professor at Gazi University in Industrial Engineering Department. She received he Ph.D. from the European University Business School in 2015. She has published more than 200 scientific articles in the areas of Finance, Economics, and Management and is an author of 5 textbooks published in English.

Edna Mngusughun Denga is a graduate student at the School of Business and Entrepreneurship, American University of Nigeria, Yola. In 2014 she finished her MBA in Business Management specializing in Marketing. Her primary research interests are in Digital Marketing, Brand Tribalism, Relationship Marketing, and other related topics.

Esra Güven is a lecturer at the University of Manisa Celal Bayar in Turkey. She holds a PhD on the impact of social media on consumer decision-makings. Her current interests include marketing communications, consumer behaviours and consumer communications in social media. Ph. Dr. Esra Guven is the author of several national and international papers and the marketing advisor of the Association of Strategic Researches in Turkey. The author still gives lectures on marketing, marketing researches, modern business, human resources at Manisa Celal Bayar University.

Muhammad Hoque is currently working as a Senior Research Associate at MANCOSA. He is a Y2-rated researcher by the National Research Foundation of South Africa. Prof Hoque's areas of research interest are in the field of leadership, entrepreneurship, and higher education.

Sophia Johnson is a senior faculty of management with more than twenty years of teaching experience in teaching both undergraduate and graduate-level courses and earned her Ph.D. in Management along with two Master's degree in Business Management and Library Science. In her more than two decades of teaching and research experience, she published around thirty research articles, book chapters, and short communication articles in the disciplines of library science, management, marketing, and human resources.

Thirunesha Naidu is a quality assurance professional currently working in the TIC sector. With a focus on identifying risks and opportunities, she develops systems to ensure compliance and promote continual improvement. Thirunesha holds a Master's Degree in Business Administration from MANCOSA.

Sfiso Nxele is a Postgraduate student at Management College of Southern Africa.

Neslişah Özdemir is an Assistant Professor at Kastamonu University in Business Administration Department. The main research interests of the author are marketing research, industrial marketing, consumer behavior and service marketing.

Sandip Rakshit is an academician of versatile talents, involved in the education field with a teaching, consulting and research experience of more than 20+ years. He received his Ph.D. in Computer Science Engineering from Jadavpur University, India. He has authored 6 books. He has gathered experience in educational institutes and universities in India, UAE, Singapore, Vietnam, and Africa. Rakshit has published articles in journals such as Technology forecasting and Social changes, Journal of business Research, Industrial Marketing Management.

Karthik Ram is a research scholar and pursuing his PhD in Retail Management Domain. He had six years of academic and research experience. He worked on several major government projects like ICSSR and SPARC. He presented several research papers at conferences and participated in workshops. He is currently pursuing his research in unorganised retail SME technology usage behaviour.

Hasini Rathnayake is a final year student of Bachelor of Business Administration at Eastern University.

Albérico Travassos Rosário, Ph.D. Marketing and Strategy of the Universities of Aveiro (UA), Minho (UM) and Beira Interior (UBI), With affiliation to the GOVCOPP research center of the University of Aveiro. Master in Marketing and Degree in Marketing, Advertising and Public Relations, degree from ISLA Campus Lisbon-European University | Laureate International Universities. Has the title of Marketing Specialist and teaches with the category of Assistant Professor at IADE-Faculty of Design, Technology and Communication of the European University and as a visiting Associate Professor at the Santarém Higher School of Management and Technology (ESGTS) of the Polytechnic Institute of Santarém. He taught at IPAM-School of Marketing | Laureate International Universities, ISLA- Higher Institute of Management and Administration of Santarém (ISLA-Santarém), was Director of the Commercial Management Course, Director of the Professional Technical Course (TeSP) of Sales and Commercial Management, Chairman of the Pedagogical Council and Member of the Technical Council and ISLA-Santarém Scientific Researcher. He is also a marketing and strategy consultant for SMEs.

Selvabaskar Sivasankara is a passionate management facilitator with a blend of industry, training, consultancy, research and academic experience with competency in developing and delivering learner-centric pedagogy. Degrees in Mechanical Engineering and Management with pre-doctoral and doctoral research in Marketing go behind his name. He has conducted several training programmes for Government and Corporate employees across the spectrum of contemporary areas such as business research, sales and customer orientation, retail branding, competitor assessment, team skills and so on. His research interest has spanned from guiding scholars, handling funded projects, and publishing research articles. He currently supervises four major funded projects at the School of Management, SASTRA and published more than 30 articles in renowned international journals. His primary area of research is related to digital technologies and their application in various aspects of management functions. He is currently engaged in several Government and Industry supported funded projects.

Index

S

T

U

V

W

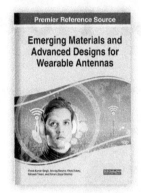

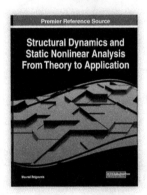

Ensure Quality Research is Introduced to the Academic Community

Become an Evaluator for IGI Global Authored Book Projects

Premier Reference Source

Stabilizing Currency and Preserving Economic Sovereignty Using the Grondona System

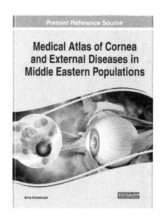

Premier Reference Source

Medical Atlas of Cornea and External Diseases in Middle Eastern Populations

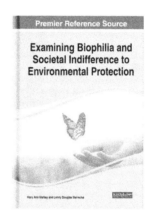

Premier Reference Source

Examining Biophilia and Societal Indifference to Environmental Protection

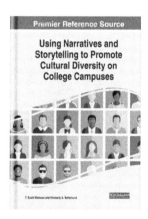

Premier Reference Source

Using Narratives and Storytelling to Promote Cultural Diversity on College Campuses

The overall success of an authored book project is dependent on quality and timely manuscript evaluations.

Applications and Inquiries may be sent to:
development@igi-global.com

Applicants must have a doctorate (or equivalent degree) as well as publishing, research, and reviewing experience. Authored Book Evaluators are appointed for one-year terms and are expected to complete at least three evaluations per term. Upon successful completion of this term, evaluators can be considered for an additional term.

If you have a colleague that may be interested in this opportunity, we encourage you to share this information with them.

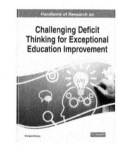

CPSIA information can be obtained
at www.ICGtesting.com
Printed in the USA
BVHW020842021222
653295BV00003B/109

9 781668 457276